COMPOSERS SINCE 1900
First Supplement

OTHER BOOKS BY DAVID EWEN

Composers Since 1900
Great Composers: 1300-1900
Popular American Composers
Popular American Composers: First Supplement
Musicians Since 1900

COMPOSERS
SINCE
1900

A Biographical and Critical Guide

First Supplement

Compiled and Edited by

D A V I D   E W E N

T H E   H . W .   W I L S O N   C O M P A N Y

NEW YORK 1981

COMPOSERS SINCE 1900 : First Supplement

Library of Congress Cataloging in Publication Data

Ewen, David, 1907-
   Composers since 1900. First supplement.
    1. Composers — Biography. 2. Music — Bio-
bibliography. I. Ewen, David, 1907-   .
Composers since 1900. II. Title.
ML390.E833   Suppl.   780'. 92'2 [B]   81-14785
ISBN 0-8242-0664-9   AACR2

Printed in the United States of America

INTRODUCTION

SINCE *Composers Since 1900* was published in 1969, a number of new composers have come to prominence whose biographies are essential in any comprehensive compendium of twentieth-century composers. Additionally, the biographies of many composers who were included in the older volume have required updating owing to continual creativity. Even for composers already deceased in 1969, new light has often been thrown on them and their music. Finally, certain composers — well-known in their own countries but at the time virtually unknown in the American music scene — were not included in the earlier volume. Some of these composers have become well-known in this country through performances or recordings, and the details of their lives and works are now required in any up-to-date reference work in the field of musical biography.

Thus, the inclusion of 47 new biographies and the updating of information on 172 composers whose biographies appear in *Composers Since 1900* are an attempt to bridge the gap of more than a decade in musical composition. The criteria for the selection of the composers in the older volume are still valid in determining the selection in the Supplement. I have taken into account (1) the significance of their work; (2) the importance of honors conferred on them; and (3) the frequency with which their music is heard in concert halls, opera houses, and on recordings.

Once again, I have gone primarily to first-hand sources for both the new biographies and the supplementary material. In the interest of accuracy and comprehensiveness, the composers were also given the opportunity to review a draft of what I had written as a final check. Where information submitted by the composers differed from that found in existing reference books (which was not unusual), I have gone to great lengths to verify the accuracy of such material by consulting publishers' catalogs, newspaper and magazine reviews, programs, and any other available sources. In these instances, information submitted by biographees has been accepted only after I have been assured by substantial evidence that it is thoroughly accurate.

I owe an immeasurable debt of gratitude to the composers themselves, who have been so generous with their time, energy, and patience in answering my deluge of queries and in reviewing the final sketches. Publishers, orchestra managements, musical societies, recording companies have also been most cooperative. A special gesture of gratitude is hereby extended to my wife, Hannah, for undertaking the taxing chore of correspondence and the typing of the first draft and final manuscript.

DAVID EWEN

Miami, Florida
September 1981

CONTENTS

Jean Absil

1893–1974

For biographical sketch, list of earlier works, and bibliography, see *Composers Since 1900*.

Jean Absil died in Brussels on February 2, 1974.

MAJOR WORKS (supplementary)

Chamber Music—Quartet, for four clarinets; Sonata for Violin Solo; Croquis Pour un Carnaval, for four clarinets and harp; Suite Mystique, for four flutes; Sonata for Violin and Piano; Esquisses, for wind quartet; Piano Trio No. 2; Images Stellaires, for violin and cello.

Choral Music—À Cloche-pied, for children's chorus and orchestra; Le Chat d'Ecole, for children's chorus.

Orchestral Music—Symphonies Nos. 4 and 5; Concerto No. 2, for violin and orchestra; Allegro Brilliante, for piano and orchestra; Fantaisie-Caprice, for saxophone and strings; Concerto for Guitar and Orchestra; Ballade, for saxophone, piano, and small orchestra; Déités, suite; Concerto No. 3, for piano and orchestra.

Piano Music—Assymetries, for two pianos; Alternances; Féeries; Poésie et Vélocité.

ABOUT (supplementary)

de Guide, R., Jean Absil, Sa Vie et Oeuvre; Wagnermée, R., La Musique Belge Contemporaine.

The Listener (England), November 1954.

Eugène d'Albert

1864–1932

For biographical sketch, list of earlier works, and bibliography, see *Composers Since 1900*.

The first New York revival in twenty-one years of d'Albert's most famous opera, *Tiefland,* and one of its infrequent revivals anywhere in the United States since its American premiere in 1908, took place on April 9, 1969 and was performed by the American Opera Society conducted by Otto Werner-Mueller. While recognizing that this opera is both hybrid and dated, Harold C. Schonberg, writing in the New York *Times,* found it "sweet, sincere and innocent . . . [with] pretty tunes and attempts at local color . . . and at times a certain kind of force." He added: "*Tiefland* is not an opera that is going to push its betters out of the repertory, but there are some nice things in it." Another rare revival of

the opera took place in England at the Wexford Festival in October-November 1978."

Franco Alfano

1876–1954

For biographical sketch, list of earlier works, and bibliography, see *Composers Since 1900*.

An infrequent American revival (and the New York premiere) of Alfano's best-remembered opera, *Risurrezione,* took place in New York on December 11, 1977, in a concert performance by the Verismo Opera Company directed by Anthony Morse. Writing in the New York *Times,* Peter G. Davis said: "*Risurrezione* can be a smashingly effective piece in the right hands." He added that the opera's strong points were those of "mood, atmosphere and pungent declamatory phrases rather than soaring tunes."

ABOUT (supplementary)

Opera News, February 24, 1962.

Hugo Alfvén

1872–1960

For biographical sketch, list of earlier works, and bibliography, see *Composers Since 1900*.

Interest in Alfvén's five symphonies was revived through recordings prepared under the auspices of the Swedish Society between 1962 and 1972, and subsequently released in the United States by the HNH Distributors in Evanston, Illinois. On the evidence of these recordings, David Hall, writing in *Stereo Review,* found that although Alfvén "was not a master to be ranked with Sibelius or Neilsen," he still proved himself to be "a creative figure of very considerable stature." Hall concluded that, on the whole, the Alfvén symphonies are "extremely beautiful and appealing music."

Between 1946 and 1952, Alfvén published his autobiography, *Memoires,* in Stockholm. A complete thematic catalog of his works, edited by Jan Olof Rudén, was published in Stockholm in 1972.

1

Allende

ABOUT (supplementary)

Hedwall, L., Hugo Alfvén; Rudén, J. O., Hugo Alfvén's Kompositionen.

Humberto Allende

1885–1959

See *Composers Since 1900.*

William Alwyn

1905–

WILLIAM ALWYN

William Alwyn was born on November 7, 1905, in Northampton, England, where his parents owned and operated a successful grocery shop. A self-educated man, Alwyn's father had a passion for literature, and he could quote from his favorite works by the page. All the children—two girls and a boy—inherited their father's love for literature, but William was the only one in the family to become interested in music. The composer recalled, "I developed an early passion for music aroused by the Sunday afternoon military band performances in the park, and my ambition was to become one of these gay-uniformed bandsmen." He was still a child when he acquired his first instrument, a piccolo, which his parents bought him because they thought it was the only instrument suitable for small hands. "A teacher was found," Alwyn recalled further, "a local boot-operative who used to come on Saturday afternoons to give me lessons, still grimy-handed and smelling of leather from the factory where he worked."

Schooling began when William was five, first at the so-called Council School, then in 1914 at the Northampton Grammar School. He was a top student in all subjects, with history, art, and English literature his particular interests. "I escaped the schoolboys' derogatory label of a 'swot' by also being good at games and I was generally popular with my schoolfellows, even though it was discovered (though I tried hard to keep it a dark secret) that I had a peculiar love for music, something regarded as both eccentric

Alwyn: ôl′ wĭn

and unmanly." Throughout those school years, Alwyn kept up with his music studies, graduating from piccolo to flute, on which he became an adept performer, and he learned to play the piano and organ.

In 1919, when Alwyn was fourteen, his schooling was ended abruptly so that he could work in his father's shop. However, he proved totally unfit for the world of commerce, and at the urging of his piano-organ teacher, Alwyn's father was induced to allow the boy to try his luck with the entrance examination to the Royal Academy of Music in London. Alwyn passed the exams and gained admittance to the Academy when he was fifteen. Now he embarked upon a new life, this time as a full-time music student, commuting by train twice a week from Northampton to London. He specialized in the flute, for which he soon earned the Ross Scholarship, with the piano as his secondary instrument. By 1922 he had become a member of the Academy orchestra, with which he performed the Beethoven Piano Concerto No. 1. He also wrote an orchestral suite which the orchestra rehearsed but its conductor, Sir Alexander MacKenzie, denounced as too modern to be playable. Nevertheless, he pursued the study of composition with J. B. McEwen (later to become principal of the Academy). Alwyn wrote, "I owe much to McEwen, who not only widened my knowledge of music into realms of Stravinsky, Schoenberg and Szymanowski, but undertook the development of my general education, particularly philosophy from the evolutionary philosophy of

2

Bergson to the more intangible philosophy of aesthetics." As a Sir Michael Costa scholarship student in composition, Alwyn wrote an opera, *Derrybag Fair,* "to an impossible libretto but one which gave me several colorful episodes on which to try my skill." The opera was never performed, but its overture survived in a number of performances. While still a student at the Academy he also completed four string quartets and *April Morn,* a piano suite that became his first published work.

The arrival of the noted conductor, Sir Henry J. Wood, to take over the Academy orchestra from MacKenzie radically altered Alwyn's development as a composer. Wood's conducting and his interest in contemporary composers greatly broadened Alwyn's musical horizon. Wood gave Alwyn his first important encouragement as a composer by performing *April Morn* at a concert at Queen's Hall; and as a performer by inviting him to appear as flute soloist at Queen's Hall, where he played Bach's Brandenburg Concerto No. 3 and Bach's B minor Suite.

With his musical life on the upswing, disaster struck. The death of his father in 1923 brought such financial duress to his family that Alwyn could no longer afford to stay at the Academy. (His two scholarships provided only tuition, not a living allowance.) Compelled to earn a living, Alwyn became music master at a private school in Surrey, supplementing this income by giving a weekly class in composition at the Royal Academy of Music. But in November 1926 he lost his job in Surrey after suffering a minor nervous breakdown.

His musical life took a new lease in 1927 with an appointment to the composition staff at the Royal Academy. At the same time, he began to perform more often as flutist in theaters, cinema houses, and also with the London Symphony Orchestra at the 1927 Three Choirs Festival in Hereford. Alwyn's music got a significant boost again when Sir Henry J. Wood conducted *Five Preludes for Orchestra* at a Promenade concert at Queen's Hall, on September 22, 1927. Alwyn revealed that his "work had a mixed reception, but Wood approved of it, said he had faith in me, and that was all that mattered."

His career developed in three ways between 1927 and 1936. As a flutist, he appeared with major orchestral and chamber-music groups, participating in some notable London premieres of works by Roussel and Ravel, among others. As a conductor, he gained his first experience with the baton in operatic performances at the Royal Academy of Music, including the British premiere of Rimsky-Korsakov's *Mozart and Salieri.* Finally, as a composer, he completed ten more string quartets, a piano concerto, a violin concerto, his first scores for motion pictures (documentaries), and a mammoth setting of William Blake's *The Marriage of Heaven and Hell* (1936) for vocal soloists, double chorus, organ, and orchestra. The *Piano Concerto* (1930) became his first work to inspire unqualified praise for its melodic inventiveness and structural skill. It was introduced at the celebrated Bournemouth Symphony concerts, with the still unknown piano virtuoso Clifford Curzon as soloist and Alwyn himself as conductor.

By 1939 he had come to the conclusion that the works he had written were unsatisfactory, and he discarded all of them. "My romantic inclinations were tentative," he explained, "and lacked both intensity and mental control. There was too much padding, too many perfunctory bars. I was now filled with the conviction that every note in a composition had to have a point, that everything unessential had to be ruthlessly pruned."

He made a new beginning by assuming a lean, disciplined neo-classical style. The first works to emerge from this new mode were the *Rhapsody,* for piano quartet, and *Divertimento,* for solo flute, both completed in 1939. The latter was given its world premiere by René Le Roy at the Festival of the International Society for Contemporary Music in New York on May 19, 1941. It was well-received at the time and has remained in the flute repertory.

With the outbreak of World War II, Alwyn volunteered his services as an air raid warden in London. The war years found him intensifying his efforts as a composer for documentary films, several of which were outstanding (*Desert Victory, Fires Were Started,* and Carol Reed's *The Way Ahead* and *The True Glory*). However, apart from some songs and the Concerto Grosso No. 1 (1942), commissioned by the B.B.C., his output of serious compositions was greatly reduced.

With the war's end, his services as a composer were sought after by commercial film makers. He became one of the most successful composers for the screen in England, the first in that coun-

3

try to be given separate screen credit for the score. Through the years, Alwyn produced over fifty motion picture scores, including *On Approval* (1944), with Clive Brook and Beatrice Lillie; *Odd Man Out* (1947), with James Mason; *The Fallen Idol* (1949), with Ralph Richardson; *The Running Man* (1961), with Laurence Harvey; and *The Naked Edge* (1961), with Gary Cooper (who was Alwyn's second cousin).

He also began directing his energies toward promoting the financial interests of British composers. In 1949 he was instrumental in founding the Composers' Guild in Great Britain, serving as its chairman in 1949, 1950, and 1964. He also helped to form the Society for the Promotion of New Music as a forum where young composers could get hearings for their works. Later, he became a member—then served on both the Council and Executive Committee—of the Council of the Performing Rights Society.

In 1950 he embarked upon his most ambitious composition up to that time: a cycle of four symphonies, each complete in itself but an integral part of the whole. His style continued to evolve. His last work, in a neo-classical vein, was the Concerto Grosso No. 2 (1951), which received its first performance at the Albert Hall in London in the same year by the London Symphony Orchestra under the direction of Sir Malcolm Sargent. From this point on, Alwyn allowed his romantic bent to reassert itself more fully, with an Elgarian breadth and feeling. This romantic attitude first emerged in the Symphony No. 1 (1951), which was premiered at the Cheltenham Festival in London in 1951, with John Barbirolli conducting. (Barbirolli also led a performance of the Symphony that year at the Royal Festival Hall in London.) Alwyn's romanticism came to full flower in his next three symphonies: Symphony No. 2 (1953) introduced by the Hallé Orchestra in Manchester under Barbirolli in 1953 and repeated at the Royal Festival Hall in London in 1954; Symphony No. 3 (1956), commissioned by the B.B.C. Symphony, which introduced it in London under Sir Thomas Beecham's direction on October 10, 1956; and Symphony No. 4 (1959), first heard at a Promenade concert under Barbirolli in London in 1959. The Symphonies Nos. 3 and 4 began to adapt the twelve-tone technique to Alwyn's creative needs, but still maintained a basic key center and a broadly diatonic melodic line. The four symphonies in the cycle have been recorded

(together with the later Symphony No. 5) by the London Philharmonic Orchestra, with Alwyn conducting. These recordings, issued between 1972 and 1977, secured worldwide recognition for him. *Penguin Stereo Record Guide* describes the four symphonies as "powerfully inventive [with] an original cast of mind," as "deeply moving" and with scoring that is "opulent and masterly."

Subsequent orchestral works added to his reputation: the Concerto for Oboe, Harp, and Strings (1951), written for Barbirolli's wife, Evelyn Rothwell, who introduced it at a London Promenade concert in 1952; *Festival March,* commissioned for the Festival of Britain in 1952; *The Magic Island,* a symphonic prelude (1953) that Barbirolli and the Hallé Orchestra introduced at the 1953 Cheltenham Festival; *Lyra Angelica,* a concerto for harp and strings (1955), a cycle of four elegiac movements each illustrating quotations from Giles Fletcher's seventeenth-century poem *Christs Victorie;* String Quartet No. 1 (1955), a work abounding with melodic invention; *Autumn Legend,* written for English horn and strings (1956), which Barbirolli conducted at the Cheltenham Festival in 1956 and again the following year at a Promenade concert in London; and the gay and bustling *Derby Day* (1962), first performed by the B.B.C. Symphony under Sir Malcom Sargent at a 1962 London Promenade concert.

Alwyn's mounting successes as a composer for both films and the concert stage encouraged him to abandon all other musical endeavors (except for his participation in organizations advancing the interests of British composers). By 1955 he had given up playing the flute in public and had resigned his teaching post at the Royal Academy of Music.

A setback in his career came in the early 1960s. For two years previously, he had suffered from a throat ailment, originally diagnosed as neurotic, that now turned out to be a growth requiring surgery. At the same time, domestic problems brought about his divorce from his first wife and his remarriage to Doreen Mary Carwithen, a former pupil and later a successful composer for both the concert hall and films. Finally, a nervous breakdown made any composition impossible for two years. However, he was back at work by 1963, and completed a String Trio and a Sonata for Clarinet and Piano.

Before his throat illness, he had already decided to give up writing music for the films, profitable though it was, in order to devote himself not only to his serious compositions but also to other artistic pursuits, such as writing poetry and prose and painting. He translated into English and edited an anthology of 20th-century French poetry (1969), completed one book on his aesthetic credo, *Daphne, or the Pursuit of Beauty* (1972), and wrote another on his personal philosophy, *The World In My Mind* (1975). When a retrospective exhibition of his paintings was held in London in 1979, he said, "At last, I was living the full life, breathing a new air and drawing in fresh inspiration."

As a personal friend of Sir Henry J. Wood, Alwyn was invited by the B.B.C. in 1964 to compose a work in tribute on the occasion of the twentieth anniversary of Wood's death. It was introduced at a Promenade concert in London under the composer's direction on August 19, 1964. A critic for the (London) *Times* described the work as "a concise, deftly scored piece . . . saving up its weight for the final threnody. In this, the composer truly mourns the loss of a friend, whereas in the two extrovert opening movements he deliberately turns his back on grief in order to pay tribute to the robuster virtues of the musician he so greatly admired." In the *Sunday Telegraph*, R. I. Henderson wrote: "Expertly written, with not a note wasted, it has a taut no-nonsense flavor."

Alwyn began to bring to realization an ambition he had been nursing for many years: to write an opera. (In addition to his student opera, *Derrybag Fair*, he had previously written a radio opera, *Farewell Companions*, which was commissioned by the B.B.C. Radio and introduced on the air in 1955.) It took him seven years (1963–1970) to complete *Juan, or the Libertine* to his own libretto. "The Don Juan I conceived, based on numerous sources, was a libertine in two senses: a hero as creative artist, as ruthless in the pursuit of his art as in the pursuit of women." As late as 1980, *Juan, or the Libertine* had not been staged; nor had Alwyn's succeeding opera, *Miss Julie*, which took him three years to write (1970–1973), using his own libretto based on the play by August Strindberg. *Miss Julie* was, however, heard over the B.B.C. Radio in London on July 16, 1977 (and subsequently recorded by the same cast). "Alwyn sets his version of the text with music exactly appropriate to it," wrote Elisabeth Forbes in *Opera*. She de-

scribed his style as "late-romantic, lyrical, often very beautiful in both texture and melody." Bryan Hesford said in *Musical Opinion* after hearing *Miss Julie* that "We must now hope that William Alwyn will be taken very seriously as a significant English opera composer. His approach is distinctly individual and this is something that perhaps puts him in a class of his own where an opera speaks directly to the listener. For all its beauty, the score is never allowed to indulge itself and hold up the story's development. This is, in my opinion, its greatness."

Alwyn described his *modus operandi* as an opera composer in these words: "The principles I laid down for myself in both operas were: the action must always be self-explanatory; there must be no lengthy soliloquies; no asides; no boring recitatives; no necessity for preliminary explanation in program notes. The plot must be uncomplicated . . . and, above all, while giving the singers ample opportunities, the vocal line must always reproduce the inflections and rhythms of the spoken word. I disagree profoundly with the use of clusters of notes decorating a single syllable which is the common practice of many opera composers today."

As relief from the tension of working on his operas, Alwyn completed a number of significant concert compositions. The most notable ones were the *Sinfonietta for Strings* (1970); Symphony No. 5, *Hydriotaphia* (1971); and the String Quartet No. 2, *Spring Waters* (1976). The Sinfonietta was commissioned for the Cheltenham Festival, where it was first performed; the composer himself described this as "one of my most important works in its harmonic freedom and contrapuntal ingenuity."

Symphony No. 5 was commissioned by the Arts Council of Great Britain for the Norwich Triennial Festival, where it was performed in 1976 by the Philharmonia Orchestra under the direction of the composer. (The subtitle "Hydriotaphia" comes from Sir Thomas Browne's essay, *Urn Burial.*) Each of the four sections of the symphony is preceded by an appropriate quotation. This work, said Alwyn, was an entirely new conception of the symphony. It is based on a three-note figure, and the four movements of the classical symphony are compressed into four short sections knitted into a single movement. The final section is a funeral march in which the full orchestra rises to an eloquent climax over

Amram

the tolling of the motto figure that had first been heard on distant tubular bells.

String Quartet No. 2 was commissioned for the Jubilee celebration of the Norwich Music Club. The Gabrieli Quartet, which performed the quartet first at a private concert of the Music Club, also gave the work its first public performance at the Aldeburgh Festival in 1976.

Since 1961, Alwyn has made his home in the village of Blythburgh, Suffolk, where freed from the stress of London professional life, he leads a serene but fruitfully creative existence, secure in the companionship of his wife, devoting his time to the writing of poetry and prose and to painting as well as to composing. He was made a Commander of the British Empire in 1978.

MAJOR WORKS

Chamber Music—2 string quartets; Divertimento, for solo flute; Sonata for Clarinet and Piano; String Trio; Naiades, fantasy sonata for flute and harp.

Operas—Farewell Companions; Juan, or the Libertine; Miss Julie.

Orchestral Music—5 symphonies; 3 Concerti Grossi; Concerto for Oboe, Harp and Strings; Festival March; The Magic Island, symphonic prelude; Lyra Angelica, concerto for harp and strings; Autumn Legend, for English horn and strings; Derby Day, overture; Sinfonietta, for strings.

Piano Music—Sonata alla Toccata; Fantasy Waltzes; Twelve Preludes; Movements.

Vocal Music—Mirages, for baritone and piano; Six Nocturnes, for baritone and piano; A Leave-Taking, for tenor and piano; Invocations, for soprano and piano.

ABOUT

London Times, September 6, 1968; Musical Opinion (London), October 1977; Opera (London), July 1977.

David Amram

1930–

David Werner Amram was born on November 17, 1930, in Philadelphia, Pennsylvania, to Philip Werner Amram and Emilie Amram. His parents' and grandparents' strong consciousness of their Jewish faith left an indelible impression on David's own religious consciousness, and in time influenced some of his endeavors as a seri-

Amram: äm' räm

DAVID AMRAM

ous composer. Another influence that ultimately affected him creatively also came early in life. An uncle who had spent a great deal of time with Indians in South America used to tell David about his experiences. "Then, when I was ten years old, I went out West to some reservations," Amram recalled. "They had traditional dancing—and I can *still* see that in my mind, it was so strong—to see something like that, to get the feeling of everybody being together, oblivious of all tourists and yet not making you feel you shouldn't be there—they were just on another level altogether."

In 1936, the illness of the elder Amram daughter, Marianna, sent the family to the warmer climate of Pas-a-Grille, Florida, where David not only began his early schooling but also acquired his first musical instrument, a bugle, a gift on his sixth birthday. "I tried it out for thirty seconds," he wrote in his autobiography (*Vibrations*, 1968), "and was able to make a sound with relative ease. This first experience was the beginning of a lifelong addiction." One year later, in 1937, the Amrams moved to the family farm in Feasterville, Pennsylvania. In addition to his academic schooling, David Amram started taking lessons on the trumpet at the Philadelphia Settlement Music School, where he began to learn the rudiments of the piano.

His love for jazz, another salient element in his evolution as a composer, dates from 1938 when he began listening to radio broadcasts of the big bands and to jazz recordings, particularly those of the cornetist, Bix Beiderbecke.

In his twelfth year, the Amram family moved from their farm to Washington, D.C., where David attended public school and served his musical apprenticeship. He played the trumpet and tuba in the school band of Gordon Junior High School. Just before he was thirteen, he made his professional debut by playing the trumpet in Louis Brown's jazz band and received a dollar a night for his work. From this time on, he said, "I knew I wanted to spend the rest of my life in music." He also added that this professional initiation into jazz "gave me a foundation, an appreciation for many attitudes that helped me enormously as a musician." At about this time, braces on his teeth made it impossible for him to play the trumpet, so he turned to the French horn which became his prime instrument (though he learned many others).

Except for music, nothing in the public school curriculum interested him. He often played hooky to indulge with other undisciplined boys in pursuits that, he said, were calculated to make him "a very bad kid." He was rescued from this fate by his enrollment in the Putney School in Vermont, an experimental school with an active music department. He took all the music courses he could and participated in the school's extracurricular musical activities. During the summer, he returned to the family in Washington and was able to study composition with Wendell Margrave and the French horn with Van Lier Lanning. He also tried his hand at composition (a horn trio, some choral pieces) with encouragement from Dimitri Mitropoulos, the distinguished conductor. He met Mitropoulos when a mutual friend brought the conductor to Amram's home to inspect some of his manuscripts, to which Mitropoulos reacted favorably.

Upon graduating from Putney School in 1948, Amram went to the Oberlin College Conservatory of Music for further training in the French horn under Martin Morris. After one year, he felt that academic existence at a music school "was killing my life." He left Oberlin in June, 1949, and found employment that summer as a sod roller.

Determined to extend his intellectual horizons, however, he matriculated that fall at George Washington University in Washington, D.C., planning to major in European history. Music remained a main preoccupation, and he continued studying the French horn with William Klang and Abe Kniaz and played the in-strument in several amateur and professional orchestras, even, at times with the National Symphony in Washington, D.C. in 1951–1952. He also wrote incidental music for plays produced at Howard University's theater in Washington in 1949–1952; helped form an ensemble that gave public performances of popular and classical music; and held jam sessions in his apartment in which musicians like Charlie "Bird" Parker and Dizzy Gillespie participated. About Parker's influence on his own musical growth, Amram said "it changed my life [making] me think of all composition as improvisation."

By transferring to evening sessions at George Washington University he could spend the daytime composing and late nights at jam sessions. Meanwhile, he supported himself for two years as a gym teacher at the Maret School and at other odd jobs.

After his graduation from George Washington University in 1952, Amram was called into military service during the Korean War. He attended the band school at Camp Breckinridge in Kentucky and then was sent overseas to play the French horn in military bands, ultimately in the Seventh Army Symphony, which toured Germany and Austria.

He completed his active military service on August 4, 1954. Instead of returning to the United States, he remained in Europe for several months, performing in concerts sponsored by the United States Department of State. He settled in Paris for a while, where he played with jazz groups (one of them, Lionel Hampton's) in various clubs and night spots. The existence was hand-to-mouth, however, and within a year he decided the time had come to return to the United States.

By September of 1955, he was living in an apartment in New York's lower East Side, maintaining what he called "a monstro crash pad" where as many as fifteen people sometimes spent the night. He attended the Manhattan School of Music in 1955 and 1956, studying with Vittorio Giannini and Ludmila Ulehla. (Subsequently he relegated music study to private teachers—mainly composition with Charles Mills and conducting with Jonel Perlea.) To support himself, he took odd jobs with jazz groups, including an engagement with Charlie Mingus at the Cafe Bohemia and another with Oscar Pettiford at Birdland. Among his activities, he played background music for the first Beat Generation poetry-reading sessions, held in New York in December, 1957, with Jack Kerouac and other poets participating; and formed his own jazz group, the Amram-Barrow Quartet (later, a quintet), which not only played at the Five Spot but also recorded an album for Decca, *Jazz Studio Number 6: The Eastern Scene.*

Beginning in this period, Amram wrote a good deal of music, such as the background music for a film documentary, *Echo of an Era* (1956) about the history of the Third Avenue El in New York; incidental music for twenty-eight Off-Broadway productions of the Joseph Papp New York Shakespeare Theater (for a long time he received only a five-dollar fee for each production); and from 1958 through the early 1960s the incidental music for the productions of the Off-Broadway Phoenix Theater, beginning with *The Power and the Glory.* He was awarded the Obie Prize in 1959 for best musical achievement in Off-Broadway Theater.

His incidental music was heard on Broadway as well: in *Comes a Day,* starring Judith Anderson (1958); in Archibald MacLeish's Pulitzer Prize winning *J.B.* (1958), directed by Elia Kazan; in Norman Corwin's *The Rivalry* (1959); in *Kataki* (1959); and in Arthur Miller's *After the Fall* (1964). Between 1963 and 1965 he was musical director of the Lincoln Center Repertory Theater.

Amram's successful ventures in composing for the New York theater brought him assignments for television and motion pictures. In television, he provided background music for such productions as *The Turn of the Screw* (1959), winner of an Emmy Award, *Something Special* (1959), *The American* (1960), and *The Fifth Column* (1960). In films, his music was heard on the soundtracks of *The Young Savages* (1961); *Splendor in the Grass* (1961); *The Manchurian Candidate* (1963); and *The Arrangement* (1969).

What he has since described as the Hollywood mentality ("Take the money and run. There's no tomorrow") upset him to such a degree that he turned down some lucrative film offers. The money he did earn from these screen chores he called "the Warner Brothers scholarships" since they enabled him to finance concerts of his own music in New York.

His first composition for the concert stage to be performed professionally was *Autobiography for Strings,* by the Washington Square Chamber Players, with Maurice Peress conducting, in June 1959. The piece was Amram's attempt to describe his own life up to that time, "the joy of playing jazz and traveling around the world . . . the feelings I had experienced as a French horn player." Another work, *Overture and Allegro,* for solo flute, was performed by John Perras in a recital at Carnegie Hall, on January 5, 1960.

On May 8, 1960, an entire evening of Amram's music was given at Town Hall in New York City. The principal items on that program were the *Autobiography for Strings* and first hearings of the *Shakespearean Concerto,* for oboe, two horns, and strings, and a violin sonata. A piano sonata, expressing Amram's feelings about the piano style of such artists as Theolonius Monk and Bud Powell, was performed in New York by Andrew Heath in December 1960. The following year, the *Sacred Service for Sabbath Eve (Shir L'Erev Shabat)* was introduced at the Park Avenue Synagogue in New York (which commissioned the work), with Maurice Peress conducting. Ross Parmentier, writing in the New York *Times,* found this music "consistently mellifluous and reverent." Two chamber music compositions—*Discussion,* for flute, cello, piano, and percussion, and *Three Songs for Marlboro,* for horn and cello—were presented at the 1961 Marlboro Festival in Vermont where Amram was guest composer that year. On February 20, 1962, the Beaux Arts Quartet offered the premiere of Amram's String Quartet in still another all-Amram concert in New York. On July 4, his cantata for narrator and orchestra, *The American Bell* (text by Archibald MacLeish) was performed at Independence Hall in Philadelphia by the Philadelphia Orchestra conducted by Amram himself. And on January 4, 1963, *Dirge and Variations,* for violin, piano, and cello, was introduced by the Marlboro Trio in Washington, D.C. Reviewing the last of these works, Paul Hume wrote in the Washington *Post:* "From the quiet manner in which the instruments are introduced at the opening, through its full presentation of the Dirge, and the imaginative treatment given the theme, it is a work of real value."

Commenting on Amram's compositions up through the early 1960s, William Flanagan wrote in the New York *Herald Tribune:* "He gives every impression of being a composer in serious search of a personal musical expression, and he writes, moreover, in a generally contemporary idiom untouched by the dictates of stylish fashion or, on the other hand, the opportunism that so often plagues the work of composers associated with the commercial theater and cinema. His work is everywhere musical, dedicated and, I should risk, passionately honest."

One of Amram's most deeply moving scores was written for a Jewish-oriented opera, *The Final Ingredient,* with a libretto by Arnold Weinstein. It was produced for television by ABC-TV on April 11, 1965, with the composer conducting. The opera's plot involves a group of Jewish prisoners in a Nazi concentration camp who plan a breakout to steal an egg from a nearby nest so they can conduct a Passover ceremony. In the New York *World-Telegram,* Louis Biancolli called it "some of the best operatic writing of our day . . . both an act of faith and a milestone for TV."

On May 13, 1965, at Town Hall, New York City, another Amram score—the cantata titled *A Year in Our Land*—received its first hearing. The work, which celebrates the four seasons of the year (text from the works of James Baldwin, John Dos Passos, Jack Kerouac, John Steinbeck and Walt Whitman), was described by Wriston Locklairin in the New York *Herald Tribune* as "a beautiful work . . . [made up of] warm, wistful vignettes . . . [and characterized by] tranquility and Copland-like cleanliness."

Let Us Remember (1965) is a cantata for solo voices, chorus, and orchestra written to a text by Langston Hughes, a memorial for all men who have died for freedom and a denunciation of the hate experienced by the Jew and the black. It was introduced in San Francisco on November 15, 1965. "The universal message set to music from the traditional '*Yiskor,*'" reported Paul Hertelendy in the Oakland *Tribune,* "is a work of moving profundity, of nobility, of compassion, and of sincerity. . . . A unifying musical motif bound the sections together with both subtlety and variety."

In 1966, Amram was chosen by Leonard Bernstein to become the first composer-in-residence in the history of the New York Philharmonic. This one-year appointment, supported by a Rockefeller Foundation grant, permitted him to attend all rehearsals, concerts, and recording sessions of the orchestra; to study all the music the orchestra was performing that season; and to do his own composing in a specially assigned office. Thus, Amram heard his orchestral

work, *King Lear Variations,* given its world premiere by the New York Philharmonic in New York on March 23, 1967. The variations were based on a melody (the "Song of the Fool") that Amram had written for a production of *King Lear* during the summer of 1962. Amram wrote: "The work begins with a statement by the timpani . . . followed by a solo bassoon stating the entire theme. All of the following variations grow directly from this statement, and each contains the theme in some form . . . I tried to use the different choirs of the unique combinations of the Wind Symphony in each of the variations. . . . Because Shakespeare's clowns are neither sad nor funny, but rather statements of the human dilemma, I tried in this piece to create many varying moods, feelings, and attitudes which would sum up a musical experience corresponding to Shakespeare's portrait of experience."

While serving his year's residence with the New York Philharmonic, Amram made his concert-hall conducting debut on January 16, 1967, with the Corpus Christi Symphony in Texas in a performance of his own *Shakespearean Concerto.* A month later he made his New York baton debut in Carnegie Hall, directing his *Sacred Service for the Sabbath Eve.*

Some of the highest praise Amram received in the 1960s was for his opera, *Twelfth Night,* in which he helped Joseph Papp prepare the libretto. The world premiere of the work was given at the Lake George Opera Festival in New York State on August 1, 1968. A critic for *Opera News* called it "an enchanting adaptation for the operatic stage." In *Musical America,* Shirley Fleming described it as "a workable and happy comic opera—a sure hit." Paul Hume, in the Washington *Post,* praised Amram for his ability to write in "a neo-Elizabethan style, both in harmonic thought and in giving natural accent to the words."

An evening of Amram's music took place in Houston, Texas, on November 10, 1968, performed by the Southern University Chorale with members of the Houston Symphony and the composer conducting. In 1969 National Education Television presented "The World of David Amram." The hour-long documentary included *Three Songs of America,* for baritone, woodwind quintet, and string quintet, with text from works by John F. Kennedy, Martin Luther King, Jr. and Robert F. Kennedy.

The world premiere of Amram's Triple Concerto took place in New York on January 10, 1971, with Kazuyoshi Akyama conducting. Scored for wind, brass, jazz quintet, and orchestra, and dedicated to "the spirit of jazz and all who create it," the work had been commissioned by Leopold Stokowski's American Symphony of New York with a grant from the Samuel Rubin Foundation. It is a modern adaptation of the baroque concerto grosso, with jazz writing prominent in the first two movements and middle Eastern music in the finale. Amram explained, "The whole Concerto is a summing up of a lifetime spent where there are no more walls in music and where playing, singing, improvising and conducting all flow back into composition." In this first performance, Amram himself played on the Pakistani flute and the Dumbek (a small near-Eastern drum). "On the Pakistani flute," Harriett Johnson wrote in the New York *Post,* "Amram astonished many of us at one point . . . by doing three things simultaneously: playing as ordinarily, singing, and clicking a different rhythm with his tongue, an effect simulating the sound of a stringed instrument."

Two works of the 1970s, *The Trail of Beauty* and *Native American Portraits,* reflect Amram's interest in ethnic music, specifically that of the American Indian, in whom he had been interested since childhood. *The Trail of Beauty,* for mezzo-soprano and orchestra, was commissioned by the Rittenhouse Square Women's Committee of the Philadelphia Orchestra as a memorial to Marcel Tabuteau, the orchestra's one-time distinguished first oboist. Tabuteau, as it happened, had been a boyhood idol for Amram, who used to listen to recordings of the Philadelphia Orchestra just to hear the oboist play. Amram decided to base his composition on the "poetry, prayers and speeches of native American people. . . . In the mystery of the spirit world of Native American people, there is the same quality of timelessness that is in the spirit of all true music." The four movements symbolize the "four signs," or "four directions," that are frequently cited in Indian lore. Authentic Indian melodies are used for oboe and orchestra, but the music for mezzo-soprano is entirely original. The world premiere took place in Philadelphia with Eugene Ormandy conducting on March 4, 1977. Ormandy said of this composition: "Amram, through his particular genius, and his hard work, digging at the sources, has built a marvelous musical tapestry full of wonderful sounds and colors."

One week later, Seymour Wakschal gave the New York premiere of *Native American Portraits,* a three-movement composition for violin, piano, and percussion, in which could be heard a buffalo dance, a woman's corn-grinding song, a hand-game song, and war dances of the Seneca, Cheyenne, and Zuni tribes.

As an ardent propagandist for concert music, jazz, folk music, and ethnic music, Amram has given outdoor concerts throughout the United States and abroad; he has performed for school children, and has served as director of youth and family concerts for the Brooklyn Philharmonic Orchestra since 1971. In giving all these concerts, it is Amram's habit to reach out and make personal contact with his audiences. After a formal concert is over, he descends from the stage and joins the audience in conversation, and sometimes even in making music if anybody in the audience has brought along an instrument. Amram explained that sometimes, "at the very end I have them join in singing Amen over and over as they clap out a variety of subtle rhythms. I like to break down the idea of a star plus onlookers. The whole hall becomes one; it's a very religious, beautiful thing."

Since 1969, Amram has traveled in twenty-five countries as a self-appointed ambassador of good will; sometimes these tours have been sponsored by the United States Information Agency. Musical ideas and instruments acquired during these travels often find their way into his concerts and his compositions. "He is the greatest ambassador the United States has ever sent to Sri Lanka," read an official report to the State Department.

When the United States lifted its restrictions against travel to Cuba in 1977, the cruise ship *Daphne* became the first vessel since 1961 to stop off at Havana. David Amram and a group of jazz musicians (including "Dizzy" Gillespie, Earl "Fatha" Hines, and Stan Getz) were aboard. Writing in *Downbeat,* Arnold Jay Smith described what happened when the boat docked at Havana: "David, Diz and Ray Mantilla got off the boat . . . and in five minutes the crowd was clapping claves to David's flute, Ray's percussion and Diz's cheerleading. The mood was set for all that took place thereafter, thirty-six hours of *descarga* [jamming]. It was a historic event, showing how dedicated musicians could transcend politics through the joy of making music together." They all gave a concert at the Teatro Mella on May 18, 1977, where David Amram's *En Memoria de Chano Pozo,* written for the occasion, received its world premiere. (Pozo, one of Cuba's leading percussionists, played with Dizzy Gillespie's band and had been a powerful influence in Afro-Cuban jazz.) Describing this work in his review of the recording *Havana/New York* (recorded live in Havana), Chris Albertson wrote in *Stereo Review:* "Amram's piano introduction ... is slow, soulful and stunningly beautiful, but the piece soon erupts into an orgiastic frenzy of rhythm. ... Throughout all this, Amram contributes a characteristic series of personal touches, switching from instrument to instrument." Amram subsequently wrote an orchestral version of *En Memoria de Chano Pozo.*

Compared to so many of his contemporaries, Amram has a traditional stance as composer. He is tonal, leans heavily on a lyricism that has fresh and spontaneous material, draws deeply from the well of jazz and varied ethnic sources, spices his music generously with discordant harmonies and exploits folk rhythms extensively. He said: "By continually learning all about forms of music throughout the world, from Eskimo throat music to newly discovered baroque composers, I become continually amazed at what a beautiful language music is."

Since June 1959, Amram has occupied a studio apartment on Sixth Avenue and 11th Street in Greenwich Village, New York. Jennifer Dunning wrote in the New York *Times,* that "his home is ... crammed with musical scores, trunks, photographs and letters in dime-store frames scattered across one wall, and instruments of all shapes and sizes, which Mr. Amram is likely to pick up in mid-sentence and play upon, intent on illustrating some principle of foreign music. The clock by the bed has stopped. The cries of the children in a nearby playground float up to mingle oddly with the sounds of such wind instruments as the Iranian *ney* and the Egyptian *shanai.*"

In April 1978 a documentary about Amram and his music was televised nationally by the Public Broadcasting Service, in which Amram conducted the Chicago Symphony in the last movement of his Triple Concerto.

He provided the music, lyrics, and "the sound of Broadway" for the non-musical play, *Harold and Maude,* which opened in New York on January 29, 1980.

On January 7, 1979, Amram married Loralee Ecobelli.

MAJOR WORKS

Chamber Music—Trio, for saxophone, French horn and bassoon; Overture and Allegro, for solo flute; Discussion, for flute, cello, piano, and percussion; Sonata, for violin and piano; String Quartet; Dirge and Variations, for violin, cello, and piano; Three Songs for Marlboro, for horn and cello; The Wind and the Rain, for violin and piano; Sonata, for solo violin; Woodwind Quintet; Triptych, for solo viola; Portraits, for violin, viola, cello, and piano; Fanfare and Processional, for brass quintet; Native American Portraits, for violin, piano, and percussion; Zohar, for unaccompanied flute.

Choral Music—Two Anthems, for a cappella voices; Sacred Service (*Shir L'Erev Shabat*) for tenor solo, vocal quartet, and organ; May the Words of the Lord, for chorus and organ; Thou Shalt Love the Lord, Thy God, for chorus and organ; A Year in Our Land, cantata for solo voices, chorus, and orchestra; Let Us Remember, cantata for solo voices, chorus, and orchestra; By the Waters of Babylon, for soprano and women's voices; Rejoice in the Lord, for a cappella chorus.

Operas—The Final Ingredient; Twelfth Night.

Orchestral Music—Autobiography for Strings; Shakespearean Concerto, for oboe, two horns, and strings; Three Dances, for oboe and strings; King Lear Variations, for wind symphony and percussion; The American Bell, for narrator and orchestra; Violin Concerto; Horn Concerto; Triple Concerto, for woodwind, brass, jazz quintet, and orchestra; Bassoon Concerto; Elegy, for violin and orchestra; The Trail of Beauty, for mezzo-soprano, solo oboe, and orchestra; En Memoria de Chano Pozo.

Piano Music—Sonata.

Vocal Music—Songs from Shakespeare, for voice and piano; Three Songs for America, for baritone, woodwind quintet, and string quartet.

ABOUT

Amram, D., Vibrations: the Adventures and Musical Times of David Amram.

BMI, The Many Worlds of Music, Winter 1976; Horizon, May 1962; Life, August 11, 1967; Musical America, February 1962; Newsday (New York), June 5, 1977; New York Times, April 14, 1978.

Hendrik Andriessen

1892–

For biographical sketch, list of earlier works, and bibliography, see *Composers Since 1900.*

Andriessen's one-act opera, *The Mirror from Venice* (1964), with a libretto by Helene Nolthenius, was performed as a television opera over the Dutch network on October 5, 1967. Two other major works were the results of commissions from the Johan Wagenaar Foundation: *Hymnus in Pentacosten* (1976), for chorus and orchestra, written in commemoration of the 150th anniversary of the Royal Conservatory at The Hague, and *De Imitatione Christe* (1977), for soprano and organ, to a text by Thomas à Kempis.

MAJOR WORKS (supplementary)

Chamber Music—Concert Spirituel, for flute, oboe, violin, and cello; Variations on a Theme of Haydn, for English horn and piano; L'Indifferent, for string quartet; Sonata for Clarinet and Piano; Divertimento à Cinque, for flute, oboe, violin, viola, and cello; Chorale Varié, for three trumpets and three trombones.

Choral Music—Te Deum Laudamus II, for chorus and orchestra; Psalm IX, for tenor, chorus, and orchestra; Lux Jocunda, for tenor, chorus, and orchestra; Carmen Seculaire, for soprano, tenor, chorus, winds, doublebass, and harpsichord; Hymnus in Pentacosten, for chorus and orchestra.

Opera—The Mirror from Venice, one-act opera.

Orchestral Music—Symphony No. 5; Concerto for Violin and Orchestra; Concertino, for oboe and string orchestra; Concertino, for cello and orchestra; Chromatic Variations, for solo quartet and string orchestra; Canzone; Chantecleer, overture; Hymnus in Pentacosten.

Piano Music—2 sonatas.

Vocal Music—Three Romantic Songs, for mezzo-soprano, flute, oboe, and piano; De Imitatione Christe, for soprano and organ.

ABOUT (supplementary)

Thurston, J. D., Hendrik Andriessen: His Life and Works.

Louis Andriessen

1939–

Louis Andriessen, at the forefront of the musical avant-garde in Holland, is the youngest son of the distinguished Dutch composer, Hendrik Andriessen, and the former Tine Anschütz, a professional pianist. Other members of the Andriessen family are also professional musicians: his older brother, Juriaan, is a composer, and his uncle, Willem, was a pianist, composer, and director of the Amsterdam Conservatory.

Louis Andriessen was born in Utrecht, Holland, on June 6, 1939. American music had a strong impact on him early in his life. Immediately after the end of World War II he became acquainted with the music of such composers as Aaron Copland, Paul Creston, and Norman Dello Joio, through the facilities of the United States Information Center established near his home. Jazz also made a powerful impression on him. When he was thirteen he heard boogie-woogie for the first time and began listening to and playing the music of Albert Ammons, Pete Johnson, and Meade Lux Lewis. The influence of boogie-woogie on Andriessen has been a continuing one and two decades later he wrote *On Jimmy Yancey* (1973), for wind instruments, doublebass, and piano, a work that used phrases from three of Yancey's boogie-woogie pieces. Between the ages of fourteen and sixteen he listened continually to American jazz over the American Armed Forces Radio, and through this listening was exposed to what he described as "a very progressive radical approach to music," and "That was a big influence."

He studied music with his father, principally between 1950 and 1956. Louis Andriessen's first published work, a sonata for flute and piano, appeared in 1956. From 1956 to 1958 he continued his music study with his brother, Juriaan, and from 1958 to 1962 with Kees van Baaren at the Royal Conservatory at The Hague. While at the Conservatory, he continued producing compositions, notably *Seriés,* for two pianos (1958) and the subtly atmospheric *Nocturnen,* for soprano and chamber orchestra (1959). Both pieces were published and began to attract interest.

Andriessen: än drē sĕn

LOUIS ANDRIESSEN

Van Baaren opened up the world of non-tonal music for Andriessen, an interest further stimulated when he studied composition with Luciano Berio in Milan and Berlin from 1962 to 1965. Under such influences, Andriessen completed *Ittrospezione II*, for orchestra, which was well received when introduced in Brussels on November 15, 1963. *Ittrospezione III* (Concepts I and II), for two pianos and instruments, was written between 1964 and 1965. Concept I received its premiere over the Hilvershum radio on September 15, 1964, and Concept II by the Concertgebouw Orchestra in Amsterdam on March 13, 1966. *Double,* for clarinet and piano, was introduced in Rotterdam on April 1, 1965.

His most impressive early work was the *Anachronie I,* for orchestra (1967); its world premiere was given in Rotterdam on January 18, 1968. It was dedicated to the memory of Charles Ives. A small orchestra (which included a piano and electric organ) was grouped in a central position around the conductor. The entire composition was based on a germinal four-note phrase. Quotations from the music of other composers (Roussel's Symphony No. 3, Bach's *Passion According to St. Matthew*) are interpolated. Andriessen said that this score "indicates more clearly than ever that any individual style is no longer ideal."

Anachronie II (1969), for solo oboe, piano, harp, four horns, and string orchestra, was *musique d'ameublement* (literally "furnishing music," or music intended not so much for active listening as for background, a notion that

Erik Satie had experimented with many years earlier). Other works of this period demonstrated the growth of Andriessen's innovative imagination and the increased significance he gave to electronics. Notable among these compositions were *Hoe Het is* (1969), written for an electronic improvisation group and fifty-two strings, and *Spektakel* (1970), written for sixteen wind instruments, six percussionists, and electronic instruments *ad libitum* (allowing the electronic instruments freedom to vary the tempo and to embark at will on improvisations).

Jazz—more specifically improvisation—appealed to Andriessen's creativity. However, the subject matter of his music has largely been dictated by his left-wing political and social ideology. Kevin Stephens wrote in *Records and Recordings:* "His compositions reflect the struggle of any composer to produce 'socialist' music whilst living and working within a capitalist economic system, and especially in a system where the supply and demand of music is controlled by factors such as the profit motive, which are totally alien to the socialist composer. His compositions are concerned with the fundamental issues of our time, but his approach to composition shows a lively sense of just what is possible and what is not. 'There is no such thing as a fascist dominant seventh', he says to illustrate the fact that, although the composer's means of handling his material are determined to a large extent socially, the abstract musical materials—pitch duration, rhythm, etc.—are supra-social; they are part of nature."

Three of Andriessen's most significant works have ideological motivations. They form a triptych: *Il Duce* (1973), inspired by a 1935 speech of Mussolini; *Il Principe* (1973–1974), whose text is derived from Machiavelli's *The Prince;* and *Der Staat* (1973–1976), based on ideas in Plato's *Republic.* "They are all settings of texts which are politically controversial, to say the least, if not downright negative," the composer explained. "The idea comes from Bertolt Brecht, whose plays feature figures from whom you can learn how not to conduct yourself and why it is that at certain moments people's political or social actions are bad. He termed this an 'asocial model.' The quotations from Machiavelli in *Il Principe* . . . were chosen first and foremost as examples of how political thinking should *not* be. But as is the case of Plato, it would be too crude to present Machiavelli as an arch reactionary pure and simple, no matter how fascist his maxim that to control a city it is necessary to destroy it."

Il Duce was written on commission from the Netherlands Broadcasting Corporation. The composer said, "I had just returned from Italy where I had seen in record shops releases of fascist songs and Mussolini speeches. The MSI [Movimento Soziale Italiano] had become the biggest neo-fascist party in Europe and this, combined with the fact that in the thirties the fascists had been the first to make systematic use of the radio as a political medium, promoted my decision to write *Il Duce*." Borrowing the last sentence of Mussolini's speech in Turin in 1935 ("This assembly signifies that the identity of Italy and of fascism is perfect, absolute and immutable"), he put it on tape. Kevin Stephens explained further: "When the tape loop is played, the signal recorded on it is switched back on itself so that it becomes a feedback loop. Thus, with successive repetitions the words become more and more garbled until finally, from the prevailing feedback roar, there emerges a musical quotation: the opening of Strauss' *Also sprach Zarathustra*. This exultant opening seems like a liberation from the oppressive electrical process which has gone before, and yet the choice of quotation contains an implicit comment on music and fascism; both Nietzsche and Strauss were artists who were used by and exploited by fascism." *Il Duce* was introduced on November 28, 1976, in Amsterdam.

The voice is used more traditionally in *Il Principe,* which is scored for two choirs, wind instruments, piano, and bass guitar, and which received its world premiere at the University of Nÿmegen on February 21, 1977. *De Staat,* scored for four female voices and orchestra, was introduced in Amsterdam by the Netherland Wind Ensemble on November 28, 1976, in a recorded performance. Andriessen said he wrote it, "as a contribution to the discussion about the place of music in politics." The entire work is based on tetrachords—groups of four notes—and is scored for groups of four. Just before the final choral section, the orchestra (split into two identical halves) plays two melodies that sound like one because their rhythms are complementary. However, polyrhythm is introduced in the coda following the choral finale by having each of the two orchestras play its own music. In 1977, *De Staat* was awarded both first prize of

the UNESCO Rostrum of Composers in Holland and the Matthijs Vermeulen Prize.

Andriessen revived a medieval musical device in *Hoketus* (1977), scored for ten instruments, and introduced at The Hague on June 31, 1976. In "Hoketus," two voices sing alternating notes of a melody. In Andriessen's piece two identical groups of musicians played groups of identical chords on alternate beats. Each group was free to repeat any measure or any number of measures as often as it wished, causing the rhythm and the harmonic pattern to change in unpredictable ways. *Hoketus* grew out of an instrumental study project at The Hague Conservatory where Andriessen was teaching instrumentation and composition.

Andriessen has also written a considerable amount of music for stage productions and films. Until 1976, he was the leader of a brass wind ensemble calling itself "De Volharding" ("Perseverance"), which he had founded in September 1972 and which specialized in new music. The group performed at universities, political rallies, and working-class and socialist meetings. Of "De Volharding" which also gave a concert at the Concertgebouw in Amsterdam in November 1974, Andriessen wrote: "We support the fight for a socialist world both in and out of our music."

Andriessen has been living with Jeanette Yanikian, a guitar player and musical therapist, since 1964—"a brilliant and liberal relationship," he said, "that has set an example for many of our friends." They have no children, but several cats. His only hobby is table tennis.

MAJOR WORKS

Band Music—Monuments of the Netherlands.

Chamber Music—Percosse, for flute, bassoon, and percussion; Sonata, for flute and piano; Paintings, for flute and piano; A Flower Song, No. 2, for oboe solo; A Flower Song, No. 3, for solo cello; Ittrospezione III (Concept I), for two pianos and three instrumental groups; Double, for clarinet and piano; Ittrospezione III, fragment for two pianos, tenor, and saxophone; Ittrospezione III (Concept II), for two pianos and instruments; De Volharding, for piano and wind instruments; On Jimmy Yancey, for wind instruments, double-bass, and piano; Hoketus, for ten instruments; Melodie, for recorder and piano.

Choral Music—Il Principe, for two choirs, wind instruments, piano, and bass guitar.

Electronic Music—Contra Tempus, for 23 musicians and electronic tapes; Hoe Het is, for electronic improvisational group and string orchestra; Spektakel,

ERRATA

Certain headings in this printing of *Composers Since 1900—First Supplement* contain typographical errors. The correct headings are printed below on gummed paper and may be cut out along the dotted line, moistened, and pasted over the incorrect headings on the pages indicated.

Page 22

Milton Babbitt

1916-

Page 229

Goffredo Petrassi

1904-

Page 69

Alfredo Casella

1883-1947

Page 231

Sergei Prokofiev

1891-1953

Page 118

Arthur Foote

1853-1937

Page 232

Henri Rabaud

1873-1949

Page 132 (paste at foot of left column)

Comargo Guarnieri

1907-

See *Composers Since 1900*

Page 234

Silvestre Revueltas

1899-1940

Page 182

Charles Martin Loeffler

1861-1935

Page 288

Karol Szymanowski

1882-1937

Page 201

Italo Montemezzi

1875-1952

Page 306

Vincenzo Tommasini

1878-1950

for 16 wind instruments, 6 percussionists, and electronic instruments ad libitum; Il Duce, for electronic tape.

Opera—Reconstructie, political opera (written with Reinbert de Leeuw, Misja Mengelberg, Peter Schat, and Jan Van Vlijmen).

Orchestral Music—Ittrospezione II; Anachronie I, Anachronie II, "musique d'ameublement" for solo oboe, piano, harp, four horns, and string orchestra; Volkslied, for an unlimited number of instruments; Worker's Union, symphonic movement for any loud sounding group of instruments; De Staat, for four female voices and orchestra; Hymne; Symphony for Open Strings.

Piano Music—Series, for two pianos; Registers; Souvenirs d'Enfance.

Theater Music—Matthew Passion; Orpheus.

Vocal Music—Nocturnen, for soprano and chamber orchestra; Mausoleum, for 2 baritones and instrumental ensemble.

ABOUT

Layton, R. and Searle, H., Twentieth Century Composers: Great Britain, Scandinavia, the Netherlands; Vinton, J. (ed.), Dictionary of Contemporary Music.

Music, July 1978; Records and Recordings (London), January 1978.

George Antheil

1900–1959

For biographical sketch, list of earlier works, and bibliography, see *Composers Since 1900.*

Both Antheil's *Ballet Mécanique* and *Jazz Symphony* (the latter originally entitled *Jazz Symphonietta*), from the 1920s, were revived on June 16, 1976, at The Hague by the Netherland Wind Ensemble conducted by Reinbert de Leeuw. This concert was repeated in Amsterdam two days later. In both cities, Antheil's music was received enthusiastically. A correspondent for *Musical America,* reported that "both works are extremely imaginative and sure-fire audience pleasers." The performance at The Hague was recorded by Telefunken, and released in 1977. *Jazz Symphony* was also revived in New York City on May 23, 1978, at a concert of the American Composers Orchestra conducted by Gunther Schuller. Writing in the New York *Times,* Raymond Ericson said: "Antheil's period piece is an entertaining curiosity. A patchwork of jazz or jazz-like phrases appro-

priately scored, it has a glittering and sophisticated veneer to keep it listenable."

Antheil's widow, Elizabeth (Böske) Markus Antheil, died in Los Angeles in 1978.

ABOUT

Opera News, December 20, 1980.

Dominick Argento

1927–

Dominick Argento was born in York, Pennsylvania, on October 27, 1927. He was the eldest of three children of Michael Argento, a tavernowner, and Nicolina Amato Argento, both Sicilian by birth.

The family was not a musical one—a brother distinguished himself as an athlete, a sister became an English teacher—and Dominick's childhood was not marked by any interest in music, his pet hobbies being model planes, trains, and reading. When he was fourteen, however, he came upon Isaac Goldberg's biography of George Gershwin. Fascinated by this story of an American musician, Argento went on to read biographies of Stravinsky and other composers and musicians. This interest, in turn, led him to explore music through textbooks on composition and harmony and to experiment at a piano keyboard in his father's inn. By the time he was sixteen he was given a piano. He later remarked, "Of course, I had to learn music to justify the present." His formal musical instruction began with piano lessons and a local teacher. While attending York High School, he completed his first composition: a one-minute polka for the piano, inspired by Shostakovich's famous polka from *The Age of Gold.*

After graduation from high school in 1945, he served two years in the United States Army as a cryptographer. Upon his release from military service in 1947, he disappointed his father's hopes for a career in medicine or law by enrolling at the Peabody Conservatory of Music in Baltimore under the G.I. Bill of Rights. At Peabody he studied piano with Alexander Sklarewski and composition with Nicolas Nabokov (later with Hugo Weisgall). During his first sum-

Argento: är′ gĕn tō

15

DOMINICK ARGENTO

mer vacation from the Conservatory, Argento became absorbed by Mozart's letters. He explained, "I don't know exactly why, but I do know that when I came back to school that fall, after reading these letters, I was a composer and had lost all interest in becoming a pianist."

In 1950, he became a co-founder of the Hilltop Opera Company in Baltimore. Receiving a Bachelor of Arts degree from Peabody in 1951, Argento went to Florence, Italy, on a Fulbright Fellowship to continue the study of composition with Luigi Dallapiccola and piano with Pietro Scarpini at the Cherubini Conservatory. He returned to Peabody for his master's degree, and further composition study with Henry Cowell, and at the same time taught composition and theory at Hampton Institute, in Virginia. On September 6, 1954, he married Carolyn Bailey, a soprano he met at Peabody, who later introduced many of his vocal works. That same year he completed *Sicilian Limes,* a one-act opera based on a play by Pirandello; it was produced only once and has since been withdrawn.

Between 1955 and 1957, Argento acquired his doctorate at the Eastman School of Music in Rochester, New York, studying with Alan Hovhaness, Bernard Rogers, and Howard Hanson. Some of his compositions began to be heard in performances at Eastman: excerpts from *The Resurrection of Don Juan,* a one-act ballet (May 5, 1956); a Divertimento, for piano and string orchestra (May 26, 1956); *Ode to the West Wind,* for soprano and orchestra (April 29, 1957).

Success came first on May 6, 1957, with the premiere of a one-act opera buffa for three characters, *The Boor,* whose text was derived from a Chekhov play. It was performed at the Festival of American Music in Rochester. Argento's talent in writing for the voice, and his sure instinct for drama and musical characterization made *The Boor* an immediate hit with audiences and critics alike. Writing in the Rochester *Times-Union,* George H. Kimball described the opera as "masterfully put together and well paced . . . full of delightful arias, duets and trios . . . and side-splitting high comedy." Since that premiere, *The Boor* has been performed frequently in the United States and has been televised in Germany.

Argento spent the next year in Florence on a Guggenheim Fellowship, working on various compositions, specifically his first full-length opera, *Colonel Jonathan the Saint.* Then, in 1958 he was appointed permanently to the music faculty of the University of Minnesota, where he has remained ever since, giving classes in theory, composition, and the history of opera. "The first few years, I didn't really like it there," he recalled, "I got involved. I made my accommodations. It nagged me that I might be jeopardizing my career as a composer by being buried there, but I had opportunities I never could have had in New York." In his palazzo-type house in Minneapolis, the Italian influence is omnipresent: in furnishings, hand-carved cabinets, statuaries, and other art objects. A large portrait of Verdi, whom he regards as his spiritual father, dominates one wall of his study. He and his wife return regularly to Florence, their second home, where they occupy an apartment at the end of Ponte Vecchio on the Pitti Palace side of the Arno River. Whether in Italy or in Minneapolis, Argento works at composing an average of eight hours a day.

The first performance of *Colonel Jonathan the Saint* was a failure when introduced by the Denver Lyric Opera on December 31, 1971. (Excerpts from this opera, a suite of dances entitled *From the Album of Allegro Harper—1867,* had previously been heard in May 1961.) Argento, himself, regarded the work as "unwieldy" and made revisions and cuts before it was performed again. *Christopher Sly,* a comic opera based on the Induction Scene from Shakespeare's *The Taming of the Shrew,* did far better in a world premiere at the University of Minnesota on May 31, 1963. "A most clever score fully in the frolicsome spirit of the burlesque" is the way John K. Sherman described it in the Minneapolis *Star.*

In 1964, Argento became co-founder of the Center Opera in Minnesota (later renamed the Minnesota Opera). The company opened its first season on January 9, 1964, with Argento's religious comedy, *The Masque of Angels,* for chorus and small orchestra, which had been commissioned by the Center Arts Council in Minneapolis. In the San Francisco *Examiner,* Arthur Bloomfield wrote that "the mark of genius is stamped all over it." To Dan Sullivan in the Minneapolis *Tribune* it was "a consummate work of art . . . a glowing masterpiece."

On June 1, 1967, the Guthrie Theater in Minneapolis offered Argento's ballad opera, *The Shoemaker's Holiday,* adapted from the Restoration comedy of Thomas Dekker. John Harvey, in the St. Paul *Pioneer Press* called it "a rich and flavorful period-style musical score of bouncy dance numbers, solo arias, trios and choruses beautifully expressing the jaunty spirits and sturdy sentiments of the work."

Between 1964 and 1969, Argento contributed incidental music to a number of plays produced by Tyrone Guthrie at his Minneapolis theater. From Guthrie, Argento revealed, he learned much about "timing, pacing of scenes, the flow from scene to scene, what's important in each scene, when to throw away music and compose less, especially the idea of unity, that setting a text is more than writing line after line of pretty harmonies and melodies."

A ninety-minute surrealistic fantasy, *Postcard from Morocco,* commissioned by the Minnesota Opera Company, brought Argento additional success in the operatic theater. Introduced in Minneapolis on October 14, 1971, it was described by John Scarborough in the Houston *Chronicle* as "action-packed as Algiers, as chilling as Chicago, as bizarre as old Bombay. . . . You're sucked into the intrigue before you know it." To Peter Altman at the Minneapolis *Star* it was "at various moments extremely funny, genuinely poignant and powerfully upsetting. It also has an extraordinary combination of sophistication and ingeniousness." Following the premiere, the opera was performed in San Francisco, Chicago, Houston, Boston, New York, and Washington, D.C., as well as Canada and Germany. It was also recorded in its entirety on the Desto label.

During these years, Argento did not confine

himself to composing for the operatic stage (though it has always been his first love). Between 1960 and 1962 he wrote two song cycles: *Songs About Spring,* for soprano and chamber orchestra, with texts from the poems of e. e. cummings, was first performed on July 14, 1960; *Six Elizabethan Songs,* for voice and piano, based on poems by Shakespeare and his contemporaries, received its premiere on May 8, 1963. (In both performances, his wife was the vocalist.) A five-part suite, *Royal Invitation, or Homage to the Queen of Tonga,* commissioned by the St. Paul Philharmonic, was produced in Minneapolis on March 22, 1964. *The Mask of Night,* variations for orchestra, was heard for the first time on January 26, 1966 in Minneapolis. *The Revelation of St. John the Divine,* a rhapsody for tenor solo, male chorus, brass, and percussion, was introduced in Minneapolis on May 16, 1966. *A Nation of Cowslips,* a choral cycle for a cappella chorus, was a setting of seven poems by John Keats; it was introduced in Minneapolis on November 12, 1968. Other non-operatic works of Argento introduced in the 1960s and 1970s were *Letters from Composers,* a cycle of seven songs for tenor and guitar, with a text derived from the letters of seven masters of music (Bach, Mozart, Schubert, Chopin, Schumann, Debussy, and Puccini (October 23, 1968); *Bravo Mozart!,* for violin, oboe, French horn, and orchestra (July 3, 1969); *A Ring of Time,* subtitled "Preludes and Pageants for Orchestra," written in homage to Gustav Mahler (October 5, 1972) and commissioned by the Minnesota Orchestra for its seventieth anniversary; *To Be Sung Upon the Water,* for high voice, piano, clarinet, and bass clarinet, a cycle based on poems by Wordsworth (October 20, 1974); and the oratorio, *Jonah and the Whale* (March 9, 1974).

National attention was focused on Argento when he received the 1975 Pulitzer Prize in music for *From the Diary of Virginia Woolf,* which Dame Janet Baker introduced in Minneapolis on January 9, 1975. Argento recalled, "It's performance was something of a fluke. The Schubert Club asked Miss Baker's agents if she would premiere a new work. They said yes, so I went to work. But when my publisher, Boosey and Hawkes, delivered the score to her in Aldeburgh, it turned out she had no idea it was coming. She didn't even know she was singing in Minneapolis. And still, with nothing to gain and much to risk—after all, a thirty-five-minute work meant dropping more than a third of her planned program—she decided to take the time and trouble to learn a new, lengthy cycle and then gave it an absolutely stunning performance. It was truly a noble gesture . . . a beautiful, selfless gesture I will always remember."

The text, as the title indicates, comes from Virginia Woolf's diary, eight excerpts beginning with 1919 and ending with a sombre entry in 1941, just before she committed suicide. The composer's aim in this monodramatic cycle, as Harold C. Schonberg pointed out in the New York *Times,* was to recreate musically "the complex, tortured, sad personality of Virginia Woolf." Though organized on a single twelve-tone row, the composition is actually a polyglot of styles ranging from the Gregorian chant to serialism and drawing from such disparate materials as the suggestion of an operatic scene, café tunes of the 1920s, and broad Edwardian melodies reminiscent of Elgar. Argento regards this as his "tightest and most emotionally mature work." The critics agreed with the composer's assessment and added praise of their own. In *The New Yorker,* Andrew Porter called it "a beautiful, moving masterly work. The text is coherent and affecting, and proves to be marvelously apt for musical treatment. The words are, as it were, 'recited' in a flexible *arioso* melodic contour, uncommonly sensitive to a natural weight, speed and inflection, embracing both recitative and full-throated lyricism. . . . Song follows song in masterly sequence."

In 1976 Argento added to his reputation with the production of his opera, *The Voyage of Edgar Allan Poe,* which was commissioned by the University of Minnesota in commemoration of the American bicentenary. He completed it in Florence in 1975–1976 during a sabbatical from the university. Its world premiere took place in St. Paul on April 24, 1976. Charles M. Nolte's libretto was based on episodes from the last, half-crazed days of Poe, who, aboard some mysterious ship, relives his past loves, sins, and misfortunes through a series of charades performed by a theatrical troupe and into which the poet himself is drawn. In the end, Poe is destroyed by the realization that he has killed the things he loved most for the sake of his muse. The critics were almost unanimous in hailing *The Voyage of Edgar Allan Poe* as the most important work of American music to emerge from the bicentennial celebration. "Argento has created not only the

perfect atmosphere for this tale but vocal lines and word-setting of remarkable know-how, mixed with stirring lyricism," reported a critic in *Opera News.* "The score has unmistakable poignancy, enhancing the sympathetic figure of the tortured, romantic Poe. In the orchestration one feels an undertow, a dark turbulence that takes the neurotic poet to his death." William Bender said in *Time*: "Argento's orchestral score . . . can be as gruff as Strauss at one moment, as ethereal as Debussy the next, sometimes underlining the drama at hand while simultaneously anticipating events to come. Most important, Argento can write for the voice."

The salient characteristics of Argento's music can be found in this opera. Argento described himself as a traditionalist "in the broadest sense," and added: "If you want a school, include me in the Mozart, Verdi, Mussorgsky school." Like Verdi, Argento's prime concern is good theater and direct contact with audiences. He seeks out opulent melodies and emotion. "I am not embarrassed by emotion," he said, "I want my work to have emotional impact and I want it to have interesting characterizations. I want to communicate, not obfuscate. I'm always thinking of what it will mean to an audience. Racine once said, 'the principal aim of the theater is to please; all other rules lead to this.' I believe that."

Argento has a deep respect and an abiding affection for the voice, for which he has written some of his major works. He explained, "the voice is not just another instrument; it is a *part* of the performer rather than an adjunct to him."

On May 19, 1977, Argento's one-act opera, *A Water Bird Talk,* was produced in Brooklyn, New York. (Its writing, however, had preceded *The Voyage of Edgar Allan Poe* by almost two years.) This is a monodrama for baritone with twelve instrumentalists, and a libretto freely drawn from Chekhov's *On the Harmful Effects of Tobacco* and J. J. Audubon's *The Birds of America.* The setting is a lecture room in a small town in Maryland in the 1880s where a lecturer provides a dissertation on birds with the help of tinted magic-lantern slides of illustrations from the Audubon book. Structurally, the score consists of a theme (a twelve-note subject), six variations (Romanza, Barcarolle, Spinning Song, Consolation, Marcia all'Italiana, and Elegy) and a coda. Argento said of this work: "It was a very concentrated two or three months of work and, as a result, seems very tight to me—compact and rich, highly organized yet free-ranging." Andrew Porter in *The New Yorker* commented: "The work is at once a tragi-comedy, a scene that provides a *tour de force* for its singer, and a shapely attractive suite. . . . The score, colorful, varied and skillful, never obscures the voice. The vocal line is lyrical; it has an expressive character."

Later the same year, on September 23, 1977, the Minnesota Orchestra offered the world premiere of Argento's *In Praise of Music,* seven "songs" without text for orchestra. The work was written on commission from the Minnesota Orchestra to commemorate its seventy-fifth anniversary. The program notes read: "Celebrating the music of the world, ingeniously borrowing from diverse idioms to build symphonic images, each episode, except the finale, is based on a song from a different culture." (These different cultures are represented by a Sephardic incantation, a Delphic hymn, a Japanese melody, a fragment of Monteverdi's *Orfeo,* an Arabian street song, and a plainchant.)

Argento's next major work was a two-act opera with prologue and epilogue, *Miss Havisham's Fire,* subtitled "Being an Investigation into the Unusual and Violent Death of Aurelia Havisham on the Seventeenth of April in the Year Eighteen Hundred and Sixty." With a libretto by John Olon-Scrymgeour loosely based on Dickens' *Great Expectations,* the work had been commissioned by the New York City Opera, which presented the world premiere in New York on March 22, 1979. Most of the critics found the opera lacking in the kind of dramatic power, intensity, and recognizable musical profile Argento revealed in earlier operas. Andrew Porter described the opera as "easy and attractive to listen to" and as "skillfully composed," but found the libretto "lacking in humor, human richness and warmth, and moral vision"—qualities, Porter added, which were equally lacking in Argento's score.

In 1976, Argento received an honorary doctorate of human letters from York College in Pennsylvania. He also received an award from, and in 1980 was elected to membership in the American Academy and Institute of Arts and Letters.

MAJOR WORKS
Ballets—The Resurrection of Don Juan; Royal Invita-

tion, or Homage to the Queen of Tonga.

Choral Music—The Revelation of St. John the Divine, rhapsody for tenor solo, male chorus, brass, and percussion; A Nation of Cowslips, for a cappella chorus; Tria Carmina Paschalia, three Latin Easter lyrics for women's voices, harp, and guitar; Jonah and the Whale, oratorio for tenor, bass, narrator, chorus, and instrumental ensemble.

Operas—Colonel Jonathan the Saint; The Boor, one-act opera buffa; Chirstopher Sly, comic opera; The Masque of Angels, one-act opera; The Shoemaker's Holiday, ballad-opera; Postcard from Morocco, one-act opera; A Water Bird Talk, one-act monodrama for baritone and twelve instrumentalists; The Voyage of Edgar Allan Poe; Miss Havisham's Fire.

Orchestral Music—From the Album of Allegra Harper—1867, a suite of dances from Colonel Jonathan and the Saint; Divertimento, for piano and string orchestra; Ode to the West Wind, concerto for soprano and orchestra; The Mask of Night, variations for orchestra; Bravo Mozart!, for violin, oboe, French horn, and orchestra; A Ring of Time, for orchestra and bells; In Praise of Music, seven songs for orchestra.

Vocal Music—Songs about Spring, for soprano and chamber orchestra; Six Elizabethan Songs, for soprano (or tenor) and baroque ensemble; Letters from Composers, for tenor and guitar; To Be Sung Upon the Water, for high voice, piano, clarinet, and bass clarinet; From the Diary of Virginia Woolf, for medium voice and piano.

ABOUT

ASCAP News, Fall 1976; High Fidelity/Musical America, September 1975; New York Times, May 6, 1975, March 18, 1979; Opera News, April 17, 1976, March 24, 1979.

Richard Arnell

1917–

For biographical sketch, list of earlier works, and bibliography, see *Composers Since 1900.*

In 1967, Arnell married Maxine Leah de Felice. In 1968 he went to the United States once again, this time to serve as visiting professor of music at Hofstra University on Long Island, New York. On February 7, 1970, Eleazar de Carvalho conducted the Pro Arte Orchestra at Hofstra in the premiere of Arnell's *The Town Crier,* for narrator and orchestra (1969). This work compared the tribulations America faced during the Revolutionary War with such twentieth-century problems as Vietnam, urban decay, and pollution.

In 1969–1970, Arnell served as Fulbright Exchange Fellow at Bowdoin College in Maine. In 1970, he was lecturer at the film school in London for two years and then was appointed music consultant. He was made Chairman of the Composers Guild of Great Britain in 1974.

Richard Arnell makes his home on Prince of Wales Road in London. His prime interests outside of music are the production of motion pictures (for which he has written many scores) and model railroads.

MAJOR WORKS (supplementary)

Multi-Media Spectacle—Combat Zone, for 2 speakers, vocal soloists, chorus, wind instruments, jazz group, and film.

Operas—The Petrified Princess, puppet opera for children; Moon Flowers, one-act opera; Rain Folly.

Orchestral Music—Piano Concerto No. 2; Food of Love, overture; Nocturne; The Town Crier, for narrator and orchestra; My Ladye Green Sleeves; Life Boat Voluntary.

Organ Music—Variations on Ein' Feste Burg.

Piano Music—Suite in D, for two pianos.

ABOUT (supplementary)

Sadie, S. (ed.), The New Grove Dictionary of Music and Musicians; Vinton, J. (ed.), Dictionary of Contemporary Music.

Malcolm Arnold

1921–

For biographical sketch, list of earlier works, and bibliography, see *Composers Since 1900.*

Arnold's Symphony No. 7 (1973), probably his most ambitious work in symphonic form, was intended to be a portrait of the composer's three children. The work was commissioned by the New Philharmonia Orchestra of London, which introduced it on May 5, 1974, with the composer conducting. "It represents his biggest gesture yet," Edward Greenfield wrote in the Manchester *Guardian,* "a massive piece of three movements of almost Mahlerian proportions. Where in earlier symphonies, any nasty grimacing, his habit of putting his tongue out at his audience, was quickly overtaken by his innate generosity, here the mood is more consistently that of disillusion. True, there are rich string melodies in each movement, and several unex-

pected passages of musical collage—a cakewalk in the first movement, an Irish jig in the last—but each time a note of defiance returns. The very end brings a simple triumphant chord and the program note suggests an optimistic resolution, but that is not the way I read it at all. Even there, Arnold is merely masking his bitterness. . . . The writing for orchestra is magnificent, never less than memorable, colorful, apt, wonderful fun to play."

In response to a London Philharmonic commission, Arnold wrote *Philharmonic Concerto,* commemorating America's bicentenary, and it was performed during that orchestra's 1976 tour of the United States. Arnold explained that his aim was "to celebrate this dramatic and joyful occasion—the birthday of the U.S.A. This piece has no quotations from war songs. It celebrates this great event with as much brilliance as I am able to muster." The world premiere took place in London on October 31, 1976, with Bernard Haitink conducting the London Philharmonic. Its American premiere followed on November 22, in New York.

Some of Arnold's subsequent outstanding works include: String Quartet No. 2 (1976), introduced by the Allegri String Quartet at the Aldeburgh Festival on June 12, 1976; *Fantasy on a Theme of John Field,* for piano and orchestra (1977), first performed by John Lill and the Royal Philharmonic Orchestra in London on May 26, 1977; *Variations for Orchestra on a Theme by Ruth Gibbs* (1977), premiered in London on February 22, 1978, with Ruth Gibbs conducting; and the Symphony No. 8 (1978), commissioned and first performed on May 4, 1979, by the Albany (New York) Symphony. A critic for *High Fidelity/Musical America* reported that "Unlike his previous symphonies, the Eighth Symphony is extremely agitated and dissonant, using tone clusters through much of the first movement, which seems less cohesive and has less formal development than is usual with this composer. After a large-scaled, brassy opening, Arnold introduces some jaunty marching tunes of a folk-like character. This movement, along with the finale, seemed to express a certain angry tension reflecting the temper of our times. The Andantino, with its rich sonorities, was the most satisfying of the three movements."

In 1969, Arnold was made Bard of the Cornish Gorsedd and received an honorary doctorate in music from Exeter University. A year later, he was named Commander, Order of the British Empire, and in 1975 he became an honorary member of the Royal Academy of Music in London.

Whimsy and the love of the quixotic have sometimes drawn Arnold close to dadaism, as evidenced in some of his orchestral works (none to be found in the listings of Major Works): *A Grand Grand Overture,* for three vacuum cleaners, one floor polisher, four rifles, and full orchestra; *Grand Concerto Gastronomique,* for eater, waiter, and large orchestra; and *A Flourish for Orchestra, Fantasy for Audience and Orchestra.*

MAJOR WORKS (supplementary)

Band Music—Fantasy for Brass Band.

Chamber Music—Trevelyan Suite, for wind instruments; String Quartet No. 2; Sonata for Flute and Piano.

Choral Music—Song of Freedom, for treble voices and brass band; Return of Odysseus, cantata for chorus and orchestra.

Orchestral Music—Symphonies Nos. 6, 7, and 8; Sinfonietta No. 3, for flute, two oboes, two horns, and strings; A Sunshine Overture; Four Cornish Dances; Peterloo, overture; Anniversary Overture; Concerto for Two Pianos (three hands) and Orchestra; Concerto for Twenty-Eight Players; Concerto for Viola and Orchestra; The Fair Field, overture; Concerto No. 2, for flute and orchestra; Concerto No. 2, for clarinet and orchestra; Fantasy on a Theme of John Field, for piano and orchestra; Variations for Orchestra on a Theme of Ruth Gibbs.

Vocal Music—Two John Donne Songs.

ABOUT (supplementary)

Greenfield, E., Layton, R., and March, I., Penguin Stereo Record Guide (2nd edition); Schafer, R., British Composers in Interview; Sadie, S. (ed.), The New Grove Dictionary of Music and Musicians.

Kurt Atterberg

1887–1974

For biographical sketch, list of earlier works, and bibliography, see *Composers Since 1900.*

Kurt Atterberg died in Stockholm on February 15, 1974.

Louis Aubert

1877–1968

For biographical sketch, list of earlier works, and bibliography, see *Composers Since 1900.*

The exact date of Aubert's death in Paris is January 9, 1968.

ABOUT (supplementary)

Landowski, M., and Morançon, G., Louis Aubert, Musicien Français.

Georges Auric

1899–

For biographical sketch, list of earlier works, and bibliography, see *Composers Since 1900.*

At the sacrifice of his works for concert hall and stage, Auric has continued to be one of France's most prolific composers for motion pictures, one of which, *Thérèse et Isabelle,* was released in the United States. While in New York in 1978 to see the world premiere of his ballet *Tricolore* (given by the New York City Opera Ballet), Auric explained this involvement with films in an interview with Royal S. Brown of the New York *Times:* "I feel it is a perfectly valid form of artistic expression. There is an immense audience. And while you can't ask every filmgoer to be a musician, you can at least reach a certain number of them." However, he later revealed: "Now that I am an old man, I've decided to return to concert music before it gets too late, since I don't work very fast."

From 1968 to 1970 Auric was president of the International Society of Authors and Composers. In 1979 he was also voted honorary membership in the American Academy and Institute of Arts and Letters. He is an Officer of the French Legion of Honor and a Commander of Arts and Letters in the Order of Academic Palms in France.

MAJOR WORKS (supplementary)

Ballet—Tricolore.

Chamber Music—Imaginées I–IV, for various solo instruments and piano (flute, cello, clarinet, and viola).

Piano Music—Double Jeux, for two pianos.

Babbitt

ABOUT (supplementary)
New York Times, June 25, 1978.

Milton Babbitt

1917–

For biographical sketch, list of earlier works, and bibliography, see *Composers Since 1900.*

Babbitt's *Relata II* received its world premiere in New York on January 16, 1969, with Leonard Bernstein conducting the New York Philharmonic Orchestra (which had commissioned the work). "Relata" is a term from philosophy and logic that signifies interrelationships or responses. *Relata II* had been preceded by *Relata I* (1965). As Babbitt explained in an interview with Joan Peyser of the New York *Times:* "*Relata I* started as one work but grew into two large related movements. I spent fifteen months writing *Relata II,* finishing it a full two months before rehearsals." The world premiere was originally scheduled for October 17, 1968. At the first rehearsal, however, composer and conductor discovered that because of the complexity of the music, numerous errors had crept into the copied parts, forcing Bernstein to make corrections while rehearsing. An additional problem was the need for highly detailed and intensive rehearsals. "There are six measures . . . no two of which are alike," explained Babbitt. "If each measure were to be practiced for only five minutes—a minimal requirement of a Chopin piano piece—we would need fifty hours to rehearse this composition." A decision was finally made to delay the premiere by several months, thereby allowing the copyist time to redo the parts correctly and making more rehearsal time possible. Babbitt said, "The piece, of course, is a difficult one; I treat the orchestra as a large ensemble with many octave doublings creating problems of intonation because they occur in intricate rhythm combinations. There are also questions of relative dynamic projection. With *Relata II,* I have tried to exploit the most subtle resources of a most sophisticated orchestra." After the premiere finally took place, Harold C. Schonberg noted in the New York *Times:* "It is one of those dense, incredibly complicated, atonal, athematic, arrhythmic pieces that were so in vogue five years ago. . . . Whatever the emotional value of *Relata II,* it is as if nothing else delicately organized, and it was obvious the orchestra was making heavy going of it. At the end, some of the audience reacted violently, as if discovering original sin. Then the cheering section set in."

Highly complex music written for traditional instruments—as opposed to Babbitt's electronic compositions—is also encountered in two significant string quartets. String Quartet No. 4 was commissioned and introduced by the Fine Arts Quartet in Chicago on May 4, 1970. A critic for *High Fidelity/Musical America* called it "an extraordinary composition, as fresh and inventive in its basic musical material as it is logical in organization of this material." No less effective in structure and originality of materials is the String Quartet No. 4, commissioned by the Elizabeth Sprague Coolidge Foundation and first performed on October 31, 1970, by the Claremont Quartet in New York.

On February 10, 1979, in New York City, Babbitt's *A Solo Requiem,* for soprano and two pianos, received its first performance, with Bethany Beardslee as soloist. The text was taken from six poems on the subject of death by Shakespeare, Dryden, and George Meredith, among others, and the work was written in memory of Bethany Beardslee's husband and the composer's friend, Godfrey Winlan. John Rockwell said in the New York *Times,* "One doesn't ordinarily think of this composer's music in emotional terms, so bristling is it with technical teeth. . . . In any case, the emotions of Mr. Babbitt's requiem—primarily anger, bitterness and a grim resignation—were more suited to his style than consoling, transcendentally hopeful lamentations might have been."

A retrospective concert of Babbitt's music was given at Columbia University in New York on March 24, 1976, in celebration of his sixtieth birthday. The program spanned forty years of Babbitt's creativity, ranging from songs written in the 1930s to the String Quartet No. 4.

While fulfilling his obligations as William Shubael Conant Professor of Music at Princeton University, Babbitt has, since 1972, served as a member of the composition faculty of the Juilliard School of Music in New York. In 1977 and 1978 he was visiting member of the faculty at the Rubin Academy in Jerusalem. He made a tour of colleges in the United States and Hawaii as a visiting scholar sponsored by Phi Beta Kappa in 1972–1973 and, in 1972, was the Whidden Lecturer at McMaster University in Hamilton, Ontario.

He received honorary doctorates in music from Swarthmore College in Pennsylvania (1969) and the New England Conservatory in Boston (1972). In addition, he was awarded the Creative Arts Medal by Brandeis University in Massachusetts (1970) and then in June 1976 the National Music Award in Chicago from the Music Industry for "extraordinary contribution to the development and performance of American music." He was appointed Fellow of the American Academy of Arts and Sciences in 1974 and a member of the committee of the Elizabeth Sprague Coolidge Foundation in 1977.

MAJOR WORKS (supplementary)

Chamber Music—String Quartets, Nos. 3 and 4; My Ends Are My Beginnings, for solo clarinet (alternating with bass clarinet).

Choral Music—More Phenomena, for mixed chorus.

Electronic Music—Occasional Variations, for synthesized tape; Phenomena, version for soprano and tape; Reflections, for piano and synthesized tape; Images, for saxophone and synthesized tape.

Orchestral Music—Arie da Capo, for chamber orchestra; Concerto for Violin and Orchestra.

Vocal Music—A Solo Requiem, for soprano and two pianos; Four Canons; Three Theatrical Songs.

ABOUT (supplementary)

Rosenberg, D. and B., The Music Makers.

New York Times, January 12, 1969; Perspectives of New Music (Babbitt Issue), vol. 15, no. 2, 1976.

Henk Badings

1907–

For biographical sketch, list of earlier works, and bibliography, see *Composers Since 1900*.

Several of Badings' principal choral works have received premieres since 1969. These include the *Cantata VII* (Johannesburg, South Africa, November 22, 1970); *Klaagsang,* for mixed chorus and orchestra (Capetown, South Africa, May 31, 1971); *St. Mark Passion* (Rotterdam, Holland, May 15, 1972); and *Cinq Poèmes Chinois* (Festival of Cork, Ireland, May 3, 1973). Among the world premieres of Badings' instrumental works, heard in the United States, were the Concerto for Three French Horns and Wind Orchestra (Pittsburgh, Pennsylvania, June 29, 1967); *Transitions,* for wind orchestra (Urbana, Illinois, January 13, 1973); and the Concerto for English Horn and Orchestra (New York City, January 25, 1978).

Among Badings' recent awards are: honorary citizenship of New Martinsville in West Virginia, United States (1965); the Wagenaar Prize in The Hague, Holland (1971); the RAI Italia Prize for *Cantata VII* (1971); and the Sweelinck Prize of the Dutch government for his overall creativity (1972).

In 1972, Badings resigned as professor of composition at the High School of Music in Stuttgart, Germany. Since 1972, he has resided at his country seat "Hugten," near Maarheese, at the southern border of The Netherlands.

MAJOR WORKS (supplementary)

Chamber Music—4 sonatas for two violins in the 31-tone temperament; String Quartet No. 4; Toccata For Marimbaphone; Piano Quartet; Trio, for alto flute, viola, and harp; Piano Quintet; Variations on Seiklos Skolion, for two violins.

Choral Music—Cantata VII, for vocal soloists and chorus; Klaagsang, for chorus; Cantata VIII, for narrator and chorus; Cinq Poèmes Chinois, for a cappella chorus; Trompetstemmung, madrigal for male chorus.

Electronic Music—Pittsburgh Concerto, for eighteen instruments and magnetic tape; Tower Music, for wind orchestra and tape; Concerto for wind orchestra, three horns, and tape; Concertino, for piano and two electronic sound tracks; Armageddon, for soprano and magnetic tape; St. Mark Passion, oratorio for vocal soloists, male chorus, and magnetic tape; Apparizioni II, for organ and magnetic tape; Kontrapunkte, for piano and magnetic tape.

Orchestral Music—12 additional symphonies; Concerto for Viola and String Orchestra; Concerto for Violin, Viola and Orchestra; Concerto No. 2, for organ and orchestra; Ragtime, for wind orchestra; Concerto for Two Violins and Orchestra; Old Dutch Christmas Carol, for wind orchestra; Five Dutch Dances; Concerto for Three French Horns and Orchestra; Sinfonietta, for chamber orchestra; Transitions, for wind orchestra; Concerto for English Horn and Orchestra; The Windmills of Lieshout, for wind orchestra; Nederlandse Dansen, for chamber orchestra.

Organ Music—Canzone, for French horn and organ; Dialogues, for flute and organ; Quempas, for violin and organ; Variations on a Dutch Theme; Apparizioni I; Ricercare; Archifonica.

Piano Music—Quaderni Sonori; Balletto Notturno, for two pianos.

Vocal Music—Oud Nederlandse Liedern, three songs

for voice, flute, and harp; Fünf Reich-Lieder, for voice and piano; Najaarsnacht, for voice and piano.

Tadeusz Baird

1928–

For biographical sketch, list of earlier works, and bibliography, see *Composers Since 1900*.

In 1966, Baird completed *Tomorrow,* a one-act lyric opera based on a story by that name by Joseph Conrad in which a love rivalry ends in the murder of the son by his father. This opera was introduced at the "Warsaw Autumn," the International Festival of Contemporary Music in Warsaw, on September 10, 1966. At the International Society for Contemporary Music, in Warsaw, on September 29, 1968, Baird's *Five Songs,* for mezzo-soprano and chamber orchestra, received its world premiere.

Baird's *Goethe-Letters,* a cantata for baritone, chorus, and orchestra, was given its first hearing in Dresden on June 6, 1971; the Concerto for Oboe and Orchestra was introduced in Warsaw on September 23, 1973, by Lothar Faber for whom it was written; and in November, 1973, *Rapsoden,* for orchestra, was premiered in Ottawa, Canada, having been commissioned by the National Arts Center of Canada.

On another commission from the Center for a piece to commemorate the 500th anniversary of the birth of the Polish astronomer, Copernicus, Baird completed the *Elegy,* for orchestra, in 1973. It was introduced that same year in Ottawa and received its American premiere on December 6, 1974, in New York. Speight Jenkins described it in the New York *Post* as "solemn and dirge-like. . . . Tone clusters can be heard, but the overall effect is of totally centered melodic writing applied to some eerie and interesting use of strings and percussion."

Concerto Lugubre, for viola and orchestra, received its initial performance in Nuremberg, Germany, on May 21, 1976. The 22nd "Warsaw Autumn" in mid-September 1978, presented the world premiere of *Scenes for Cello, Harp and Orchestra,* performed by Klaus and Helga Storck with Antoni Wit conducting the Cracow Radio and TV Orchestra. Bain Murray reported on it in *High Fidelity/Musical America:* "Against a shimmer orchestral background of

minimal, sustained clusters and occasionally sparkling colors, the solo cello soared with much splendid material encompassing the instrument's entire range, with the harp often echoing it. Baird's penchant for quick shifts of mood—from declamatory to lyric—was evident."

Among Baird's awards are the Prize of the Union of Polish Composers (1966); the Polish State Prize (1970); the Prize of the Alfred Jurzykowski Foundation in New York (1971); the Koussevitzky International Award (1974); and the Arthur Honegger Prize (1974).

MAJOR WORKS (supplementary)

Chamber Music—Play, for string quartet; String Quartet Variations.

Choral Music—Goethe-Letters, cantata for baritone, chorus, and orchestra.

Opera—Tomorrow, one-act lyric drama.

Orchestral Music—Sinfonia Breve; Symphony No. 3; Psychodrama; Elegy; Concerto for Oboe and Orchestra; Concerto Lugubre, for viola and orchestra; Scenes, for Cello, Harp, and Orchestra; Concerto for Oboe and Orchestra; Rapsoden.

Vocal Music—Four Love Sonnets, for baritone and chamber orchestra.

ABOUT (supplementary)

Maciejewski, B. M., Twelve Polish Composers.

Cleveland Orchestra Program, September 23, 1965; New York Philharmonic Program, December 1, 1963.

Sir Granville Bantock

1868–1946

For biographical sketch, list of earlier works, and bibliography, see *Composers Since 1900*.

ABOUT

Bantock, M., Granville Bantock: a Personal Portrait

Samuel Barber

1910–1981

For biographical sketch, list of earlier works, and bibliography, see *Composers Since 1900*.

Heinz Hall, a new concert auditorium, was inaugurated in Pittsburgh, on September 10,

1971, with a performance by the Pittsburgh Symphony Orchestra under William Steinberg. For this occasion, Barber, commissioned by the Alcoa Foundation, wrote *Fadograph of a Yestern Scene* (the title is from a line in James Joyce's *Finnegan's Wake*). "The composer seems to have taken it [Joyce's line] literally," noted Allen Hughes in the New York *Times,* "producing a quiet impressionistic work that might have come from a musical era long since past. It is pretty music, skillfully wrought."

On September 22, 1980, another Barber world premiere took place, in Philadelphia: *The Lovers,* for baritone, chorus, and orchestra, was performed by the Philadelphia Orchestra, conducted by Eugene Ormandy. The work had been commissioned by the Girard Bank of Philadelphia. At first, the directors of the bank balked at accepting a work that set to music the poetry of an avowed Communist, the Chilean poet, Pablo Neruda. However, Barber finally convinced them that the message of the nine poems was love and not Communism. Irving Kolodin in *Saturday Review* wrote, "His involvement with Neruda's celebrations of erotic love, in which the body of the beloved becomes a world of symbolism and a temple of pleasure, is replete with lovely sounds, artful exploitation of a motival element and finely shaded colorations."

Barber wrote *Three Songs,* Op. 45, for Dietrich Fischer-Dieskau, on commission from the Chamber Music Society of Lincoln Center in New York City and its world premiere took place on April 30, 1974. Speight Jenkins, in the New York *Post,* described the work as follows: "The first, 'Now Have I Fed and Eaten Up the Rose,' had a mysterious quality; the second, 'A Green Lowland of Pianos,' was filled with light bubbling humor; and the third, 'O Boundless Evening,' made lyric the substance of dreams."

When Zubin Mehta made his first appearance as musical director of the New York Philharmonic Orchestra on September 14, 1978, he presented the world premiere of Barber's *Essay No. 3,* which Barber had written in Italy earlier that summer on commission from the Merlin Foundation. This orchestral work was somewhat longer and more thematic than two earlier *Essays,* introduced in 1937 and 1942. Barber described the third *Essay* as "absolutely abstract music which is essentially dramatic in character," and explained that his aim above all was "to create a unity."

Barber's opera, *Antony and Cleopatra,* which had suffered a critically disastrous premiere on September 16, 1966, when it opened the new auditorium of the Metropolitan Opera, was radically revised and drastically cut both in libretto and music. The new version was introduced by the Juilliard American Opera Center in New York on February 6, 1975. What emerged, said Harriett Johnson in the New York *Post,* "was a music drama of greatly heightened power and effectiveness."

A revised production of Barber's first opera, *Vanessa* (first produced at the Metropolitan Opera in 1958) enjoyed a substantial success at the Spoleto Festival at Charleston, South Carolina, on May 27, 1978. The performance was filmed for television and later shown over the facilities of the Public Broadcasting Service in January 1979.

"Capricorn," the two-winged house in Mt. Kisco, New York, which Barber shared with Gian Carlo Menotti for thirty years, was sold in 1973. Barber then acquired an apartment in New York City and a villa at Santa Cristina in the Italian Dolomites near the Brenner Pass. Barber confessed, "It has affected me very much, this business of selling 'Capricorn.' Of course, I love the place in the Dolomites . . . but I can't stay there for more than three months in the summer and a few weeks in the winter. It's just too boring. So, in a way, I'm homeless."

Barber's seventieth birthday was celebrated by the Chamber Music Society of Lincoln Center in New York several weeks prematurely on January 13, 1980, with a performance of his *Summer Music,* for wind octet. On the actual date of his birth (March 9) the Curtis Institute in Philadelphia presented two all-Barber concerts. Further commemoration of his birthday took place at the White House on March 11 when Rosalynn Carter presented him with the Wolf Trap Award. Among many other birthday tributes in the United States and Europe were an all-Barber chamber-music concert in London in July and a Barber program later that summer at the Festival of Naples. On August 24, 1980, Barber was presented with the MacDowell medal.

In his last years, Barber suffered from cancer, making composition difficult and reducing his productivity. Released from the University Hospital in New York City on January 18, Barber died in his New York apartment five days later, on January 23, 1981.

Barraud

MAJOR WORKS (supplementary)

Chamber Music—Sonata, for two violins and piano.

Orchestral Music—Fadograph of a Yestern Scene; The Lovers, for baritone, mixed chorus, and orchestra; Meditations from Bach; Essay No. 3; Canzonetta, for oboe and orchestra.

Piano Music—Ballade.

Vocal Music—Three Songs, Op. 45, for voice and piano.

ABOUT (supplementary)

Musical America, September 1974; New York Times, October 3, 1971, January 26, 1979, January 24, 1981 (obituary); Opera News, May 1978.

Operas—La Fée aux Miettes (radio); Le Roi Gordogane, chamber opera; Alceste; Tête d'Or.

Orchestral Music—Symphonie Concertante, for trumpet and orchestra; Three Etudes for orchestra; Une Saison en Enfer, suite; Variations à Treize, for chamber orchestra; Ouverture pour un Opéra Interdit; Concerto for Strings.

Vocal Music—La Divine Comédie, cantata for vocal quartet and an ensemble of old and modern instruments.

ABOUT (supplementary)

Goléa, A., Vingt Ans de Musique Contemporaine; Vinton, J. (ed.), Dictionary of Contemporary Music.

La Table Ronde (Paris), special Barraud Issue, July 1961.

Henri Barraud

1900–

For biographical sketch, list of earlier works, and bibliography, see *Composers Since 1900.*

Barraud's *Symphonie Concertante,* for trumpet and orchestra, and his *Three Studies,* for orchestra, received their world premieres in Paris on April 10, 1966, and February 1969, respectively, in performances by l'Orchestre Philharmonique de l'ORTF (Ensemble Ars Nova), with Charles Brück conducting. The cantata, *L'Enfance à Combourg,* after a work by Chateaubriand, was given its first hearing over Radio-France on March 17, 1976, and *Alceste,* an opera based on the tragedy by Euripides, was broadcast by Radio-France in December 1977. The chamber opera, *Le Roi Gordogane,* with a libretto by Radovan Irsie, was first produced on January 4, 1979, by the Bordeaux Opéra.

Since 1969, Barraud has written and published *Les Huit Chefs d'Oeuvres de Théatre Lyrique* (1971) and *Les Cinq Grand Opéras* (1972).

In 1967, Barraud received the Grand Prix National de la Musique. In 1976, the Société des Auteurs, Compositeurs et Editeurs de Musique (SACEM) awarded him the Grand Prix de la Musique Symphonique.

MAJOR WORKS (supplementary)

Chamber Music—Quartet, for saxophones.

Choral Music—L'Enfance à Combourg, cantata for children's chorus, two pianos, and two percussion instruments.

Béla Bartók

1881–1945

For biographical sketch, list of earlier works, and bibliography, see *Composers Since 1900.*

The centenary of Bartók's birth was commemorated in 1981 with performances of his major works throughout the music world. In New York, on March 23, 1981, the Detroit Symphony under Antal Dorati presented an all-Bartók program, followed two days later (Bartók's actual birthday) with another Bartók program by the New York Philharmonic under Rafael Kubelik. Toward the end of May, the Abraham Goodman House in New York presented a Bartók festival covering all but his orchestral music.

A complete catalog of Bartók's works was published in London in 1970. All of Bartók's compositions were recorded in a thirty-nine disk edition in Budapest, and released in 1979.

ABOUT (supplementary)

Bartók, B., Béla Bartók's Essays; Demeny, J. (ed.), Béla Bartók's Letters; Dommett, K., Bartók; Helm, E., Bartók; Lendvai, E., Béla Bartók: An Analysis of His Music; Suchoff, B. (ed.), Béla Bartók's Essays; Szabolocsi, B. (ed.), Béla Bartók, Leben und Werk.

High Fidelity/Musical America (Bartok Issue), March 1981. Musical Quarterly, October 1972.

Leslie Bassett

1923–

For biographical sketch, list of earlier works, and bibliography, see *Composers Since 1900.*

Since receiving the 1966 Pulitzer Prize in music for his *Variations for Orchestra,* Bassett enjoyed his greatest success with *Echoes from an Invisible World,* three movements for orchestra (the title comes from Giuseppe Mazzini's definition of music). *Echoes from an Invisible World* was one of six compositions commissioned from six major American composers by the National Endowment for the Arts to commemorate America's bicentennial. Bassett completed this work in 1974 while on sabbatical leave from the University of Michigan and on a Guggenheim Fellowship. Its world premiere took place on February 27, 1976, with Eugene Ormandy conducting the Philadelphia Orchestra. It was subsequently performed by the Chicago Orchestra, the Los Angeles Philharmonic, the New York Philharmonic, the Boston Symphony, and the Cleveland Orchestra.

In describing his composition, Bassett said he aimed "to evoke something of the mystery of music and inviting possible reflections by the listener (perhaps after hearing the work) upon the remarkable force and eloquence of an art which, in spite of many illuminative studies of its physical properties and hundreds of scholarly analyses, remains elusive." He then added: "The title is suggestive, not descriptive. Only a few sounds could, by any stretch of the imagination, be called echoes: quiet tones that remain after a sharp attack in another instrument, repeating sounds that diminish in intensity following a sharp attack, etc. Much of the music springs instead from sources that are implanted within the score, yet are comparatively insignificant. One of the more obvious of these is the opening three-chord figure whose twelve tones recur in many guises throughout the work, and contribute to the formation of other sounds and phrases. The principle of unfolding and growth from small elements is basic to the work, as is the principle of return to them."

Characteristic of the acclaim with which the critics received this work is this review by James Felton in the Philadelphia *Evening Bulletin:* "Bassett uses his tone palette fully, sometimes weaving brasses or woodwinds in separate meshes of sound, beautiful to the ear." In the Philadelphia *Inquirer,* Daniel Webster noted that "the whole work is made from such attractive sounds and alteration of those sounds that it beguiles and soothes the listener and asks some poetic response."

In 1974, Bassett's Sextet for Piano and Strings (introduced by the Juilliard Quartet with John Graham and William Masselos at the Library of Congress in Washington, D.C., on April 17, 1972) received the Naumburg Foundation Recording Award.

In 1976 festivals of Bassett's music were held at Drake University in Des Moines, Iowa, and the University of Wisconsin at River Falls. The Drake festival was climaxed by *Forces,* whose world premiere had taken place at Drake University on May 1, 1973, for the dedication of its new Fine Arts Building.

Between 1969 and 1973, Bassett was the director of the Contemporary Music Performance Project at the University of Michigan; and from 1967 to 1970 he was a member of the policy committee of the Contemporary Music Project at the University. Since 1970, Bassett has been the chairman of the composition department at the University of Michigan School of Music, where, in 1977, he was named Albert A. Stanley Distinguished University Professor; and in 1973, he was guest composer at the Berkshire Music Center at Tanglewood in Massachusetts. He received a Guggenheim Fellowship in 1980 and in 1981, he was elected to membership in the American Academy and Institute of Arts and Letters.

Bassett's extra-musical interests are reading and gardening.

MAJOR WORKS (supplementary)

Band Music—Sounds, Shapes and Symbols.

Chamber Music—Music for Saxophone and Piano; Sextet, for piano and strings; Sounds Remembered, for violin and piano; Soliloquy, for solo clarinet; Twelve Duos, for two or four trombones; Wind Music, for wind sextet; String Quartet No. 4.

Choral Music—Moon Canticle, for chorus, narrator, and solo cello; Celebration in Praise of Earth, for narrator, chorus, and orchestra; Notes in the Silence, for chorus and piano; Hear My Prayer, O Lord, for two-part children's or women's chorus and organ; Of Wind and Earth, for chorus and piano; Prayers for Divine Service, for four-part male chorus and organ.

Electronic Music—Collect, for chorus and electronic tape; Three Studies in Electronic Sounds; Triform.

Orchestral Music—Colloquy; Forces, for solo violin, cello, and piano and orchestra; Echoes from an Invisible World; Concerto for Two Pianos and Orchestra.

Piano Music—Elaborations.

Vocal Music—The Jade Garden, four songs for soprano and piano; Time and Beyond, for baritone, clarinet, cello, and piano; Love Songs, for soprano and piano.

ABOUT (supplementary)

Asterisk, a Journal of New Music, May 1976; BMI, Many Worlds of Music, July 1966; Bulletin of the National Association of Teachers of Singing, December 1975; Who's Who in America, 1980–1981.

Marion Bauer

1887–1955

See *Composers Since 1900.*

Sir Arnold Bax

1883–1953

For biographical sketch, list of earlier works, and bibliography, see *Composers Since 1900.*

To honor the memory of Bax on the twenty-fifth anniversary of his death, the newly founded Society for British Music in New York featured one of his compositions at each of six concerts in 1978–1979. The first concert, on November 17, 1978, offered Bax's Sonata for Viola and Piano, performed by Emanuel Vardi and Abba Bogin. The work was described by Peter G. Davis in the New York *Times* as "a piece of some harmonic originality and melodic power conjuring up the kind of mysterious Celtic atmosphere that was Bax's stock in trade."

ABOUT (supplementary)

Sadie, S. (ed.), The New Grove Dictionary of Music and Musicians; Scott-Sutherland, C., Arnold Bax.

Music and Letters (London), January 1971; Recorded Sound (London), January-April 1968.

Conrad Beck

1901–

For biographical sketch, list of earlier works, and bibliography, see *Composers Since 1900.*

Beck's *Die Sonnenfinsternis,* cantata for solo alto and instruments, was first performed in Lucerne, Switzerland, on August 25, 1967; his *Fantasie,* for orchestra, was introduced by the Basel Chamber Orchestra under Paul Sacher on March 19, 1970; *Élégie,* a cantata for solo soprano and orchestra, with a text taken from the poetry of Friedrich Hölderlin, was given its first hearing in Basel on December 13, 1973; and the Concerto for Wind Quintet and Orchestra was first heard on August 31, 1977, in Baden-Baden, Germany.

In 1964, Beck was awarded the Kunstpreis der Stadt Basel. He is a Commandeur de l'Ordre du Merité Culturel in Monaco and an honorary member of the Basler Kammerorchester.

His principal hobby is mountaineering.

MAJOR WORKS (supplementary)

Chamber Music—Sonata a Quattro, for violin, flute, oboe, and clarinet; Dialogue, for two doublebasses; Facetten, three impromptus for trumpet and piano; Sonatine, for viola and piano; Duettino, for two clarinets.

Orchestral Music—Concerto for Clarinet and Orchestra; Fantasie; Kammerkonzert; Mouvements Lyriques, for cello and chamber orchestra; Drei Episoden, for chamber orchestra; Concerto for Wind Quintet and Orchestra.

Vocal Music—Die Sonnenfinsternis, cantata for solo alto, flute, clarinet, harpsichord, and string orchestra; Élégie, cantata, for solo soprano and chamber orchestra.

ABOUT (supplementary)

Larese, D. and Schuh, W., Conrad Beck: eine Lebenskizze der Komponist und sein Werk.

Melos (Germany), June 1971.

Paul Ben-Haim

1897–

For biographical sketch, list of earlier works, and bibliography, see *Composers Since 1900.*

In 1968 Ben-Haim was decorated by the German Federal Republic with the Cross of Merit,

First Class. He has served as honorary president of the League of Israeli Composers.

Since 1972, when he was a victim of a traffic accident that caused serious injury, Ben-Haim has withdrawn from all teaching and other professional obligations.

MAJOR WORKS (supplementary)

Chamber Music—Divertimento Concertante, for flute solo and instruments; Three Pieces, for cello solo; Prelude, Fugue and Epilogue, for violin, viola, cello, and harp; Chamber Music, for flute, viola, and harp.

Choral Music—Friday Evening Service, for soprano, baritone, chorus, and organ; Six Sephardic Songs.

Orchestral Music—Fanfare for Israel; Rhapsody, for piano and chamber orchestra; Symphonic Metamorphosis of a Bach Chorale; Sonata for String Instruments.

Piano Music—Music for Piano.

Vocal Music—Myrtle Blossoms from Eden, for soprano, alto, and piano.

ABOUT (supplementary)

Paul Ben-Haim (a brochure which does not identify the author, published in Tel-Aviv in 1967).

Arthur Benjamin

1893–1960

For biographical sketch, list of earlier works, and bibliography, see *Composers Since 1900.*

Benjamin's one-act opera, *The Prima Donna,* was successfully revived at the Salzburg Festival in Austria on August 1, 1971. In the United States, his *Romantic Fantasy,* for violin, viola, and orchestra, was revived on February 27, 1976, by the Philadelphia Orchestra, conducted by Eugene Ormandy, with Joseph de Pasquale and William de Pasquale as soloists. The Concerto for Harmonica and Orchestra was revived on August 27, 1978, by the Cleveland Orchestra under Richard Hayman, with Larry Adler as soloist.

Richard Rodney Bennett

1936–

For biographical sketch, list of earlier works, and bibliography see *Composers Since 1900.*

Richard Rodney Bennett's opera, *Victory,* commissioned by the Friends of Covent Garden, had a successful introduction at the Royal Opera House at Covent Garden in London on April 18, 1970. The libretto, written by Beverly Cross, was adapted from Joseph Conrad's novel. Frank Granville Barker reported in *Opera* that "The score is cleverly cast in three atmospheric styles —percussion and rhythmically harsh for the outer world represented by the sailors' hotel in Surabaya; voluptuous in its string sonorities for Heyst's island [Polynesian] retreat in the Java Sea; and racily tuneful in Victorian musical comedy pastiche for the hotel's ladies' band. The composer has turned in a skillful atmospheric score conceived in lyrical, serialism-without-tears terms. As a piece of theater which holds the attention, it certainly works."

Bennett's Concerto for Guitar and Chamber Ensemble was heard for the first time on November 18, 1970, in London; the Concerto for Oboe and Strings, on June 6, 1971, at the Aldeburgh Festival in England; and the Concerto for Viola and Orchestra, on July 3, 1973, at York University in England.

As a tribute to Benjamin Britten on his sixtieth birthday, Bennett wrote *Concerto for Orchestra,* whose world premiere took place in Denver, Colorado, on February 25, 1974, in a performance by the Denver Symphony Orchestra conducted by Brian Priestman. This Concerto borrows its principal theme from a twelve-tone row from Britten's *Cantata Academica,* and a fox-trot and blues are some of the diverse material included in the opening movement, "Aubade." "The Bennett work is filled with tensions and contrasts," wrote Harriett Johnson in the New York *Post* when the visiting Denver Symphony introduced the Concerto in New York. "There is nothing jolly or really relaxed in this music, and if the high strings do momentarily seem to have moments of repose, they are not for long. The work is constantly in action. . . . The music is packed with dissonance and uses serial technique freely, linking them at points with an obscure sense of tonality."

To honor the American bicentennial, Bennett wrote *Zodiac,* on commission, for the National Symphony Orchestra of Washington, D.C., which introduced it on March 30, 1976, with Antal Dorati conducting. For the occasion of Queen Elizabeth II's silver jubilee, Bennett was commissioned by the London Celebration Committee to write a three-movement orchestral work, *Serenade.* It was heard first on April 24, 1977, in a performance by the orchestra of the Royal College of Music under Sir David Willcocks. Bennett was the soloist in the world premiere of his Concerto for Harpsichord and Orchestra which he wrote for the St. Louis Symphony. It was introduced on December 4, 1980.

Bennett's *Actaeon,* for horn and orchestra, had its American premiere in December 1979 by the Cincinnati Symphony Orchestra under Walter Susskind, with Barry Tuckwell as soloist. This performance was taped on December 7, 1979, for transmission in October 1980 by the National Public Radio System.

Bennett remained a prolific and significant contributor of music to the screen. Some of the later notable motion pictures for which he provided the background music were: *Secret Ceremony; The Go-Between; Nicholas and Alexandra,* (the score was nominated for an Oscar); *Lady Caroline Lamb; Sherlock Holmes in New York; Murder on the Orient Express* (the score received the Ivor Novello Award in England and was nominated for an Oscar); *Equus* (the score received a British Association of Film and Television Arts [BAFTA] nomination); *The Brinks Robbery;* and *Yanks.* From the score of *Nicholas and Alexandra* came the popular hit song, "Too Beautiful to Love," made successful by Engelbert Humperdinck; and from the score of *Murder on the Orient Express,* the popular song, "Silky."

Bennett served as visiting professor at the Peabody Conservatory in Baltimore in 1971. In 1977 he received the decoration of Commander of the Order of the British Empire.

Efficient and methodical, Bennett is also gregarious, a lively conversationalist, and interested in books, the movies, calligraphy, and American popular music. "I love to play old Tin Pan Alley tunes on the piano," he revealed. "I have a collection of old sheet music of Gershwin,

Porter, Arlen and all those are the epitome of the lyric approach."

MAJOR WORKS (supplementary)

Chamber Music—Wind Quintet, Scena II, for cello; Oboe Quartet; Travel Notes, Books I and II, for string quartet; Scena III, for solo clarinet; Sonata for Horn and Piano; Sonata for Violin and Piano.

Choral Music—Two Carols; The House of Sleep, for six male voices; Devotions, for a cappella chorus; Spells, for soprano, chorus and orchestra.

Electronic Music—Night Piece, for soprano and magnetic tape.

Guitar Music—Impromptus.

Opera—All the King's Men, children's opera; Victory.

Orchestral Music—2 piano concertos; Jazz Pastoral; Concerto for Oboe and String Orchestra; Concerto for Guitar and Chamber Orchestra; Party Piece, for piano and orchestra; Commedia I and II; Concerto for Orchestra; Concerto for Viola and Chamber Orchestra; Commedia III and IV; Concerto for Violin and Orchestra; Zodiac; Serenade; Actaeon (Metamorphosis I), for horn and orchestra; Music for Strings; Concerto for Double Bass and Orchestra; Sonnet to Orpheus; Concerto for Harpsichord and Orchestra.

Organ Music—Alba.

Piano Music—Scena I; Four-Piece Suite, divertimento for two pianos; Kandinsky Variations, for two pianos; Eustace and Hilda.

Vocal Music—Crazy Jane, for soprano, clarinet, cello, and piano; A Garland for Marjory Fleming, for soprano and piano; Tenebrae, for baritone and piano; Sonnet Sequence, for tenor and strings; Times Whiter Series, for countertenor and lute; The Little Ghost Who Died for Love, for soprano and piano.

ABOUT (supplementary)

Foreman, I. (ed.), British Music Now.

High Fidelity/Musical America, June 1977.

Robert Russell Bennett

1894–1981

For biographical sketch, list of earlier works, and bibliography, see *Composers Since 1900.*

Bennett wrote *The Fun and Faith of William Billings,* for chorus and orchestra, to commemorate the American bicentenary. It was introduced by the National Symphony Orchestra of Washington, D.C., and the University of Maryland Chorus at the Kennedy Center for the Performing Arts in Washington, D.C., on April 29, 1975. *Four Carol Cantatas,* for chorus, were written to celebrate the one hundredth anniversary of the First Presbyterian Church of Orlando, Florida, where the work was first heard on December 24, 1976. *Easter Story,* a cantata for chorus and orchestra, was introduced in Orlando during Easter Week of 1978.

Bennett is the author of *Instrumentally Speaking* (1975), a textbook on the subject of orchestration. He died in New York City on August 18, 1981.

MAJOR WORKS (supplementary)

Band Music—Four Preludes; Autobiography.

Choral Music—The Fun and Faith of William Billings, for chorus and orchestra; Four Carol Cantatas; The Easter Story, cantata, for chorus and orchestra.

Orchestral Music—Concerto for Guitar and Orchestra.

Alban Berg

1885–1935

For biographical sketch, list of earlier works, and bibliography, see *Composers Since 1900.*

The world premiere of the completed *Lulu,* staged by Patrice Chereau, took place on February 24, 1979, at the Paris Opéra, with Pierre Boulez conducting; a recording of this production was awarded the World Disk Prize by an international jury of music critics during the 1980 Festival in Montreux, Switzerland.

Up until this time, *Lulu* had been heard only in a truncated version that included only a fragment of the third act, which is the way it had been performed the first time by the Metropolitan Opera on March 18, 1977. Actually, Berg left a considerable amount of material for the third act, about three-fifths of it completely orchestrated and the rest with detailed sketches and specific indications of his intentions. In 1977 George Perle, an American composer and authority on Berg, had inspected the manuscripts at the office of Berg's publisher, and thought that it would be relatively simple to complete the opera. However, Berg's widow, Helene, refused to allow any of the third-act material to be released. One report was that she insisted she was in regular communication with her dead husband who had expressed the wish that the opera be performed only in its unfinished state.

Another report maintained that Helene Berg had always considered the subject matter of *Lulu* repulsive and a reminder of her husband's infidelity and for this reason stubbornly withheld any of the third-act manuscript.

Helene Berg died on August 10, 1976 and her will reaffirmed her refusal to allow anyone to see the original third-act material. In spite of the will, Universal Editions called upon Friedrich Cerha to prepare a complete third act from Berg's manuscripts, and it was with Cerha's adaptation that the opera was produced in its Paris world premiere. "Naturally, the third act makes a difference to *Lulu*—rather several differences," wrote David Hamilton in his review of the recording made of the Paris premiere in *High Fidelity/Musical America:* "First of scale: *Lulu* is now an opera of nearly three hours' length, some forty minutes longer than the old version with its ersatz Act III. Then, a difference of shape, for the palindromic aspect of the action—Lulu's symmetrical rise and fall—now comes into its own as the opera's principal structural motion. Previously, we had all of her rise, but only parts of the fall." The American premiere of the completed opera, *Lulu,* took place in Santa Fe, New Mexico, on July 28, 1979. The Metropolitan Opera premiere of the revised opera in New York on December 12, 1980, was telecast from its stage over the facilities of the Public Television Service eight days later.

Recent musicological research on Berg's chamber-music masterwork, the *Lyric Suite,* long considered an abstract work with no extramusical implications, revealed that the piece actually is a deeply felt personal document, testimony to the great secret love of Berg's life, Hanna, wife of Prague industrialist, Herbert Fuchs-Robettin. Berg first met her in 1925 when he was forty and had been married to Helene for fourteen years. Although few people were aware of the affair, and although no mention of it occurs in earlier Berg biographies, his passion for Hanna evidently dominated the rest of his life. This revelation, and the strange relationship between the *Lyric Suite* and Berg's secret love, was detailed by Peter G. Davis in the New York *Times* on March 27, 1977. Evidence to support this contention was found by the musicologist, Douglass M. Green, who deciphered a handwritten text for a never-performed last movement: a complete setting for voice of Baudelaire's poem *"De Profundis Clamavi,"*

31

which was a tortured expression of hopeless love and by George Perle in January 1977 in an annotated pocket score of the *Lyric Suite* which Berg had presented to Hanna and which was in the possession of her daughter.

ABOUT (supplementary)

Berg, E. A. (ed.), Alban Berg, Leben und Werk in Daten und Bildern; Carner, M., Alban Berg: The Man and the Work; Grun, B. (ed.), Alban Berg: Letters to His Wife; Jarman, D., The Music of Alban Berg; Monson, K., Alban Berg; Perle, G., The Operas of Alban Berg, vol. I.

New York Times, March 27, 1977, July 9, 1978, October 5, 1980, January 11, 1981; Opera News, April 12, 1969, April 2, 1977.

William Bergsma

1921–

For biographical sketch, list of earlier works, and bibliography, see *Composers Since 1900.*

Bergma's *Wishes, Wonders, Portents and Charms,* for chorus and instruments—commissioned by the New York State Council on the Arts and the National Chorale—received its world premiere at Lincoln Center for the Performing Arts in New York on February 12, 1975. With lyrics drawn from the works of Walt Whitman, Herman Melville, Sir Walter Scott, and from Ecclesiastes, this three-part choral work touches successively on the themes of childhood, maturity, and death. John Rockwell reported in the New York *Times* that "All three interrelate, and there is something simultaneously childlike and despairing throughout. . . . The music is simply diatonic and supported by only a few instruments, but the way Mr. Bergsma makes use of his forces sounds fresh and attractive."

With *In Space,* for soprano and instruments, Bergsma made an excursion into wit and whimsy. The arrangement inside the Seattle (Washington) studio where the piece was introduced on May 21, 1975, was unusual: "a cube draped in black, with catwalks running around its sides and projecting across the ceiling," as Wayne Johnson described it in the Seattle *Times.* "Bergsma placed four woodwind players on the catwalks. The rest of the dozen players (strings, percussion, oboe and harmonica) are placed far

apart from each other in clusters on the stage floor." At the beginning of the piece, the players seemed to be tuning up. When the soloist (Marni Nixon) appeared, she walked around the catwalk imitating the various sounds of the woodwinds. Then, after coming to the stage, she delivered a vocalise. Wayne Johnson called the opening "witty and amusing" and the vocalise, "attractively lyrical and engaging."

Bergsma's *Second Symphony: Voyages* was introduced in Montana by the Great Falls Symphony Orchestra and Symphonic Choir, with H. Harvey Jewell as conductor, on May 11, 1976. On April 10, 1978, the Seattle Symphony, directed by Rainer Miedel and with Donald McInnes as viola soloist, performed *Sweet Was the Song the Virgin Sung: Tristan Revisited.* The work is in two unrelated parts, the first being a series of variations on a song by the seventeenth-century lutenist-songwriter, John Attey. The second part, a fantasia, was taken from Wagner's *Tristan and Isolde* and altered so radically that at times the original Wagnerian themes become unrecognizable. "The beauty of the work, which is tonal and conservative by contemporary avant-garde measures, lies not so much in its overall impact but in the smaller moments: the juxtaposition of instrumental colors, the interplay between viola and orchestra, the bravura writing for that much-neglected instrument," wrote R. M. Campbell in the Seattle *Post-Intelligencer.*

Bergsma was director of the School of Music at the University of Washington (Seattle) until 1971, after which he served there as professor of music. In 1972–1973 he was visiting professor of music at Brooklyn College in New York.

MAJOR WORKS (supplementary)

Chamber Music—Illegible Canons, for clarinet and piano; String Quartet No. 4; Clandestine Dialogues, for cello and percussion; Blatant Hypothesis, for trombone and percussion; Four All, for three instruments and percussion.

Choral Music—The Sun, The Soaring Eagle, The Turquoise Prince, The God, for chorus, brass, and percussion; Wishes, Wonders, Portents, Charms, for chorus and instruments.

Opera—The Murder of Comrade Sharik.

Orchestral Music—Concerto for Violin and Orchestra; Documentary Two: Billie's World; Changes, for solo woodwind quintet, harp, percussion, and strings; Changes for Seven, for solo woodwind quintet, harp, percussion, and strings; Second Symphony: Voyages;

Sweet Was the the Song the Virgin Sung: Tristan Revisited, variations and fantasy for viola and orchestra.

Vocal Music—In Space, for soprano and instruments.

ABOUT (supplementary)

Slonimsky, N. (ed.), Baker's Biographical Dictionary of Musicians (6th edition); Vinton, J. (ed.), Dictionary of Contemporary Music; Who's Who in America, 1980–1981.

Luciano Berio

1923–

For biographical sketch, list of earlier works, and bibliography, see *Composers Since 1900.*

To commemorate the 125th anniversary of the New York Philharmonic, Berio wrote one of his greatest successes: the *Sinfonia,* which was introduced in New York on October 10, 1968, with the collaboration of the Swingle Singers (a French pop vocal group, one of whose specialties was the "scat" singing of baroque and classical instrumental music in its own arrangements), and with the composer conducting. Berio pointed out that the four movements of this work "are not analogous to the movements of a classical symphony. The title, in fact, must be taken only in the etymological sense of 'sounding together' (of eight voices and instruments)." The first movement makes use of fragments from Claude Lévi-Strauss's *Le Cru et le Cuit,* an anthropological work that analyzes the symbolism of Brazilian myths. The second movement is a tribute to Martin Luther King. The third movement draws on a bewildering variety of sources, including excerpts from Samuel Beckett and James Joyce, political graffiti, recorded dialogue, brief quotations from various composers (among them, Schoenberg, Mahler, Berg, Debussy, and Stravinsky) and snatches of solfeggio. This part of the *Sinfonia* is, in fact, a tribute to both Gustav Mahler, "whose work seems to bear within it the weight of the entire history of music," Berio explained, and Leonard Bernstein "for his unforgettable performance of the *Resurrection Symphony. . . .* Quotations and references were chosen, not only for their real but also for their potential relation to Mahler." The final movement is a kind of coda, with texts drawn from material used in the preceding three parts. "How to describe all this?" inquired Harold C. Schon-

berg in the New York *Times.* "Music of the absurd, perhaps, or a new kind of *Walpurgisnacht.* But it moves, and it has a force and it never lets the attention down. In a way, this kind of composition is a synthesis making use of many of the schools of music that have come up since World War II, including serialism, Dada, electronic music and a touch of aleatory. It marks the beginning of consolidation. Berio's *Sinfonia . . .* is one of the musics of the future."

Berio later added a fifth movement to *Sinfonia,* and the entire five-movement composition was first heard in Los Angeles in May 1970, with Zubin Mehta conducting the Los Angeles Philharmonic Orchestra. The entire score of *Sinfonia* was also used for the ballet *That Is the Show,* produced by Norman Morrice for Ballet Rambert and first performed in London on May 7, 1971.

In 1971, Berio completed *Ora,* a companion piece to *Sinfonia,* with lyrics adapted by Berio and Maurice Essam from Virgil's *The Aeneid.* The work, commissioned by the Detroit Symphony Orchestra, was first performed on November 18, 1971, with the Swingle Singers as collaborating artists and the composer as conductor.

A much less successful experiment than *Sinfonia* was *This Means That,* presented at Carnegie Hall, New York, on February 17, 1970. The work was a mixture of lecture recital, vocal demonstration, and transcriptions from Bach, Satie, and Ravel, sung by the Swingle Singers. Members of the audience expressed their dissatisfaction by booing; some even left the hall midway in the performance. "This was a premiere unlike the ones attended by great demonstrations of the past," reported Harold C. Schonberg in the New York *Times,* "for there seemed nobody to demonstrate for the composer." A second performance of *This Means That* had been scheduled for a May 4 concert of the Composers Showcase Series in New York, but apparently discouraged by the reaction to the Carnegie Hall premiere, Berio decided to replace it with a concert of some of his earlier and more familiar works.

A generally negative reaction on the part of audience and critics alike greeted Berio's mixed-media spectacle, *Opera,* introduced on August 12, 1970, by the Santa Fe Opera (which had commissioned it). The title does not refer to the musico-dramatic structure but to the plural of "opus," and was intended by its composer to suggest a synthesis of ideas functioning on several different theatrical levels. Berio's libretto uses the sinking of the *Titanic* in 1912 as a symbol of the destruction of human society in a technological age. Using verbal, musical, and choreographic means, Berio places the action on three main levels, respectively entitled "Orpheus," "Titanic," and "Terminal." John Rockwell wrote in *Opera News,* "The first was a little hard to perceive at a first hearing; references to the sinking of the *Titanic* and the crushing of modern man's technological hubris recur constantly; and 'Terminal' is a remarkable theater piece created by Joseph Chaikin's Open Theater, parts of which (using the New York troupe) have been incorporated into *Opera.* There are many other persistently reappearing ideas—themes, short scenes, gestures and quotations, many of them overtly or slyly parodistic."

On March 12, 1971, Berio's *Memory for Electronic Piano and Electronic Harpsichord* was introduced in New York and performed by the composer and Peter Serkin. A few weeks later, on April 5, *Prayer,* a speech-sound event, was heard in New York in a premiere performance. The Concerto for Two Pianos and Orchestra (another commission from the New York Philharmonic) was heard on March 15, 1973, with Pierre Boulez as conductor and Bruno Canino and Antonio Ballista as soloists. Berio looks upon this work as "a voyage through a variety of instrumental roles and relationships, different functions and processes, during which each of the two pianos keeps returning to reexamine paths already trodden in order to repeat each step under a different perspective, thus transforming each repeated event into something unrecognizably new." In *The New Yorker,* Andrew Porter called it "a distinguished and attractive composition, easily enjoyed . . . [displaying] all of Berio's virtues. His command of graphic musical gesture and his control of musical time conspire to make the score unfold before us like so many 'scenes' of a drama." The RCA recording of this concerto (with Canino and Ballista as soloists, but with the composer conducting the London Symphony) received the Koussevitzky International Recording Award in 1977.

On April 21, 1976, the Cleveland Orchestra, with the composer conducting, offered an all-Berio program that featured the American premiere of *Calmo.* This work, for voice and thir-teen instruments, was completed in 1974 in memory of the Italian avant-garde composer and conductor, Bruno Maderna, who died one year earlier.

In 1975–1976, on commission from the West German Radio, Berio composed *Coro,* for voices and instruments, and its world premiere took place in Donaueschingen, Germany, on October 10, 1976, with the composer conducting. Berio subsequently revised this work, and the new version received its first hearing in London on September 1, 1977, again under the composer's direction. The American premiere took place on October 1, 1980, with Lorin Maazel conducting the Cleveland Orchestra and the Cologne Radio Chorus.

Scored for forty singers and forty instruments, this is not a traditional choral work, but, in the words of the composer, "an ensemble of forty musicians with forty singers, more like forty couples." Each singer, Andrew Porter explained in *The New Yorker,* has his own separate line. "Each singer sits or stands beside an instrument of roughly equivalent range, to constitute a symbiotic duo. The instruments plus two percussion batteries, an electric organ and a piano make up the orchestra." The music sets fragments of folk songs dealing with love, death, and work, combined with some of the writings of the Chilean poet, Pablo Naruda, "There are no quotations or transformations of actual folk songs (with the exception of Episode VI where a Yugoslav melody is used and Episode XVI where I quote a melody from my *Cries of London*)," the composer explained, "but rather here and there, there is a development of folk techniques and modes which are combined without any reference to specific songs. It is the musical function of those techniques and modes that is continuously transformed." In his review in *The New Yorker,* Andrew Porter said: "*Coro* . . . is a vastly ambitious score, simple in its ground plan, simple in its textual juxtapositions, but far from simple in its musical procedures. In ages hence, it may perhaps come to be regarded as a twentieth-century masterpiece—by a visionary, a creator, and a poetic, all-embracing and yet intensely personal musician with a wonderful ear."

Berio appeared as guest conductor of the Los Angeles Philharmonic Orchestra on January 25, 1979, to present the American premiere of his *Il Ritorno Degli Snovidiana,* for cello and orchestra. In *High Fidelity/Musical America,* Melody Peterson said it "proved a mellow exercise in acoustic contemporary techniques. ... Spun along on an often plaintive, always tortuous cello line and frequently shadowed by rumbling piano figurations, *Ritorno* crossed the line into outright demonstration only seconds before its ending."

On a commission from Dr. and Mrs. Ralph I. Dorfman for the San Francisco Symphony Orchestra in 1980, Berio wrote *Entrata,* which was introduced by Edo de Waart on October 1, 1980. The word "entrata" suggests a short opening ceremonial piece. Berio's work is a brilliant exercise in sonoric effects, "a joyous celebration of the modern symphony orchestra," Michael Steinberg, the program annotator for the San Francisco Symphony, wrote.

Berio left the faculty of the Juilliard School of Music in 1971 to take charge of the Electro-Acoustic Department of the Institut de Recherche et de Coordination Acoustique (IRCAM) in Paris. In 1976, he became the artistic director of the Accademia Filarmonica Romana in Rome.

MAJOR WORKS (supplementary)

Ballet—Per la Dolce Memoria di Quel Giorno.

Chamber Music—Sequenza V, for solo trombone; Sequenza VII, for solo oboe; Sequenza VIII, for percussion; Sequenza IX, for solo violin; Linea, for two pianos, vibraphone, and marimba; Points on the Curve to Find . . ., for piano and twenty-two instruments.

Choral Music—Questo Vuol Dire Che, for three female voices and small chorus; Magnificat, for two sopranos, chorus, and instrumental group; Coro, for forty voices and forty instruments.

Electronic Music—A-Ronne; Chants Paralleles; Prayer, a speech-sound event with magnetic tape.

Mixed-Media—Opera.

Orchestral Music—Sinfonia; Chemins IIb, Chemins IIc, for bass clarinet and orchestra; Chemins III, for viola, nine instruments, and orchestra; Chemins IV, for oboe and strings; Ora, for soprano, mezzo-soprano, flute, English horn, small chorus, and orchestra; Bewegung II, for baritone and orchestra; Concerto for Two Pianos and Orchestra; Still; Eindrücke; Il Ritorno Degli Snovidiana, for cello and ten instruments; Concerto for Cello and Orchestra; Entrata.

Piano Music—Wasserklavier; Erdenklavier; Memory, for electronic piano and electronic harpsichord.

Vocal Music—Melodrama, for tenor and instruments; El Mar Var, for mezzo-soprano and seven instruments; Agnus, for two sopranos and three clarinets; Folk Songs, for mezzo-soprano and large orchestra; Recital I, for mezzo-soprano and seventeen instru-ments; Cries of London, for six voices; Calmo, for soprano and instruments.

ABOUT (supplementary)

Sternfeld, F. W. (ed.), Music in the Modern Age.

Musical Quarterly, July 1975; New York Times, December 14, 1969, February 15, 1970, March 8, 1970, October 19, 1980.

Sir Lennox Berkeley

1903–

Sir Lennox Randal Francis Berkeley was born in Boars Hill, near Oxford, England, on May 12, 1903. He was the son of Captain Hastings George Berkeley, a naval officer, and Alina Carla Harris Berkeley. Through his mother, the boy learned to speak French at an early age: her parents had for many years lived in France and she often took him on visits to her family. Through his father, a music lover, who owned an entire set of Beethoven's piano sonatas on piano rolls, Lennox learned to love music. As a child, he could improvise on the piano and he developed the ability, without any instruction, to compose music. However, his parents did not intend a musical career for him, and thus he received a comprehensive academic education at Gresham's School in Holt, St. George's School in Harpenden, and, between 1922 and 1926, at Merton College in Oxford where he studied philology, French, and Old French. Nevertheless, he did not neglect his talent for composing, and while at Merton he even managed to take lessons on the organ from W. H. Harris.

Maurice Ravel saw some of Berkeley's compositions and advised him to go to France for formal musical instruction. In Paris, between 1927 and 1932, Berkeley studied counterpoint, ear training, and musical analysis with Nadia Boulanger. During these years, his friendship with Ravel ripened. He also became a close friend of Francis Poulenc and through him made the acquaintance of Stravinsky, Honegger, Milhaud, and Roussel. The influence of the neo-classical Stravinsky and of Ravel and Poulenc was pronounced on Berkeley's Paris compositions, which included songs, piano pieces, the First String Quartet, Overture for light orches-

---

Berkeley: bärk′ lĭ

SIR LENNOX BERKELEY

tra, and an oratorio, *Jonah.* The first string quartet, three impromptus for piano, and the song "How Love Came In," all written in 1935, were published.

The Overture was performed at the International Society for Contemporary Music Festival in Barcelona on April 23, 1936. It was at this festival that Berkeley met the twenty-two year old Benjamin Britten, one of whose compositions had been performed two days before. While in Barcelona Britten and Berkeley decided to collaborate on a four-movement suite for orchestra based on Catalan folk tunes they had heard one day in a park. Each composer wrote two movements. "It would only be possible for two composers who are fairly close to each other in style and outlook to do something like this successfully," Berkeley remarked. This suite, named *Mont Juic* for the Barcelona park, was published in 1937.

Berkeley returned to England in 1935, settling in London where, on June 17, 1938, a psalm for chorus and orchestra, *Domini est Terra,* was introduced at the International Society for Contemporary Music Festival. Later in the 1930s his ballet, *The Judgement of Paris,* was given in London by Sadler's Wells. His most important work for orchestra during this period was the *Serenade,* for string orchestra (1939).

Between 1942 and 1945 Berkeley was employed at the B.B.C., in charge of programs in the music division. In his wartime compositions his creative individuality was beginning to emerge, particularly in its virile harmonic writing and in the individuality and expressiveness of his melodic line (although the French influences of clarity, transparency, and light texture, and that of Stravinsky's neo-classicism, still prevailed).

One of his most significant works of the war period was the Symphony No. 1, whose world premiere Berkeley conducted at a Promenade concert in London on July 8, 1943. When a recording of this symphony was released in 1978, Richard Freed, writing in *Stereo Review,* called it "a splendid work. . . . While this symphony is thoroughly of its time in terms of coloring and the shapes of themes, a classical character is felt in the broadly expressive opening movement, the dancelike Allegretto that takes the place of a scherzo, the impassioned slow movement and the brilliant and boisterous finale." Other wartime compositions of note were his second string quartet, a Nocturne for orchestra, a piano sonata (written for and introduced by Clifford Curzon), a string trio and a viola sonata. Discussing these compositions, Wilfred F. Mellers wrote in Grove's *Dictionary of Music and Musicians:* "While the influence of Stravinsky remains dominant . . . the music has acquired much greater lyrical force than is observable in his Parisian works. At times this lyricism suggests the remote influence of the late work of Mahler. The melodic element is now convincingly fused with the harmony; indeed the subtlety and occasional richness of the harmony depend on the melodic freedom of the inner parts."

In 1946, the year in which he married Elizabeth Freda Bernstein, with whom he later had three sons, Berkeley received the Collard Fellowship in Music and was appointed professor of composition at the Royal Academy of Music in London where he remained until 1968. After World War II, Berkeley turned more actively to writing music for the voice, for which he demonstrated an uncommon aptitude. In 1946, he wrote *Five Songs,* Op. 26 (to poems by Walter De la Mare) for Pierre Bernac, who introduced it at one of his recitals with Francis Poulenc at the piano. In 1947 he wrote the *Four Poems of St. Teresa,* for contralto and strings, which was introduced by Kathleen Ferrier, and the *Stabat Mater,* for six solo voices and twelve instruments, dedicated to Benjamin Britten. In instrumental music, he produced a distinguished Concerto for Piano and Orchestra (1947) and a

Concerto for Two Pianos and Orchestra (1948). Reviewing the latter work from its recording in 1978, Richard Freed said in *Stereo Review* it was "an entirely different sort of work [than the Symphony No. 1], though almost equally fascinating. There are only two movements. The first more or less corresponds to the old French overture . . . and the second, three times as long, in the form of a theme (of vaguely folklike character) and eleven variations, the seventh of which is a big luscious waltz *à la Ravel.*"

The *Four Ronsard Sonnets,* for two tenors and piano, was written in 1953 for Peter Pears who helped to introduce it in London on March 8, 1953; Berkeley revised it in 1977. On July 29, 1953, Concerto for Flute and Orchestra had its world premiere in London. A second symphony, commissioned by the Feeney Trust for the City of Birmingham Symphony—completed in 1958, and revised in 1977—was heard for the first time on February 24, 1959, in Birmingham.

The decade of the 1950s is often singled out by English musicologists as the opera decade for Berkeley. His first opera was *Nelson,* with a libretto by Alan Pryce-Jones, which was previewed in London on February 14, 1953 (with piano accompaniment), and given a complete stage presentation with orchestra by Sadler's Wells in London on September 22, 1954. "He has written music that is hearty and honest, without becoming cheap," remarked Cecil Smith in reporting on the premiere for *Musical America.*

His second opera, *A Dinner Engagement,* was a one-act comedy (libretto by Paul Dehn) in which an encounter takes place over the dinner table at the home of a former ambassador and his wife, the guests including a Grand Duchess and her son from the country to which the ambassador had once been accredited. Much of the dialogue concerns gastronomy but the librettist left room for a good deal of purely lyrical music. The world premiere, which took place at the Aldeburgh Festival, was performed by the English Opera Group on June 17, 1954. Since then, the little opera has become popular in performances in schools and over television. When the English Opera Company performed it in London not long after the Aldeburgh premiere, Cecil Smith spoke of the "lightness of its humor and the urbanity of Paul Dehn's blithe libretto," in *Musical America.*

Ruth, Berkeley's third opera of the 1950s, was also in one act. The work, introduced by the English Opera Group in London on October 2, 1956, has a libretto by Eric Crozier which was based on the Book of Ruth.

A fourth opera, again in one act, appeared a decade later. *Castaway,* with a libretto by Paul Dehn, concerned the amatory involvement of Odysseus and Nausicaa. The world premiere took place at the Aldeburgh Festival on June 3, 1967.

Since 1960, Berkeley has continued to produce major works for the concert hall. Yehudi Menuhin presented the world premiere of the Concerto for Violin and Orchestra at the Bath Festival in 1961. Symphony No. 3, commissioned by the Cheltenham Festival, was also introduced there in 1969. Symphony No. 4, commissioned by the Royal Philharmonic Orchestra of London, was given its premiere by that orchestra in May 1978. *Magnificat,* for chorus and orchestra, was heard at the City of London Festival in 1968. *Windsor Variations* for orchestra was written in 1969; the third string quartet in 1970; *Sinfonia Concertante,* for oboe and orchestra, in 1973; the guitar concerto in 1974, performed as part of the City of London Festival in 1975; some vocal music, including "Judica Me," between 1975 and 1978.

Berkeley visited Australia in 1975 in connection with his presidency of the Performing Rights Society in Great Britain. In 1976 he visited the United States for the first time to attend the world premiere of his Quintet for Piano and Winds, commissioned and introduced by the Lincoln Center Chamber Music Society of New York on January 30, 1976. During this visit he also attended a performance of his *Mass for Five Voices* (1964) at St. Thomas' Church in New York and a concert of his chamber music in Minneapolis where he lectured music students at the University of Minnesota.

Lennox Berkeley has written incidental music to two Shakespearean plays produced at Stratford-on-Avon: *The Tempest* (1946) and *A Winter's Tale* (1960); music for two B.B.C. documentaries in 1943 and 1952; and music for the British films *Hotel Reserve* (1944); *Out of Chaos* (1944); *The First Gentleman* (1947–1948), and *Youth in Britain* (1957).

As one of Great Britain's leading composers, Berkeley has been the recipient of many honors. In 1957 he was made a Commander, Order of the British Empire, and in 1962, he received the

Cobbett Medal in London for his contributions to chamber music. In 1967, he was given the Ordre de Merite Culturel from Monaco and in 1973 the Papal Knighthood of St. Gregory in Italy. He was knighted in 1974, the year in which he was also made honorary fellow of Merton College, Oxford. In 1975 he was given an honorary professorship at the University of Kiel where he had opened a new department of music.

On his seventieth birthday, in 1973, he was named Composer of the Year by the Composers Guild of Great Britain. On his seventy-fifth birthday, a concert of his music was held at the Queen Elizabeth Hall in London, and there were additional performances of his works given over the B.B.C. and at the Cheltenham Festival (together with the world premiere of his already mentioned Symphony No. 4 by the Royal Philharmonic Orchestra of London).

For many years, Sir Lennox Berkeley has lived with his family in a riverside part of London known as Little Venice. He maintains that his sole form of recreation is reading.

MAJOR WORKS

Ballet—The Judgement of Paris.

Chamber Music—3 string quartets; String Trio; Viola Sonata; Theme and Variations, for violin solo; Elegy, for violin and piano; Toccata, for violin and piano; Trio, for violin, horn, and piano; Sextet, for clarinet, horn, and string quartet; Concertino, for flute (or treble recorder), violin, cello, and harpsichord (or piano); Sonatina, for oboe and piano; Diversions, for eight instruments; Quartet, for oboe and string trio; Introduction and Allegro, for double-bass and piano; Duo, for cello and piano; In Memoriam Igor Stravinsky, for string quartet; Quintet, for Winds and Piano.

Choral Music—Jonah, oratorio for solo voices, chorus, and orchestra; Domini est Terra, psalm for chorus and orchestra; Gibbons Variations, for tenor, chorus, strings, and organ; Salve Regina, for unison voices and organ.

Guitar Music—Sonatina; Theme and Variations.

Opera—Nelson; A Dinner Engagement (one act); Ruth (one act); Castaway (one act).

Orchestral Music—4 symphonies; Serenade, for string orchestra; Concerto for Piano and Orchestra; Sinfonietta; Concerto for Flute and Orchestra; Suite for Orchestra; Concerto for Piano and Double String Orchestra; Overture, for light orchestra; A Winter's Tale, suite; Five Pieces, for violin and orchestra; Concerto for Violin and Chamber Orchestra; Partita, for chamber orchestra; Signs in the Dark, for soprano, tenor, alto, bass, and strings; Magnificat, for soprano, tenor, alto bass, and orchestra; Windsor Variations, for

chamber orchestra; Dialogue, for cello and chamber orchestra; Palm Court Waltz; Sinfonia Concertante, for oboe and orchestra; Voices of the Night; Antiphon, for string orchestra; Suite for Strings; Concerto for Guitar and Orchestra.

Organ Music—Three Pieces; Fantasia.

Piano Music—Theme and Variations; Mazurkas; Scherzo; Sonatina, for two pianos; Improvisations on a Theme of Falla; Prelude and Fugue, for clavichord; Theme and Variations, for piano duet; Prelude and Capriccio.

Vocal Music—Five Songs, to poems by Walter De la Mare, for medium voice and piano; Four Poems of St. Teresa of Avila, for contralto and strings; Stabat Mater, for six solo voices and twelve instruments; Three Greek Songs, for medium voice and piano; Four Ronsard Sonnets, Sets 1 and 2, for two tenors and piano; Five Poems of W. H. Auden, for medium voice and piano; Missa Brevis, for soprano, alto, tenor, bass, and organ; Mass, for five voices; Songs of the Half-Light, for high voice and guitar; Three Songs, for four male voices; Chinese Songs, for medium voice and piano; Hymn for Shakespeare's Birthday, for soprano, alto, tenor, bass, and organ; Herrick Songs, for high voice and harp; The Lord Is My Shepherd, for soprano, alto, tenor, bass, and organ; The Hill of Graces, for soprano, alto, tenor, bass, and organ; Another Spring, for voice and piano; Judica Me, for soprano, alto, tenor, and bass.

ABOUT

Dickenson, P., Lennox Berkeley, Composer; Dickenson, P., Twenty British Composers; Schafer, M., British Composers in Interview; Searle, H., and Layton, R., 20th Century Composers: Britain, Scandinavia, the Netherlands.

The Listener (London) May 10, 1973; Musical Times (London), November 1968, May 1978; New York Times, February 1, 1976.

Leonard Bernstein

1918–

For biographical sketch, list of earlier works, and bibliography, see *Composers Since 1900*.

The Kennedy Center for the Performing Arts in Washington, D.C. was formally opened on September 8, 1971, with the world premiere of Bernstein's *Mass*, written on commission for this occasion. The text came from the liturgy of the Roman Mass with additional material by Bernstein and Stephen Schwartz. Described as "a theater piece for singers, players and dancers," the *Mass* probes the function of religion in the modern world, with a score that encompasses folk music, church chorales, show tunes, rock, revivalist hymns, band music, and ballads, in styles reminiscent of Ives, Stravinsky and others. The central character is named Celebrant who has been seen variously to represent the clergy, Christ, Everyman, Youth, and Religion. He appears on the stage dressed in blue jeans and a denim work shirt, singing "A Simple Song," a hymn of praise to God, accompanying himself on the guitar. As the *Mass* progresses, the voices of doubt and protest are loudly sounded, touching on such subjects as the Vietnam War, the assassinations of President Kennedy, Senator Kennedy and Reverend Martin Luther King, and the response of the Establishment to the pacificism of the Berrigan brothers.

Probably no Bernstein composition up to this time provoked such conflicting reactions among the critics. Some regarded the *Mass* as vulgar, pretentious, or sacrilegious; the music, a confusing hodge-podge of many disparate styles and idioms, frequently made intolerable through over-amplification and the frequent use of loud pre-recorded tape. Others found the *Mass* to be a spellbinding spectacle, an overwhelming emotional and theatrical experience, and a penetrating commentary on religion and orthodoxy.

On the whole, the affirmative voices outnumbered the negative ones. Peter G. Davis wrote in *High Fidelity* Magazine, "the *Mass* is a brilliant piece of theatrical entertainment—the original dramatic creative exuberance of it all literally leaves one's head spinning. But there is a great deal more operative here than smooth show-biz glitter, and aside from the deeper emotional responses provoked by the piece's spiritual tone. ... *Mass* functions as an extremely sophisticated, carefully controlled musical entity that repays close scrutiny."

In the Washington *Post,* Paul Hume did not hesitate to call the *Mass* "the greatest music Bernstein has written" and described the work as "a shattering experience that signally honors its creator, the Center, and the memory of the man for whom the Center is named."

The *Mass* was staged by the Vienna State Opera in Austria on February 16, 1981, with the text translated into German. Bernstein suffered two serious musical setbacks after the *Mass.* A ballet, *The Dybbuk Variations,* with choreography by Jerome Robbins, was introduced by the New York Ballet Theater in New York on May 16, 1974. Based on a Yiddish play by S. Ansky,

its plot involved exorcism in a Hassidic community in Eastern Europe. This theme was not treated literally in the ballet, but various aspects were suggested in choreographic sequences, the emphasis being on atmosphere and mysticism. The music was in the form of free variations based on note sequences Bernstein identified as "rows," but not related in any way to the rows in serial music. While conceding that some of the ensemble dances were very well done, Clive Barnes wrote in the New York *Times,* that "elsewhere Mr. Robbins adopts the showbiz style padding of his composer, where the texture is too unvarying and the dance just a little too slick. Once in a while—not often but disconcertingly—you get a fleeting impression of seeing dance routines rather than choreography." Neither the ballet nor the symphonic suite derived from this score have acquired a foothold in the repertory. Later, in an interview by John Arodin of the New York *Times,* Bernstein admitted that *The Dybbuk Variations* was "a failure as the work I wanted it to be. This is not a criticism of Jerome Robbins, but of the fact the marriage between music and dance I had hoped for didn't occur."

The reception was even worse for Bernstein's first new score for Broadway since his 1957 *West Side Story.* The new musical was *1600 Pennsylvania Avenue,* with book and lyrics by Alan Jay Lerner. It opened in New York on May 4, 1976, and closed after seven performances. Subtitled "a musical about the problems of housekeeping," *1600 Pennsylvania Avenue* tried to tell the story of the White House during its first one hundred years through a backstairs view of the First Families. Last-minute doctoring and out-of-town rewriting failed to get the show in shape when it arrived. The critics were unanimous in their denunciation. Clive Barnes called it "tedious and simplistic"; in the New York *News,* Douglas Watts referred to it as "an impossible enterprise ... just one more bicentennial burden"; William B. Collins, writing for the Knight newspapers, called it "a heavy bloated gloom cloud of a show ... with no little spirit."

But if a new Broadway production was a failure, revivals of three older Bernstein musicals on Broadway proved to be successes: *On the Town* (October 31, 1971); *Candide* (March 8, 1974) with a new book by Hugh Wheeler and additional lyrics by Stephen Sondheim; and *West Side Story* (February 13, 1980).

Bernstein

Two Bernstein songs were heard at the Inaugural concert for President Carter at the Kennedy Center for the Performing Arts in Washington, D.C., on January 19, 1977. One, "Take Care of This House," was taken from *1600 Pennsylvania Avenue.* The other one was new: "To My Dear and Loving Wife" (with a 17th-century text by Anne Bradstreet), which Bernstein dedicated to President Carter's wife, Rosalynn.

On October 14, 1977, the National Symphony Orchestra in Washington, D.C. (conducted alternately by Mstislav Rostropovich and Bernstein) presented an all-Bernstein program with three works receiving their world premieres. *Slava!,* completed just four days before the performance, was a tribute to Rostropovich who is affectionately called "Slava" by his friends and family. Basic thematic material for the piece was taken partly from the score of *1600 Pennsylvania Avenue* and partly from the symphonic suite Bernstein had previously adapted from his background music for the 1954 motion picture *On the Waterfront.* The second new work, *Meditations,* for cello and orchestra, was based on musical ideas from Bernstein's *Mass.* The third premiere was the only work that was not derived from earlier Bernstein compositions. It was called *Songfest,* a cycle of twelve pieces (three sextets, two duets, six solo songs, one trio) for six singers and orchestra. The work, employing poems by Anne Bradstreet, Walt Whitman, Edgar Allan Poe, Gertrude Stein, Conrad Aiken, and other poets spanning some three hundred years, provided a picture of America's artistic past. It also served as a kind of psychological biography of Bernstein himself, touching on his creativity, loves, marriage, and sundry problems in a Puritan society. Andrew Porter wrote in *The New Yorker,* "Songfest has its own character—urban, just a shade slick, maybe, and a shade sentimental, but very attractive as soon as one decides that it has an honest heart. ... Any musician must respond to the sheer technical skill, the felicity of the facture—but it is more than that. It was rather like meeting someone who's been to charm school—and discovering a genuine, innate charm and warmth behind the polished formulae."

In celebration of its centennial season, the Boston Symphony commissioned Bernstein to compose *Divertimento for Orchestra.* It opened the orchestra's concert season on September 25, 1980, with Seiji Ozawa conducting. This work is a fifteen-minute suite comprised of eight short movements, including a mazurka, waltz, samba, turkey trot, blues, and a rousing march. Writing in the New York *Times,* Donal Henahan said: "The piece puts its tongue in cheek and keeps it there. ... Mr. Bernstein is a born entertainer of a superior sort, and a score such as his *Divertimento* is likely to outlive some of the more cerebral pieces that the orchestra's commissioning project will produce."

Although Bernstein had retired as music director of the New York Philharmonic Orchestra in 1969, he did not lack conducting assignments either in the United States or in Europe. (Moreover, as lifetime "laureate" conductor of the New York Philharmonic he often returned to its podium for guest performances.) In 1970, the Austrian government asked him to conduct Beethoven's *Fidelio* at the Theater-an-der-Wien in Vienna where the opera had been introduced as part of the festivities surrounding the two hundredth anniversary of Beethoven's birth. In April and May of 1971 he led the London Symphony in a special concert commemorating the first anniversary of Stravinsky's death, and the Vienna Philharmonic Orchestra in a Brahms cycle which was filmed for later transmission over television. On September 19, 1972, conducting a new production of *Carmen,* he inaugurated what had been planned as the Göran Gentele managerial epoch at the Metropolitan Opera in New York but which, due to Gentele's tragic death in an automobile accident, became the Schuyler G. Chapin regime. As Bernstein's protest against the Vietnam War he led a free concert of Haydn's *Mass in Time of War* at the Washington Cathedral in Washington, D.C. on January 19, 1973, at the same time as the official inaugural concert for President Nixon at the Kennedy Center. On June 23, 1973, he conducted his own *Chichester Psalms* from 1955 (sung in Hebrew) at the Vatican in Rome to honor the tenth anniversary of the ascension to the papacy of Pope Paul VI. On July 26, 1975, he made his debut at the Salzburg Festival in Austria in the dual role of conductor and pianist. In the fall of 1979, he conducted the visiting Vienna State Opera in performances of *Fidelio* in Washington, D.C. and New York City.

During the 1972–1973 academic year, Bernstein was Charles Eliot Norton Professor of Poetry at Harvard University. Six of his lectures, entitled "The Unanswered Question," were taped for television transmission by the Public Broadcasting Service and were published in book form in 1976.

In the spring of 1977, the Israel Philharmonic, on the occasion of its fortieth anniversary and in honor of Bernstein's thirty-year affiliation with it, presented a retrospective two-week festival of Bernstein's music in Tel-Aviv, Jerusalem and several smaller Israeli communities. During the course of the festival, every major Bernstein work was heard either in its entirety or in excerpts, including a revised version of his third symphony, *Kaddish* (1963).

Two other all-comprehensive Bernstein festivals were held in 1978 and 1979, at the Fine Arts Center of the University of Massachusetts in Amherst (June-July 1978) and in Kansas City, Missouri (May 1979).

Some of America's leading musicians gathered to celebrate Bernstein's sixtieth birthday in Washington, D.C., on August 25, 1978. Six conductors collaborated in performing Bernstein's music at a concert of the National Symphony, a live performance over the television network of the Public Broadcasting Service. After a movement from Beethoven's *Triple Concerto* had been performed by Menuhin, Rostropovich, and Arrau (with Bernstein conducting), they received a frenetic ovation and the audience burst into singing "Happy Birthday." William Schuman, host for the evening, recalled personal experiences with Bernstein at a reception for friends and colleagues which followed. Once again in celebration of Bernstein's birthday, Deutsche Grammaphon released new recordings of his three symphonies and the *Chichester Psalms* in a commemorative album.

In 1971, Bernstein earned a special "Grammy" from the National Academy of Recording Arts and Sciences for "bringing musical understanding to children and adults alike." Two years later, when the Israel Philharmonic celebrated the twenty-fifth anniversary of the founding of the state of Israel, Bernstein was presented with the King Solomon Award of the American-Israel Cultural Foundation. Bernstein became the first classical artist ever to receive the Golden European Trophy, an annual award usually given to popular musicians.

In addition, on December 7, 1980, Bernstein was one of the recipients of the third annual Kennedy Center Honors in Washington, D.C.,

for his significant contributions to American culture in the artistic field.

Bernstein's wife, Felicia Montealegre Cohn Bernstein, a former actress, died in East Hampton, New York on June 16, 1978. As a memorial, Bernstein established three scholarships in her name, one each for $50,000 at Columbia University, New York University, and the Juilliard School of Music to benefit students of acting, since Mrs. Bernstein had been an actress.

MAJOR WORKS (supplementary)

Ballet—The Dybbuk Variations.

Choral Music—Mass, a theatrical production for actors, singers, chorus, and orchestra.

Orchestral Music—Slava!, "a political overture"; Meditations, for cello and orchestra; Divertimento for Orchestra; Halil, for flute and orchestra.

Vocal Music—Songfest, song cycle for six voices and orchestra.

ABOUT (supplementary)

Ames, E. P., Wind from the West: Bernstein and the New York Philharmonic Abroad; Ewen, D., Musicians Since 1900: Performers in Opera and Concert; Gottlieb, Jack (ed.), A Complete Catalogue of Bernstein's Works.

High Fidelity/Musical America, August 1978; New York Times, January 25, 1970, April 17, 1977, December 11, 1977, November 26, 1978; New York Times Magazine, December 19, 1971.

Harrison Birtwistle

1934–

Harrison Birtwistle was born in Accrington, Lancashire, England, on July 15, 1934. His music study began with lessons on the clarinet. He entered the Royal Manchester College of Music on a scholarship in 1952 where he studied composition with Richard Hall. While he was at the College of Music, he and several other progressive young musicians (including Peter Maxwell Davies and John Ogdon) formed the New Music Manchester Group, dedicated to the performance of new music, with emphasis on the Viennese dodecaphonic school. Following a short period of military service, where he played in the Army band, Birtwistle entered the Royal Academy of Music in London and completed his

Birtwistle: bĕrt′ wĭsl

41

Birtwistle

HARRISON BIRTWISTLE

musical training in 1962. From 1962 to 1965 he was director of music at the Cranborne Chase School near Salisbury. A Harkness International Fellowship in 1966 made it possible for him to visit the United States for two years, the first one as visiting Fellow at Princeton University.

One of Birtwistle's earliest compositions, *Refrains and Choruses* (1957), for wind quintet, provides a clue to his later mature style. According to Bill Hopkins in the *Dictionary of Contemporary Music,* the work anticipates later compositions "in its processes of growth from a single note, its many homophonic passages, and its persistent use of repeated notes, unison sounds and octave relationships." Similar development, though with increasing complexity of style, can be found in *Monody for Corpus Christi* (1959) and in an untitled twelve-minute piece (1959) for soprano, flute, violin, and horn based on a text of 16th century English songs and presented at the Festival of the International Society for Contemporary Music in Vienna on June 15, 1961. Dominic Gill, writing in the London *Financial Times,* found the work to have the "same toughness and sharp lyrical edge, the same concentration of lyrical gesture which we have come to associate with his later music." Another of Birtwistle's early compositions that was well received was *The World Is Discovered* (1960), an instrumental motet for chamber ensemble, first heard on June 2, 1964, at the Festival of the International Society for Contemporary Music, held in Copenhagen.

Birtwistle attracted international attention with his one-act chamber opera, *Punch and Judy,* based on a children's puppet play. Commissioned by the English Opera Group, it was introduced at the Edinburgh Festival in Scotland on August 22, 1968; it received its American premiere in Minneapolis on January 30, 1970. The librettist, Stephen Pruslin, described this work as "a totally stylized and ritualistic drama" whose basis is "the opera of cruelty" in which Mr. Punch, in quest of his sexual ideal, murders his wife, throws a baby into a fire, murders a doctor and a lawyer, and manages to elude the hanging he deserves. For the score, Birtwistle borrowed material from his own *Tragoedia* (a work for wind quintet, harp, and string quartet which he had written in 1966 while he was at Princeton) and employed for the most part a post-Webern serialistic style. Peter Heyworth, reporting from Edinburgh to the New York *Times,* wrote that "Birtwistle's score is not really assimilable at first hearing. ... But on the second hearing the music seemed to open up like a flower in the sun. Where before there had been a predominant impression of aggressive harsh sounds, I began to perceive lyricism and even tenderness. Slowly the subtlety of some of the instrumental writing became apparent, and notably in little toccatas which serve as interludes of calm in this tale of violence. The vocal writing also begins to reveal an unsuspected melodic strength."

On commission from the London Sinfonietta, and through a grant from the Calouste Gulbenkian Foundation, Birtwistle completed *Verses for Ensembles* in 1969. This is an instrumental work for twelve players who are broken up into smaller groups and distributed spatially across the stage in seven different positions. When the work was introduced in London by the London Sinfonietta under David Atherton on February 12, 1969, the London *Daily Telegraph* wrote that it was "as engrossing in content as it is thrilling and shattering in sound—a color, variety and control of sound that leaves any electronic composition yet heard far behind." It was performed again on June 20, 1971, during the June festival weeks in Vienna, with Pierre Boulez conducting the London Sinfonietta. The London Sinfonietta also commissioned and introduced *Meridian* (1971), a forty-minute score for mezzo-soprano, chorus, and instruments, with text by Thomas Wyatt and Christopher Logue.

Among Birtwistle's most successful compositions are those he describes as "landscapes in music," in which his style consists of blocks of sounds (he calls them "objects") that he manipulates into extraordinary transformations. *An Imaginary Landscape,* for chorus and orchestra, had its premiere on June 2, 1971, at the Festival of the International Society for Contemporary Music in London with Pierre Boulez conducting the B.B.C. Symphony and Women's Chorus. Harold C. Schonberg described this work in the New York *Times* as "an angry sounding piece, with muttered interjections and powerful tonal jabs."

On June 2, 1972, the Royal Philharmonic Orchestra of London, conducted by Lawrence Foster, introduced another "musical landscape," *The Triumph of Time,* a prolonged funeral procession that had been commissioned by the Royal Philharmonic. This work had originally been set for a performance in 1971, but Birtwistle was dissatisfied with it and began over again. His inspiration for this music was a gruesome allegorical painting by the 16th century Flemish artist, Pieter Bruegel. "We are invited to watch a slow funeral cortège as it passes us by," according to program notes by Michael Hall. "As spectators and listeners we are involved and yet uninvolved with the action at one and the same time. . . . The funeral cortège may be symbolic and activate our empathy or horror, but it may also be an event moving towards us at a speed which allows us to contemplate only the gradual metamorphosis of visual planes. In other words we are observers of an event in slow motion." Birtwistle transferred the grim images of Bruegel's painting to highly discordant music that contained passages of affecting lyricism. In the London *Observer,* Peter Heyworth called this composition "one of the most important new works I have heard at the Festival Hall in recent years. . . . The music's real triumph lies in its unfaltering sense of movement. To sustain this over so long a period and at so slow a tempo . . . is an amazing achievement. From start to finish, the work treads like some implacable giant. . . . There are elements of greatness in this work." *The Triumph of Time* has become one of Birtwistle's most popular compositions. It was given its American premiere by the Houston Symphony in Texas, conducted once again by Lawrence Foster.

Another "musical landscape," *Melancolia I,* for clarinet, harp, and two string orchestras, was first performed in September 1976 at the University of Glasgow by Alan Hecker, clarinetist, with Alexander Gibson conducting the Scottish National Orchestra. This is a comparatively simple work in a sustained slow tempo. It involves an extended melody for the clarinet, with the harp as partner, to which antiphonal strings provide embroidery. "It proved enthralling, tremendous in performance," wrote Andrew Porter in *The New Yorker.*

Silbury Air, which Birtwistle wrote in 1977 on commission from the Koussevitzky Music Foundation, had its premiere in London in March 1977. It was introduced in the United States by the Chamber Music Society of Lincoln Center in New York City on October 14, 1977. This "musical landscape," which calls for eighteen instrumentalists, takes its title from Silbury Hill, a man-made prehistoric mound in Wiltshire whose origin is cloaked in mystery. The composer disavows any attempt to portray this particular landscape, insisting that the music presents a mysterious landscape of its own. While the earlier "landscape" pieces are in a slow tempo, *Silbury Air* moves so swiftly that it almost resembles dance music.

Birtwistle returned to the United States in 1973 to serve for a year as visiting professor of music at Swarthmore College in Pennsylvania and in 1975–1976 he was visiting Slee Professor at the State University of New York at Buffalo. In 1975 he was appointed Associate Director of Music at the National Theater in London, where he lives with his wife, Peggy, and their three sons.

MAJOR WORKS

Ballet—Frames, Pulses, and Interruptions.

Chamber Music—Refrains and choruses, for wind quintet; Three Lessons in a Frame, for flute, clarinet, violin, and cello; Linoi, for clarinet and piano; Verses, for clarinet and piano; Some Petals from the Garland, for piccolo, clarinet, viola, cello, and bells; Verses for Ensembles, for twelve players; Tombeau (in memory of Stravinsky), for flute, clarinet, and harp; Dinah and Nick's Love Song, for three saxophones and harp (or three English horns and harp); Grimethorpe Aria, for brass ensemble; Chorales from a Toyshop, for variable instruments; For O For O the Hobbyhorse is Forgot, for six percussion instruments.

Choral Music—Narration: the Description of the Passing of a Year, for a cappella chorus; Carmen Paschale, for chorus and organ; The Mark of the Goat, school cantata, for vocal soloists, narrators, chorus, and instruments; Meridian, for two sopranos, chorus,

Blacher

and instrumental ensemble; The Fields of Sorrow, for two sopranos, chorus, and instruments.

Electronic Music—Four Interludes from a Tragedy, for clarinet and pre-recorded tape; Chronometer: Chanson de Geste, for sustaining instruments and pre-recorded tape.

Opera—Punch and Judy, one-act chamber opera; Orpheus.

Orchestral Music—The World is Discovered, motet for chamber ensemble; Chorales; Three Movements with Fanfares, for chamber orchestra; Tragoedia, for wind quintet, harp, and string quartet; Nemos; Medusa, for chamber orchestra and percussion; The Triumph of Time; An Imaginary Landscape; Melancolia I, for clarinet, harp, and two string orchestras; Silbury Air, for woodwind quintet, trumpet, horn, trombone, string quintet, piano, harp, and percussion; Carmen Arcadiae Mechanicae Perpetuum.

Piano Music—Précis.

Theater—Down by the Greenwood Side, dramatic pastoral for soprano, mimes, speaker, and chamber ensemble; Bow Down, improvisational music-theater for musicians and actors.

Vocal Music—Monody for Corpus Christi, for soprano, flute, violin, and horn; Entr'actes and Sappho Fragments, for soprano, flute, oboe, violin, harp, and percussion; Ring a Dumb Carillon, for soprano, clarinet, percussion; The Visions of Francesco Petrarca, seven sonnets for baritone, chamber ensemble, and school orchestra; Cantata, for soprano, flute or picolo, clarinet, violin or viola, cello, piano or celesta; Nenia on the Death of Orpheus, for soprano, clarinet, crotales, and piano; Prologue, for tenor, bassoon, and instruments; Epilogue, "Full Fathom Five," for baritone, horn, and percussion; La Plage, eight arias of remembrance, for soprano, three clarinets, piano, and marimba.

ABOUT

Sternfeld, F. W. (ed.), Music in the Modern Age; Vinton, J. (ed.), Dictionary of Contemporary Music.

New York Times, June 23, 1968.

Boris Blacher

1903-1975

For biographical sketch, list of earlier works, and bibliography, see *Composers Since 1900.*

In 1971, Blacher resigned as director of the High School for Music in Berlin, and came to the United States in 1972 to lecture at the University of Southern California.

Blacher's last significant works included *Collage,* for orchestra, completed in 1968, and introduced by the Vienna Philharmonic on

October 5, 1969; and *Blues Espagnola and Rumba Philharmonica,* for twelve cellos, written in 1972–1973 at the suggestion of the cellist of the Berlin Philharmonic. In this work, Blacher once again revealed interest in popular idioms (having previously written several works in the jazz style). The work was premiered at the Waseda University in Tokyo on October 28, 1973; the German premiere followed on November 28, 1973, at a concert of the Berlin Philharmonic; and it was first performed in the United States by the Cleveland Orchestra under Lorin Maazel on January 8, 1976. (A tape of the Berlin Philharmonic performance had already been heard in the United States on December 27, 1975, over radio station WCLV in Cleveland.)

Blacher died in Berlin on January 30, 1975. "I saw Boris Blacher just a few weeks before his passing," recalled Lorin Maazel. "He had returned from the hospital, delighted to be able to make plans for the future. ... Blacher led the way for the Darmstadt darlings (Stockhausen, Boulez, Zimmermann, etc.); his was a primary influence in the use of music for films and television specials. ... Some of us are born to be young forever. Boris was one of these fortunate beings. He loved work, champagne, dogs, children, sounds, life, laughter." In Blacher's memory, Maazel directed the Cleveland Orchestra in an all-Blacher program on January 8, 1976.

Blacher was survived by his wife, Gerta Herzog, a concert pianist, whom he had married in 1945; they had four children.

Speaking of his own direction as a composer, Blacher once said: "Basically, a composer should write what is fun for him. In this, there exist many kinds of music: some easy, some hard to comprehend; some purely entertaining, some experimental. There are composers who take only one path or the other. That is ultimately a question of fateful determination. And then again there are others—among whom I count myself—who depending upon how it pleases them, compose sometimes in this way, sometimes in the other."

MAJOR WORKS (supplementary)

Chamber Music—String Quartet No. 4; Four Ornaments, for violin and piano; Piano Trio; Sonata for Two Cellos; Blues Espagnola and Rumba Philharmonica, for twelve cellos; Duo, for flute and piano; Quintet, for flute, oboe, and string trio.

Choral Music—Anacona; Vocalises.

Operas—Yvonne, Princess of Burgundy; The Secret of the Purloined Letters, chamber opera.

Orchestral Music—Collage; Concerto for Clarinet and Orchestra; Stars and Strings, for jazz ensemble and strings; Poème; Pentagram.

Piano Music—Twenty-Four Preludes.

ABOUT (supplementary)

Cleveland Orchestra Program, January 8, 1976.

Easley Blackwood

1933–

For biographical sketch, list of earlier works, and bibliography, see *Composers Since 1900*.

Blackwood's Piano Concerto was commissioned by the Illinois Arts Council and introduced on July 26, 1970, by the Chicago Symphony under the direction of Gunther Schuller at the Ravinia Festival. When this concerto was played at a concert of the New York Philharmonic under Pierre Boulez, Harold C. Schonberg of the New York *Times* wrote that it was a "strong work. . . . It has a great deal to say and is indicative of one way music is going these days."

Collaborating with Elliott Kaplan and Frank Lewin, Blackwood completed a multi-media opera in 1972, scored for 12-, 15-, 16-, and 23-note equal tempered tuning, produced on a Moog synthesizer. It was called *Four Letter Scenes from Gulliver*, with a text by Robert Karmon and Louis Phillips, based on Jonathan Swift's work. The world premiere was held on February 22, 1975, in Minnesota.

The Symphony No. 4, for 14 wind instruments, was introduced by the Chicago Symphony under the direction of Sir Georg Solti on November 22, 1978. The work was commissioned in 1970 by the Chicago Symphony to celebrate its eightieth anniversary. However, it took Blackwood six and half years to complete it, and the premiere had to be delayed. The composer explained, "I was able to advance only one or two measures a day, spending at least three hours in the process. At several points during the composition I felt it necessary to pause for a substantial period in order to weigh carefully the inferences of the continuation I was considering." Blackwood added that the three move-

ments in his symphony were "all conceived thematically, with transformations, variations and fluctuations in modality that are not unlike traditional classical forms. Uppermost in my mind as I composed the work was the creation of a harmonious musical design. . . . No conscious effort was made to express anything other than musical ideas."

Since this symphony was written for Solti and the Chicago Symphony, Blackwood was always conscious of the virtuosity and special sound of that orchestra. "That sound," observed John Von Rhein in the Chicago *Tribune*, "is predicated on a huge instrumentation that emphasizes the low winds. . . . If one takes away some of the layers of dissonance and readjusts the spacing of the various chords, many of Blackwood's great, striding climaxes would sound, I suspect, rather like Mahler or Strauss. The Romantic desire to create a big musical statement using mammoth forces clearly is there, even if the underlying esthetic is studiously anti-Romantic."

Robert C. Marsh discussed in the Chicago *Sun-Times* the immediate aspects of the music on first hearing: "the forceful beginning, for example, with some impressive brass writing and a strong counter-melody in the strings, and the soft, melodic pages with which the middle movement (a sort of combined slow movement and scherzo) fades away. The immediate impact of these pages was probably a major factor in the cordial reception the music received from the audience."

Blackwood, on the music faculty of the University of Chicago since 1958, was made a full professor in 1968. In 1978–1979 he left to serve as visiting professor of music at Webster College in St. Louis, on a grant from the National Endowment for the Humanities, in order to explore equal tempered tuning for thirteen through twenty-four notes, and to compose a piece in each of the twelve tuning systems.

MAJOR WORKS (supplementary)

Chamber Music—Sonata No. 2, for violin and piano.

Multi-media—Four Letter Scenes from Gulliver (with Elliott Kaplan and Frank Lewin).

Orchestral Music—Concerto for Piano and Orchestra; Symphony No. 4, for 14 wind instruments.

BIBLIOGRAPHY (supplementary)

Slonimsky, N., (ed.), Baker's Biographical Dictionary

Bliss

Sir Arthur Bliss

1891–1975

For biographical sketch, list of earlier works, and bibliography, see *Composers Since 1900.*

Bliss celebrated his seventy-fifth birthday on August 2, 1966, by attending a performance of his Piano Concerto, performed by John Ogdon at the Promenade concert in London; and a reception followed that evening. Bliss returned to the United States in 1968 to direct the New York Philharmonic on November 19th in the American premiere of his oratorio, *The Beatitudes,* written seven years earlier.

Mstislav Rostropovich conducted the premiere of Bliss's Concerto for Cello and Orchestra at the Aldeburgh Festival in England on June 24, 1970. On April 21, 1973, Bliss's *Variations for Orchestra* was introduced in London, with Leopold Stokowski conducting.

In 1971, Bliss was made Commander, Order of the British Empire. His last composition was *Shield of Faith,* a choral work whose premiere took place posthumously in 1975 at Windsor, England, in a ceremony celebrating the 500th anniversary of the St. George's Chapel. Bliss died in London on March 27, 1975.

MAJOR WORKS (supplementary)

Choral Music—Shield of Faith, oratorio for solo voices, chorus, and orchestra; Sing, Mortals!, for chorus and organ.

Orchestral Music—Concerto for Cello and Orchestra; Metamorphoric Variations, for orchestra.

Vocal Music—Angels of the Mind, song cycle for voice and piano; The World Is Charged With the Grandeur of God, cantata for voice and piano.

ABOUT (supplementary)

Bliss, A., As I Remember; Foreman, L. (ed.), Arthur Bliss: a Catalogue and Critical Survey.

Marc Blitzstein

1905–1964

For biographical sketch, list of earlier works, and bibliography, see *Composers Since 1900.*

Blitzstein's one-act opera, in thirteen short scenes, *Idiots First,* was left unfinished by his death and completed by Leonard Lehrman. It was introduced at Indiana University in Bloomington on March 14, 1976, and produced in New York on January 22, 1978. One of Blitzstein's most deeply emotional and human works, it is based on a short story of Bernard Malamud in which the central character is an old Jew who will not succumb to Death before making provisions for his thirty-five-year old demented son. In *Opera News,* Stephen Casale wrote: "The music for this powerful story does it full justice, and its unlikely mixture of Viennese expressionism and American musical-theater lyricism, particularly in the sensitive setting of the speech rhythms of Yiddish-American English, is expertly handled." In the New York *Times,* Peter G. Davis described the music as "unusual for Blitzstein" in that it was "in a chromatically dissonant idiom, yet it is always effective, intensely expressive and eminently vocal."

Blitzstein's opera *Regina* (1949) was revived at the Houston Grand Opera in Texas on April 25, 1980.

ABOUT (supplementary)

Gruen, J., Close-Up; Mellers, W. H., Music in a New Found Land; Sadie, S. (ed.), The New Grove Dictionary of Music and Musicians.

Opera News, April 12, 1980.

Ernest Bloch

1880–1959

For biographical sketch, list of earlier works, and bibliography, see *Composers Since 1900.*

Bloch's *America,* an epic rhapsody for chorus and orchestra—rarely heard since its premiere in 1928—was revived for the American bicentennial by the Cleveland Orchestra under the direction of Lorin Maazel on April 13, 1976. This performance was taped and televised in a ninety-minute tribute to Bloch by the Public

Broadcasting Service series, "Music in America."

Bloch's archives were established at the Library of Congress in Washington, D.C., in July 1975. His Guadanini violin was presented to the American-Israel Cultural Foundation on December 5, 1967, to be loaned to a gifted Israeli scholarship violinist selected by violinist Isaac Stern.

In commemoration of the centenary of Bloch's birth, an exhibit of his memorabilia, including rare pictures of and by the composer, was held in 1980 at the Music Museum in Haifa, Israel, at the Spoleto Festival, in Charleston, South Carolina, and in Miami Beach, Florida. Performances of Bloch's music were given in the United States in his honor, including an all-Bloch concert in New York City on April 21, 1980.

ABOUT (supplementary)

Heskes, I., and Bloch, S., Ernest Bloch: Creative Spirit; Kushner, D. Z., Ernest Bloch and His Music; Strassburg, R., Ernest Bloch: Voice in the Wilderness.

Music Magazine (Toronto), December 1980; New York Times, April 20, 1980.

Karl–Birger Blomdahl

1916–1968

For biographical sketch, list of earlier works, and bibliography, see *Composers Since 1900.*

Blomdahl died of a heart attack in Kungsängen, Sweden and his ashes were strewn over nearby Lake Mälaren. His *Altisonans,* an electronic sound-picture (1966), which combines ornithological sounds and static noise from outer space, received its world premiere at the Festival of Art and Technology in Stockholm on September 4, 1966. It was performed posthumously at the Festival of the International Society for Contemporary Music in Warsaw on September 27, 1968.

MAJOR WORKS (supplementary)

Electronic Music—Altisonans.

ABOUT (supplementary)

Musical Quarterly, January 1972.

Pierre Boulez

1925–

For biographical sketch, list of earlier works, and bibliography, see *Composers Since 1900.*

Although the critics accepted Boulez's *Pli Selon Pli,* a portrait of Mallarmé, as his masterwork, sixteen years passed before its world premiere in the United States. It took place in New York on February 15, 1978, at a concert of the Contemporary Chamber Ensemble conducted by Arthur Weisberg. Andrew Porter of *The New Yorker* called it "a towering masterpiece. . . . It is the best piece that came out of those adventurous and prolific years—not just the work in which new techniques were most elegantly and lucidly refined and formulated, but the most beautiful, most poetic, richest product of the time."

Boulez explained that in translation, the title means "fold by fold, a portrait of Mallarmé." In this five-part composition of one hour's duration, Improvisations I, II and III, the middle three movements, are fantasias rather than specific settings of three poems by Mallarmé, for soprano and chamber ensemble. The two remaining movements, scored for orchestra, are "Don" ("Gift") and "Tombeau" ("Tomb"), which begin and end respectively with a line from Mallarmé, sung by the soprano. "It builds slowly from the initial vocal 'announcement' through the hesitant music of the 'Don,' through the three sonnets (the last of which is the most discursive, summing up, as it were, the first two) to the final 'Tombeau,' which is the structural analogue to the final movement of a nineteenth-century symphony," wrote a critic in *Musical America.* "Here the full orchestra, with its shifting layers of sound, sweeps all before it and draws all that preceded into a conclusive statement."

Boulez made his debut in electronic music with *Explosante/Fixe* (dedicated to Stravinsky). It is scored for flute, clarinet, trumpet, violin, viola, cello, harp, vibraphone (each equipped with a floor microphone), and an electronic machine called the Halaphone, which was invented for Boulez by Peter Haller, a German engineer. The Halaphone was described by Jane Perlez in the New York *Post* as "a cross between a telephone operator's switchboard and a sophisticat-

47

ed computer housed in a gray cabinet casing. . . . From the programming of the machine, the sounds are projected in various directions and at various speeds—moving in circles around the hall or moving diagonally across the hall."

The British music journal, *Tempo,* commissioned Boulez (and several other composers) to write music in memory of Stravinsky. In August 1971, a visit to an 18th century castle in Scotland and an improvisation on a flute inspired Boulez, who recalled, "It was quite impressive, . . . I had the idea then of the work beginning with a flute solo." The title came from a line by André Breton: "La beauté will be explosante-fixe or it will not be." A part of Boulez's composition was heard in London in June 1972, but it was not premiered until January 5, 1973, when the Chamber Music Society of Lincoln Center in New York first presented it. "In this music," explained Harold C. Schonberg in the New York *Times,* "the medium rather than the message is the thing. Now that electronic music has broken away from abstract noises, composers more and more are beginning to utilize it as merely another instrument in the ensemble. That is what Mr. Boulez has done. . . . In this work [he] is pointing to one element of the electronic future." In the *Saturday Review,* Irving Kolodin found that "enough did emerge to persuade me that the line of thought to which Boulez has directed himself has a functional future. It makes the machine not the master of man but his servant. It does not, as so much tape recording does, make the performer merely an extension of an instrument but its living, breathing, creative pulse."

On commission from the B.B.C., Boulez wrote *Rituel,* for orchestra, in memory of Bruno Maderna, the Italian avant-garde composer and conductor. The world premiere took place on April 2, 1975, with Boulez conducting the B.B.C. Symphony; the American premiere followed on August 14, 1975, at Tanglewood in Massachusetts, with Gunther Schuller conducting the Berkshire Music Center Orchestra. In *Rituel,* the orchestra is broken up into nine segments (including a group of nine percussion performers) and scattered as widely as possible to emphasize solo segments. A critic for *Musical America* described the work as "bleak and dour . . . evoking the eternal lamentations of a wake in a wasteland. As such, it represents a piece apart—and not immediately comparable—to Boulez's other music, reminding the listener of the compositional gestures of other composers: the mystic rituals of Stockhausen, the rapt otherworldliness of Messiaen, and the voids of Ligeti. . . . The pessimistic emotional tone is very much that of a composer and not of Maderna, and singular within the corpus of Boulez's nonsubjective work."

Not until five years after *Rituel* did Boulez complete another work for orchestra. The new composition called *Notations* was an adaptation for large symphony orchestra, with extended brass and percussion sections, of four of twelve little piano pieces Boulez had written in 1945 while attending the Paris Conservatory as a pupil of Messiaen. Each of the pieces is built from a single central theme. "The character of each piece is defined, isolated, fixed in a single expressive mode," the composer explained. "The relationship between the pieces is essentially one of contrast." Daniel Barenboim, conducting the Orchestre de Paris, presented *Notations* at its world premiere in Paris in June 1980. The American premiere followed on December 11, 1980, with Zubin Mehta directing the New York Philharmonic Orchestra. After the American premiere, John Rockwell, of the New York *Times,* called *Notations* "one of the most significant premieres in Philharmonic history." He added: "Each [of the four pieces] had elements that were rhythmically kinetic or repetitive or melodic. Yet the music is built up with an almost incredible wealth of detail and with a remarkable ear for clarity and pictorial vividness too." To Andrew Porter, writing in *The New Yorker,* the four pieces represented "a small symphony. The first of them is a thing of sudden attacks, swells and decays. The second is a scherzo. The third is a lyrical slow movement of almost Messiaenic lushness, with yearning melodies that wind their way across a richly scored background. The finale is a terse modern 'Rite'—a percussion-dominated dance of bright colors which sets the pulses racing."

While Boulez was music adviser to the Cleveland Orchestra from 1970 to 1972, he was also music director of the B.B.C. Symphony from 1971 to 1975. Between 1971 and 1977, his tenure as director of the New York Philharmonic was marked by a variety of brilliant performances (Berlioz, Debussy, Stravinsky, the Viennese expressionists, the avant-gardists), adventure, and innovation. However, his emphasis on new and unorthodox programming aroused criticism; in some quarters it was felt that Boulez had slighted the classics. His programming included "Major Perspectives," performances by composers in depth (Liszt, Alban Berg, Haydn, Stravinsky) and also "Prospective Encounters," performances and discussions of avant-garde music in "pre-concert recitals" which attempted to bridge the gap between the audience and new works appearing on the regular subscription program. In addition, "rug concerts" allowed the audience to listen to music informally, at special performances, sprawling on the floor and free of the usual concert rituals.

In the spring of 1975, Boulez made his only tour of Europe with the New York Philharmonic, presenting fifteen successful concerts in twelve cities.

Boulez was acclaimed in Bayreuth, Germany, where he conducted the complete *Ring* cycle of Wagner, during the summer of 1976, to celebrate the centenary of that world-renowed Wagnerian festival. On February 24, 1979, he conducted the world premiere of Berg's *Lulu* with its reconstructed third act at the Paris Opéra. (For further information about *Lulu* see the biography of Alban Berg in this volume.) Boulez has received "Grammy" awards from the National Academy of Recording Arts and Sciences as well as other recording awards from Japan. He has also appeared on television in documentaries, including one on Alban Berg and another on Mahler.

Since the termination of his New York Philharmonic appointment, Boulez has been serving as director of the Institut de Recherche et de Coordination Acoustique/Musique (IRCAM), a branch of the Centre National d'Art et de Culture Georges Pompidou, an organization formed to explore resources of electronic, and particularly computer-made, music. He went back to his home in Paris, his house in Baden-Baden, Germany, and a vacation place in the French Alps in southern France, near Avignon. Other than a secretary and a valet, Boulez prefers a solitary existence, avoids publicity, and dresses conservatively. "The good thing about not having a family," he said, "is that one does not have to make conversation at meals." He composes in fragments, pulling them together into an overall design, continually revising, and often taking several years to complete a major work. "I think quickly," he said, "but it takes a long time for my thoughts to ripen." He added:

"The more I grow, the more I detach myself from other composers, not only from the distant past but also from the recent past and even from the present. Conducting has forced me to absorb a great deal of history, so much so, in fact, that history seems more than ever to me a great burden. In my opinion, we must get rid of it once and for all."

MAJOR WORKS (supplementary)

Chamber Music—Livre pour Quatuor, string quartet.

Choral Music—e. e. Cummings ist der Dichter, for sixteen solo voices and orchestra.

Electronic Music—Éxplosante/Fixe.

Orchestral Music—Domaines, for clarinet and orchestra; Figures, Doubles, Prismes; Éclat-Multiples; Mémoriales; Rituel; Notations.

ABOUT (supplementary)

Ewen, D., Composers of Tomorrow's Music; Ewen, D., Musicians Since 1900: Performers in Concert and Opera; Griffiths, P. A., A Concise History of the Avant Garde Music from Debussy to Boulez; Myers, R. H., Modern French Music from Fauré to Boulez; Peyser, J., Boulez: Composer, Conductor, Enigma.

Esquire, February 1969; High Fidelity/Musical America, August 1971, January 1978; New York Times, March 9, 1969, June 20, 1971, May 15, 1977, June 4, 1978, December 7, 1980; New York Times Magazine, March 25, 1973; The New Yorker, March 14, 31, 1973, January 31, 1977, March 20, 1978; Saturday Review, October 18, 1975.

Henry Brant

1913–

For biographical sketch, list of earlier works, and bibliography, see *Composers Since 1900.*

In his continuous exploration of spatial music, Brant wrote his work, *Kingdom Come,* for two orchestras (one on the stage, the other in the balcony), organ, and such noisemakers as buzzers, sirens, slide whistles, and bells. It was introduced on April 14, 1970, in Oakland, California, in the Desto recording with Brant himself playing the organ. In *Machinations,* for ceramic flute, double flageolet, double ocarina, organ, harp, and percussion written in 1970, Brant plays all of the instruments.

In response to the Watergate hearings in Washington, D.C., Brant wrote *An American Requiem,* for soprano and orchestra, in 1974. It was premiered in Mt. Lebanon, Pennsylvania, on June 8, 1974, in a performance where seventeen instrumentalists sat on stage, backs to the audience, and five other instrumental groups were scattered around the concert hall. Brant took his text from the Old Testament in which a holocaust and ultimate redemption are predicted.

Homage to Ives, for baritone, orchestra (requiring three conductors), and noisemakers, was written in 1975 in commemoration of the centenary of Charles Ives's birth. After its world premiere by the Denver Symphony on February 21, 1975, a critic for *Musical America* commented that "the music subtly evoked the emotional line of Emerson's complex poem, 'Illusions.' In an effort to recreate Ives in today's terms, Brant enriched his score with vertical textures produced by blocks of instruments located in unusual locations in aisle C, trumpets in aisle D, trombones in aisle B, winds in the balcony and strings on the stage."

An ambitious program of Brant's spatial music took place at a six-week concert at the Buffalo Contemporary Music Festival, directed by Morton Feldman, in June 1978. Herman Trotter wrote about it in *Musical America:* "Brant was every bit the musical pixie as he performed intently on both the vibraphone and organ, smiled benignly at the thunderous reception his music was given, and offered devastatingly fey, though not uninformative, commentary about his various works."

For forty years, Brant earned his living mostly as a commercial composer-arranger. Added teaching duties at Bennington College (Vermont) where, since 1957 he taught group composition and "space music," made it necessary for him to compose in "snatches, whenever and wherever I could find the time, even in subway rides." A $15,000 composing fellowship from the Thorne Music Fund in 1972 released him from commercial work, and he accepted the Santa Fe Opera's commission to write an opera (*Everybody*) to his wife's libretto. Hilde Somer, the concert pianist, also commissioned him to write the *Spatial Concerto* ("Questions From Genesis") for piano and voices, which was introduced at the Massachusetts Institute of Technology in 1978.

Brant received grants from the New York State Council on the Arts (1974) and the National Endowment for the Arts (1976). In 1979,

Brant was elected to membership in the American Academy and Institute of Arts and Letters. He and his wife now live in an apartment in New York City; they are childless.

MAJOR WORKS (supplementary)

Band Music—Immortal Combat, for spatial band; American Debate, for spatial band.

Chamber Music—Windjammer, for woodwind quintet; Machinations, for ten instruments; Hieroglyphics, for solo violin, harp, celeste, organ, offstage soprano, and percussion; Consort for Two Violins, for a consortium of assorted vari-sized violins; Crossroads, for four violins; Divinity, for harpsichord and brass quintet; Prevailing Winds, for woodwinds; Piano Sextet.

Choral Music—Solomon's Gardens, for solo voices, chorus, and orchestra; Vita de Sancto Hieronymo, for chorus and instruments; A Plan of Air, for singers, percussion, and brass; Spatial Concerto, for solo voices and orchestral groups; Long Life, for a cappella chorus; American Weather, for chorus and orchestra.

Opera—Everybody Incorporated (libretto by Patricia Brant).

Orchestral Music—Odyssey—Why Not?, for flutes and orchestra, to a wordless text; Verticals Ascending, for two separate instrumental groups; Chanticleer; Kingdom Come, for orchestra, circus band, and organ; An American Requiem, for soprano and orchestra; Sixty; Nomads, for brass and percussion, to a wordless text; Homage to Ives, for baritone, orchestra, and noisemakers; American Debate, for winds and percussion; Antiphonal Responses, for three solo bassoons, eight isolated instruments, and orchestra; Trinity of Spheres, for three orchestral groups.

ABOUT (supplementary)

Sadie, S. (ed.), The New Grove Dictionary of Music and Musicians; Yates, P., Twentieth Century Music; Vinton, J. (ed.), Dictionary of Contemporary Music.

Sir Benjamin Britten

1913–1976

For biographical sketch, list of earlier works, and bibliography, see *Composers Since 1900.*

Britten's first full-length opera in over a decade, and his penultimate opera, was *Owen Wingrave.* It was commissioned for television by B.B.C. and produced jointly by the B.B.C., National Education Television in the United States, and members of the European Broadcasting Union. Its world premiere took place on May 16, 1971, in a broadcast to a dozen countries including the United States. Based on a story by

Henry James (libretto by Mifanwy Piper), *Owen Wingrave* repeated textual themes that Britten had developed so effectively in former masterworks, *Peter Grimes* and *Billy Budd:* man's inhumanity to man; the tragedy of the innocent who becomes an outcast; the struggle of the individual against a hostile world; and pacifism. In the opera, Owen Wingrave is being schooled for a military career, to follow in the footsteps of his ancestors, but renounces militarism as immoral, barbaric, and criminal. Branded a coward, Wingrave stands ready to prove his courage by allowing himself to be incarcerated for a night in a haunted room, where he, like an earlier Wingrave, is destroyed for failing to live up to family standards of courage.

Reporting in the New York *Times,* Peter Heyworth wrote that the score was "a highly skillful piece of work that accommodates itself to a chosen medium without prostrating itself before it. . . . He [Britten] has worked his material with cunning flexibility, so as to take advantage of the camera's ability to move to and from scenes with a rapidity impossible in the opera house. But he stood his ground on the essential matter that the music needs time to make a point. *Owen Wingrave* is a work that is also able to exist outside the TV studio." This point was convincingly proven in the spring of 1973 when *Owen Wingrave* was staged at Covent Garden in London, and when it was premiered in America by the Santa Fe Opera in New Mexico that summer.

In spite of heart surgery and partial paralysis, Britten was able to complete his last opera, *Death in Venice,* with a libretto by Myfanwy Piper in 1972. His textual source was Thomas Mann's novella of the same name. The central character, the aging German author Aschenbach, as Peter Heyworth described him in the New York *Times,* "is clearly modeled on Mann himself . . . is not a conventional middle-aged homosexual with a taste for small boys. He is a stern, self-disciplined married man, dedicated to his art, and part of the temptation lies in the fact that in self-abandonment he recognizes a stimulus for his flagging creativity."

The world premiere of *Death in Venice* took place at the Aldeburgh Festival in England on June 16, 1973. Peter Pears, Britten's lifelong friend, housemate, and principal interpreter of vocal music, assumed the exacting role of Aschenbach. Britten, unable to conduct the premiere, turned the baton over to Stewart Bedford.

"The score," reported Martin Cooper in the London *Daily Telegraph,* "shows all Britten's accustomed aptitude, versatility and sense of atmosphere."

Death in Venice received its American premiere at the Metropolitan Opera in New York on October 18, 1974, and Irving Kolodin wrote about it in the *Saturday Review:* "Like Mann's story, it exists on many levels: The deeper one probes, the clearer are the purposes of the extraordinary colorations invented by Britten for an orchestra smallish in size but extensive in such uncommonly heard instruments as vibraphone. These are the instruments that give the music for Tadzio and his companions a singularly bright, pure sound. The darker shades, for Aschenbach, are drawn from the more conventional instruments. Of the many levels on which Mann communicated, Britten has reflected the aesthetic, the erotic, the purely classical." In the New York *Times,* Peter G. Davis wrote that the "opera unfolds with an unerring sense of fluidity and sustained motion. And yet for all the free-flowing mobility of the opera's seventeen scenes, there is a tightly structured progress from the clear premise set in the opening Munich scene, an unfolding design in both the intricately related thematic material, and the development of Aschenbach's nature and destiny as he gradually deserts his Apollonian principles of self-discipline and succumbs to the Dyonisiac ideal of beauty through the senses."

The first creative work Britten undertook after completing *Death in Venice* was to revise two of his early compositions, the first string quartet, and his first opera, *Paul Bunyan.* The opera was written in 1941 to a libretto by W. H. Auden while both were residing in the United States. It had only a single performance—at Columbia University in New York—and it was a failure. Britten then decided to withdraw the work, never to be performed again or published, but thirty-five years later his friends convinced him to revise it. The new version was heard first over B.B.C. Radio in February 1976, then staged at the Aldeburgh Festival on June 4 of that year. The style was polyglot—jazz, blues, ballads, show tunes, simulations of American folk songs, even parody. Harold C. Schonberg wrote in the New York *Times* that "*Paul Bunyan* is brashly tuneful, with an old fashioned consonant tunefulness. . . . One other interesting fact about *Paul Bunyan:* the vocal settings are much more idi-

Brott

omatic and the sung language flows in a much more natural manner than in almost anything to be found in his later operas."

Canticle V, completed in 1974, was Britten's first new work after *Death in Venice.* It was scored for tenor and harp, and set to an early poem by T. S. Eliot, "The Death of St. Narcissus." It was followed in November 1974 by *Suite on English Folktunes,* a five-movement composition based on several folk tunes ("Cakes and Ale," "Lord Melbourne," "The Bitter Withy," "Nankin Booby," and "Hunt the Squirrel"). In 1975, Britten completed *Sacred and Profane,* based on eight medieval lyrics for unaccompanied voices, and introduced it at the Aldeburgh Festival on September 14, 1975. *A Birthday Hansel* (Scottish for "gift"), for tenor and harp, to poems by Robert Burns, was written for the seventy-fifth birthday of the Queen Mother of England and the solo cantata for soprano and orchestra, *Phaedra,* was composed for Janet Baker.

Britten's last major works were String Quartet No. 3, first heard posthumously on December 19, 1976, at the Aldeburgh Festival and performed by the Amadeus Quartet for whom it was written, and *Welcome Ode,* for "young voices" and orchestra, a greeting to Queen Elizabeth II on her Jubilee visit to Ipswich.

On December 4, 1976, Benjamin Britten died at his seaside farmhouse at Aldeburgh, after being hospitalized for a deteriorating heart condition. Funeral services took place at the Aldeburgh Parish and he was buried near his home. Memorial performances of his works took place throughout Europe and the United States: in London, the B.B.C. canceled its scheduled program to offer *Sinfonia da Requiem,* and other compositions; the New York Philharmonic presented Shostakovich's Symphony No. 14, since it was dedicated to Britten, and Pears presented a concert of his works, when a memorial was unveiled in Westminster Abbey on November 21, 1978.

In June 1976, Britten was granted a life peerage by Queen Elizabeth II for service to music, becoming the first musician ever so honored.

MAJOR WORKS (supplementary)

Chamber Music—Suite No. 3, for solo cello; Suite, for harp solo; String Quartet No. 3.

Choral Music—Children's Crusade, for chorus and or-

chestra; Sacred and Profane, for a cappella voices; Welcome Ode, for "young voices" and orchestra.

Operas—Owen Wingrave, television opera; Death in Venice.

Orchestral Music—Suite on English Folktunes; Phaedra, dramatic cantata for mezzo-soprano and small orchestra; Lachrymae, for viola and string orchestra.

Vocal Music—Canticle IV, for countertenor, tenor, and baritone; Who Are These Children?, song cycle for tenor; Canticle V, for tenor and harp; A Birthday Hansel, for tenor and harp; Phaedra, solo cantata for soprano and orchestra.

ABOUT (supplementary)

Evans, P., The Music of Benjamin Britten; Herbert, D. (ed.), The Operas of Benjamin Britten; Howard, P., The Operas of Benjamin Britten; Kendall, A., Benjamin Britten; Mitchell, D., Benjamin Britten; Mitchell, D. and Evans, J. (eds.), Benjamin Britten: 1913–1976, Pictures from a Life; Mordden, E., Opera in the 20th Century: Sacred, Profane, Godot; Young, P. M., Britten.

The Listener (London), December 16, 1976; New York Times, May 16, 1971, January 9, 1972, July 1, 1973, October 13, 1974, December 5, 1976; Opera (London), February 1977; Opera News, February 5, 1977, December 10, 1977.

Alexander Brott

1915–

Alexander Brott was born in Montreal, Canada, on March 14, 1915, to Samuel Brott, a tailor, and Anna (Fixman) Brott. "I was born in very humble circumstances," he recalled, "and I believe that my parents, particularly my mother, looked upon music as the salvation from deprivation both practically and emotionally." According to Brott, he began taking violin lessons when he was about five, and he recalled "practising diligently, and by the time I was about twelve I had established a format of practising for one hour before leaving for school each day." His most powerful musical influences came from attending concerts by such violinists as Fritz Kreisler, Jascha Heifetz, and Mischa Elman, who became his idols. "I made my exit from their concerts bewitched and dazed." He began to compose when he was twelve, and at thirteen he won three scholarships to the McGill Conservatium of Music.

Brott: brŏt

52

ALEXANDER BROTT

When Brott was fifteen he became a member of the newly organized Montreal Symphony. While in that orchestra, he came into contact with Georges Enesco, Nicolai Medtner, Serge Prokofiev, and other world-famous musicians who visited Montreal. "They mirrored for me the concept of the whole man, the total musician. I have endeavored to follow that path consistently."

By the time Brott was eighteen, he had earned a licentiate in music from McGill University (1932) and a laureate degree in music from the Quebec Academy of Music (1933). Between 1935 and 1939 he attended the Juilliard School of Music in New York on scholarship, to study composition with Bernard Wagenaar, violin with Sascha Jacobson, and conducting with Willem Willeke. To support himself during these years he played violin with a concert trio for room and board; commuted to Richmond, Virginia, to play in its symphony orchestra; gave violin lessons; copied music; and occasionally appeared with the Musical Art String Quartet when it required an additional violin.

While at Juilliard, Brott was awarded the Elizabeth Sprague Coolidge Award for chamber-music composition and the Loeb Memorial Award for chamber-music performance. His first noteworthy composition at this time was *Oracle* (1938), for orchestra, introduced by the Montreal Symphony Orchestra under the direction of Sir Thomas Beecham in 1939. A critic for *Le Canada* in Montreal wrote: "*Oracle* is a symphonic work which admirably reflects the trou-

bled epoch in which we live. Written with an audacious modern harmony, and orchestrated in a remarkable fashion, this symphonic poem is without doubt the most advanced piece of music attempted by a Canadian composer."

Upon completing his studies at Juilliard, Brott received the Lord Strathcona Award for further study at the Royal College of Music in London. However, World War II frustrated these plans and he joined the faculty of McGill University as teacher and lecturer instead, rising to the post of professor. He also became concertmaster and assistant conductor of the Montreal Symphony, a position he held until 1963. In 1939, Brott had founded the McGill String Quartet which, eleven years later, became the nucleus of the McGill Chamber Orchestra, under his direction. The orchestra gave annual concerts in Montreal and toured Canada, Europe, South America, Mexico, and the Near East; it was recorded and broadcast over Canadian radio and TV; and it introduced more than fifty new Canadian works.

In addition, Brott founded the "Montreal Concerts Under the Stars" in 1955; conducted the Montreal Pops Orchestra in 1960 and the McGill student orchestra from 1950 to 1975; and in 1964 he became director of the Kingston Orchestra in Ontario, Canada. He also made numerous guest appearances as conductor with European orchestras (including the London Symphony and the B.B.C. Symphony in England, the Royal Swedish Philharmonic, the Bolshoi Orchestra of Moscow, and the Mexico National Orchestra).

His career as a composer prospered too. His String Quartet (1940) received a favorable reaction from the Montreal *Gazette:* "It is an extremely well-written work, clear and concise in the setting forth of the material, expertly couched in contrapuntal terms and advanced in idiom. ... He has used devices for color and contrast that match favorably with such redoubtable colorists as Debussy and Ravel. And his thinking, in these respects as in what he has to say, is independent."

In 1944 he conducted *War and Peace,* his symphony for orchestra, at its first performance on the Canadian Broadcasting Company network. Subsequent performances were given by the Toronto Symphony under Sir Ernest McMillan, the Montreal Symphony under Desiré Defauw, and the Royal Philharmonic Orchestra of

Brott

London under Sir Thomas Beecham. In 1945, *War and Peace* received the Canadian Performance Rights Award for serious music, and in 1948, the Olympic Medal for composition in London. Hector Challesworth reported in the Toronto *Globe and Mail* that "the symphony is inspired by the present conflict, and it may be said at the outset that it is quite as good as anything of similar inspiration produced by any other country. Mr. Brott's brilliant technical powers and individuality are evident throughout. He is sufficiently a master of orchestral resources to create his own idioms, and underneath passages typifying the chaos of the world are evidences of serene melodic inspiration. The suggestion of mechanized warfare is very deftly handled without blatancy, and in the section typifying peace are moments of singular beauty." The distinguished Soviet critic, Grigori Schneerson, called Brott's *War and Peace* "a monumental work."

From Sea to Sea (1946) was the first composition to be commissioned by the International Service of the C.B.C. (Canadian Broadcasting Company), and showed Brott's interest in the folk music of Canada. In 1947 the work was premiered in a worldwide performance by the C.B.C. Montreal Orchestra, which was conducted by the composer, in a UNESCO-sponsored broadcast. Sir Thomas Beecham later took *From Sea to Sea* to London on a United Kingdom tour of the Royal Philharmonic. The work was also recorded by RCA, with the composer conducting.

Another Brott orchestral work to gain international attention in the 1940s was *Concordia,* which was performed at the Prague Music Festival, in 1946.

On March 28, 1944, Brott married Lotte Goetzel who was the cellist for the McGill String Quartet and later the McGill Chamber Orchestra. The Brotts settled in Montreal where their two sons, Boris became a conductor and Denis, a concert cellist. Lotte Brott, now manager of the McGill Chamber Orchestra and the Kingston Symphony, also handles publicity and writes program notes for both orchestras.

Commissions in the 1950s brought forth a number of new compositions. The Concerto for Violin and Orchestra, based on folk melodies and rhythms, was commissioned by George Schick and the Little Symphony in Montreal. Its world premiere took place on March 7, 1950,

with Noel Brunet as soloist and George Schick as conductor. "It contains several genuinely moving moments (the wonderful solo and cadenza for the violin in the opening movement) and some striking orchestral effects, particularly for the brasses," said Brian MacDonald in *The Herald* of Montreal. This concerto was later heard in New York with Leopold Stokowski conducting, and in 1952 it was awarded the Olympic medal for composition in Helsinki.

Delightful Delusions, for orchestra, was commissioned by conductor Desiré Defauw, in 1951, who presented its first performance with the Montreal Symphony soon after it was completed. *Royal Tribute,* commissioned by the C.B.C. in 1953 to honor the coronation of Queen Elizabeth II, was introduced in London at the Royal Albert Hall with the composer conducting. *Fancy and Folly,* for orchestra, was commissioned in 1953 by conductor Vladimir Golschmann, who led its premiere with the St. Louis Symphony on January 16, 1948. *Sept for Seven,* for narrator, strings, and winds, was commissioned in 1959 by the Faculty of Music of McGill University for the University's fiftieth anniversary. *Analogy in Anagram,* for orchestra, was commissioned in 1959 by conductor Pierre Monteux, who premiered it with the Montreal Symphony.

Brott's later outstanding compositions follow: *The Prophet* (1960) a cantata for tenor, soprano, and piano, was commissioned and introduced by Leopold Simoneau and Pierrette Alarie; *Martlet's Muse* (1962), an orchestral overture, was commissioned by McGill University and performed by the Boston Pops Orchestra, conducted by Arthur Fiedler; *Le Corriveau* (1967), a ballet, was commissioned by Canada's Centennial Commission and performed by Les Grand Ballets Canadiens throughout Canada, the United States, and Europe; *Pristine Prisms* (1967) for solo violin was commissioned by the Canadian Council and performed at Expo '67 in Montreal; and *The Emperor's New Clothes* (1970), based on Hans Christian Andersen's children's story, was commissioned and introduced by the Hamilton Philharmonic Orchestra in Canada under the direction of Boris Brott, the composer's son, on February 21, 1971.

Brott was awarded medals from the Arnold Bax Society in London (1961), the Canadian Music Council (1976), and the Queen's Anniversary Silver Jubilee (1978). He received honorary doctorates in music from the University of Chicago (1955) and McGill University (1980), and an honorary doctorate (LLD) from Queen's University in Canada. On November 16, 1980, a documentary on the "Brott Family" was telecast in Canada and throughout the French-speaking world.

MAJOR WORKS

Ballet—Le Corriveau.

Chamber Music—Invocation and Dance, for violin and piano; String Quartet; Rhapsody, for cello and piano; 3 Acts for 4 Sinners, for saxophone quartet; Three on a Spree, for flute, oboe, and harpsichord; Mutual Salvation Orgy, for brass quintet; Pristine Prisms, in Polychromes, for solo violin; Centennial Colloquy, for thirteen wind instruments; Spasms for Six, for six percussion players; Tout de Suite, for solo cello.

Choral Music—Canadiana, for a cappella chorus; Israel, for choir and strings; The Prophet, cantata for tenor, soprano, and piano; Elie, Lama Sabachtani, for female voices and piano; Esperanto, for female voices and piano; Badinage, for mixed voices and piano.

Orchestral Music—Oracle; Lament, for string orchestra; Ritual, for string orchestra; War and Peace; Laurentian Idyl, for symphonic band and strings; From Sea to Sea; Concordia; Critics Corner, for string orchestra and percussion; Concerto for Violin and Orchestra; Delightful Delusions; Royal Tribute; Fancy and Folly; Sept for Seven, for narrator, strings, and winds; Arabesque, for cello and orchestra; Analogy in Anagram; Three Astral Visions, for string orchestra; Spheres in Orbit; Martlet's Muse, overture; Triangle, Circle, 4 Squares, for strings; Profundum Praedictum, for solo bass and string orchestra; Paraphrase in Polyphony (on a Beethoven canon); Mini-Minus, for chamber orchestra; The Emperor's New Clothes, for narrator and orchestra.

Piano Music—Suite; Vignettes.

Vocal Music—Songs of Contemplation, for soprano and strings; Vision of the Dry Bones, for baritone and strings; World Sophisticate, for soprano and brass quintet.

ABOUT

MacMillan, K. and Beckwith, J. (eds.), Contemporary Canadian Composers; Vinton, J. (ed.), Dictionary of Contemporary Music; Who's Who in America, 1980–1981.

Earle Brown

1926–

Earle Brown, leading avant-garde composer, was born in Lunenburg, Massachusetts, on December 26, 1926. For generations, the Browns owned and operated a general store in Lunenburg. In addition, Earle's father, Earle Appelton Brown, was town postmaster, a position he inherited from his father. Earle's mother, Grace Freeman Brown, came to the United States from Nova Scotia when she was a year old. Both parents loved music: his father sang in the choir of the Congregational Church in Lunenburg and his mother played the piano competently, though never professionally.

While neither his brother nor sister were musical, Earle was very interested in the Sunday afternoon broadcasts of the New York Philharmonic Orchestra which his father listened to. Of having to take piano lessons, he recalled, "I really hated it. I didn't like the teacher, or I didn't like the piano, or I was just too restless to sit down and practice. Neither one of my parents was of the kind to insist in a dictatorial way that I should practice. When the time for piano lessons came, I would sort of disappear in the woods where I loved to walk. As a kid, I spent lots of time alone because there were not that many kids living near me."

Popular music influenced Earle, since this was the heyday of the big bands. Fascinated by such musicians as Louis Armstrong, Bunny Berrigan, and Harry James, Earle abandoned the piano for a trumpet while still in grammar school and studied trumpet at the local music store for $1.25 a week (one dollar for the lesson and twenty-five cents toward the purchase of the instrument). At Lunenburg High School, he played baseball and basketball when he did not have to help out in his father's store and he joined a small dance band in nearby Fitchburg. He organized and led a dance band of his own and recalled, "We used to make as much as eight dollars a night, and it was great fun. It was also valuable training for me in that it gave me the confidence that I could work with and even lead people in making music." He also played in the town band, eventually joining a large dance orchestra that played all over Massachusetts.

Some of his experiences with serious modern

EARLE BROWN

music during his boyhood days left an indelible impression on him. Charles Ives's *Concord Sonata*, he said, "was the most impressive serious music of my early life. I just didn't believe that music of such complexity and power could be written." Other early favorites were Bartók, and later Stravinsky and Schoenberg.

Aside from music, Brown's boyhood interests included airplanes and flying, a love he had acquired from a favorite uncle, a test pilot for Curtiss-Wright. A fascination for aeronautics, combined with excellence in mathematics and physics, induced him to enter Northeastern University in Boston, as an engineering student after high school in 1944. "Becoming an engineer was not important to me, but the idea of flying was, so that when I applied to Northeastern University it was with the hope that I would eventually enter the field of aeronautical engineering."

While at Northeastern University, he joined the Army Air Force in 1945 as a pilot officer trainee, during World War II. When the war was over and the program was terminated, he was retained for about a year and a half to play the trumpet in Army Air Force bands, which performed concert pieces, marches, popular songs, and jazz. "That was a tremendous training," he recalled, "playing the trumpet all day long and frequently at night as well, and so many different kinds of music." At times he also filled a trumpet chair with the San Antonio Symphony where he received his first training in symphonic literature. Along with this practical training, he studied harmony, counterpoint, ar-

ranging, etc., from books borrowed from the library.

Such musical experiences convinced Brown to devote himself to music, and although he made an attempt to continue his studies at Northeastern University, he left to study music. From 1946 to 1950 he attended the Schillinger School of Music in Boston where his studies included the history of music, polyphony, composition privately with Dr. Rosalyn Brogue Henning, lessons on the trumpet with Fred Berman, and arranging and orchestration with Jesse Smith. The method there appealed to him because of, as he put it, "my predilection for mathematics— the Schillinger method being based on mathematical concepts or, to put it somewhat more accurately, numerical concepts. I learned a great deal about the manipulation of pitches, rhythms, and many of the things unique to Schillinger." Brown became interested in pre-classic polyphony and in twelve-tone music through Henning. All the varying influences upon him, Brown maintained, "left me with a far more open mind than if I had gone the usual conservatory route. My music background is curious and diverse and I think that is very good, and I feel very fortunate in the way I came into becoming a composer."

On June 28, 1950, Brown married Carolyn Rice, whom he met at ten years of age at a social-dancing school. (Carolyn later became a famous dancer as a member of the Merce Cunningham company.) They moved to Denver where Brown opened a studio to teach arranging and Schillinger technique and during those years, he met John Cage for the first time. He said, "We had marvelous discussions. He saw the music I was then writing and became for me a tremendously supportive figure."

Brown developed as an avant-garde composer, as evidenced in his first published works, composed between 1950 and 1952, which derived their style and technique from the Schillinger method and the twelve-tone system: *Three Pieces*, for piano (1951), *Perspectives*, for piano (1952), and *Music for Violin, Cello and Piano* (1952). David Tudor, pianist, received from Cage a copy of *Three Pieces* and performed the work in New York early in 1952.

In 1952, Cage invited Brown to join him in New York to work on a small grant ($40 a week) for three years on the "Project for Music for Magnetic Tape," the first American experiment with magnetic tape for musical production. When this grant was terminated, Brown found a job selling books at Brentano's, at the same salary, but he confided, "I got fed up spending forty hours a week of my life making $40 a week. If I was going to spend all that time I might as well make money at it." His technical background and recent experience with magnetic tape, made him well-suited for the recording industry and he was employed by Capitol Records as editor and recording engineer, from 1955 to 1960. Then he became an independent producer and director of artists and repertory for "Contemporary Sound Series" of Time-Mainstream Records, producing a total of eighteen records.

Abandoning the twelve-tone technique, he sought a new kind of 20th century music with few, if any, precedents. He had been influenced by experiences in jazz and wished to carry over to his own music the freshness and spontaneity of jazz improvisation. He was also impressed by the abstract expressionism of Jackson Pollock's paintings and the mobiles of Alexander Calder whose interrelationships and juxtapositions change constantly while component parts remain totally fixed and predetermined. In his attempt to imitate these elements of the visual arts in his music, he developed the concept of "open form" in which conductor and performers are given latitude to perform pages of a composition in any order they wish (e.g., pitch, directions, and dynamics are specified in *25 Pages,* written in 1958 , but it can be performed either side up, due to the absence of clefs). Brown described his notational procedures as "time notation," where the duration of each section is indicated in seconds with the performer exercising his "time-sense perception" of the scored relationships; and "graphic notation," where a score suggests in purely visual terms the kinds of actions to be taken by the musicians as well as the relationships between such actions.

Morton Feldman described Brown's "time-notation" as follows: "The sound here is placed in its approximate visual relationship to that which surrounds it. Time is not indicated mechanistically, as with metric notation. It is articulated for the performer, but not interpreted for him. The effect is twofold. When the performer is made more intensely aware of time he also becomes more intensely aware of the action or sound he is about to play. The result is a

heightened spontaneity which only performance itself can convey. Brown's notation, in fact, is geared to counteract just this discrepancy between the printed page and the realities of performance."

Brown's new approach to music was first evident in *Folio* (1952–1953), which is made up of six compositions: three of them are *November 1952,* or *Synergy, December 1952,* and *December 1953,* all for an indeterminate number of musicians. This is one of the earliest works in classical music in which the performer is so deeply involved in the creative process. The mobile character of *December 1952* is apparent in the instructions of the graphically notated published score. "The composition may be performed in any direction from any point in the defined space for any length of time and may be performed from any of the four rotational positions in any sequence." Brown explained further: "This seems to be the first truly 'graphic' score—a score which does not give specific or precise information as to what its sound-content must be or exactly how it is to be read. It is simply a field of graphic events which are to suggest visually a kind of activity and possible relationships between them and the parameters (in this case of frequency, duration or loudness)." In *December 1952* the directions in the score read as follows: "To have elements exist in space . . . space as an infinitude of directions from an infinitude of points in space; to work (compositionally and in performance) from right to left, back, forward, up, down and all points between. The score being a picture of this space in one instant, which a performer must set into motion (time), which is to say, realize that it is in motion and step into it, either sit or let it move or move through it at all speeds."

In March 1953 Brown completed his first composition for magnetic tape: *Octet I,* for eight loud-speakers surrounding the audience. A year later, he presented *Twenty-Five Pages* (New York, April 14, 1954) in which "open form" and "time notation" were realized more fully than in *Folio.* In this work, twenty-five sheets of music are performed in any sequence or inversion by from one to twenty-five pianos. *Indices,* for chamber orchestra (1954, Brooklyn, New York, 1954) and *Music for Cello and Piano* (1954–1955; New York, 1959) are written in closed form and "time notation."

At the end of 1956, Brown visited Europe for

the first time and renewed acquaintances with such avant-garde composers as Pierre Boulez and Luciano Berio, whom he had previously met in New York. He also came in contact with such European avant-gardists as Bruno Maderna and Karlheinz Stockhausen. Brown said Maderna "was a tremendous influence in my life. He instantly recognized and admired my music, and did a great deal to perform it all over Europe." In 1958, at Boulez's request, Brown wrote *Pentathis,* for nine soloists, which was conducted by Maderna that summer at the Darmstadt Festival in Germany. Commenting on his composition, Brown said: "It is standard notation and unremarkable except, I hope, as a very personal expression of my subjective taste and musicality. The work reaffirmed my interest in attempting to expand the possibilities of the Schillinger technique and of getting even closer to my personal vision of a new world of sound and performance and compositional condition."

In 1960, Brown left his position with Capitol Records to devote most of his working hours to composition. "I still don't know how I lived from 1961 to 1968, but in one way or another, with lectures, commissions—mostly in Europe —I was able to make it," he told Donal Henahan in an interview for the New York *Times.*

Commissions helped to give Brown's compositions worldwide exposure in the 1960s. The city of Darmstadt commissioned him to write *Available Forms I,* for eighteen instruments, which was introduced by the International Kranichsteiner Kammer Ensemble in Darmstadt on September 8, 1961. Within two years of this premiere the work was also heard in Hamburg, Palermo, Helsinki, Paris, The Hague, Zagreb, Kansas City, and twice in New York. In this score each of the six pages contains five "musical events" which are played on specific instructions from the conductor. "In front of the podium is a numbered board with sliding red arrows; the conductor moves the arrows to give the page and holds up one or more fingers to indicate the 'event' he wants played," explained *Time* Magazine when the work was heard in Baltimore in January 1969.

Available Forms II, for ninety-eight instruments and two conductors, was written by Brown on commission from the Rome Radio Orchestra; its first performance took place at the Venice Biennale in April 1962. Commenting on it, the composer explained: "The title refers to the availability of many possible forms which these composed elements may assume, spontaneously directed by the conductors in the process of performing the work. The conductors work independently of one another. . . . No two performances will arrive at the same formal result but the work will retain its identity from performance to performance through the unchanging basic character of the events." After it was performed in Cologne in 1963, Cornelius Cardew wrote in the London *Financial Times* that "The vital interaction brought about by the fact of there being two conductors thinking independently ensures a constant awareness on the part of the musicians and audience and the raw coincidences of sonority, and the desperate individual efforts made by musicians to keep and play their parts, were like a gust of fresh air sweeping through the audience." *Available Forms II* was performed by the New York Philharmonic in 1964, with the composer conducting one section and Leonard Bernstein the other.

Novara for eight instruments was written in the spring of 1962 at the request of Lukas Foss for the Tanglewood Festival in Massachusetts where it was performed that summer under the composer's direction. *Novara* is comprised of twenty fixed "sound elements" which the conductor can summon in any sequence or juxtaposition. The musical content is invariable though the formal shape changes with each performance. When *Novara* was heard at the second Hellenic Week of Contemporary Music in Athens, Greece, George Leotsakis commented in the *Ta Nea Enimerotis:* "With Brown, the sound which he admirably knows how to bring into existence from the instruments is not only simply decorative but has a profound function, interior and human."

From Here, for chorus and twenty instruments, was commissioned by the Foundation for the Performing Arts, and had its first hearing in New York in October 1963. When *From Here* was performed in Paris three years later at a concert of the Domaine Musical (a concert organization founded in Paris by Pierre Boulez to promote new music), with the composer conducting. Martin Cachen said in *Lettres Françaises:* "It dominated the evening like a pleasantly smiling hill . . . imagination in all its forms . . . intelligent, sensitive and a keen sense of perception. Brown knows the art of understatement . . . fragments of sonority which twirl, float slowly on an element as gentle as water, and as fleeting. Everything is transparent, subtle and shot through with humor, a true touchstone of joy in writing."

Also in the 1960 s, commissions were responsible for a number of works. The Service de la Recherche of the Paris Radio commissioned Brown to write *Times Five,* an open form piece for five instruments and four channels of tape in 1963; the Bremen Radio commission in 1964 led to the writing of *Corroboree,* for three pianos; a commission from Sudwestfunk, the radio of Baden-Baden in Germany, in 1965, brought forth String Quartet, which was performed at the Donaueschingen' Festival by the La Salle Quartet; and the French Radio commissioned *Event: Synergy II,* for two chamber orchestras, performed at the Festival of Royan in France. All of these compositions were introduced in the year they were composed. On January 21, 1972, Bruno Maderna conducted *Event: Synergy II* at the New York Philharmonic Prospective Encounter concert. On this occasion, two performances of the same work were given, each using a different running order, combinations of orchestras, and starting and finishing points.

Modules I and II was still another noteworthy work by Brown in the 1960s. It was written in 1966 and performed in February 1967 by the Orchestre Nationale de Paris on the Paris Radio. The American Symphony Orchestra, under the joint direction of the composer and Ainslee Cox, offered the work for the first time in the United States in New York on April 9, 1972. "It shimmered; it swayed like a ship at mooring; it danced solemnly in place; it spun webs of sound and hung them in the air," reported Donal Henahan in the New York *Times.* He added: "The material available evidently was restricted to five chords, but an enormous variety of sonorities and rhythmic byplay was generated from this simple scheme, and a mood of gentleness, strength and stability was sustained in an alert, seemingly superb orchestral performance." *Modules III,* "for one-half large orchestra" was introduced in 1969 at the Festival de Zagreb in Yugoslavia.

In 1964 and 1965, Brown was guest composer and lecturer at the Darmstadt summer courses in Germany, and in 1969 he assumed similar roles at the Berkshire Music Center at Tanglewood, Massachusetts. In 1968, he was appointed composer-in-residence at the Peabody Conservatory in Baltimore for five years and in the middle year of that appointment, he was a guest composer of the West Berlin government in the Deutscher Akademischer Austausdienst "Künstler programm."

While at Peabody, Susan Sollins, then curator of Education at the Smithsonian National Collection of Fine Arts invited Brown to lecture and do a concert at the Institution. As Brown's first marriage had failed, Susan became his second wife and they have lived in Rye, New York, since 1973.

Since 1970, Brown's major commissioned works also included *Sytagm III,* for eight instruments, performed at the Festival at St. Paul de Vence in France in 1970; *New Piece Loops,* for large orchestra and chorus was completed in 1972 and first performed at the Venice Biennale that September; *Centering,* for solo violin and chamber orchestra was written for Paul Zukovsky and the London Sinfonietta who introduced it in London in December 1973; and *Cross Section and Color Fields,* for orchestra, was commissioned by the Koussevitzky Music Foundation and first performed by the Denver Symphony under Brian Priestman during the 1975–1976 season. In referring to the latter work, a critic in *High Fidelity/Musical America* wrote: "The music is not hard to absorb. Its character is one of general suavity—a neo-Schubertian spirit of brooding drama within a gentle mood, well-paced with contrasts."

In the late 1970s, on a grant from the National Endowment for the Arts, Brown worked on *Patchen,* for large orchestra and chorus, and on commission from the Fromm Music Foundation he completed *Windsor Jambs,* for voice and seven instruments, which was introduced in New York on January 8, 1981.

Brown made numerous appearances both in Europe and the United States as composer, conductor, and lecturer. In 1971 he was composer-in-residence and conductor at the Aspen Music Festival; in 1974, composer-in-residence with the Rotterdam Philharmonic and Conservatory in Holland; in 1974–1975, guest professor at the Basel Conservatory in Switzerland, again composer-in-residence at the Aspen Summer Festival, and also composer-in-residence at Tanglewood; in 1975, visiting professor of music at State University of New York in Buffalo; in 1976, visiting professor of music at the University of Southern California in Los Angeles, and at the California Institute of Arts in Valencia, in fall 1979.

Brown received an honorary doctorate in music from the Peabody Conservatory in 1970; and he received awards from the American Academy and Institute of Arts and Letters (1972); from the New York State Council on the Arts (1974); and the Creative Arts Award from Brandeis University (1977).

MAJOR WORKS

Chamber Music—Music for Violin, Cello, and Piano; Pieces, for string quartet; Music for Cello and Piano, Nos. 1, 2, 3; Folio, for any number of instruments; Pentathis, for nine instruments; Hodograph, for six instruments; Novara, for nine instruments; String Quartet; Chef d'Orchestre/Calder Piece, for four percussionists and Calder mobile; Syntagm III, for eight instruments; Centering, for violin and ten instruments.

Choral Music—From Here, for twenty instrumentalists and four optional choruses; New Piece Loops, for large orchestra and chorus; Patchen, for large orchestra and chorus; Small Pieces for Large Chorus.

Electronic Music—Octet I, for eight magnetic tapes; Octet II, for eight magnetic tapes; Light Music, for electric lights, electronic equipment, and a variable number of instruments; Times Five, for five instruments and magnetic tape; Untitled, for large orchestra and magnetic tape.

Orchestral Music—Indices, for chamber orchestra; Available Forms I, for eighteen instruments; Available Forms II, for ninety-eight instruments and two conductors; Event: Synergy II, for chamber orchestra; Modules I and II; Module III, for one-half orchestra; New Piece, for eighteen instruments; Time Spans; Sign Sounds, for chamber orchestra; Cross Sections and Color Fields; Windsor Jambs, for soprano and chamber orchestra.

Piano Music—Three Pieces; Perspectives; Four More, for one or more pianos; Four Systems, for one or more pianos; Fugue; More Systems, for one or more pianos; Strata, suite for two pianos; Twenty-Five Pages, for one to twenty-five pianos; Corroboree, for three pianos; Nine Rarebits, for one or two harpsichords.

ABOUT:

Peyser, J., The New Music; Rosenberg, D. and B., The Music Makers; Russcol, H., The Liberation of Sound: an Introduction to Electronic Music; Salzman, E., Twentieth Century Music: an Introduction.

New York Times, June 21, 1970; Time, January 24, 1969; Washington Post, October 19, 1973.

Willy Burkhard

1900–1955

For biographical sketch, list of earlier works, and bibliography, see *Composers Since 1900.*

ABOUT (supplementary)

Mohr, E., Willy Burkhard: Leben und Werk; Zurlinden, M., Willy Burkhard.

Alan Bush

1900–

Alan Dudley Bush was born in London, England, on December 22, 1900, the last of three sons. His father, Alfred Walter Bush, was founder and a director of the firm of W. J. Bush & Company, manufacturer of essential oils. His mother, Alice Maud Brinsley Bush, a talented painter, was never permitted to practice the art professionally. For the first eleven years of his life, Alan was educated privately; then he entered Highgate Grammar School where he finished in the Sixth Form and passed the London Matriculation in 1917. At four years of age he started instruction in piano; at eleven, in harmony, and at fifteen, organ. When he was fourteen, he composed piano pieces, which he later destroyed.

Bush described his first visit to a library as a "momentous" event: "I did not know that such an institution as a public library existed. Full of curiosity I walked in and was allowed to wander among the shelves. I discovered that a lot of people had written serious books concerning the problem of what the world was really about (philosophy) and what human beings had made or were making of their lives (politics). This was the beginning of my general education. I continued to swim fascinated among the book-islands of the Hornsey Branch Library." Thus he came upon the first books which were to help shape and give dimension to his thinking: Ernst Haeckel's *Riddle of the Universe,* Darwin's theory of natural selection, and the sociological writings of H. G. Wells, among others.

In January 1918, Bush enrolled in the Royal Academy of Music in London to study piano with Tobias Matthay and Lily West, organ with

ALAN BUSH

piano with Artur Schnabel and between 1929 and 1931 he attended the Berlin University as a student of philosophy and musicology, with Johannes Wolf and Friedrich Blume. In 1929, he succeeded Rutland Boughton as conductor of the London Labor Choral Union for the next eleven years. In 1929, he also wrote his first extended composition which was organized thematically as well as harmonically and rhythmically. It was entitled *Dialectic,* a string quartet, whose five sections are all derived from the opening unifying passage. In considering his work, Bush said, "that the way in which these subjects swing from fast to slow and then from faster to slower was reminiscent of the developing contractions of Hegelian dialectic. Furthermore, there is dialectic of theses, antitheses and synthesis in the objective character of the exposition, the agitated emotionalism of the development and the purposeful optimism of the recapitulation and coda." *Dialectic* was premiered on March 22, 1935, in London by the Brosa String Quartet.

A number of Bush's works brought him worldwide recognition: *Dialectic* on September 2, 1935, at the festivals of the International Society for Contemporary Music in Prague and in Paris on June 21, 1937; *Concert Piece,* for cello and piano, in London in January 1937; *Symphonic Impression* (1926–1927), introduced at a Promenade concert in London on November 11, 1930; and *Dance Overture* (1935) at a London Promenade concert on August 30, 1935.

On March 31, 1931, Bush married Nancy Rachel Head, with whom he had two daughters (one is deceased). His wife, who received her Master of Arts degree at Cambridge University, was a translator of songs and librettist of operas.

In 1934, Bush participated in the Hunger Marches of the Unemployed in London which inspired him to write "The Hunger March Song." After joining the Communist Party, he helped organize the Workers Music Association in 1936, serving as its president for the next forty years. In a number of his compositions he made a conscious effort to present aspects of the working-class struggle either through actual singing texts or by means of titles of either movements or the whole work: for example, the Concerto for Piano and Orchestra (1934–1937), with baritone solo, where in the last movement there is a male voice choir singing the text by Randall Swingler. The work was introduced on March 4,

Reginald Steggall, and composition with Frederick Corder. In 1920 he was awarded the Thalberg Scholarship and the Matthew Phillimore Prize for piano playing. He was also awarded the Battison Haynes and Philip Agnew prizes for composition, having already written his first opus, *Three Pieces for Two Pianos* (1921; London, March 2, 1921). This work was followed by the Sonata in B minor, for piano (1921; London, July 6, 1921). Upon graduation from the Academy in July 1922, he was elected Associate of the Royal Academy and a Fellow in 1938. In 1925 he was appointed professor of harmony and composition at the Royal Academy where (except for two hiatuses) he remained until his statutory retirement in July 1978. In the meantime, he received a Bachelor of Music degree there in 1934, a doctorate in music in 1968, and was awarded an honorary doctorate from Durham University in 1971.

In 1927, Bush began a five-year period of instruction in composition with John Ireland, a distinguished English composer, combined with the study of the piano with Benno Moiseiwitsch. Beginning in the 1920s, he started to be involved in the political activities of the British working class. As a composer for the proletariat, he wrote political songs and conducted amateur working class choruses in Great Britain. However he also produced music for the professional concert hall. His String Quartet in A minor (1923; London, December 4, 1924) received the Carnegie Award in 1924.

In 1928, Bush continued his study of the

1938, at a concert of the B.B.C. Orchestra, conducted by Sir Adrian Boult, with Dennis Noble as vocal soloist and the composer at the piano. Kaikhosru Sorabji reported in the *New English Weekly,* that "the entire work has about it the aura of an epic struggle and almost the grandly sombre air of one of the minatory Old Testament prophets. . . . It is lean, muscular, ascetic even, but with a fine integrity of utterance and convincing power of expression that are indicative of a work of major importance."

In 1927 Bush adopted total thematization as his method of composition. In the classics, with such rare exceptions as Beethoven's *Grosse Fugue,* musical tones, organized thematically, harmonically, and rhythmically, were combined with others, not thematically organized. He believed that the the principle of total thematization was an aesthetic advance and he adopted it in principle, even in his folk-song harmonizations where the accompanying voice parts are developed from the motifs of the particular melody. Until 1948 his accompanying voice parts had included chromaticism, sometimes at variance with the basic theme of the work which was characterized as English in idiom. A twelve-tone row is organized tonally, in the first movement of the Symphony No. 1 in C (1939–1940) and in the second movement of the Violin Concerto (1948). The programmatic First Symphony is arranged to reflect Bush's social and political consciousness: the Prologue is intended to evoke "the striving upward of humanity, vague and ending unresolved"; the first movement is called "Cliveden," meaning the headquarters of the pro-Hitler monopoly-capitalists called "the Cliveden Set"; the second movement, "Dowlais," is named after a former industrial town in South Wales where the population was totally unemployed and dependent on national assistance; the concluding movement is entitled "Harworth" after the industrial town in the Midlands, where in 1938–1939 a fierce struggle against exploitation was smothered by police action. "This movement," said the composer, "represents the feelings and outlook of the revolutionary working class and its leadership in the person of the working-class professional revolutionary." The First Symphony was first heard at a Promenade concert in London on July 24, 1942.

In 1938, Bush formed the London String Orchestra and served as its conductor until 1950.

From 1941 to 1945, during World War II, Bush served in the Royal Army Medical Corps and was stationed in London where he composed during his free hours at a hideaway on Baker Street. Much of this writing was influenced by the war. *Meditation on a German Song of 1848,* for orchestra (1941; London, December 6, 1941) contrasts the ancient revolutionary spirit of Germany with that of the Nazis. *Fantasia on Soviet Themes,* for orchestra, was written in 1942 and introduced at a London Promenade concert on July 27, 1947, and in 1943 Bush completed a song to honor the Red Army called "The Great Red Army." *Britain's Part* (1943), a large war-oriented work, was for chorus, narrator, piano, and percussion.

After the war, in his effort to appeal to the general music public, Bush simplified his writing, making it more consistently English in style, more consonant and commercial, his textures more transparent, and his material more easily assimilable. At the same time, he maintained a high artistic level. As a critic noted in *Musical Events* in 1962: "Alan Bush's music is one of the most serious and solid achievements that England can boast in our time. One of the distinguishing factors of his music as a whole is the thorough-going and unremitting professionalism which emanates from every bar of it." And, in the fifth edition of *Grove's Dictionary of Music and Musicians,* Colin Mason said: "His range is wide, the quality of his music consistently excellent. He has the intellectual concentration of a Tippett, the easy command and expansiveness of Walton, the nervous intensity of Rawsthorne, the serene leisureliness of Rubbra. . . . He is surpassed only in melody, as are all the others, by Walton, but not even by him in harmonic and orchestral richness, nor by Tippett in contrapuntal originality and the expressive power of rather austere musical thought, nor by Rawsthorne in concise, compelling utterance and telling instrumental invention, nor by Rubbra in handling large forms well."

One of the first results of a new striving for realization of a national style was the *English Suite,* for string orchestra (1945–1946; London, February 9, 1946) in which the common chord progressions found in English music are fully used. "Each individual's faculty of self-expression is developed within a particular national and cultural framework," Bush wrote in a 1969 paper entitled *National Character an Essential*

Ingredient in Musical Art Today, which was read to the Congress of the International Folk-Music Council on August 12, 1969. He indicated in it how a national style is evolved: "When he expresses himself in words, he does so, unless artificially required or conditioned to do otherwise, in his own language with its particular metrical accentuation, tempo, rise and fall. . . . Music, which began with singing, developed from the start its turn of melody peculiarities of rhythm and accentuation which are brought about by its association with the words of whatever language is being sung; and instrumental music is nothing other essentially than a technically elaborated representation of vocal music. From this it follows that a composer, if he is to express himself truthfully and without yielding to the pressures of fashion or without being deceived by superficial and false theorizing about the necessity of internationalism in art in the present technological age, will do so without the framework of musical turns of phrases which have resulted from the basic vocal music of his own nationality."

Besides using nationalism, Bush appealed to a larger audience through his operas for children and school productions. The first was *The Press-Gang* (1945), performed at St. Christopher's School in Letchworth, Herts, England on March 7, 1947. It was followed by *The Spell Unbound,* an opera for girls, in an Elizabethan setting (1953; Sunderland, England, March 11, 1955), and *The Ferryman's Daughter,* an opera of the Thames Waterside (1961; Letchworth, March 6, 1964). Bush's wife, Nancy, provided the libretti for all three operas.

A number of Bush's works continued to have social, economic, or political overtones. On commission from the Nottingham Cooperative Society for its quincentenary celebration, Bush wrote *The Nottingham Symphony* (1949; Nottingham, June 27, 1969), with Robin Hood, in the first movement called "Sherwood Forest," symbolizing the rebellion of the poor against the rich. The remaining movements had other Nottingham place names, representing aspects of past and present life, without social implications: "Clifton Grove" describes the peaceful flow of the River Trent below a beautiful cliff favored by courting young couples of Nottingham. "Castle Rock" portrays Nottingham Castle which is built on a rock and dominates the city. "Goose Fair" is descriptive of the oldest

surviving fair in Britain. Structurally, this symphony followed the "thematic method" in which every note has thematic significance (much in the same way it has in the twelve-tone system). All the various elements—melody, harmony, and bass—emanate from the original themes of the work as well as having their harmonic and rhythmic parts to play.

Song of Friendship, a cantata for bass solo, chorus, and orchestra, with a text by Nancy Bush (1949; London, November 6, 1949), was dedicated to international cooperation with the socialist countries of Europe. *Defender of Peace,* a politically oriented "character portrait for orchestra" (1957), was a plea for pacificism; *The World Is His Song,* with a text by Nancy Bush, was dedicated to Paul Robeson (1958; London, February 15, 1959); and *The Tide That Will Never Turn,* a "declaration by Hugh McDiarmid," was for two speakers, bass or baritone solo, chorus, strings, percussion, and piano (1961; London, April 1, 1961).

Bush's third symphony dealt with a literary subject with social and political implications. It was *The Byron Symphony* (1959–1960) which was introduced in Leipzig on March 20, 1962. As in the previous symphonies, Bush gave place names associated with Byron's life to each of the movements: "Newstead Abbey," characterizes the youthful Byron with boundless energy, love of life, and fiercely critical attitude toward tyranny and the social conventions of the day; "Westminster," refers to Byron's address to the House of Lords, condemning the political oppression of the common people by the House of Lords; "Il Palazzo Savioli," celebrates Byron's happy idyll with Teresa, Countess Guiccioli; and, finally, "Missolonghi" deals with Byron's participation in the Greek struggle for liberation from the Turks, and his death. The text for the last movement, for mixed chorus and baritone solo, was taken from the *Ode on the Death of Lord Byron,* written in 1824 by the Greek national poet, Dionysos Solomos and the melody of the battle music was derived from a Greek folk dance.

Bush also wrote opera to call attention to social and political issues. *Wat Tyler* (1948–1950) —winner of the Arts Council Competition Prize in London in 1951 and produced in Leipzig on September 6, 1953—speaks of the struggle of the English peasants for liberation in 1381. *Men of Blackmoor* (1954–1955; Weimar, November 18, 1956) describes the hardships of the Northumbrian miners at the beginning of the 19th century. The *Sugar Reapers* (1961–1964; Leipzig, December 11, 1966), known in Europe as *Guyana Johnny,* was based on the struggle of the Guyanese people against British imperialism in 1953. *Joe Hill: The Man Who Never Died* (1965–1967)—produced at the Deutsche Staatsoper in Berlin on September 29, 1970—had Joe Hill for its hero. He was the celebrated American labor leader who, on a slim thread of circumstantial evidence, was convicted of murder and, after a trial charged with anti-labor hysteria, was executed in spite of the protests of world leaders. Four labor songs by Joe Hill are incorporated into the score. The four operas by Bush have been performed in twelve professional productions in ten European opera houses and one hundred performances; they have all been broadcast by the B.B.C. The libretti of the first three operas are by Nancy Bush, the fourth by Barrie Stavis.

In 1947–1948, Bush was the chairman of the Composers Guild of Great Britain. For his fiftieth birthday, the Workers Music Association issued *A Tribute to Alan Bush,* to which many leading English composers and critics made contributions. His sixtieth birthday was celebrated with a concert of his works at Morley College in England. In 1962, Bush was awarded the Handel Prize by the City Council of Halle of the German Democratic Republic.

Bush and his wife make their home at Radlett, Hertfordshire, England. His extra-musical interests include travel, reading, graphic arts, chess, bridge, and watching tennis matches at Wimbledon. Bush is the author of *Strict Counterpoint in the Palestrina Style* (1948) and a book of reminiscences, *In My Eighth Decade* (1980).

MAJOR WORKS

Chamber Music—String Quartet in A minor; Quartet, for piano, violin, viola, and cello; Dialectic, for string quartet; Concert Piece, for cello and piano; Three Concert Studies, for piano, violin, and cello; Autumn Poem, for horn and piano; Three African Sketches, for flute and piano; Three Raga Melodies, for unaccompanied violin; Prelude Air and Dance, for solo violin, string quartet, and percussion; Serenade, for string quartet; Suite of Six, for string quartet; Sonatina, for viola and piano.

Choral Music—Britain's Part, for chorus, narrator, piano, and percussion; The Winter's Journey, cantata for soprano and baritone solos, chorus, string quartet, and harp; Song of Friendship, cantata for bass solo, chorus, and orchestra; The Ballad of Freedom's Soldier, for tenor, bass-baritone solos, chorus, and orches-

tra; The World Is His Song, for mezzo-soprano or baritone solo, chorus, and instruments; The Tide That Will Never Turn, for the two speakers, bass or baritone solo, chorus, strings, percussion, and piano.

Operas—Wat Tyler; The Spell Unbound, children's opera; Men of Blackmoor; The Ferryman's Daughter, children's opera; The Sugar Reapers (Guyana Johnny); Joe Hill: The Man Who Never Died.

Orchestral Music—3 symphonies; Piano Concerto, with baritone solo and male voice chorus; Meditation on a German Song of 1848, for solo violin and string orchestra; Fantasia on Soviet Themes; Resolution, overture; English Suite; Piers Plowman's Day, symphonic suite; Concerto for Violin and Orchestra; Concert Suite, for cello and orchestra; Defender of Peace: Character Portrait for Orchestra; Dorian Passacaglia and Fugue; Variations, Nocturne and Finale on an English Sea-Song, for piano and orchestra; Partita Concertante; Time Remembered, for chamber orchestra; Scherzo, for wind orchestra with percussion; Africa: Symphonic Movement, for piano and orchestra; Concerto Overture for an Occasion; The Liverpool Overture.

Piano Music—2 sonatas; Esquisse Le Quatorze Juillet; Nocturne; Two Ballads of the Sea; Suite, for harpsichord or piano; Suite, for two pianos; Correnty ne Kwe-Kwe; Letter Galliard; Twenty-Four Preludes.

Vocal Music—Pages from the Swallow Book, for mezzo-soprano and piano; Voices of the Prophets, cantata for tenor and piano; Seafarers' Songs, for baritone and piano; The Freight of Harvest, song cycle for tenor and piano; Life's Span, song cycle for mezzo-soprano and piano; De Plenos Poderes, song cycle for baritone and piano; Woman's Life, song cycle for soprano and piano.

ABOUT

Bush, A., In My Eighth Decade; Clare, E. (ed.), A Tribute to Alan Bush on his Fiftieth Birthday: A Symposium; Sadie, S. (ed.), The New Grove Dictionary of Music and Musicians; Schafer, M., British Composers in Interview.

Ferruccio Busoni

1866–1924

For biographical sketch, list of earlier works, and bibliography, see *Composers Since 1900.*

Busoni's rarely performed opera, *Arlecchino,* was revived in Vienna by the Vienna Chamber Opera on November 26, 1978, and in San Francisco by the Berkeley Promenade Orchestra on January 28, 1980. In 1979 all six Busoni piano sonatas were recorded in a single album by Paul Jacobs and released by Nonesuch Records. The two-piano team of Philip Lorenz and Ena Bronstein revived the monumental *Fantasia Contrappuntistica* in an all-Busoni program in New York on March 18, 1980.

ABOUT (supplementary)

Ley, R. (ed.), Busoni's Letters to His Wife; Stuckenschmidt, H. H., Ferruccio Busoni: Chronicle of a European.

New York Times, March 16, 1980.

Charles Wakefield Cadman

1881–1946

For biographical sketch, list of earlier works, and bibliography, see *Composers Since 1900.*

After more than half a century, Cadman's opera, *Shanewis* (1918) was revived by the Central City Opera in Denver, Colorado, during the summer of 1979. Reviewing this revival in *The New Yorker,* Andrew Porter found the opera to be "tunefully Puccinian with an occasional hint of Griegian exoticism. It flows, it sounds fresh, and it is affecting."

ABOUT (supplementary)

Dictionary of American Biography, Supplement 4.

John Cage

1912–

For biographical sketch, list of earlier works, and bibliography, see *Composers Since 1900.*

HPSCHD ("harpsichord" in computer language) was a four-hour multimedia conception which Cage had devised with Lejaren Hiller, a computer-music expert, between 1967 and 1969. Scored for one to seven amplified harpsichords and one to fifty-one monaural tape machines, the music is accompanied by films, including one of the Apollo moon landing, and slides in brightly colored patterns. It was first performed at the University of Illinois in Urbana on May 16, 1969, with subsequent performances in Albany, New York, San Francisco, Berlin, London, and Brooklyn, New York.

Cheap Imitation was written in 1969 as a piano solo. It was then developed in 1972 for an orchestra of from twenty-four to ninety-five in-struments (with or without conductor) on a commission from the Koussevitzky Music Foundation, and in 1977 was redone as a violin solo. It is essentially an "alteration" of Erik Satie's *Socrate,* to quote the composer. Cage explained: "In the fall of 1969 I completed the two-piano version of Satie's *Socrate* for Merce Cunningham. But the copyright owner did not give permission to publish it. The dancers had already rehearsed it so I made a piano solo based upon I Ching chance operations which preserves the rhythms and phraseology of *Socrate.* I produced a new melody for the rhythm—and I hope the spirit—of the original." The orchestral version was first heard in Munich, Germany, on August 28, 1972, before receiving its American premiere on January 21, 1973 in New York. Donal Henahan wrote in the New York *Times,* that "like *Socrate,* it disdained to excite in any way, dealing at length in a static, passionless unrolling of sound tapestry made up of fairly brief, sometimes fragmentary, statements. Rarely did more than half a dozen instruments play at once so that a chamber-music texture was maintained."

In *Sixty-Two Mesostics Re Merce Cunningham* (1971), for unaccompanied voice using microphone, Cage replaced conventional musical symbols with arrangements of six hundred typefaces to suggest sonority, pitch, time durations, and timbre. This music accompanied the Merce Cunningham dance company in a choreographic concept in New York on March 19, 1978.

In *Score (40 Drawings by Thoreau) and 23 Parts,* "for any instruments and/or voices," in 1974, Cage went one step further in his "art is life" theory by using a "recording of the dawn at Stony Point, New York, on August 6, 1974." Following a performance at the Celebration of Contemporary Music at the Juilliard School of Music in March 1976, Andrew Porter described this work in *The New Yorker:* "The piece consists of twelve sound flurries, each followed by a silence of equal length; after all that is done, player and audience spend an equivalent time listening in silence to the Stony Point recording (no dawn chorus sang—only one dull, repetitive bird)."

Child of Tree (1975), for percussion solo with "amplified plant materials" derived its sound from contact microphones being attached to cactus, seeds, branches, and other flora, as Joan La Barbara explained in *Musical America,* "and then plucking the spines, striking or stroking the object to produce delicate pitched clicks, pops and rattles."

Cage wrote *Renga* and *Apartment House 1776* ("material for a musical happening") on a joint commission from the National Endowment for the Arts in conjunction with six major American symphony orchestras to commemorate the American bicentennial. Two separate works for orchestra, *Renga* is for an orchestra of seventy-eight musicians and *Apartment House 1776* (named to suggest many happenings at once) is for an orchestra of twenty-four musicians and four voices (representing Protestant, Sephardic, American Indian, and Negro people who lived in this country two hundred years ago). Though different, *Renga* and *Apartment House 1776* can be played separately or one after the other or simultaneously. It was first heard when the Boston Symphony under Seiji Ozawa introduced it in Boston on September 10, 1976, and then in performances by the New York Philharmonic, Los Angeles Philharmonic, the Cleveland Orchestra, the Philadelphia Orchestra, and the Chicago Symphony.

Cage explained that the seventy-eight musicians performing *Renga* "act on the suggestion of graphic notation. In Western tradition, tones are musical when they are fixed with respect to their characteristics. In folk and Oriental traditions tones are musical when they change pitch and quality in their course. Graphic notation suggests such changes. By being conducted, *Renga* is given time-length, since the conductor may introduce silences at the end of most of the lines and since his changing tempi are his own he must first of all attempt to know fairly closely how long *Renga* is when he conducts it. . . . Then he must decide whether *Apartment House 1776* is to begin before or after *Renga* and which of these pieces is to end first. Then he will be able to tell the four singers and the twenty-four musicians of *Apartment House 1776* how long their programs which they themselves make are to be; and he will establish means for them to know when to begin and when to conclude their performances." Cage explained further: "*Apartment House 1776* is a body of material (sixty-four pieces, any number of which may be performed in any sequence and any superimpositions) for the rest of the orchestra . . . and four voices. . . . The twenty-four musicians make four quartets (each with an assistant time beater) and

four soloists: a drummer, a string player, a fife or flute player and a keyboard player." At one point in this composition, one of the vocalists, representing Chief Swift Eagle, indulges in belly-slapping laughter.

The stimulus for *Renga* and *Apartment House 1776* was 361 drawings by Thoreau and it was composed by the I Ching method of chance determination. Reporting for the New York *Times,* Donal Henahan wrote: "Mr. Cage weaves a remarkable intricate texture, but also allows singers and instrumentalists to achieve genuine touching results. In this work one finds Mr. Cage giving more attention than in the past to shaping recognizable musical profiles, and he is not at much pains to obscure overlapping tempos and layers of sonority." The audiences in Boston and New York responded with competing boos and cheers. During the New York performance, a mass exodus by the audience took place while the work was still in progress, "the likes of which," said Allen Hughes in the New York *Times,* "this reporter has never witnessed in twenty-five years of professional concertgoing."

Cage was honored on his sixty-fifth birthday (a bit belatedly) on April 24, 1978 in New York with a "retrospective concert" featuring the world premiere of *Freeman Etudes I-VIII,* for solo violin, performed by Paul Zukofsky whom Cage frequently consulted in the course of its composition. The program also included a performance by Grete Sulton of eight of the thirty-two études comprising *Études australes* which Cage had written in 1974–1975. In composing these piano études, Cage used a book of star maps and numerology (based on the number 64), translated these into note values, the I Ching method of chance determination to determine intervallic structure, and harmonic drones produced by using rubber wedges to depress certain keys in the bass register.

In 1970, Cage served as Fellow at the Center for Advanced Studies at Wesleyan University in Middletown, Connecticut (a post he previously held in 1960). Since 1970 he has been composer-in-residence at the University of Cincinnati; an Associate at the Center for Advanced Study at the University of Illinois where he received a Thorne Music Fund grant; and artist-in-residence at the University of California in Davis. He was elected to membership in the American Academy of Arts and Sciences.

Cage is the author of *Notations,* with Alice Knowles (1969); *Not Wanting to Say Anything about Marcel,* with Calvin Sumsion (1969); and *The Mushroom Book,* with Lois Long and Alexander Smith (1974). He also wrote *M* (1973), *Writings through Finegan's Wake* (1978), and *Empty Words,* a collection of his writings between 1973 and 1978 (1979). His graphic works include *Seven Day Diary* (1978) and *Signals* (1978).

MAJOR WORKS (supplementary)

Chamber Music—Score (40 Drawings by Thoreau) and 23 Parts, for any instruments and/or voices; Cheap Imitation (solo violin version); Études boreales, for cello solo and piano solo; Freeman Études I–VIII, for violin solo; Nine Microtonal Chorals, for violin solo.

Multi-media—HPSCHD, for 1–7 harpsichords and 1–51 tape machines.

Orchestral Music—Quartets I–VIII, for three different orchestras, also for band and twelve amplified instruments; Cheap Imitation (orchestral version); Etcetera, for chamber orchestra; Renga, for 78 instruments; Apartment House 1776, a mixed-media event.

Percussion Music—Child of Tree, percussion solo with "amplified tree materials"; Inlets, for 4 performers with conch shells.

Piano Music—Cheap Imitation (original version); Etudes australes, thirty-two études.

Vocal Music—Sixty-Two Mesostics Re Merce Cunningham, for unaccompanied voices using microphones; Song Books I, and II, for 3–92; Hymns and Variations, for twelve amplified voices.

Miscellaneous—Sound Anonymously Received; Bird Cage, 12 tapes; Lecture on the Weather, for twelve spoken vocalists; A Dip in the Lake; Letters to Erik Satie; Variations III and IV, for any number of people performing any actions.

ABOUT (supplementary)

Charles, D., Gloses sur John Cage; Ewen, D., Composers of Tomorrow's Music; Griffiths, P., A Concise History of Avant-Garde Music: from Debussy to Boulez; Kostelanetz, R., (ed.), John Cage; Nyman, M., Experimental Music: Cage and Beyond.

High Fidelity/Musical America, November 1972; Musical Quarterly, October 1979; New York Times, September 3, 1972, October 22, 1976; People, October 15, 1979; Stereo Review, May 1969.

John Alden Carpenter

1876–1951

See *Composers Since 1900.*

Elliott Carter

1908–

For biographical sketch, list of earlier works, and bibliography, see *Composers Since 1900.*

Carter's *Concerto for Orchestra* was written on a commission from the New York Philharmonic Orchestra to celebrate its 125th anniversary in 1969. Because of the unusual complexity of the work's organization and scoring, Carter was unable to finish it on schedule. He worked on it as composer-in-residence at the American Academy in Rome (a stay interrupted only to attend an all-Carter concert in New York on February 16, 1969, on his sixtieth birthday). The Concerto was finally finished and performed on February 5, 1970 with Leonard Bernstein conducting. Although it made exacting demands on the listener, the work was well-received by the audience.

The Concerto's inspiration came from the Nobel Prize-winning poem *Vents* ("Winds") by the French poet St. John Perse. "The poem had attracted me by its expansive, almost Whitmanesque, descriptions of a United States constantly swept by forces like winds, forces that are always transforming, remolding or obliterating the past and introducing the fresh and the new," Carter revealed, and he added that the music does deal "primarily with the poetry of change, transformation, reorientation of feelings and thoughts," but it does not follow the poem literally. The Concerto, played without interruption, is mainly in a serial technique, in four contrasting movements and the orchestra is subdivided into four sound groupings. "Each movement comes into focus against a background of the other three," the composer explained, "each with its own character and development." Writing in *High Fidelity/Musical America,* David Hamilton said: "The virtuosic treatment of the sound groups, the constant flux and interplay of color, tempo and density are obviously governed by an argument more organic than schematic, with the overall rate of change functioning as a kind of large-scale counterpoint in the local movement. At crucial points, the various elements seem to collide—the recitative-like double-bass ensemble colored by horns, tubas and low drums; the cello group, with its 'outriders' of piano, harp and wooden percussion; the arabesque-dominated violin-and-flute group, with its glittering accents of metallic percussion and the midrange unit built around the violas, which begins slowly and gains tempo as the Concerto proceeds. After the last climax, the music gradually disintegrates into fragments, ending on a questioning resonance of glockenspiel, bells and vibraphone."

In 1971, Carter was awarded the Pulitzer Prize in music for the second time for a string quartet—the String Quartet No. 3. This work was commissioned by the Juilliard School of Music for its Quartet, which introduced it in New York on January 23, 1972. In this single-movement work, the four instruments are divided into pairs: one duo for violin and cello playing in rubato style, and the other duo for violin and viola in regular rhythm. Carter said, "the violin-cello duo presents four different musical characters: an angry intense Furioso, a fanciful Leggerissimo, a Pizzicato giocoso with a lyrical Andante expressivo in short sections one after the other in various orders, sometimes with pauses in between. The violin-viola duo, meanwhile, presents the six contrasting characters listed in the program (Maestoso; Grazioso; Pizzicato, Giusto mechanico; Scorrevole; Largo tranquillo; and Appassionato). During the quartet each character of each duo is presented alone and also in combination with each character of the other duo to give a sense of ever-varying perspective of feeling, expression, rivalry and cooperation." So unorthodox in style, structure, and technique is this quartet that when the Juilliard Quartet rehearsed it, its first violinist remarked: "We had to forget everything we ever learned about playing together and perform it in a new way." Though intricate and abstruse, Harriett Johnson in the New York *Post* found it "a finely wrought and conceived composition, the antithesis of chaos, but it looks out at a long horizon with anger, detachment, even mystery in the process and always questioning, provoking." In *Time*, William Bender noted that "Ex-

periencing the drama of its dense inner layers and illusory surfaces . . . is like viewing late Beethoven through an atonal prism. . . . The power is there. So is the higher mathematics of Carter's intricate organizational scheme."

The one-movement Brass Quintet (1974) is as multilayered as the third string quartet, with totally individualized parts for each instrument. It was written for the American Brass who presented it first in London on October 20, 1974 (the anniversary of the one hundredth birthday of Charles Ives) before bringing it to New York on December 15 of that year.

On March 21, 1975, *Duo for Violin and Piano* (1974), commissioned by the Library of Congress, received its premiere with Paul Zukofsky and Gilbert Kalich as soloists at a "Prospective Encounter" concert under the auspices of the New York Philharmonic and its music director, Pierre Boulez. *A Mirror on Which to Dwell*—a setting of six poems by Elizabeth Bishop for soprano and nine instrumentalists—was commissioned by the Speculum Musicae in honor of the American bicentennial. Its world premiere took place in New York on February 24, 1976, with Susan Davenny Wyner as soloist and Richard Fritz as conductor.

Carter's *A Symphony of Three Orchestras* was also written for the bicentennial. Commissioned jointly by the National Endowment for the Arts and several of America's leading orchestras, the world premiere took place on February 17, 1977, with Pierre Boulez conducting the New York Philharmonic Orchestra. The orchestra was divided into three smaller orchestras: the first, made up of brass, strings and timpani; the second—clarinets, piano, vibraphone, chimes, marimba, solo violins, basses, and a group of cellos; the third—flutes, oboes, bassoons, horns, violins, violas, basses, and non-pitched percussion. The joining of three ensembles carries out the baroque concept of the symphony rather than the classical concept. Irving Kolodin in *Saturday Review* pointed out that not only is Carter's aim in "the redistribution of resources possessed by our symphony orchestra to unshackle the ties to long-established concepts of tonal weight, dynamic distribution and coloristic identity," but also "it serves the purpose of distributing sound from the directions and in the combinations that take shape in his mind, in a manner much harder to achieve under normal circumstances." The work begins with an introduction, continues with twelve short movements (four for each of the three orchestras, with each orchestra playing its four movements twice but not in regular order) and ends with a coda.

Carter's seventieth birthday was the occasion for a number of performances of his work. On October 28, 1978, an all-Carter program was presented by the League of Composers–International Society of Contemporary Music in New York. On December 1, the New York Philharmonic revived his 1965 Piano Concerto, with Ursula Oppens as soloist. On December 10, an all-Carter program was given in New York featuring members of the Speculum Musicae, who combined earlier Carter works and the world premiere of a new composition, *Syringa,* for mezzo-soprano, bass, and eleven instruments. This work is set to a poem by John Ashbery based on the Orpheus legend and various literary quotations. "As in every new Carter composition," commented Peter G. Davis in the New York *Times,* "there is a great deal to digest here, surely more than most people can grasp during the initial hearing. First of all, one must attend to the Ashbery poem itself, which is densely packed with imagery and subtle allusions. Then there is the extra overlay of the Greek passages. Finally, there is Mr. Carter's own supercharged musical syntax with its metrical fluidity, vertical restlessness and coloristic variety."

On December 11, 1978, Carter's actual birthday, he was presented with the Handel Medallion, New York's highest cultural award, by Mayor Koch. An "Elliott Carter Day" was declared in the City of Los Angeles on April 27, 1979, with an evening concert of his music. In 1981, Carter was awarded the prestigious West German Siemens Music Prize of $78,500 for his contributions to orchestral music.

Bayan Northcott, the English musicologist, in the 70th birthday catalog tribute, wrote "if one had to single out Carter's most characteristic gift, it would surely be the sheer power of invention which has unfailingly carried him through the grandest structures with a momentum and purposefulness equal to any composer of this century."

In 1969, Carter was elected to membership in the American Academy of Arts and Sciences; that year he also received the Premio delle Muse, "Polimnia," award from the Associazione Artistico Letteraria Internazionale in Florence, Italy. The National Institute of Arts and Letters pre-sented him with a gold medal for Eminence in Music in 1971. Honorary doctorates in music were conferred on him by Boston University, Princeton University, Oberlin College, and Yale and Harvard Universities in 1970, the year in which he was also made honorary member of the Akademie der Kunst in Berlin. An exhibition of his manuscripts was held at the Library and Museum of the Performing Arts in New York in 1973–1974.

MAJOR WORKS (supplementary)

Chamber Music—Canon for 3; In Memoriam Igor Stravinsky; Duo for Violin and Piano; Brass Quintet; Fantasy on Purcell's Fantasia on One Note, for two trumpets, horn, and trombones.

Orchestral Music—Concerto for Orchestra; A Symphony of Three Orchestras; Birthday Fanfare.

Piano Music—Night Fantasies.

Vocal Music—A Mirror on Which to Dwell, six songs for soprano and chamber orchestra; Syringa, for mezzo-soprano, bass, and eleven instruments.

ABOUT (supplementary)

Edwards, A. F. and E. C. Flawed Words and Stubborn Sounds: a Conversation with Elliott Carter; Stone, E., and Stone, K. (eds.), The Writings of Elliott Carter: an American Composer Looks at Modern Music.

BMI, Many Worlds of Music, Issue 4, 1978; High Fidelity/Musical America, August 1973; Music and Musicians (Juilliard School), August 1972; New York Times, February 3, 1969; December 10, 1978; The New Yorker, February 5, 1973, April 24, 1978; Stereo Review, December 1972; Time, February 10, 1975.

Alfredo Casella

1881–1947

See *Composers Since 1900.*

Mario Castelnuovo-Tedesco

1895–1968

For biographical sketch, list of earlier works, and bibliography, see *Composers Since 1900.*

In 1973, an international contest for guitar music named after Castelnuovo-Tedesco was formed in Ancona, Italy, by the publishing house of Berben.

Chadwick

In commemoration of Castelnuovo-Tedesco's eightieth birthday, a seven-part festival of his compositions was held at the LaGuardia Community College in New York City beginning on February 2, 1975. Two world premieres were heard at the initial concert of the festival: the comedy opera *The Importance of Being Earnest* (1962), based on Oscar Wilde's play and the scenic oratorio, *Tobias and the Angel* (1965), for high school production. The latter work was based on the Old Testament story of the youth, Tobias, who was guided by a traveling companion who turned out to be an angel. Jack Heimenz reported in *High Fidelity/Musical America,* that "there is much to enjoy in ... [this] work. ... One soprano aria involving shimmering strings and a haunting oboe obbligato is pure Rimsky; but the presiding influence is pretty much Puccini. It's all ingratiating enough, sometimes quite impressive."

A complete catalog of Castelnuovo-Tedesco's works, compiled by Nick Rossi, was issued by the Castelnuovo-Tedesco Society of New York in 1977.

ABOUT (supplementary)
High Fidelity/Musical America, May 1975.

George Chadwick

1854–1931

For biographical sketch, list of earlier works, and bibliography, see *Composers Since 1900.*

Chadwick's String Quartet No. 4 (1896) was resurrected and performed by the American String Quartet in New York on January 18, 1977. In the New York *Times,* Allen Hughes described it as "fashioned with considerable skill out of materials that often seem just one step removed from the folk idiom. Melodic contours, harmony, even rhythms, are close to those of hymns and the popular songs and dance music of the time."

Another long forgotten Chadwick composition—the opera-oratorio *Judith*—was revived at the Hopkins Center of Dartmouth College, in Hanover, New Hampshire, on January 29, 1977. Reviewing it in *High Fidelity/Musical America,* a critic wrote that it "includes a variety of vocal combinations and sumptuous orchestral score

which is the work's most impressive feature. ... Chadwick's admirable workmanship was apparent throughout, although listeners had to concede a variety of musical styles. ... Some of *Judith's* most effective movements came when the composer threw off his German-oriented learning and reverted to a simpler style."

ABOUT (supplementary)
Musical Quarterly, January 1975.

Gustave Charpentier

1860–1956

See *Composers Since 1900.*

Carlos Chávez

1899–1978

For biographical sketch, list of earlier works, and bibliography, see *Composers Since 1900.*

Chávez returned to the United States from Mexico in 1969 to conduct the New York premiere of *Elatio* with the Little Orchestra Society. Scored for large orchestra and augmented percussion, *Elatio,* written in 1967 on commission from the Mexican government, had received its world premiere in Mexico City on July 15, 1967.

Among Chávez's subsequent principal works for orchestra are *Discovery,* introduced in Aptos, California, on August 24, 1969; *Clio,* a symphonic ode, first heard in Houston, Texas, on March 23, 1970; and *Initium,* commissioned for the inaugural of the Performing Arts Hall in Akron, Ohio, where it received its world premiere on October 9, 1973 with Louis Lane conducting. John Von Rhein in reviewing the premiere of *Initium* for the Knight newspaper chain, wrote that "as in most recent Chávez works, the writing is basically linear, the sonorities hard and bright. ... The dissonant content is high and the piece is almost totally athematic. ... There are haunting sustained trills, and a wonderful capricious mid-section full of compressed energy."

Chávez disclosed his modus operandi as a composer to Von Rhein: "I think of every work as an experiment. But when I say experimentation I do not mean calculation because composition involves a great deal of intuition. I start with a general idea of what I wish to express, then, through intuition, particularize that idea. Thus, for me, creation is going from the general to the particular."

From 1960 to 1965, Chávez was the director of the composers' workshop which he founded in the National Conservatory. In 1973 he resigned as artistic director of the National Symphony and the National Opera in Mexico City.

A complete catalog of his works, edited by Rodolfo Halffter, was published in Spanish, English, and French in Mexico City in 1971.

Chávez died of a heart attack at the home of his daughter, Anita, in Mexico City, on August 2, 1978. After lying in state for several hours on August 3 at the Palace of Fine Arts, he was buried there, in the Rotunda of Illustrious Men.

MAJOR WORKS (supplementary)

Ballet—Piramíde.

Chamber Music—Variations, for violin and piano.

Orchestral Music—Elatio, for large orchestra and augmented percussion section; Discovery; Clio, a symphonic ode; Initium.

Piano Music—Estudio a Rubinstein; Caprichios.

ABOUT (supplementary)

New York Times, August 4, 1978.

Samuel Coleridge-Taylor

1875–1912

See *Composers Since 1900*.

Michael Colgrass

1932–

Michael Charles Colgrass was born in Chicago on April 22, 1932. His father, Michael Clement Colgrass—a postmaster in Brookfield, Illinois, for thirty-seven years—came from Foggia, Italy; his mother, Ann Hand Colgrass, was Irish.

Colgrass: kōl′ gràs

MICHAEL COLGRASS

"The thing that made me want to become a musician," Colgrass revealed, "was seeing a jazz drummer, Ray Bauduc, play the drums in Chicago." As proof of his determination to play the drums, he took on a job caddying at a golf course. When, he had saved twenty-five dollars at summer's end, his father provided the rest of the money for a drum. Michael began to play without instruction and played drum solos at many grammar school student programs. When he was twelve, he formed a jazz band.

Since he was also talented in drawing and painting, Colgrass said, "actually there was some question of whether I would go to the Art Institute in Chicago or to the University of Illinois to study music. There was no real question in my mind, but my father, who thought I was a good artist, tried to push painting. At thirteen I was drawing jazz musicians." It was through these drawings that Colgrass came to know some of the foremost jazz musicians of the time. Whenever one of the jazz greats performed in Chicago, Colgrass would make the forty-five-minute trip from Brookfield, to hear the performance and go backstage to present the artist with a portrait. Thus he came to meet Benny Goodman, the Dorsey brothers, Gene Krupa, Buddy Rich, and others. "They'd sit and talk to me for a long time, and I'd ask a thousand questions about the things they did, the pieces they played, where they traveled in the country and could I have a job in their band. There I was, thirteen, and ready for them."

A few years later he was sitting in on jazz

71

bands in South Side Chicago cafes and he didn't even know where "C was on the treble clef." He decided to study classical music to get a solid grounding for his jazz activities and in 1950, after graduating from Riverside-Brookfield High School, he enrolled in the University of Illinois in Urbana.

At the University, he was such an unsatisfactory student in classes other than music that twice he was put on probation, but he received formal musical training for the first time from Paul Price (percussion) and Eugene Weigle (composition). He also received instruction from Lukas Foss at the Berkshire Music Center in Tanglewood, Massachusetts, and during the summer of 1953 he studied composition with Darius Milhaud at Aspen. His summers of 1952 and 1954 were spent as percussionist in the Berkshire Music Center Orchestra at Tanglewood.

In a wish to extend the all too limited repertory for percussion, he wrote *Three Brothers* (1950–1951) for nine percussions, following it in the next few years with *Percussion Music* (1953), *Concerto for Percussion and Brass* (1953), *Chamber Music for Percussion Quintet* (1955), *Inventions on a Motive,* for percussion ensemble (1956), *Variations for Four Drums and Viola* (1957), and *Fantasy Variations,* for percussion ensemble (1960). *The Variations for Four Drums and Viola* was given its initial hearing at the Five Spot Cafe in New York City in 1957 with the composer as drummer and Emanuel Vardi as violist.

He served in the United States Army between 1954 and 1956, and played the timpani in the Seventh Army Symphony Orchestra in Germany. After receiving his Bachelor of Music degree at the University of Illinois in 1956, he went to New York to study composition privately; with Wallingford Riegger in 1958–1959 and Ben Weber between 1959 and 1962, under whose influence he became interested in serial music. "I wanted to stretch my muscles," he said.

A rhapsody, for clarinet, violin, and piano, was commissioned in 1963 by clarinetist Arthur Bloom, who helped to introduce it in February of that year. *Rhapsodic Fantasy* for fifteen drums and orchestra, received its world premiere with Colgrass as soloist in Copenhagen, in an October 1965 performance of the Danish Radio Orchestra with Tamas Veto conducting.

Colgrass earned his living by playing percus-sion instruments with dance and opera orchestras, new music ensembles, in films and recordings, in the pit of musical theaters and ballet companies (including *West Side Story* and the Bolshoi Ballet), with jazz groups (including the New York Philharmonic Jazz Quartet), and in serious musical performances (Igor Stravinsky's Columbia Recording Orchestra, for example). He received two Guggenheim Fellowships, in 1964–1965 and 1968–1969.

Aware that these extensive performing appearances were competing with his ambitions as a composer, he reassessed what he was doing in music and where he was going. He realized that up to now he had been just "going through the motions. . . . My pieces were played primarily for audiences of the avant-garde, who were interested mainly in what was fashionable. Any desire to communicate on the part of the composer was considered unsophisticated. . . ." He turned away from serialism to the principles of composition that he had been rejecting for about seven years and he renounced the conviction that tonality and melody were dead. He began to write in the more traditional techniques and the more formal approaches of pre-Schoenbergian music.

"I knew I had to restore that relationship with an audience or that I would as a creative musician stop existing. I didn't care what Pierre Boulez was saying or Karlheinz Stockhausen on how to write music. I'd rather look at Charlie Parker."

According to Colgrass, establishing contact with the music public became a compulsion—the need to communicate with audiences instead of writing music solely for his own delectation or that of a limited elite group. "How to bridge the gap that has developed between the artist and people became the biggest challenge I knew," he declared.

He decided to write "stories" about life in multimedia productions involving singing, acting, dancing, and mime. One of these was a short opera, *Virgil's Dream,* to his own text in which a child prodigy is given an insurance policy to protect his dream of success. Four actor-singer-dancers were involved, and four instrumentalists and "with the singers we worked 'masks,' a technique of locking your face in an expression and trying to sing through it in a natural way. With the instrumentalists we practiced mime movements." The first performance took place at the

Brighton Festival in Brighton, England, in April 1967 and four years later there were performances in Fort Wayne, St. Louis, Columbus (Ohio), and Huntington (West Virginia).

Colgrass enjoyed his first success as a composer in America with a seven-movement suite for orchestra, *As Quiet As* (1965–1966). Written on commission from the Fromm Music Foundation for the Berkshire Music Center at Tanglewood, it was introduced on August 18, 1966, under Gunther Schuller's direction. This work was performed by other major American symphony orchestras including the Boston Symphony (February 17, 1967) which recorded it for RCA Victor under Erich Leinsdorf.

In composing the work, Colgrass started with "Let's be as quiet as. ..." From twenty one completions by fourth graders, listed by Constance Fauci in the New York *Times* in December 1961, Colgrass chose seven, he said, "to make a nature study as might be perceived by a child. My purpose was to depict the very nature of each metaphor as if I were demonstrating to a blind person the essence of a leaf as it changes color, of a creek abandoned even by birds and of an ant—or many ants—skittering about." The fourth and fifth sections of the work ("Children Sleeping" and "Time Passing") are dream sequences in which Colgrass quotes from a Beethoven sonatina, then arranges the tune in musical styles from 1800 to the present time (Haydn, Sibelius, Ravel, Stravinsky, Webern, Count Basie), "as if one were taking a fleeting glance at music history moving through time," according to the composer. The program annotator of the Chicago Symphony described this composition as "a continuous set of seven pieces which are highly expressive in the most subtle musical manner with the most delicate of musical means; its musical style reflects his own experiences as a performer with many elements of today's music. His eclecticism has created a score of great charm and imagination."

On November 25, 1968, Colgrass married Ulla Damgaard Rassmusen. They spent one year in Europe on a Rockefeller grant studying the theater arts—taking classes in acting technique, scene study, directing voice, mime, fencing, ballet, gymnastics, Yoga, and Commedia dell' arte. "My goal," he explained, "was not to become an expert in these arts but to try to understand them, and to see how a performer's training and my writing could feed each other."

During the summer he attended a course in physical training for the arts at the Odin Theater in Denmark where Jerzy Grotowski, director and founder of the Theater Laboratory in Poland, and others trained him in nonverbal theater techniques.

These studies helped him in later years when he gave training sessions in schools in composing, acting, singing, dance, and mime to teachers, artists, students, and laymen. Characteristic of his approach was a 1971 session held in a Fort Wayne school gymnasium for a class of junior high school students which included the school wrestling team. He told them: "Your body is the first musical instrument ever invented. Like any instrument, it has to be tuned. That's what I just did and I'm going to show you how to do it." By the time the session ended, he had the wrestling team dancing to the music of Stravinsky's *The Rite of Spring*.

In 1969, the Boston Symphony Youth Concerts commissioned him to write a work for young audiences to be performed by a teenage orchestra and he wrote *The Earth's a Baked Apple*, to his own text comprising six poems about American life as it might have been reported by a young person. Harry Ellis Dickson, conductor of the Youth Concerts, suggested that Colgrass read his own poems to the youngsters just before the premiere on March 29, 1969, by the Boston Symphony and the Lincoln-Sandbury High School Chorus. Colgrass reported, "After my reading ... the audience response was so lively that Mr. Dickson had to stop the piece several times to let the children quiet down. When I left the hall after the performance I felt something *new* as a composer: a real contact with the public, and a terribly important public—young people."

On another commission, from the Chamber Music Society of Lincoln Center in New York, he wrote *New People*, a setting of seven Colgrass poems for soprano, viola, and piano. The world premiere took place at Lincoln Center on October 17, 1969, with Shirley Verrett as vocalist. To Harold C. Schonberg, in the New York *Times*, the poems as well as the music were "very imaginative. The songs are short, sometimes haunting, full of a strange kind of tenderness. Mr. Colgrass has the lyric flair in a modern idiom, and of very few composers can that be said."

For the opening of the Opera House in Spokane, Washington, for Expo' 74, Colgrass composed *Image of Man* whose first performance on May 1, 1974, was by the Spokane Symphony under Donald Thulean. Colgrass provided his own poetic text which Joann Gibbs said in the Spokane *Daily Chronicle* "may be the definitive look at the irony, the insanity of the race through life on a finite planet. Spring demands the credit which goes to summer, a man becomes invalid because he has no debts, a penguin knows that vegetable gardens and roses grow beneath his white environment because his leaders told him so." The unconventional scoring called for, in addition to the more traditional instruments, a cooking pot, a car horn, various kitchenware, and sleighbells. "The work is pure delight," Gibbs added.

In world premieres, the year 1976 proved to be the most productive of Colgrass' career. On January 29 *Concert Masters,* for three violins and orchestra, commissioned by the Detroit Symphony, was introduced with Aldo Ceccato conducting. The Concerto is written in four styles through which the concerto form has passed, beginning with the baroque concerto *à la* Vivaldi, and progressing through the romantic, impressionistic, and post-Weberian periods. The Detroit Symphony brought this work to New York on February 4, 1976. Calling it "an ingenious and substantial creation," Raymond Ericson wrote in the New York *Times* that "its parodistic elements might have led to a more entertaining work, perhaps, if they had been developed, but Mr. Colgrass is being serious here. He is also very lyrical, and there are many fine moments when the soloists are quietly going it alone or together. The orchestra is used resourcefully."

Ronald Thomas, cellist, performed in the premiere of Colgrass' *Wolf,* for unaccompanied cello, in New York on February 17, 1976. The title is named after an imaginary American-Indian and, as the program note explained, the music follows the Indian "through various situations —playing, meditating, singing, talking to plants (sometimes getting high on them) and hunting and being hunted." Allen Hughes of the New York *Times,* thought it was not "hearts-and-flowers music, but it is not often abrasive either. . . . The harmonics, pizzicatos, glissandos, unvibrated bowed tones and slashing doublestops . . . are rather fascinating in themselves and in the way he used them as building blocks in the architecture of the piece as a whole."

On March 10, 1976, the Minnesota Orchestra and the Bach Society Chorus, directed by Stanislaw Skrowaczewski, offered the premiere of *Theatre of the Universe,* for five soloists, chorus, and orchestra. In seven sections, with a text based on Colgrass' own poems on the subject of "the alienation of human feelings in a fast changing world," the work is witty, satiric, wistful, melancholy, and atmospheric. In the Minneapolis *Tribune,* Michael Anthony described it as "eclectic without being a patchwork of styles, and by virtue of the attractiveness of its lyricism and occasional jazzy syncopations (in the sixth section) it is accessible without seeming shallow."

A couple of weeks later, on March 30, the world premiere of *Best Wishes, U.S.A.,* for solo voices, black and white choruses, jazz band, and orchestra, received its first hearing in Springfield, Massachusetts, under the direction of Robert Gutter. The text was again by Colgrass (except for quotations from an after-dinner speech by Mark Twain, a Civil War song, and the closing lines of Thoreau's *Walden*). This work was jointly commissioned by the orchestras of Springfield, Portland (Maine), Providence, Hudson Valley (New York) and Albany (New York) and the National Endowment for the Arts to commemorate the American bicentennial. In response to a request for music that would "show us where we've been, where we are and where we're going," Colgrass wrote, according to a critic for *High Fidelity/Musical America,* "the panoramic view of America's musical and social history. . . . At one point transistor radios are also used. With the exception of fragments of church hymns and twentieth-century jazz styles, all the music is Colgrass' own. The listener, however, can readily identify a typical Indian tune, a cowboy song, a modern folk song and black influenced pop idioms."

Before the end of 1976, another world premiere to Colgrass' credit was *Letter from Mozart,* a tribute to Mozart, performed by the Musica Aeterna Orchestra under the direction of two conductors (Frederic Waldman and José Serebrier) on November 29, 1976. Harold C. Schonberg described it in the New York *Times* as "a collage of Mozartean ideas filtered through the clever mind of Mr. Colgrass in a very modern manner." A Mozart-like theme on the piano opens the composition, but "soon," Schonberg said, "references to Mozart disappear. . . . A spot of jazz is succeeded by a touch of serialism, followed by aleatory, by marches, by tuneful lyricism, by the percussion effects so beloved by the new generation. It's all skillful, terribly clever and without much substance. But fun."

In 1978, Colgrass was awarded the Pulitzer Prize in music for *Déja Vu,* written for percussion quartet and orchestra. The New York Philharmonic commissioned and introduced it on October 20, 1977, with Erich Leinsdorf conducting. The composer tells us: "In *Déja Vu,* I wrote four separate concertos for four soloists—Elden Bailey, Walter Rosenberger, Morris Lang and Roland Kohloff. I knew that each of them played in a certain way, and I wanted to write music that would fit the personalities of four different instrumentalists. So Buster Bailey's vibraphone solo, for instance, makes a mutation into jazz. Walt is playing the marimba, and I think of a large marimba with those ringing rosewood bars as having an impressionistic character. And so his part is impressionistic—it has runs that are almost whole-tone scales. Roland's part, the timpani part, is quite romantic. I was really surprised—I just let myself go to see what would happen. I wrote romantic melodies because it turned out that was the best way to get the timpani to sound melodically. When you write for kettledrums in thirds, sixths and octaves, you pick up the overtones and they ring nicely. And those melodies could be supported in trombones and low strings." Harriett Johnson of the New York *Post,* reported the piece "a triumph with the audience," and "an engaging whole." *Times* critic Harold C. Schonberg thought that "Mr. Colgrass understands the entire potential of percussion, and some of his mixtures were very beautiful. ... Despite the frequent dissonance and tremendous surges of energy, the music did hit the ears easily."

On February 6, 1979, the Canadian Brass presented the world premiere in New York of Colgrass' *Flashbacks,* subtitled *A Musical Play for Five Brasses.* In this fragmented composition the composer, an artist lost between two cultures, recalls some of his experiences in music from working on advertising "jingles" to a visit to India. Donal Henahan commented in the New York *Times,* that *Flashbacks* "added up to unpretentious entertainment, even though at times the composer hinted that he was aiming higher than that." Later in the year the National Arts Center Orchestra of Canada introduced *Delta,*

for orchestra, a work Colgrass described as three concertos based on the same material but going on simultaneously, intended to symbolize the three rivers that meet in Ottawa. This music, strongly influenced by Indian music, utilizes primitive percussion and Raymond Ericson described it in the New York *Times* as "a kind of Surrealist collage, although the material is all original. It reflects a concern with dramatic surfaces, which infuse much of Mr. Colgrass' work. There are elements of primitivism. ... There are jazzy interludes and an amusingly satirical exchange between violin soloist and orchestra. The ending has a nostalgia aroused by a softly strummed fiddle."

Colgrass, his wife, Ula, and their son, Neal, maintain an apartment on Riverside Drive in New York and a home in Toronto, Canada. Ula Colgrass is the editor of *Music Magazine,* published in Toronto.

MAJOR WORKS

Ballet—Sea Shadow.

Chamber Music—Three Brothers, for percussion; Percussion Music; Chamber Music, for percussion quintet; String Quintet; Concertino, for timpani and brass; Inventions on a Motive, for percussion; Variations, for four drums and viola; Fantasy Variations, for percussion; Wind Quintet; Rhapsody, for clarinet, violin, and piano; Light Spirit, for flute, viola, guitar, and percussion; Wolf, for solo cello; Flashbacks, A Musical Play for Five Brasses.

Choral Music—Chant, for vibraphone and chorus; The Earth's a Baked Apple, for chorus and orchestra; Best Wishes, U. S. A., for solo voices, chorus, jazz quartet, and orchestra; Image of Man, concert piece for chorus and orchestra; Theater of the Universe, for solo voices, chorus, and orchestra.

Opera—Virgil's Dream; Nightingale, Inc., a satiric fantasy; The Tower, a musical play for child performers.

Orchestral Music—Divertimento, for eight chromatic drums, piano, and strings; Seventeen; Rhapsody, fantasy for fifteen drums and orchestra; As Quiet As; Auras, for harp and orchestra; Concert Masters, for three violins and orchestra; Letter from Mozart; Déja Vu, for percussion quartet and orchestra; Delta, for percussion, violin, clarinet, and orchestra.

Piano Music—Tales of Power.

Vocal Music—New People, song cycle for mezzo-soprano, viola, and piano; Mystery Flowers of Spring, for soprano and piano; Night of the Raccoon, five songs for soprano and four players.

ABOUT

High Fidelity/Musical America, November 1978;

Music Journal, September 1977; New York Times, April 1, 1969, May 18, 1972.

Frederick Shepherd Converse

1871–1940

See *Composers Since 1900.*

Aaron Copland

1900–

For biographical sketch, list of earlier works, and bibliography, see *Composers Since 1900.*

Since 1970, Aaron Copland has been far more active as a conductor than a composer. He has appeared with about one hundred major symphonies in the United States and abroad, in programs made up mainly of his own works but sometimes those of other composers. He was guest conductor for the Boston Symphony when it toured Japan, the Philippines, and Australia, and for more than a decade he has appeared annually with the London Symphony Orchestra in England.

As a composer, Copland's output has dwindled, and it is not of the scope and dimension of earlier works. Elaine Schaffer and Hephzibah Menuhin introduced his *Duo for Flute and Piano* in Philadelphia on October 2, 1971. In the New York *Times,* Peter G. Davis described it as "a lightweight affair . . . in Mr. Copland's friendliest lyrical tonal style. . . . Beneath the surface charm lies the composer's sophisticated sense of narrative development, rhythmic ingenuity and keen ear for instrumental color."

The first public performance of *Three Latin American Sketches* (previously heard at the EMI studios of CBS during a recording session) was given by the New York Philharmonic Orchestra in New York under André Kostelanetz on June 7, 1972. Its first and third movements ("Estribillo" and "Danza de Jalisco") had originally been written in 1959 with the title *Two Mexican Pieces.* The third piece, "Paisaje Mexicano" was new.

Threnody I: Igor Stravinsky in Memoriam and *Threnody II: Beatrice Cunningham in Memoriam,* both for flute and three strings, received their world premiere at the Ojai Festival in Ojai, California, on June 2, 1973.

"I've bogged down a bit," Copland told an interviewer in 1977, referring to the sparcity of his creative output. "I might start up again, but I am seventy-seven years old and most composers didn't have the luck to live that long, so they didn't have the problem of going on. When you've been composing for more than fifty years it gives you quite a long time to express yourself."

In spite of his creative relaxation, Copland has received numerous honors befitting one who for many years has been looked upon as "the dean of American composers." On his seventieth birthday, major American orchestras, and several in Europe, performed his works in tribute: a concert of his chamber music by the Aldeburgh Festival in England; and a gala Copland concert at the Juilliard School of Music, with a birthday supper reception given by his publisher, Boosey and Hawkes; awards included: the Commander's Cross of Merit from the Federal Republic of Germany; the Howland Prize from Yale; and honorary doctorates in music from Ohio State University and New York University.

In 1971, Copland was elected president of the American Academy of Arts and Letters. A week in November 1974, was proclaimed "Aaron Copland Week" by the Mayor of Cleveland and at an all-Copland concert by the Cleveland Orchestra conducted by the composer, on November 14, an official proclamation was presented to him. During that week, his music was heard over the radio and there was an hour-long television documentary (WKYC-TV) about him. In addition, two award-winning Hollywood films with his music were shown at the Cleveland Museum; public concerts of his chamber and vocal music were presented, and an open rehearsal was given by the Cleveland Institute of Music Orchestra under his direction.

His seventy-fifth birthday brought further accolades: four major New York concerts of his compositions were performed, two conducted by Copland himself; at the Kennedy Center for the Performing Arts, Copland directed the National Symphony Orchestra in a Copland program; he was awarded the Brandeis Creative Award for Notable Achievements; the Norlin Foundation (of the Norlin Corporation, manufacturers of musical instruments) presented the MacDowell Colony at Peterborough, New Hampshire with a grant of $250,000 for fellowships in his name; and honorary doctorates in music were awarded to him by Brooklyn College in New York and the University of Portland in Oregon.

In 1978, the American Symphony Orchestra League presented him with the Golden Baton Award for distinguished service to music. On December 2, 1979, Copland was the recipient of the second annual Kennedy Center Honors in Washington, D.C., for "a lifetime of significant contribution to American Culture in the artistic arts."

Copland's eightieth birthday once again inspired nationwide commemorations, including a concert of his works at the Berkshire Music Festival during the summer of 1980 in which he conducted the Boston Symphony; an all-Copland concert performed by the American Symphony in New York on November 9, 1980, conducted by Copland and Leonard Bernstein; and a Copland program by the National Symphony Orchestra of Washington, D.C., on November 14.

In addition to honorary doctorates in music already mentioned, Copland also received doctorates from Columbia University (1971), York University in England (1971), University of Florida (1972), Long Island University (1974), University of Ottawa (1976), University of Rochester (1976), University of Leeds in England (1976), and Tulane University in New Orleans (1976).

MAJOR WORKS (supplementary)

Chamber Music—Duo for Flute and Piano; Threnody I: Igor Stravinsky in Memoriam, for flute, violin, viola, and cello; Threnody II: Beatrice Cunningham in Memoriam, for flute, violin, viola, and cello.

Orchestral Music—Three Latin American Sketches, for small orchestra.

Piano Music—Night Thoughts.

ABOUT (supplementary)

Dobrin, A., Aaron Copland, His Life and Times; Peare, C. O., Aaron Copland: His Life; Rosenberg, D. and B., The Music Makers; Thomson, V., American Music Since 1910.

High Fidelity/Musical America, November 1975; New York Times, November 8, 1970, November 9, 1980; Stereo Review, February 1981; Tempo (Copland Issue) Winter 1970–1971.

John Corigliano

1938–

John Corigliano was born in New York City on February 16, 1938, to a very musical family. His father, John Corigliano Sr., was the concertmaster of the New York Philharmonic Orchestra from 1943 to 1966. His mother, Rose Buzen Corigliano, was a piano teacher.

Despite this musical background, the younger John never learned to play any instrument well. His early musical training seemed always to end in disaster: one lesson on the piano by his mother ended in a fight, and two lessons on the clarinet from Stanley Drucker, clarinetist of the New York Philharmonic, ended when Corigliano's instrument was stolen from his high-school locker. At no time was the boy ever interested in developing as a virtuoso; it was some time before he even became interested in serious music at all. A recording of Copland's *Billy the Kid* stimulated his interest in music and he bought other records and eventually even their scores to better appreciate the music. "That's how I learned orchestration," he revealed. His love for music was further developed through frequent attendance at rehearsals and concerts of the New York Philharmonic Orchestra.

Gradually music began to occupy a prominent role in his life and he decided to become a composer, against the wishes of his father who felt that the works of American composers were rarely performed or appreciated.

John Corigliano received his academic education at Midwood High School, in Brooklyn, New York (where his interest in music was noted and encouraged). He enrolled at Columbia University in 1955 to study composition with Otto Luening. After graduating in 1959 with a BA degree, he worked for the next five years as a programmer and writer for the New York City radio station, WNYC, and then as musical director for the New York radio station WBAI. During these years several of his compositions received public performances: *Kaleidoscope*, for two pianos, at the festival in Spoleto, Italy (July 1961); *Fern Hill*, for mezzo-soprano, chorus, and orchestra, based on a poem by Dylan Thomas, in New York City (December

Corigliano: kȯr el yä′ nō

JOHN CORIGLIANO

19, 1961); and *What I Expected Was . . .,* for chorus, brass, and percussion, based on a poem by Stephen Spender, in New York City (August 16, 1962).

In 1962, Corigliano studied composition privately with Vittorio Giannini. The composition that launched his career, Corigliano said was completed one year later. It was *Violin Sonata,* written for his father, who refused to look at it. The piece won first prize in a competition at Spoleto, Italy, in 1964, where the jury included Gian Carlo Menotti, Samuel Barber, and Walter Piston. Its world premiere took place in Spoleto on July 10, 1964, under the direction of Yoko Matsuda. Only after two other concert violinists performed it successfully did Corigliano's father program it at one of his concerts in 1966 in New York, and a critic for *Stereo Review* praised it: "I was completely caught up by the lyrical sensitivity of the piece, its considerable command over traditional musical disciplines, and its engaging sweetness and honesty. Its second-movement Andantino is perfectly beautiful: it manages to be utterly fresh in its expressive effect."

Although this sonata utilized 20th century harmonic, rhythmic, and metric practices, the style was comparatively conservative in its concern for a basic tonality, lyricism, clarity of design, overall romantic outlook, and expressivity. "I felt like a rebel," Corigliano told an interviewer for the New York *Times,* "writing unfashionably Romantic, tonal music when the musical establishment was run by people who did not see

that as a valid idiom." Its romanticism, lyricism, and above all, communicability—without any lowering of standards—have remained identifying traits of Corigliano's music, and probably the reason why it found an early and enthusiastic acceptance.

The *Violin Sonata* was followed by several other compositions demonstrating Corigliano's rapid creative and technical growth. *Elegy,* for orchestra, was introduced by the San Francisco Symphony on June 1, 1966, and *Christmas at the Cloisters,* for chorus and organ (or piano), was premiered in a telecast over the NBC network on Christmas Day, 1967. The *Concerto for Piano and Orchestra*—written in 1968 on a Guggenheim fellowship—was heard first at the inaugural concert of the San Antonio Worlds Fair in Texas on April 7, 1968, performed by Hilde Somer and the San Antonio Symphony conducted by Victor Alessandro. *Poem in October,* for tenor and piano (or orchestra), based on a nostalgic poem of childhood by Dylan Thomas, was written in 1970 on commission from the Chamber Music Society of Lincoln Center for the Performing Arts in New York, where it was first heard on October 25 of that year. The orchestral version was introduced in Washington, D.C., on April 24, 1976, by members of the National Symphony conducted by Robert White. Alan Rich, in *New York,* said it was "never less than attractive, put together with great skill and superior sense of musical declamation."

Corigliano's first major success was the *Concerto for Oboe and Orchestra,* commissioned by the New York State Council on the Arts in commemoration of the American bicentennial. It was performed on November 9, 1975, by the American Symphony in New York, with Kazuyoshi Akiyama conducting and Bert Lucarelli as soloist. This Concerto opens in a somewhat jocular vein with "Tuning Fame," a fantasy based on an orchestra's tuning up just before a concert. Two slow movements follow ("Song" and "Aria"), then a high velocity and polyrhythmic Scherzo featuring multiphonics, and a finale, "Rheita Dance," an imitation of a Moroccan dance played on a Moroccan oboe called the "Rheita" or "Rhaita." (The sound of the "Rheita" can be simulated on the Western oboe by playing with lips or tongue not against the reeds but on the string that binds the two reeds together.) Paul Kresh, in *Stereo Review,* called the Concerto "an intriguing complex piece of work, brilliant in its exploitation of the solo instrument and daring—though seldom dissonant—in its adroit use of immense orchestral forces, in its strong rhythms and in its surprising turns of phrases." A shouting ovation was accorded this work at its premiere.

Corigliano's *Concerto for Clarinet and Orchestra* enjoyed even greater success. The New York Philharmonic commissioned it on a grant from Francis Goelet for Stanley Drucker, the first clarinetist of the orchestra. On December 6, 1977, Drucker and the New York Philharmonic Orchestra, with Leonard Bernstein conducting, presented its world premiere and inspired a standing ovation. Four performances of the work that followed were similarly received. During its tour of Europe in the summer of 1980, the New York Philharmonic featured this Concerto frequently on its program. Written for the New York Philharmonic, and its principal clarinetist, the Concerto had a special meaning for Corigliano, owing to his father's long association with the orchestra as concertmaster. "My regard for the musicians ... shaped their roles in the accompaniment to this concerto," Corigliano explained. "In it, each player has a chance to display solo virtuosity; often the work approaches being a concerto for orchestra in its demands." The first movement of the Concerto is made up of two clarinet cadenzas, inspired by Stanley Drucker's virtuosity, separated by an interlude. The second movement, "Elegy," was written in memory of the composer's father who died in 1975. "I still find it hard to think of the orchestra without him sitting in the first chair. So the idea of an extended dialogue for clarinet and violin seemed not only natural but inevitable. This duet has a special poignancy for me when I remember the many years that my father and Stanley Drucker were colleagues under the baton of Leonard Bernstein." The Concerto ends with a two-section finale entitled "Antiphonal Toccata," the first section of which alternates calls on the stage as well as motion across the stage, and the second section involves players around the hall.

Following its premiere, the Concerto was successfully performed in Los Angeles, Toronto, Kansas City, Syracuse, and again at a concert of the New York Philharmonic on May 2, 1980. In *New York,* Alan Rich thought the Concerto was written "with great skill. ... The slow movement is a long sustained elegy of considerable

beauty. The finale is a real rouser [with the] ability to let his music flow naturally and powerfully off a stage and into a large hall." A Dallas *Morning News* critic wrote: "The concerto is a dazzling and remarkable piece ... brilliant and deeply moving. What makes it so vital is its ability to play immediately upon the imagination of a listener and to involve him in the fullest."

A new work, *Poem on His Birthday,* for baritone solo and chorus, was commissioned and premiered by the Washington Cathedral on April 24, 1976. Since this was the final work in *A Dylan Thomas Trilogy,* it was combined with the two earlier works, *Fern Hill* and *Poem in October,* in the same concert program. Joseph McLellan of the Washington *Post,* wrote, "They work well together as a single piece of music, depicting the poet in his youth, at maturity and finally in his confrontation with the approach of death. ... The final section is the climactic masterpiece of the work, though both of the earlier sections are excellent in their own way."

Etude Fantasy, written in 1976, on commission from the Edyth Bush Foundation, stands out as one of Corigliano's principal works for the piano. A fantasy made up of five etudes, the piece was introduced by James Tucco in Washington, D.C., on October 9, 1976. Paul Hume of the Washington *Post,* called it "a work of unusual strengths both in design and content. ... There are pages that have the ferocity of Bartók, others that sing in quiet repose."

Between 1960 and 1973, Corigliano contributed to musical "Specials" for CBS-TV; he was head of the composition department at the College of Church Musicians in Washington, D.C. (1967–1968); he worked with the Lincoln Center Student Programs in city high schools (1969–1970); and since 1971 he has been associate professor of music at Lehman College in New York and a member of the composition department at the Manhattan School of Music. In addition he served as a producer of several Masterwork Recordings in 1972–1973 and as director of the Corfu Festival of Music in 1973–1974.

Corigliano's first score for motion pictures was the background music for *Altered States* (1980), a film based on a novel by Paddy Chayefsky.

John Corigliano resides on West End Avenue in New York City. Aside from music, his interests include traveling and Italian cooking. Cooking, he confided, "is the only thing I am really confident about."

MAJOR WORKS

Chamber Music—Sonata for Violin and Piano; Scherzo, for oboe and percussion.

Choral Music—Fern Hill, for mezzo-soprano, chorus, and orchestra; What I Expected Was . . ., for chorus, brass, and percussion; Christmas at the Cloisters, for chorus and organ, also for chorus and piano; Poem in October for tenor and orchestra, also for tenor and piano; L'Invitation au Voyage, for a cappella chorus; A Black November Turkey, for a cappella chorus; Poem on His Birthday, for baritone, chorus, and orchestra; Psalm No. 8, for chorus and organ.

Mixed-Media Opera—The Naked Carmen.

Orchestral Music—Elegy, Tournaments; Concerto for Piano and Orchestra; Creations, two scenes from Genesis, for narrator and chamber orchestra; A Williamsburg Sampler, suite; Gazebo Dances, also for piano four hands and piano and band; Overture to the Imaginary Invalid; Concerto for Oboe and Orchestra; Aria, for oboe and strings; Soliloquy, for clarinet and orchestra; Voyage, for string orchestra; Concerto for Clarinet and Orchestra; Pied Piper, for flute and orchestra.

Piano Music—Kaleidsocope, for two pianos; Etude Fantasy.

Vocal Music—Petit Fours, cycle of four songs; The Cloisters, for mezzo-soprano and piano, also for orchestra; Wedding Song, for voice, instruments, and organ.

ABOUT

Vinton, J. (ed.), Dictionary of Contemporary Music. Composers of America, vol. 9.

New York Times, April 27, 1980; Village Voice (New York), February 21, 1977; Virtuoso, March–April, 1980.

Henry Cowell

1897–1965

For biographical sketch, list of earlier works, and bibliography, see *Composers Since 1900*.

Prior to his death, Cowell attended the world premiere at Dartmouth College in New Hampshire of two new works: *The Koto Concerto No. 2* and a Piano Trio.

On April 13, 1977, a retrospective concert of Cowell's works was heard at Columbia University in New York. Early in 1978, the Speculum Musicae offered the world premiere of his *Quar-*

tet Romantic which had been written in 1917, but not performed because no chamber-music ensemble of the time was capable of playing such atonal music, where tonal durations and pitches were coordinated according to the ratios of the overtone series.

The American premiere of Cowell's *Piano Concerto* took place in Omaha, Nebraska, on October 12, 1978, with the Omaha Symphony Orchestra conducted by Thomas Briccetti and Doris Hays as soloist.

In an appreciative article on Cowell in the New York *Times* in 1978, Harold C. Schonberg wrote: "Cowell always was in advance of his day. He was one of the authentically big men of American music. . . . He was an 'electronic' composer long before the Columbia-Princeton boys got into the act. His metrical experiments led into Elliott Carter. His use of American elements, as in his *Hymn and Fuguing Tune* pieces, attracted the interest of Virgil Thomson and such young composers as Lou Harrison. His concept of the tone cluster was studied by Bartók. His piano sonorities influenced John Cage. He was one of the first of the ethnomusicologists and made intensive research into Oriental music."

MAJOR WORKS (supplementary)

Chamber Music—Piano Trio No. 2.

Orchestral Music—Symphonies, Nos. 20 and 21; Concerto for Harp and Orchestra; Concerto No. 2 for Koto and Orchestra.

ABOUT (supplementary)

Saylor, B., The Writings of Henry Cowell: a Descriptive Bibliography.

New York Times, May 28, 1978; Stereo Review, December 1974.

Paul Creston

1906–

For biographical sketch, list of earlier works, and bibliography, see *Composers Since 1900*.

In November 1969, Creston's *Hyas Illahee* (Chinook Indian, meaning "Great Land"), a three-movement suite for chorus and orchestra, was introduced in Seattle by the Central Singers and Orchestra, and conducted by the composer. At that time, the composition's title was *The*

Northwest. But, as the composer explained, "the qualities in the three movements—Majesty, Serenity, Vigor—are applicable to the entire nation, and since the names used are preponderantly Indian, the Indian title was substituted." As there is no text, the voice is used as an instrument. Voice parts in the first movement are syllables and Indian words; in the second, vowels and syllables; in the third, syllables and geographical names of the United States and Canada. "The syllables and names," the composer said, "were selected for their tonal and rhythmic values; and were adapted to the music rather than the contrary."

In 1969, Creston also completed a *Concertino,* for piano and woodwind quintet, commissioned by the pianist Rose d'Amore and premiered by Ascher Temkin in Brookport, New York, on April 15, 1972. Its first movement (Maestoso–Allegro) is alternately majestic and rhapsodic; the second movement (Poco lento) is romantic, and the third movement (Allegretto) is rhythmic with flashes of buffoonery, gaiety, and even ferocity.

The Central Singers, directed by Wayne S. Hertz, and with the composer at the piano, presented the world premiere of *Leaves of Grass,* a cycle of five songs for chorus and piano based on Walt Whitman's poetry, in Seattle on February 28, 1971. *Thanatopsis,* for orchestra, was commissioned and introduced by the Chappaqua Orchestral Association of New York (in memory of Boris Koutzen, the American composer) under the direction of Wolfgang Schanzer on December 4, 1971.

In response to a request by Colonel Samuel R. Loboda, director of the United States Army Band for a symphonic band piece, Creston wrote *Jubilee,* the most ambitious of ten such works he has written. The work had its first hearing at the Kennedy Center for the Performing Arts in Washington, D.C., on January 24, 1972 and the announcer introduced it as follows: "Creston's Italian heritage comes to the fore in the copious melodies and lyric vigor of his music. He writes with a rich harmonic palette, alert rhythms and a keen sense of brilliance. All these qualities, plus an unabashed display of patriotism, are apparent in the work."

At a two-day festival of Creston's music at Ithaca College, New York, his tenth work for symphonic band—*Liberty Song*—was introduced on February 9, 1976 with the composer conducting. In July of that year, at the World Saxophone Congress in London, Jean-Marie Londeix was heard in a work he had commissioned, the *Rapsodie,* for saxophone and organ. A four-movement Suite, for string orchestra, had its world premiere in San Diego, on May 21, 1978, with David Amos conducting the Jewish Community Chamber Orchestra of San Diego for whom it was written.

Creston is the author of several theoretical texts on music: *Principles of Rhythm, Creative Harmony,* and *Rational Metric Notation.* He has explored the world of rhythm in the ten-book *Rhythmicon.*

In 1975, Creston retired as professor of music and composer-in-residence at Central Washington State College in Seattle, becoming professor emeritus. He has since acquired a new home—in Rancho Bernardo in northern San Diego—with a private study overlooking the mountains—such a private sanctum that even his wife does not intrude.

In 1964, Creston received an "Emmy" for his score for TV documentary, *In the American Grain.* In 1966, he received the Achievement Award from the New York College of Music, and in 1970, the Composers Award from the Lancaster Symphony in Pennsylvania.

MAJOR WORKS (supplementary)

Band Music—Jubilee; Liberty Song.

Chamber Music—Concertino, for piano and woodwind quintet; Ceremonial, for eight percussion players; Rapsodie, for saxophone and organ; Piano Trio.

Choral Music—Leaves of Grass, for chorus and piano; Calamus, for brass and percussion.

Orchestral Music—Hyas Illahee (The Northwest), for soprano, alto, tenor, bass, and orchestra; Thanatopsis; suite, for string orchestra.

Piano Music—Romanza.

ABOUT (supplementary)

Music Journal, December 1976; San Diego Magazine, June 1979.

George Crumb

1929–

George Henry Crumb was born in Charlestown, West Virginia, on October 24, 1929. Both his parents were trained musicians: his father, George Henry Crumb, was a bandmaster and clarinetist, and his mother, Vivian Reed Crumb, was a cellist. The family, including their other son, William Reed Crumb, a flutist, made music at home their prime form of entertainment in the depression years. Thus music became a powerful influence upon young George from childhood on and he started playing the piano by ear by the age of nine, and soon after writing little pieces. At Charleston High School (where he was a member of the track team) he upset his teachers by composing in class.

On graduating from high school in 1947, he decided to devote himself completely to music and entered Mason College, a music conservatory in Charleston. In harmony class, he met Elizabeth May Brown, a piano student, and married her on May 21, 1949, while they were still students. Crumb earned his Bachelor of Music degree in 1950 and his Masters degree in Music at the University of Illinois in Urbana two years later. During 1953 he attended the University of Michigan at Ann Arbor.

In 1954, he wrote his first composition, marking the beginning of creative maturity. In *String Quartet,* he showed an appreciation for modern compositional processes by emulating the stylistic traits of Bartók, Hindemith, and Alban Berg. This work and a *Sonata,* for solo cello, in 1955, won him the BMI Prize for composition in 1957.

He spent the summer of 1955 at the Berkshire Music Center at Tanglewood in Massachusetts. Then, on a Fulbright fellowship to Germany, he attended the Berlin High School of Music where he studied composition with Boris Blacher (1955–1956). Crumb returned to the University of Michigan for his doctorate in music which he received in 1959 and where he studied composition with Lee Ross Finney. (He also received musical instruction from Eugene Weigel in composition and from Stanley Fletcher and Benning Dexter in piano.)

In 1958–1959, Crumb taught theory at Hollins College of Music in Virginia and left in 1959 to become assistant professor of piano at the

GEORGE CRUMB

University of Colorado, for five years. At this time, he produced his first orchestral work, *Variazioni,* a twenty-minute composition, partially in the twelve-tone technique. When the Philadelphia Orchestra under Eugene Ormandy revived *Variazioni,* Harold C. Schonberg noted in the New York *Times* in 1973, "the twelve-tone Schoenbergian elements are used in a personal manner. Mr. Crumb had a built-in lyricism from the beginning."

At the request of pianist David Burge, Crumb's colleague at the University of Colorado, he wrote *Five Pieces,* for piano, in 1962. Burge introduced it, then performed it on an extended concert tour, and recorded it. The composer Richard Wernick wrote, "It possesses an unpretentious musicality best expressed in the composer's remark that 'music can exist only when the brain is singing.' The influence of Webern is evident in the economy and compactness of musical gesture." Wernick commented on some of the new sounds and sonorities that would characterize Crumb's music from this point on: "The use of exotic percussion effects are evocative of Oriental theater and dance (water gong, fifth-partial piano harmonics 'like tiny bells,' piano strings struck with the palm of the hand, antique cymbals and the like)."

While attending the University of Michigan for his doctorate, Crumb heard a song setting of a Spanish poem by Federico García Lorca, "Casida of the Boy Wounded by the Water." He discovered a spiritual affinity between the poem and his own musical inclinations and proceeded to use Lorca's poetry as settings for compositions between 1963 and 1966, notably *Night Music,* I and II (1963, 1964), *Madrigals,* Books I and II (1965), and *Eleven Echoes of Autumn, 1965* (1966).

Night Music, I (1963) "nocturnes," introduced in Paris in 1964, is made up of seven pieces, five of them instrumental (piano, celesta, and percussion), and two of them settings in a kind of Sprechstimme style of poems by Lorca ("The Moon Rises" and "Gacela of the Terrible Presence"). Irving Kolodin said in the *Saturday Review* that, "Generically, *Night Music,* I strikes me as descended in a family fashion from *Pierrot Lunaire,* especially in the manner of writing evolved for the soprano. However Crumb has evolved his own way of juxtaposing resonant values. . . . It defines Crumb as a man of poetic impulse, responsive to the symbolism of García Lorca and questioning for a way to shape sound to an image of his own." To achieve unusual sound qualities and timbres, the score requires "a bit of human whistling here and there, a gong whose vibrations are transformed when it is immersed or withdrawn from a tub of water, patterings on a drum head, staccato punctuations by a woodblock, etc." *Night Music,* II (1964) was scored solely for violin and piano.

The first two books of *Madrigals* were commissioned by the Koussevitzky Music Foundation, dedicated to Serge and Natalie Koussevitzky, and performed in July 1968 by the Festival Chamber Ensemble at the Lincoln Center for the Performing Arts. The Lorca texts from which each madrigal was taken consist of from one to three short sentences touching on life, death, water, rain, and earth. Book I is scored for mezzo-soprano, vibraphone, and contrabass, and Book II for mezzo-soprano, percussion, and flute. The voice sometimes sings in Sprechstimme style, at other times in quarter tones, coloratura, or *senza vibrato.* Alfred Frankenstein, in *High Fidelity/Musical America,* remembers it "for its ethereal effects, its integrity and fineness and fragility." Crumb wrote two more books of *Madrigals* in 1969, for Elizabeth Suderburg, the soprano who introduced and recorded them.

In *Eleven Echoes of Autumn, 1965,* for violin, alto flute, clarinet, and piano, Crumb created a novel effect by having the flutist speak across the mouthpiece of his instrument.

Crumb left the University of Colorado in 1964

to teach composition at the University of Pennsylvania, first as assistant professor in 1966, and later as full professor in 1970. In 1965 he received a grant from the Rockefeller Foundation and in 1967 and 1973, he received Guggenheim Fellowships.

Comparatively unknown to the musical establishment until 1968, Crumb was awarded the Pulitzer Prize in music for a composition of remarkable imagination and fantasy. This composition with novel sound textures and performing procedures was *Echoes of Time and the River* (1967), "four processionals for orchestra." It was commissioned by the University of Chicago for the 75th anniversary of the Chicago Symphony and introduced on May 26, 1967. (Despite its title, the work has no connection, either in content or theme, with the Thomas Wolfe novel of the same name.) The composer said, "The central unifying theme is 'time' (including psychological and philosophical time). The *continuum* of time (or the 'river of time') is expressed by the concept of the 'processional' and there are, in fact, many actual processionals (involving various sections of the orchestra)." To create a ritualistic flavor, Crumb had his wind players or percussionists march across the stage while performing, though at one point, nine wind players do position themselves in front of the orchestra, blow into their instruments to produce the rising and falling sound of wind, and then walk off. At the world premiere in Chicago, these "processionals" were omitted, but at the Berkshire Music Center Festival of Contemporary Music in Massachusetts in August 1970, which Gunther Schuller conducted, they were included. "The ritualistic aspect had touches of vaudeville fun," according to Donal Henahan in the New York *Times.* But they "did add a theatrical dimension. . . . As in the earlier performances, however, one was caught and held in the grip of Mr. Crumb's fantasy by the art with which he exploited the orchestra's sound potential. This is 'ear music' . . . a four-movement masterpiece."

Novel effects were introduced throughout: In the first movement, "Frozen Time," members of the orchestra whisper or shout *"Montani semper liberi?"* ("Mountains are always free?" the state motto of West Virginia to which Crumb added the question mark); or in the second movement, "Remembrance of Time," García Lorca's phrase, "the broken arches where time suffers"; or in the third movement, "Collapse of Time," the meaningless syllables "Krek-tu-dai," a purely phonetic invention by Crumb; or in the fourth movement, "Last Echoes of Time," another phonetic sound, "Koitais." There is occasional aleatory music; clarinets play into an open, undamped piano; a small tambourine is placed over bass strings of the piano to produce metallic sounds; two groups of whistlers, placed at the right and left of the stage, are heard towards the end of the work.

Esoteric subject matter and sounds—and the poetry of Lorca—continued to dominate Crumb's creativity. *Songs, Drones and Refrains of Death* (1968), for baritone, guitar, piano, and doublebass (all amplified) are combined with a variety of percussion instruments for two players. Commissioned by the University of Iowa, it was written between 1962 and 1968 and introduced there in the spring of 1969. The score calls for sleighbells, a jew's-harp, water-tuned crystal glasses, a Chinese temple gong, antique finger cymbals, Japanese hand bells, and sundry other noise-producing implements. The baritone sings much of his music through a cardboard tube; the instrumentalists are required to whisper, shout, and chant. Four Lorca poems are the setting: "The Guitar," "Casida of the Dark Doves," "Song of the Rider, 1860," and "Casida of the Boy Wounded by the Water," and each is prefaced by an instrumental refrain which, in the words of the composer, "presents in various guises the rhythmic, fateful *motif* heard at the beginning of the work." The music, for all its unconventionalities, manages to convey the bleakly desolate, anguished, violent, and sometimes ironic tones of the Lorca texts. After the New York performance in April 1972, Donal Henahan of the New York *Times* wrote, "astonishingly beautiful. . . . The necessary dark Lorca mood was struck at once on the crystal glasses. A ten-second silence that preceded the last phrase was so profound that the audience's involvement in the world created by Mr. Crumb could not be doubted."

Lorca texts were also the settings for *Night of the Four Moons* (1969) and *Ancient Voices of Children* (1970). *Night of the Four Moons,* for alto and a chamber ensemble including a banjo, electric cello, and a percussion group that includes Japanese kabuki blocks, alto Africa thumb piano (mbira), tam-tam, Chinese temple gong, and bongo drums, was commissioned by the Philadelphia Chamber Players. The work was inspired by man's first landing on the moon. "The first three songs," Crumb wrote, "with their very brief texts are, in a sense, merely introductory to the dramatically sustained final song. The *moon is dead, dead* . . . is primarily an instrumental piece to a primitive rhythmical style, with the Spanish words stated almost parenthetically by the singer. The conclusion of the text is whispered by the flutist over the mouthpiece of his instrument. . . . The concluding poem (inspired by an ancient Gypsy legend)— Run away, moon, moon, moon! . . . provides the climactic moment of the cycle."

Ancient Voices of Children, for mezzo-soprano, boy soprano, oboe, mandolin, harp, electric piano (or toy piano), a musical saw, and percussions including Tibetan prayer stones and Japanese temple bells, is a poetic conception of life and death. Commissioned by the Elizabeth Sprague Coolidge Foundation for the 14th Festival of Chamber Music in Washington, D.C., it was triumphantly introduced by the Contemporary Chamber Ensemble under Arthur Weisberg, with Jan DeGaetani as soloist, on October 31, 1970. The boy soprano is heard offstage throughout the whole score until he joins the mezzo-soprano on the stage for the concluding vocalise. At one point in the music an unusual echo effect is produced by the mezzo-soprano singing a vocalise based on purely phonetic sounds into an amplified piano. Following its premiere the work was widely performed: in May 1971, at the International Roster of Composers presented by UNESCO in Paris; in March 1972, at the Library of Congress with choreography; in January 1973 by the New York Philharmonic under Pierre Boulez; in March 1974, at an all-Crumb concert in Toronto. Alan Rich wrote in *New York* that "It belongs to a growing repertory of intensely quiet pieces notable for an extraordinary ability to draw an audience toward them. . . . Its sounds are fashioned with a degree of imaginativeness that leaves me spellbound. . . . Crumb's piece is not sound effects or tricks. It is a work that combines the utmost transparency, and inventiveness . . . I cannot begin to explain rationally, a sense of daring that challenges everyone involved in performing or listening. I am not sure that mere words on paper can explain why Crumb's music makes sense; but it remains to me as powerful and moving a contemporary creation as I know." In 1971 the International Rostrum of Composers in Paris voted it the most distinguished of 89 works heard there (the first American composition ever thus honored), and that same year it received the Koussevitzky International Recording Award.

No less striking is *Black Angels* (Images I), "thirteen images from the Dark Land," for electric string quartet, written in 1970. Four musicians are required not only to play their own instruments but also percussion instruments (including maracas, tam-tams, and water-tuned crystal glasses played with a bow) and to vocalize in French, German, Russian, Japanese, and Swahili. The striking and often morbid musical reflections on death have no text; they were "conceived," the composer says, "as a kind of parable on our troubled contemporary world. . . . The image of the 'black angel' was a conventional device used by early painters to symbolize the fallen angel. . . . The work portrays a voyage of the soul. The three stages of this voyage are Departure (fall from grace), Absence (spiritual annihilation) and Return (redemption)." The work was commissioned by the Stanley Quartet (resident quartet of the University of Michigan) which introduced it soon after its completion.

Crumb's imagination, seeking new directions, turned to tape-recordings of songs of the humpback whale which he tried to imitate instrumentally. *Vox Balaenae* ("Voice of the Whale"), for electrified piano, cello, and flute was written in 1971 for the New York Camerata and consists of an opening vocalise as prologue, five variations (each named for a geological era), and a "Sea-Nocturne" as epilogue. The instrumentalists are required to wear masks and to play in a darkened auditorium in order, said Crumb, "to efface the sense of human projection." When it was first performed in New York on September 30, 1972, by the Aeolian Chamber Players, Donal Henahan, in the New York *Times,* was impressed by "Mr. Crumb's exceptional ability to draw evocative sonorities out of the instruments. . . . suggestive of gulls' cries or surf or the echoes of the vast deep. . . . One also heard many a sound not usually connected with whales or water: a drone rather like that of an Indian tabla from the strummed piano strings, or melisma that might have come from a Moorish throat." A documentary on *Vox Balaenae* and George Crumb was telecast by the Public Broadcasting Service.

In *Lux Aeterna* (1971) Crumb called upon his five instrumentalists to wear masks again, as well as robes, and group themselves around a burning candle on a stage illuminated by a red light. Subtitled "for the Children of Night," it is scored for soprano, bass flute, sitar, and two percussion players, and it was premiered by the Philadelphia Composers Forum at New York University in April 1972.

In *Makrokosmos* (meaning "the universe in its entirety") I and II, Crumb wrote a major work for amplified piano (1972–1973). Each volume consists of twelve fantasy-pieces corresponding to the Zodiac, which are divided into three groups of four numbers and played without interruption. The first volume was dedicated to David Burge, who introduced it in Colorado Springs on February 8, 1973. It was performed nine times after its premiere before being heard at the International Piano Festival and Competition at the University of Maryland on August 14, 1973, and then was given thirteen more performances by David Burge before he recorded it. The second volume was written for Robert Miller (Crumb's lawyer, an excellent pianist) who presented its world premiere in New York on November 12, 1974, and recorded it.

The work is a study of every aspect of manipulating piano strings and keys, as well as an exploration of harmonic and sonic shadings. The instrumentalist must not only manipulate the piano but also whistle, speak, and sing. In Book I, every fourth piece is notated symbolically: No. 4 is shaped like a cross; No. 8, in circular design; No. 12, as a spiral. Crumb conceived Book II "as a very gradual intensification in tempo and dynamics up to the climactic eighth piece ("A Prophecy of Nostradamus") and a subsequent spinning out to the beautifully sustained and almost hypnotic '*Dona nobis Pacem*' conclusion."

Noting features that can be identified with Crumb's style, a critic for *High Fidelity/Musical America* wrote: "The piano sound is altered through the use of such external props as paper, glass tumblers and a wire brush; strings are played pizzicato; harmonics are employed. . . . Yet for all these sonic innovations, the piano writing is closely bound to the nineteenth-century virtuoso tradition; the kinds of figurations and textures used . . . have their close parallels in Schumann and Liszt. The spell of such later composers as Debussy and Bartók can also be frequently detected. These associations are no doubt intended by the composer, and they provide the work with a 'historical resonance' that supplied an interesting accompaniment to those acoustical resonances that gradually die out while being sustained by the pedal, etc. . . ."

Makrokosmos III, entitled *Music for a Summer Evening* (1974), is scored for two amplified pianos and two percussion players and no longer adheres to the Zodiac, but is in five movements entitled "Nocturnal Sounds," "Wanderer-Fantasy," "The Advent," "Myth," and "Music of the Starry Night." The three larger movements are preceded by poetic quotations: "Night Sounds," has an inscription by Quasimodo ("I hear ephemeral echoes, oblivion of full night in the starred water"); "The Advent" has a Pascal quotation ("The eternal silence of infinite space terrifies me"); and "Music of the Starry Night" cites lines by Rilke ("And in the night the heavy earth is falling from all the stars down into loneliness. We are all falling. And yet there is One who holds this falling endlessly, gently in His hands"). In this score, the piano strings are covered with sheets of paper to produce a distorted, almost surrealistic effect.

Music for a Summer Evening was commissioned by the Fromm Music Foundation for Swarthmore College in Pennsylvania where it received its first performance on March 30, 1974, by Gilbert Kalish, James Freeman, Raymond Des Roches, and Richard Fritz, to all of whom it was dedicated. Its New York premiere followed on January 9, 1975, at "An Evening with George Crumb," and renamed *Mask of the Night*, it was introduced by the Juilliard Dance Ensemble in New York in April 1975, as dance music.

Makrokosmos IV (1979), for amplified piano, four hands, is subtitled "Celestial Dances," as each of its four movements is named after a star. It was commissioned by the Chamber Music Society of Lincoln Center in New York, and had its world premiere by Gilbert Kalish and Paul Jacobs on November 18, 1979. Harold C. Schonberg reported in the New York *Times* that it "is something of a throwback to a style that was very popular twenty years ago, when so many composers were exploiting hitherto unheard-of techniques. . . . He has asked the two artists . . . to spend as much time poking inside the piano as on the keys themselves. . . . The emphasis is on pure sound."

Crumb's first work for large orchestra since *Echoes of Time and the River* was written in 1977 on a Ford Foundation grant for the New York Philharmonic and the soprano, Irene Gubrud. The first performance of *Star-Child* took place on May 5, 1977, with Pierre Boulez conducting the New York Philharmonic Orchestra. The work bore the subtitle, "a parable for soprano, antiphonal children's voices, and large orchestra." (Later a male choir and handbells were added.) This performing group was the largest in any Crumb work, requiring four conductors (one each for an autonomous string section in the rear right corner of the stage; for brass and percussion; and for clarinets, flutes, and vibraphone). The principal conductor stood at the head of the instrumental and vocal array which included the traditional instruments and eight percussionists performing on about seventy unusual instruments (such as iron chains, metal thunder sheet, log drums, pot lids, sleigh bells, hand bells, and a wind machine). They performed on stage, in the balcony, and on the sides of the auditorium. In addition to the soprano solo, the score called for two children's choirs, grouped around the conductor rather than at the rear of the stage.

Crumb described his music as having "a sense of progression from darkness (or despair) to light (or joy and spiritual realization) . . . that, after a struggle or after dark implication, there is something beyond." Six sections are played without interruption, focusing on three main themes: "Voices Crying in the Wilderness," "Music of the Apocalypse," and "Advent of the Children of Light." Two medieval texts are used: *Dies Irae* and the *Massacre of the Innocents.*

An influence on Crumb's overall creativity, besides that of Garciá Lorca, was his West Virginian origin. It is evident in his use of "Montani semper liberi?," the state's motto, in *Echoes of Time and the River,* in the Appalachian revival hymn, "Will There Be Any Stars in My Crown? " whistled by the pianist in the "Nightspell" section of *Makrokosmos II,* and in his use of such unconventional instruments as the musical saw, banjo, jew's harp, blowing on the mouth of a stone jug, and playing the electric guitar the way hill country musicians do (sliding a glass rod over the frets).

Influences of other composers can also be traced in Crumb's music, most significantly Webern and Charles Ives. In *Night of the Four Moons,* an offstage singer sings "Berceuse in stilo

Mahleriano" ("Berceuse in the style of Mahler"); in the second movement of *Echoes from Time and the River,* the Negro spiritual, "Were You There When They Crucified My Lord?" is heard (though distorted); in the "Ancient Voices" section of *Night of the Four Moons* a snatch of Ravel's *Bolero* is heard; in *Makrokosmos I* Chopin's *Fantaisie Impromptu;* in *Vox Balaenae* the stirring opening measures of Richard Strauss's *Thus Spake Zarathustra;* in *Black Angels,* Saint-Saëns's *Dance Macabre* and Schubert's *Death and the Maiden* are referred to; in *Music for a Summer Evening* the D-sharp minor Fugue from the second volume of Bach's *Well Tempered Clavier* is heard. "Crumb uses the technique so deftly," said Donal Henahan in *Dialogue,* "and with such sure instinct for dramatic impact that one can experience not only a twinge of nostalgia but something like the sense of irretrievable loss that arises when one leafs through an album of family pictures or yellowing snapshots of half-forgotten friends in half-forgotten wars."

Crumb's first purely vocal composition in almost a decade is *Apparition,* for mezzo-soprano and amplified piano, completed in 1979. Jan DeGaetani introduced it on January 13, 1981, in New York. Subtitled "Elegiac Songs and Vocalises," *Apparition* uses as text six excerpts from Walt Whitman's poem, "When Lilacs Last in the Dooryard Bloom'd." In writing his cycle, Crumb successfully achieved a return to the traditions of 19th century song. Vocalises employing only phonetic sounds appear after the first, third, and fourth songs. "The interweaving of vocalise with words proved to be an effective device," reported Donal Henahan of the New York *Times.* He added: "The vocalise sometimes allowed the cycle to retain an overall tone of abstract modernity, while still fulfilling Mr. Crumb's aim."

Crumb, his wife, and three children, live in Media, a suburb of Philadelphia, in a house described as "a warehouse of exotic instruments, if not a hardware store." All kinds of implements, contraptions, utensils, and esoteric musical instruments of exotic lands are stored there (the more cumbersome ones in an addition built for that purpose). Crumb experiments with them for new sound effects and many are used in his compositions. Apart from this fascination, Crumb enjoys reading books about astronomy and archaeology.

Dallapiccola

Crumb has been awarded honorary doctorates in music by Norris Harvey College in Charleston, West Virginia, in 1969, by Marshall University in Huntington, West Virginia, in 1973, and by Oberlin College in Ohio in 1978. He is a member of the National Institute of Arts and Letters.

MAJOR WORKS

Chamber Music—String Quartet; Sonata, for solo cello; Night Music I, for soprano, piano, celesta, and percussion; Night Music II, four nocturnes, for violin and piano; Eleven Echoes of Autumn, for violin, alto flute, clarinet, and piano; Vox Balaenae, for three masked players, electric flute, electric cello, and electric piano; Dream Sequences, for violin, cello, piano, and percussion; Lux Aeterna, for five masked musicians, soprano, bass flute (or soprano recorder), sitar, and two percussion players.

Orchestral Music—Variazioni; Echoes of Time and the River, four processionals; Star-Child, a parable for soprano, antiphonal children's voices, and large orchestra.

Piano Music—Makrokosmos, I, for amplified piano; Makrokosmos, II, for amplified piano; Music for a Summer Evening (Makrokosmos III) for two amplified pianos and two percussion players; Makrokosmos IV, for amplified piano, four hands.

Vocal Music—Madrigals, Book I, for soprano, contrabass, and vibraphones; Madrigals II, for soprano, flute (or piccolo, or alto flute), and one percussion player; Songs, Drones and Refrains of Death, for baritone, electric guitar, electric contrabass, electric piano (or electric harpsichord), and two percussion players; Madrigals III, for soprano, harp, and one percussion player; Madrigals IV, for soprano, flute (or piccolo, or alto flute), harp, contrabass, and one percussion player; Apparition, song cycle for mezzo-soprano and amplified piano.

ABOUT

BMI, Many Worlds of Music, May 1972; Dialogue, vol. 9, no. 2, 1976; High Fidelity/Musical America, September 1968; New York Times, December 13, 1970; New York Times Magazine, May 11, 1975; Wall Street Journal, August 15, 1974.

Luigi Dallapiccola

1904–1975

For biographical sketch, list of earlier works, and bibliography, see *Composers Since 1900.*

When Dallapiccola's opera, *Ulisse,* based on Homer to his own libretto, received its world premiere at the Berlin Festival on September 29,

1968, it was performed in German with the title *Odysseus*. As *Ulisse*, in Italian, it was heard at La Scala in Milan a year later. The idea for this opera came to the composer at age twelve when he saw a film based on the Homeric legend. He began to make notes for a libretto in 1952, and spent several years reducing Homer's epic into a prologue and two acts. The world premiere attracted attention all over Europe in a broadcast by the networks of thirteen nations. Everett Helm reported in *Musical America*, that "it was a score of surpassing beauty that spoke of eternal truths in an atmosphere of concentrated, cogent serenity. It is not an 'outward' but a profound 'inward' music—one that in a sense stands in opposition to the noisy crassness of our times. . . . There is little 'action'. . . . While retaining the setting in antiquity, Dallapiccola has consciously transformed the Odysseus of Homer into a tormented man of our time, whose wanderings are of the spirit and whose search is not for homeland and family but for truth."

Dallapiccola's *Sicut Umbra*, for mezzo-soprano and twelve instruments—a cycle of three songs to Spanish poems by Juan Ramón Jiminez—was introduced in Washington, D.C., on October 30, 1970. *Tempus Destruendi/Tempus Aedificandi*, for soprano, alto, and chorus—written for an Israeli choral society—touches on the symbolism of Solomon's temple. "*Tempus Aedificandi*," wrote David Drew in *Tempo*, "seems to epitomize his conception of the artist's duties in a troubled age whose potentialities are nevertheless immense. It also reflects his relationship to the traditions of Italian music which he so splendidly renewed, and to the ancient craft of composition which he practised with such meticulous and loving precision." *Commiato*, for soprano and orchestra (his last completed work) received its world premiere in Murnau, Austria, on October 15, 1972, and its American premiere in New York on March 27, 1974.

"Few composers of our time", wrote David Drew, "have been so consistently truthful in their art, and few have managed to reconcile such veracity with the discovery of so much that is beautiful—whether serenely . . . or fiercely . . . It is music that always reflects the indomitable courage of his own convictions, even in, or especially in, its darkest and most violent moments."

In July 1969, Dallapiccola was composer-in-residence at the Congregation of the Arts at Dartmouth College in Hanover, New Hampshire, where a wide cross-section of his works was performed. That summer he also taught composition at the Aspen Music School in Colorado.

Failing health in 1972 compelled Dallapiccola to abandon all composition (except for a few random sketches), travel, and public activity. Suffering from a pulmonary condition, Dallapiccola was taken to a hospital in Florence, Italy, in February 1975, where he died on February 19. Soon after his death, the Milanese publishing house, Edizioni Suvini Zerboni, issued a brochure, *In Ricordi di Luigi Dallapiccola*, in which many outstanding musicians of America and England paid tribute to him.

Dallapiccola was the author of *Appunti, Incontri, Meditazioni* (1970).

MAJOR WORKS (supplementary)

Choral Music—Tempus Destruendi/Tempus Aedificandi, for soprano, contralto, and chorus.

Orchestral Music—Commiato, for soprano and orchestra.

Vocal Music—Sicut Umbra, three songs for mezzo-soprano and twelve instruments; Commiato, for soprano and fifteen instruments.

ABOUT (supplementary)

Goldbeck, F., Twentieth Century Composers: France, Italy and Spain; Zanolini, B., Luigi Dallapiccola: la Conquista di un Linguaggio.

New York Times, February 20, 1975; Persepectives of New Music, vol. 15, no. 2; Revue Musicale de Suisse Romande (Dallapiccola Issue) July–August 1975; Tempo (London), June 1975.

Peter Maxwell Davies

1934–

Peter Maxwell Davies was born in Manchester, England, on September 8, 1934, to Thomas Davies, a manufacturer of surveyor's instruments, and Hilda Howard Davies. He received his academic education at Leigh Grammar School in Salford, Lancashire. Since the school did not encourage music study, Davies (who was musical from childhood on) took outside music lessons, making such progress that he earned a county music scholarship. Between 1952 and

Davies: dä′ vĕz

PETER MAXWELL DAVIES

1957 he attended the Royal Manchester College of Music and Manchester University. At the College he received thorough musical training, acquiring an honorary Bachelor of Music degree. Before graduating in 1957, he completed writing his first compositions: Sonata, for trumpet and piano (1955) and *Five Pieces for Piano* (1956), both complex in their rhythmic and textural structures. *Alma Redemptoris Mater,* for wind sextet (1957), was a 20th-century interpretation of a 15th century motet, Davies' first work indicating a lifelong interest in medieval polyphonic music. The work represented Great Britain at the festival of the International Society for Contemporary Music in Strasbourg, France, on June 12, 1958.

On a grant from the Italian government, Davies studied composition with Goffredo Petrassi in Rome between 1957 and 1959. In 1958 he composed *St. Michael Sonata,* for seventeen wind instruments, which was introduced at the Cheltenham Festival in England in 1959. In this year he was also awarded the Olivetti Prize for *Prolation,* for orchestra (1958), whose world premiere took place at the festival of the International Society for Contemporary Music in Rome on June 10, 1959.

Back in England in 1959, Davies was director of music at the Cirencester Grammar School in Gloucestershire where he instructed children in avant-garde music and encouraged them to improvise. For those three years, he wrote some music for young people and was responsible for a series of television programs broadcast by the B.B.C. to schools.

His serious music already showed a tendency that Davies would follow throughout his career: bridging the distance between music's distant past and the 20th century. On the one hand, he wrote works in a neo-expressionist idiom, using the advanced methods of serialism. On the other hand, he wrote works of a deeply religious nature which reached back to medieval times and early baroque music through the simulation of early polyphonic methods and forms, and the use of medieval modes, at times even resorting to quotation from early works. In his religious, quasi-medieval vein, such early compositions (in addition to *Alma Redemptoris Mater*) as *Ricercar and Doubles,* for eight instruments (1959), based on an old English song, "To Many a Well," reverted to 16th and 17th century contrapuntal forms; this work was featured at a festival of the International Society for Contemporary Music in Cologne, Germany, on June 18, 1960. In *Frammenti di Leopardo,* for soprano, contralto, and instruments (1962)—a setting of poetry by Count Leopardi of the early 18th century—Davies quoted fragments from Monteverdi's *Vespers* (1620). As a voice of the 20th century, he wrote *Sextet* (1958) and *String Quartet* (1961), the latter performed at the festival of the International Society for Contemporary Music in London on June 2, 1962. Sometimes the old and the new were combined in the same work. For example, *Five Motets,* for vocal soloists, double chorus, and instruments (1959), was in the expressionist atonal idiom of Webern and Stravinsky, and also possessed the mysticism and religiosity of medieval church music. Two other early works are characteristic of the later Davies: *Sinfonia,* for chamber orchestra (1962), commissioned by the English Chamber Orchestra and his first orchestral fantasia based on Travener's *In Nomine* (1962), on a commission from the B.B.C.

On his first visit to the United States in 1963, Davies, on the recommendation of Aaron Copland, was a Harkness Fellow at Princeton University, studying composition with Roger Sessions. He completed a major choral work, *Veni Sancte Spiritus* for vocal soloists, chorus, and orchestra (1963), written for and introduced by the Princeton High School Choir; and during his absence from England he wrote a second fantasia on Travener's *In Nomine* (1964), which was commissioned and premiered by the London Philharmonic Orchestra in April 1965. In symphonic form, it was made up of thirteen sections played without interruption.

Davies embarked on a lecture tour of Europe, Australia, and New Zealand in 1965 under the sponsorship of UNESCO. That year, he was commissioned by the Koussevitzky Music Foundation, to write *Revelation and Fall,* for soprano and sixteen instruments, set to six expressionist poems by Georg Trakl. Its Sprechstimme writing for the voice and atonal style resembled Schoenberg's *Pierrot Lunaire* and *Erwartung,* and the soprano, screaming into a bullhorn, and weird percussion sounds contributed to the feeling of frenzy and violence suggested by the poems. In the *Observer* (London), Peter Heyworth described the music as "a prolonged scream of agony for which there is no precedent in English music." When the work was introduced at the Lincoln Center Festival '68 in New York City on July 10, a critic for *American Record* suggested that it "may not be everyone's dish, but there is simply no escaping its power."

No less dramatic was *Eight Songs for a Mad King* for male singer and chamber orchestra (1969), whose text actually consisted of words of the insane George III. Combining theater with music, the king appeared in costume and four of six musicians, in symbolic cages, represented some facet of the king's madness. In a serial idiom, the score called for instrumental sounds produced by rattling fragments of glass in a large biscuit tin. This work was first performed in London on April 22, 1969; in December 1970, after its American premiere, Harold C. Schonberg wrote in his review in the New York *Times,* that the work "hits the listener like a collective shriek from Bedlam."

In 1966, Davies was composer-in-residence at Adelaide University in Australia. Two years later, with Harrison Birtwistle, he founded and directed the Pierrot Players in London, a small instrumental group giving public concerts. Several of his works were heard at these concerts. (In 1971, this concert group was reorganized and renamed The Fires of London.)

Davies' first opera, *Travener* (1970), was introduced on July 12, 1972, at Covent Garden in London. Davies wrote his own libretto based on the dramatic life of John Travener, the 16th century English church composer who was accused of heresy and subsequently supported Oliver Cromwell in his persecution of monks. Davies drew most of his material directly from Tudor documents and letters, again combining the old and new. Though his musical style was neo-expressionistic, he included in his orchestration a medieval instrument (regal) and a baroque one (harpsichord). Ethan Madden said in *Opera in the 20th Century,* "*Travener* works as theater, certainly—as an experience but not as an organism. There is no growth in it, no inner definition, just the pictures and the patter in the post-expressionist style that Davies had utilized more effectively . . . in smaller terms." But Andrew Porter wrote in the *Financial Times* of London that the opera was "a powerful and brilliant piece of music theatre, product of a fiery imagination wedded to a prodigious craft."

Davies spent a summer holiday in 1970 in the Scottish Orkney Islands and their remoteness, serenity, and bleakness so intrigued him that a year later he acquired a permanent cottage in a rebuilt isolated seaside croft in Hoy. Living in Spartan simplicity, his cottage is without electricity and water and he has to go outdoors to a spring, and to chop firewood. Speaking of his austere isolation, Davies said: "Living in London, travelling, one's sense of hearing becomes dulled and distorted; a single jet taking off blurs one's hearing for hours afterwards. . . . But after a few days of solitude at Hoy I begin to hear again."

Some of Davies' major works since 1971 reflect the somber landscapes of these islands, in their music, which is more austere, emotionally more subdued, and more introspective than so many of his earlier compositions. Even his subject matter was derived from the islands, as occasionally, Davies reached to George Mackay Brown, an Orcadian poet, for his texts. This was the case with *From Stone to Thorn* (1971), for mezzo-soprano and chamber ensemble, introduced at Oxford on June 30, 1971, and *Fiddlers at the Wedding* (1973–1974), which was descriptive of Orkney life in the 19th century. Several runic inscriptions found on prehistoric Orkney monuments were set to music in *Stone Litany: Runes from a House of the Dead,* for mezzo-soprano and orchestra (1973). Written for mezzo-soprano Jan DeGaetani and the Scottish National Orchestra (on a joint commission from Glasgow University and the Scottish National Orchestra), it was introduced in Glasgow on September 22, 1973 with Alexander Gibson conducting. When Pierre Boulez conducted its New York premiere with the New York Philharmonic Orchestra on March 12, 1976, Andrew Porter of *The New Yorker* thought it was "a highly organized, picturesque and very beautiful composition. . . . The ear delights in the sounds . . . in the 'atmospheric' effect suggesting sigh of wind, play of light, surface movement over grand, ancient stillness. The instrumentation is magical. Davies is not afraid to use the childhood toy, the flexatone . . . or, through the closing pages, wineglasses tuned to E-flat and C, stroked with a damp finger into soft-shining sound. The voice enters as the most colorful and sensitive of all instruments, uttering first the letters of the runic alphabet, then . . . singing a duet with itself—one line apparently continuous against the quick flourishes of another."

In 1977, Davies founded the St. Magnus Festival, an annual mid-summer event, in the Orkney Islands. The main attraction of the first festival was Davies' second opera, *The Martrydom of St. Magnus,* produced on June 18, 1977, at the 12th century St. Magnus Cathedral at Kirkwall. Although the opera was commissioned by the B.B.C. for the Silver Jubilee of Queen Elizabeth II, Davies' own libretto was from a novel by George Mackay Brown about the patron saint of the Orkney Islands. The story of Magnus, the martyr, was first told in the 13th century *Hymn to St. Magnus.* (In the opera, however, the setting and time were changed to the place and time where the opera was being produced.) This small-scale one-act work requires only four male singers and a mezzo-soprano who are called upon to sing various roles, accompanied by ten instrumentalists, including The Fires of London group. Following the American premiere in Aspen, Colorado, on July 18, 1978, Andrew Porter wrote in *The New Yorker:* "The score becomes a nightmare phantasmagoria of distorted dance music through the centuries from the twelfth to the twentieth; transformation and parody techniques pioneered in Davies' expressionist compositions of the sixties become alarmingly potent. Then, in the final scene, the 12th century and the present are merged: monks chant a litany that Magnus himself might have sung but the resonances around that melody and the visionary solo song of a timeless Orkney woman are heard and set down with a twentieth-century ear."

At the second St. Magnus Festival in 1978,

Davies' masque, *Le Jongleur de Notre Dame,* with a libretto based on the famous medieval French legend, was introduced. More functional was *The Two Fiddlers,* a little opera deriving its text from an old island myth which called for the participation of the pupils of Kirkwall Grammar School.

The geography of the Orkneys also left a subtle imprint on Davies' first full-length symphony and his most ambitious orchestral work up to that time. He completed it in 1976 on commission from the Philharmonia Orchestra in London. Davies expanded a one-movement orchestral piece, *Black Pentecost,* which he had written for the Philharmonia in 1973 but it was not performed. He revealed that many of his technical procedures in writing a four-movement symphony stemmed from Sibelius's Fifth Symphony and Schumann's Second Symphony, while the overall shape and detailing of the formal structure of the last movement came "on the surface level" from Boulez's *Pli Selon Pli.* The premiere of the Symphony took place in London on February 2, 1978, with Simon Rattle conducting the Philharmonia, and it was hailed by Alan Blyth in the London *Daily Telegraph* as "one of the major orchestral works in the last quarter of this century." In *The New Yorker,* Andrew Porter, who reviewed the American premiere by the New York Philharmonic under Zubin Mehta on October 12, 1978, described it as "a romantic and picturesque work that holds evocations of sea, sky and storm, of bright-edged light and unpolluted natural sound on the Orcadian Island. . . . It is the largest manifestation of its composer's almost medieval devotion to 'secret' structures governing details of pitch and duration, his rapt transformations of plainchant melodies in a way to make modern listeners one with the ages, and his professed concern 'to evolve a musical language simple and strong enough to make the complex forms with which I have become involved, meaningful and audible.' "

In 1977, in honor of Roger Sessions' eightieth birthday, Davies wrote *A Mirror of Whitening Light,* for a chamber orchestra of fourteen players. The title refers to the alchemy by which base metal is transformed into gold, or, metaphorically, the process by which the soul becomes purified. When this work received its American premiere on April 4, 1978, in New York, a critic for *High Fidelity/Musical America* said: "If there is magic in music, it is in the splendid instrumentation.... The clarity of the writing is impressive, with the percussion providing a cloud of shimmering timbre above the intricate maze of counterpoint.... The music ... seems at once the most sophisticated and the most accessible of Davies' recent works that have been heard here."

In November 1978, Davies' ballet, *Salome*, stirred up considerable controversy at its world premiere at the Circus Theatre in Copenhagen (which commissioned it). The reason for the uproar was the twelve-minute "Dance of the Seven Veils," choreographed by Fleming Flindt and performed by Vivi Flindt in the nude. Amid accusations of pornography and sensationalism, Clive Barnes of the New York *Post* noted that "The controversy at this outrage has unfortunately drawn attention away from Flindt's very considerable artistic achievement, which goes far beyond a strip-tease, however artfully contrived. What Flindt has done is to produce a popular ballet of considerable power." As far as Davies' music was concerned, Barnes praised it as "one of the most engrossing new ballet scores for years, possibly ... it may well be the final statement needed to win for Maxwell Davies the more general audience he deserves and to confirm his place as England's foremost composer since Britten."

On commission from the Boston Symphony Orchestra and its musical director, Seiji Ozawa, in commemoration of the orchestra's centenary, Davies wrote the Symphony No. 2. It was introduced in Boston on February 26, 1981. Inspired by the scene from Davies' window in the Orkneys, this symphony is, as the composer describes it, "a direct response to the sounds of the ocean's extreme proximity." He further explained that in this music he tried to translate two basic wave types, "that where the waveshape moves through the seas, while the water remains basically static, and that where the wave-shape is static and constant while the water moves through it." A comparatively recent fascination with Haydn's music helped Davies to shape much of the developmental symphony, while plainsong became the source of thematic unity.

Davies contributed the background music to two British-made films: *The Devils* (1971) and *The Boy Friend* (1971). *Fires of London* is a concert suite derived from *The Devils*. It was introduced in London on December 11, 1971, with the composer conducting, at a concert that also featured the premiere of a concert suite from the score of *The Boy Friend*.

MAJOR WORKS

Ballet—Visalii Icones, for dancer, solo cello, and ensemble; Salome.

Chamber Music—Sonata for Trumpet and Piano; Alma Redemptoris Mater, for wind instruments; St. Michael Sonata, for seventeen wind instruments; Sextet; Ricercar and Doubles, for eight instruments; String Quartet; Seven in Nomine, for instruments; Solita, for solo flute; Hymnus, for clarinet and piano; Stedman Caters, for instruments; Bell Tower, for percussion; Ara Coeli; Lullaby for Ilian Rainbow, for guitar; Psalm 124, for instruments; Ave Maria Stella, for instruments; The Door of the Sun, for viola; The Kestrel Paced Round the Sun, for flute; The Seven Brightnesses, for clarinet; Three Studies, for percussion; Runes from a Holy Island, for various instruments (one player); Our Father Which in Heaven Art, for instruments.

Choral Music—Five Motets, for vocal soloists, double chorus, and instruments; Ecce Manus Tradentis, for chorus and instruments; The Shepherd's Calendar, for young singers and instrumentalists; Missa Super l'Homme Armé, for speaker and chamber orchestra; Solstice of Light, for solo tenor, chorus, and organ.

Opera—Travener; Blind Man's Buff, masque; The Martyrdom of St. Magnus, chamber opera; The Two Fiddlers, opera for children; Le Jongleur de Notre Dame, masque; Cinderella, children's opera; The Lighthouse, one-act opera.

Orchestral Music—2 symphonies; Prolation; 2 Fantasias on a *In Nomine* by John Travener; Sinfonia, for chamber orchestra; Shakespeare Music, for chamber orchestra; Antechrist, for chamber orchestra; St. Thomas Wake, fox-trot for orchestra on a pavane by John Bull; Worldes Blis; Eram Quasi Agnus, instrumental motet; Fool's Fanfare, for speaker, mime, and chamber orchestra; Stone Litany: Runes from a House of the Dead, for mezzo-soprano and orchestra; Five Klee Pictures, for youth orchestra; A Mirror of Whitening Light, for chamber orchestra.

Organ Music—Three Preludes.

Piano Music—Five Pieces; Five Little Pieces; Sub Tuam Protectionem; Stevie's Ferry to Hoy, beginner's piano solo.

Vocal Music—Te Lucis ante Terminum, for soprano, alto, tenor, bass, and chamber orchestra; Four Carols, for soprano, alto, tenor, and bass; Frammenti di Leopardi, for soprano, contralto, and instruments; The Lord's Prayer, for soprano, alto, tenor, and bass; Veni Sancte Spiritus, for soprano, alto, tenor, bass, and small orchestra; Ave Plena Gratia, for soprano, alto, tenor, and bass, with optional organ; Revelation and Fall, for soprano and sixteen instruments; Shall I Die for Mannis Sake?, for soprano, alto, and piano; Notre Dame de Fleur, for vocal soloists and instruments;

Delius

Five Carols, for unaccompanied soprano and alto; Eight Songs for a Mad King, for male singer and chamber orchestra; From Stone to Thorn, for mezzo-soprano and chamber ensemble; Hymn to St. Magnus, for soprano and chamber ensemble; Tenebrae Super Gesualdo, for mezzo-soprano and chamber ensemble; Fiddlers at the Wedding, for mezzo-soprano and instrumental ensemble; Dark Angels, for soprano and guitar; Miss Donnithorne's Maggot, for mezzo-soprano and chamber ensemble; Anakreontika, Greek songs for mezzo-soprano and instruments; The Blind Fiddler, for soprano and instruments; Westerlings, for unaccompanied soprano, alto, tenor, and bass.

ABOUT

NGDMM; Foreman, L. (ed.), British Music Now; Sternfeld, F. W. (ed.), Music in the Modern Age.

High Fidelity/Musical America, January 1981; Musical Times (London), October 1961; New Yorker, October 30, 1978; New York Times, March 1, 1981; Tempo (London), June 1975, No. 124, 1978 (Davies Issue).

Claude Debussy

1862–1918

For biographical sketch, list of earlier works, and bibliography, see Composers Since 1900.

In 1909, Debussy attempted to make an opera of Edgar Allan Poe's story, "The Fall of the House of Usher," to his own libretto. He managed to complete the libretto, but only scattered parts of the score. In 1962, some of the sketches were published, and presented for the first time over the B.B.C. in England and over the French radio. A decade or so later, two students at Yale (Carolyn Abbate and Robert Kyr) reconstructed and orchestrated these sketches and presented them at a world premiere at the Great Hall of Jonathan Edward College at Yale, in New Haven. The program consisted of about twenty minutes of music followed by the remainder of Debussy's libretto as spoken drama. In December 1977, the Frankfurt Radio in Germany broadcast still another reconstruction of Debussy's sketches, which was twice as long as the version at Yale. Then, in April 1978, the Yale score was revived and revised, this time solely by Carolyn Abbate, for a performance at Tully Hall in New York by the Bronx Arts Ensemble conducted by Johannes Somary.

In 1974, a periodical devoted exclusively to Debussy, Cahiers Debussy, was published by the

Centre Documentation Claude Debussy in St. Germaine-en-Laye near Paris.

ABOUT (supplementary)

Holloway, R., Debussy and Wagner; Jarocinski, S., Debussy: Impressionism and Symbolism; Wenk, A.B., Debussy and the Poets.

New Yorker, March 14, 1977, May 8, 1978; Opera News, March 4, 1978.

Frederick Delius

1862–1934

For biographical sketch, list of earlier works, and bibliography, see Composers Since 1900.

The American premiere of Delius's opera, Koanga (seventy years after its world premiere, and rarely heard since), was by the Opera Society of Washington (D.C.) on December 18, 1970. Carman Moore said in the New York Times that its value "resides almost totally in its music." As regards the whole opera, the critical consensus was negative, with one reviewer describing it as a corpse that could not be resurrected.

A more significant musical experience resides in the dramatic and visual appeal of the American premiere of Delius's opera, A Village Romeo and Juliet, by the Opera Society of Washington, on April 26, 1972. Enhanced by films and unusual lighting projections, this production added a new dimension to the opera. When it came to the stage of the New York City Opera at Lincoln Center on October 6, 1973, Harold C. Schonberg reported in the New York Times that "When everything comes together ... the results are exquisitely beautiful. ... As for the music, it is one lone, sensuous outburst—the kind of unending melody Wagner was always talking about. ... The score is not everybody's dish. ... But don't say that to Delius lovers who adore every note of the score. In any event, the final scene, starting with the 'Walk to the Paradise Gardens' is as moving, throat-clutching and imaginative as anything in 20th century opera."

Delius's second opera, The Magic Fountain (1893) had its world premiere in London on July 30, 1977, in a concert version performance by the B.B.C. Orchestra and vocal soloists, with Norman Del Mar conducting.

Dello Joio

ABOUT (supplementary)

Carley, L., Delius: The Paris Years; Carley, L., and Threlfall, R., Delius: a Life in Pictures; Jahoda, G., The Road to Samarkand: Frederick Delius and His Music; Jefferson, A., Delius; Palmer, C., Delius, Portrait of a Cosmopolitan; Redwood, C. (ed.), A Delius Companion.

Virginia Magazine of History and Biography, July 1971 ("Delius in America").

Norman Dello Joio

1913–

For biographical sketch, list of earlier works, and bibliography, see *Composers Since 1900.*

Dello Joio's *Homage to Haydn* had its world premiere in June 1969, at Little Rock, during ceremonies celebrating the Arkansas sesquicentennial. It was performed by the Philadelphia Orchestra under the direction of Eugene Ormandy. Early in 1970, Dello Joio was guest composer at the third Contemporary Music Festival at Del Mar College in Corpus Christi, Texas, where six of his compositions were performed. Later in that year, on October 2, Dello Joio conducted the premiere of his *Evocations* (with texts by Robert Hillyer and Richard Hovey), for chorus, a youth chorus, and orchestra, at Tampa, Florida.

Lyric Fantasies (1973), for viola and string ensemble, was introduced in the "New and Newer Music Series" at the Lincoln Center for the Performing Arts in New York on February 23, 1975, with Michael Tree as soloist and Efrain Guigui as conductor.

Dello Joio was commissioned to write *Colonial Variants,* for orchestra, by the Farmers Bank of the State of Delaware for the opening of the restored Grand Opera House at Delaware's Center for the Performing Arts in Wilmington, as an American bicentennial project. The Philadelphia Orchestra, under Eugene Ormandy, presented the work there on May 27, 1976. The composer described it as "thirteen profiles of the original Colonies, based on an ancient tune." The ancient tune, "In Dulci Jubilo," is heard in English horn and bassoon in the opening section, after which it is elaborated upon by strings and woodwinds. Thirteen variations follow, each representing one of the original colonies, beginning with Rhode Island and ending with

Massachusetts. The composer explained that these variations "progress into one another in a cycle of fifths, with the final variant closing in a chorale-like manner. It should be noted that Variations VI and VII are connecting—North and South Carolina. The work is in no way to be thought of as programmatic. It is an exercise in structured musical fancies and impressions, with no literal connotations." Otto Dekom wrote in the Wilmington *Morning News,* that the music "has a very special quality. The emphasis is not ... so much on the clever turns of musical phrases, but on creating the spirit and mood of the American experience. ... He makes us see the people."

Dello Joio received a number of other commissions for music in celebration of the American bicentennial: for William H. Carrigan he wrote the *Mass to the Blessed Virgin,* for baritone, chorus, and organ, which was premiered at the National Shrine of the Immaculate Conception in Washington, D.C., on December 8, 1975; for J.C. Penney Co. he completed *Notes from Tom Paine,* for chorus and piano, intended for high schools; for the historic town of Concord, Massachusetts, he wrote *Satiric Dances,* for band, which the Concord Band performed on July 17, 1975; for the Saratoga Festival in New York, Dello Joio composed *Songs of Remembrance,* for baritone and orchestra, which was premiered by the Philadelphia Orchestra under Eugene Ormandy on August 26, 1977, with Alan Wagner as soloist.

The last-named work is a setting of four poems by John Hall Wheelock. Peter G. Davis wrote in the New York *Times,* that the feeling "is one of nostalgia for lost love, youth, and friends, all tinged by a strong identification with nature, especially the sea. ... Mr. Dello Joio has produced a skillful score couched in a conservative idiom and decked with gracefully curvacious melodic lines."

The 41st International Eucharistic Congress commissioned Dello Joio to write *Mass in Honor of the Eucharist* for chorus, brass, organ, and strings (1976). It was heard for the first time at the John F. Kennedy Stadium in Philadelphia in August 1976. The composer discussed it, "The Mass was very definitely written with a wide public in mind. To me it seemed to be a return to the tradition that the artist is a servant of the Church—or, if one may risk sounding pretentious, of mankind."

In 1958, Dello Joio became chairman of the Contemporary Music Project for Creativity in Music Education, financed by the Ford Foundation. The project which he originated was the placement of composers in junior high and high schools around the country, and, beginning in 1968, in residence with various middle-sized communities, where they were called upon to write new music for school and community cultural groups. Dello Joio left the project in 1972, when he became dean of the School for the Arts at Boston University in Massachusetts. In 1974, he married Barbara Bolton (having divorced his first wife in 1973). With his three children from his first marriage, he maintains homes in Boston, Massachusetts, and East Hampton, New York. Dello Joio received an honorary doctorate in music from the University of Cincinnati (1967) and St. Mary's College of South Bend, Indiana (1969).

MAJOR WORKS (supplementary)

Ballet—A Time of Snow.

Band Music—Songs of Abelard; Fantasies on a Theme by Haydn; Concertante for Wind Instruments; Satiric Dances; Colonial Ballads.

Chamber Music—Suite, for flute and piano; Suite, for clarinet and piano; Sonata, for trumpet and piano.

Choral Music—Proud Music of the Storm, for chorus, brass, and organ; Mass, for baritone, chorus, brass, and organ; Evocations, for chorus, youth chorus, and orchestra; The Poet's Song, for chorus and piano; Leisure, for chorus and piano; Mass to the Blessed Virgin, for cantor, chorus, brass, and organ; Mass in Honor of John XXIII; Mass in Honor of the Eucharist, for chorus, brass, and strings; Notes from Tom Paine, for chorus and piano; The Psalmist's Meditation, for chorus and piano.

Orchestral Music—Homage to Haydn; Choreography, three dances for string orchestra; Lyric Fantasies, for viola and string orchestra; Colonial Variants; Southern Echoes; Songs of Remembrance, for baritone and orchestra; As of a Dream, for narrator, chorus, vocal soloists, orchestra, and dancers.

Organ Music—Suite.

Piano Music—Capriccio on the Interval of a Second; Stage Parodies, for piano four hands.

Vocal Music—Songs of Abelard, for baritone and band.

ABOUT (supplementary)

BMI, Many Worlds of Music, Winter 1976; New York Times, July 9, 1972.

David Del Tredici

1937–

David Walter Del Tredici was born in Cloverdale, California, on March 16, 1937. His father, Walter, was Italian; his mother, Helen Wegele was German. When he was eleven, David appeared as the White Rabbit in a public school presentation of a musical based on *Alice's Adventures in Wonderland.* That appearance, he said, "left a mark on me," as his later mature works based on the same work may attest. He started playing the piano without any formal instruction when he was twelve. "I'm the freak in an unmusical family," he told Robert Jacobson in an interview in *After Dark.* "And I loved the piano! All I wanted to do was play, play, play. It never occurred to me to compose."

His piano training took place between 1953 and 1959 in Berkeley, California, with Bernard Abramowitsch. Del Tredici demonstrated such talent that he gave public recitals and made five appearances with the San Francisco Symphony under Enrique Jorda and Arthur Fiedler. While attending the University of California at Berkeley between 1955 and 1959, Del Tredici studied composition with Seymour Shifrin, Andrew Imbrie, and Arnold Elston.

During the summer of 1958 he attended the Aspen Music Festival in Colorado to study the piano with Leonard Shure. Del Tredici recalled, "He took all the fun out of playing. My early teacher had been just the opposite. So I looked for something else to do, something more pleasant. And I started writing piano pieces." One of these, *Soliloquy,* was performed at Aspen in August. Del Tredici played a few of his pieces for Darius Milhaud, who taught composition at Aspen and the French master said: "My boy, you are a composer," and urged him to reconsider his ambitions and concentrate on composition rather than playing the piano. Del Tredici remembers that "It was very nice hearing that, so I kept doing it," but he admitted that it was also "a traumatic time. After all the energy I have invested in playing, I had to make a' nebulous start as a composer. It was difficult until I felt confident with it." A String Trio and *Songs on Poems of James Joyce,* for voice and piano,

Del Tredici: dĕl trĕ′ dĭ chē

95

Del Tredici

DAVID DEL TREDICI

were completed in 1959; the latter was performed that same year at the University of California at Berkeley. Two piano pieces in atonal style, influenced by Schoenberg and Webern, were written in 1960 and 1962: *Scherzo,* for four hands, and *Fantasy Pieces,* introduced by Del Tredici in San Francisco.

After receiving his Bachelor of Arts degree and membership in Phi Beta Kappa at Berkeley in 1959, Del Tredici entered Princeton University on a Woodrow Wilson Scholarship, to study composition with Roger Sessions and Earl Kim (1959–1960). Between 1962 and 1964, he continued studying piano in New York with Robert Helps, but returned to Princeton in 1963–1964 to complete requirements for a Master of Fine Arts degree.

Aaron Copland heard some tapes of Del Tredici's music and arranged for the young composer to appear in Tanglewood, Massachusetts, as pianist with the Fromm Fellowship Players during the summers of 1964 and 1965. It was at the Berkshire Music Festival at Tanglewood on August 12, 1964, that Del Tredici's *I Hear an Army* was introduced. The text for the work, for soprano and string quartet, is based on a poem from James Joyce's *Chamber Music.* Michael Steinberg described its style in the Boston *Globe* as "highly intense, non-serial, almost atonal chromaticism most effectively handled. There is effective contrast between the tightly curled utterances and repetitions of the string quartet against the broadly swinging vocal line. The work is very effective."

Night Conjure-Verse (1965), a setting of two poems by James Joyce, for soprano, mezzo-soprano (or counter-tenor), woodwind quintet, and string quartet, was first performed on March 4, 1966, in San Francisco, by Carol Bogard, John Thomas, and instrumental members of the San Francisco Symphony Orchestra under the direction of the composer. James Joyce's poetry also provided the text for another successful vocal composition, *Syzygy* (1966), for soprano, French horn, and chamber orchestra. ("Syzygy" comes from astronomy, zoology, and mathematics, indicating a strong union of elements hitherto in no such juxtaposition.) Commissioned by the Koussevitzky Music Foundation, the work was premiered on July 6, 1966, in New York.

In 1966, Del Tredici was awarded a Guggenheim Fellowship and during the summers of 1966 and 1967, he was invited by composer Leon Kirchner to be resident composer at the Marlboro Festival in Vermont and in 1967, on Kirchner's recommendation, to be assistant professor of music at Harvard University for the next four years.

In 1967–1968 Del Tredici completed two electronic compositions for a solo rock group. The first, *The Last Gospel* (1967), with a text from the Confraternity of Christian Doctrine of the Bible (John 1:1–18), was scored for amplified soprano, a solo rock group comprising two amplified saxophones and two electric guitars, a mixed chorus, and orchestra. After its introduction by the San Francisco Symphony under the direction of the composer on June 15, 1968, Robert Commanday wrote in the San Francisco *Chronicle* that it was "a marvelously imaginative ritual setting of the text. In exploring the Word as Ritual, Del Tredici turns the phrases around and mixes the syllables to create a rich scramble, with new rhythms and sound values evolving another meaning."

The second work was *Pop-Pourri* (1968), for amplified soprano solo (and counter-tenor or mezzo-soprano ad libitum), solo rock group of two amplified saxophones, and two electric guitars, chorus, and orchestra. Its first performance in 1968 was at La Jolla, California and it was conducted by Milton Katims. Del Tredici described the five-section work as "a kind of cantata of the Sacred and the Profane, with the two elements mingled on many levels: the 'crazy' *Alice in Wonderland* texts and *Chorale;* the amplification and 'rock instruments' besides the unamplified 'normal' orchestra sections of tonality juxtaposed to quasi-tonal and atonal materials. The first treatment, completely tonal, is a quotation—the chorale, *'Es ist genug'* by Johann Sebastian Bach—and has this scale as its opening phrase, ... The *Litany* dwells on an intermediate, quasi-tonal version of the same notes; and the 'Turtle Soup I and II' are based on a completely atonal treatment. The 'Jabberwocky' movement is the only part of the piece which does not involve this process."

Pop-Pourri was the first of several major works by Del Tredici based on *Alice's Adventures in Wonderland,* in which he moved away from atonality (without totally abandoning it) toward tonality. As he explained: "Tonality is really a surprise to me, but the subject of Alice is not atonal. It has a 'crazy' tonality all the time, a funny context, and juxtaposition of traditional devices." Although Del Tredici's first acquaintance with Lewis Carroll came when he played the role of the White Rabbit as a boy, it was not until many years later that he was impressed by the information in Martin Gardner's *The Annotated Alice.* It read "Most of the poems in the *Alice* books are parodies of poems or popular songs that were well known to Carroll's contemporary readers. With few exceptions, the originals had been forgotten, their titles kept alive only by the fact that Carroll chose to poke fun at them." The idea of setting to music these Carroll poem-parodies, in conjunction with their Victorian originals, "struck fire in my imagination," Del Tredici revealed. Beginning with *Pop-Pourri,* he undertook a series of independent compositions, based on episodes in the Carroll book.

Pop-Pourri was followed by *The Lobster Quadrille* (1969), from the Carroll chapter in which the Mock Turtle and the Gryphon describe, and then in an awkward manner, perform a quadrille, and the Mock Turtle sings his own little song. The composer said, "What particularly caught my fancy in this scene, was the possibility of musically blending together both its humor and grotesquerie." To accomplish this, the score called for the normal symphony orchestra plus such instruments as the mandolin, banjo, and accordion, and two saxophones. It also called for a solo folk group with optional soprano (or tenor) solo. The seven-sectioned *Lobster Quadrille* contained two dances, three songs, and a coda, —Dance I and Dance II were played contrapuntally in a separate section after being played independently. Aaron Copland conducted the world premiere of this work with the London Symphony Orchestra on November 14, 1969.

Vintage Alice (1972) was premiered at Music at the Vineyards, California, on August 5, 1972, with the composer conducting. A "fantascene" based on *A Mad Tea Party,* Alice, the Mad Hatter, March Hare, and Dormouse are all sung by the same soprano. Del Tredici's composition, *Adventures Underground* (Carroll's original title for the book) was commissioned by the New York State Council on the Arts, and the Buffalo Philharmonic Orchestra which introduced it under Michael Tilson Thomas (to whom it was dedicated) on April 13, 1975. The consecutive chapters in Carroll, "The Pool of Tears" and "The Mouse's Tale," are connected by a narrative which, though a Del Tredici original, is very characteristic of Carroll; thus the two songs together form one complete "adventure." Del Tredici wrote music for "The Mouse's Tale" on the page graphically so that it looked like a mouse's tail, similar to Carroll's page.

For *In Wonderland* (1974), Del Tredici revised *The Lobster Quadrille* of 1969 and joined it to two other sections, "'Tis the Voice of the Sluggard" and "Dream—Conclusion." Commissioned by the National Endowment for the Arts and dedicated to Aaron Copland, it had its initial hearing on July 29, 1975, at the Aspen Music Festival with Richard Dufallo conducting.

In celebration of the American bicentennial, the National Endowment for the Arts commissioned Del Tredici, as one of the six composers to write new works to be performed by six of America's major orchestras. In 1975, Del Tredici prepared the largest and most ambitious in musical content of all his compositions inspired by *Alice's Adventures in Wonderland—Final Alice.* The score called for an amplified soprano, narrator, a solo concertante group of folk instrumentalists, and a greatly expanded orchestra. *Final Alice* is a series of five extended arias, interspersed and separated by dramatic episodes taken from the last two chapters of Carroll's fantasy, with emphasis on the "Trial in Wonderland" and Alice's last reawakening to "dull reality." The Del Tredici composition, almost operatic in its dramatic continuity, arias, and characterizations, resembles a concerto for voice

97

and orchestra, since a single person performs all the parts. Del Tredici said, "I would call *Final Alice* an opera written in concert form."

Final Alice was premiered by the Chicago Symphony under Sir Georg Solti on October 7, 1976, with Barbara Hendricks as soloist. Thomas Willis reported on its success in the Chicago *Tribune:* "The audience broke into sustained applause which quickly grew into a standing ovation. Cheers and bravos mingled with handclaps. ... It was the most enthusiastic reception of a new work that I ever heard at a symphony concert." Soon after, *Final Alice* was performed in New York, Los Angeles, and Boston. Martin Bernheimer of the Los Angeles *Times* called it "possibly the most valuable product of the bicentennial." In all these performances the work was cut; the first complete performance took place in St. Louis on December 17 and it was followed by one in Minneapolis on April 20, 1978.

Del Tredici was awarded the Pulitzer Prize in music in 1980 for *In Memory of a Summer Day,* for amplified soprano and orchestra (1979). The poem that opens "Through the Looking Glass" was used as text for two large arias, "Simple Alice" and "Ecstatic Alice," separated by an orchestral march. The work was commissioned and given its world premiere by the St. Louis Symphony, under Leonard Slatkin's direction, with Phyllis Bryn-Julson as soloist, on February 23, 1980. "Nobody but he [Del Tredici] could have produced *In Memory of a Summer Day,*" reported Frank Peters in *High Fidelity/Musical America.* "It may be slick, clever and ingratiating, but on the other hand it isn't pretentious and boring."

Happy Voices, for amplified (off-stage) soprano and orchestra (1980) continued Del Tredici's preoccupation with *Alice.* He wrote it on commission for the opening of the Louise M. Davies Symphony Hall in San Francisco, where it was premiered by the San Francisco Symphony conducted by Edo de Waart with Judith Blegen as soloist, on September 16, 1980. In this composition, five themes make up an extended fugue.

Del Tredici planned both *Happy Voices,* and its immediate precedessor, *In Memory of a Summer Day,* as parts of a large three-part composition collectively entitled *Child Alice,* including *All in the Golden Afternoon,* for large orchestra and amplified soprano voice (1981).

In speaking of his attraction to *Alice,* Del Tredici told Raymond Ericson of the New York *Times* that "the texts or poems seem to belong to me. I'm not sure why. It may be an identification with the writer, with his combination of whimsey and mathematical exactitude. I believe this is an exact metaphor for my music, with its tight procedures that intend to sound natural. ... I was pulled screaming and hollering back to tonality, but it happened almost inadvertently. I just couldn't relate atonality to setting the humor and charm of the *Alice* texts."

In a discussion of Del Tredici's *Alice* compositions, Nicholas Kenyon said in *The New Yorker:* "Del Tredici has something to say, about childhood, tenderness, memory, innocence, and the nature of love. Also about nightmares, and possible dark currents beneath these tales told on a sunny river. He is a generous and romantic composer."

Aaron Copland said that Del Tredici "is that rare find among composers—a rare creator with a truly original gift. ... I venture to say that his music is certain to make a lasting impression on the American musical scene. I know of no other composer of his generation, at least among those who write within the normal concert idiom, who composes music of greater freshness and daring, or with more personality."

In 1973, Del Tredici was appointed teaching associate at Boston University; that year he received the Creative Arts Citation from Brandeis University. In 1975 he was composer-in-residence at the Aspen Music Festival.

MAJOR WORKS

Chamber Music—String Trio; String Quartet.

Choral Music—The Last Gospel, for amplified soprano, solo rock group of two amplified saxophones, and two electric guitars, chorus, and orchestra; Pop-Pourri, for amplified soprano solo (and counter-tenor or mezzo-soprano ad libitum), solo rock group of two amplified saxophones, and two electric guitars, chorus, and orchestra.

Orchestral Music—The Lobster Quadrille, folk group and orchestra, with optional soprano (or tenor) solo; Vintage Alice, for amplified soprano solo and solo folk group of two saxophones, mandolin, tenor banjo, accordion, and chamber orchestra; Adventures Underground, for amplified soprano solo with solo folk group of two saxophones, mandolin, tenor banjo, accordion, and orchestra; In Wonderland, Part I, for amplified soprano solo with a solo folk group of two saxophones, banjo, accordion, and orchestra; In Wonderland, Part II, for amplified soprano solo and orchestra; Final Alice, for amplified soprano solo with a solo folk group of two saxophones, mandolin, tenor banjo, accordion, and orchestra; Annotated Alice, for amplified soprano solo with a solo folk group of two saxophones, mandolin, tenor banjo, accordion, and orchestra; In Memory of a Summer Day, for amplified soprano and orchestra; Happy Voices, for amplified soprano and orchestra; All in the Golden Afternoon, for amplified soprano and orchestra.

Piano Music—Soliloquy; Scherzo, for piano four hands; Fantasy Pieces.

Vocal Music—Six Songs on Poems of James Joyce, for voice and piano; I Hear an Army, for soprano and string quartet; Night Conjure-Verse, for soprano, counter-tenor (or mezzo-soprano), woodwind septet and string quartet; Syzygy, for soprano, French horn, chimes, and chamber ensemble.

ABOUT

After Dark, August 1973; Chicago Symphony Program Notes, October 7, 1976; High Fidelity/Musical America, September 1980; New Yorker, April 11, 1977, October 6, 1980; New York Times, May 4, 1980, October 26, 1980.

David Diamond

1915–

For biographical sketch, list of earlier works, and bibliography, see *Composers Since 1900.*

The Thorne Music Fund commissioned the writing of Diamond's *Concerto No. 3,* for violin and orchestra. Completed in 1968, it was introduced on April 1, 1976, by the New York Philharmonic Orchestra under Leonard Bernstein, with Piotr Janowski as soloist. An orchestral *Overture (No. 2), A Buoyant Music* (1970) was heard for the first time on March 14, 1971, in a performance by the National Gallery of Washington Orchestra under Richard Bales.

For the dedication of a new auditorium at the Manhattan School of Music's new location near Columbia University in New York, the Thorne Music Fund commissioned Diamond to write a choral symphony, To Music. The dedicatory concert took place on January 31, 1970, with the composer conducting. Scored for solo tenor, solo baritone, chorus, and orchestra, this symphony was based on the texts of two poems, "To Music," by John Masefield and Longfellow's "Dedication." *High Fidelity/Musical America* reviewed the performance: "Diamond's new three-movement work is another in the long line of inspirational orchestral-choral works extoll-

ing Art, Beauty, Love, Brotherhood and other assorted Muses. Diamond uses a somewhat conservative-oriented idiom—his material is contrapuntally conceived, symphonically developed and traditionally orchestrated—but with vitality and spontaneity. And he treats the poems' sentiments expressively."

While he was composer-in-residence at the American Academy in Rome in 1971–1972, Diamond completed the *Quintet for Piano and Strings,* begun three years earlier. He explained, "Although the work is in the traditional four-movement sonata form played without interruption, the developmental and episodic sections are very tightly condensed to permit the clarity of the thematic substance the right-of-way at all times, so that when the final Fugue is reached, the subject itself seems to be the fulfillment (which it is, in fact) of the opening introductory materials." The first performance was by the Concord Quartet, with Beveridge Webster at the piano, at Lincoln Center in New York on November 13, 1972.

As in so many of Diamond's earlier vocal and choral compositions, *A Secular Cantata* (1976), for soloists, chorus, and small orchestra, was based on poetry by James Agee, a close friend according to Diamond: "It is of the world, yes, secular in that sense, but like Jim's poetry and prose in general it is deeply religious in the human essence. All of man's suffering is in it, as is Jim's and my own. And Man's glory, too, when he emerges from the dark. . . . It is a statement of faith composed in a time of transition. . . . There are terrible things and wonderful things in them [Agee's poems]. Life and Death, Love and Hate, Suffering, Redemption. All there. In a way, it is my spiritual testament, as much as these poems were for Jim his confessional." The cantata sets to music nine poems in nine parts, with the first part serving as a prelude, and the last as an epilogue. One movement, the second, is for an a cappella eight-part chorus, and the fifth is for a tenor solo and organ. The seventh movement is a chaconne (a series of variations on a ground bass) for baritone solo and orchestra. The Cantata was introduced on February 5, 1977, by the Collegiate Chorale under Richard Westenburg in Carnegie Hall, New York.

Between 1971 and 1975 Diamond was working on his first opera—*The Noblest Game,*—with a libretto by Katie Louchheim, on a commission

Von Dohnányi

from the National Opera Institute, which was never performed.

Diamond has been professor of composition at the Juilliard School of Music in New York since 1973. A bachelor, he makes his home in Rochester, New York.

MAJOR WORKS (supplementary)

Chamber Music—String Quartet No. 11; Piano Quintet; Concert Piece, for horn and string trio.

Choral Music—A Secular Cantata, for chorus and small orchestra; Ode on the Morning of Christ's Nativity, for a cappella chorus.

Opera—The Noblest Game.

Orchestral Music—Concerto No. 3, for violin and orchestra; Choral Symphony, "To Music," for tenor, baritone and orchestra; Overture No. 2, "A Buoyant Music."

Piano Music—Sonata No. 2.

Vocal Music—The Fall, a cycle of nine songs to poems by James Agee, for voice and piano.

ABOUT (supplementary)

New York Times, July 6, 1975.

JACOB DRUCKMAN

Ernst Von Dohnányi

1877-1960

See *Composers Since 1900.*

Sem Dresden

1881–1957

See *Composers Since 1900.*

Jacob Druckman

1928–

Jacob Raphael Druckman was born in Philadelphia on June 26, 1928. Neither his father, Samuel Druckman (a garment manufacturer) nor his mother, Miriam Golder Druckman, was a professional musician, though his father was a music lover and amateur musician. Jacob was interested in music from very early childhood on, but formal violin study did not come until he was six and at ten he began training with Louis Gesensway, violinist with the Philadelphia Orchestra. By the time Druckman was fifteen, he was already composing without any previous instruction; but Gesensway felt he was not ready for instruction in composition. Before long he was studying with a pupil of Hindemith at the local settlement school in Philadelphia and he composed a woodwind quintet which was performed and recorded. Gesensway was then so impressed with the quintet that he accepted Druckman as a composition student. Druckman recalled, "His was really a unique kind of training to find in America because it was thorough and completely traditional conservatory discipline. I was not even allowed to utter the word 'chord' until I had written a five-voiced mass in 16th century style." Composition study was supplemented by lessons in solfeggio with Renée Longy.

As a teenager, Druckman was also busy as a jazz trumpeter and he remembered that "Growing up during World War II, I found myself too young to be in the service but not old enough to be in the musicians' union. There was a lot of money about and a good deal of employment for musicians so I had quite a bit of professional experience playing jazz. This, combined with excellent classical training, made a kind of magic greenhouse for musicians of that time."

During the summer of 1948 he attended the Berkshire Music Center at Tanglewood in Massachusetts as a violinist, to support himself as a

100

composer by playing violin in the orchestra. Tiring of the anonymity of an orchestra string player, and losing interest in a jazz career, he became discouraged and decided to quit music in spring 1949. On a "fluke," as he described it, he sent one of his compositions to Aaron Copland who invited him to Tanglewood as a scholarship pupil in composition. "This brought me back to music. I think that if Copland hadn't done that, I would have ended up in some other field." The summers of 1949 and 1950 were spent at Tanglewood under Copland.

Between 1949 and 1954 he attended the Juilliard School of Music where he studied composition with Bernard Wagenaar, Vincent Persichetti, and Peter Mennin. In Norman Singer's sociology class at Juilliard, Druckman met and later married Muriel Helen Topaz, a dance student, on June 5, 1954, and they had two children. Muriel Topaz, an authority on dance notation, was for several years on the faculty of the Juilliard School before becoming executive director of the Dance Notation Bureau in New York.

After Druckman received his Bachelor of Science degree at Juilliard in 1954, a Fulbright Fellowship enabled him to go to Paris to attend L'École Normale de Musique as a composition student of Tony Aubin. Returning to the United States for his Master of Arts degree at Juilliard in 1956, he joined that faculty as a teacher of music literature and the materials of music from 1957 to 1972. In 1957, he was awarded a Guggenheim Fellowship (and a second one in 1968) and from 1961 to 1967 he taught music part-time at Bard College in New York.

His composition, *Dark Upon the Harp,* set to verses from the biblical psalms, for mezzo-soprano, brass quintet, and percussion, was completed and first performed in New York in 1962. Andrew Porter wrote in *The New Yorker* more than a decade later, that it was "a progression from fierceness in adversity through rejoicing to serenity. Druckman's setting is vivid too, and the close is particularly beautiful. By various mutes, the range of brass colors is skillfully extended. By delicate attention to balance, the voice remains unobscured." *The Sound of Time,* for soprano and orchestra, to a text by Norman Mailer, was introduced in Provincetown, Massachusetts, on July 7, 1965. String Quartet No. 2 (1966) was performed by the Concord Quartet in the opening program of the third Annual May Festival of the Composers Theater on May 1, 1972. At that time, Donal Henahan, described the quartet in the New York *Times,* as a "strong-minded and relentlessly serious work, in one extended movement [which] called on an endless variety of fiddling techniques and compositional permutations. ... Its rigorous statements and spasmodic impulses combined to sustain a definite, rather grim, mood."

In 1965–1966 Druckman was invited to work at the Columbia-Princeton Electronic Music Center at Columbia University in New York. His first electronic composition in 1966 was *Animus I,* for trombone and solo tape, written for Davis Shuman, trombonist, who died before he could introduce it (the work was dedicated to his memory). It was introduced by André Smith at Bard College in Annandale-on-the-Hudson, New York, on May 23, 1966, and has since been performed dozens of times throughout the world. Alfred Frankenstein wrote in *High Fidelity/Musical America,* that the work "is a dialogue, debate or battle royal between tape and trombone. It is a bit of a masterpiece, partly because Druckman knows so much about electronic sound and what it can do that a trombone can't; partly because he is equally past master of everything the wind instrument can do that is beyond the possibilities of tape."

In 1968–1969, Druckman wrote two more electronic compositions, bearing the title *Animus. Animus II,* for mezzo-soprano, two percussionists, and tape, was heard for the first time at a concert of Domaine Musical in Paris on February 2, 1970. In *The New Yorker,* Andrew Porter described it as "the sexiest music I have ever heard. ... The singer leads, lures, stimulates, cajoles the two instrumentalists who respond to her siren song with trembling, quivering, pattering, shimmering, excitable eruptions of fierce or flickering sound and sometimes a low vocal moan of desire. ... Perhaps it is all rather shameless; it is also delicately and subtly constructed in its musical and dramaturgical incidents." *Animus III,* commissioned by the Groupe de Recherches Musicales of Radiodiffusion-Télévision Française was introduced in Paris on October 23, 1969. *Animus IV,* for tenor, instruments, and tape, was also commissioned by the Groupe de Recherches Musicales and its premiere performance took place in Paris on September 29, 1977, under the direction of the composer. In this work, Druckman borrowed thematic material from Chabrier's *Villanelles des Petits Canards* and Liszt's *Die drei Zigeuner* for a fantasia-type composition.

In the early 1970s, Gerald Arpino, choreographer for the Joffrey Ballet, chose several of Druckman's scores for ballets: *Animus* (1969), *Solarwind* (1970), and *Valentine* (1971).

Druckman achieved national recognition when he won the Pulitzer Prize in music for *Windows,* a one-movement work for orchestra in 1972. Commissioned by the Koussevitzky Music Foundation and the Library of Congress in Washington, D.C., its world premiere took place on March 16, 1972, with Bruno Maderna conducting the Chicago Symphony Orchestra. *Windows* was also performed with Maderna conducting the Berkshire Music Centre Orchestra at the Festival of Contemporary Music at Tanglewood the following August. Pierre Boulez introduced it at a concert of the New York Philharmonic Orchestra on January 16, 1975, and Lorin Maazel conducted it both with the Cleveland Orchestra and with the Berlin Philharmonic.

According to Druckman, "The title *Windows,* came from the original premise of the piece which is that the normal sound is a very thick, complex, contemporary structure which occasionally opens up—almost like clouds parting, and one catches a glimpse of very simple music behind the thick textures. The simple music is, I suppose, a kind of nostalgia flitting on the edge of memory, music that never was but that has the perfume of things remembered." As the music progresses, stylistic suggestions of waltz music or ragtime can be heard. Since Debussy was one of Druckman's favorite composers, Debussy is brought in with echoes from *Jeux* and *La Mer,* and there are also passing references to Ravel and Richard Strauss. Donal Henahan reported in the New York *Times* that "It is a big, steely work . . . that sets its fragmentary ideas swirling at the start and never relaxes. There is . . . a kind of pulsating breathlessness that . . . never permits . . . allusions to develop past the germinal stage."

Druckman wrote *Lamia* in 1974 for soprano Jan DeGaetani, who introduced it with the Albany Symphony Orchestra on April 20, 1974. Lamia was a Greek mythological sorceress, and Druckman's composition attempts to evoke the abnormal and supernatural with a suggestion of sorcery. Drawing on five languages (Latin,

French, Malay, Italian, and German), it began with Ovid evoking Medea; continued with a French folk conjuration; went on with a Malaysian invocation against "death or other absence of the sour"; then passed on to Italian (with a quotation from the 17th century opera, *Il Giasone* by Cavalli), and German (calling upon the sorcery in the death potion that Isolde prepares for Tristan in the Wagner music drama). Performed with two orchestral groups, one larger than the other, *Lamia* was presented abroad by the Berlin Philharmonic Orchestra and the Netherlands Radio Orchestra and its American performances included those at the Aspen Music Festival in Colorado and a revised and enlarged version by the New York Philharmonic Orchestra under Pierre Boulez. Raymond Ericson wrote about it in the New York *Times:* "*Lamia* is as magical as it should be. Taking incantatory texts, the composer has immersed them in orchestral sound that sometimes shimmers, sometimes commands. . . . It is a haunting score."

On March 4, 1976, the St. Louis Symphony under Leonard Slatkin offered the world premiere of *Mirage.* In this work, Druckman explained that he dealt with "different but simultaneous layers of consciousness. Images, more or less veiled . . . memories reflected and echoed. Identities change, as do persons and locales in dreams." Druckman conceded the influence of Debussy by taking three quotes from *Sirènes.* In an unconventional handling of the orchestra, the work calls for an offstage ensemble of twenty-four players with its own conductor, and the main orchestra, on stage, including a large percussion group with an electric harmonium and piano. *Musical America* described the works as follows: "The sounds from here and there brush, collide, fade. Contrast is implicit in *Mirage*—contrasts of timbre, of dynamics, of consonance with dissonance. . . . In developing the piece across a little more than a quarter of an hour, Druckman thickens and intensifies the sound layers. Most of the offstage players return one by one to the main orchestra, according to Druckman's instructions."

To celebrate the American bicentennial, Druckman wrote *Other Voices* (1976), for the American Brass Quintet on commission from the New York Council on the Arts and its world premiere took place at the Aspen Festival in Colorado on July 20, 1976. According to Druckman, two of his artistic concerns in this composition were "adoration of virtuosity" and the search "for sounds that deal with flesh and blood rather than intellect." Raymond Ericson of the New York *Times* thought the work was "simply beautiful. . . . The echoing voice of an offstage trumpet, for example, is used subtly and hauntingly."

Chiaroscuro (1976), for orchestra, was another American bicentennial tribute. It was commissioned by the Cleveland Orchestra as one of a series of joint commissions for six major American orchestras, funded by a grant from the National Endowment for the Arts. Inspired by the Italian Renaissance painting term, "chiaroscuro," the composer related it to his music: "By analogy, this work deals with musical equivalents of *chiaro* ('clear,' 'light') and *oscuro* ('obscure,' 'dark'): the opening dense dark sound slowly clarifies and reveals simpler sounds within it almost as a dark gem slowly turned will reveal each of its facets. Fragments of bright unison melody are reflected and echoed to the point where they are obscured by their own memory. One image returns several times: that of a bright single note which gradually disintegrates into a shimmering dust." In combining the sounds of a large orchestra, an electric piano, an electric organ, and a percussion section that includes wood and temple blocks, conga, tam-tam, vibraphone, claves, maracas, marimba, bell tree, gong, and chimes, Druckman has according to a critic for *Musical America,* "taken all these instruments and created a new glossary of sounds, many of which on first hearing defy identification or description. In a masterful way he has woven them together into sheets of sound, into masses and blocks and combinations of instruments which thus become a web of colors both light and dark, as the title suggests." The world premiere of *Chiaroscuro* took place on April 14, 1977, with Lorin Maazel conducting the Cleveland Orchestra. Soon after, repeat performances of the work were given by many orchestras, including the Boston Symphony, Chicago Symphony, the New York Philharmonic, and the Berlin Philharmonic.

On November 2, 1978, the premiere of Druckman's *Viola Concerto* was presented by the New York Philharmonic, under James Levine. The work had been commissioned by the Orchestra for soloist Sol Greitzer, the principal violist, with funds provided by Francis Goelet. Andrew Porter, of *The New Yorker,* wrote that the *Viola Concerto* demonstrated "all the big-orchestra virtuosity of *Chiaroscuro.* . . . Druckman has long been a master orchestrator, adept at creating thin, luminous washes of sound, rich impastos and transformations of texture, sudden or slow. A clear sonic sky may swiftly blacken, grow dense with menace, and be rent by lightning bolts. Darkness almost visible may begin to spark with twinkling points of light."

Leonard Bernstein and the New York Philharmonic Orchestra commissioned Druckman to write *Aureole* for orchestra (1979), and it was premiered on June 9, 1979. The composer discussed the work: "There is a single line running throughout *Aureole,* a constant but shifting, shimmering melody from which all the music springs. . . . At the center of this line is the 'Kaddish tune' from the Third Symphony of Leonard Bernstein." The title points to the music's intent, in alluding to the three definitions of aureole: a halo, a circlet of light around the head of a sacred person, and the sun's corona observed through a mist. The score calls for a large percussion section including tam-tams, tom-toms, conga drums, bongos, temple blocks, and other exotic instruments. Peter G. Davis wrote in the New York *Times* that "As pure sound experience, *Aureole* produces precisely the effect the composer had intended. It is virtually a textbook demonstration of how to achieve shimmering, vaporous, iridescent textures from a full symphony orchestra through such familiar devices as string harmonics, purling woodwind sonorities and the manipulation of many exotic percussion instruments."

Andrew Porter discussed Druckman's music in general, in *The New Yorker:* "Jacob Druckman . . . is a composer whose music is always carefully worked out and set down. There is nothing slap-dash, nothing shoddy or imprecise in the facture. His fancy is fertile and exuberant; his natural accents are dramatic. The ideas can be extravagant, exciting and entertaining. The themes often sound like the musical embodiment of gestures; they have a 'graphic' quality. . . . These gestures are expressive of emotions keenly felt, which the composer is eager to share."

In 1967, Druckman joined the faculty of the Juilliard School, and from 1972 to 1976 he directed the Electronic Music Studio at Brooklyn College, in New York. In 1976 he was appointed professor of composition, chairman of the composition department, and director of the Electronic Music Studio at Yale University.

Druckman was awarded the Creative Arts Award and Citation from Brandeis University in Waltham, Massachusetts, in 1975. He was appointed to the board of directors of the American Society for Composers, Authors and Publishers (ASCAP) in 1976, and in 1978 he was elected to the American Academy and Institute of Arts and Letters. He has been on the board of directors of the Koussevitzky Music Foundation since 1972 and on the New York State Council on the Arts during 1975. In 1980 he was appointed co-chairman of the National Endowment for the Arts composer-librettist project.

MAJOR WORKS

Ballets—Animus; Valentine; Solarwind; Jackpot.

Chamber Music—String Quartet No. 2; Incentors, for thirteen players; Valentine, for doublebass solo; Other Voices, for brass quintet.

Choral Music—Four Madrigals, for a cappella chorus; Antiphonies I, II and III, for two a capella choruses; Sabbath Eve Service, "Shir Shel Yakov," for tenor, chorus, and organ.

Electronic Music—Animus I, for trombone and tape; Animus II, for mezzo-soprano, two percussionists, and tape; Animus III, for clarinet and tape; Orison, for organ and tape; Synapse, for tape; Delizie Content Che l'Alme Beate, for woodwind quintet and tape; Animus IV, for tenor, instruments, and tape.

Orchestral Music—The Sound of Time, for soprano and orchestra; Windows; Lamia, for soprano and orchestra; Mirage; Chiaroscuro; Concerto for Viola and Orchestra; Aureole; Prism.

Vocal Music—Dark Upon the Harp, for mezzo-soprano, brass quintet, and percussion; Bo, for marimba, harp, bass clarinet, and three accompanying voices.

ABOUT

Vinton, J. (ed.), Dictionary of Contemporary Music.
ASCAP Today, January 1974.

Paul Dukas

1865–1935

See *Composers Since 1900.*

Henri Dutilleux

1916–

For biographical sketch, list of earlier works, and bibliography, see *Composers Since 1900.*

In response to a commission from Mstislav Rostropovich to write a work for him, Dutilleux wrote a cello concerto entitled *Tout un Monde Lointain* ("An Entire Faraway World"). Rostropovich introduced it at the Aix-en-Provence Festival in France on July 25, 1970, with Serge Baudo conducting L'Orchestre de Paris and it proved very successful. The American premiere was given on February 3, 1980, by the Cleveland Orchestra, with Lorin Maazel conducting. A poem by Baudelaire on the total escape by mind and senses was Dutilleux's inspiration for the music made up of five interrelated movements. He employed a structural technique used in writing some of his earlier works, "reverse variation," in which thematic fragments are suggested, then developed in variations, before emerging in full statement. The Concerto received the Grand Prix de Musique de la Ville de Paris in 1974, and its recording on the Angel label two years later won the Koussevitzky Recording Award.

Rostropovich also commissioned *Timbres, Espace, Mouvement* ("Tones, Space, Movement"), a diptych for orchestra (but without violins or violas). It was for Rostropovich's first season as musical director of the National Symphony in Washington, D.C., but only the first of two parts was ready in time to be heard on January 10, 1978. The entire work was finally heard in Washington, D.C., on November 7, 1978. Inspired by Van Gogh's paintings, particularly "Starry Night" and "Road with Cypresses," the mood found an echo in the composer's "inner resonance," and he confided, "While entirely rejecting any notion of merely making a necessarily ineffectual musical version of the paintings, it has seemed . . . that the intense pulsation that is the life of Van Gogh's canvases, the sense of space that dominates them, the trembling quality of the material and above all the effect of the quasi-comic swirling the paintings give off, could indeed have their counterparts in sound." The three subsections in part one of the work are contrasts in rhythms with "some static portions —almost 'lulls'—alternating with blazes of violence." In the second part, "even more than in the first, the exploration of contrasts between extreme registers of the orchestra has been one of the preoccupations of the composer."

Theodore W. Libbey Jr. wrote in the Washington *Star* that "It is a fascinating score with an abundance of captivating sonorities and musical gestures—spiraling scale ascents, fortuitous little crescendos, moments of seemingly static vibration. ... The writing is exotic, deliciously atmospheric. ... The idiom remains highly original and impressively refined. Dutilleux possesses a keen sense of timing—he knows how to pace a movement and when to end it. There was no wasted material."

The Koussevitzky Music Foundation commissioned the string quartet No. 3, entitled *Ainsi la Nuit* ("Thus the Night"), first performed in Paris on January 6, 1977, by Quatuor Perrenin, a string quartet. The Juilliard Quartet gave the American premiere of the work at the Library of Congress in Washington, D.C., on April 13, 1978. Joan Reintheiler, writing in the Washington *Post,* found that this seven-movement composition was "a direct descendant of Debussy. ... A feast of textures is displayed, explored and contemplated. ... Throughout, Dutilleux maintains the glowing transparency that characterizes French music."

Dutilleux is active in Paris arranging programs for the French Radio and with teaching, and administrative duties at the École Normale de Musique. He came to the United States for the third time in August 1975 to serve as President of the Jury in the First Robert Casadesus International Piano Competition which was held at the Cleveland Institute of Music, and again in 1980 to attend the American premiere of *Tout un Monde Lointain.*

In *Les Nouvelles Littéraires,* Dutilleux discussed his creative *modus operandi:* "I work very slowly. I have an obsession with rigorousness, and I seek always to insert my thought into a formal frame, precise, abstracted, strict. On the other hand, I have such a curiosity that I cannot detach myself—before the work in me is completely mature—from all the diverse temptations of form, and often after that which I discover or hear in the course of my search and my work. ... These desires for rigor and this curiosity—I believe they both live in me. I am very sensitive to all that occurs in the world, to events, to journals, to books which make their appearance.

I can enclose myself in my ivory tower to compose, only when my work has become imperious, that is to say when I have chosen the form it will have. There evidently exists a form particular to each work, according to an interior evolution. The problem of forms, of structures which are far removed from prefabricated frames, preoccupies me more and more."

MAJOR WORKS (supplementary)

Chamber Music—Ainsi la Nuit, for string quartet; Hommage à Paul Sacher, for cello solo.

Orchestral Music—Tout un Monde Lointain, concerto for cello and orchestra; Timbres, Espace, Mouvement, diptyque.

Piano Music—Figures de Resonances, for two pianos; Preludes.

ABOUT (supplementary)

Humbert, D., L'Oeuvre d'Henri Dutilleux; Jacobs, R., Henri Dutilleux; Mari, P., Henri Dutilleux.

High Fidelity/Musical America, September 1976.

Klaus Egge

1906–1979

For biographical sketch, list of earlier works, and bibliography, see *Composers Since 1900.*

Egge's *Symphony No. 4,* "Sopra B-A-C-H, E-G-G-E," had its world premiere with the Detroit Symphony on March 28, 1968. This is one of several works in which the composer used the musical notes of "E-G-G-E" as a motto theme. He also liked to sign many of his scores with the same notes. This symphony, and the *Fifth Symphony,* "Quasi dolce Passacaglia"—introduced in 1969 in Oslo on September 27—are in a serial technique.

Klaus Egge died in Oslo on March 7, 1979.

MAJOR WORKS (supplementary)

Chamber Music—Sonatina, for harp; Woodwind Quintet No. 2.

Opera—Olaf Lijekrans.

Orchestral Music—Symphonies Nos. 4 and 5; Concerto for Cello and Orchestra; Concerto No. 3, for piano and orchestra.

Egk

Werner Egk

1901–

For biographical sketch, list of earlier works, and bibliography, see *Composers Since 1900.*

Egk's comic opera, *17 Days and 4 Minutes,* which had its world premiere in Stuttgart, Germany, on June 2, 1966, received its American premiere in Minneapolis on January 17, 1970, by the Center Opera Company. This burlesque on the story of Ulysses and Circe was adapted from Calderón's *El Mayor Encanto Amor.* Harold C. Schonberg reported from Minneapolis to the New York *Times,* that "Unfortunately, the opera turned out to be heavily Teutonic in humor, composed in a neutral conservative style, and lacking one original musical idea."

Die Verlobung in Santa Domingo ("Engagement in Santo Domingo"), an opera based on a story by Heinrich von Kleist, was written in 1963 and introduced in Munich on November 27 of that year. The first performance in the United States was by the St. Paul Opera in Minnesota, on July 20, 1974. Reviewing it in the New York *Times,* Donal Henahan wrote: "With its touches of Germanic jazz, Puccini, Berg and so on, and its arias and duets and other set pieces, the opera is eclectic and conservative. . . . *San Domingo* worked very well."

Egk's ballet, *Casanova in London,* was premiered in Munich, Germany, on November 23, 1969, and his orchestral piece, *Moria,* was heard for the first time on January 12, 1973, in Nuremberg, Germany.

What had been planned as a birthday tribute to Egk turned out to be a fiasco: his opera, *Der Revisor,* which is based on Gogol's *The Inspector General,* was revived by the Bavarian State Opera in Munich on May 19, 1976, with the composer conducting. After the second performance, Egk angrily withdrew it explaining, in an open letter to the local press, that noisy and busy stage business interfered seriously with his music. The stage director, Dietrich Haugk, countered with the accusation that *Der Revisor* so mutilated Gogol's play that it could only be staged as an outright farce. The controversy— *pro* and *con* Egk—raged hotly in Munich throughout the summer.

MAJOR WORKS (supplementary)

Ballet—Casanova in London.

Orchestral Music—Moria.

Gottfried von Einem

1918–

For biographical sketch, list of earlier works, and bibliography, see *Composers Since 1900.*

Two important works by von Einem were introduced in 1970: the *Violin Concerto in D* (1966) in Vienna on May 31, 1970, and *Hexameria,* for orchestra (1969) in Los Angeles on February 19, 1970.

His opera, *Der Besuch der Alten Dame* ("The Visit of the Old Lady") was hailed as "an opera with the musical and dramatic qualities certain to make it a modern classic," by Donald R. Shanor in the Chicago *Daily News* following its world premiere at the Vienna State Opera on May 23, 1971. The opera was based on the famous play by Friedric Dürrenmatt which had been successfully produced on Broadway and in film under the title, *The Visit.* The libretto, by the composer, dealt with human avarice and the way immense wealth can corrupt an entire society. *Variety* reported: "Von Einem's score adds much to the play's striking material, making it a highly effective opera and even more so a fascinating piece of theater which holds the audience's attention throughout. The rhythmic patterns carry the action well as does the lyric declamation; and the instrumental interludes, between the ten scenes, were more than adequate to explain the characters and their diverse emotions."

In 1973 and again in 1974, this opera was produced in English translation at the Glyndebourne Festival in England. When it was first performed in the United States—by the San Francisco Opera on December 25, 1972—von Einem revisited the United States, not only to attend the performance, but also to undertake a tour of American universities, lecturing on the subject of "Composers and Society."

A cantata, *An die Nach Geborenen* ("To Those Yet Unborn"), for chorus, vocal soloists, and orchestra, was written on commission from Kurt Waldheim, the Austrian-born Secretary-General of the United Nations, to celebrate its thirtieth anniversary. Seven texts are set to music—principally Bertolt Brecht's poem of the same title, two Biblical psalms, excerpts from Sophocles' *Antigone* and *Oedipus at Colonnus,* and two lyrics by Hölderlin. The Vienna Symphony under Carlo Maria Giulini, the Temple University Choirs, and soloists Dietrich Fischer-Dieskau and Julia Hamari performed the cantata at the General Assembly Hall of the United Nations in New York on October 24, 1975, and the composer was present. Raymond Ericson of the New York *Times* considered it "unusually successful for an occasional work," but noted, "It is not notably original, but it accomplishes its aims with the skill expected from the 57-year-old composer."

A new von Einem opera was produced at the Vienna State Opera on December 17, 1976: *Kabale und Liebe,* with a libretto based on Schiller's drama of protest, by Boris Blacher, the eminent composer, and von Einem's wife, Lotte Ingrisch. According to Joseph Wechsberg of the London magazine, *Opera,* "it is an effective libretto which Einem turns into an effective opera. Einem translated the poet's pathos into his own musical pathos. . . . It is always adroitly structured music."

Wiener Symphonie, commissioned by the Gesellschaft der Musikfreunde in Vienna, had its world premiere in the United States, not Austria. It was performed by the Minnesota Orchestra under Stanislaw Skrowaczewski on November 16, 1977. Written as a tribute to Vienna, the Symphony refers to music of three of Vienna's adopted sons—Beethoven, Bruckner, and Mahler. A critic for *Musical America* thought that it "is worked naturally into von Einem's style rooted in the Germanic tradition. The many melodic ideas in the piece are immediately appealing without being at all simplistic— the sort that wears well." The symphony was first heard on December 1, 1977, in Vienna.

On May 18, 1980, von Einem's religious opera, *Jesu Hochzeit,* was introduced in a television performance at the Theater-an-der-Wien in Vienna. Lotte Ingrish's provocative libretto aroused demonstrations of protest and prayer meetings among devout Catholics outside the theater, and caused a furor within. There were objections to the portrayal of Mary and Joseph as simpletons who rejected the Annunciation, and to other "sacrilegious scenes." Christopher Norton-Welsh reported in *Opera News* that the music was "neoromantic and sparse-textured,

with melodic lines and distinct tonalities for the leading figures."

Von Einem and his wife, Lotte Ingrisch, a gifted playwright and short-story writer, occupy his Vienna apartment about six weeks a year; the balance of the time they live in a remodeled old barn in the village of Rindlberg, in the province of Lower Austria. Lotte Ingrisch described it to Robert Breuer of *Opera News.* "Our place looks as if it were in the midst of Vermont, . . . surrounded by woods—not foliage trees but fir trees. Each of us works at his own desk, undisturbed by the other. I believe I throw much more writing paper into the wastebasket than my husband." In addition to her work on the libretto for *Kabale und Liebe,* she wrote the text for von Einem's opera *Jesu Hochzeit,* and his song cycle, *Lieb and Seelen.*

Von Einem received the Austrian and State of Vienna Highest Order, and in 1973 was appointed by the Austrian government professor emeritus in composition. He is honorary president of the Austrian Akademie der Kunst and Musik and honorary member of the Gesellschaft der Wiener Musikfreunde und Direktion. He also belongs to the Akademie der Kunst von West und Ost Berlin, of the Austrian Kunstsenat, and of the Wiener Konzerthaus Gesellschaft.

MAJOR WORKS (supplementary)

Chamber Music—String Quartet, Op. 45; Wind Quintet; Sonata for Solo Violin; String Quartet, Op. 51.

Choral Music—Die Träumenden Knaben; An die Nach Geborenen, cantata for soprano, baritone, chorus, and orchestra.

Opera—Der Besuch der Alten Dame; Kabale und Liebe; Jesu Hochzeit.

Orchestral Music—Hexameron; Bruckner Dialog; Rosa Mystica, for vocal soloist and orchestra; Wiener Symphonie; Arietten, for piano and orchestra.

Piano Music—Two Capricios, for cembalo.

Vocal Music—Geistliche Sonate, for soprano, trumpet, and organ; Leb' Wohl, Frau Welt, song cycle for mezzo-soprano, baritone, and piano; Liebes- und Abendlieder, for tenor and piano.

ABOUT (supplementary)

Stuckenschmidt, H. H., Die Grossen Komponisten unseres Jahrhunderts.

Opera News, December 4, 1976.

Elgar

Sir Edward Elgar

1857–1934

For biographical sketch, list of earlier works, and bibliography, see *Composers Since 1900*.

An Elgar Society newsletter is published triennially by the Elgar Society in Northwood, Middlesex, England.

ABOUT (supplementary)

Burley, R. and Carruthers, F. C., Edward Elgar: the Record of a Friendship; Hurd, M., Elgar; Menuhin, Y., Sir Edward Elgar: My Musical Grandfather; Moore, J. N., Elgar on Record; the Composer and the Gramophone; Moore, J. N., Elgar—A Life in Photographs.

Musical Times, (London) November 1969; Stereo Review, April 1977.

DONALD ERB

Georges Enesco

1881–1955

For biographical sketch, list of earlier works, and bibliography, see *Composers Since 1900*.

ABOUT (supplementary)

Menuhin, Y., Unfinished Journey; Voicana, M., and others (eds.), Georges Enescu: a Symposium.

Donald Erb

1927–

Donald Erb was born in Youngstown, Ohio, on January 17, 1927. Neither his father, Tod Erb (who retired as head of the Order Department of Republic Steel Corporation after fifty years), nor his mother, Janet Griffith Erb, was a musician. The musician in the family was a maiden aunt who lived in western Kansas where she taught school in a one-room schoolhouse. When Donald was eight he spent a summer with her, and she gave him his first lessons on the trumpet. Erb recalled: "She was no great musician, but she had a sensitivity to music. She had a little trailer that she would hook to her car and drag out to the schoolhouse where she taught. In that trailer

---

Erb: ĕrb

were beat-up instruments: guitars, trumpets, and folk instruments. She lived to be eighty-five and she never stopped teaching school." On returning home, Erb began taking lessons on a cornet his aunt had given him from a W.P.A. worker who charged fifteen cents a lesson.

The family moved to Cleveland and Donald was educated in its public schools, graduating from Lakewood High School in 1944. He served in the Navy from 1944 to 1946, and upon discharge, he enrolled at Kent State University to study composition with Harold Miles and Kenneth Gaburo, specialize in trumpet, and earn a Bachelor of Science degree in 1950. Influenced by Hindemith and Bartók, two of his favorite composers, he started serious composition in 1949, producing juvenilia in a neo-classical idiom for a short time. During these years he supported himself by doing jazz arrangements and playing trumpet for touring dance bands, and he admitted, "I got my basic training in music in bars." These jazz experiences influenced some of his later mature compositions.

The decline of big bands caused hardship and a financial struggle to support his continuing studies in music, which intensified when he married Lucille Hyman on June 10, 1952, and the first of their four children was born in 1953. Between 1950 and 1952 he attended the Cleveland Institute of Music where he studied composition with Marcel Dick who taught the disciplines of serial music, and he received his Master's degree in 1952. Then, with funds from pawning his wife's wedding silverware, they went to Paris where he studied composition with Nadia Boulanger. But this investment was not worthwhile, for he found Boulanger to be "too rigid and academic for me, with an approach to teaching that was too regimented." Returning to Cleveland he continued studying with Marcel Dick and began an eight-year teaching stint at the Cleveland Institute. He said that in 1961, "I hocked everything—my insurance policy and my teacher's retirement pension" to do graduate work with Bernard Heiden at Indiana University in Bloomington, and he received his doctorate in music in 1964. Meanwhile, a 1962 Ford Foundation Fellowship enabled him to serve as composer-in-residence for the Bakersfield, California, school system.

Discarding his early compositions, Erb started anew by writing *Dialogue,* for violin and piano (which Giorgio Ciompi introduced in 1958 at the Cleveland Institute) and *Correlations,* for piano, which was performed many times by the noted Cleveland pianist, Arthur Loesser. These were followed by *Music for Violin and Piano,* premiered by Max Pollikoff on "Music in Our Time" in New York.

His continuing interest in innovative methods, in unusual sonorities and tone colorings, in rapidly shifting rhythms, and in fragmented textures became evident in his compositions of the early 1960s: the *String Quartet No. 1* (1960); *Sonneries,* for brass and choir (1961); *Cummings Cycle,* for chorus and orchestra (1963); *Hexagon,* for flute, alto saxophone, trumpet, trombone, cello, and piano (1963); and *Antipodes,* for string quartet and percussion (1963).

His most significant work in the early 1960s (and the first to draw attention to his talent in the United States) was his doctoral dissertation, *Symphony of Overtures,* completed in 1964. Its first performance was given by the Indiana University Orchestra in Bloomington on February 11, 1964, with Tibor Kozsma conducting. The Seattle Symphony in Washington performed it in 1965 under the direction of Milton Katims (on a Rockefeller Foundation grant). The Cleveland Orchestra under Louis Lane presented it on November 11, 1965 as have most other major orchestras, and it was recorded by the Dallas Symphony Orchestra under Donald Johanos.

Each movement of the Symphony is an overture to a contemporary play: Jean Gênet's *The Blacks,* Samuel Beckett's *Endgame,* Jean Gênet's *The Maids,* and Eugene Ionesco's *Rhinoc-*

eros. The composer explained, "The form of each movement is in a general way dictated by the dramatic structure of the play upon which it is based. In essence, the work marks a return to the long dishonored ways of 'program music'; yet it can be heard on purely musical terms. The motives and textures which begin each overture are almost immediately treated in developmental fashion. The divisions of each movement into sections are created more by changes in texture than by other traditional means, such as cadences or changes in tonal areas. Texture, then, is of primary importance and is used as a basic organizing factor, rather than as an effect." The symphonic pattern unfolds with the first movement approximating the opening-movement Allegro of a symphony; the second is a conventional Adagio; the third is a Scherzo with trio; and the fourth (described by the composer as "a brutal march-like movement") is the climactic finale.

In 1964–1965, Erb was assistant professor of composition at Bowling Green State University in Ohio. In addition he was composer-in-residence at Roosevelt University in Chicago during the summer of 1966, and since then he has held a similar post with the Cleveland Institute of Music where, in 1973, he became head of the theory and composition departments. In 1966, Erb was awarded the Cleveland Arts Prize from the Women's City Club of Cleveland and in 1966–1967 he was one of ten musicians to win a fellowship from the National Council on the Arts. In 1968 he headed a composition workshop at the Centennial Alaska Festival.

On a Guggenheim Fellowship (1965–1966), he became involved in electronic music as visiting professor for Research in Electronic Music at the Case Institute of Technology in Cleveland (now Case Western Reserve University) from 1965–1967. His experiments with the creation of electronic music began with *Reticulation* (1965), for symphonic band and electronic tape, and continued with *Stargazing* (1966), for elementary band and electronic tape; *Kyrie* (1967), for chorus, piano, and percussion with electronic tape; and *Reconnaissance* (1967), for violin, string bass, piano, percussion, and two electronic-performance set-ups.

In *Kyrie,* first performed at the Birmingham Unitarian Church in Michigan, in the fall of 1967, the tape was a collage of sounds taken from the news, sound effects (police whistles, screams, etc.), and a quote from *Deutschland über Alles.* Costuming, slides, and stage movement were specified. The composer said, "The total effect is created by the sacred text side by side with a great deal of aural and visual violence. It attempts to expose the face of hate, an outgrowth of my growing concern for our lack of ability to listen to one another. A well-known quote from Yeats is what I have often used as the only program note for the piece: 'Things fall apart; the centre cannot hold; mere anarchy is loosed upon the world.' "

Erb's *Reconnaissance* calls for live electronic instruments on the stage—a Moog synthesizer, and a smaller Moog with a four-octave keyboard, supplemented by violin, string bass, piano, and percussion. This work was written and performed, in 1967, in the "Music In Our Time" series in New York, and performed later at Expo '67 in Montreal and at the Monday Evening Concerts in Los Angeles. Erb, who has since revised and extended it by seven minutes, indicated, "I simply wrote a piece for six instruments, and regarded the electronic ones as equal partners, no more, no less. To me the electronic instruments in conjunction with our traditional ones are capable of producing a chamber music that is rich in possibilities."

Regarding his use of the Moog instruments as opposed to electronic tapes, Erb explained in 1967 "that the new instruments with their extreme versatility and portability could be used on stage rather than committed to tape. Live musicians add drama to music that a tape recorder simply cannot duplicate. This allows a real give-and-take quality (which is one of the attractions of chamber music). The biggest drawback of live electronic music is that the electronic instruments are limited (temporarily at least) to fewer possibilities than when the music was committed to tape."

Erb's continued explorations in electronic music resulted in *Fission* (1968), where he entered the multi-media field by utilizing dancers and lighting as well as electronic tape and a soprano saxophone; *Klangfarbenfunk* (1970), translated loosely as "low down tone color," had its world premiere with the Detroit Symphony under Sixten Ehrling on October 1, 1970 and featured, in addition to electronic sounds, an orchestra and a rock band. . . . *And Then Toward the End* . . . (1971) was written for trombone and four-track pre-recorded trombone; *The Purple*

Roofed Ethical Suicide Parlor (1972), combined a wind ensemble with electronic sounds; and *Autumnmusic* (1973), where electronic music was merged with a full symphony orchestra, was commissioned by the William Inglis Morse Trust Fund for a premiere with the New Haven (Connecticut) Symphony Orchestra under Frank Brieff, on November 20, 1973. In three movements, the last two played without pause, *Autumnmusic,* in spite of its electronic sound and aleatoric procedures, is written in the classical tradition—its second movement is similar to a symphony finale. The work was again performed by the National Symphony Orchestra of Washington, D.C., under Leonard Slatkin on December 19, 1978 and Theodore W. Libbey Jr. wrote about it in the Washington *Star:* "Erb's music is brilliantly conceived in terms of sound rather than theory, and keenly exploits the less well-known capabilities of standard instruments. It is music of experience, always reaching out to involve the listener as an unfolding of sense sound, never dwarfing him in obscurities. It is also music of a human dimension, with gestures that are both natural and spontaneous."

To celebrate the American bicentennial and on commission from the TRW Corporation for its 75th anniversary, Erb's *Music for a Festive Occasion,* for orchestra, electronic tape, and forty water-goblet players, was performed by the Cleveland Orchestra under Lorin Maazel on January 11, 1976.

Erb's interest in electronic music did not preclude his writing traditional music. *Christmas Music* was commissioned to celebrate the 50th anniversary of the Cleveland Orchestra which performed it under Louis Lane's direction on December 21, 1965. At Lane's suggestion, Erb based the composition on a Christmas carol, "O Come, O Come Emmanuel," which appears as a musical motif before it is quoted in its entirety towards the end. Bain Murray of the Cleveland *Sun Press* wrote: "The mysticism, wonder and excitement are there, but also the little pangs of anguish and sadness, crass commercialism and the zany hilarity of the office party. . . . Above all, there is a whimsical fantasy—a fascination with minute, original constellations of new sonorities which are integrated into an all-encompassing orchestral texture."

As composer-in-residence with the Dallas Symphony on a Rockefeller Foundation grant in 1968–1969, Erb wrote *The Seventh Trumpet,* for orchestra, which was premiered by that orchestra under Donald Johanos on April 5, 1969. Although the title refers to the Book of Revelations, the composer preferred "not to make any specific comparisons between this section of the Bible and what occurs in music." *The Seventh Trumpet,* in a single movement (in three sections), opens with a free cadenza for flute, oboe, clarinet, bass clarinet, bassoon, and string bass, which is repeated in various guises. Citing the "static quality" of the beginning, the composer informs us that "The strings enter stand by stand and proceed to hold the note they land on for the rest of the section. Other musical figures are superimposed on this relatively inactive mass. The second section is very rhythmic and consists of most of the players in the orchestra performing their instruments in unusual ways. The last section begins slowly and gradually speeds up. It is basically cumulative in nature."

The Seventh Trumpet is one of Erb's most frequently played compositions, and probably one of the most frequently performed orchestral works by an American in over a quarter of a century. Its two hundred odd performances by fifty major orchestras were worldwide, and it received the UNESCO Award in 1971. In the New York *Times,* Harold C. Schonberg said: "It is a whiz-bang of a piece, the work of a composer who knows exactly how to get what he wants and, furthermore, a work that has real communicative power."

New England's Prospect, an oratorio for narrator, triple chorus, children's chorus, and orchestra (1974), is Erb's most massive composition—some 16,000 pages long. Titled after an 18th century pamphlet describing the New World, it's eight sections are based on the texts of American speeches (including Thomas Jefferson, William Lloyd Garrison, Anne Bradford, William Carlos Williams, Julian Bond, and others). Commissioned for the 100th anniversary of the Cincinnati May Festival and on a grant from the Julifs Foundation, it opened the festival on May 17, 1974, with James Levine conducting and the Georgia legislator, Julian Bond, as narrator. In the Cleveland *Plain Dealer,* Wilma Salsburg described the musical language as "eclectic with an emphasis on overwhelming sonorities [absorbing] influences as diverse as Gregorian chant, tonal counterpoint, multiphonics and jazz licks." She found the message to be "universal in theme and rele-

vant, [dealing] with the feelings of outrage against war, love of liberty, faith in the future and a deep desire for peace."

Erb wrote his *Trombone Concerto* in 1976 as a showcase for trombonist Stuart Dempster, on a grant from the Martha Baird Rockefeller Fund for Music. The first performance was given by soloist Dempster with the St. Louis Symphony Orchestra under Leonard Slatkin on March 11, 1976. In four movements, the composition exploits aspects of the trombone in a variety of timbral effects produced through the use of beautifully sounding mutes, the lip trill, and its capacity to produce effective staccato passages of elegant character and double stops through playing one note and at the same time singing through the instrument. In the trombone finale, the composer borrowed a technique known as circular breathing from the didjeridoo, a wind instrument of Australian bushmen. Warren Prince, a critic in Omaha, said the aural result "was a kaleidoscope of whirring, thumping, humming and buzzing that examined the possibilities of sound from the most rowdy to the most delicate."

While working on this Concerto, Erb was writing another one, Concerto for Cello and Orchestra, for Lynn Harrell, cellist, on a Ford Foundation Young Artists Commission. Harrell performed it on November 4, 1976, with the Rochester Philharmonic under David Zinman, again displaying the performance of the solo instrument. The work, in three sections, each with a cadenza, is played without interruption. Still another Concerto, for trumpet and orchestra (1980), was commissioned by Don Tison, principal trumpeter of the Baltimore Symphony Orchestra, who introduced it on April 29, 1981.

Erb was visiting professor of composition at Indiana University in 1975–1976 and visiting distinguished professor at California State University in Los Angeles during the spring quarter of 1977. He also made appearances as composer-lecturer-conductor at numerous educational institutions throughout the United States.

He was staff composer for the Bennington Composers Conference in Bennington, Vermont, between 1969 and 1974; on the composer-librettist panel of the National Endowment for the Arts between 1973 and 1977, and chairman from 1977 to 1979; and he was board member of the American Music Center from 1979 to 1982.

His home is in Cleveland Heights, Ohio,

De Falla

where, aside from music, his hobbies are gardening, fishing, and birdwatching. Three of his favorite composers are Mozart, Edgard Varèse, and Charles Ives.

MAJOR WORKS

Band Music—Bakersfield Pieces, for trumpet, percussion, piano, and strings; Compendium; Spacemusic; Concert Piece I, for saxophone and band.

Chamber Music—Dialogue, for violin and piano; Music for Violin and Piano; String Quartet No. 1; Music for Brass Choir; Quartet for flute, oboe, alto saxophone, and string bass; Sonata for Harpsichord and String Quartet; Sonneries, for brass choir; Four for Percussion; Dance Pieces, for violin, piano, trumpet, and four percussion; Hexagon, for six instruments; Antipodes, for string quartet and percussion quartet; VII Miscellaneous, for flute and string bass; Phantasma, for flute, oboe, string bass, and harpsichord; Andante, for piccolo, flute, and alto flute; Diversions for Two, for trumpet and percussion; Trio, for violin, electric guitar, and cello; Three Pieces for Brass Quintet and Piano; Trio for Two, for alto flute, percussion, and string bass; Music for Mother Bear, for alto flute; Fanfare, for three trumpets, two French horns, two trombones, tuba, timpani, and one percussion; Quintet, for violin, cello, flute, clarinet, piano, and electric piano; Trio for violin, piano or electric piano or celesta or organ, and percussion; Mirage, for flute, bassoon, trumpet, trombone, piano or electric piano or harpsichord or organ, and percussion.

Choral Music—Cummings Cycle, for chorus and orchestra; Fallout, for narrator, chorus, string quartet, and piano; N, for chorus, percussion, cello, string bass, and piano; God Love You Now, for chorus, percussion, and harmonicas; New England's Prospect, oratorio, for narrator, triple chorus, children's chorus, and orchestra.

Electronic Music—Reticulation, for symphonic band and electronic tape; Kyrie, for chorus, piano, percussion, and electronic sounds; Stargazing, for elementary band and electronic tape; Reconnaissance, for violin, string bass, piano, percussion, and two electronic-performance set-ups; In No Strange Land, for electronic tape, trombone, and string bass; Basspiece, for string bass and four tracks of pre-recorded bass; Klangfarbenfunk I, for orchestra, rock band, and electronic sounds; . . . And Then, Toward the End . . ., for trombone and four tracks of pre-recorded trombone; Z Milosci Do Warszawy, for piano, clarinet, cello, trombone, and electronic sounds; The Purple Roofed Ethical Suicide Parlor, for wind ensemble and electronic sound; Autumnmusic, for orchestra and electronic sounds; The Towers of Silence, for electronic quartet; Music for a Festive Occasion, for orchestra and electronic sound.

Multi-Media—Fission; Souvenir.

Orchestral Music—Chamber Concerto, for piano and chamber orchestra; Concertante, for harpsichord and strings; Symphony of Overtures; Concerto for Solo Percussion and Orchestra; Christmas Music; The Seventh Trumpet; Treasures of the Snow; Concerto for Cello and Orchestra; Concerto for Trombone and Orchestra; Concerto for Keyboards, for piano or electric piano or celesta and orchestra; Concerto for Trumpet and Orchestra.

Piano—Correlations; Summermusic.

ABOUT

Anderson, E. R., Contemporary American Composers: A Biographical Dictionary; Reimer B. and Evans, E., The Experience of Music; Thompson, W., Music for Listeners; Vinton, J. (ed.), Dictionary of Contemporary Music.

BMI, Many Worlds of Music, Winter 1976; Cleveland Plain Dealer, October 23, 1977; Cleveland Press, October 29, 1976.

Manuel De Falla

1876–1946

For biographical sketch, list of earlier works, and bibliography, see *Composers Since 1900.*

ABOUT (supplementary)

Crichton, R., Manuel de Falla: Descriptive Catalogue of his Works; Falla, M. de, On Music and Musicians; Franco, E., Manuel de Falla.

New York Times, June 18, 1978.

Gabriel Fauré

1845–1924

For biographical sketch, list of earlier works, and bibliography, see *Composers Since 1900.*

To honor the fiftieth anniversary of Fauré's death (three years late), two recorded sets of his complete songs, originating in France, were released in the United States in 1977: A Connoisseurs Society album featuring Gérard Souzay and Elly Ameling; and a recording released by Musical Heritage Society with Anne-Marie Rodde, Sonia Nigoghossian, and Jacques Herbillon.

ABOUT (supplementary)

Vuaillat, J., Gabriel Fauré.

Stereo Review, August 1977.

Morton Feldman

1926–

Morton Feldman, a prominent figure in the American avant-garde movement in music, was born in New York City on January 12, 1926. His earliest recollection of musical activity was sitting at the piano and having his mother pick out with one of his fingers the melody of the Jewish song, "Eili, Eili." He began to study piano early, suffering through a succession of what he recalled as incompetent teachers who did little more than teach him to read notes. The first teacher to whom he is respectfully grateful was Vera Maurina-Press, a pupil of Busoni, with whom he began to take piano lessons at twelve. She instilled in him, he said, "a vibrant musicality rather than musicianship." At fifteen, Feldman was studying composition and counterpoint with Wallingford Riegger and three years later, composition with Stephan Wolpe. Riegger and Wolpe both helped to arouse and stimulate in him an interest in such modern concepts as atonality and twelve-tone music. Feldman's first published piece of music was *Journey to the End of the Night,* written in 1949. It was atonal, inspired by a novel by Céline, and scored for soprano, flute, two clarinets, and bassoon.

During the 1949–1950 music season, Dimitri Mitropoulos conducted the New York Philharmonic in a performance of Webern's twelve-tone Symphony that aroused a good deal of audience antagonism. Feldman was at that concert as was John Cage, the avant-gardist, and they met for the first time. Mutual admiration of Webern and contempt for the way the audience reacted produced an instant friendship. While visiting Cage in his apartment on Grand Street in New York City, Feldman showed him the manuscript of a string quartet that he had just written. Cage asked the question, "How did you make this?" to which Feldman could not reply but he recalled, "John jumped up and down and with a high kind of monkey squeal screeched, 'Isn't that marvelous. Isn't that wonderful. It's so beautiful and he doesn't know how he made it.' " Feldman regarded his association with Cage as a turning point in his creative life and confided, "I sometimes wonder how my music would have turned out if John had not given me

MORTON FELDMAN

those early permissions to have confidence in my instinct."

Through Cage Feldman came in contact with other avant-gardists—in music and art—who introduced him to a new freedom of expression and technique which released him from tradition and long-accepted theories. The artists Philip Guston (who became one of his closest friends), Jackson Pollock, and Willem de Kooning, more than the composers Earle Brown and Pierre Boulez, made Feldman aware of the kind of music he wanted to create, as he indicated. "The new painting made me desirous of a sound world more direct, more immediate, more physical than anything that had existed hitherto. . . . The new structure required a concentration more demanding than if the technique was that of a still photograph, which for me is what precise notation has come to imply." His new concept embodied sound whose elements were intentionally unrelated and disassociated; the new aleatory process, partially controlled; and graphic notation, which he described: "The discovery that sound *in itself* can be a totally plastic phenomenon, suggesting its own shape, design and poetic metaphor, has led me to devise a new system of graphic notation—an 'indeterminate' structure allowing for the different utterance of the sound, unhampered by compositional rhetoric." The purpose of the graph, as distinguished from traditional notation, is that it directs action in terms of sound itself.

Among his earliest experiments in graphic notation are five compositions collectively entitled

Projections, completed between 1950 and 1951; *Projection I,* for cello solo; *Projection II,* for violin, cello, flute, trumpet, and piano; *Projection III,* for two pianos; *Projection IV,* for violin and piano; and *Projection V,* for three cellos, three flutes, trumpet, and two pianos. In these works, the register is indicated (high, middle, low) but not the pitches within each register; this is left to the performers themselves to select. Time values are also given and so are the dynamics (always soft). *Projection II* was first heard at an avant-garde festival in New York on September 3, 1963.

Feldman extended his method further between 1951 and 1953 in working with larger masses of sound—the large symphony orchestra —in *Intersection I* and *Marginal Intersection.* The title suggests a street intersection at the moment when a traffic light changes from red to green. Both of these graph-scored pieces also designate the register within a given time structure, with the players selecting the exact pitch for themselves. Within this structure, entrances are also freely chosen by performers.

Feldman attempted to explain to Brian O'Doherty of the New York *Times* that his score was "my canvas, this is my space. What I do is try to sensitize this area—this time-space. The reality of lock-time comes later in performance, but not in the making of the composition. In the making of a composition the time is frozen. The time structure is more or less in vision before I begin. I know I need eight or ten minutes like an artist needs five yards of canvas." Referring to a complexly-designed score, he pointed out: "I can start here or there wherever the point is I want to work in or around or from." A score made up of boxes resembled, O'Doherty said, "a crossword puzzle by Mondrian " and Feldman explained further: "Each box has a number, the number of sounds that instrument plays on or within the duration—that's up to the instrumentalist. I don't tell him the note to play either— just the general area of sound. ... It's like a painter. What has a painter got? Form and ... touch, frequency, intensity, density, ratio color. It's just the spatial relationship and the density of the sounds that matter. Any note will do as long as it's in the register."

O'Doherty related Feldman's work to art: "Like the action painters, he makes one aware of his medium as if it were a substance. Silence and intervals have different tensions and structure, created by the sounds that blurt and spray and slip around them. Attention switches from silence to sound and back again in a way reminiscent of figure-ground relationships in the painting he admires. To a conventional musician, his work must often seem like automatic random choice. To a painter, aware of the discipline against which he creates tension, his music makes sense."

In 1951 Feldman experimented with electronic music in *Intersection,* for magnetic tape, which received its world premiere at the Donaueschningen Festival in Germany on October 17, 1954. The score, a topographical diagram, indicated the number of notes to be used as well as the register.

In *Out of "Last Pieces,"* for orchestra (1958), Feldman again allows members of the orchestra to select their own pitch within given registers, but the duration of the work, its tempo, rhythm, and texture are controlled. The conductor can combine the thirty-eight sound units ("events") that made up the composition into any combinations, sequences, or juxtapositions that he desires. The score is written on coordinated paper "with each box equal to 80mm. The number of sounds to be played within each box is given, with the player entering in or within the duration of each box. Dynamics throughout are very low. The amplified guitar, harp, celesta, vibraphone, and xylophone may choose sounds from any register. All other sounds are played in the high registers of the instrument except for brief sections in which low sounds are indicated." After its world premiere in March 1961 in New York, Raymond Ericson wrote in the New York *Times* that "A pattern in the texture is not apparent, and in its muted way the music bubbled along like a wayward stream, now quietly, now bubbling up. An overall elegiac mood may or may not have been the key to the title." *Out of "Last Pieces"* was performed by the New York Philharmonic Orchestra under Leonard Bernstein on February 6, 1964, when it was well received by the audience.

At a New York City concert of avant-garde music on October 11, 1963, two new Feldman compositions were introduced: *Vertical Thoughts III* (1963), for soprano, violin, tuba, percussion, and celesta, where the musicians enter the performance at will in four of the five moments, and play when the sound of the preceding instrument is finished. Silences and simultaneous sounds are predetermined. The second world premiere was *The Straits of Magellan,* for seven instruments (including amplified guitar). In this work, the duration of the notes and the number of sounds to be played within a given interval of time as well as the register, dynamics, and color are predetermined. Theodore Strongin reported in the New York *Times,* that the composer "freed his players from the restrictions of the conventionally printed score and encouraged them to listen and decide for themselves what to play next. . . . Mr. Feldman's music is all soft. It is extremely soothing and extremely intriguing, all at once. In a way, as suggested, it makes a composer out of the listener, just as it does of the player. The listener is free to make whatever musical or other association he pleases from it." Two other Feldman works on this program were given their New York premieres: *For Franz Kline,* a threnody for the abstractionist painter, for soprano, violin, cello, horn, chimes, and piano (1962); and *The Swallows of Salangan,* for large chorus and instruments (1960) to a text by Boris Pasternak. According to Strongin, in the latter work, Feldman "parceled out his freedoms among the players so that the sounds collect together in surprisingly fascinating combinations. The purity of his sound sense is impressive."

Feldman's predilection for the softest possible dynamics and for silences in contrast to sound—both characteristic of earlier compositions—were again evident in *Four Instruments,* for violin, cello, piano, and chimes (1965). It was performed at an "Evening for New Music" concert in New York conducted by Lukas Foss on December 21, 1965. (There is another and much later Feldman composition entitled *Four Instruments* which was written in 1976 for four pianos and was introduced on January 18, 1976, by the Cantilena Chamber Players in New York.)

In April 1966, Feldman provided the score for a ballet, *Summerspace,* produced by the New York City Ballet, with choreography by Merce Cunningham. In regard to Feldman's music, Clive Barnes wrote in the New York *Times:* "Mr. Feldman scorns, or at least neglects, conventional music notation and prefers to indicate his musical preferences loosely on graph. . . . The resulting squibbles of sound are so pretty and arresting—with musical oohs, ahs, and timely silences blossoming like daisies in a field —that it may be wondered whether (but only for

a moment) music has been wrong all these centuries."

Feldman's *First Principles,* for brass, strings, pianos, and percussion (1967), played pianissimo throughout, was premiered in San Francisco in April 1968. The musicians, arranged spatially in different parts of the auditorium, "uttered single notes and cluster chords measured in time, not in meter, often at the very threshold of audibility," according to Alfred Frankenstein of the San Francisco *Chronicle.* "The work was really a mosaic of subtly stained silences, creating a curious mixture of tension and trance as it proceeded. You could feel your ear growing out of your head to take it all in." Feldman's *False Relationships and the Extended Ending,* for cello, violin, trombone, three pianos, and chimes (1968), was featured at the Festival of New Music in Palermo on December 31, 1968.

Feldman's premieres of new works in the 1970s included *Mme. Press Died Last Week At 90,* for orchestra, which was introduced on July 29, 1970, at St. Paul de Vence, France, with Lukas Foss conducting; *The Rothko Chapel,* for orchestra, viola, and percussion, was written in memory of the artist, Mark Rothko, and was first performed by the Corpus Christi Orchestra in Houston under Maurice Peress in 1972; and Concerto for String Quartet and Orchestra was commissioned and premiered in Buffalo in 1974 by the Cleveland Quartet (who were then artists-in-residence at the State University of New York in Buffalo), and the Buffalo Philharmonic and its music director, Michael Tilson Thomas. It was introduced in New York on February 2, 1975.

In 1976 Feldman, on commission from the Rome Opera, wrote his first "opera," *Neither,* to an original text by Samuel Beckett. It was premiered by the Rome Opera in the spring of 1977. Not a true opera, it is a fifty-minute monodrama for soprano and orchestra. Joan La Barbara described it in *High Fidelity/Musical America* as "a poignant expression of a particular state of aloneness, when one has left the world of others and entered the private torment of an endless search for a resting place." The American premiere of this work took place at the Manhattan School of Music in New York on November 21, 1978, performed by the Group for Contemporary Music with Charles Wuorinen conducting.

Dore Ashton, art critic, described the music

as follows: "Feldman is a symbolist in the sense that he prefers the ambiguous, . . . the imprecise. He also understands ornament . . . the basis for all arts. In the gravity and delicacy of tracery in primitive music, one finds Feldman's spiritual genealogy."

Feldman was awarded a Guggenheim Fellowship in 1966, the National Institute and American Academy of Arts and Letters Award in 1970, and a commission from the Koussevitzky Music Foundation in 1975. In the early 1970s he served as the Edgard Varèse Professor of Music and director of its Center of the Creative and Performing Arts at the State University in Buffalo where, in June 1974, he inaugurated an annual festival of contemporary music. A retrospective concert of Feldman's work, covering twenty-three years, was given at the New York Cultural Center on March 26, 1971.

MAJOR WORKS

Ballet—Summerspace.

Chamber Music—Piece for Violin and Piano; Projection I, for cello solo; Projection II, for violin, cello, flute, trumpet, and piano; Structures, for string quartet; Projection IV, for violin and piano; Projection V, for three cellos, three flutes, trumpet, and two pianos; Extentions I, for violin and piano; Intersection IV, for cello solo; Two Pieces, for violin, cello, flute, alto flute, horn, and trumpet; Three Pieces, for string quartet; Two Instruments, for cello and horn; Durations I, for violin, cello, alto flute, and piano; Durations II, for cello and piano; The Straits of Magellan, for flute, horn, trumpet, amplified guitar, harp, piano, and bassoon; Durations III, for violin, piano, and tuba; Durations IV, for violin, cello, and vibraphone; Durations V, for violin, cello, horn, vibraphone, harp, piano (or celesta); Two Pieces, for clarinet and string quartet; De Kooning, for horn, percussion, piano, violin, and cello; The King of Denmark, for percussion solo; Four Instruments, for violin, cello, chimes, and piano; False Relationships and the Extended Ending, for violin, cello, trombone, three pianos, and chimes; Between Categories, for two pianos, two chimes, two violins, and two cellos; The Viola in My Life, for viola and six instruments; Why Patterns, for violin, piano, and percussion; Spring of Chosroes, for violin and piano.

Choral Music—The Swallows of Salangan, for large chorus and instrumental ensemble; Chorus and Instruments, for chamber chorus and instruments; Christian Wolff in Cambridge, for a cappella mixed chorus; Chorus and Instruments II, for chorus, chimes, and tuba; The Rothko Chapel, for viola, percussion, and chorus; Chorus and Orchestra I and II; Voices and Instruments, for chorus and instruments; Elemental Procedures, for soprano, chorus, and orchestra.

Electronic Music—Intersection, for magnetic tape.

Opera—Neither, one-act monodrama.

Orchestral Music—Intersection I; Marginal Intersection; Atlantis; Out of the "Last Pieces"; Structures; Numbers, for instrumental ensemble; In Search of an Orchestration; First Principles, for large instrumental ensemble; Mme. Press Died Last Week at 90, for instrumental ensemble; Concertos: Cello and Orchestra; String Quartet and Orchestra; Piano and Orchestra; Oboe and Orchestra; Flute and Orchestra; Orchestra.

Piano Music—Two Intermissions; Projection III, for two pianos; Intersections II; Intermission V; Extensions III; Piano Piece; Extensions IV, for three pianos; Intermission VI, for one or two pianos; Intersection III; Piano Pieces; Piano, for three hands; Piece for Four Pianos; Two Pianos; Piano, for four hands; Last Pieces; Vertical Thoughts, for three pianos; Vertical Thoughts II, for violin and piano; Vertical Thoughts III; Two Pieces, for three pianos; Four Instruments, for piano quartet.

Vocal Music—Journey to the End of Night, for soprano, flute, clarinet, bassoon; Four Songs, for soprano, cello, and piano; Intervals, for bass-baritone, cello, vibraphone, and percussion; For Franz Kline, for soprano, violin, cello, horn, chimes, and piano; The O'Hara Songs, for bass-baritone, violin, viola, cello, chimes, and piano; Rabbi Akiba, for soprano, flute, English horn, trumpet, trombone, percussion, piano (or celesta), cello, and bassoon; Vertical Thoughts III, for soprano, flute, horn, trumpet, tuba, piano (or celesta), two percussions, violin, cello, and bassoon; Vertical Thoughts V, for soprano, violin, tuba, percussion, and celesta; Voice, Violin, and Piano.

ABOUT

Ewen, D., Composers of Tomorrow's Music; Machlis, J., Introduction to Contemporary Music.

New York Times, February 2, 1964; Saturday Review, February 13, 1960.

Irving Fine

1914–1962

See *Composers Since 1900.*

Ross Lee Finney

1906–

For biographical sketch, list of earlier works, and bibliography, see *Composers Since 1900.*

Since 1970, Finney's compositions continued to be written in the twelve-tone technique, though in later works there is a greater concern for traditional harmonic sound. Many of the later works were also written in abstract form, such as Symphony No. 4 (1972), whose world premiere in Baltimore on May 9, 1973, was performed by the Baltimore Symphony under Sergiu Comissiona; the Violin Concerto No. 2 (1973), introduced by Robert Gerle and the Dallas Symphony Orchestra on March 31, 1976; and the Concerto for Strings (1976), whose first performance by the American Composers Orchestra in New York was under Dean Dixon on December 5, 1977. Some of his music is aleatory in nature, Finney explained, "to get sound results that would be impossible for performers to read if they are exactly notated." The two compositions where this practice is best demonstrated are *2 Acts for 3 Players* (1970), for clarinet, percussion, and piano, and Symphony No. 4.

Between 1962 and 1978, Finney wrote a choral trilogy which he regards as a major creation. *Still Are the New Worlds,* for speaking voice, vocal soloists, chorus, orchestra, and tape, *The Martyr's Elegy,* for tenor, chorus, and orchestra, and *Earthrise,* for tenor and contralto soloists, chorus, and orchestra, are all concerned with the human dilemma. The first work is based on texts from Kepler, Milton, Donne, Camus, and others; the second is on Shelley's *Adonais;* and the third is on Teilhard de Chardin and Lewis Thomas. This trilogy was composed in such a way that it can be performed in its entirety or separately.

Paul Cooper wrote in *Musical Quarterly* that Finney's music "is appealing to a large audience because of a surface simplicity and directness; fellow composers are attracted by his innate curiosity for the totality of musical sound ... and by the sophistication with which he examines vital and relevant musical ideas."

In 1973, Finney retired as professor of composition and composer-in-residence at the School of Music of the University of Michigan. He has spent his retirement lecturing extensively and serving on the editorial board of New World Records and Composers Records, Inc., on the board of Composers Orchestra in New York, and as head of the music division of the American Academy and Institute of Arts and Letters. Since 1973, Finney has divided his year between New York City, where he maintains an apartment in Greenwich Village, New York City, and his home in Ann Arbor.

MAJOR WORKS (supplementary)

Band Music—Summer in Valley City; Skating on the Sheyenne.

Chamber Music—Four Acts for Three Players, for clarinet, percussion, and piano; Two Ballades, for flute and piano; Tubes I, for one to five trombones; Easy Percussion Pieces, for four percussion players; Variations on a Memory, for winds, piano, and percussion; Piano Quintet.

Choral Music—The Remorseless Rush of Time, for chorus and thirteen instruments; Still Are the New Worlds, for speaking voice, vocal soloists, chorus orchestra, and tape; The Martyr's Elegy, for tenor, chorus, and orchestra; Earthrise, for tenor, contralto, chorus, and orchestra.

Orchestral Music—Symphony Concertante; Concerto No. 2 for Piano and Orchestra; Landscapes Remembered, for chamber orchestra; Spaces; Symphony No. 4; Concerto for Alto Saxophone and Wind Orchestra; Concerto No. 2 for Violin and Orchestra; Narrative, for cello and chamber orchestra; Concerto for Strings.

Organ Music—Organ Fantasies.

Piano Music—Thirty-two Piano Games; Twenty-four Inventions; Waltz.

ABOUT (supplementary)

Vinton, J. (ed.), Dictionary of Contemporary Music.

Carlisle Floyd

1926–

For biographical sketch, list of earlier works, and bibliography, see *Composers Since 1900.*

Carlisle Floyd's opera, *Of Mice and Men,* to his own libretto based on John Steinbeck's novel, received its world premiere in Seattle, Washington, on January 22, 1970. The critical consensus was that his treatment of the two migratory ranch hands who dream of owning a farm demonstrated his growth as a musical dramatist. Robert Commanday wrote in *Opera News*: "The text and vocal line ride high; the play is still the thing, the handle for the audience. Floyd's own libretto is good, the setting of it excellent. The lyrics sing and there are strong and distinctive arias and ensembles. Most important, Floyd's musical style has made significant strides away from his earlier square-metered phrasings and methodical prosody; it now provides a flexible, more subtle rhythmic current, more interesting textural variety and accent." Since the premiere, *Of Mice and Men* has had numerous performances in the United States and Europe.

After *Of Mice and Men* Floyd wrote both the music and libretto for the opera *Bilby's Doll,* introduced by the Houston Grand Opera in Texas on February 29, 1976. It was commissioned by the Houston Grand Opera, with a grant from the National Endowment for the Arts, in commemoration of the American bicentennial. The opera was based on Esther Forbes's *A Mirror for Witches,* the tragedy of a French orphan raised in the Puritan home of a sea captain in colonial New England, who is accused of having an alliance with the devil and ends up dying in jail awaiting salvation. In *Musical America,* Carl Cunningham wrote that "Floyd has largely forsaken his formerly direct tonal musical language for an atonalism that has a certain self-conscious sterility and occasionally conflicts with badly diatonic means." But he also found that "Floyd's skill as a composer and musical dramatist is still stamped in scene after scene of the score. His vocal lines are masterfully and lyrically shaped and he has drawn powerful, deeply faceted portraits of the opera's two main characters."

On April 24, 1981, the Houston Opera in Texas celebrated its twenty-fifth anniversary, in Washington, D.C., with the premiere of *Willie Stark,* which Floyd wrote on joint commission from the opera and the Lincoln Center for the Performing Arts in New York. The libretto, by the composer and Harold Prince, is based on Robert Penn Warren's novel, *All the King's Men,* and traces the colorful career of a ruthless American politician.

In 1976, Floyd resigned as professor at Florida State University in Tallahassee, Florida, to become W. D. Anderson Professor of Music at the School of Music at the University of Houston, in Texas, where he now lives. He also became co-director of the Houston Opera Studio, a joint venture of the University of Houston and the Houston Grand Opera to provide training and performances for young professional singers. In November 1977, Floyd was honored with a plaque at Indiana University in Bloomington by the National Opera Association for his contribution to American opera at a program of scenes from his opera. Floyd served as chairman of the Opera Musical Theater Panel of the National Endowment for the Arts.

MAJOR WORKS (supplementary)

Choral Music—The Martyr.

Opera—The Flower and the Hawk, monodrama; Bilby's Doll; Willie Stark.

Orchestral Music—In Celebration, An Overture for Orchestra.

ABOUT (supplementary)

High Fidelity/Musical America, February 1978; New York Times, May 28, 1972; Opera News, Spetember 6, 1969, February 7, 1976.

Arthur Foote

1835–1937

For biographical sketch, list of earlier works, and bibliography, see *Composers Since 1900.*

A number of rarely performed compositions by Foote were recorded in the 1970s: the 1891 orchestral overture, *Francesca da Rimini* (Louisville Orchestra label); the three string quartets (Vox); Piano Quintet, Op. 38 (Turnabout); Violin Sonata in G, Op. 20 (Orion); Piano Trio in C, Op. 5 (Golden Crest); and Organ Suite in D, Op. 54 (Orion).

ABOUT (supplementary)

Foote, A., An Autobiography; Dictionary of American Biography, Supplement 2.

Wolfgang Fortner

1907–

For biographical sketch, list of earlier works, and bibliography, see *Composers Since 1900.*

Fortner's three-act opera, *Elisabeth Tudor,* with a libretto by Mattias Braun and the composer, is comprised of scenes from the political struggle between Elizabeth I of England and Mary Stuart of Scotland. Its world premiere was performed by the Berlin State Opera during the Berlin Festival Weeks in 1972. *That Time,* a setting of a text by Samuel Beckett, for female narrator, mezzo-soprano, baritone, and instruments, was first heard in Baden-Baden on April 24, 1977, and in New York on February 18, 1979. *Triptychon*—a three-part suite including *Hymnus I,* for six wind instruments, *Improvisationen,* for large orchestra, and *Hymnus II,* for eighteen string instruments, was introduced in Düsseldorf on April 6, 1978.

In 1972, Fortner resigned after fifteen years as professor of composition at the High School for Music in Freiburg, Germany, and was named professor emeritus. On his seventieth birthday, in 1977, he was awarded the Grosses Bundesverdiensterkreuz mit Stern by the Federal Republic of Germany and was given honorary doctorates in music by the Universities of Heidelberg and Freiburg. Earlier awards included the Grosse Kunstpreiz in Northein-Westfalen, the Bach Prize of Hamburg, the Spohr Prize in Braunschweig, and the Reinhold-Schneider Prize in Breisgau.

MAJOR WORKS (supplementary)

Ballet—Carmen.

Chamber Music—Zyklus, for cello, winds, harp, and percussion; String Quartet no. 4; Hymnus, for three trumpets and three trombones; Neun Inventionen und ein Anhang, for two flutes; Piano Trio; Madrigal, for twelve celli.

Choral Music—Gladbacher Te Deum, for bass, voices, orchestra, and magnetic tape; Petrarca-Sonette, for a cappella chorus.

Opera—Elisabeth Tudor.

Orchestral Music—Immagini, for strings with optional soprano; Marginalien; Prismen, for solo instrument and orchestra; Versuch eines Agon um . . . ? for seven singers and orchestra; Machaut-Balladen, for voice and orchestra; Prismen, for five solo instruments and orchestra; Triptychon; Variations.

Piano—Triplum, for three pianos.

Vocal Music—That Time, for female narrator, mezzosoprano, baritone, and instruments.

ABOUT

Vinton, J. (ed.), Dictionary of Contemporary Music.

Lukas Foss

1922–

For biographical sketch, earlier list of works and bibliography, see *Composers Since 1900.*

Paradigm (1968)—first heard in Buffalo, New York, in 1969—requires the members of the orchestra to hum, whisper, and talk (sometimes unrelated words or just consonants and vowels). On March 19, 1970, Harold C. Schonberg described its first New York performance in the New York *Times:* "Two of the four brief movements were jazzy, rhythmic, witty, combining old and new techniques, using instruments in a wonderfully outlandish way. One of the movements was almost like a nocturne, slow and evocative. The remaining movements had the instrumentalists reciting into microphones, throwing preselected words in random patterns that made crazy sense. A tape recorder was called into play, and there was one delirious moment where, at the end of the piece, the violinist alone continued to fiddle insanely."

In *Geod* (1969)—an abbreviation for geodesics —"a non-improvisation" musical action introduced in Hamburg, Germany, on December 6, 1969, with the composer conducting, Foss divided his orchestra (augmented by organ, harmonica, accordion, and mandolin) into four groups directed by four conductors in addition to the principal one. Foss explained that each group has "its own music, which appears and fades away as through a distance." Klaus Wagner reported in *Melos,* a publication in West Germany, that the sound "changing sharply in location, cheerfully allusive and wanting in accent in terms of dynamics, portrays in its own peculiar way a model of antimusic. Nothing happens, or in any case no more than with a mobile which turns around itself, balances itself off, retracts every movement it makes, and thus never moves from its place." The score is a collage of familiar tunes in quiet tones ("Battle Hymn of the Republic," "Going Home," "Taps," "Merrily We Roll Along") and the entire work ends climactically with symphony orchestra and rock groups performing an improvised jam session under the conductors' spoken directions. Throughout the performance, laser beams produce designs in four colors (green, blue, yellow, and red) over the ceiling and across the walls.

Foss described his multi-media composition, *MAP* (1970)—an acronym for "Men at Play"—as follows: "For the performer it is a game, for the listener-viewer it is a piece of music. The game was an afterthought on my part, designed to make the 'piece of music' *happen.*" *MAP* was premiered in Vence, in southern France, in 1970, and in America on December 14, 1970, in New York. A reviewer for *Musical America* described what actually happened: "Five musicians, each in charge of separate instrumental groups (strings, winds, brass, percussion, and plucked instruments) are kept busy moving about the stage and auditorium when they are not improvising from electronic tapes. The game rules also require the players to huddle together like doctors at an operating table, take turns conducting, and monkey around with a bull horn and a stringed instrument bow. There was a fascinating assortment of bells hung from the ceiling which were struck all too rarely and usually by accident as the players groped around in the semi-darkness."

Two noteworthy premieres took place in 1976: *Folksong for Orchestra* was commissioned by the Baltimore Symphony which introduced it on January 21, with Sergiu Comissiona conducting. In this work, Foss quoted American folk tunes from his youth (notably "On Top of Old Smoky") and a reviewer for *Musical America* thought he "exploited them brilliantly. . . . It is a fascinating work—impressionistic music in the most contemporary terms—a montage of echoes and antiphonies." The String Quartet No. 3, which was commissioned jointly by the New York State Council on the Arts and the Brooklyn Philharmonic Orchestra, was first performed on March 15 by the Concord String Quartet at the Lincoln Center for the Performing Arts in New York. Joseph Horowitz in the New York *Times* called it "an obsessive, driving piece that strings together short, repeated figures in densely overlapping layers." It was performed in Brooklyn, New York, on April 29, 1977, as *Quartet Plus,* with the addition of a second string quartet ensemble, a narrator, and videotape.

Foss wrote the *American Cantata* (with text by Arieh Sachs and Foss from quoted material) in 1976 on a grant from the National Endowment for the Arts, and it was heard for the first time at Interlochen, Michigan, on July 24, 1976. After extensive revision, the new version had its first hearing on December 1, 1977, with Leonard Bernstein conducting the New York Philharmonic Orchestra. This work—scored for two speakers, vocal soloists, chorus, and orchestra—quotes seven American folk tunes and a Negro spiritual. Harold C. Schonberg wrote in the New York *Times* that it was "smart, slick, and very, very thin. . . . There is some jazz. There are some Coplanesque settings. There are snatches of spirituals, whispered choruses, a rather constipated type of old-fashioned melody, and some cacophony. . . . The *American Cantata* impresses

one as the work of a man pretending to feel rather than actually feeling."

Leaving the Buffalo Philharmonic Orchestra in 1970, after seven years as its music director, Lukas Foss became music advisor and principal conductor of the Brooklyn Philharmonic in New York, where he instituted two innovations: "Marathon Concerts" devoted to a single master (Bach, Mozart, Beethoven, etc.) or to American music in 4-hour concerts without intermission which allowed the audience to drift in and out at will to listen; and "Meet the Moderns," to better acquaint audiences with contemporary composers and their music. He was also music advisor and principal conductor of the Jerusalem Symphony Orchestra between 1972 and 1975 and musical director of the Milwaukee Symphony Orchestra beginning with the 1981–1982 season. He has appeared as guest conductor of major orchestras in the United States, Canada, Europe, the Middle East, the Far East, and the Soviet Union.

Foss was also active in music education. In 1969–1970 he was visiting professor of music at Harvard University; in 1972–1973 he was visiting professor at the Manhattan School of Music in New York; and in 1975 he was composer-in-residence and visiting professor at the University of Cincinnati College Conservatory of Music. Foss also appeared as lecturer at numerous other American and Canadian colleges.

Foss, his wife Cornelia, and their two sons live in an apartment in New York City.

MAJOR WORKS (supplementary)

Chamber Music—Paradigm, for percussion and five instruments; Cave of the Winds, for woodwind quintet; Divertissement, "Pour Mica," for string quartet; String Quartet No. 3 (expanded into Quartet Plus, for two string quartets, narrator, and videotape); Music for Six, for any six instruments; Brass Quintet; Round a Common Center, for piano, three or four strings, and optional voice.

Choral Music—Three Airs for Frank O'Hara's Angels, for soprano, female chorus, and instruments (or soprano, flute, piano, and two percussions); American Cantata, for tenor, chorus, and orchestra; Lamdeni, for chorus and six instruments; . . . And the Rocks on the Mountain Begin to Shout (choral version of Brass Quintet).

Mixed-Media—M.A.P., (Men At Play) a musical game for any four players, five instruments, and tape.

Orchestral Music—Geod, for orchestra with optional voices; Orpheus, for viola (or cello, or guitar), and orchestra; Fanfare; Concerto for Solo Percussion and

Orchestra; Folksong for Orchestra; Salamon Rossi Suite; American Cantata.

Piano Music—Ni Bruit Ni Vitesse, for two pianos and two percussion.

Vocal Music—Thirteen Ways of Looking at a Blackbird, for voice, distant flute, piano, and percussion.

ABOUT (supplementary)

Thomson, V., American Music Since 1910.

High Fidelity/Musical America, January 1981; New York Times, October 13, 1971, January 27, 1978, October 21, 1979.

Jean Françaix

1912–

For biographical sketch, list of earlier works, and bibliography, see *Composers Since 1900*.

Jean Françaix added several major concertos to his list from 1965 on. The Concerto for Two Pianos and Orchestra (1965) was performed by the Orchestre Radio-Lyrique in Paris on March 31, 1967, with the composer and his daughter, Claude Françaix, soloists, under the direction of Hirovuki Iwaki. The Concerto for Flute and Chamber Orchestra (1967) had its premiere in Schwetzingen, Germany, on May 13, 1967, with Jean-Pierre Rampal as soloist and Helmut Müller-Bruhe as conductor. The world premiere of the Concerto for Clarinet and Chamber Orchestra (1967) took place in Paris on November 17, 1968, at a performance of the Concerts Symphoniques de Chambre, with Louis Fourestier conducting and Jacques Lancelot as soloist. The Concerto for Violin and Orchestra (1968) was introduced by Roger Andre, soloist, and l'Orchestre Symphonique de Quebec under the direction of Pierre Dervaux in Canada, on January 26, 1970. The Concerto for Doublebass and Orchestra (1974) received its first hearing in Frankfurt-on-Main, Germany, on January 11, 1974, with soloist Günter Klaus and the Symphonic Orchestra of Frankfurt Radio under Hirovuki Iwaki. And the Concerto Grosso (1976) was first performed in Mainz, Germany, on February 6, 1977, by the Orchestra of the state of Mainz, conducted by Dietfried Bernet.

Other significant later works by Françaix include the following: *Les Inestimables Chroniques du Grand Gargantua*, for narrator and orchestra (1971), whose first performance was in Paris on May 17, 1971, by Pierre Bernac and l'Ensemble André Colson; the Octet (1972), presented by l'Octuor de Paris in Vienna on November 7, 1972; *La Ville Mystérieuse* (1973), a fantasy for large orchestra inspired by Jules Verne's *Dr. Ox,* had its premiere in Nuremberg, Germany, on March 15, 1974; *Cassazione,* for three orchestras, was heard first at the Salzburg Festival in Austria on August 12, 1975, with Leopold Hager conducting the Mozarteum Orchestra; *La Promenade à Versailles,* for two tenors, baritone, bass, and string orchestra (1975), was a feature of the Versailles Festival on June 23, 1976; and *La Cantate des Vieillards,* for tenor, baritone, and eleven string instruments (1978), based on a story by Guy de Maupassant, was first performed at Vevey, Switzerland, in 1978.

During a return visit to the United States in 1981, Jean Françaix appeared as a guest speaker and conductor at a concert of Melos Sinfonia in New York on May 6. On that occasion, his Concerto for Clarinet and Orchestra, performed by Gervase de Peyer, received its New York premiere.

MAJOR WORKS (supplementary)

Ballet—Le Croupier Amoureux, for television.

Chamber Music—Quartet, for English horn and string trio; Octet; Neuf Pièces Caracteristiques, for two flutes, two oboes, two clarinets, two bassoons, and two horns; Le Gay Paris, for trumpet and winds; Aubade, for twelve cellos; Quasi Improvisando, for eleven wind instruments; Theme Varié, for solo doublebass; Variations Sur un Thème Plaisant, for piano and wind ensemble; Quintet, for clarinet and string quartet.

Orchestral Music—Concerto for Two Pianos and Orchestra; Concerto for Flute and Chamber Orchestra; Concerto for Clarinet and Chamber Orchestra; Concerto for Violin and Orchestra; Jeu Poétique, for harp and orchestra; Les Inestimables Chroniques du Grand Gargantua, for narrator and string orchestra; Theme and Variations; Quinze Portraits d'Enfants d'Auguste Renoir, for string orchestra; La Ville Mystérieuse, fantasy; Cassazione, for three orchestras; Concerto for Doublebass and Orchestra; La Promenade à Versailles, for two tenors, baritone, bass, and string orchestra; Chaconne, for harp and string orchestra; Double Concerto; Concerto Grosso, for wind quintet, string quartet, and orchestra.

Vocal Music—La Cantate des Vieillards, for tenor, baritone, and eleven string instruments.

ABOUT (supplementary)

New York Times. June 21, 1981.

Gershwin

1898–1937

For biographical sketch, list of earlier works, and bibliography, see *Composers Since 1900.*

On December 29, 1969, as part of the annual international concert season of the European Broadcasting Union, the B.B.C. Radio in London broadcast an hour and a half of Gershwin music to twelve countries. It was unusual for the English, in their turn, to choose Gershwin instead of one of their own serious composers such as Britten, Walton, or Tippett. Writing in *The Listener* (London), Ronald Stevenson said: "Paraphrasing the song from *Porgy and Bess,* 'I Got Plenty of Nuthin', we might say of its creator, George Gershwin, he got plenty of sump'n and it would still be an understatement. This sump'n was genius. . . . The sequence of some thirty Gershwin songs went by like the musical equivalent of a rail journey through scenery revealing a new beauty every minute. The total impression was of a prodigality of melody matched only by Schubert and Johann Strauss."

Songs by Gershwin inspired the ballet *Who Cares?,* introduced by the New York City Ballet on February 5, 1970, at the Lincoln Center for the Performing Arts, with choreography by George Balanchine. The plotless ballet was a forty-five minute performance with dancers Patricia McBride and Jacques d'Amboise. The entire ballet consisted of dances to seventeen Gershwin melodies by the corps ensemble and soloists. Clive Barnes commented in the New York *Times* that this ballet offered "the fresh musical echoes of a faded age . . . evoking a world of warm notes, Manhattan penthouses, cold martinis, and the Astaires smiling at one another with cheerful camaraderie." Hubert Saal in *Newsweek* was convinced that the ballet renewed "Gershwin's lease on immortality."

In April 1970, the naming of a college in the State University of New York, at Stony Brook, Long Island, after Gershwin, was celebrated by performances of Gershwin's music and an exhibition of Gershwin memorabilia.

All of Gershwin's concert and operatic music was presented in a three-day festival in Miami, Florida (October 27, 28, and 29, 1970). It was initiated and planned by David Ewen and presented under the auspices of the University of Miami School of Music. The program included both well-known and less-familiar works, such as the one-act opera, *135th Street,* the *Lullaby* (originally for a string quartet), the art song, "In a Mandarin's Orchid Garden," *A Short Story,* for violin and piano, and the orchestral *Promenade.* This festival was broadcast by Voice of America throughout the world.

The first production of *Porgy and Bess* in Charleston, South Carolina (its locale) was given on June 25, 1970, to commemorate the 300th anniversary of the founding of the city. The performance in a desegregated theater with an integrated cast proved to be a first in Charleston.

After forty years of performances, the first uncut presentation of *Porgy and Bess*—with recitatives replacing the spoken dialogue of the Broadway production and omitted segments restored—took place at the Blossom Music Center of Cleveland, on August 16, 1975, in concert form, by the Cleveland Orchestra, chorus, and with distinguished soloists, under Lorin Maazel. At this performance, "Summertime" did not follow the introduction, but "Jazzbo Brown Blues" played on the piano did; this was followed by a chorus singing "Da—da—da Wa—wa." "The Buzzard Song," the patter song for Maria, and the introductions to the second and third scenes of Act II were restored. Other long-omitted original pieces included: "Oh Doctor Jesus," "O Hev'nly Father," and "Dere's Somebody Knockin' at de Do'." Reviewing the London recording of this performance, Edward Greenfield wrote about it in *Gramophone,* a London publication: "It emerges triumphantly on the grand operatic side of the fence, a work in its way as moving and revealing of human nature as *Wozzeck* on the one hand and *Peter Grimes* on the other. . . . The bigness can here be appreciated fully for the first time."

The first staged performance of the complete *Porgy and Bess* (in two acts instead of three) took place at the Houston (Texas) Grand Opera in the spring of 1976, and then on tour, in New York on September 25, 1976, and then Europe. This production was recorded by RCA.

In February 1973, the United States Post Office issued an eight-cent stamp bearing an engraving of Gershwin and Mayor John V. Lindsay of New York City decreed February 28 as George Gershwin Day. The seventy-fifth anniversary of Gershwin's birthday the following September inspired numerous tributes here and

122

abroad. His eightieth birthday anniversary was also remembered in a special exhibition in November 1978 at the Yale Music Library, entitled "George Gershwin: His Career in Retrospect"—a collection of historical photographs and an original life-size portrait of Gershwin by Judy Cimaglia.

ABOUT (supplementary)

Ewen, D., George Gershwin: His Journey to Greatness (rev. and enl. 1970 ed.); Kimball, R. and Simon A. (eds.), The Gershwins; Schwartz, C., George Gershwin: a Selective Bibliography and Discography.

American Record Guide, September, 1978; High Fidelity/Musical America, January 1974; New York Times, September 10, 1973, September 16, 1973; New York Times Magazine, October 19, 1980; Saturday Review, December 9, 1973.

Vittorio Giannini

1903–1966

For biographical sketch, list of earlier works, and bibliography, see *Composers Since 1900.*

Giannini's opera, *The Taming of the Shrew,* first produced in 1933, received one of its rare revivals in a performance by the Houston Grand Opera at Wolf Trap, in Vienna, Virginia, on August 9, 1979.

ABOUT (supplementary)

New York City Opera Program, March 8, 1967.

Miriam Gideon

1906–

For biographical sketch, list of earlier works, and bibliography, see *Composers Since 1900.*

The Seasons of Time, ten songs based on ancient Japanese Tanka poetry—for voice, flute, cello, and celesta alternating with piano—was first heard in New York in February 1970. Composed in memory of the cellist Otto Deri, this cycle reflected a poignancy in living as well as in relinquishing life. As Paul Hume said in *Book World:* "The delicacy of the texts is mirrored in the sounds [of the instruments] each used with a shimmer like that of silk screening."

In 1970, Miriam Gideon became the first woman to be commissioned to write music for a complete synagogue service. The commission, from David Gooding, music director of the Cleveland Temple, gave her complete freedom to compose in her own "freely atonal" style. She said, "I wanted to express my feelings for the text in terms of a personal idiom." No stranger to sacred music, she is professor of music at the Cantors Institute of the Jewish Theological Seminary of America since 1955. She explained, "I found that there was a background which I could draw upon positively and negatively: positively in desiring to communicate freshly the inspiration of the marvelous poetry of the Psalms and the inspiration of the wonderful sonorities of the Hebrew language; negatively, in wishing to avoid cliches." Scored for vocal soloists, choir, trumpet, flute, oboe, bassoon, violin, cello, and organ, *Sacred Service for Sabbath Morning* was introduced in Cleveland on April 18, 1971, under the musical direction of David Gooding. Writing in *Congress Bi-Weekly,* the organ of the American Jewish Congress, Albert Weisser called it a "work of extraordinary significance. ... It is easily the finest service yet composed by a native-born American-Jewish composer and very probably the most important advance in the form since Darius Milhaud's *Service Sacré* (1947). ... Miss Gideon's style and approach to the liturgy is so deeply personal that its contemporary habiliment proves no barrier at all to the sophisticated listener—or one should say worshiper if so one should be inclined—and what one is mainly aware of is a profoundly felt work of piercing beauty."

A second religious service, for Friday evening—*Shirat Miriam L'Shabbat (Miriam's Song for the Sabbath),* for cantor, choir, and organ—was commissioned later by David Putterman, cantor of the Park Avenue Synagogue in New York, which presented it on May 3, 1974. In this work, the composer wrote in several cantillation motives without abandoning her own personal style.

Fantasy on Irish Folk Motives, for oboe, viola, bassoon, and vibraphone, was commissioned by the New York State Music Teachers Association, under whose auspices the first performance was given in Albany, on October 26, 1975. The *Fantasy* echoed three ancient Irish melodies which the composer had known since childhood, and elaborates on the essential motives in each

Gideon

with instruments chosen to reflect the folk character of each song.

Nocturnes, for voice, flute, oboe, violin, cello, and vibraphone, is based on poems by Shelley, Jean Starr Untermeyer, and Frank Dempster Sherman. It was premiered in St. Paul, Minnesota, on February 21, 1976, at a concert of the St. Paul Chamber Orchestra with Judith Raskin as soloist. The composer said the work, "Written on commission from Mr. and Mrs. Sidney Siegel of New York, in celebration of the eighteenth birthday of their daughter, Rena, *Nocturnes* is a cycle of poems whose transmutation into music seemed an appropriate evocation of youth and its awakening to the magical forces of nature." In reviewing a recording of *Nocturnes* in *American Record Guide,* a critic said: "Setting of three poems . . . in the form of a chamber piece with instrumental interludes between poems creates a magical atmosphere dominated by the sounds of oboe and vibraphone. Gideon's familiar technique of writing lovely melodies played by two instruments in minor seconds here sounds bittersweet rather than astigmatic."

On December 5, 1977, the American Composers Orchestra, under the direction of James Dixon, with Judith Raskin as soloist, presented in New York the premiere of *Songs of Youth and Madness.* Written on a National Endowment for the Arts grant, the work was set to four poems by Friedrich Hölderlin, each one heard twice, (in English translation and in original German). Raymond Ericson noted in the New York *Times* that "The music is quite different for the two versions of the text; and the mood can be distinctly varied. The effect of an emotional depth and color would not be possible in a single language setting. . . . The music emerged nostalgic, troubling and beautiful."

In her Piano Sonata (commissioned by Lillian and Irwin Freundlich in 1977), Gideon took motives of favorite songs by Hugo Wolf and Robert Schumann. *Voices from Elysium,* an evocation of Greek antiquity, with tender and whimsical reflections upon life and death, for voice, flute, clarinet, violin, cello, and piano, was commissioned by the Da Capo Players, who introduced it in New York on April 18, 1979.

"In recognition of the high achievement of one of our outstanding composers," the Elizabeth Sprague Coolidge Foundation in the Library of Congress in Washington, D.C., commissioned a new work from Gideon in 1980

in a medium to which she had long been partial, a poetry setting for voice and instruments. Entitled *Spirit Above the Dust,* a song cycle for solo voice and eight instruments, the text was based on American poems. The world premiere took place at Yale University on February 11, 1981.

In addition to her appointment as professor of music at the Cantors Institute of the Jewish Theological Seminary of America since 1955, Miriam Gideon has been on the music faculty of the Manhattan School of Music in New York since 1967, and from 1971 to 1976 she was visiting professor of music at City College, in New York (professor emeritus since 1976).

In 1975, she was the second woman to be elected to membership in the American Academy of Arts and Letters. She has also served on the board of governors of the American Composers Alliance, the International Society for Contemporary Music, and the American Music Center.

MAJOR WORKS (supplementary)

Chamber Music—Suite for Clarinet and Piano; Fantasy on Irish Folk Motives, for oboe, viola, bassoon, and vibraphone; Trio, for clarinet, cello, and piano.

Choral Music—Sacred Service for Sabbath Morning, for soloists, choir, flute, oboe, bassoon, trumpet, violin, cello, and organ; Shirat Miriam L'Shabbat, for cantor, choir, and organ.

Orchestral Music—Songs of Youth and Madness, for voice and orchestra.

Piano Music—Of Shadows Numberless, suite; Sonata.

Vocal Music—The Seasons of Time, song cycle for voice, flute, cello, and celesta alternating with piano; Nocturnes, for voice, flute, oboe, violin, cello, and vibraphone; Voices from Elysium, for voice, flute, clarinet, violin, cello, and piano; Spirit Above the Dust, song cycle for voice, flute, oboe, bassoon, horn, and string quartet.

ABOUT (supplementary)

Rosenberg, D. and R. (eds.), The Music Makers; Vinton, J. (ed.), Dictionary of Contemporary Music.

Dimensions, Spring 1970; Music Journal, April 1976; Who's Who in America, 1980–1981.

Henry F. Gilbert

1868–1928

See *Composers Since 1900.*

Paul Gilson

1865–1942

See *Composers Since 1900.*

Alberto Ginastera

1916–

For biographical sketch, list of earlier works, and bibliography, see *Composers Since 1900.*

On commission from the Opera Society of Washington, D.C., Alberto Ginastera wrote the opera, *Beatrix Cenci,* for the inaugural of the Kennedy Center for the Performing Arts in Washington, D.C., where it was performed on September 10, 1971, with Julius Rudel conducting. As in earlier Ginastera operas, its text dealt with sex, revels, and lurid violence. The historical plot (used by others, including Shelley in his tragedy, *The Cenci*) involves 16th century incest, murder, and torture and "offers Ginastera bountiful opportunity to do what he does so well—create what can best be described prosaically as horror-movie spook music," observed a critic for *High Fidelity/Musical America.* "All this is done with sophisticated contemporary means—tone clusters, serial rows . . . recurring motifs, and a great range of adventurous instrumental effects. It leaves no doubt that Ginastera is extremely skillful in manipulating the modern tools of his trade. He does more. He writes in addition to dramatic declamation singable vocal line. . . . There is, too, a cool transparent chorus for Beatrix's ladies-in-waiting and a perfect, self-contained Renaissance dance during the masked ball."

Irving Kolodin wrote about *Beatrix Cenci* in *Saturday Review*: "There are many marks of Ginastera's craftmanship in the first act which is mainly devoted to revels and the rape, . . . An intermission later, the mood is totally different. . . . Through much more inspired declamation, sometimes veering on arioso . . . and a dazzling display of visual effects . . . movement and action flow together and the work moves to its appointed end with gathering tension and theatrical force."

On March 22, 1973, Hilde Somer, soloist with the Indianapolis Symphony Orchestra under Izler Solomon, was heard in the first performance of the Piano Concerto No. 2, which she had commissioned. Ginastera described this music as "tragic and fantastic." In the first movement, he borrows a chord from the finale of Beethoven's Ninth Symphony for the tones of his serial structure and in the finale, Chopin's music is suggested. The second movement is unusual in that it is for left hand piano alone. In *High Fidelity/Musical America,* Byron Belt described the Concerto as "a brilliant showpiece in the grandest Lisztian manner. The writing of both keyboard and orchestra (especially rich in striking percussion and wind effects) is Ginastera at his best. This means that daring sounds mingle with traditional contemporary tonal and harmonic devices to produce a fresh work astonishingly rich in variety, excitement and even poetry."

Milena, a cantata for soprano and orchestra, has a Spanish text, taken from Kafka's letters to Milena Jesenka. Commissioned by the Institute of International Education for its fiftieth anniversary, *Milena* was introduced by the Denver Symphony under Brian Priestman, with Phyllis Curtin as soloist, on April 6, 1973.

Love poems by the Chilean poet Pablo Naruda, provided Ginastera with the text for *Serenata,* for bass-baritone, solo cello, and ten instrumentalists. It was written on commission from the Chamber Music Society of Lincoln Center in New York which introduced it on January 18, 1974, with Justin Diaz as vocal soloist. Ginastera explained that he used the term "serenata" in its original sense of "night music." Allen Hughes wrote in the New York *Times* that the music suggested "a night in the tropics. . . . [evoking] the sensuousness, mystery and occasionally the violence of a tropical jungle." The three sections of the work are entitled "Poetico," "Fantastico," and "Dramatico."

Ginastera's String Quartet No. 3, for soprano and string quartet, with a Spanish text, was based on the poetry of Alberti, Lorca, and Jimenez. It was commissioned in Dallas by the Chamber Music Society and the Public Library in memory of John Rosenfeld, the distinguished music critic; its first performance, in Dallas, took place on February 4, 1974, by the Juilliard Quartet with Benita Valente as soloist.

Turbae, a choral work of massive structural dimensions, requiring a giant ensemble, was written for the centenary of the Mendelssohn Club in Philadelphia on a grant from the Community Federal Savings and Loan Association and the Club. The Philadelphia Orchestra under the direction of Robert Page, three "Gregorian singers," and a treble choir gave the first performance in Philadelphia on March 20, 1975. The work retells the Passion story of Holy Week —Jesus's arrival in Jerusalem, His Crucifixion, and Resurrection.

Ginastera discussed "turbae," the Latin word, in relation to his work, "I wish to give this work an essentially dramatic character of that muddled and scattered crowd, with everything this work may call up: our troubled, excited, convulsive times; this is an existentialist reality which distresses us today." The four sections of the work (I, Solemnis Introitus in Jerusalem; II, Passio D.N. Jesu Christ; III, Golgotha; IV, Resurrectio D.N. Jesu Christi), are subdivided into forty-four parts. In *Turbae,* with a Latin text, the three "Gregorian singers" represent the biblical characters and perform in recitative-like passages that alternate with choral parts. The chorales of Bach's Passions are replaced by the Psalms and the Lamentations of Jeremiah from the Bible, but a fragment of Bach's *Passion According to St. Matthew* is quoted in the Barabbas section. We learn from the program notes of the Philadelphia Orchestra, that "There are no solo arias as such, only differing strengths and divisions of the choral forces, whose function is to expand upon, illustrate or otherwise react to the utterance of the Evangelist and the other Gregorian soloists. Accordingly, the character of the chorus varies from one section to another: in some sections it assumes a participatory role —that of the *turbae* in the drama itself—while in others it provides a commentary on the action, rather in the manner of the chorus in the Greek tragedy." The chorus is required not only to sing, but also to talk, whisper, whistle, shout, groan, and, in one instance, to produce sounds by "knocking the mouth with the hand." Exotic background sounds are produced by the percus-

sion section, made up of four players, performing on such instruments as bongo drums, cowbells, tambourine, whip, flexation, maraca, gongs, tom-toms, wood blocks, gourd, ratchet, temple blocks, and crotales. *High Fidelity/Musical America* found that Ginastera's "sense of drama keeps this music from becoming predictable and moves the story along deftly. No section repeats a mood or device. There are stunningly difficult moments in which the singers soar chromatically to the top of their ranges and press beyond into microtones. There are some dramatic devices taken intact from his operas. ... The continual contrast of that cool Gregorian narrative ... with the explosiveness of the choral writing providing a dazzling virtuoso work for chorus."

Glosses, for string orchestra (1976), was commissioned by the Festival Casals of Puerto Rico and the Puerto Rican Bicentennial Commission for its first performance in San Juan on June 14, 1976, with Alexander Schneider conducting the Festival Orchestra. Ginastera said he composed this work in memory of Pablo Casals and in its musical themes, he "tried to bring back to life with love and friendship certain of Casals' imaginary memories of Catalonia." Ginastera subsequently rescored this work for full symphony orchestra and the new version had its first hearing on January 24, 1978, in Washington, D.C., in a performance by the National Symphony Orchestra directed by Mstislav Rostropovich.

In 1977, Ginastera revised his Concerto No. 1 for Cello and Orchestra (1968) and Aurora Nátola-Ginastera, the composer's wife who is a cellist, introduced it at a concert of the National Symphony Orchestra under Rostropovich in Washington, D.C., in February 1978.

To commemorate the 400th anniversary of the founding of the City of Buenos Aires (on commission from the Directors of Teatro Colón), Ginastera composed *Iubilum,* for full orchestra, which he described as "a symphonic celebration." This three-movement composition begins with a "Fanfare" highlighting the brass; continues with a slow-movement "Chorale," whose principal theme is presented by muted strings; and ends with a rhythmically compelling "Finale" which reaches its culmination in full orchestra with the hymn, "Laudate Dominum de Caelis, Alleluia." The composer explained that "This final sequence, together with the theme 'Kechua,' with which *Iubilum* starts, symbolizes the character and eternity of the city of my birth." When *Iubilum* had its world premiere on April 12, 1980, in Buenos Aires, with the Teatro Colón Orchestra conducted by Bruno D'Astoli, it was highly acclaimed. A critic for the Buenos Aires *Herald* spoke of it as "music of enormous vitality which makes its point—its three different although related points—convincingly and ... with originality and the personal commitment which, among other things, dictates that the music should not last one moment longer than he [Ginastera] needs to state his case."

During the 1980–1981 season, the Atlanta Symphony paid tribute to Ginastera by featuring one of his works in each of seven programs.

Ginastera has received honorary doctorates in music from Yale University in 1968 and from Temple University in Philadelphia in 1975. His home is in Geneva, Switzerland. Divorced from Mercedes de Toro, on September 24, 1971 he married Aurora Nátola, an Argentine cellist from Greenwich, Connecticut.

MAJOR WORKS (supplementary)

Chamber Music—String Quartet No. 3, for soprano and string quartet; Puneña, No. 1, for flute; Puneña, No. 2, for cello.

Choral Music—Turbae, ad Passionem Gregorianam, for three Gregorian singers, treble choir, mixed chorus, and orchestra.

Guitar Music—Sonata.

Opera—Beatrix Cenci; Barabbas.

Orchestral Music—Milena, cantata for soprano and orchestra; Piano Concerto No. 2; Glosses, for string orchestra, also for full orchestra; Iubilum.

Piano Music—Toccata.

Vocal Music—Serenata, for bass-baritone, solo cello, and ten instrumentalists.

ABOUT

Sadie, S. (ed.), The New Grove Dictionary of Music and Musicians; Vinton, J. (ed.), Dictionary of Contemporary Music; Cleveland Orchestra Program Book, January 15, 1981.

Umberto Giordano

1867–1948

See *Composers Since 1900.*

Peggy Glanville-Hicks

1912–

For biographical sketch, list of earlier works, and bibliography, see *Composers Since 1900.*

In 1969, Peggy Glanville-Hicks was afflicted with a brain tumor which was operated on at the New York Medical Center and she went to Greece to recuperate. In 1971, she suffered a setback, but she has since recovered her eyesight. Her prolonged illness has kept her from composing.

In 1976, on an invitation from the Australian Arts Council, she returned to her native country to set up the East-West Department at the Australian Music Center. In 1977, when Queen Elizabeth II visited Australia, she decorated Peggy Glanville-Hicks with the Royal Medal for distinguished service in music (even though she was an American citizen).

ABOUT

Murdoch, J., Australia's Contemporary Composers; Sadie, S. (ed.), The New Grove Dictionary of Music and Musicians; Vinton, J. (ed.), Dictionary of Contemporary Music.

Philip Glass

1937–

Philip Glass, one of America's most successful avant-garde composers, was born in Baltimore, Maryland, on January 31, 1937. He was the son of Benjamin Glass, owner of a small record shop, and Ida Gouline Glass, teacher and librarian. Glass's musical education began with lessons on the violin when he was six, but finding little interest in that instrument he changed to the flute. He enrolled at the Peabody Conservatory in Baltimore when he was eight, to study the flute with Britton Johnson for the next seven

PHILIP GLASS

years. Meanwhile, his academic education took place in Baltimore's grade schools and at Baltimore City College (a high school), where he played the flute in the school orchestra and band. In 1952, at fifteen, he enrolled in the University of Chicago and received a Bachelor of Arts degree four years later. The summer of 1955 was spent studying harmony with Louis Cheslock.

Between 1958 and 1962, Glass attended the Juilliard School of Music, and studied composition under William Bergsma and Vincent Persichetti. He was also able to study composition with Darius Milhaud—at the Aspen School of Music in Colorado—during the summer of 1960. He now composed music in styles popular with Juilliard pupils: twelve-tone music, or music in the harmonic, rhythmic, and motivic idioms of Stravinsky, Copland, or Elliott Carter. He had as many as seventy-five compositions performed at the Juilliard School of Music. "I had twenty published pieces, and I was getting things into print as soon as I wrote them," he recalled. Some of his works won prizes from Broadcast Music Inc. (BMI) in 1960, the Lado Prize (1961), the Benjamin Award (1961 and 1962), and in 1964 he was presented with the $10,000 Young Composers Award from the Ford Foundation.

After earning his Master of Science degree at Juilliard in 1962, Glass became composer-in-residence for public schools in Pittsburgh on a Ford Foundation grant (1962–1964). At the same time he produced music in traditional idi-

oms which were successful enough to be published in Pittsburgh. But, in spite of this, he was dissatisfied with what he was writing. He told an interviewer: "I had reached a kind of dead end with music. I couldn't do it any more. Not that I couldn't; I could turn it out easily. That was the problem. I just didn't believe in it anymore."

In reassessing both his aims and values, he decided they could best be realized with further study abroad. On a Fulbright Fellowship in 1964 he went to Paris, in hopes of finding new directions through the study of harmony and counterpoint with Nadia Boulanger. Not composing for a while and concentrating on his studies, he found time to travel extensively to places in North Africa, India, Tunisia, and Tibet, where he became acquainted with Eastern music which made a profound impression on him.

In Paris, he learned more about Indian music during the winter of 1965–1966 from Ravi Shankar, the famous virtuoso of the sitar, who was in France to make a film and hired Glass to change Eastern music notation to notation for French musicians. Glass also received instruction from Alla Rahka, a famous tabla player. His immersion in Eastern music impelled him to develop a new style based on the Eastern principles of motivic repetitions, and he concentrated on forming rhythmic structures where short units were joined into larger ones of thirty and more beats, the larger cycles then becoming "like wheels within wheels." Glass explained: "Everything going at the same time and always changing."

By the time Glass returned to the United States in 1967 he had totally converted to Eastern music. "Ravi, not drugs, was my acid trip," he later told an interviewer. "Overnight I began writing a completely different kind of music." To promote his compositions, he formed in 1968 the Philip Glass Ensemble, a seven-man unit in which he was one of the performers (three saxophonists doubling on flutes, three electronic organists, and a sound engineer). The Ensemble made its debut at Queens College in New York on April 13, 1968, and in 1969 embarked on the first of many European tours. In 1970, the group performed at the Royal College of Art in London where it was heard by a leader of the progressive rock movement who responded enthusiastically to the new sounds, thereby enlarging Glass's audience.

Glass's earliest Eastern-influenced composi-

128

tions, which had their initial performances by his Ensemble, included *Piece in the Shape of a Square* (1968; New York, May 19, 1968), *Music in Fifths* (1969; New York, January 16, 1970), and *Music with Changing Parts* (1970; New York, October 10, 1970). In 1971, Glass formed his own record company, Chatham Square Productions, whose first release was *Music with Changing Parts.*

One of Glass's highly structured works in the early 1970s was *Music in Twelve Parts:* Parts 1 to 6 (1971), Parts 7 through 9 (1973), and Parts 10 through 12 (1974). In 1974 the first parts were recorded in England by Virgin Records, which specializes in rock music, thus extending Glass's influence to rock circles. The entire 4-hour work received its first hearing at Town Hall, New York, on June 1, 1974 (the Ensemble's first appearance in a conventional concert hall instead of an empty loft or other available place). The concert began at six in the evening and ended at midnight, with time off for dinner.

Glass had concerned himself primarily with developing Eastern rhythmic structures in *Music in Twelve Parts,* but now he began to develop a style in which harmony and modulation were incorporated with Eastern rhythmic patterns in a series of works collectively entitled *Another Look at Harmony:* Parts 1 and 2 (1975), Part 3 (1976), and Part 4 (1977). "It is music that consciously reduced its means harmonically and melodically in favor of structural clarity," Glass explained. "Music that tends to be fairly consistent in terms of meter and tempo," which has come to be known as "minimalism." The first two parts of *Another Look at Harmony* were first heard on May 6, 1975, in New York. Part III was an organ piece Glass had written for a production of Samuel Beckett's *Cascando* by Mabou Mines in 1975, and Part IV was a choral composition commissioned by and introduced at the Holland Festival in 1977. Parts III and IV were heard when Philip Glass made his debut at Carnegie Hall on June 1, 1978.

Glass's reputation widened with a surrealistic multi-media production, *Einstein at the Beach,* which is sometimes called an "opera." Actually it is just an abstract series of montages, stage pictures, and surrealistic episodes running some four and half hours on stage. Glass wrote the work in collaboration with Robert Wilson who provided the staging, direction, and decor. There is no solo singing on the stage, since all singing is confined to a chorus of twelve members and actors who speak in recurrent solfège syllables, sometimes meaningless phrases and numerical counts, sometimes speeches, and often clichés, much of it in a dull sing-song chant. The accompanying orchestra is made up of eight instrumentalists (two soprano saxophones doubling with two flutes, a tenor saxophone, three electric organs, and a solo violin) and a vocal soprano as part of the ensemble. While there are no lyrics to the music, there is a series of "events" combining sound, dancing, pantomime, and simplistic episodes. Einstein is represented by several characters: an old man playing a violin solo in the orchestra pit; another man symbolizing science; and a third one writing a mathematical formula on an imaginary blackboard. In one scene, a character does nothing more than walk up and down the stage; another sits in a space ship; another delivers a monologue about bathing caps in an air-conditioned supermarket, a boy sits atop a tower flying paper airplanes, and a man and woman stand on a caboose. John Rockwell wrote in the New York *Times,* "Einstein crosses the conventional barriers effortlessly, without any artificial straining towards 'fusion' music. ... *Einstein* represents a *genuine* fusion—new music that stays true to itself yet appeals in different directions. ... The static harmonies ... provide a backdrop for the fascinating rhythms and coloristic interest of this music. The dances and other basically instrumental sections are closest to his [Glass's] earlier pieces—pulsing, highly kinetic exercises for his basic ensemble of amplified electronic keyboards, winds and wordless female voice. But there are also accompanied and a cappella choruses, violin solos ... an eerie soprano aria preceded by a mysterious electric organ improvisation and a demonic, intensely chromatic penultimate scene that attempts to portray nothing less than the end of the world. All this comes across with enormous force. ... There can be little doubt that *Einstein on the Beach* offers some sort of greatness for the present."

The *Einstein* world premiere took place at the Avignon Festival in France on July 25, 1976, where it proved such a sensation that there were productions all over Europe during the next few months, where it appealed to old and young, avant-gardists, and rock enthusiasts alike. At the American premiere at the Metropolitan

Opera House on November 21, 1976, the house sold out so quickly in advance that a second performance was scheduled a week later which also sold out before curtain time. The composer said, "It almost never played to an empty seat. That music just had a way of drawing people out of the woodwork. There were people who would follow us around Europe; there were people who saw sixteen or eighteen performances!" *Einstein on the Beach* was awarded an "Obie," an off-Broadway prize given by the *Village Voice* (Glass's second "Obie;" the first was in 1975 for the theatrical production, *Cascando,* by the Mabou Mines Company). In 1979, *Einstein on the Beach* was recorded in its entirety by Tomato Records, a new record company Glass formed in 1978 for his compositions and those of members of his Ensemble to replace the earlier Chatham Square Productions.

Dance is Glass's score for a choreographic sequence comprising five solo and ensemble dance numbers, conceived and choreographed by Lucinda Childs, with films to accompany the dancers. It was premiered in Amsterdam, Holland, on October 19, 1979. After its American premiere at the Brooklyn Academy of Music on November 29, 1979, David Bither wrote in *Horizon:* "Musically, *Dance* is a further exploration of the rhythmic and harmonic techniques used in *Einstein.*"

In 1980, Glass completed writing the music for an opera, *Satyagraha,* based on the early life of Gandhi. Constance DeJong wrote the libretto from the text, *Bhagavad-Gita,* which is sung in Sanskrit. Utilizing a chorus of forty and an orchestra of sixty, Glass became more conventional in his operatic procedures than in *Einstein* and as he revealed: "The instrumentation is fairly traditional: a string orchestra—winds and strings—and one electric organ. The orchestration, however, is quite unusual; it sounds kind of like the Philip Glass Ensemble.... There are no solo instruments in it at all, so all the sounds are mixed, the way timbres on an electric organ are mixed. But apart from that, it's very traditional and very tuneful." *Satyagraha* had its world premiere in Rotterdam, Holland, on September 5, 1980, by the Netherland Opera. In his review in *Opera News,* Menno Feenstra said of the score that "Glass's hallucinatory music reduces time speed to nearly zero, intensifying the audience's sensitivity to the tiniest change in harmony, rhythm, melody or color and to the drama's undercurrents." In the New York *Times,* John Rockwell commented: "What is new is first of all the use of the orchestra. ... There are also breathed, intensely lyrical vocal lines that arrive out of the instrumental texture. And there is a considerable amount of slow, contemplative music along with Mr. Glass's more familiar, busily burbling, motoric style. But the last impression is of a floating lyricism, cushioned in soft strings and dulcet winds."

Glass received grants or commissions from the Foundation for Contemporary Performance Arts (1970–1971), Changes, Inc. (1971–1972), the National Endowment for the Arts (1974, 1975, 1978–1979), and the Mentil Foundation (1974), the last of these matching the 1974 National Endowment grant. He was awarded one of the largest individual grants by the Rockefeller Foundation in 1981, a three-year grant of $90,000 which did not involve commissions.

In 1975, Glass wrote the music for a documentary film about the sculptor Mark de Suvero entitled *North Star.* A four-evening retrospective of his music was presented in New York between February 12 and 15, 1981, and included two complete performances of *Einstein on the Beach* and *Music in Twelve Parts.*

Glass made numerous appearances as organist performing his own compositions. Following one concert—in Brooklyn, New York, on June 8, 1980—Robert Palmer wrote in the New York *Times:* "One left feeling that the composer has found a compelling new mode of presentation for his music and that solo performance will prove more and more fruitful for him."

Glass, who makes his home in New York City, is the father of two children, by a first marriage to JoAnn Akaltis, actress and theatrical director. He was married a second time to Luba Burtyk, an internist, in October 1980.

MAJOR WORKS

Ballet—Dance.

Chamber Music—Pieces in the Shape of a Square; Music in Fifths; Music in Eight Parts; Music in Similar Motion; Music with Changing Parts; Music in Twelve Parts; Music for Voices; Another Look at Harmony; Geometry of Circles.

Multi-Media (theater or opera)—Einstein on the Beach; Satyagraha.

Organ Music—Music in Contrary Motion; Fourth Series.

ABOUT

Sadie, S. (ed.), The New Grove Dictionary of Music and Musicians; Vinton, J. (ed.), Dictionary of Contemporary Music.

High Fidelity/Musical America, April 1979; Horizon, March 1980; People, October 6, 1980; New York Times, May 28, 1978, June 19, 1978; Quest, November 1980.

Alexander Glazunov

1865–1936

See *Composers Since 1900.*

Reinhold Glìere

1875–1956

See *Composers Since 1900.*

Morton Gould

1913–

For biographical sketch, list of earlier works, and bibliography, see *Composers Since 1900.*

Morton Gould's *Soundings,* a two-movement work for orchestra, was commissioned by the Junior League of America and introduced on September 18, 1969, with Robert Shaw conducting the Atlanta Symphony. Its first movement, "Threnodies," is elegiac in mood, "a memorial movement reflecting that particular period in our society, and the second movement, 'Paeans' is affirmative and assertive," according to the composer.

Several of Gould's later works were written to commemorate the American bicentennial. *Symphony of Spirituals* was commissioned for the bicentennial by the National Endowment for the Arts. Its premiere was given by the Detroit Symphony, with Aldo Ceccato conducting, on April 1, 1976. While all the melodic material of this four-movement composition is original, it nevertheless evokes and transforms the vernacular of the spiritual idiom which, in itself, is seeded in jazz, ragtime, blues, etc. On April 24, 1976, David Katz, conducting the Queens Symphony Orchestra in New York, presented the first performance of *American Ballads,* a commission from the New York State Council on the Arts and the United States Historical Society. These ballads are settings of American "chestnuts," six movements playable collectively or individually, incorporating "The Star-Spangled Banner," "America the Beautiful," "Year of Jubilo," "Taps," "The Girl I Left Behind Me" and "We Shall Overcome." A choral-theater piece, *Something to Do,* with a text by Carolyn Leigh, was commissioned by the United States Department of Labor through the National Endowment for the Arts. It was produced at the Kennedy Center for the Performing Arts in Washington D. C. on September 6, 1976, with Pearl Bailey as vocal soloist. This composition celebrated work and human productivity.

The paintings of Charles Burchfield were the inspiration for Gould's *Burchfield Gallery,* for orchestra, written in 1980. The Cleveland Orchestra premiered it on April 9, 1981 with Lorin Maazel conducting.

Since 1970, Gould wrote two outstanding scores for television; one was for *F. Scott Fitzgerald in Hollywood,* broadcast by the ABC-TV network on May 16, 1976. Two years later, Gould wrote the background music for the provocative and much publicized four-night TV mini-series, *The Holocaust,* broadcast by the NBC-TV network in April 1978. A concert suite, derived from this score, was premiered the same month in Midland, Michigan, at the Matrix Music Festival; it was recorded by RCA with Gould conducting the National Philharmonic Orchestra.

In 1976, Gould toured Australia as composer-conductor. In 1978 he was the recipient of the New York City Mayor's Award of Honor in the Arts. He is a member of the board of directors and chairman of the Symphony Concert Committee of the American Society for Composers, Authors, and Publishers (ASCAP) and on the board of directors of the American Symphony Orchestra League, and the American Music Center.

MAJOR WORKS (supplementary)

Miscellaneous—Something to Do, a choral theatrical piece.

Orchestral Music—Troubadour Music, for four guitars and orchestra; Soundings; Vivaldi Gallery, for string quartet and divided orchestra; Venice, audio-graph for double orchestra and brass choirs; Festive Music, with offstage trumpet; Columbia, Broadsides on Columbian Themes; Symphony of Spirituals; American Ballads; Cheers, Celebration March; Burchfield Gallery.

ABOUT (supplementary)

New York Times, April 14, 1978.

Percy Grainger

1882–1961

For biographical sketch, earlier list of works, and bibliography, see *Composers Since 1900.*

An all-Grainger concert was presented on July 13, 1980, at the Caramoor Festival in Katonah, New York.

A complete catalog of Grainger's works, edited by Teresa Balough, was published by the University of Western Australia Press in 1975. Grainger's widow, Ella Viola Grainger, died in 1979 at the age of ninety.

ABOUT (supplementary)

Bird, J., Percy Grainger: the Man and the Music; Slattery, T. C., Percy Grainger: the Inveterate Innovator.

New York Times, July 13, 1980.

Enrique Granados

1867–1916

See *Composers Since 1900.*

Alexander Gretchaninoff

1864–1956

See *Composers Since 1900.*

Charles Tomlinson Griffes

1884–1920

See *Composers Since 1900.*

Louis Gruenberg

1884–1964

For biographical sketch, list of earlier works, and bibliography, see *Composers Since 1900.*

The first fully-staged revival of Gruenberg's opera, *Emperor Jones,* since the performance by the Chicago Opera Company in 1946 and a production by the Rome Opera in 1951, took place in Detroit on February 9, 1979, by the Michigan Opera Company. Reviewing that performance, Andrew Porter wrote in *The New Yorker:* "It is almost athematic. The only tune is the three-note spiritual, and that lasts only eleven measures. The rest is declamation, cries, plain speech, rhythms and sounds. And yet the first impression that there is 'no music' . . . is soon modified by the discovery that something is holding one's attention—propelling, shaping and articulating the drama and making it vivid in a way that a plain spoken performance would not be. Probably, it is Gruenberg's control of timbres, density and rhythmic tensions."

ABOUT (supplementary)

Opera News, February 10, 1979.

Gene Gutchë

1907–

Gene Gutchë was born in Berlin, Germany, on July 3, 1907. His father, Maximilian Gutsche, who came from Alsace-Lorraine, was a wholesale fruit merchant with branches in Germany, Switzerland, and Italy; his mother, Flora von Zerbst Gutsche, was of Polish descent. Gene Gutchë's name at birth was Maximilian Eugene Ludwig Gutsche. As he grew older, he dropped not only the "s" from his name (because he felt

---

Gutchë: go͞o chā´

GENE GUTCHË

it would be easier to pronounce) but also his given names, substituting the simple one Gene.

The Gutsche family—including Gene's sister, Eleanora—lived in Berlin and Zurich. Gene began to show a sensitive response to good music by the time he was four and started taking piano lessons with Marie Magnani in Zurich, continuing with Ferdinand Conrad and Ferruccio Busoni in Switzerland. Though Busoni was encouraging, Gutchë's father was not, because he wanted nothing to keep the boy from pursuing a business career. In Zurich, Gene broke his wrist while roller-skating, putting to rest his ambitions to be a concert pianist. Not until he was thirty-eight did he finally come to the realization that he wanted to be a composer.

In universities in Heidelberg, Lausanne, and Padua, Gutchë received an education in business and economics. At eighteen, he decided to break all ties and come to the United States, arriving in Galveston, Texas in 1925, with five hundred dollars and not knowing a word of English (though he was fluent in five European languages). To support himself he worked on a Texan ranch, shocking wheat, then moved north as a migrant worker, and finally landed in St. Paul, Minnesota. In the late 1920s and early 1930s he gave piano lessons, became a church organist, and arranged music for jazz bands. At that time, he decided to continue his music with Donald Ferguson, distinguished music educator, to study theory. Ferguson found him "bewildered, untrained and uncertain of everything but his consuming desire to compose. . . .

I did what I could. Then he disappeared for several years."

On December 1, 1935, Gutchë married Frances Buchan, and the two, in search of a new life, went to New York for eight years. Gutchë's linguistic abilities and his European business training secured for him a position as foreign correspondent, purchasing agent and, later, vice-president in public relations of Essential Oil Company. World War II forced him to abandon business and he decided to resume his musical education. On a creative scholarship, he enrolled at the University of Minnesota, in 1947, to spend three years studying again with Donald Ferguson and James Aliferis. Ferguson recalled: "Gene returned sadder, wiser and more determined than ever. Dr. Aliferis in harmony and counterpoint, and I in basic theory and history of music, did something I suppose to shape his musical thought." In 1950, Gutchë received his Master of Music degree, submitting as his theses his Symphony No. 1 and his third string quartet.

The presence of the Minneapolis Symphony and its musical director, Dimitri Mitropoulos, on the grounds of the university became an all-important musical stimulus for Gutchë. He attended orchestral rehearsals and profited from the advice and guidance of orchestra members during his study of orchestration.

Gutchë's First Symphony was introduced by the Minneapolis Symphony under James Aliferis on April 11, 1950. His String Quartet, No. 3 was premiered by the Arts Quartet in Minneapolis on May 16, 1958, and received the Minnesota State Prize in that year. These two works were followed by Symphony No. 2 (1950–1954), Symphony No. 3 (1952), and *Rondo Capriccioso,* for orchestra (1953), which showed that he had advanced from the neo-Romantic tendencies of his apprentice years to modern techniques and innovative experimental writing. He employed the twelve-tone row flexibly in his String Quartet No. 3, polytonal, polyrhythmic, and dissonant writing in his symphonies, and in the amusing *Rondo Capriccioso* (premiered at Cooper Union by the New York Chamber Orchestra on February 19, 1960), he employed not only the twelve-tone row (modified) but also microtonal music through separating two groups of woodwinds tuned a quarter tone apart. *Musical America* said the string quartet displayed "fine skills with twelve-tone writing . . . plus the ability to provide musical substance. . . . The work is profound in its slow movement." John Sherman wrote in the Minneapolis *Journal* that *Rondo Capriccioso* was an "amusingly prankish escapade with a lyric mid-section." John H. Harvey added in the St. Paul *Pioneer Press:* "The music is full of chuckles and outright laughs, abounding in out-of-focus quotations from familiar music in a general spirit of mockery. Far from being forbidding, the coloration achieved is pungent, iridescent and unusually attractive."

From 1950 to 1953 Gutchë studied composition and conducting with Philip Greeley Clapp at the University of Iowa, receiving his doctorate in music with Symphony No. 3. Gutchë became a full-time composer, but for the next decade he was able to pursue his artistic career only through the support of private benefactors. Working in obscurity and with little recognition, he confessed that much music that he wrote during those three years—and more afterwards—he destroyed because it did not represent him. A satisfactory work that did survive was the Concerto for Piano and Orchestra (1955). It was introduced in Minneapolis on June 19, 1956, by the Minneapolis Symphony under Aliferis with Bernhard Weiser as soloist, and it was awarded the Louis Moreau Gottschalk Gold Medal fourteen years later. John Sherman of the Minneapolis *Star* called it "a furious and angular work with a highly hazardous but interesting piano role . . . made up of harmonic ingenuities, much of it of fascinating texture."

Subsequent performances and awards not only added to Gutchë's musical stature in the latter 1950s but put him on the road to financial self-sufficiency as a composer. These works included the Piano Sonata (1958); the *Holofernes Overture* (1958) which he wrote for the Luria Competition where it won an award and then was introduced by the Minneapolis Symphony under Antal Dorati on November 17, 1959; the microtonal *Judith Prologue,* for speaker and strings (1959); and the Concertino for Orchestra (1959), performed by the Minneapolis Symphony under David Zinman on June 13, 1961. In *Holofernes,* Gutchë advanced the dodecaphonic technique by using the twelve-tone row motivically and implementing the row to such a degree that a feeling of polarity is manifested. This departure from strick serialism Gutchë called "romantic expressionism."

Two of Gutchë's later symphonies were premiered in 1962: the Symphony No. 4, winner of the Albuquerque National Composition Competition in 1961, was introduced there on March 8, 1962; and Symphony No. 5, for strings, winner of the Oscar Espla International Award in 1962 was first heard in Chautauqua, New York, on July 29, 1962, with Walter Hendl conducting. With Symphony No. 5, Gutchë was most successful up to that time. Following its premiere, it was performed by several other American orchestras, including the Cincinnati Symphony; it was broadcast by ABC nationwide on radio; in 1964 it was telecast nationally over the facilities of the National Education Television; and in 1967 it was broadcast over the Luxembourg Radio-Television in Europe. "The work may be difficult," said John H. Harvey in the St. Louis *Sunday Pioneer Press,* "but it's well worth the trouble, for it exploits the string medium in a wonderfully vigorous and colorful way. Ideas jostle each other in lively rhythms and leap about from group to group, from instrument to instrument. Everything is woven into a cogent and compact whole which runs a wide expressive range." Gutchë described the symphony: "Compositionally, the work is based on the time-honored principle of motif-exposition and variations. Structurally, the main weight of the symphony falls in the two outer movements. The first movement is almost perpetual motion, essentially based on one sinuous melody. . . . The inner movements, despite their intrinsic interest, act almost as foils for the much more complex and expansive first and last movements. The second movement, *Burletta* (musical farce) . . . is relaxed and ever sardonic. The compact slow movement is a distillation of carefully conceived lyricism. The finale is a combination of the powerful rhythmic drive of the first movement with a touch of the jocularity of the *Burletta.*"

There was an eight-year hiatus between the writing of the Fifth Symphony and the Sixth in which Gutchë concentrated on programmatic music. Symphony No. 6 was commissioned by the Detroit Symphony which, under Sixten Ehrling's direction, presented its premiere in Detroit on October 7, 1971. The first movement of this symphony is a kind of prolog of fanfares, solely for brass; the second (an emotional slow movement) is for strings; the third movement is a scherzo for woodwinds; and the energetic and intense fourth movement is for the entire orchestra. In the Sacramento (California) *Bee,* Elliott W. Galkin wrote about it: "Gene Gutchë writes truly modern music that makes a connection with the general concert-going public. In its dissonance, in its vigorous pursuit of musical ideas that seem boldly the product of an individual mind, in its unusual transformation of an old form (the concerto grosso), in its general personality—in all these things the work seems modern. . . . The work's larger distinctions are a sense of drama, the energetic pursuit of ideas that are recognizable, and a fine sense of the sonorities of the instruments."

Gutchë was awarded two Guggenheim Fellowships between 1963 and 1965. On December 6, 1963, the Minneapolis Symphony Orchestra, under the direction of Stanislaw Skrowaczewski, premiered one of his orchestral works, *Genghis Khan,* for winds and string bases. In this work, Gutchë's pronounced gift for programmatic writing within well-integrated structures is evident in his description of the exploits, barbarism, treachery, and murders of Genghis Khan, conqueror. Later, on March 23, 1969, Leopold Stokowski directed a performance of *Genghis Khan* in New York with the American Symphony Orchestra, which was broadcast over the Voice of America. The Indianapolis *Star* said: "Gutchë lavished imaginative and technical gifts on a challenging score. . . . It has moments of jagged power relieved by passages of lyrical excitement. Beneath it beats a strong rhythmic pulse."

The series of other successful programmatic works for orchestra included *Raquel* (1963), which tells the story of Raquel, beautiful Jewess of Toledo, and Alfonso VIII, King of Castile. It was first performed on December 2, 1963 by the Tulsa (Oklahoma) Philharmonic Orchestra, with Franco Autori conducting. *Hsiang Fei,* for brass and percussion (1965), is based on the Oriental tale of Hsiang Fei, who is brought to the emperor for his harem against her will. Max Rudolf conducted the Cincinnati Symphony in its world premiere on October 21, 1966. *Epimetheus U.S.A.* (1968) was commissioned and premiered by the Detroit Symphony Orchestra on November 13, 1969, under the direction of Sixten Ehrling who subsequently led the European premiere, with the Stockholm Philharmonic, and gave it eighteen more performances on a Detroit Symphony tour of the American midwest. The Symphony is based on the Greek myth in which Epimetheus, husband of Pandora, fool-

ishly allows his wife to open the box that releases evil in the world. Epimetheus is symbolic of America's highly industrialized society, and Gutchë infers that industry might easily be a menace as well as a blessing.

In commemoration of the American bicentennial, Gutchë wrote three more programmatic works for orchestra, all on grants from the National Endowment for the Arts. *Icarus* (1975) was commissioned and premiered by the National Symphony Orchestra in Washington, D.C. on October 26, 1976, with Antal Dorati conducting. Then David Zinman and the Rochester Philharmonic Orchestra performed the work on an extended tour, and recorded it on a Ford Foundation Recording-Publishing Program grant. In this composition, Icarus, representing Columbus, matches his wits against the sea and his rebellious crew in his goal to find a new continent. *Bi-Centurion* (1976) was commissioned by David Zinman and the Rochester Philharmonic Orchestra who introduced it in New York, on January 8, 1977. This composition, appropriately titled, traces two hundred years of American growth and development. *Perseus and Andromeda* (1976) was commissioned by the Cincinnati Symphony and its musical director, Thomas Schippers. Due to Schippers' illness, the world premiere was conducted in Cincinnati by Kenneth Schermerhorn on February 25, 1977. Described by the composer as "an asymetric dance suite in three movements," this is a 20th-century version of the old Greek legend with special reference to the world today. In the first movement, "Immolation," Andromeda's despair becomes our present-day weltschmerz. In the second movement, "Enter Perseus," a monster symbolizes the future. The concluding movement, "Festival," portrays the 20th-century creation of a pragmatic Procrustean multitude with which we must come to grips.

On December 4, 1978, the Florida Philharmonic under the direction of Brian Priestman, presented the premiere of *Helios Kinetic,* which it had commissioned. In writing this programmatic piece, the composer, influenced by "sunny Florida," describes Helios, the sun god in Greek mythology, in a four-horse chariot, rising in the morning from the ocean in the east, driving across the heavens, and descending at evening into the western sea.

Eleanor Bell wrote in the Cincinnati *Post and*

Haieff

Star about Gutchë's programmatic *Hsiang Fei,* but it can apply as well to his other works. "Mr. Gutchë's music grabs the attention and holds it simply by being a masterpiece of orchestral manipulation, of harmonic inventiveness and rhythmic resourcefulness. . . . One doesn't need to know the story to be carried away by Mr. Gutchë's authority. His music is lively and forceful. He is an expert craftsman whose work is far from being obscure or inaccessible."

Though Gutchë had the opportunity to teach in universities, he did not want to assume the dual role of composer-teacher. As he explained: "Even in his most precocious achievement the academic artist cannot of necessity create and teach at the same time."

The Gutchës, Gene, his wife Marian, and their English setter, Peppi, reside in a secluded house in White Bear Lake in Minnesota, far from the madding crowd. In a setting of sylvan beauty, Gutchë found a welcome year-round retreat conducive to continuous work, interrupted only by gardening, taking long walks, and cooking gourmet meals. He leaves to attend important performances of his music, but never for vacations. Empty champagne bottles, labeled with dates and titles of awards, are lined up in his studio alongside his books, music, recordings, and sound equipment.

MAJOR WORKS

Chamber Music—4 string quartets.

Opera—Yodi.

Orchestral Music—6 symphonies; Rondo Capriccioso; Concerto for Piano and Orchestra; Concerto for Cello and Orchestra; Holofernes, overture; Judith Prologue; Concertino for Orchestra; Timpani Concertante; Bongo Divertimento; Gemini; Concerto for Violin and Orchestra; Genghis Khan; Raquel; Rites in Tenochtitlán; Hsiang Fei; Aesop Fables Suite; Concerto for Chamber Orchestra; Prometheus U. S. A.; Icarus; Bi-Centurion; Perseus and Andromeda; Helios Kinetic; Akhenaten.

Piano Music—3 sonatas.

ABOUT

Vinton, J., (ed.), Dictionary of Contemporary Music.

BMI, Many Worlds of Music, December 1966; Miami Herald, December 3, 1978; Minnesota Daily, August 11, 1978.

Alexei Haieff

1914–

For biographical sketch, list of earlier works, and bibliography, see *Composers Since 1900.*

Haieff composed *Eloge,* for nine instruments, in 1967 on commission from the Koussevitzky Music Foundation. It was introduced in 1968 at the Library of Congress in Washington, D.C.

Between 1967 and 1970, Haieff was composer-in-residence at the University of Utah.

Haieff spends each spring and summer in Rome and the winters in an apartment in New York City.

MAJOR WORKS (supplementary)

Chamber Music—Eloge, for nine instruments.

Guitar Music—Rhapsodies, for guitar and harpsichord.

ABOUT (supplementary)

Vinton, J. (ed.), Dictionary of Contemporary Music.

Iain Hamilton

1922–

Iain Ellis Hamilton, son of James and Catherine Hamilton, was born in Glasgow, Scotland, on June 6, 1922. When he was seven, his family moved to London where he attended the Mill Hill School and was trained as an engineer. Music was an early interest and he began taking piano lessons. By the time he reached his teens, he had written "six to ten operas for piano and voices" for which he also considered their production. His penchant for opera was nourished by attendance with his parents at Sadler's Wells opera performances, and frequent visits to the theater and the cinema.

After graduating from the Mill Hill School, Hamilton was employed as an engineer by Handley Page, Ltd., between 1939 and 1946. Deciding in 1947 that music was to be his vocation as well as avocation, he entered the Royal Academy of Music on scholarship for the next four years. In the course of studying composition with William Alwyn and piano with Harold Craxton, he began to reveal a marked talent for composition. His Clarinet Quintet (1949), his

IAIN HAMILTON

Christopher Grier in the *Dictionary of Contemporary Music.* Nicolas Slonimsky said they could be distinguished "by an incisive rhythmic manner and terse melodic expressions within a framework of broadly tonal harmony with strident dissonant contrapuntal lines adding up to the impression of advanced modernity."

After receiving his Bachelor of Music degree from London University in 1950, Hamilton served for six years as Lecturer at Morley College in London and, between 1956 and 1960, at London University. During these years he was chairman of both the Composers Guild in London (1958) and the Music Section of the Institute of Contemporary Arts (1958–1960), the British branch of the International Society for Contemporary Music.

Hamilton was one of the earliest British composers to employ the serial technique, found in his *Sinfonia for Two Orchestras* (1959). Written in 1959 on commission from the Edinburgh Festival, it was premiered there on August 28, 1959; also in Cello Sonata (1959), presented at the Edinburgh Festival in 1965; in the Piano Concerto (1960), which was given performances in Berlin as well as London; and in *Pharsalia* (1961), written to commemorate the centennial of the American Civil War, which the B.B.C. introduced in London in April 1961. The composer added a dramatic commentary with a text derived from the Roman poet, Lucan, to this work.

Commissions from the British Broadcasting Company (B.B.C.) led to the writing of a number of other works in the late 1950s, including *The Bermudas,* for baritone, chorus, and orchestra (1956); *Five Love Songs,* for tenor and orchestra (1957); and Concerto for Jazz Trumpet and Orchestra (1957), programmed for the Edinburgh Festival in 1965.

Hamilton represented Great Britain at the International Composers Conference in Stratford, Ontario, in 1960 and at the Los Angeles Music Festival where he presented the American premiere of his Sinfonia for Two Orchestras in 1961. This visit to the United States developed into a prolonged residence which enabled him to be composer-in-residence at the Berkshire Music Center at Tanglewood, Massachusetts in the summer of 1962 and to be appointed Mary Duke Biddle professor at Duke University where he was chairman of the music department from 1966 to 1971.

first Symphony (1949), and his first String Quartet (1950) were followed in 1951 by the *Nocturne,* for clarinet and piano; a ballet, *Clark Saunders;* a Viola Sonata; and the Symphony No. 2. Some of these early works were first heard at concerts sponsored by the Society for the Promotion of New Music in London. Evidence of success came in April 1952 when he was acclaimed for his Concerto for Clarinet and Orchestra (1949) at its introduction by the Royal Philharmonic Orchestra. His String Quartet No. 1, winner of the Clements Memorial Prize, was a British representative at the Festival of the International Society for Contemporary Music in Oslo on June 3, 1953; and the Symphony No. 2 received its world premiere at the Cheltenham Festival in England on June 9, 1953.

Awards in recognition of his talent included the Dove Prize, the highest award that the Royal Academy could give a student, and the Koussevitzky Music Foundation Award, which was for his Second Symphony in 1951, a year in which he also won the Royal Philharmonic Society Prize in London for his clarinet concerto. In the 1950s, he also received the Butterworth Prize in 1954 and the Arnold Bax Gold Medal in 1956. In 1960 he was named Fellow of the Royal Academy of Music.

In his early compositions, Hamilton was influenced by Stravinsky, Hindemith, and Bartók; his early works were characterized as having "thrusting vigor, seriousness, dark-tinged scoring, formal innovations and individual flavor of rhetorical and sometimes harsh beauty," by

Hamilton

Commissions were also responsible for a number of noteworthy works in the 1960s, including Sextet, for flute, two clarinets, violin, cello, and piano (1962) and Concerto for Organ and Small Orchestra (1964), both written for the Mary Duke Biddle Foundation at Duke University; the five-section *Cantos,* for orchestra (1964) was commissioned by the B.B.C. and its first performance took place on August 4, 1965, at the Promenade concert in London by the B.B.C. Symphony. In 1966, in celebration of the 900th anniversary of Westminster Abbey, Hamilton wrote *Threnos—In Time of War,* for organ. Another B.B.C. commission resulted in the writing of *Circus,* for two trumpets and chamber orchestra (1969).

It was not until the closing years of the 1960s that Hamilton turned to opera. His first one was *Agamemnon* (1967–1969), for which he also wrote the libretto. His first opera to be performed, *The Catiline Conspiracy,* with a libretto by the composer based on a play by Ben Jonson, was written in 1967–1969. It was commissioned and introduced by the Scottish Opera in Stirling, Scotland, on March 16, 1974. Noel Goodwin wrote in *Opera* that the opera "is, in my view, an outstanding work in its incisive theatrical character and immediate musical rewards for the listener," and that in its clarity and directness, it "was the closest modern equivalent to Verdi that I had come across." The opera was successful with critics and audiences.

This encouraged the English National Opera to produce Hamilton's *The Royal Hunt of the Sun,* with a libretto by Hamilton based on Peter Shaffer's play of the same name, in London on February 3, 1977. This work was actually written in 1967 for a performance by the Santa Fe Opera in New Mexico, which never took place. Hamilton did not return to it until 1975, for the 1977 performance. The original text for this opera told of the plunder of the Incas' gold in Peru by the Spaniards and the ensuing destruction of a civilization and Hamilton felt it had relevance to modern-day problems. Some critics detected a parallel to Wagner's *Ring of the Nibelungs,* though Hamilton discounted it.

Hamilton abandoned the serial technique in favor of a tonal one, explaining that he had previously used serialism as an essential discipline in ordering his thoughts and organizing the sound structure. "Obviously, some of this is left on one's musical thinking, but a year before *The Royal Hunt of the Sun,* I realized I no longer needed to use serial technique and I became increasingly interested in how I could use tonality again—how to use its qualities relative to the discipline in serial thinking." Noel Goodwin noted the difference in *Opera: "The Royal Hunt of the Sun* is an important work in Hamilton's development, marking a change from his previous austerities to a more exotic and colorful means of expression. His orchestra is basically that of a Verdi opera with added percussion and keyboard. It involves some organ and a good deal of piano, not as a soloist but in adding deep clusters of notes. . . . There is a limited use of pre-recorded tape for specifically theatrical effect, but Hamilton says this technique is no primary element."

In *Tamburlaine,* the composer's libretto was based freely on Marlowe's tragedy. Written on commission from the B.B.C. as a radio opera, it was completed in 1976, and heard over the B.B.C. Radio on February 14, 1977. "Choosing to view the conqueror's career in flashbacks from his deathbed, Hamilton has anchored each remembered episode clearly and unambiguously to the main moment of narration," reported Arthur Jacobs in *Opera,* and added, "It must be rated musically above *The Royal Hunt of the Sun* and possibly above *The Catiline Conspiracy,* at any rate in more smoothly accommodating the lyric or passionate element."

During the first American tour of the Scottish National Orchestra in November 1975, Hamilton's *Aurora* (1972) had its world premiere in New York on November 12, with Alexander Gibson conducting. Raymond Ericson wrote in the New York *Times* that "in its color, brevity and clear form, it is easy to like. . . . It is only twelve minutes long and simple in its basic structure since it moves from a relatively quiet nocturne to bursting brilliance at the end."

In the 1960s, Hamilton was a visiting professor in the United States at the University of Alabama, Syracuse University, Salem College, and Converse College. He was appointed professor of music at Lehman College at the City University of New York in 1971 but resigned after one day because of teaching conditions. That year he held the Crumb Lectureship at Glasgow University. In 1970 he was awarded an honorary doctorate by Glasgow University and in 1975 he was presented with the Ralph Vaughan Williams Award by the Composers Guild of Great Britain.

MAJOR WORKS

Ballet—Clerk Saunders.

Band Music—The Chaining of Prometheus; Overture, 1912 (arranged from orchestral version).

Chamber Music—2 string quartets; 2 cello sonatas; Clarinet Quintet; Viola Sonata; Nocturne, for clarinet and piano; Aria, for horn and piano; Capriccio, for trumpet and piano; Clarinet Sonata; Piano Trio; Sextet, for flute, two clarinets, violin, cello, and piano; Sonata and Variants, for winds; Quintet for Brass; Sonata Notturna, for horn and piano; Five Scenes, for trumpet and piano; Sonata for Five, for wind quintet; Flute Sonata; Sea Music (Quintet No. 2), for clarinet and string quartet; Violin Sonata; The Alexandrian Sequence, for 12 instruments; Hyperion, for clarinet, horn, violin, cello, and piano.

Choral Music—The Fray of Support; The Bermudas, for baritone, chorus, and orchestra; Nocturnal, for eleven voices; Four Border Songs, for a cappella chorus; Epitaph for This World and Time, for three choruses and two organs; Te Deum, for chorus, wind instruments, and percussion; To Columbus, for chorus, three trumpets, three trombones, and percussion.

Opera—Agamemnon; Pharsalia, dramatic commentary; The Royal Hunt of the Sun; The Catiline Conspiracy; Tamburlaine, radio opera; Anna Karenina.

Orchestral Music—2 symphonies; 2 violin concertos; Variations on an Original Theme, for string orchestra; Clarinet Concerto; Overture, Bartholomew Fair; Symphonic Variations; Scottish Dances; Sonata for Chamber Orchestra; Five Love Songs, for tenor and orchestra; Concerto for Jazz Trumpet and Orchestra; Overture, 1912 (also for band); Sinfonia, for two orchestras; Piano Concerto; Arias, for small orchestra; Cantos; Concerto for Organ and Small Orchestra; Circus, for two trumpets and chamber orchestra; Alastor; Voyage, for horn and orchestra; Concerto for Orchestra, "Commedia"; Aurora.

Organ Music—Fanfares and Variants; Aubade; Threnos—In Time of War; A Vision of Canopus.

Piano Music—3 sonatas; Three Pieces; Nocturnes with Cadenzas; Palinodes.

Vocal Music—Cantata, for tenor and piano; Dialogues, for coloratura soprano and chamber orchestra.

ABOUT

Sadie, S. (ed.), The New Grove Dictionary of Music and Musicians; Schafer, M., British Composers in Interview.

Listener (London), October 24, 1957; Musical Times (London), July 1958; Opera (London), February 1977.

For biographical sketch, list of earlier works, and bibliography, see *Composers Since 1900*.

On February 19, 1976, Hanson Hall was dedicated at the Eastman School of Music in honor of Howard Hanson. The following May 2, Hanson's oratorio, *New Land, New Covenant,* received its world premiere in Bryn Mawr, Pennsylvania. It had been commissioned by the Bryn Mawr Church, the Brick Presbyterian Church in New York, and the Princeton (New Jersey) Theological Seminary. Howard Clark Kee, who wrote the text, drew a parallel between America's founding and the biblical founding of Israel, drawing his material from writings of various colonial authors (including Isaac Watts and John Winthrop) as well as from the Bible and T. S. Eliot. *High Fidelity/Musical America* reported: "A narrator draws together the meaning of the texts; children sing reminders of the innocence of the American dream. The music, symphonically constructed, moves under the narration and the solos and chorales. ... His music builds its present on the antique past; at least four centuries of musical style stay in the air through anthems and chorales and the rich orchestral writing. Some of the settings are his own; some are exhumations from old hymn books."

On his eightieth birthday, in 1976, Hanson was honored with two concerts. On October 19, at the opening of its concert season, the Rochester Philharmonic under David Zinman presented an all-Hanson program culminating with his Symphony No. 6, which was first performed on February 29, 1968, by the New York Philharmonic Orchestra. On October 28, the Eastman Philharmonic Orchestra under Willis Page offered a musical tribute in the form of *Nine by Nine: Variations on a Theme by Howard Hanson.* Taking the opening from Hanson's *Nordic Symphony* (Symphony No. 1), each of nine composers on the faculty of the Eastman School of Music prepared a variation.

Hanson's Symphony No. 7, subtitled "The Sea," for chorus and orchestra, was based on Walt Whitman's poetry and written to commemorate the fiftieth anniversary of the Music Camp at Interlochen in Michigan where it was

Harris

introduced on August 7, 1977. Hanson provided the score for the ballet *Nymph and Satyr,* which was premiered on August 16, 1979, by the Chautauqua Ballet and Festival Orchestra in Chautauqua, New York.

In 1980, Hanson was elected to the fifty-member American Academy and Institute of Arts and Letters. He died in Rochester, New York, on February 26, 1981.

MAJOR WORKS (supplementary)

Ballet—Nymph and Satyr.

Band Music—Dies Natalis I.

Chamber Music—Young Persons' Guide to the Six-Tone Scale, for solo piano and wind ensemble; Laude, for wind ensemble.

Choral Music—The Mystic Trumpeter, for narrator, chorus, and orchestra; Two Hymns for the Bicentennial; New Land, New Covenant, oratorio for solo voices, children's chorus, and adult chorus. Prayer for the Middle Ages, for a capella chorus; Symphony No. 7, "The Sea," for chorus and orchestra.

ABOUT (supplementary)

ASCAP Today, March 1971.

Roy Harris

1898–1979

For biographical sketch, list of earlier works, and bibliography, see *Composers Since 1900.*

In commemoration of the American bicentennial, Roy Harris wrote the five-section Symphony No. 14, entitled "Bicentennial" for speaker, chorus, and orchestra on the theme of "America." It was premiered on February 10, 1976, by the National Symphony Orchestra (which had commissioned it), in Washington, D.C., with Antal Dorati conducting.

A week later, on February 16, the Long Island Chamber Ensemble of New York honored Roy Harris at a Lincoln Center for the Performing Arts concert. William Schuman, one of Harris' most distinguished students, read a citation and Harris gave a brief talk. His 1927 Concerto for Piano, Clarinet and String Quartet was revived.

Additional honors were bestowed on Harris for his eightieth birthday in 1978. The town of Chandler, Oklahoma, where he was born, dedicated a commemorative sign reading: "Birthplace of Dr. Roy Harris, All American

Composer, February 12, 1898." (Up to this time, the exact location of his birthplace in Lincoln County was not known.) Mayor Ben Walkingstick read a proclamation from the City Council and at a dinner in Harris's honor, Governor Boren of Oklahoma spoke; that evening an all-Harris concert was given in the town's Methodist Church.

Harris's birthday was also commemorated by the Los Angeles Philharmonic, which opened its 78th season with a performance of his *Horn of Plenty* (1964); by the California State University in Los Angeles with an all-Harris program; by the University of California in Los Angeles with a presentation of some of Harris's choral and band music; and by a broadcast of his Symphony No. 4 throughout Canada. Harris was also named honorary Chief of the Ponca Indian tribe.

In 1973, a Roy Harris Archive was established at the Kennedy Memorial Library at California State University in Los Angeles, housing his manuscripts, sketches, recordings, correspondence, etc. He retired from the University of California in Los Angeles in 1973 as professor emeritus. Between 1973 and 1976 he was composer-in-residence at the California State University in Los Angeles and was also appointed Composer-Laureate of the State of California and of the City of Covina in California, in 1975.

Roy Harris died in Santa Monica, California, on October 1, 1979.

MAJOR WORKS (supplementary)

Band Music—Bicentennial Aspirations.

Chamber Music—Piano Sextet; Concerto for Amplified Piano, Brasses, and Percussion; Folk Song Suite, for harp, winds, and percussion.

Choral Music—Peace and Good Will to All, cantata for chorus, brass, organ, and percussion; Whether This Nation, for chorus and band; America We Love Your People, for chorus and band; Symphony No. 14, "Bicentennial," for speaker, chorus, and orchestra; Peace and Good Will to All, cantata for chorus, brasses, organ, and percussion.

Orchestral Music—Symphonies Nos. 13 and 15.

Organ Music—Studies for Pedals.

Vocal Music—Life, for soprano, winds, and percussion; Rejoice and Sing, cantata for soprano or bass, string quartet, and piano.

ABOUT (supplementary)

American Record Guide, May-June 1979; BMI, Many Worlds of Music, Winter 1976; High Fidelity/Musical America, June 1978, August 1980; New York Times (obituary), October 4, 1979.

Lou Harrison

1917–

Lou Silver Harrison was born in Portland, Oregon, on May 14, 1917, one of two sons of Clarence Maindenis Harrison (a lumberman), and Lilian Silver Harrison. As a child of three, Lou made stage appearances as "the littlest orphan" with two stock companies in performances of *Daddy Long Legs*. His mother, however, harbored no ambitions for him either in Hollywood or on Broadway, and she made sure that he got a well-balanced public school education, supplemented with piano lessons, social-dancing lessons, and Sunday School.

When Lou was nine, the family moved to Stockton, California, where he wrote his first pieces of music that he confided were a "kind of corny waltz in a minor key," and "sort of transcendental childhood things, you know, *Visions,* for piano and that sort of thing and they were very corny indeed, I see now, but with an air of mysticism."

The Harrison family made a number of moves to different parts of California. In spite of these frequent changes, neither Harrison's academic nor musical education was affected. He skipped two grades, he continued to study the piano with various private teachers, and was found to have an appealing boy soprano voice, so he sang in the church choir and performed in Sequoia High School programs. During his high school years, he continued to study composition and piano with Howard Cooper, graduating from Burlingame High School in 1934, when he wrote the first of six cembalo sonatas.

While attending San Francisco State College for two years, Harrison studied French horn, clarinet, recorder, percussion instruments, and the harpsichord; he sang in a madrigal group; served as accompanist; and wrote music for various dance groups. He also studied composition informally with Henry Cowell, and through him, he was brought in contact with Charles Ives, whose music interested him. Ives sent Harrison a crate of his music including the Symphony No. 3, the first Piano Sonata, one version of the *Concord Sonata,* and the first two quartets, which influenced Harrison's musical growth and served as a stimulus for innovative musical thinking. In appreciation, Harrison edited much

LOU HARRISON

of Ives's music; wrote liner notes for Ives's recordings; on April 5, 1946, in New York, he conducted the world premiere of Ives's Symphony No. 3; and he composed *At the Tomb of Charles Ives.*

After college, Harrison got a teaching position at Mills College in Oakland, California, from 1936 to 1939, and commuted regularly to it from his apartment on Jackson Street in San Francisco. In addition he worked as accompanist and composer for dance troupes and part-time in a San Francisco music store. His composing included *France 1917—Spain 1937,* for strings and percussion, completed in 1937, and *Two Pieces,* for piano, called Saraband and Prelude, published in 1938 in *New Music,* a quarterly journal edited by Cowell.

Meeting with John Cage, at Cowell's suggestion, led not only to a lasting friendship, but opened up new musical horizons for Harrison, who decided in 1941 to study with Arnold Schoenberg, apostle of the twelve-tone technique in Los Angeles. He was employed in the dance department of the University of California in Los Angeles and attended Schoenberg's seminars at the University. "It was very instructive," the composer recalled. "He was a marvelous man." Schoenberg praised some of Harrison's compositions, among them a piano suite in the twelve-tone technique, a method Harrison would favor in many of his compositions.

Moving to Newark in 1943, he earned his living for three years writing feature articles for *Modern Music* and music reviews for the New

York *Herald Tribune* in addition to serving as editor of *New Music* in 1945–1946. His friendship with Ives, Virgil Thomson, Carl Ruggles, and Edgard Varèse, members of the avant-garde in American music, was stimulating, but work in New York did not prove to be productive creatively. He complained, "I am a westerner and I expect to be able to walk ten straight feet without having bodies in front of me and being frustrated at not being able to walk. And also the noise! The entire island of Manhattan roars day and night. There's no stopping it." In 1947 (the year in which he was awarded a grant from the American Academy of Arts and Letters), he suffered a breakdown, requiring hospitalization and psychotherapy.

In 1949, Harrison left New York for Portland, Oregon, to accept an appointment as a music member of a dance, music, and drama workshop at Reed College. During that summer he wrote two compositions for dancer Bonnie Bird: *Marriage at the Eiffel Tower,* with a text by Jean Cocteau (in English translation) and *The Only Jealousy of Emer,* derived from a poetic drama by Yeats. The former work was reintroduced in New York on February 7, 1977, with Lou Harrison and Virgil Thomson serving as the two narrators (on opposite ends of the stage) by the American Composers Orchestra conducted by Denis Russell Davies. Harold C. Schonberg wrote in the New York *Times* that the score was "French, frothy, sophisticated, peppy and lightweight."

In the fall, Harrison, back in New York, accepted a teaching position at the Greenwich Settlement Music School for two years. He wrote Suite for Cello and Harp for the debut of the New York Trio in fall 1949; Suite No. 2, for string quartet, for Fritz Rikko's chamber-music ensemble at the Greenwich Settlement Music School; and *Seven Pastorales,* for orchestra (1950), among other works.

In 1951, on Cage's recommendation, Harrison was appointed to the music faculty of Black Mountain College in North Carolina for two years. During that time he not only became the recipient of a Guggenheim Fellowship, but he wrote *Hummingbirds and Hawks,* a dance suite for Shirley Broughton; *Western Dance,* for dancer Merce Cunningham; *Solstice,* for flute, oboe, trumpet, celesta, tack piano, two cellos, and double-bass for dancer Jean Erdman; and Suite for Solo Violin, Solo Piano and Orchestra, introduced under the composer's direction in New York on January 11, 1952. Reviewing a recording of this Suite, conducted by Stokowski, Arthur Cohn wrote in *American Record Guide* that its place in American composition "is assured. . . . His [Harrison's] mingled colors and lines are a synthesis of West meeting the East in a codification that can be termed exotic but minus all aspects of vulgarization."

Two principal works completed in 1952 were an opera, *Rapunzel,* and a Mass. *Rapunzel,* with a text from a poem by William Morris, is a short opera in five acts, written in the twelve-tone technique. It required three characters and a small instrumental ensemble; when it was finally produced in New York on May 14, 1959, it received a review from Francis D. Perkins in the New York *Herald Tribune:* "*Rapunzel* was remarkable both for the way in which the varied array of instrumental sonorities contributed to the atmosphere sought by the composer, and for the masterly use of the twelve-tone row on which the score is based. There is no austerity, no setting off in brief segments, but a continuity which was lyric and when desired, pungent, along with a pervasive and convincing sensitiveness." Howard Taubman wrote in the New York *Times:* "There are places in *Rapunzel* that sing with a freshness that is quite magical. . . . Even on first acquaintance there is no doubt about its originality and poetry."

The Mass (in honor of St. Anthony) for chorus, trumpet, harp, and strings, though completed in 1952, was begun as early as 1939. Since Harrison happened to begin the first movement on the day Hitler invaded Poland, the composer wrote it as a "cry for mercy. I set it originally over a military march for percussion, drums and snares—very shocking, as shocking as Hitler's march into Poland was." From 1939 on, the Mass underwent various transformations and rewritings, but was performed for the first time publicly in New York in February 1954. The final definitive version of the work is modal, and it is written in linear form. In *Twentieth Century Music,* Peter Yates called it "a tower of tonal emancipation in the post-dodecaphonic landscape . . . distinguished by its restraint, the individuality of each section without recourse to drama, with no effort to display contrapuntal ingenuity."

In 1952, Harrison received the first of two Guggenheim Fellowships. In February 1953, his

Canticle No. III (1940–1941)—for flute, guitar, and seven percussion players—was performed in New York. In this work Harrison's interest in Far Eastern music is evident and would become a potent influence on later works. Virgil Thomson said in the New York *Herald Tribune* that it was "one of those delicate and delicious symphonies masterfully sustained that are a unique achievement of the composer. The most instantaneously recognizable effects come from the Far East, but one can not call it a piece about Java or Bali or India. It is Western in its drama and structure, though many of its rhythmic and instrumental devices have been learned from the lands where percussive orchestration is the norm of music. . . . The work is subtle, lovely to listen to and powerful in expression, a memorable experience."

Harrison began his Symphony on G in 1947 and completed it in 1953. Its world premiere did not take place until some years later (August 1964) by the Cabrillo Festival Orchestra, conducted by Gerhard Samuel, in Aptos, California. Dean Wallace said in the San Francisco *Chronicle* that "it makes its mark upon first hearing. One feels confident that it will not wear thin with repeated exposure. It is, in fact, one of the most obviously durable pieces written since composers began trying to make the twelve-tone row more generally palatable." Afterwards, Harrison wrote a new finale for the symphony, and its second premiere followed on February 8, 1966, by the Oakland Symphony under Gerhard Samuel. Carl Cunningham reported on it in the San Francisco *Chronicle:* "Written eighteen years after the rest of the piece, Harrison's new finale naturally spoke in a more sophisticated language, employing thicker textures, more pungent harmonies, and greater discretion in its thematic recurrences. It propelled itself forward with an energy bordering on vehemence."

In April 1953, Harrison was officially invited to compete in the international composers' contest in Rome, sponsored by the Committee for Cultural Freedom. Later in the year, in Rome, a scene from his *Rapunzel,* a long aria for soprano in a chamber-music version, was sung by Leontyne Price, and won the Twentieth Century Prize for the best composition for voice and chamber orchestra. The composer also learned that he had been awarded a second Guggenheim Fellowship. On his return to San Francisco, he rented a small studio on Hayes Street in 1954.

On commission from the Louisville [Kentucky] Orchestra, he wrote *Four Strict Songs,* for eight baritones and orchestra (1955), and it was introduced under Robert Whitney in January 1956, and recorded. Harrison's own text hymned the beauties of the world, touching upon the subjects of Holiness, Nourishment, Splendor, and Tenderness. Each song in the work is tuned to a different five-note scale requiring special tuning for piano and harp, but the rest of the orchestra comprised of the string section, two trombones, and percussion does not have a fixed pitch. In the Louisville *Courier Journal,* Dwight Anderson said: "Harrison has constructed a score that is charged with spiritual expression, weaving spells and enchantments." When *Four Strict Songs* was heard in San Francisco, Alfred J. Frankenstein of the *Chronicle* called it "a knockout of a piece. . . . The music takes us to new frontiers—the revival of our intonation and the mingling of Western and Oriental idioms."

In 1955, Harrison was awarded a Fromm Music Foundation grant for the recording of his Mass. During the summer of 1956, while fighting fires with the Forestry Service, he wrote *Simfony, from Simfonies* in free style. While employed in an animal hospital, he worked on his Concerto for Violin with Percussion Orchestra (title in Esperanto, in which Harrison became interested, was *Koncerto por la Violono Kun Perkuna Orkestro*), completed in 1959. It was introduced in New York City on November 19, 1959, by Anahid Ajemian and performed at the Cabrillo Festival in Aptos, California, in August 1965. Dean Wallace reported on it in the San Francisco *Chronicle:* "First and foremost, Harrison knows with uncanny sensitivity what music is all about. His rhythms . . . are complex but never vague; the solo melody highly sophisticated but never abstruse. . . . He is an absolute master in the employment of one elusive element which renders music meaningful: silence."

A Rockefeller Foundation grant for Asian studies enabled Harrison to travel to the Far East in 1961–1962. He visited Japan, Korea, and Taiwan where he studied Oriental modalities, rhythms, and instruments and one result of his research in Korea and other Sinitic classical music was a premiere heard at the Composers' Workshop in San Francisco. Sponsored by the San Francisco Conservatory in December 1962, it was the second part of *Nova Odo* (1961–1963), for chorus, orchestra, and special Oriental instruments. Its text (by the composer), both in English and Esperanto, was a protest against nuclear weapons. The scoring in the work was for Western strings, Korean percussion instruments, and seven *piris* (the Korean form of the ancient Greek double read *aulos*). Harrison designed improved lucite piris, adapting them to Western pitch standards, and taught a group of Californians how to play them. He explained that the second part of *Nova Odo* was a combination of Gagaku and Ah-ak (the Japanese and Korean terms, respectively, for ceremonial or recreational court music). The complete *Nova Odo* was presented for the first time in Aptos, California, in 1963 with Gerhard Samuel conducting the Cabrillo Festival Orchestra and chorus.

In 1963, Harrison was invited to be senior scholar-in-residence at the East-West Center of the University of Hawaii. On commission from both, he wrote *Pacifika Rondo* (Esperanto for the Pacific Circle), a seven-movement composition for an orchestra combining Western and Oriental instruments. It was introduced at the Festival of Arts of the 20th Century in Hawaii in May 1963. Each movement of the work refers to a Pacific Ocean area: "The Family of the Court" is Korean; "Play of the Dolphins" is mid-ocean music; "Lotus" is a Buddhist temple piece; "In Sequoia's Shade" refers to California; "Netzhualcoyoti" describes Mexico and the Aztecs; and "From the Dragoon's Pool" refers to Chinese Asia.

An award from the Phoebe Ketchum Thorne Music Foundation in 1966 enabled Harrison to concentrate on composition for the next three years. He spent a year in Mexico working on *Political Primer,* for vocal soloists, chorus, and orchestra. Then, in California again in 1967, he joined the music faculty of the San Jose State College (now a University), teaching, lecturing, and giving concerts. In 1968 he served as a panel member of the World Music Council and UNESCO conference in New York City.

In 1969, a concert of Harrison's compositions was given at San Jose State College by the music faculty. Premieres of several of his compositions were also heard on that campus, including *Music for Violin with Various European, Asian and African Instruments,* written for Gary Beswick who was soloist when it was introduced in 1967; *Orpheus—For Singer to the Dance,* for chorus and percussion orchestra, written for Anthony

Cirone, percussionist, who helped in its premiere with the San Francisco Symphony in 1969; *Organ Concerto,* for organ with tuned and abstract percussion, written for Philip Simpson who presented it on April 30, 1973.

Other premieres of Harrison's works occurred elsewhere. For a 1971–1972 contemporary music series at the California Institute of Technology in Pasadena, Harrison wrote *Young Caesar,* a chamber opera for puppets. The text, by Robert Gordon, traced the life of Julius Caesar from adolescence to the time of his friendship with Nicomedes, King of Bithynia. The premiere took place in Aptos, California, on August 21, 1971, and John Rockwell of the Los Angeles *Times* wrote: "The occasion left one refreshed in one's admiration of Harrison's music. The many instrumental interludes and the occasional set pieces sound wonderful: simple, colorful, tuneful, in every way a reaffirmation of Harrison's preeminent status among American composers." Alfred J. Frankenstein wrote in *High Fidelity/Musical America* that he had "witnessed the baptism of a major event. In an area of the repertoire—American opera—characterized by the cheapest kind of opportunism, Harrison sounds a whole fluteful of new notes—fresh, charming, often very moving, totally original and totally right."

La Koro Sutro, or "Peace Piece IV" (1972), for chorus and American gamelan, with text in Esperanto, reflected the composer's interest in world religions. It was given its first performance on August 11, 1972, at the San Francisco State University, with Donald Cobb conducting. *Festive Movement* (1972), commissioned by the Thorne Music Fund, was performed at the Lincoln Center for the Performing Arts in New York on November 13, 1972, by the Aeolian Chamber Players. *Elegiac Symphony,* commissioned by the Koussevitzky Music Foundation, was performed first on December 7, 1975, by the Oakland Youth Symphony under Denis de Coteau. Harrison himself introduced his *Serenade,* on the suling (Far-Eastern flute) at the Cabrillo Music Festival in 1978.

Explaining his modus operandi as a composer, Harrison said: "I have to be home one whole day before I can start composing. The busy of the world, the buzz in the ear, the driving, all that has to stop. Sometimes I have to coax myself into it. Sometimes I can start quite deliberately and with pleasure. Reading is a way I found for keeping a suitable mental condition. If I start reading, before long I find that I'm not really reading, the music has started. Then I get up and start working. When the music sort of goes down underneath again, resumes itself interiorly, then I start reading again and so on.

"I used to be a night worker, go on all night long. Now I'm living a more regular life. I don't permit myself the Dionysiac quality quite so much anymore. I'm becoming Apollonian as I'm becoming more socially disciplined—domesticated, let's say. When my writing goes easily, it shows in the manuscript: there are often very finely done notes, all clear and light. But if I struggled, there are lots of erasures and messes; then the music isn't really very good. It's what comes easily that is the perfect expression of the mind, ears and heart."

Harrison lives in a house in Aptos, California, where there is a veritable storehouse of Oriental instruments, and a workshop to build instruments, as well as all kinds of soundmakers used in various compositions. He is a man of many talents and many interests: he speaks Esperanto fluently, and is a student of world religious philosophy; he has written plays and poetry; and he has a talent for calligraphy and for painting. During one summer (1974) he designed eight panels depicting eight musical modes, for decoration in the concert hall of the Music Department at San Jose University. He also once developed a process for direct composition for a photo-phonograph. Building instruments for many years, he discovered two new principles in the construction of the clavichord. He also built a Phrygian aulos, and huge Javanese-style gamelans.

In 1973, Harrison was appointed a member of the National Institute of Arts and Letters.

MAJOR WORKS

Chamber Music—France 1917—Spain 1937, for strings and percussion; Schoenbergiana, for string sextet; Trio, for violin, viola, and cello; Suite, for cello and harp; Solstice, for flute, oboe, trumpet, celesta, tack piano, two cellos, and double-bass; Serenade to Frank Wiggelsworth, for guitar or harp; At the Tomb of Charles Ives, for chamber ensemble; Ductia in the Form of a Jahla.

Choral Music—Mass (in honor of St. Anthony), for vocal soloists, chorus, trumpet, harp, and strings; A Joyous Procession and a Solemn Procession, for high and low voices, trombone, and percussion; Nova Odo, for chorus, orchestra, and special instruments; Easter Cantata, for soloists, chorus, and small orchestra;

Peace Piece I, for chorus; Orpheus—For Singer to the Dance, for chorus and percussion orchestra; A Political Power, for vocal solos, chorus, and orchestra; Peace Piece IV, for chorus and American gamelan.

Operas—Rapunzel; Young Caesar; puppet opera.

Orchestral Music—Suite for Symphonic Strings; Flute Concerto; Suite No. 2, for strings; 7 Pastorales, for chamber orchestra; The Only Jealousy of Emer; Suite, for violin, piano, and small orchestra; Four Strict Songs, for eight baritones and orchestra; Simfony I, in free style; Concerto for Violin and Percussion Orchestra; Concerto in Slendro, for violin, celesta, and percussion; Pacifika Rondo, for chamber orchestra and Western and Asian instruments; Symphony on G; Music for Violin, with various European, Asian, and African instruments; Festive Movement, for chamber orchestra; Elegiac Symphony.

Organ Music—Organ Concerto, for organ and tuned abstract percussion.

Percussion Music—Bomba; Labyrinth; Canticles I and III; Suite; Thirteen Symphonies, for percussion; Double Music (with John Cage); Song of the Zetzalcoatl; Fugue.

Piano Music—3 sonatas; Prelude and Saraband; Tribunal, for piano four hands; six Sonatas for cembalo or piano; Praises for Michael the Archangel; Little Suite.

Vocal Music—Song Project No. 2, for voice and percussion; Sanctus, for contralto and piano; David's Lament for Jonathan, for voice and piano; Pied Beauty, for voice, trombone, cello, flute, and percussion; Fragment from Calamus, for low voice and piano; Alma Redemptoris Mater, for voice, violin, trombone, and tack piano; Holly and Ivy, for voice, harp, and strings; Peace Piece Two, for dramatic tenor with percussion, harp, and string quintet; Peace Piece Three, for voice with violin, harp, and drone strings; Soundings I, No. 1, for voice, prepared piano, and tam tam.

ABOUT

Peyser, J., The New Music; The Sense Behind the Sound; Thomson, V., American Music Since 1910; Yates, P., 20th Century Music.

American Record Guide, November 1979; Musical America, December 1962; New York Times, October 26, 1969.

Roman Haubenstock–Ramati

1919–

Roman Haubenstock-Ramati, a leading figure in European avant-garde music, was born of German-Jewish extraction in Cracow, Poland, on February 27, 1919. He revealed a strong predi-

Haubenstock–Ramati: hoú bn′ stôk rä′ mä tē

ROMAN HAUBENSTOCK–RAMATI

lection for both music and art in his youth, and while attending high school, he also studied music composition at the Cracow Conservatory with Arthur Malawski from 1934 to 1938. After graduation from high school in 1937, he entered the University of Cracow for the study of musicology and philosophy. Haubenstock-Ramati's earliest compositions—a string quartet, a violin sonata, and some pieces for the piano—reflected neo-baroque influences of Stravinsky and Szymanowski. But in 1938, he became acquainted with the twelve-tone music of Anton Webern, which encouraged him to write in that technique.

When World War II began, he left Cracow for Lemberg, to resume the study of composition with Jósef Koffler at the Academy of Music from 1939 to 1941. During the early part of the war, Haubenstock-Ramati spent a year in a Soviet prison camp in Tomsk, Siberia, as a prisoner of the Soviets. In June 1942 he returned to Poland for the remainder of the war, where he was musical director of the Cracow Radio, between 1947 and 1950. During this period he was also a music critic and editor of a music journal. In 1950, because of anti-Semitism in Poland, he went to Israel where he became director of the music library in Tel Aviv and from 1954 to 1956 served as professor of music at the Tel Aviv Academy of Music.

He developed a personalized style in compositions written in Israel, including *Blessings,* for voice and nine players (1951) and, more important, *Recitativo ed Aria,* for cembalo and orches-

tra (1954), which combined serialism with a neo-baroque structure. *Recitativo ed Aria* was performed at the Festival of the International Society for Contemporary Music in Zurich on June 3, 1957. John S. Weissmann wrote in *The Listener* (London): "This music speaks of considerable independence of mind in the emancipated treatment of its formal conventions which involve a reversal of the customary roles associated with complementary movements."

He left Israel for Paris in 1956, where he became vitally interested in *musique concrète,* electronic music, through experiments in which taped sounds were distorted and altered to form newer and more unusual sound textures. In 1957 he finally settled in Vienna, which became his permanent home, and he was employed as reader and adviser for the publishing house of Universal Editions. His composition, *Les Symphonies de Timbres,* was written in 1957, and heard at the Festival of the International Society for Contemporary Music in Amsterdam on June 8, 1963. This work in a totally serialized style, is made up of three episodes, sharply contrasting in speed, metric structure, and orchestral timbres. In *Sequences,* for violin and four orchestral groups, written in 1958, the linear song of the solo voice is in sharp contrast to the richly textured orchestral part. The orchestra is divided into four groups providing a stereophonic effect, which John S. Weissmann said, "envelops the listener from all sides with tiny flecks of constantly moving golden-powered sound. . . . This is music of gentle delights of a fundamentally melancholic temperament. But this tender quality, as well as its intellectual refinement and the consummate degree of compositional skill, remains a permanent hallmark of Haubenstock-Ramati's music." *Sequences* was successfully performed at the Festival of the International Society for Contemporary Music in Vienna.

Interpolation, for solo flute, written in 1958, was one of Haubenstock-Ramati's earliest electronic works, a pioneer effort in combining the music of a solo performer with his own performance on tape. *Liaisons,* written in 1958, went further in combining the playing of a percussionist (vibraphone and marimba) with his own taped performance. Both compositions were also Haubenstock-Ramati's first pioneer experiments with "musical mobiles," where, as Howard Hersh explained, "the score is divided into small parts that in the player's imagination spin and rotate in constantly varying relationships to one another. Haubenstock-Ramati's mobiles contain spare, distinctive material that is to be played over a long period of time. Here, in more than any other form, is the performer forced to study and devour every minute notation on the page, to realize every possible permutation of the material, so that in making his way through the mobile he can continue to express new aspects of the musical cells as they rotate and appear in ever-changing patterns and contexts."

Credentials, or 'Think, Think, Lucky" (1960), for narrator and eight players, from a text by Samuel Beckett, is a "musical mobile," introduced at the Donaueschingen Festival of Contemporary Music in Germany on October 21, 1961. With no traditional score, each player has his own mobile to guide him, and the conductor to indicate the entrances and exits of performers, and to suggest dynamic and expressive effects.

In composing music, Haubenstock-Ramati devised a revolutionary kind of graphic notation made up of a variety of illustrative figurations, designs, and free and spontaneous drawings which are visually attractive. In 1959, he organized the first exhibition of graphic notation in musical scores in Donaueschingen.

Electronics continued to give new dimensions to Haubenstock-Ramati's creativity. *Vermutungen Über ein Dunkles Haus* (1963), for three orchestras (two on pre-recorded tape), marked a significant advance in his electronic experimentation, for it combined live orchestral and recorded sounds. Electronics and advanced serialism characterized his opera, *Amerika* (1962–1964), with a libretto based on Kafka by Max Brod. It had its world premiere at the Berlin Festival in West Germany on October 8, 1966. *Symphony K* (K represents Kafka's oppressed "everyman"), written in 1967, took three sections from the instrumental portions of *Amerika.* The work was featured at the Festival of the International Society of Contemporary Music in Hamburg on June 5, 1969.

Haubenstock-Ramati also produced compositions exclusively for percussion groups in a series of works collectively entitled *Jeux*. The first of these (for six percussion groups) was written in 1961. *Jeux 2*, a Divertimento (1968) with a text by Plato and others, is a multi-media stage work for two percussionists, two actors, dancer, and/or mime.

In 1967, Haubenstock-Ramati was one of several composers invited to write music for an oratorio, *Testimonium*—a history of Jerusalem in text and music—which inaugurated the Festival of Israel in Jerusalem on July 30, 1968. In 1967 he also completed the score for *Comedie,* described as a one-act "anti-opera," with a text by Beckett, for two women, two men, and three percussionists. It was introduced on July 21, 1969, at the International Festival of Music and Art at Saint Paul, France.

Haubenstock made numerous appearances as lecturer and leader of seminars on avant-garde music in Bilthoven, Holland, Buenos Aires, Stockholm, Tel Aviv, San Francisco, and elsewhere. In 1973 he was appointed professor of composition at the Musikhochschule in Vienna.

PRINCIPAL WORKS

Chamber Music—2 string quartets; Multiples I–VI, for instruments; Ricercari, for string trio; Jeux I, for six percussionists; Jeux II, for two percussionists; Jeux IV, for four percussionists; Jeux VI, for six percussionists; Hexachord I, II, for one or two guitars; Song, for percussion; Self, for two clarinets and saxophone.

Choral Music—Madrigal; Chorographie; Sonatas for six solo voices.

Electronic Music—Vermutungen Über ein Dunkles Haus, for three orchestras, two on recorded tape.

Opera—Amerika; Comedie, one-act.

Mobile Music—Interpolation, for solo flute, Liaisons, for vibraphone and marimba; Petite Musique de Nuit, for orchestra; Mobile for Shakespeare, for voice and six instruments; Credentials, or 'Think, Think, Lucky,' for narrator and eight instruments.

Multi–media—Divertimento (Jeux II), for two percussionists, narrator, dancer, and/or mime; Alone, for trombone and mime.

Orchestral Music—Recitativo ed Aria, for cembalo and orchestra; Papageno's Pocket Size Concerto, for orchestra and glockenspiel; Chants et Prismes; Séquences, for violin and orchestra in four groups; Tableau I, II, and III; Psalm; Concerto for Three Pianos, Percussion, Trombone, and Orchestra; Symphonien.

Organ Music—Catch III.

Piano Music—Klavierstücke I; Catch I, for harpsichord; Catch II, for one or two pianos.

ABOUT

Sadie, S., (ed.), The New Grove Dictionary of Music and Musicians; Slonimsky, Nicolas (ed.), Baker's Biographical Dictionary of Musicians (6th edition); Vinton, J. (ed.), Dictionary of Contemporary Music.

The Listener (London), February 2, 1967.

Hans Werner Henze

1926–

For biographical sketch, list of earlier works, and bibliography, see *Composers Since 1900*.

In the latter half of the 1960s, Henze began to develop Marxist sympathies that powerfully affected both his musical ideology and political outlook. In interviews and published writings previous to 1965, he had shown no particular political leanings, but in 1966, his new political direction and social orientation were crystallized by contact with the radical student left in Germany and Marxist associations formed on a trip to Cuba. Inspired with the ideal of making his music the voice of the New Left, he used texts loudly proclaiming his newly found political commitment. He told Joan Peyser in an interview for the New York *Times*, "My operas all written before 1967 were personal complaints about being lonely. I am lonely no longer and that is because of socialism." His demarcation of his compositional life was as follows: 1948–1954, twelve-tone music and serialism; 1954–1966, freely invented composition without serial parameters; from 1966 on, the displacement of opera by "action music" in which musical instruments became instruments of action and musicians became stage players.

In 1968, the North German Radio commissioned Henze to write a multi–media oratorio, *Das Floss der Medusa (The Raft of Medusa),* which he dedicated to the memory of the Cuban revolutionary, Che Guevera, who had been assassinated in Bolivia. The dramatic text, by Ernst Schnabel, was based on the infamous shipwreck of the French vessel, *Medusa,* en route to Africa, and the drama that followed. The elite passengers and crew seized the lifeboats while the others had to save themselves on a raft attached to the lifeboat. Hampered by the raft, the occupants of the lifeboat set it adrift, allowing the survivors to perish. The finale of the oratorio was a summons for revolution.

In Henze's score the dead are represented by string instruments and the living by wind and percussion. "Written in Henze's eclectic, postromantic style," Robert P. Morgan wrote in *High Fidelity/Musical America,* "it has the quality of music turned out in great haste. The whole oratorio, in fact, has something of the character of an endless recitative, a monotone punctuated only by occasional dramatic high points, achieved by such primitive means as the use of shouting in the chorus and the massing of percussion and wind in the orchestra. The only consistent lyrical element is to be found in the role of Death as she attempts to seduce the living to her side. As a result, the work is rather like a melodrama in which music is accorded a distinctly subsidiary role. Experienced on this level, it is admittedly not without certain effect; but in terms of its musical substance there is much to be desired."

The premiere of *Das Floss der Medusa* was scheduled for a Hamburg performance on December 9, 1968, with Henze conducting. It had been planned as left-wing propaganda for international socialism, with a huge poster of Guevara, framed by red and black flags, and inscriptions of the word "Revolution!" Some performers (including Dietrich Fischer-Dieskau) refused to perform in front of a red flag and the poster and Henze would not conduct unless they were replaced. A disturbance broke out and the police were called. The premiere was cancelled, but a dress-rehearsal performance was later heard over the Hamburg Radio and recorded by Deutsche Grammophon.

Versuch Über Schweine (Essay on Pigs)—the reference to left-wing students by West Berlin reactionaries—is a multi–media production written in 1968 calling for a baritone, a chamber orchestra including an electric guitar, an electronic organ, and additional brass. The text, a call for revolutionary action, based on a poem by Gaston Salvatore, a Chilean who was a leader of radical students in West Berlin, is pessimistic in tone. The premiere of the work was held in London, with the composer conducting, on February 14, 1969. The vocal line is in the style of Schoenbergian song-speech (Sprechstimme) and "its predominant characteristic," wrote Peter Heyworth in the New York *Times,* "is a neo-expressionist fervor. . . . On first hearing, it is prodigiously exciting."

In 1969, the Cuban Ministry commissioned Henze to write the large-scale orchestral work, *Sinfonia No. 6,* for two chamber orchestras, which celebrated world revolution. In it, he quoted Cuban folk music and two revolutionary songs, one sung by the National Liberation Front in Vietnam, and the other, "The Song of Freedom" written by Mikos Theodorakis in an

Athens jail. Henze conducted both the Cuban National Symphony in the world premiere of *Sinfonia No. 6* in Havana on November 18, 1969, and the American Symphony Orchestra when he made his New York debut on March 9, 1970. According to *High Fidelity/Musical America,* "The quoted material is so submerged in the rich web of the contrapuntal writing, that it is unable to have any significant impact upon the total compositional effect. . . . It is still possible, I am certain, to write first-rate music within the 'dialectical' framework. But in the case of this piece, one has the impression that the composer 'protests too much,' that he is trying too hard to achieve a desired effect which is simply not germane to his musical materials."

Henze described his multi–media work, *El Cimarrón (The Runaway Slave),* as "a recital of four musicians," and some critics spoke of it as a "one-man opera." It is scored for three instrumentalists (flute, guitar, and percussion), and the singer (a baritone) who is also required to play percussion instruments, and serve as conductor, sing, whistle, shout, scream, and moan. Each of the three instrumentalists is a one-man orchestra who performs on a variety of percussion instruments and in the case of the flutist, a harmonica or a Japanese instrument called a "nyuteki." The Schoenbergian song-speech is accompanied by controlled aleatory music. The text, from Esteban Montejo's *Autobiography of a Runaway Slave,* consists of the recollections of a hundred year-old survivor of slavery who has learned that the only basis for living is human-kindness which is worth fighting for.

The world premiere of *El Cimarrón* took place at the Aldeburgh Festival in England on June 22, 1970, and proved so successful that it was performed at festivals in Spoleto, Edinburgh, and Berlin, and received its American premiere in Pittsburgh in March 1971.

Peter Heyworth of the New York *Times* said *El Cimarrón* was "a decisive step in Henze's evolution. The uncanny sure-footedness with which he has here taken possession of an immense range of sounds and devices and made them serve his own purposes, suggests that his creative eclecticism is as potent as ever. . . . The presence of a composer who moves across the whole field with cavalier confidence is surely a cause for rejoicing." The work was scheduled for performance at the Caramoor Festival at Katonah, New York, on July 16, 1971, but the per-

formance was cancelled because left-wing propaganda and profanity might prove too objectionable to festival audiences.

Henze's socialist leanings were evident in his multi–media work, with *Der langwierige Weg in die Wohnung der Natascha Ungeheuer (The Tedious Journey to the Flat of Natascha Ungeheuer).* Its first performance took place in Rome on May 17, 1971. Taken from Gaston Salvatore's text, Natascha symbolizes those "false utopias" that lure revolutionaries away from their true mission. Eighteen performers, in surgical and military garb (including a baritone soloist and taped voices) are split into small groups: a brass quintet representing the police, a piano quintet, a jazz quartet representing hippies, and an organist and percussionist. The "real world" sound, on tape, is superimposed by the seductive counter-revolutionary voice of Natascha and the condemnation of cowardly Marxist intellectuals who are not active in the class struggle. Strains of Schoenberg's *Pierrot Lunaire* represent bourgeois decadence. The work ends with the hero realizing that Natascha is a fraud and that he must become a more active revolutionary. Peter Heyworth reported to the New York *Times* that "the work fails to make the sort of impact Henze clearly intended. The music is direct and effective, but it fails to provide a dramatic articulation that is only intermittently present in the text. There are many striking passages in the score. But too often the listener is left insufficiently clear about the precise relevance to the point the drama has reached."

Sir Georg Solti and the Chicago Symphony Orchestra commissioned Henze to write an orchestral work for their eightieth anniversary. *Heliogabalus Imperator,* a tone poem based on the career of the decadent Roman emperor Heliogabalus is atonal, in serial form, aleatory, microtonal, and allegorical, according to the composer. The work was first performed by the Chicago Symphony under Solti on May 6, 1972, and Arthur Satz of *High Fidelity/Musical America* wrote "much of the piece is exceedingly loud, but it is always entertaining. Indeed, there may be more humor in the work than a serious and concentrating critic hearing it for the first time would be willing to admit."

Henze's *Rachel, La Cubana,* is an important operatic piece for television, whose premiere took place in New York over the NET network on March 4, 1974. The text for the work, by

Hans Enzenberger, was based on Miguel Barnet's novel, *La Canción de Rachel.* In the work, the heroine, Rachel, a dramatic actress, must accept the reality of the Castro revolution.

Henze returned to opera fully in *We Come to the River,* his "action in music." Commissioned by Covent Garden, the work had its world premiere at the Royal Opera House in London on July 12, 1976. Edward Bond, the British playwright, wrote the allegorical libretto which contrasts power and liberty. In the plot a tyrannical emperor orders the blinding of an anti-militaristic general, who has visions of a brighter tomorrow.

Henze described this huge opera as dramatic in the first part and ritualistic in the second part. With a cast of fifty-nine singers assuming well over a hundred roles, three separate orchestras, and a military band, the work takes place in eleven scenes, on three staging areas. Writing in *Opera News,* Frank Granville Barker said: "The score is skillfully put together, a mixture of the composer's earlier lyrical style and his more recent spicy one, with a dash of Weill here and Puccini there to spice the brew. The music is remarkably articulate. . . . So much action is crammed into Act I that rapid speech-song is inevitable, but in Act II Henze is able to spread himself lyrically and provide more memorable music, including an expressive women's sextet, a duet for the general and a soldier, and a truly haunting final ensemble of the victims of war. There is also a captivating aria for the emperor, a travesty role." When this opera was produced by the Cologne Opera on May 30, 1977, it made a deep impression upon an enthusiastic audience; in fact, two people were overcome by the general's blood-soaked face.

Some of Henze's other major compositions in his abundant and widespread body of works include: Piano Concerto No. 2 (which pianist Christoph Eschenbach commissioned and introduced for the opening of the Richard Kaselowsky Kunsthaus in Bielefeld, Germany, in September 1968); *Royal Winter Music* (1976) a sonata on Shakespeare for guitar was written for Julian Bream, who commissioned a large-scale work equivalent in dimension and virtuosity to Beethoven's *Hammerklavier Sonata. Aria de la Folia Española* was commissioned and premiered by the St. Paul, Minnesota, Chamber Orchestra, under Dennis Russel Davies on September 17, 1977. Of two violin concertos, Nos.

2 and 3, the Second had its American premiere on August 25, 1974, at the Cabrillo Festival in California (with Romula Tecco as soloist) and the Third on January 31, 1979, in San Francisco (with Stuart Canin as soloist and Bernhard Klee as conductor of the San Francisco Symphony).

Henze's fiftieth birthday was officially celebrated in September 1976 at the West Berlin Festival, with a mini-festival of Henze's works in which fifteen compositions were heard. Two all-Henze programs by the Berlin Philharmonic were conducted by the composer. At this festival, the world premiere of String Quartets Nos. 3, 4, and 5 was given on September 12 by the Concord String Quartet (for whom they were written) and the German premiere of *We Come to the River* took place on September 18, 1976.

In 1975, Henze became director of the International Workshop of Art at Montepulciano which is actually a festival in which operas are produced, and some are staged by Henze.

MAJOR WORKS (supplementary)

Ballet—Orpheus.

Chamber Music—String Quartets Nos. 3, 4, and 5; Campases Para Preguntas Ensimismadas, for viola and twenty-two instruments; Wind Quintet; Violin Sonata; Amicizia, for clarinet, trombone, cello, percussion, and piano.

Guitar Music—Royal Winter Music 1976.

Multi-Media or *Operas*—Das Floss der Medusa; Versuch Über Schweine; El Cimarrón; Der Langwierige Weg in die Wohnung der Natascha; Rachel, La Cubana, for television; We Come to the River; Don Chisciotte della Mancia.

Orchestral Music—Symphonies Nos. 6 and 7; Violin Concertos Nos. 2 and 3; Piano Concerto No. 2; Heliogabalus Imperator; Tristan; Ragtimes and Habañeras, for brass band; Aria de la Folia Española, for chamber orchestra; Musik, for cello and chamber orchestra; Il Vitalino Raddopiato, for violin and chamber orchestra.

Vocal Music—Voices, for two voices and instruments.

ABOUT (supplementary)

Geitel, K., H. W. Henze; Mordden, E., Opera in the 20th Century: Sacred, Profane, Godot; Sadie, S. (ed.), The New Grove Dictionary of Music and Musicians.

High Fidelity/Musical America, December 1969, June 1978; Opera News, March 31, 1973; New York Times, July 16, 1972, March 3, 1974.

Paul Hindemith

1895–1963

For biographical sketch, list of earlier works, and bibliography, see *Composers Since 1900*.

In the 1970s, an independent Los Angeles record company (GSC) recorded on thirty disks all of Hindemith's chamber music, consisting of about one hundred and twenty-five compositions (many never recorded before). Seven volumes appeared in 1977. Peter G. Davis wrote in the New York *Times:* "One of the interesting features of these disks is the opportunity they give to trace Hindemith's development over the years as he clarified his harmonic and contrapuntal thinking from the explosive, energetic, occasionally helter-skelter works of the '20s to the suaver, more refined and carefully calculated creations of his later years. What these recordings illustrate above all is that Hindemith has not disappeared from view as a composer of highly enjoyable and relevant music. ... Hindemith left a host of imitators whose pale copies mirror a dull reflection of the genuine article. But his own works live on with undiminished vigor."

In 1971, the annual publication of *Hindemith —Jahrbuch* was launched by the Hindemith Stiftung in Germany. Hindemith's 1929 *Neues vom Tage* was revived in New York in 1979 and Santa Fe in 1981.

ABOUT (supplementary)

Briner, A., Paul Hindemith; Rösner, H., Paul Hindemith; Katalog seiner Werke, Diskographie, Bibliographie, Einführung in das Schaffen; Sadie, S. (ed.), The New Grove Dictionary of Music and Musicians; Skelton, G., Paul Hindemith: the Man Behind the Music.

New York Times, August 14, 1977.

Gustav Holst

1874–1934

For biographical sketch, list of earlier works, and bibliography,, see *Composers Since 1900*.

In connection with the centenary of Holst's birth in 1974, several books were published: *The Collected Essays,* edited by Edmund Rubbra and S. Lloyd in London; *A Thematic Catalogue of*

Gustav Holst's Works, by Imogene Holst in London; and *Holst: A Centenary Documentation,* by M. G. Short in New York. A centenary edition of Holst's compositions was also issued in London.

ABOUT (supplementary)

Short, M. G., Gustav Holst: a Centenary Documentation.

American Record Guide, September 1978.

Arthur Honegger

1892–1955

For biographical sketch, list of earlier works, and bibliography, see *Composers Since 1900*.

ABOUT (supplementary)

von Fischer, K., Arthur Honegger; Meylan, P., Arthur Honegger, Humanitare Botschaft der Musik.

Alan Hovhaness

1911–

For biographical sketch, list of earlier works, and bibliography, see *Composers Since 1900*.

Hovhaness is one of America's most prolific serious composers. He has continued to compose extensively and the body of his works had already exceeded well over three hundred compositions by 1980.

Fra Angelico, a fantasy for orchestra was written as a tribute to the celebrated Italian painter; it was commissioned by the Detroit Symphony which introduced it under Sixten Ehrling's direction on March 21, 1968. Since Fra Angelico's paintings are associated with angels playing celestial trumpets, Hovhaness wrote parts for trumpets, horns, and trombones in music he called "adorational cantorial music" and "voices of celestial messengers." Fra Angelico's painting, "In the Eastern Spirit," gave the composer free rein to indulge in his natural bent for musical Orientalism. "The score goes along in great washes of color, ostinatos and instrumental solos," wrote Harold C. Schonberg in his review in the New York *Times.* "Much of it is delicate and sensitive, but there is one wild section where everything erupts in an aleatoric-like mass of sound."

Conductor André Kostelanetz, impressed with tapes of the humpback whale made by Professor Roger S. Payne off Bermuda, suggested to Hovhaness that he compose a symphony based on their song. He wrote *And God Created Great Whales,* for orchestra, which Kostelanetz premiered at a New York Philharmonic Promenade concert on June 11, 1970. The moaning, howling, and whining of humpback whales became a part of the orchestral fabric. "Free rhythmless, vibrationless passages, each string player playing independently, suggest waves in a vast ocean," was Hovhaness's own description of the music. "Pentatonic melody sounds openness of wide ocean sky. Undersea mountains rise and fall in horns, trombones, and tubas. Music of whales also rises and falls like mountain ranges. Song of the whales emerges like giant mythical sea bird. Man does not exist, has not yet been born in the solemn oneness of nature."

In October 1970, the North Carolina School of the Arts introduced a new ballet to Hovhaness's music entitled *A Rose for Emily* which was based on a short story by William Faulkner. The following December 30, the American Ballet produced the ballet in New York.

Hovhaness considers one of his most significant works since 1970 to be *The Way of Jesus,* an oratorio performed by the St. Patrick Cathedral Choir in New York and the All City Concert Choir, conducted by Laszlo Halasz on March 7, 1975. Halasz had commissioned a nondenominational composition appealing to young adults. Finding echoes of Handel, Fauré, and Scriabin in the work, Robert Sherman of the New York *Times* called it "a glowing, deeply expressive, often eloquent testimony of faith and love. . . . It holds the attention throughout, both musically and in Mr. Hovhaness' evocative sequencing of Biblical and other texts."

Yehudi Menuhin commissioned a large work for violin and orchestra in honor of the American bicentennial and Hovhaness wrote *Ode to Freedom* which was presented by Menuhin and orchestra under the direction of André Kostelanetz at Wolf Trap Farm in Virginia, on July 3, 1976. On October 24, 1976, Hovhaness conducted the premiere of his Symphony No. 26 with the San Jose (California) Symphony which commissioned it. This four-movement composition was described by the composer as follows: "The first movement is a lament for the victims of twentieth-century man's cruelty reinforced by the diabolical power of science. The second is a prayer for resurrection. The third is a dance of nature—celebrating growth and life of trees and living creatures. The final movement is a psalm to the glory of mountains and the starry universe. Out there in far space among billions of distant solar systems where the hand of man can never touch, there is hope." In *High Fidelity/Musical America,* Marta Morgan wrote that the symphony was "extremely subtle in its variety of melodic and rhythmic elements but . . . easy to assimilate, since the composer's idiom creates an atmosphere of utter serenity."

Hovhaness's Symphony No. 29 was commissioned by Henry Charles Smith, associate conductor and horn player of the Minnesota Orchestra. Since the work is more of a concerto for baritone horn and orchestra than a symphony, the composer subtitled it "Euphonium Concerto." A critic for *High Fidelity/Musical America* noted that "Hovhaness' penchant for long, winding melodies is very much in evidence in his use of modal chant and his interest in Indian and Far Eastern music in a piquant blend with Western musical traditions." Its premiere, by the Minnesota Orchestra under Stanislaw Skrowaczewski, took place on May 4, 1977.

Slightly more than two weeks later, André Kostelanetz led the first performance of *Rubáiyát,* for narrator, accordion, and orchestra, in which the narrator read selections by Omar Khayyám, at a Promenade concert of the New York Philharmonic. In the New York *Times,* Peter G. Davis said that the work has "its share of exotic Middle Eastern touches, splashy orchestral color and Hollywood soundstage tinsel, all of it digestible."

On January 16, 1979, the National Symphony in Washington, D. C., under the direction of Mstislav Rostropovich, with Jean-Pierre Rampal as soloist, premiered Hovhaness's Symphony No. 36, for solo flute and orchestra. A critic for *High Fidelity/Musical America* reported, "Hovhaness achieves with the symphony a subtle play of texture in the juxtaposition of the flute with various orchestral and instrumental groups. When he calls upon the full orchestra to play, it invariably makes a beautiful sound, the hallmark of one who has written for this medium extensively. . . . The sweetness and regularity of the writing remain ... just one step away from platitude."

In March 1979, Hovhaness's opera, *Tale of the Sun Goddess Going to the Stone House,* for four vocal soloists, chorus, "a spoken and stamping chorus," and orchestra, was presented for the first time in Salinas, California. This work was followed in 1980 by a monumental cantata for soprano, tenor, baritone, chorus, and orchestra entitled *Revelations of St. Paul.* Its New York world premiere took place on January 28, 1981, by Musica Sacra (which commissioned it), with Richard Westenburg conducting. Hovhaness used a text by Donald V. R. Thompson, taken from St. Paul's writings, for the work. In the New York *Times,* Donal Henahan remarked: "*St. Paul* does not deviate much from that settled idiom [a compositional style that is at once quite sophisticated and quite agreeable to the large concert going and record-buying public], unless it can be said to be slightly less self-consciously exotic in flavor than many previous Hovhaness pieces."

In the early 1960s, Hovhaness and his first wife, Elizabeth Whittington Hovhaness, founded Poseidon Records in order to record all of Hovhaness's works. This plan was frustrated by a divorce and ultimate exclusive ownership by the wife.

Since 1972, Hovhaness has lived in Seattle, Washington with his present wife, Hinako Fujihara, a coloratura soprano. Regarding his productivity, Hovhaness told Richard Kostelanetz, in an interview for the New York *Times,* that he composes every day, wherever he happens to be—even while he is sleeping. "After feeling drowsy in an early evening, I get more and more creative as the night goes on. By dawn, I'm wildly creative; it gets stronger all the time. I don't know how to compose slowly. I correct and revise later, but composing goes in a sweep. Sometimes I just get the beginning idea, but more often the entire score complete with orchestration comes into my head at once. ... I have more ideas than I can use."

Hovhaness was elected to the American Academy and Institute of Arts and Letters in 1977.

MAJOR WORKS (supplementary)

Ballet—A Rose for Miss Emily; Circe.

Band Music—Symphonies Nos. 20 and 23.

Chamber Music—String Quartets Nos. 4 and 5; Mountains, Rivers Without End, for ten instruments; Island of Mysterious Bells, for four harps; Nagooran, for cello and percussion; Yakamochi, for cello; Sonata for Trumpet and Organ; The Garden of Adonis, for flute and harp; Sonata for Cello and Piano.

Choral Music—Magnificat, for soprano, tenor, bass, chorus, and orchestra; In the Beginning Was the Word, for alto, bass, chorus, and orchestra; Adoration, for women's or men's chorus and orchestra; Praise the Lord with Psaltery, cantata for mixed chorus and orchestra; Lady of Light, cantata for soprano, baritone, chorus, and orchestra; A Rose Tree Blossoms, for chorus and organ; The Way of Jesus, oratorio for three soloists, chorus, and orchestra. Revelations of St. Paul, for soprano, tenor, baritone, chorus, and orchestra.

Guitar Music—Sonata.

Operas—The Travellers; Burning House; Pericles; Pilate, Leper King; Tale of the Sun Goddess Going to the Stone House.

Orchestral Music—Symphonies Nos. 24 through 40; Return to Rebuild the Desolate Place, concerto for trumpet and wind orchestra; Ode to the Temple of Sound; The Holy City, for trumpet solo, large chime or Bell in A, and strings; Fra Angelico; Requiem and Resurrection; And God Created Great Whales, with recorded humpback whale solo; Concerto for Cello and Orchestra; Ode to Freedom, for violin and orchestra; Rubaiyát, for narrator, accordion, and orchestra; Fanfare for the New Atlantis, for brass, strings, and percussion.

Piano Music—5 Visionary Landscapes; Bardo Sonata; Lake of Van Sonata; Sonata "Ananda."

Vocal Music—Five Songs, for low voice and piano; The Flute Player of the Armenian Mountains, Op. 239; Four Songs, for low voice and piano, Op. 242; Saturn, for soprano, clarinet, and piano; Glory Sings the Setting Sun, for soprano, clarinet, and piano; Celestial Canticle, for soprano and piano; Presentiment, for soprano and piano.

ABOUT (supplementary)

Vinton, J. (ed.), Dictionary of Contemporary Music.

BMI, Many Worlds of Music, Winter 1976; New York Times, November 12, 1978.

Karel Husa

1921–

Karel Husa was born on August 7, 1921, in Prague, Czechoslovakia, to Karel Husa Sr., the owner of a small shoe business, and Bozena Dongresova Husová. His early education was in

Husa: ho͞o sä

Husa

KAREL HUSA

technical schools—where he specialized in mathematics and engineering—because his parents, particularly his mother, wanted him to be an engineer. Although he was adept at his studies, especially mathematics, he escaped from what he calls "mathematical strictness" to painting, in which he was gifted. Neither parent was musical, but they insisted that he and his sister learn to play an instrument. Karel began to study the violin at eight and, at his mother's urging, took lessons on the piano from his sister at thirteen. He finds it incredible that both parents were so insistent that he get a musical education, since as he recalled, "they were from modest families, but they paid for nine years of lessons, twice a week, for two children. It was expensive. They felt it was important (even for an engineer!)" However, he was eighteen before he attended a concert, because "my parents didn't go. My father's business kept him at work from 7:00 in the morning to 8:30 at night. They also had the impression that one didn't go to a concert without an evening jacket, that concerts were for high society only."

During the Nazi occupation of Czechoslovakia, Husa was attending college as an engineering student. A Nazi killing of a student caused unrest in universities in Prague which led to student deportations to Germany to work in factories. All the universities were closed, but art schools and conservatories were allowed to remain open. Husa tried to apply for entrance to an art school, only to discover that he was not eligible. He was then able to gain admittance to

the Prague Conservatory in 1941, as a student in composition, even though he had no formal training in harmony and counterpoint. Before entering the Conservatory he had studied theory privately with Jaroslav Rídký for a year and from the time he was twelve he had made efforts at composing. He was admitted to the second year of a five-year program to study composition with Rídký and conducting with Pavel Dĕdeček. He also attended concerts for the first time, thrilling to the music of Debussy, Smetana, Dvořák, and Bartók. He recalled: "Everything was new, everything was fantastic. I lived only for music. But I must honestly say I was also escaping. We did not consider the Nazi occupation to be permanent—we knew it would end some day. But that six years seemed incredibly long at that time. Still, life goes on under nearly any conditions, if one wants it to."

By the time Husa graduated *summa cum laude* from Prague Conservatory in 1945, he was well on the way to becoming a composer. As a Conservatory student he had written his first work, a sonatina for piano in classical form which was published and performed in 1945 at a concert of the Czech branch of the International Society for Contemporary Music. A critic for *Kulturní Politika* called it "a delightful work, remarkably fresh, magnificently written for the piano," and Dr. Jan Hradecký of *Tempo* (Prague) said it "expressed remarkably the clarity, conception and economy of expression which should be typical for such diminutive forms." His second composition was an orchestral Overture, written to fulfill requirements for a Master's degree. Influenced by such Czech masters as Suk and Janáček, the work was performed in 1945 by the Prague Symphony Orchestra under Husa's direction.

Husa attended the Academy of Musical Arts in Prague for additional graduate work in 1945–1946, but then decided to study music in Paris at the École Normale de Musique. He studied composition under Arthur Honegger and Nadia Boulanger and conducting under Jean Fournet and André Cluytens. Returning to Prague in 1947, he received his doctorate from the Academy of Musical Arts with credit for his year's work in Paris and a composition entitled Sinfonietta, for orchestra. The work was performed by the Prague Symphony, and won Husa's first award, the Czech Academy of Sciences and Arts Prize in 1948. In addition, a newspaper in

Prague, *Práce,* referred to him on May 30, 1948, as "one of the greatest hopes of Czech music."

Husa also developed as a conductor in performances on Czech radio, but in spite of this, he returned to Paris to continue on a French scholarship at the École Normale de Musique where he received a *licence* in conducting and to study conducting with Eugène Bigot at the Paris Conservatory.

While in Paris, Husa wrote several works that testified to his continual creative growth and expansion of technical facility. They included: *Fresques,* (1947), for orchestra, *Divertimento,* (1948), for string orchestra, String Quartet No. 1 (1948), and Piano Sonata No. 1 (1949) which received its first performance in Paris by Louise Vosgerschian in the spring of 1950. When she performed it again in Boston, a critic for the Boston *Globe* described it as "a massive and demanding work. . . . Husa seems to have a sense of logic that enables him to develop a large structure from slight material with good sense and musical imagination."

Husa wrote a string quartet for the Smetana Quartet which introduced it during the Spring Festival in Prague in 1948. The work was not only presented later at the Festival of the International Society for Contemporary Music in Brussels on June 29, 1950, but also at festivals in Darmstadt, Holland, and Salzburg and it won the Lili Boulanger Award in 1950 and the Bilthoven Festival Prize in Holland in 1952. A Stockholm critic reporting from Brussels said that Husa was "the discovery of the music festival" and his quartet was "a storming success" and "an altogether brilliant work, exceptionally well written for the instruments and with its own tonal color which captivated one throughout the three movements."

Deciding to remain in France, Husa established residence in Royaumont, north of Paris. On February 2, 1952, he married Simone Perault in Paris and they had four daughters. While in France, he appeared as guest conductor of numerous orchestras in Europe, including the Grand Orchestre Symphonique of the Belgian Radio-Television Corporation in 1951–1952 and the Chamber Orchestra in Lausanne, Switzerland, in 1952–1953. In 1953–1954 he conducted the Orchestre des Solistes de Paris in a number of recordings. He also served as a member of the jury at the Paris Conservatory in 1952–1953 and

at the Fontainebleau School of Music and Fine Arts in 1953.

The compositions continued to flow in Paris. *Evocation of Slovakia,* for clarinet, viola, and cello, written in 1951, was first performed in May 1952 on French Radio. The three movements of the work—"Mountain," "Night," and "Dance"—are variations of Slovak folk songs and Husa selected those particular instruments because they resembled the colors and combinations of small folk-dance ensembles heard throughout Slovakia.

In 1953 alone, Husa wrote *Musique d' Amateurs* (four easy pieces for oboe, trumpet, percussion, and strings) on commission from UNESCO; *Portrait,* for orchestra, commissioned by the Donaueschingen Festival; String Quartet No. 2, written for the Parrenin Quartet which introduced it in Paris at a Festival of the Centre de Documentation sur la Musique Internationale in October 1954; and Husa's most ambitious work to date, *Symphony No. 1,* premiered over Radio Brussels with Daniel Sternfield conducting, on March 4, 1954. This Symphony was performed throughout Europe and it was introduced in the United States in April 1965 with the composer conducting the Baltimore Symphony Orchestra.

In 1954, Husa accepted a three-year teaching position in theory at Cornell University in Ithaca, New York, and leadership of the University orchestra in the absence of its regular conductor. (He had originally planned to study conducting with Serge Koussevitzky at the Berkshire Music Center at Tanglewood, Massachusetts in 1950, but a leg ailment frustrated this plan.) At Cornell Husa became associate professor in 1957, full professor in 1961, and in 1973 was given the distinguished Kappa Alpha Professorship. Between 1956 and 1975, he was the musical director and conductor of the University orchestra and between 1954 and 1961, the conductor of the Ithaca Chamber Orchestra. He became a permanent resident of the United States, receiving his American citizenship in 1959.

His first important composition in the United States was *Fantasies,* for orchestra (1956), commissioned by the Friends of Music at Cornell. The work, in three sections, opens with an Aria in contrapuntal style primarily for strings; the second movement is a Capriccio in "concertante style" for three trumpets, piano, and several woodwind instruments with strings in the background; the final movement is a Nocturne in which new colors and potentials in orchestration are evident. The first performance was at a Festival of Contemporary Arts at Cornell University in April 1975 with the composer conducting the Cornell University Orchestra. Husa also conducted the Paris Chamber Orchestra in France, when the work was recorded.

Poem, for viola and orchestra (1959), had its premiere at the Festival of the International Society for Contemporary Music in Cologne, Germany, on June 12, 1960. Ulrich Koch was viola soloist and the Southwest German Radio Orchestra was conducted by Hans Roshaud. In this work, the composer employs the twelve-tone technique with, as a critic noted in the *Deutsche Zeitung,* "uncommon melodic sensitivity."

In 1961, Husa revisited Paris on a sabbatical from Cornell. While there, he was commissioned by the Hamburg Radio to write *Mosaïques,* in partial serial technique. The composer explained: "Groupings of 2, 3, or 4 notes are used in a similar way as the different stones or other materials of different colors are used in constructing a mosaic." Of the five parts in all, the full orchestra is used only in the fourth and fifth parts and the fourth mosaic climaxes the work with dissonant groupings of notes in a kind of ostinato, a dramatic portrayal of tragedy. Phrases and sounds from earlier movements are recalled in the concluding mosaic. *Mosaïques* was first heard on Hamburg Radio on November 7, 1961, with Husa conducting the NDR (Nordeutsche Rundfunk) Hamburg Orchestra.

Husa's international reputation was enhanced in 1969 when he was awarded the Pulitzer Prize in music for String Quartet No. 3. The Fine Arts Quartet commissioned this work through the Chicago Fine Arts Music Foundation, after the ensemble had successfully performed Husa's String Quartet No. 2 in Europe and the United States. Husa composed it in two weeks in mid-February of 1968 from sketches he had written on European conducting assignments. In this quartet, Husa concentrated on highlighting solo performance, "spotlighting the several instruments in rather free forms: the viola in the first movement, the cello in the second, the two violins in the third," he explained. "I feel I have been able to find some unusual paths for bow and finger. As for the rest, I have used all the possibilities hitherto available. The forms of the

four movements are free, based mostly on contrasting colors and inner tensions." When the Fine Arts Quartet presented the world premiere in Chicago on October 14, 1968, the audience cheered it. The Chicago *Daily News* said it "deserved the warm ovation it received. It is an exciting, imaginative piece, superbly written for the instruments and fresh though not revolutionary in its tonal and textural exploration."

What is thought to be Husa's most famous composition—*Music for Prague 1968*—was inspired by the tragic uprising in Czechoslovakia in August 1968 and the Soviet takeover. Poignant and nostalgic memories came back to Husa when the Ithaca band director commissioned him to write a composition for a convention in Washington, D. C., in January 1969. The band version became a permanent staple in the band repertory, with four to five thousand performances. The orchestral version, written in 1969, was acclaimed in Europe and the United States following its premiere in Munich on January 31, 1970. Husa conducted the performance by the Munich Philharmonic, Sergiu Comissiona conducted it with the Cleveland Orchestra at his Carnegie Hall debut in New York on February 17, 1972, and Jorge Mester conducted it with the Louisville Orchestra when it was recorded on the Louisville Records label.

In four short movements (Introduction and Fanfare, Aria, Interlude, and Toccata and Chorale), *Music for Prague 1968* is an emotional and stirringly dramatic work. In the opening measures an old Hussite religious song, "Ye Warriors of God and His Law" is suggested by the timpani and it serves as one unifying element throughout. This theme, symbolizing resistance, recurs later in various forms and is used in the last movement as a final climax. Another unifying element is a chorale-like motive of three harmonized notes. The ringing of bells recalls the churches of Prague, a city of "a hundred towers," while masterful and frequent use of brass and percussion enhances tensions and a piccolo suggests the Czech bird-calls of liberty. Robert Shaw conducted this work in Atlanta, Georgia, in January 1975, and a critic for the Atlanta *Journal* thought it was "music of searing intensity. . . . After a quiet introduction and vigorous fanfare in the brass, the strings sing out a great anguishing song which depicts the tragedy in Prague's history. A ghostly interlude for percussion instruments alone leads to an energetic driving toccata which, together with a mighty chorale played by the entire orchestra in unison, ends the work."

In 1970, Husa's motivation in writing *Apotheosis of this Earth* (originally for wind band; rewritten in 1973 for chorus and orchestra), was as he revealed, "the present desperate stage of mankind and its immense problems with everyday killings, war, hunger, extermination of fauna, huge forest fires and critical contamination of the whole environment. Man's brutal possession and misuse of nature's beauty—if continued at today's reckless speed—can only lead to catastrophe."

The composer described the movements in the work: "In the first movement, 'Apotheosis,' the Earth first appears as a point of light in the universe. Our memory and imagination approach it in perhaps the same way as it appeared to the astronauts from the moon. The Earth grows larger and larger, and we can even remember some of its tragic moments (as struck by the xylophone near the end of the movement). The second movement, 'Tragedy of Destruction,' deals with the actual brutalities of man against nature, leading to the destruction of our planet, perhaps by radio-active explosion. The Earth dies, a savagely, mortally wounded creature. The last movement is 'Postcript,' full of the realization that so little is left to be said: The Earth has been pulverized into the universe, the voices scattered into space. Towards the end, these voices—at first computer-like and mechanical—unite into the words *this beautiful Earth*, simply said, warm and filled with regret . . . and one of so many questions comes to our mind: 'Why have we let it happen?' "

The *Apotheosis of this Earth* was commissioned by the Michigan School Band and Orchestra and performed for the first time at the University of Michigan at Ann Arbor on April 1, 1971, with the composer conducting. Writing in *High Fidelity/Musical America*, Richard Freed said: "*Apotheosis of this Earth* has everything—power, passion, mysticism, even peace and ecology."

Husa's fiftieth birthday was celebrated in 1971–1972 with performances of his music in numerous colleges and universities throughout the United States. These tributes included a Husa Festival at the University of Wisconsin in Madison during the week of March 20, 1972, when eleven of his works, covering virtually every phase of his career, were heard under his own direction. There were two new compositions during his fiftieth year, including *Two Sonnets from Michaelangelo*, written in 1971 on a commission from the Evanston (Illinois) Symphony which, under Frank Miller's direction, introduced it on April 28, 1972; and the *Concerto for Percussion and Wind Ensemble*, commissioned by Ludwig Industries and first performed by the Baylor University Symphonic Ensemble under Gene C. Smith with Larry Van Landingham as soloist in Waco, Texas, on February 7, 1972.

The Koussevitzky Music Foundation commissioned the writing of the Sonata for Violin and Piano in 1972–1973. The composer said he "was influenced—though not voluntarily—by some events of the past years such as continuous wars, senseless destruction of nature, killing of animals and, on the other hand, man's incredible accomplishments in space." Both instrumental parts, in virtuoso style, are equally important and sometimes independent of each other. The first performance of the work was at a concert of the Chamber Music Society of Lincoln Center in New York on March 31, 1974, by Ani Kavafian, violinist, and Richard Goode, pianist.

To commemorate the American bicentennial, the National Endowment for the Arts and the Jordan College of Music of Butler University commissioned and sponsored the music for *Monodrama*, a ballet, choreographed by Bud Kerwin. It was first produced in Indianapolis, Indiana, on March 26, 1976, by the Butler Ballet, with Oleg Kovalenko conducting the Indianapolis Symphony Orchestra. Husa said *Monodrama* "portrays the American artist, his aloneness, isolation from society which he feels does not understand him and constantly battles with him."

Also to celebrate the American bicentennial —and the 125th anniversary of the founding of Coe College in Cedar Rapids, Iowa—is Husa's *An American Te Deum*, for baritone solo, chorus, and band. Its world premiere took place on December 5, 1976. Husa used a variety of sources for his text, including poems by Paul Engle, parts of Rölvaag's immigrant novel, *Giants in the Earth*, and assorted writings by Henry David Thoreau. The score quotes a motive from Dvořák's Quintet in E major, an Indian melody, "Chippewa Lullaby" and includes an opening drum section reminiscent of an Afro-

American and Indian dance song and a hymn tune from the Amana Colonies in Iowa. In 1978, Husa rewrote *An American Te Deum* for orchestra and chorus and this version was premiered during the Inter-American Music Festival at the J. F. Kennedy Center in Washington, D. C., on May 10, 1978, with the composer conducting.

Husa writes functional music *(Gebrauchsmusik)* and virtuoso music with equal facility and aptitude in styles of 20th century music that meet the demands of the composition. There is no imitation, only a feeling of assimilation in his eclectic style, which embraces Debussy's Impressionism, Bartók's neo-primitivism, Schoenberg's dodecaphony, Alois Hába's microtonal writing, as well as the Slavic lyricism and emotionalism of his own Czech predecessors. He absorbs all these idioms "without destroying or belittling the aesthetics and devices of his musical forebears," wrote Dr. Harold Simmons in his liner notes for the recording of *Music for Prague 1968.* Husa explained: "What I have been trying to do is to preserve what little is still viable and useful from the past, but mostly my concern is to write music of today, and also find some new paths for tomorrow. Most of the works of the past and present mirror the period in which they were composed, so I hope my music can reflect the exciting, passionate and also tragic times of today."

Husa lives in a house with his wife and family in Ithaca, New York. He does his composing in a studio above the garage to the side of his house and in a cottage on a lake near Ithaca which the family has for summer relaxation.

Considering his prodigious productivity, Husa works slowly, usually producing no more than twelve measures a day. Not having the form of a piece in mind, he has only an idea of something he would like to write—two or three staves in the manner of a piano reduction, with notations about instrumentation, and he said that "if I get tired and don't know where to go, if I come to an impasse in some way, I will go back and start to do the complete orchestration. Then, when I come to the same spot, it will open up and I will know how to progress."

Husa was awarded two Guggenheim Fellowships in 1964 and 1965. In 1974 he was elected Associate Member of the Royal Belgian Academy of Arts and Sciences, and in 1976 he received an honorary doctorate in music from Coe College.

Teaching and composing do not keep Husa from appearing as guest conductor of major orchestras in Europe and the United States. He also finds time for the reconstruction of French baroque compositions, and other interests aside from music, such as sports (soccer, tennis, ice hockey, and swimming), reading, painting, architecture and nature preservation.

MAJOR WORKS

Ballet—Monodrama.

Band Music—Divertimento, for brass and percussion; Concerto for Alto Saxophone and Concert Band; Music for Prague 1968 (also for orchestra); Apotheosis of This Earth (also for chorus and orchestra); Concerto for Percussion and Wind Ensemble; Concerto for Trumpet and Wind Orchestra; Al Fresco.

Chamber Music—3 string quartets; Evocations of Slovakia, for clarinet, viola, and cello; Four Little Pieces, for strings; Poem, for viola and piano; Élégie et Rondeau, for saxophone and piano (also for saxophone and orchestra); Serenade, for woodwind quintet and piano (also for woodwind quintet and orchestra); Concerto for Alto Saxophone and Piano (also for alto saxophone and concert band); Two Preludes, for flute, clarinet, and bassoon; Divertimento, for brass quintet; Sonata for Violin and Piano; Landscape, for brass quintet.

Choral Music—Festive Ode; Apotheosis of This Earth; American Te Deum, for baritone solo, chorus, and orchestra.

Orchestral Music—Divertimento, for string orchestra; Fresques (revised 1963); Symphony no. 1; Concertino for Piano and Orchestra; Musique d'Amateurs, for oboe, trumpet, percussion, and strings; Portrait, for string orchestra; Fantaisies; Poem, for viola and chamber orchestra; Élégie at Rondeau, for alto saxophones and orchestra; Mosaïques; Serenade, for woodwind quintet solo with string orchestra, xylophone, and harp; Music for Prague 1968; Two Sonnets from Michaelangelo; Concerto for Trumpet and Wind Orchestra; The Steadfast Tin Soldier, for narrator and orchestra.

Piano Music—2 piano sonatas; Sonatina; Eight Czech Duets, for piano four hands; Élégie.

ABOUT

BMI, Many Worlds of Music, January 1970, Winter 1976; High Fidelity/Musical America, August 1969; Musical Quarterly, January 1976.

Jacques Ibert

1890–1962

See *Composers Since 1900.*

Andrew Imbrie

1921–

Andrew Welsh Imbrie was born in New York City on April 6, 1921, to parents of Scottish descent, Andrew C. Imbrie, a businessman, and Dorothy Welsh Imbrie. Andrew began taking piano lessons before he was five and his first teacher was Ann Abajian who, in addition to giving him piano lessons, encouraged him to compose music. "I owe to her my present attitude toward composition as an entirely natural form of expression," he said. "She knew how to start a young pupil composing before he was ready to acquire a real technique, so that his interest was kept alive and his search for self-expression ultimately led him to the acquisition of technique."

He was six when his family moved to Princeton, New Jersey, and he attended Princeton Country Day School. From 1930 to 1942 he traveled once a week to Philadelphia for piano studies at the Philadelphia Music Academy and later the Ornstein School of Music with Leo Ornstein, a one-time concert pianist and one of America's earliest modernist composers. He told us, "Leo Ornstein taught me by example. One learned from what he did even more than from what he said, though he was highly articulate and at times even fascinating in his conversation."

He also told of his early associations with orchestras which left an indelible impression on him, notably, playing the piano with the orchestras at school and the Conservatory, and, in 1933, with the Philadelphia Orchestra as one of the two pianists performing Saint-Saëns' *Carnival of the Animals.* "What remained in my mind is a strong impression of the orchestra, not only as a support for my piano playing, but as an exciting milieu, surrounding me with music, and

Imbrie: ĭm′ brē

ANDREW IMBRIE

infinitely subtle and powerful in its musical utterance. This 'gut' feeling of being in the midst of the orchestra has always guided me back to writing for the orchestral medium."

He was conscious of another powerful influence at about ten or eleven years of age, when he first heard Wagner's *Parsifal* and *Die Götterdämmerung.* "The music haunted me for years, as well as the power of the drama which I perceived simply as an adventure story, disregarding the philosophical content. I collected leitmotives the way most children collect stamps."

By the time he was sixteen he knew that he wanted to become a composer rather than a pianist and during that summer he studied composition with Nadia Boulanger at the American Conservatory in Fontainebleau, France. On his return to the United States he went on to study harmony and composition privately with Roger Sessions (1937–1938).

Graduating from the Lawrenceville School, a private preparatory school, in 1939, he enrolled at Princeton University to study the fugue, musical analysis, and composition with Sessions who was a member of the music faculty. For his senior thesis, Imbrie wrote his first string quartet which was performed at Princeton in June 1942. It was successful enough to be performed by several well-known string-quartet ensembles, to receive the New York Music Critics' Circle Award following its performance in New York City by the Bennington Quartet on April 10, 1944, and eventually to be recorded by the Juilliard String Quartet.

Imbrie

Imbrie graduated from Princeton with a Bachelor of Arts degree in 1942 and from 1942 to 1946 served in the Army Signal Corps, near Washington, D.C. During the war years, his sole musical activity was providing original music for informal musical shows which he improvised on the piano—mainly in the style of Gershwin. He never wrote it down, but taught it to the performers by rote.

After the war, Imbrie followed Sessions to the University of California in Berkeley, where he was then on the music faculty. On an Alice M. Ditson Fellowship from Columbia University, Imbrie earned his Master's degree in music in 1947. An outstanding composition written during these years was the Piano Trio, composed for the Princeton bicentennial and performed there in March 1946.

After receiving his degree, Imbrie was appointed instructor of music at the University of California in Berkeley on condition that he be allowed to take advantage of his prize, the Prix de Rome, and reside at the American Academy in Rome between 1947 and 1949 before the appointment. In 1947, both his Piano Sonata and *Ballad in D,* for orchestra were introduced in Rome, the *Ballad* on the Rome Radio (RAI) before its first public hearing in Florence on June 20, 1949. In 1948 he completed a *Divertimento* for six instruments (also performed in Rome on May 5, 1949) and a choral work to a poem by Walt Whitman, *On the Beach at Night,* which was introduced by the University chorus and orchestra at Berkeley in April 1952.

Back in the United States in 1949 as an instructor of music at the University of California, he rose to the rank of assistant professor in 1951, associate professor in 1957, and since 1960, a full professor. He said, "Teaching has been an indispensable part of my life. It keeps me from taking things for granted, and it has kept me in contact with what each new generation is thinking about and doing."

Both the String Quartet No. 2 (1953) and the Concerto for Violin and Orchestra (1954) showed decided growth in Imbrie's technical skill and articulation. The String Quartet was introduced in Cambridge, Massachusetts, on May 12, 1952, by the Kroll Quartet. Virgil Thomson of the New York *Herald Tribune* called both string quartets "the work of a master talent." After four years, the Violin Concerto was performed by the San Francisco Symphony,

under Enrique Jorda with Robert Gross as soloist, in Berkeley on April 22, 1958; it won the Naumburg Recording Award a year later and was released on Columbia Records. Both works reflect the powerful influence of Bartók and Sessions in their rhythmic drive, strong-fibered and dramatic lyricism, and forceful and frequently dissonant harmony.

On January 31, 1953, Imbrie married Barbara Cushing, and they live in Berkeley where they raised two sons. Imbrie received two Guggenheim Fellowships, in 1953 and 1960–1961. In 1955 he earned the Merit Award from the Boston Symphony and in 1958 the Creative Arts Award from Brandeis University in Waltham, Massachusetts.

Imbrie's String Quartet No. 3 (1957), commissioned by the University of Illinois in Urbana and the Fromm Music Foundation, received its first hearing in Urbana on March 29, 1957. When the Quartet was performed in New York on October 13, 1958, Allen Hughes described it in the New York *Herald Tribune:* "Contrapuntal writing is sinewy; the frank, rugged dissonances are expressive, and the concurrent play of lyricism and dramatic interjection is telling." Ingolf Dahl of *Musical Quarterly* (1960) praised all three Imbrie quartets for their "combination of clear, classically oriented form with the spontaneity of those welcome comments in which the music bursts out of the established patterns in free declamation."

On December 9, 1959, the San Francisco Symphony under Enrique Jorda commissioned and premiered Imbrie's first composition solely for orchestra—*Legend,* for the American Music Center Commission Series. This short composition, with no programmatic content, was described by Arthur Bloomfield of *Musical America:* "The most fascinating aspect of the score is its sound texture—very transparent in its use of pure, lustrous colors—for Imbrie had a superb ear . . . highly chromatic, quite fragmentary and complex in part-writing and rhythm . . . not difficult to listen to."

In 1960, on commission from the Interracial Chorus in New York, Imbrie composed *Drum Taps,* for chorus and orchestra with a text from Walt Whitman. The Interracial Chorus performed the work in New York in the spring of 1961. Another composition in 1960 was a one-act chamber opera, *Three Against Christmas* (retitled *Christmas in Peebles Town*) for five principal singers, double chorus, and orchestra, first performed in Berkeley on December 3, 1964. This opera's libretto, by Richard Wincor, is a fantasy about the abolition of Christmas and its consequence in the mythical town of Peebles.

Imbrie's Symphony No. 1 was written in 1966 at the request of Josef Krips, musical director of the San Francisco Symphony Orchestra, after he had conducted one of Imbrie's works. Krips and the San Francisco Symphony introduced it on May 11, 1966.

In 1967–1968, Imbrie, as composer-in-residence at the American Academy in Rome, wrote the *Chamber Symphony* which was premiered at the Congregation of the Arts at Dartmouth College in Hanover, New Hampshire, on August 11, 1968. Robert Commanday of the San Francisco *Chronicle,* in reviewing the West Coast premiere in 1970 said it "is so rich in implication, it insists on deeper, further involvement. This music is to stay with us. . . . There is a passion here in the rhythmic thrusts which, phrase by phrase, builds to a hair-raising crisis, then lets off in gradual release of tension. This ecstatic, highly personalized style marks the composer in his maturity, writing from a vital compulsion and evincing a minimal sense of labor."

Before the 1960s were over, Imbrie had further strengthened his position in American music with String Quartet No. 4 and his Symphony No. 2, both completed in 1969. The string quartet was commissioned by the Pro Arte String Quartet which introduced it in Madison, Wisconsin, on November 17, 1969, and in San Francisco in April 1971. Robert Commanday praised it in the San Francisco *Chronicle:* "A sense of genuine passion is the essence of the Fourth Quartet. Imbrie launches the challenge immediately, into a fiery complex of compacted ideas and broad-reaching melodic statement. This insists on exploration before the softer, almost vocal, section can assert its nature, later rediscovered as a fulfillment of the impassioned business."

Imbrie's Symphony No. 2 was performed for the first time on May 21, 1970, by the San Francisco Symphony under Josef Krips. This time Robert Commanday noted the symphony's "charge of ideas, impulses, the generation and regeneration of motion from every orchestral resource. This is not the bruitisme of the avant-garde; it has a power far more urgent than that because of inner forces."

Indicative of Imbrie's growing international status was a 1970 commission from the Hallé Orchestra of Manchester to write a new symphony, his third. It was performed in Manchester on December 3, 1970, with Maurice Hanford conducting, and it won the Walter Hinrichson Award to finance a recording by the London Symphony under Harold Farberman. The Symphony opens with an expansive eighty-nine measure introduction before the three movements begin to unfold. A London critic for *Tempo* commented on the recording: "The quality I admire above all in this music is its toughness; by which I mean strength without brutality or stupidity. The general character is active, flexible, energetic: splendidly athletic and sinewy, both in the long-uncurling lyrical themes and the brisk rhythmic tuttis. The particular character of each movement defines itself more vividly with closer acquaintanceship. The first movement proper is a type of allegro increasingly dominated by lyrical content, and as such it contrasts with the more forceful allegro finale, which develops into a vigorous and prolonged contrapuntal tutti. . . . Between them is a perfectly-judged slow movement: a prolonged cantilena for clarinet, rising to a tutti, and returning a renewed solo to the peacefulness of the opening."

In the early 1970s, Imbrie returned to the concerto form which he had abandoned for almost two decades. The Concerto for Cello and Orchestra (1973) was commissioned and performed by the Oakland Symphony in California, with Sally Kell as soloist, on April 24, 1973. Piano concertos were written in 1973 and 1974: the First Piano Concerto was written for Hélène Wickett who performed it at Saratoga, California, on August 4, 1973 and the Second Piano Concerto, commissioned by the Ford Foundation, had its first performance by the Indianapolis Symphony on January 29, 1976, with Gita Karasik as soloist and Oleg Kovalenko as conductor. In a brochure on Imbrie issued by BMI (Broadcast Music, Inc.), James G. Roy Jr. described the First Piano Concerto as "playful, provocative and witty," the Second Piano Concerto as leaning "to the sterner side" and the Cello Concerto, by contrast, "as haunting and ethereal."

Imbrie later added the Concerto for Flute and Orchestra (1977), which was commissioned by Francis Goelet, chairman of the New York Philharmonic music policy committee, for the first flutist, Julius Baker who premiered it with the Philharmonic under the direction of Erich Leinsdorf on October 13, 1977. A critic for *High Fidelity/Musical America* noted that "the most effective moments are those involving reduced forces—the solo in the first movement or its nocturnes with horn and strings at the beginning and end of the slow movement."

To commemorate the American bicentenary, Imbrie wrote his first full-length opera (his second work for the stage) on commission from the San Francisco Opera with additional funds from the National Endowment for the Arts. *Angle of Repose,* with a libretto by Oakley Hall, is based on Wallace Stegner's 1972 Pulitzer Prize novel. The plot, set in Western U. S. A., follows a Western mining-camp family from the 1870s to the present. In a flashback a half-century later, the crippled Lyman Ward and his daughter, Shelley, review the erratic history of his grandparents' marriage (Oliver Ward to Susan Burling) and their varied misfortunes. In considering this source for his bicentennial opera, Imbrie thought it would "be suited for the occasion, dealing as it does with our national and regional heritage. It impressed me particularly because it exemplified so poignantly the paradoxes inherent in our recurrent American dream of opening and civilizing new frontiers." It took Imbrie two full years to write his opera and on November 6, 1976, it was produced in San Francisco. Although the music is atonal and dissonant, Imbrie has introduced into his score miners' choral pieces, waltzes, Virginia reels, and other American folk elements. "Imbrie has fashioned a score with great variety and consistency," wrote Alan Rich in *New York,* "and a melodic power that any intelligent hearer can easily grasp. He has found a neat, subtle manner for differentiating the style of characters from past and present. . . . The opera is beautifully written for singers, handsomely scored for a large orchestra. It . . . doesn't seem to waste a moment in the telling of an absorbing and compelling story."

Speaking of his composing procedures, Andrew Imbrie said: "My way of working is to begin at the beginning. I start with an idea—by this I don't mean an abstract idea but a rhythm, a chord, a part of a melody, or perhaps just an inkling of some combination of these things. By trial and error I attempt to nail down this idea, to establish its speed, duration, color, loudness, shape and texture—in short its character. Then I listen to it to discover where it wants to go next. By this process the idea begins to grow. Very soon, however, things get stuck, the bigger problems begin to loom up. One can't proceed very far without knowing in a general way what kinds of contrast are going to be needed and about how long it should take to get to the next big change in the music. In other words, the demand for proportion—of large rhythmic shape—begins to assert itself, again not as an abstract principle, but as an urgent necessity. That's why I almost never use the word 'form' because to me the word implies that the music is poured like cement into a pre-fabricated mold, then allowed to harden. For me the shape of the finished product of the *musical* imagination is more like the *outcome* of tendencies present in the ideas. Musical ideas, then, have not only shape, color, duration, etc., but also implications for the future. The composer is both leader and follower: the ideas are his own, but while he writes, he listens—and the ideas make their own demands."

MAJOR WORKS

Chamber Music—4 string quartets; Piano Trio; Divertimento, for six instruments; Serenade, for flute, viola, and piano; Impromptu, for violin and piano; Sonata for Cello and Piano; Three Sketches, for trombone and piano; Dandelion Wine, for oboe, clarinet, piano, and string quartet; Here We Stand, fanfare for double bass choir; A Hawk for Peace, fanfare for three trumpets, three trombones, and a tuba; To a Traveler, for violin, clarinet, and piano; Fancy for Five, for five trombones.

Choral Music—On the Beach at Night, for chorus and string orchestra; Introit, Gradual and Offertory, for chorus and organ; Two Christmas Carols, for male chorus and piano; Drum Taps, for chorus and orchestra; Psalm 42, for male chorus and organ; The Serpent, for mixed chorus and organ; *a* Wind Has Blown the Rain away, for mixed chorus and piano; Let All the World, for chorus and organ; Prometheus Bound, dance cantata for three singers, double chorus, orchestra, and dancers.

Opera—Christmas in Peebles Town, one-act chamber opera; Angle of Repose.

Orchestral Music—3 symphonies; 2 piano concertos; Ballad in D; Three Songs, for soprano and small orchestra; Concerto for Violin and Orchestra; Little Concerto, for piano four hands and orchestra; Legend, tone poem; Chamber Symphony; Concerto for Cello and Orchestra; Concerto for Flute and Orchestra.

Piano Music—Sonata; Waltz; O Moment's Reflection.

Vocal Music—Tell Me Where Is Fancy Bred, for soprano, clarinet, and guitar; Three Roethke Songs, for soprano and piano.

ABOUT

Vinton, J. (ed.), Dictionary of Contemporary Music.
Music Journal, February 1977; Oakland Tribune, December 4, 1977.

Vincent D'Indy

1851–1931

Fro biographical sketch, list of earlier works, and bibliography, see *Composers Since 1900*.

ABOUT (supplementary)

Davies, L., César Franck and His Circle.
Musical Quarterly, January 1972.

John Ireland

1879–1962

For biographical sketch, list of earlier works, and bibliography, see *Composers Since 1900*.

ABOUT (supplementary)

Longmire, J., John Ireland: Portrait of a Friend; Searle, M. V., John Ireland: the Man and his Music.

Charles Ives

1874–1954

For biographical sketch, list of earlier works, and bibliography, see *Composers Since 1900*.

On February 9, 1974, the world premiere of the full orchestral version of Ives's masterwork, *Three Places in New England* (previously performed only in the chamber-orchestral version), took place in New Haven with John Mauceri conducting the Yale Symphony Orchestra. Ives had originally written the work for full orchestra, and then adapted it for chamber orchestra to encourage more performances. The original version disappeared, but one movement was recovered in the fall of 1973 from a pile of manuscripts Ives had presented to Goddard Lieberson, president of Columbia Records. Parts and sources of the other two movements were located by James Sinclair who had come to Yale University in 1977 as an assistant to John Kirkpatrick, director of the University's Ives Collection. Sinclair completed full restoration of the work by January 1974 and reported: "In this study I have compared the published chamber-orchestra score with surviving portions of the original score for full orchestra and with earlier sources and sketches, in order to develop a new score for full orchestra which retains both the work's original color and the advantages of Ives's later revisions."

The centenary of Ives's birth, in the fall of 1974, brought forth worldwide tributes in many different forms. Festivals of Ives's music were held in various parts of the United States including New Haven (Yale University) and Danbury, Connecticut, Minneapolis, New York City, and Miami, Florida. The festival in Miami lasted nine months with all local musical organizations and most major musicians participating. Works by Ives were presented by virtually every major symphony orchestra in America and many in Europe. In commemoration, Columbia Records issued a volume of five disks: three were devoted to Ives's works; one to Ives himself, performing his works; and a fifth, "Charles Ives Remembered," consisted of reminiscences of the composer by relatives, friends, and associates. Books about Ives and innumerable articles in newspapers and magazines were published in the United States and abroad and there were television documentaries on his life, personality, and works, and individual documentaries on his *Concord Sonata* and Symphony No. 4. *Meeting Mr. Ives,* a theater pageant with dialogue, choreography, and music was produced at the Lenox Arts Center in Lenox, Massachusetts, on August 20, 1975.

Charles Ives's widow, Harmony Twichell Ives, died in a nursing home in West Redding, Connecticut, on April 4, 1969, in her ninety-second year.

ABOUT (supplementary)

Hitchcock, H. W., Ives; Kirkpatrick, J. (ed.), Charles E. Ives: Memos; Perlis, V., Charles Ives Remembered: an Oral History; Perry, R. S., Charles Ives and the American Mind; Rossiter, F. R., Charles Ives and His America; Wooldridge, D., From the Steeples and Mountains: a Study of Charles Ives.

High Fidelity/Musical America (Charles Ives Issue), October 1974; New York Times Magazine, April 21, 1974; Yale Alumnae Magazine, October 1974.

Leoš Janáček

1854–1928

For biographical sketch, list of earlier works, and bibliography, see *Composers Since 1900.*

Interest in Janáček's music, had waned, but was revived throughout the music world after World War II. It gained momentum in the 1960s and early 1970s and reached its peak in 1979 with commemoration of the fiftieth anniversary of the composer's death.

Soon after World War II, the Janáček Archive was established by the Institute of Musical History of the Moravian Museum in Brünn, Czechoslovakia, and became a major repository of Janáček memorabilia, housing over six hundred items, including manuscripts, published music, sketches, proofs, personal and family documents, over seventy notebooks, and Janáček's library.

In the middle 1960s, an increasing number of performances of Janáček's music in the United States and Europe indicated the rekindling of interest in his music and a determination to rediscover much of it. In 1965, Janáček's long-neglected *Glagolitica Mass (Slavonic Mass)* was recorded by the Deutsche Grammophon in a performance by the Bavarian Symphony Orchestra and Radio Chorus under Rafael Kubelik. The same year—on November 4—Robert Shaw conducted the Cleveland Orchestra in a performance of the same Mass. Both events drew fresh attention to this choral masterwork of the 20th century, which was, according to Alan Rich of *High Fidelity,* "a kind of tone poem on the dimensions of faith," and "a blazing affirmation of life," in the words of David Hall of *Hi Fi/Stereo Review.*

The American premiere of Janáček's opera, *The Makropulos Affair,* was produced by the San Francisco Opera on November 22, 1966 and the performance was well-received. In 1967, a recording of the opera *From the House of the Dead,* performed by the Prague National Theater, was released in the United States by CBS and in 1969, it was televised by the NET Opera Company. In 1968, under Walter Felsenstein's direction, a remarkable production of the opera, *Cunning Little Vixen,* was produced in East Berlin and filmed for television, and on April 9, 1981, the New York City Opera produced it for

the first time. All of Janáček's works for the piano (many little known) were recorded by Rudolf Firkusny on a two-record Deutsche Grammophon release in 1972. That year, Janáček's deeply moving and almost never-performed *Diary of One Who Vanished,* for tenor and orchestra, was revived by the Seattle (Washington) Symphony Orchestra under Milton Katims. On November 15, 1974, Janáček's operatic masterwork, *Jenůfa* (the most popular Janáček opera) was revived in a new production by the Metropolitan Opera in New York.

On September 17, 1977, the San Francisco Opera presented a performance of *Katya Kabanova* in English translation, which was taped for television. Three years later, on October 1, 1980, the same company offered the first performance of *Jenůfa* in the United States in its original language. The American premiere of *The Excursions of Mr. Broucek,* in a semi-staged production, was given on January 23, 1981, by the Berkeley Symphony in California, with Kent Nagano conducting. The New York City Opera's first presentation, in English, of *The Cunning Little Vixen* was given on April 9, 1981.

Many outstanding events during the fiftieth anniversary year of 1978 testified to Janáček's so newly acquired high esteem. Supraphon Records in Czechoslovakia recorded everything that Janáček had written, and many older and outdated recordings were replaced by new ones. They also published a new edition of all Janáček's music, and the first two volumes appeared in 1978, and the next two in 1979.

The 13th Annual International Festival in Brünn was devoted completely to Janáček's music, from September 29 through October 13, 1978, and included every one of his completed works such as the operas *Sarka, The Beginning of a Romance,* and *Fate* which had not been heard in decades. Prague held its own Janáček Festival, in the spring of 1978, presenting a vast cross-section of his symphonic, chamber, and choral works, and eight of his nine operas. In Czechoslovakia, Janáček was represented on concert platforms, opera stages, and on radio and television.

On September 13, 1979, the Czech Philharmonic, with Vaclav Neumann conducting, presented the world premiere of Janáček's music for Gerhart Hauptmann's play, *Schluck und Jau.*

Outside Czechoslovakia, the Lucerne Festival in Switzerland devoted much of its programming between August 16 and September 7, 1978, to Janáček's music, including performances of *The Makropulos Affair,* and an exhibition of Janáček memorabilia at the Lucerne Central Library. Frankfurt Opera in Germany offered a new production of *Katya Kabanova* at the Edinburgh Festival in September 1978 where the Scottish Opera and the Welsh National Opera presented a Janáček opera cycle. A new production of the opera in Vienna became the first recording of a Janáček opera outside Czechoslovakia; it was released in 1978, and received the International High Fidelity-Record Critics Award in Salzburg, Austria. On September 6, 1978, the Cardiff New Theatre in Wales presented *The Makropulos Affair* for the first time. In December 1978, the Zurich Opera presented a new production of *From the House of the Dead,* and on December 28, 1978, the English National Opera offered *Adventures of Mr. Broucek* in London.

In the United States, the American Spoleto Festival at Charleston, South Carolina, highlighted a Janáček retrospective on June 9 and 10, 1978, with concerts (that included the *Glagolitic Mass*), lectures, ballets to Janáček's music, and the filmed presentation of the Walter Felsenstein production of *The Cunning Little Vixen.* On November 17, 1978, the Houston Opera in Texas mounted a new production of *Jenůfa.*

ABOUT (supplementary)

Chisholm, E., The Operas of Leoš Janáček; Ewans, M., Janáček's Tragic Operas.

High Fidelity/Musical America, June 1978.

André Jolivet

1905–1974

For biographical sketch, list of earlier works, and bibliography, see *Composers Since 1900.*

Jolivet's Concerto No. 2 for Cello and Orchestra (1966) was introduced in Moscow on January 6, 1967; his *Twelve Inventions for Twelve Instruments* (1966) was presented in Paris on January 23, 1967; and Concerto for Violin and Orchestra (1972) was performed in Paris on February 28, 1973. A complete catalog of Jolivet's works was compiled by V. Fedorov and P. Guinard and published in Paris in 1969.

André Jolivet died in Paris on December 20, 1974.

MAJOR WORKS (supplementary)

Chamber Music—Twelve Inventions for Twelve Instruments; Five Eclogues, for solo viola; Ascèses, five pieces for solo flute and clarinet; Cérémonial Hommage à Varèse, for six percussion; Controversia, for oboe and harp; Heptade, for trumpet and percussion; Arioso Barocco, for trumpet and organ; La Flèche du Temps, for solo strings; Yin-Yan, for eleven solo strings.

Guitar Music—Tombeau de Robert de Visée, suite.

Orchestral Music—Cello Concerto No. 2; Violin Concerto.

Organ Music—Mandala.

Piano Music—Patchinko, for two pianos.

Vocal Music—Songe à Nouveau Rêvé, for soprano and orchestra.

ABOUT (supplementary)

Jolivet, H., Avec André Jolivet.

Joseph Jongen

1873–1953

See *Composers Since 1900.*

Paul Juon

1872–1940

See *Composers Since 1900.*

Dmitri Kabalevsky

1904–

For biographical sketch, list of earlier works, and bibliography, see *Composers Since 1900.*

MAJOR WORKS (supplementary)

Chamber Music—Rondo, for violin and piano.

Choral Music—A Game Chorus for Children, for chorus and piano; A Letter to the 30th Century, oratorio for solo voices, chorus, and orchestra.

Opera—The Sisters.

Khatchaturian

ABOUT (supplementary)

Krebs, S. D., Soviet Composers and the Development of Soviet Music; Schwarz, B., Music and Musical Life in Soviet Russia 1917–1970.

Aram Khatchaturian

1903–1978

For biographical sketch, list of earlier works, and bibliography, see *Composers Since 1900.*

The Bolshoi Ballet presented the American premiere of Khatchaturian's *Spartacus,* with the new Yuri Grigorevich choreography and a revised score, in New York on April 22, 1975. A screen production of *Gayane,* created and choreographed by Boris Eifman and performed by the Ballet Company of Riga, Latvia, was released in the United States in 1979 by Special Event Entertainment; this was the first time that Khatchaturian's famous ballet was seen in the United States.

Aram Khatchaturian died in his native Caucasus on May 1, 1978, after a prolonged illness.

ABOUT (supplementary)

Krebs, D., Soviet Composers and the Development of Soviet Music; Schwarz, B. Music and Musical Life in Soviet Russia: 1917–1978.

New York Times, May 3, 1978.

Leon Kirchner

1919–

For biographical sketch, list of earlier works, and bibliography, see *Composers Since 1900.*

Kirchner wrote *Music for Orchestra* on commission from the New York Philharmonic Orchestra to celebrate its 125th anniversary in 1967–1968. However, the work arrived two years late for that event when it was completed on October 7, 1969, and introduced by the New York Philharmonic under the composer's direction on October 17. "It was a case of better late than never," wrote Harold C. Schonberg in his review in the New York *Times.* "On the whole . . . this is a score so different from what we have been getting lately, so definitely derrière-garde that it actually sounds new. It takes a stand, it

has a point, goes some place and stops when it has had its say. Surges of orchestral power alternate with quieter sections and there is a feeling of personality. In short, Mr. Kirchner has contributed a well-written piece to the repertory." The initial success led to performances by the Los Angeles Philharmonic, the Chicago Symphony, the Philadelphia Orchestra, the Minnesota Symphony, and other orchestras. The work was repeated by the New York Philharmonic Orchestra in October 1972 with Pierre Boulez conducting. Harriett Johnson, critic of the New York *Post,* added to her initial praise of it: "The almost hypnotically imaginative piece is one of the most significant works to come from any American composer."

A Chicago program note described the work: "The music flows in one continuous piece, all growing out of the interval of the second, with which it begins in the oboe. It is not thematic in the usual sense, but it builds with textures, instrumental color, dynamic levels and particularly in the use of fluctuating tempos as the music moves from one musical event to another. Toward the end, the piece used controlled improvisation in which the speed is left to the discretion of the conductor."

It took Kirchner eighteen years to write his first opera, *Lily.* On commission from the Fromm Music Foundation in 1959, Kirchner began work on his libretto based on Saul Bellow's novel, *Henderson, the Rain King,* which took four years to complete. For the next fourteen years he worked on the score. In the course of working on the opera, a more direct use of the material resulted in a twenty-minute chamber-music work entitled *Lily,* for soprano, chamber orchestra, and electronic tape. The Ensemble introduced it in New York in March 1973, then recorded it for Columbia. The program described the composition as "a segment, self-contained but part of a larger theatrical piece based on Saul Bellow's novel." It was heard by Julius Rudel, director of the New York City Opera, who made it worthwhile for Kirshner to take leave from his professorial duties at Harvard to complete his opera. With this new commission, Kirchner spent 1973 working on the music as composer-in-residence in Rome and as Fellow of the Institute for Advanced Musical Studies at Stanford University in California in 1974–1975. The orchestration was completed in 1977 and the opera was finally performed by the New

York City Opera, with the composer conducting, on April 14, 1977.

Lily, a ninety-minute opera, without intermission, has as its main character Henderson, a vigorous, violent American multimillionaire who is dissatisfied with life and full of self-doubts. He goes on a trip to Africa to seek solutions to his personal problems and while there, he tries to remedy the sufferings of the Arnewi tribe. His failure to solve their problems can be compared to the failure of American culture and technology, which tries to intrude upon and change the culture of others. Lily, Henderson's wife, symbolizes Western decadence as opposed to African innocence in this pessimistic opera.

Writing in *Newsweek,* Hubert Saal said: "Kirchner's music has always disdained rigid formalism in favor of strong feeling and *Lily,* especially in the early episodes, is colorful, explosive and exotic in its angularity and dissonance. The music for Lily's scenes has an appropriately brittle and jaded quality. Henderson's music is jangling and febrile, befitting Bellow's cosmological complainer. For Arnewi, the music is generally serene, using woodwinds and percussion to evoke the untroubled jungle. In the Arnewi scenes, Kirchner employs amplified tape music that supports or blends with the live orchestra. The score is most successful in its efforts to contrast two cultures, alternating between the wordy ravings of the distraught Henderson and the non-verbal but highly articulate croonings of the noble savage."

Before the premiere of this opera in New York on March 18, 1976, the Performers Committee for 20th Century Music staged a Kirchner retrospective concert of his work from his 1948 Piano Sonata through excerpts from *Lily,* written in 1973. On May 2, 1979, the Baltimore Symphony under Sergiu Comissiona presented the premiere of Kirchner's *Metamorphosis,* for orchestra.

Despite his duties as Walter Bigelow Rosen Professor of Music at Harvard University since 1965, Kirchner had numerous commitments as conductor and pianist. He was pianist and conductor at the Marlboro Music Festival in Vermont (1965–1973); principal conductor of the Boston Philharmonia (1969–1971); conductor of the Harvard Chamber Players (since 1973); and the Harvard Chamber Orchestra (since 1978); he helped guide the Rockefeller Contemporary Music Program at the Marlboro Music Festival (1963–1973); he was appointed a member of the Board of Overseers of the Boston Symphony (1971); and was guest professor at the University of California in Los Angeles (1970–1971).

Kirchner was awarded the National Music Award from the Music Industry of America in 1976 "in honor of extraordinary contribution to the development and performance of American Music." He was also the recipient of the Brandeis University Creative Arts Award in Waltham, Massachusetts in 1977.

Kirchner said, "The thing that really strikes me more than anything else in music is not the intellectual concept or the structural material. I am attracted to the imagery, the humanistic aspect of the work and how it ignites my soul, my feelings. It's that which I adore in Webern and Schoenberg or in Messiaen: that touch, that smell—all the physical stuff."

MAJOR WORKS (supplementary)

Opera—Lily.

Orchestral Music—Music for Orchestra; Lily, for soprano, chamber orchestra, and electronic tape; Metamorphosis; Music for Flute and Orchestra.

ABOUT (supplementary)

High Fidelity/Musical America, January 1971, April 1977; New York Times, March 11, 1973, April 10, 1977; New Yorker, May 2, 1977; Opera News, April 16, 1977.

Zoltán Kodály

1882–1967

For biographical sketch, list of earlier works, and bibliography, see *Composers Since 1900.*

Kodály's *Dances of Galanta* and *Marosszék Dances* provided inspiration and music for a ballet, *Kodály Dances,* which received its world premiere in New York in January 1971 in a performance by the New York City Ballet.

Virtually all of Kodály's songs, beginning with Op. 1 (sixteen settings of folksongs) were performed by leading Hungarian singers and recorded for the first time (on the Qualiton label and released in 1978).

The writings of Kodály were assembled in *Selected Writings of Zoltán Kodály,* edited by Ferenc Bonis, published in London in 1974.

Krenek

ABOUT (supplementary)

Eösze, L., Zoltán Kodály: His Life in Pictures.

Ernst Krenek

1900–

For biographical sketch, list of earlier works, and bibliography, see *Composers Since 1900.*

Since 1970, Krenek has continued to be one of the most prolific composers of our time, his opus number exceeding two hundred twenty-five by 1980.

Sardakai (If Sardakai Goes Traveling), a comic opera to the composer's own libretto (1969–1970) was produced by the Hamburg State Opera on June 27, 1970, with the composer conducting; his Mass, *Gib uns den Frieden,* for vocal soloists, chorus, instrumentalists, and organ was premiered in the same city at the Holland Festival in 1971; and Heinz Holliger, Swiss oboist, helped to introduce *Kitharaulos,* for oboe, harp, and string orchestra which was written for him on commission. A version of *Kitharaulos* called *Aulokithara*—in which the string orchestra is replaced by electronic tape— was first heard on February 4, 1973, in Baltimore.

Flaschenpost vom Paradies (Bottled Message from Paradise), a humorous take-off on science set on the fictitious island of Migo-Migo (found previously in *Sardakai*) is a play for television, utilizing electronic tape, and it was shown in Vienna in 1974. *Spaetlese (Late Harvest),* a cycle of six songs for baritone and piano (to poems by Krenek) was written for Dietrich Fischer-Dieskau who presented it for the first time in 1974 at the Munich Festival. *Feierstag-Kantate (Anniversary Cantata)* for speaker, two vocal soloists, chorus, and orchestra with a text by Krenek and additional quotations from the writings of Hans Arp, Karl Kraus, and Walter Mehring, was written for the Berlin Festival where it was heard in September 1975. Krenek dedicated it "to myself for the jubilee year of 1975."

Krenek conducted the world premiere of *Dream Sequence,* for symphonic band, at the 19th National Conference of the College and Band Directors National Association at the University of Maryland at College Park in 1976. *They Knew What They Wanted,* three English stories adapted for narrator, oboe, piano, percussion, and electronic tape (with a text by Krenek) was premiered in New York City in 1978. This work proved to be "an entertainment executed with a master's touch: witty, laconic, neatly understated, not serious," wrote Andrew Porter in *The New Yorker. The Dissembler,* for baritone and chamber orchestra (with another Krenek text) was commissioned by the Chamber Music Society of Baltimore which premiered it on March 11, 1979. This work is a monologue by one who pretends to be an actor and impersonates various characters.

A week-long Krenek festival was held in the fall of 1975 in Palm Springs, California (where Krenek now makes his home) to honor his seventy-fifth birthday. Similar events took place in Minneapolis-St. Paul, Minnesota around the same time and at Santa Barbara, California, in April 1979. Twelve concerts spanned six decades of Krenek's creativity.

Krenek's 1930 opera, *Leben des Orest,* was performed first in America on November 14, 1975, by the Portland (Oregon) Opera. His provocative and highly successful jazz opera of *Jonny Spielt Auf* (1927) was performed in the United States, for the first time since its Metropolitan Opera premiere in 1929, by the New England Conservatory in Boston, conducted by Gunther Schuller, on May 12, 1976; it was its first time in English, in a translation by the composer and his wife.

Krenek received the Order of Merit for Science and Art by Austria in 1975; he was awarded an honorary doctorate in music by the New England Conservatory in Boston in 1976; and the state of Hesse, Germany, presented him with the Goethe Plaque in 1978.

In 1974, Krenek's book, *Horizons Circle,* comprised of lectures he gave at the University of California in San Diego, was published in California. Three years later, the university established a Krenek archive for all his manuscripts, personal papers, letters, etc., accumulated since his arrival in the United States in 1938. Earlier memorabilia can be found at the City Library in Vienna.

MAJOR WORKS (supplementary)

Band Music—Dream Sequence.

Choral Music—Gib uns den Frieden, Mass for vocal soloists, chorus, instrumentalists, and organ; Feierstag-Kantate, for speaker, two soloists, chorus, and orchestra.

Electronic Music—Tape and Double, for two pianos and electronic tape; Aulokithara (a version of Kitharaulos), for oboe, harp, and electronic tape; Flaschenpost vom Paradies, TV play with electronic tape; They Knew What They Wanted, three English stories adapted for narrator, oboe, piano, percussion, and electric tape.

Opera—Sardakai, comic opera.

Orchestral Music—Fivefold Enfoldment; Kitharaulos, for oboe, harp, and string orchestra; Static and Ecstatic, ten short pieces for chamber orchestra; Von Vorn Herein, for chamber ensemble; Auf und Ablehnung; Concerto for Organ and String Orchestra.

Organ Music—Four Winds Suite.

Vocal Music—Two Time Songs, for soprano and string quartet; Three Songs, for soprano and piano; Spaetlese, song cycle for baritone and piano; The Dissembler, monologue for baritone and chamber orchestra.

ABOUT (supplementary)

Knessl, L., Ernst Krenek; Rogge, W., Ernst Kreneks Opern—Spiegel der Zwanziger Jahre.

EZRA LADERMAN

Ezra Laderman

1924–

Ezra Laderman was born in Brooklyn, New York, on June 29, 1924, to Isidor and Leah Stock Laderman. He began composing at the High School of Music and Art in New York City and one of his earliest works was a piano concerto (1940) which brought him a prize at graduation. He served for four years (1942–1946) in the American armed forces during World War II, as a technical sergeant. His spare time was used to compose and he wrote a symphony called *Leipzig* (1945). In 1946, after being mustered out, he entered Brooklyn College in New York, where he wrote *Meditation on Isaiah,* a cello partita with the structure of a baroque suite. In this work he portrayed the moods of Isaiah as described in the Bible, at the same time reflecting on his own experiences on entering college.

Laderman received his Bachelor of Arts degree at Brooklyn College in 1950 and went on to Columbia University for post-graduate work in composition with Otto Luening, in prosody and opera with Douglas Moore, and in musicology with Paul Henry Lang. He also studied composition privately with Stefan Wolpe. While attending Columbia, Laderman married Aimlee H. Davis, a research biologist, on December 9, 1951 and his son, Isaiah, was born in 1955, the first of three children. His birth served as an incentive to Laderman to write Piano Sonata No. 2. Three years after receiving his Master of Arts degree at Columbia in 1952, Laderman was awarded the first of three Guggenheim Fellowships (the other two were in 1958 and 1964).

In the late 1950s, Laderman completed several chamber music works in which a mature style began to emerge. Elliott Schwarts analyzed Laderman's Sonata for Flute and Piano, and Sonata for Clarinet and Piano (written in 1957) in *Notes* as follows: "In both works, Laderman deals with highly chromatic themes, distinct in profile and endowed with unique intervallic characteristics. Within individual movements, the traditional arc of intensity (climaxes, contrasts, restatements) and tonal-harmonic scheme are skillfully achieved, and a cyclic use of identical material from one movement to the next is also evident. . . . One might note as well that the piano parts are not mere 'accompaniments,' but technically and musically match the sophisticated level of the woodwind writing; in each piece, therefore, both performers are to be regarded as equal partners." Reviewing Laderman's *Theme, Variations, and Finale,* for four woodwinds and four strings (1957), John Rockwell wrote in the New York *Times:* "The piece is unusual for its undoctrinaire stylistic freedom as well as light-hearted charm."

In addition to chamber music (which included his first string quartet in 1958–1959), Laderman

169

wrote three operas in the late 1950s: *Jacob and the Indians* (1956–1957), introduced in Woodstock, New York, on July 26, 1957; *Sarah* (1958), a one-act opera, first heard on November 30, 1958, in New York; and *Goodbye to the Clowns* (1959–1960) premiered in New York on May 22, 1960.

In 1960–1961 Laderman became a member of the music faculty at Sarah Lawrence College in Bronxville, New York. His children's opera, *The Hunting of the Snark,* based on a Lewis Carroll story, was heard in New York on March 25, 1961. That year he also wrote an oratorio, *The Eagle Stirred,* to a text by Clair Roskam, and a violin concerto. In 1962–1963 he completed *Songs for Eve,* a song cycle to poems by Archibald MacLeish; one of its songs, "The Riddles," became one of his most popular compositions.

Winning the Prix de Rome (1963) enabled Laderman to attend the American Academy in Rome. In that year, too, he completed his first symphony and the second string quartet, which had its world premiere at the Third Inter-American Music Festival in Washington, D.C., on May 8, 1965. He also wrote the score for the motion picture *The Eleanor Roosevelt Story,* which won an "Oscar" as the year's best documentary. After a year back at Sarah Lawrence College in 1965–1966, he became professor of composition and composer-in-residence at the State University of New York in Binghamton, New York in 1966–1967. He spent the summers of 1967 and 1968 as staff composer at the Bennington Composers Conference in Vermont.

The Six-Day War in the Middle East in 1967 inspired Laderman to write *From the Psalms* (1967–1968), for soprano and piano, a cycle of five songs with texts made up of words, phrases, and ideas from twenty psalms. Laderman later rewrote the composition for soprano and instruments (piano, violin, cello, flute, and clarinet). The new version was introduced by the Da Capo Chamber Players in New York on January 12, 1977.

On commission from CBS News, Laderman completed a biblical television opera, *And David Wept,* with a libretto by Joe Darion in 1970. It was based on the story of David's love for Bathsheba and his sending off to war and certain death Bathsheba's husband, Uriah. The premiere, on the CBS-TV network, was so successful that it was repeated and its first staged

performance took place in New York on May 31, 1980. In this score, speech (over an instrumental accompaniment) is as prominent as lyrical songs, duos, and trios. Peter G. Davis reported in the New York *Times* that "for this opera he has smoothed out the dissonant edges of his musical language considerably. The score is tonal, melodic and clearly the work of a craftsman who never makes a false step. While the style is quite eclectic . . . it is all blended skillfully."

CBS again commissioned Laderman to write Symphony No. 3, "Jerusalem," for the twenty-fifth anniversary of the State of Israel and it was introduced by the Jerusalem Symphony in 1973 (during the Middle East war). In four movements entitled "Beginning," "Exile," "Longing," and "Return," Laderman presented four different stages in Jewish history culminating in the establishment of Israel. *High Fidelity/Musical America* described the work as follows: "The first movement, built around a single motif which begins in the flutes and proliferates through the entire orchestra, is the easiest to appreciate on a single hearing. But I also liked the bitter outbursts near the end of the second movement, a Concertanto section for solo violin with liturgical overtones in the third movement, and some moments for hushed tremolo strings in the finale." The American premiere was heard over CBS-TV on April 3, 1977, during the Passover holiday.

In 1973, Laderman composed *Elegy* for unaccompanied viola on commission from Toby Appel, violist, who introduced it in New York on February 17, 1974. The composer wrote it to assuage his grief at the death of his eighty-three year old mother, a tragedy that was so traumatic, he could do no composing for some time. He rewrote the composition as a trio for three unaccompanied violas and renamed it *Other Voices.* Appel played all three parts on tape, then dubbed them into a single montage which was introduced over CBS-TV on March 20, 1977.

On February 3, 1979, at Binghamton, New York, the Tri-Cities Opera presented the world premiere of Laderman's opera, *Galileo Galilei.* This work had started out as a ninety-minute oratorio, *The Trials of Galileo,* with a text by Joe Darion. It was originally commissioned by CBS-TV and introduced on May 14, 1967; then the composer and librettist decided to enlarge it into a full-length opera, tracing the career of Galileo:

the Papal Council condemnation of his unorthodox teachings, his trial before the Inquisition, his torture, and recantation. In the epilogue Galileo, old and blind, dispatches his last book to Holland for publication. The score skillfully combined tonal and atonal elements, creating the high tensions and drama of the libretto by means of expressive declamations and discordant harmonies. The score also abounded with jingles, chants, refrains, "brought back," said Andrew Porter of *The New Yorker* "to underpin the free passages of recitative and lyrical arioso" as well as to build up extended scenes. He added, "The score is arresting. . . . The music is . . . decent, satisfying, intelligently and strongly made." In the New York *Times,* Harold C. Schonberg maintained that *Galileo Galilei* "will occupy an honorable place in the annals of American opera."

Laderman's Piano Concerto (1978) was premiered in Washington, D. C., in May 1979, and performed again in New York on May 14, 1979, by the American Composers Orchestra, with José Serebrier conducting, and Walter Ponce as soloist. Raymond Ericson reported on it in the New York *Times,* "It is a traditional three-movement piece, in which the piano makes many of the grand gestures to be found in 19th-century concertos. It is, to oversimplify the composer's description, about battles and reconciliations between tonal and atonal material. The conflict and resolutions are easy to follow and certainly hold the interest the first time around, and the frequent moves from simple to complex musical situations are often ingenious. This is a shrewdly made piece and a likable one."

Laderman continued to favor the concerto form with rewarding results. He wrote a violin concerto in 1979 for Elmar Olviera, who premiered it on December 12, 1980, as soloist with the Philadelphia Orchestra conducted by the composer. This was Laderman's first violin concerto for a full symphonic ensemble, since his earlier violin concerto (1963) was scored for chamber orchestra. Describing the second concerto in *High Fidelity/Musical America,* Daniel Webster said: "Laderman's concerto style vividly evoked that of the nineteenth-century virtuosi, for it made the soloist a dashing figure whose bravura carries him over all hazards." Obeisance to the past is again made in Laderman's Concerto for String Quartet and Orchestra (1980), which revives baroque and classical approaches. The

Alard String Quartet, for which it was written, introduced it with the Pittsburgh Symphony Orchestra, under André Previn on February 6, 1981.

Laderman's late compositions included String Quartet No. 6, written in 1976, for the Alard String Quartet which premiered it on November 24, 1980, in New York; *Music for Cain,* a large choral work (1979), was introduced at the Riverside Church in New York on Christmas Eve, 1979, and televised by CBS; and *Summer Solstice,* for orchestra (1980), which was commissioned by the Saratoga Performing Arts Center in New York, where it was first performed on August 15, 1980, with Michael Tilson Thomas conducting the Philadelphia Orchestra.

Laderman was president of the American Music Center in 1973–1976. In 1979 he resigned as professor and composer-in-residence at the State University of New York at Binghamton to become the director of the music program for the National Endowment for the Arts in Washington, D. C.

MAJOR WORKS

Chamber Music—6 string quartets; Sonata for Flute and Piano; Sonata for Clarinet and Piano; Theme, Variations, and Finale, for four woodwinds and four strings; Sonata for Violin and Piano; Nonette; Octet, for winds; Elegy, for solo viola (also for three solo violas, renamed Other Voices); Meditations on Isaiah, for cello; Celestial Bodies, for flute and string quartet; Cadence, for double string quartet, two flutes, and double-bass.

Choral Music—The Eagle Stirred, oratorio; The Trials of Galileo, rewritten as an opera; Thrive Upon the Rock; Music for Cain.

Operas—Jacob and the Indians; Sarah, television opera; Goodbye to the Clowns; The Hunting of the Snark, children's opera; Shadows Among Us; Galileo Galilei; And David Wept, television opera.

Orchestral Music—3 symphonies; 2 violin concertos; Concerto for Bassoon and Strings; Stanzas, for chamber orchestra; Magic Prison, for two narrators and orchestra; Satire; Concerto for Orchestra; Columbus for solo bass-baritone and orchestra; Concerto for String Quartet and Orchestra; Concerto for Piano and Orchestra; Summer Solstice; Concerto for String Quartet and Orchestra; Concerto for Viola and Orchestra.

Organ Music—Twenty-Four Short Preludes.

Piano Music—2 sonatas; Duo Concertante, for two pianos; Momenti.

Vocal Music—Songs for Eve, song cycle for soprano and piano; From the Psalms, song cycle for soprano

La Montaine

and piano (also for soprano and instruments); Songs from Michelangelo, for bass and piano.

ABOUT

Slonimsky, N., (ed.), Baker's Biographical Dictionary of Musicians (6th edition); Vinton, J. (ed.), Dictionary of Contemporary Music.

High Fidelity/Musical America, March 1980; New York Times, May 25, 1980.

John La Montaine

1920–

JOHN LA MONTAINE

John La Montaine was born in Chicago, Illinois, on March 17, 1920, to Sidney James La Montaine, civil engineer, and Rhoda Dulcina Wright La Montaine; his first eighteen years were spent in Oak Park, Illinois. One of his earliest recollections of music came from hearing his mother play hymns on the piano. Music, he said, was a compelling interest as far back as he could remember, and—in spite of extended study of the piano—he had the ambition to be a composer rather than a professional pianist from before the age of five. His early piano teachers included neighbors, Muriel Parker, Margaret Farr Wilson, and later, Max Landow at the Eastman School of Music. In 1931 he gave his first piano recital in Bloomington, Indiana, which featured the first piece of music he composed.

In 1935 he enrolled at the American Conservatory of Music in Chicago where, for three years, he studied theory with Stella Roberts. From 1938 on he attended the Eastman School of Music in Rochester, New York, where his principal composition teachers were Howard Hanson and Bernard Rogers, and where he received a Bachelor of Music degree in 1942.

Between 1942 and 1946, La Montaine served in the United States Navy and in 1945, while in uniform, he studied with Rudolph Ganz at the Chicago Musical College. Following his discharge from the Navy, he studied composition with Bernard Wagenaar at the Juilliard School of Music in New York and later with Nadia Boulanger at the American Conservatory in Fontainebleau, France.

At the same time, he was writing music beginning with Op. 1, a Toccata, for piano, and con-

La Montaine: lä mǒn' tān

tinuing with Op. 2, *Four Songs,* for soprano, piano, and violin or flute, Op. 3, Sonata, for piano, and Op. 4, *Invocation,* for voice and piano. Although essentially romantic in nature, these pieces differ radically from each other. Such a variety of approaches is characteristic of all of La Montaine's works.

His first major work was *Songs of the Rose of Sharon,* Op. 6. Conceived for soprano and orchestra, the composer later wrote a version for voice and piano. This work is a cycle of seven songs performed without interruption, with a text from the King James version of the Bible (Chapter 2, *Song of Solomon*). Eight years after its completion the work was finally introduced in Washington, D.C., by Leontyne Price with the National Symphony Orchestra under Howard Mitchell on May 31, 1956. It has subsequently been widely performed: by Leontyne Price (Australian premiere), Eleanor Steber (first recorded performance), Jessye Norman (first performances with the Philadelphia and Chicago Symphony orchestras). The latest New York performance was in 1975 with the American Symphony Orchestra and soloist Jessye Norman. "The work holds up quite well after all these years," commented Donal Henahan in the New York *Times.*

Between 1950 and 1954 La Montaine was pianist and celestist with the NBC Symphony Orchestra under Arturo Toscanini who encouraged him as a composer. For eight years (1950–1958), La Montaine's compositional output was meager, but included his Op. 7, a piano suite

172

entitled *A Child's Picture Book,* and Op. 8, a Sonata for Violoncello and Piano, neither of which portended his soon-to-blossom creativity. In 1958, on commission from the Ford Foundation, he was able to devote himself to completion of his Concerto for Piano and Orchestra, Op. 9, his most ambitious work to date. When Jorge Bolet, pianist, and the National Symphony under Howard Mitchell, introduced the work on November 25, 1958, it was received enthusiastically by both audience and critics, and it won the Pulitzer Prize in 1959. In addition, on a grant from the American Academy of Arts and Letters it was recorded in 1962 by the Oklahoma City Symphony Orchestra under Guy Fraser Harrison, with Karen Keys as soloist. Jorge Bolet performed it again with the Boston Symphony under Charles Munch, and it was performed by the Cincinnati Symphony, the San Francisco Symphony, and other orchestras in the United States and Europe. The composer described the work as follows: "The concerto affirms both the lyric and virtuoso capabilities of the piano. The first movement is bold and decisive, classic form, romantic in content. The second movement is slow and introspective, rising to an overwhelming climax. It is an elegy in memory of the composer's sister, Isabel La Montaine. The Finale, in quadruple meter, is brilliant, rhythmic and marchlike, with some jazz influence, interrupted twice by an extended songful passage of great intensity in triple meter. All the thematic and passage material in the final movement is derived from the opening of first movement."

In 1959 La Montaine was awarded a Guggenheim Fellowship which was extended to a second year when he immersed himself in medieval literature and music, planning to compose a trilogy of liturgical operas based on medieval miracle plays. Interrupted by an extended illness, he completed the first of these operas, *Novellis, Novellis,* Op. 31, in 1960, and its premiere took place at the Washington Cathedral, on December 24, 1961, under the direction of Paul Callaway. *Novellis, Novellis* is a forty-five minute work that deals with the Annunciation and Birth of Jesus. Under a grant from the Martha Baird Rockefeller Foundation, the opera was later performed at the Riverside Church in New York and has since been performed somewhere in the United States every year.

In spite of illness, he completed a number of successful works. On commission from the New Haven Symphony Orchestra and a grant from the William Inglis Morse Trust for Music, La Montaine composed a large work for orchestra in 1959. Encouraged by the success of the *Rose of Sharon,* he decided to set the entire Song of Solomon to music, resulting in *Fragments from the Song of Songs,* Op. 29, for soprano and orchestra. The premiere took place on April 14, 1959, with Adele Addison as soloist, and the New Haven Symphony under Frank Brieff. The work was highly acclaimed, and later performed by Adele Addison with the New York Philharmonic and the San Francisco Symphony Orchestras.

In 1960 La Montaine won the Rheta Sosland Chamber Music Competition for his String Quartet, Op. 16, which extensively employs inversion of thematic elements and motive development. A year later, as the first composer to be commissioned to compose a work for a Presidential Inauguration, he wrote *Overture: From Sea to Shining Sea,* Op. 30. It was performed by the National Symphony under Howard Mitchell on January 20, 1961, at the Inaugural Concert for President and Mrs. John F. Kennedy.

In 1961 La Montaine was Visiting Professor of Composition at the Eastman School of Music, his alma mater, which later awarded him the Distinguished Alumni Award. In 1962 he was composer-in-residence at the American Academy in Rome.

An effort to analyze bird calls, while visiting friends in Mount Kisco, New York, in 1963 proved so fascinating that he later pursued it widely in travels to Africa, India, Nepal, and New Guinea, where he lived with natives, recording every sound in nature. This was in preparation for composing a work for piano and orchestra, *Birds of Paradise,* Op. 34, which was premiered by the Eastman-Rochester Symphony under Howard Hanson in Rochester, New York, in April 1964. It was later performed by the Los Angeles Philharmonic under Zubin Mehta. In an article for the *Music Journal,* La Montaine wrote: "What would happen if we opened our ears to the fresh, unsullied sounds that nature makes—the real sounds—not simplified and vulgarized imitations? What would happen if we were to accept these materials and let our imagination roam from that premise? . . . The true notation of a song sparrow or a western meadow lark, or the croaks of a family of frogs would astound us all. . . .Nature is a legitimate source of raw material . . . perhaps the most nourishing, the healthiest, the richest, the most delightful and most needed source of raw material for the making of art."

From the Kazinga Channel in Africa and hundreds of other remote spots, La Montaine's catalog of bird and animal sounds would become source material for some of his later works, including the *Mass of Nature,* Op. 37, for narrator, chorus, and orchestra. Although the complex work was completed in 1966, it was not performed until May 26, 1976, at the Washington Cathedral by the Cathedral Choral Society under the direction of Paul Callaway. The two related works on the program were based on the same thematic material, *Te Deum,* Op. 35, for narrator, chorus, wind orchestra, and percussion, and *Birds of Paradise,* Op. 34, forming the trilogy of works called *Sacred Service.*

In 1966, *Birds of Paradise* came to the attention of Gerald Arpino who choreographed the work for the Joffrey Ballet with the title *Nightwings.* The premiere of the ballet, which remained in the company's repertory four years, took place on September 7, 1966, in New York. According to Clive Barnes of the New York *Times, Nightwings* "has a nightmarish quality between fantasy and reality . . . The work has an atmosphere so strong you could almost reach out and touch it."

The warm reception of the first ballet score encouraged another work for the dance. Jean Woodbury had choreographed an early set of *Twelve Relationships for Piano,* Op. 10, for the Repertory Dance Theater of Utah, and the company then commissioned *Incantation for Jazz Band,* Op. 39, an intense, vibrant ballet. It was premiered in New York City in 1971 and was later performed at the Arcosanti Festival in Arizona.

In 1966, an anonymous benefactor and Washington Cathedral commissioned the completion of the remaining two operas of La Montaine's projected *Christmas Trilogy,* that began with *Novellis, Novellis. The Shephardes Playe,* Op. 38, had its premiere at the Washington Cathedral on December 24, 1967, produced by Richard Kirksen and directed by Paul Callawat. As with the other opera librettos of the *Trilogy, Shepardes Playe,* was adapted from medieval miracle plays, and used only original texts. The opera was televised nationally by the ABC Network a

year later, and awarded the 1969 Sigma Alpha Iota National Television Award as the year's best single TV musical. Critics reviewed the three operas: *Musical America* described *Novellis, Novellis* as "sensitive, truthful, beautiful," Paul Hume in the Washington *Post* called a scene in the *Shephardes Playe* "one of the loveliest moments in the history of music in the theater," and Hume wrote that in the grandest of the three operas, *Erode the Greate,* Op. 40, "La Montaine has caught the singular spirit of simplicity of the humble, the majesty of the baby King, the exotic journeying of the Three Kings, and the terrible envy of the killer-king Herod." The opera, introduced at the Washington Cathedral on New Year's Eve, 1969, was based on a medieval ballad by Guillaume de Machault, with part-writing of the song of the shepherd boy Trowle intact. In addition, the extant music originally associated with performances of the medieval miracle plays is incorporated in various ways into the operas. A doctoral thesis analyzing the Trilogy and its medieval influence was written by Harold Alexander Daugherty at the University of Southern California in 1976.

In January 1969 Mrs. Jouett Shouse commissioned a work for the opening of the Kennedy Center for the Performing Arts, in Washington, D.C., and the dedication of the Filene organ which she donated, with the sounds of nature and based on the writings of Thoreau. La Montaine wrote what he feels to be his most important work up to that time, *Wilderness Journal,* Op. 41, whose premiere opened the second season at the Kennedy Center on October 10, 1972, with Donald Gramm as bass baritone, Paul Callaway at the organ, and the National Symphony conducted by Antal Dorati. In the Washington *Star,* Irving Lowens noted that the Thoreau texts were "clothed . . . in a sound-web of surpassing loveliness, embroidered with bird calls and other sounds of nature. His achievement is perhaps all the more remarkable because he elected to base the piece on a tone row developed in strictly serial fashion. Despite this dedication to dodecaphony, the work sounds quite consonant and rings pleasantly in the ear."

In February 1973, the Institute of the Arts and Humanistic Studies of the Pennsylvania State University commissioned a major work to commemorate the American bicentennial. La Montaine gradually evolved the idea of a documentary opera-extravaganza entitled, *Be Glad*

Then America, Op. 43, subtitled "A Decent Entertainment from the Thirteen Colonies." The text of the opera-spectacle was assembled from letters, speeches, journals, newspapers, and broadsides from 18th-century colonial America and La Montaine spent two years tracing events leading to the signing of the Declaration of Independence. A chorus represents "We the People," and other main characters include King George, a Town Crier, and one singer who plays the parts of eight different American Patriots. Daniel Webster of the Philadelphia *Inquirer* said, "He avoided the usual dramatic means. No three-dimensional characters emerge. Tom Paine speaks, King George fumes ... Sam Adams ignites the colonists and Patrick Henry gives the incendiary speech. The first-act finale is a reenactment of the Boston Tea Party; the second act recreates the Battle of Lexington; and the opera ends with the singing of William Billings' 'Chester' (the most popular song inspired by and written during the Revolutionary War) on a stage filled with soldiers and flags." (Another Billings anthem, "An Anthem for Fast Day," gave La Montaine the title of his opera.) The opera was performed by Donald Gramm, Richard Lewis, David Lloyd, and Odetta, with the Pennsylvania State University Choirs and the Pittsburgh Symphony Orchestra under the direction of Sarah Caldwell on February 6, 1976. *Be Glad Then America* was, according to Allen Hughes in his review in the New York *Times,* "definitely not an opera in any conventional sense. But it is filled with drama, both implied and overt, and it would be a hard-hearted American indeed who did not feel a lump in his throat as the signing of the Declaration of Independence began the climactic conclusion of the work. ... It is a vivid and eloquent celebration of a momentous era in the founding of the nation." It was televised nationally by the Public Broadcasting System on July 4 and 10, 1977.

A new facet of La Montaine's creative ability was stimulated in 1977 by a Hymn Society of America commission resulting in *Three Hymns and an Anthem.* Severely diminished eyesight due to cataracts kept La Montaine from work on large orchestral scores and he became deeply interested in composing hymns, in fact, an entire hymn book. The second set of hymns, based on texts of John Greenleaf Whittier soon followed. *The Whittier Service,* Op. 43, for chorus, organ, and guitar had its premiere on May 20, 1979, at

the Washington Cathedral by the Washington Cathedral Choral Society under the direction of Paul Callaway.

John La Montaine was visiting professor of composition at several educational institutions, including the Eastman School of Music, in Rochester, New York, the University of Utah in Salt Lake City, and Whittier College in California, where he held the Nixon Chair as the Nixon Distinguished Scholar in 1977. In July 1975, La Montaine and composer Paul J. Sifler founded Fredonia Press for exclusive publication of the works of both composers. They extended their activities two years later by establishing Fredonia Discs to record their works.

La Montaine divides his time between New York and Hollywood, California. His hobbies are amateur carpentry, mountain climbing, and fishing.

MAJOR WORKS

Chamber Music—Sonata for Violoncello and Piano, Op. 8; String Quartet, Op. 16; Sonata for Flute Solo, Op. 24; Quartet for Woodwinds, Op. 24A; Incantation for Jazz Band, Op. 39; Scherzo for Four Trombones; Conversations, Op. 42; Twelve Studies, for two flutes, Op. 46; Canonic Variation, for flute and clarinet, Op. 47; Come into My Garden, and My Beloved, Let Us Go Forth, for flute and piano, Op. 49.

Choral Music—Songs of the Nativity, Op. 13, for a cappella chorus; Nonsense Songs from Mother Goose, Op. 19, for chorus and piano; God of Grace and God of Glory, Op. 22, for chorus and organ; Wonder Tidings, Op. 23, for soloists, chorus, harp, and percussion; Te Deum, Op. 35, for narrator, chorus, wind orchestra, and percussion; Three Psalms, Op. 6, for chorus and small orchestra; Mass of Nature, Op. 37, for chorus, narrator, and orchestra; The Nine Lessons of Christmas, Op. 44, for chorus, soloists, narrator, harp, and percussion; Holiday Greeting, for chorus with piano or organ; Merry Let Us Part, and Merry Meet Again, for chorus with piano; Nativity Morn, for voices with organ and chimes or handbells.

Operas—Spreading the News, Op. 27, one-act opera; The Christmas Trilogy (three pageant operas based on medieval miracle plays); Novellis, Novellis, Op. 31, The Shephardes Playe, Op. 38, and Erode the Greate, Op. 40; Be Glad Then America, Op. 43.

Orchestral Works—Songs of the Rose of Sharon, Op. 29, biblical cycle for soprano and orchestra (or piano); Concerto for Piano and Orchestra, Op. 9; Canons for Orchestra, Op. 10A; Ode for Oboe and Orchestra, Op. 11; Sonata for Orchestra, Op. 12A; Jubilant Overture, Op. 20; Symphony No. 1, Op. 28; Fragments from the Song of Songs, Op. 29, Biblical Cycle, for soprano and orchestra; Overture: From Sea to Shining Sea, Op. 30; A Summer's Day, Op. 32; Canticle for Orchestra, Op.

33; Birds of Paradise, Op. 35, for piano and orchestra; Incantation for Jazz Band, Op. 39; Wilderness Journal, Op. 41, for bass-baritone, organ, and orchestra; Overture: An Early American Sampler, Op. 43A; Concerto for Flute and Orchestra, Op. 48.

Organ Music—Evensong for Organ; Processional; Wilderness Journal, Op. 41, for bass-baritone, organ, and orchestra.

Piano Music—Toccata, Op. 1; Sonata for Piano, Op. 3; A Child's Picture Book, Op. 7; Twelve Relationships, Op. 10, a set of canons; Fuguing Set for Piano, Op. 14; Concerto for Piano and Orchestra, Op. 9; Six Dance Preludes, Op. 18; Sonata for Piano, four hands, Op. 25; Copycats, Op. 26 (canons for young pianists); A Summer's Day, sonnet for piano; Jugoslav Dance; Venice West Blues.

Vocal Music—Four Songs, Op. 2, for soprano, with piano and violin or flute; Invocation, Op. 4, for medium voice and piano; Six Sonnets of Shakespeare, Op. 12, for high or medium voice and piano, orchestral version for high voice only; Songs of Nativity, Op. 13A, for medium voice, organ, and small percussion; Three Poems of Holly Beye, Op. 15, for medium voice and piano; Stopping by Woods, for voice and piano.

ABOUT

Slonimsky, N., (ed.) Baker's Biographical Dictionary of Musicians (6th edition); Vinton, J. (ed.), Dictionary of Contemporary Music.

Benjamin Lees

1924–

For biographical sketch, list of earlier works, and bibliography, see *Composers Since 1900.*

Lees's Symphony No. 3, commissioned by and dedicated to the Detroit Symphony Orchestra, was first performed on January 16, 1969, with Sixten Ehrling conducting. While writing this symphony, Lees had in mind "a world of computers, satellites and space exploration," he revealed, and he tried to find some new meaning "in a period of revolutionary social upheaval unprecedented in history." His symphony, "in a different garb and, coincidentally, with a contemporary instrument—the tenor saxophone," has three movements. Each movement is preceded by a slow interlude for tenor saxophone and percussion and the final movement melds in a Postlude where elements of earlier movements are recalled while the saxophone is played in opposition to them. Thus the saxophone, a "modern" instrument, is played solo versus tutti.

Medea in Corinth, a one-act opera completed in 1970, received its world premiere in London on January 10, 1971, by the Grosvenor Ensemble and on May 26, 1974, it was telecast over the CBS network in the United States. An adaptation of the Euripides drama by Robinson Jeffers, the half-hour work calls for a cast of four.

The Trumpet of the Swan, for narrator and orchestra was first performed by the Philadelphia Orchestra under William Smith on May 13, 1972. The composer used a poetic and whimsical text by E. B. White in which a father swan, determined to give his mute cygnet a voice, breaks into a music shop, steals a trumpet, and teaches his cygnet how to play it. The cygnet's ability to make music not only brings him a love, Serena, but also an engagement with the Philadelphia Orchestra. The score calls for the actual breaking of glass, a merry gigue when the cygnet learns to play the trumpet, and provides for haunting songs by the lovers. "His music," wrote Nicolas Slonimsky in *Tempo,* "tells the swan's story on his own terms and in his own personal idiom."

In a more serious vein are Sonata No. 2, for violin and piano, and the *Etudes,* for piano and orchestra. The Sonata was commissioned by the McKim Fund of the Library of Congress and was introduced in Washington, D.C., by Rafael Druian (violinist) and Ilse von Alpenheim (pianist) on May 8, 1973. In *High Fidelity/Musical America,* George Gelles called it "a work of enormous craft and confidence, traditional in the tonal bias of its language, conventional in the interplay of its themes, yet vital and interesting." *Etudes* was commissioned by Joe L. and Barbara B. Albritton for pianist James Dick. The Houston Symphony Orchestra under Lawrence Foster presented the world premiere with Dick as soloist on October 28, 1974. The five Etudes alternate between fast and slow tempi and between rhythmic drives and lyrical outpourings. The first Etude has a harmony dominated by an interval in second and rapid motion on the piano, while the second Etude is more leisurely, offering a cantabile melody by the flute over broken chord figures on the piano. In the third, devices of the past recall etudes by Chopin and Debussy, the fourth is a study in sixths, and the fifth, in thirds. Irving Lowens placed the music in our time, in reporting from Houston to the Washington *Star-News,* "but its connection with the past is just as evident. In this particular piece, there seems to be an underlying sense of malaise, a hint of suppressed anger, that makes it peculiarly a product of the United States in 1974. . . . It has the immediacy of appeal which marks genuine, passionately felt music."

The National Symphony Orchestra in Washington, D.C., commissioned Lees to write an orchestral work in honor of the American bicentennial. *Passacaglia for Orchestra* was performed by the National Symphony under Antal Dorati on April 13, 1976. Paul Hume described it in the Washington *Post* as "one of the finest and most impressive scores Lees has created. The theme is highly chromatic, slightly Tristanesque in tone and one that immediately inspires the compoer to a rich variety of ideas. Eloquent solos, notably for clarinet and deeper brass, share the spotlight with massed strings and wind choirs. The familiar matter of augmentation becomes the means to superb effects. The music has power and lyric beauty."

Premieres of two other impressive works by Lees took place in 1976: *Variations for Piano and Orchestra,* was presented by the Dallas Symphony under Louis Lane and Eugene List as soloist on March 31. It was commissioned by the Music Teachers National Association for its 100th anniversary and consisted of an original theme, eleven variations (each with a specific technical study for the pianist), and a coda. *Concerto for Woodwind Quintet and Orchestra* was commissioned and introduced on October 7 by Aldo Ceccato conducting the Detroit Symphony for the American bicentennial. In this work, the orchestra's first-desk woodwind players (flute, oboe, clarinet, bassoon, and horn) are highlighted against the background of a large orchestra (minus woodwinds) and an expanded percussion section. A reviewer for *High Fidelity/Musical America* wrote, "The fast opening section introduced and developed two thematic ideas. The material was treated to some jolting shifts in meter and extremes in volume and timbre. . . . The second section's opening sounded like a unique vintage of Bartókian night music. . . . Near the end, each of the soloists . . . displayed his virtuosity in a series of cadenzas punctuated by insistent staccato jabs from the orchestra."

Lees, who was professor of composition at the Peabody Conservatory in Baltimore and Queens College in New York, resigned from both positions in 1969. He was composer-in-residence at the Manhattan School of Music in New York in

1970–1972; composer-in-residence at the University of Wisconsin in Milwaukee during the summer of 1973 and at the International Piano Festival Institute in Round-Top, Texas, in 1974; and visiting professor at the Juilliard School of Music in New York in 1976–1977.

Lees married Leatrice Banks in 1948 and they have a daughter, Janet. His sole hobby is photography but he explained it "is usually limited to summer snapping."

MAJOR WORKS (supplementary)

Chamber Music—Sonata No. 2, for violin and piano; Collage, for string quartet, woodwind quintet, and percussion; Dialogue, for cello and piano; String Quartet No. 3.

Opera—Medea in Corinth, one-act opera.

Orchestral Music—Symphony No. 3; The Trumpet of the Swan, for narrator and orchestra; Etudes, for piano and orchestra; Labyrinths, for symphonic wind ensemble; Passacaglia for Orchestra; Variations for Piano and Orchestra; Concerto for Woodwind Quintet and Orchestra; Scarlatti Portfolio, seven piano sonatas by Domenico Scarlatti in an orchestral transformation; Mobiles, for chamber orchestra.

Vocal Music—Staves, song cycle for soprano and piano.

ABOUT (supplementary)

Tempo (London), June 1975.

Anatol Liadov

1855–1914

See *Composers Since 1900.*

Rolf Liebermann

1910–

For biographical sketch, list of earlier works, and bibliography, see *Composers Since 1900.*

Administrative duties as general director of the Hamburg Opera allowed Liebermann little time for composition, and his creative endeavors since 1969 have been sparse. From 1969 to 1980 Liebermann was the artistic director of the Paris Opéra where he ended his tenure with a farewell performance of the same opera with which it had

Ligeti

begun, *The Marriage of Figaro,* on July 14, 1980, in a free performance for the people of Paris.

In 1974, Liebermann was designated Commander of the French Legion of Honor and in 1975 he received an honorary doctorate in philosophy from the University of Bern in Switzerland. He is the author of *Actes et Entr'actes* (1976).

ABOUT (supplementary)

Riess, C., Rolf Liebermann; Nennen Sie mich Einfach Musiker; Scharberth, I., and Paris, H. (eds.), Rolf Liebermann zum 60 Geburstag.

New York Times, July 15, 1970.

GYÖRGY LIGETI

György Ligeti

1933–

György Sándor Ligeti, a major figure in European avant-garde music, was born of Hungarian parentage in Dicsöszentmarón, a city south of Cluj, Transylvania (Rumania), on May 28, 1923. His family moved to Cluj soon after his birth, and it was there that he received his early musical and academic schooling. He attended the Cluj Conservatory between 1941 and 1943, as a composition pupil of Ferenc Farkas. During the summers of 1942 and 1943 he studied composition with Pál Kadosa in Budapest. Then, from 1945 to 1949, he attended the Academy of Music in Budapest where his teachers included Farkas and Sándor Veress, among others. He recalled, "It was a time of isolation from the music of Western Europe. My greatest influences were Bartók, Stravinsky and Berg, the three modern composers I knew best. It was not until 1952–1953 that I even heard indirectly of new ideas, that electronic music existed, and serial music, and that in America there was a man called Cage."

Inspired by Bartók, Ligeti toured Rumania for a year, after graduation from the Academy, to do research in folk music. In 1950 he realized that he was no longer interested either in a post-Bartókian idiom nor in folk music; that, as composer, he would have to seek out an altogether new language, new methods, and a new musical ideology. He added, "I was twenty-seven, and living in Budapest totally isolated from all com-

positional ideas, trends, and techniques which had emerged in the West since the war. It was at that time I first conceived the idea of a static, self-contained music, without either development or traditional rhythmic configurations. These ideas were vague at first, and then I lacked the courage and the compositional and technical powers to realize them in sound. Although traditional modes of thought appeared questionable, I still clung to regular metrical groupings."

In 1951 he began experimenting with a new kind of music, simple in structure, rhythm, and sonority, but, he said, "starting from nothing. My approach was virtually Cartesian, in that I treated all the music I knew and loved as irrelevant, indeed invalid, to my purpose. I posed myself such problems as: what can I do with one single note? with its octave? with an interval? with two intervals? with specific interrelationships which could serve as the basic elements of a formation of rhythms and intervals?" He tried out his new ideas in composing a few pieces which had something in common with the twelve-tone system—even though at that time he was totally unfamiliar with Schoenberg's method and the music of Webern. He admitted, "My supposed self-liberation was, of course, doomed to partial frustration by the isolation in which I was working, for the worthy Bartókian idiom still came through as a stylistic feature. . . . So my works of that period strike me as being thoroughly heterogeneous; in style, naive in their absence of orientation, inadequate and half-baked as solutions."

Ligeti: lĭ′ gĕ tē

178

From 1950 to 1956, Ligeti taught harmony, counterpoint, and analysis at the College of Music in Budapest. At the same time, he was being profoundly affected by new scores, recordings, and musical ideas that were beginning to invade Hungary. "It was as though air was rushing into a vacuum and suddenly had been released," he said. *Metamorphoses Nocturnes,* for string quartet (1953–1954), premiered in Vienna in 1958, and the choruses, *Night* and *Morning* (1955) represented a break with Bartókian influences and folk traditions.

According to Ligeti, the Hungarian uprising in 1956 sent him fleeing from that country. "We had no passports. The frontiers were guarded and mined." Suffering untold hardships in escaping, he settled permanently in Vienna, and in 1967 became an Austrian citizen. He chose Vienna "not out of sentiment," he revealed. "It was just that we had no reason to go farther. It was the first city we came to. It was close to Hungary."

In 1957, he went to Cologne to work at the Studio for Electronic Music, living at first with Karlheinz Stockhausen, his good friend who encouraged him in his initial electronic experiments. In 1959, Ligeti became instructor at the Summer International Courses for New Music in Darmstadt.

In actually composing electronic music for the first time in *Artikulation* for four-track tape in 1958, which was introduced in Cologne in March of that year, Ligeti also clarified his own goals in music. Rejecting serialism, he explained, "I soon came to realize that serial music brought in its wake an indifferent attitude to harmony and a leveling-out of interval characteristics." An even more radical direction seemed necessary to him: "Intervals and rhythms were to be completely disintegrated. This was no mere iconoclasm: it was to make room for the creation of fine-spun musical networks where the formative function should devolve primarily upon the way in which the structure is woven. . . . This is done by the rather . . . complex product of interlacing numerous strands of intervals and rhythm. The musical event is thus no longer manifest on the plane of harmony and rhythm, but as a web-like sound complex. I thus penetrated a realm of subtle sonorities forming an area intermediate between sound and noise; the sounds were hidden and effected by the complex interweaving of parts." Thus he developed "micropolyphony," an elaborate polyphonic texture of many individual parts.

His first work in what is known as "Klangenflaschencompositen"—or composition utilizing blocks of sounds—was *Apparitions,* for orchestra, completed in 1959. The title, according to Nicolas Slonimsky, suggests "a transitory manifestation of ephemeral phenomenon." When the new work was first performed at the Festival of the International Society for Contemporary Music in Cologne on June 19, 1960, it created a sensation. *Atmosphères,* for large orchestra, no percussion, and two pianos, was completed in 1961 and introduced at the Donaueschingen Festival of Contemporary Music under Hans Rosbaud on October 22 of that year. Both works brought Ligeti recognition as a leader in Germany's musical avant-garde, the first to break with the serialists in favor of new horizons.

Atmosphères, Ligeti said, "presumably occupies an extreme position, which possibly may be interpreted as dead end. But often it is the apparent dead end that conceals a gateway opening into fresh fields." It was commissioned by the Southwest German Radio in Baden-Baden and was dedicated to the memory of the composer's compatriot and friend, composer Matyas Seiber, who had been killed in a car accident. Writing in the Edinburgh Festival program (where it was performed in 1977), Gerald Larner explained: "*Atmosphères* is all color, a series of stripes painted down the canvas, some wider than others, some overlapping, some with horizontal bands, some splashed by different colors, each one varying in shade and giving the illusion of a play of light moving on the surface . . . There are perhaps ten distinguishable bands of color, none of them lasting more than a minute." Leonard Bernstein and the New York Philharmonic performed this work in 1964; Seiji Ozawa and the Philadelphia Orchestra performed it in 1965; and both Leonard Bernstein and Herbert von Karajan recorded it. A brief segment from the composition is used in the Stanley Kubrick picture, *2001: A Space Odyssey* (as well as two other Ligeti excerpts).

In *Aventures* (1962; Hamburg, Germany, April 4, 1963) and *Nouvelles Aventures* (1962–1965; Hamburg, Germany, May 26, 1966), both for three voices and seven instruments, Ligeti explored the expressivity of the human voice. In Nouvelles, three people imprisoned in a room are subjected to extreme pressures and they voice despair, fear, boredom, loathing. (Ligeti planned this work as concert music, but it was also staged.) Every possible sound of which the human voice is capable is heard: falsetto, inhaling, exhaling, shouts, gasps, moans, groans, laughs, gulps. Sounds from a bursting paper bag or the rubbing of sandpaper on a suitcase, are interpolated, and singers and instrumentalists engage in discussions, voices against instruments. A critic wrote about it in *Stereo Review:* "The effect is at first comic rather than dramatic. Yet in the end these are curiously abstract works which use some of the most evocative forms of human expression to make a kind of pure chamber music. The instruments pick up where the voices leave off and both instrumental and vocal interjections take place in a curiously empty universe—as if it were more difficult and even more necessary than ever to make art and artistic expression in the void."

Ligeti became even more provocative (and more prominent in music circles) with *Poème Symphonique* (1962), which caused a stir at its world premiere in Hilvershum, Germany, in September 1963, and at its American premiere at the Buffalo (New York) Festival of Arts Today on March 4, 1965. This composition is scored for one hundred metronomes, manipulated by ten musicians, who perform at different speeds, and end the composition when the last sounding metronome is heard. As the composer told Nicolas Slonimsky: "I composed my piece . . . as a sort of persiflage of chance music (believing that little automatons can do this job better than human performers) partly as an experiment in 'continuous form' resulting in a gradual 'rhythmic diminuendo,' the metronomes stopping one by one."

Ligeti's interest in the music of the absurd led him into becoming a participant in "24 Hours," a festival of environmental anti-music featuring "non-events," in Wuppertal, Germany, on June 5, 1965. Ligeti's contribution was *The Future of Music* in which the composer stood on the stage in front of his audience with a stopwatch; he scrutinized the audience; then he used audience-reaction as the material for his composition.

Requiem, a setting of three sections of the Mass, for soprano, mezzo-soprano, chorus, and orchestra, received its world premiere in Stockholm on March 14, 1965. (It was later heard on September 21, 1968, at the Festival of the International Society for Contemporary Music in Warsaw.) Parts of *Kyrie* were used in the motion picture *2001: A Space Odyssey* (as well as the already-mentioned brief abstract from *Atmosphères* and another abstract from the sixteen-part chorus, *Lux Aeterna,* composed in 1966), much to Ligeti's displeasure, for he felt that his music had been distorted and emasculated and he successfully sued for adequate financial compensation. A critic for the New York *Times* wrote: "Far from being restricted to the kind of fearsome stridency heard in *Kyrie,* his *Requiem* explores a full, liturgically valid range of emotions and sonorities, while holding onto a unity of mood by means of a few marvelously effective devices. Ligeti often augments note values to the point where the ear no longer grasps words or realizes that the textures are achieved by ancient polyphonic techniques." Instead, Ligeti lays down "a complex tone cluster and then slowly moves the voices around in steps and half steps."

In 1961 Ligeti was appointed visiting professor of composition at the Musical High School in Stockholm, and in 1964 he was given an honor rarely bestowed on a foreigner when he was elected to the Royal Swedish Academy. In Stockholm he came into friendly contact with Goeran Gentele, director of the Stockholm Opera who, in 1966, commissioned an opera for his company and his own direction. When Gentele became director of the Metropolitan Opera in New York in 1970, a problem arose, since Ligeti's opera was contracted to Stockholm Opera and Gentele could no longer direct it. Gentele's sudden death before he assumed his Metropolitan position frustrated intentions to produce the opera in New York. Ligeti then decided to abandon the opera as planned, and write a new one with a new libretto which took several years to be written and produced.

Meanwhile, Ligeti's international fame was growing through major works in the late 1960s. Concerto for Cello and Orchestra—a two-movement, fourteen-minute composition completed in 1966—was introduced in Berlin on April 19, 1967. When this Concerto was performed on October 28, 1971, by Siegfried Palm and the New York Philharmonic Orchestra under Michael Gielen, Harold C. Schonberg described it in the New York *Times* as follows: "The first [movement] consists almost entirely of long-held, static notes, mostly pianissimo. Occasionally, mysterious dots of sound vary the texture and there is one build-up. The second movement makes use of oscillating rather than held notes. The big moment is the silent cadenza, with the cellist's fingers dancing nimbly over the fingerboard, the bow slowly moving, but without any sound."

Of all Ligeti's works, *Lontano,* for orchestra, gained American recognition following its premiere at the Donaueschingen Festival on October 22, 1967 because it was performed most often in the United States. Both the title and Ligeti's intent suggest a feeling of remoteness in a composition totally devoid of melody, harmony, or rhythm. A similar feeling is aroused in *Ramifications,* for twelve solo instruments, and also for chamber orchestra, written in 1967 on commission .from the Koussevitzky Music Foundation. It was introduced in Berlin on April 23, 1969, and heard in New York on April 13, 1971.

The *Chamber Concerto (Kammerkonzert),* for thirteen instruments, was completed in 1970 and performed on October 1, 1970, at the Festival Weeks in Berlin and at the Warsaw Autumn Festival two years later. The program book at its world premiere said, "Many of Ligeti's earlier traits and ideas are found: the sustained sonoric masses of *Atmosphères* and the fireworks of sound bursting forth over a subtle, hazy background from *Lontano.* The *Chamber Concerto* is a compendium of everything Ligeti introduced to contemporary composition technique and our musical imagination."

In 1969, Ligeti left Vienna to settle in West Berlin. In the early 1970s, he began to emphasize melody and rhythm, though much of his older style remained. Many divergent melodic strands are woven together and can be heard together or separately, a tendency first made evident in *Melodien,* a chamber concerto either for sixteen instrumentalists or for a large chamber orchestra. Written in 1971 for the Dürer Festival in Nuremberg, Germany, it was first heard on December 10, 1971. Ligeti was present at its American premiere by the Los Angeles Philharmonic under Zubin Mehta on April 13, 1972, because he had been invited by Stanford University in California to come to the United States to serve as composer-in-residence in the spring, 1972. However, Ligeti was not satisfied with this performance because he failed to hear the different melodic voices clearly. A subsequent performance by the San Francisco Symphony under Seiji Ozawa, in May 1972, was, he said, "the first

real performance my work has received. Each orchestral player studied his individual part before the first rehearsal, and Ozawa rehearsed the piece perfectly coordinating the separate melodies to an overall and harmonious unity of musical form." He was so pleased with Ozawa and the San Francisco Symphony that he decided to dedicate a one-movement symphonic work to them, calling his new composition *San Francisco Polyphony.* The new work, with a complex contrapuntal structure, was introduced on January 8, 1975. The composer compared it to *Melodien* which was a "soft and rather 'beautiful' piece. The new *San Francisco Polyphony* is more 'dry,' sometimes even harsh. The musical texture is made up of a large number of melodic lines, which are more or less independent in rhythm, meter and movement. . . . The different and divergent melodic lines, i.e., parts, are held together by an overall intervallic structure, so that the result is never chaos but a well-ordered structure in spite of the 'disorder' of the melodic lines. There is a combination of order and disorder (which I like in everyday life too)." In his review in *High Fidelity/Musical America,* Alfred Frankenstein said: "The involvement, the brilliance and the virtuoso demands of the work are fabulous; so is its vertiginous finale, which reminds you of nothing so much as running into a haystack in a hurricane."

Ligeti made a second visit to the United States during the summer of 1973, after attending an all-Ligeti concert in Toronto. For two weeks he gave master classes in composition at the Berkshire Music Center at Tanglewood, Massachusetts. In 1973 he was appointed professor of composition at the High School of Music in Hamburg. Ligeti has lectured extensively in Europe and the United States.

On April 23, 1977, Ligeti's long-delayed first opera, commissioned so many years before by the Swedish Royal Opera, was finally produced. *Den Stroen Makabre (The Grand Macabre),* whose overture is a fanfare of twelve car horns, has a Swedish libretto by the composer and Michael Meschke, which was based loosely on *Ballade du Grand Macabre* by the Flemish dramatist, Michel de Ghelderode. A parody on things people take seriously, it takes place in the world of the absurd in the fantasy kingdom of Breughelland. Final extinction of the kingdom is planned by Nikrotzar (representing the Macabre or Death), but the holocaust never takes place because Nikrotzar gets drunk and falls asleep. Characters include the triumphant lovers, Clitoria and Spermando, and the Chief of Police who appears dressed as a giant peacock, traveling about either on roller skates or on stilts. Dominic Gill of the *Financial Times* of London, reported from Stockholm: "Ligeti fills out this elaborate comic script . . . with a richly elaborate comic score. . . . The manner is wholly individual: a brilliant, exotic music-box of medleys, set pieces, recurrent motifs, quotation and references proposed with the greatest delicacy, bound together with a quick, taut thread. There are a few obvious quotations: from Beethoven's *Eroica*, the Offenbach Can-Can, a snatch of Scott Joplin. But there is no direct pastiche. Instead, Ligeti weaves a web that is very much his own, setting small parts of it only, as it were, in quotation marks. . . . They permeate the score, and explain much of its variety and complex resonance." In *High Fidelity/Musical America*, Camilla Lundberg wrote: "Here you will find a concentrate of Ligeti's music: the clockworks out of order, an op-art for the ears with audial points constantly shifting place. Ligeti created new colors with elaborate blends of mouth-organs, maracas, low strings and a multitude of clocks and bells." The first German production took place on February 7, 1979, in Hamburg. Excerpts from this opera were heard for the first time in the United States at an all-Ligeti concert on January 15, 1981, performed by the Cleveland Orchestra and soloists, with Lorin Maazel conducting.

Ligeti became the vice-president of the Austrian section of the International Society of Contemporary Music in 1971. Four years later he was awarded both the French decoration, *"pour le mérite,"* and the Bach Prize of the city of Hamburg.

MAJOR WORKS

Chamber Music—2 string quartets; Six Miniatures, for wind ensemble; Six Bagatelles, for wind quintet; Ten Pieces, for wind quintet; Chamber Concerto, for thirteen instruments.

Choral Music—Morning, Night, for two a cappella choruses; Requiem, for soprano, mezzo-soprano, two choruses, and orchestra; Lux Aeterna, for sixteen-part a capella chorus; Clocks and Clouds, for women's chorus and orchestra.

Electronic Music—Glissandi; Pièce Electronique; Artikulation.

Harpsichord Music—Continuum.

Opera—The Grand Macabre.

Orchestral Music—Apparitions; Atmosphères; Fragment, for chamber orchestra; Concerto for Cello and Orchestra; Lontano; Ramifications, for twelve solo instruments or string orchestra; Melodien; Double Concerto for Flute, Oboe and Orchestra; San Francisco Polyphony.

Organ Music—Two Etudes; Volumina.

Piano Music—Three Objects, for two pianos; Monument, for two pianos.

Vocal Music—Aventures, for three voices and seven instruments; Nouvelles Aventures, for three voices and seven instruments.

ABOUT

Sadie, S. (ed.), The New Grove Dictionary of Music and Musicians; Salmenhaara, E., György Ligeti; Sternfeld, F. W. (ed.), Music in the Modern Age; Vinton, J. (ed.), Dictionary of Contemporary Music.

High Fidelity/Musical America, December 1973.

Charles Martin Loeffler

1851–1935

See *Composers Since 1900.*

Nikolai Lopatnikoff

1903–1976

For biographical sketch, list of earlier works, and bibliography, see *Composers Since 1900.*

Lopatnikoff resigned as professor of music at the Technological Institute in Pittsburgh in 1968, becoming professor emeritus. His Symphony No. 4, commissioned by the Pittsburgh Symphony, was performed by that orchestra under William Steinberg's direction on January 21, 1972.

Nikolai Lopatnikoff died in Pittsburgh on October 7, 1976.

MAJOR WORKS (supplementary)

Ballet—Melting Pot.

Orchestral Music—Symphony No. 4.

ABOUT

Vinton, J. (ed.) Dictionary of Contemporary Music; Who's Who in America, 1974–1975.

Witold Lutoslawski

1913–

For biographical sketch, list of earlier works, and bibliography, see *Composers Since 1900.*

Lutoslawski's Concerto for Cello and Orchestra, completed in 1970, was commissioned by the Royal Philharmonic Orchestra of London, and introduced by Mstislav Rostropovich and the orchestra conducted by Edward Downes on October 14, 1970. In this work the composer utilized controlled aleatory processes. When the Concerto was broadcast in Glasgow during the Edinburgh Festival nine years later, Malcolm Raymont, in the Glasgow *Herald,* called it "one of the few masterpieces in that medium. The concerto is unique in conception and it is doubtful whether the dramatic idea behind it can ever be employed again. We are presented with a personality conflict and contest between soloist and orchestra. ... This theatrical approach makes demands on the soloist of the type to be found in no other concerto. Much of the time both the cellist and the orchestra are allowed to interpret their parts freely, although nothing is left to chance as regards the overall effect." A reviewer for *High Fidelity/Musical America,* in reviewing another performance, spoke of the music's "mystery, nonchalance, warm lyricism and angry dialogue."

In June 1971, Lutoslawski returned to the United States to receive an honorary doctorate in music from the Cleveland Institute of Music and to appear as lecturer, conductor, and leader of symposia on composition. At this time, two all-Lutoslawski concerts presented programs including the American premiere of his *Livre pour Orchestre* (1968). Bain Murray wrote in the quarterly *Polish Music,* "that in America as elsewhere, Lutoslawski is considered an absolute master of his art and that each of his works is regarded as a masterpiece with the *Livre* perhaps receiving the highest laurels of all."

Les Espaces du Sommeil (1975), for baritone and orchestra to a text by Robert Desnos, received its world premiere in West Berlin on March 12, 1978, with Dietrich Fischer-Dieskau as soloist. This work was to have been performed at the 22nd Warsaw Autumn Festival of Contemporary Music in mid-September 1978, but had to be cancelled because of the illness of the baritone soloist, John Shirley-Quirk. As a replacement, Lutoslawski conducted a performance of his Cello Concerto with Roman Jablonski as soloist.

Lutoslawski completed *Mi-Parti,* for orchestra, in 1976 on commission from the Amsterdam Municipality for the Amsterdam Concertgebouw Orchestra in Holland. The composer conducted the premiere performance on October 22, 1976, and on September 17, 1977, it was performed at the opening concert of the 21st Autumn Festival of Contemporary Music in Warsaw. The American premiere on December 15, 1977 by the Chicago Symphony Orchestra and a New York Philharmonic performance on February 15, 1979, were both conducted by Daniel Barenboim. The composer described the work as follows: "The title *Mi-Parti,* according to Quillet's dictionary, means composed in two parts, equal but different. However, this does not concern the form of the whole piece, but rather the way of developing the musical thought. Here, the phrase often consists of two parts, the second of which is combined with a new element when the whole phrase is repeated."

In 1977, Lutoslawski's *Variations on a Theme of Paganini* (1941) for two unaccompanied pianos—based on a theme from Paganini's Caprice No. 24 for solo violin—was rewritten for solo piano and orchestra. The world premiere took place on November 20, 1979, in Miami, in a performance by the Florida Philharmonic Orchestra conducted by Brian Priestman with Felicja Blumenthal as soloist. A commission from Rostropovich, music director of the National Symphony Orchestra of Washington, D.C., led to the writing of *Novelette,* for orchestra, in 1979, and its first performance on January 29, 1980. The five movements of the work are entitled "Announcement," "First Event," "Second Event," "Third Event," and "Conclusion." The composer described the movements: "The first movement is so called because in it I present as it were samples of the 'events' which follow. The three are contrasting in character, the slow middle one being *buffo,* and the third one being a fast and sparkling scherzando. The 'Conclusion' consists largely of a slow heterophonic cantilena of two groups of violins with accompaniment of other instruments playing *ad libitum.*" Reviewing this performance in *The New Yorker,* Nicholas Kenyon said: "Lutoslawski has written an intricate, carefully patterned, and

Malipiero

atmospheric score, unpretentious in content and satisfying in effect.... He makes imaginative use of a range of devices drawn from the world of musical avant-garde: controlled indeterminacy, non-coordination between different groups of players, sections guided by time rather than by rhythm, passages in which individual instrumentalists control the progress of the music.... Lutoslawski makes them fresh and purposeful."

Lutoslawski was made an "extraordinary member" of the Academy of Arts in West Berlin in 1968, honorary member of the International Society for Contemporary Music in 1969, and associate member of the German Academy of Arts in East Germany in 1970. He received the Maurice Ravel Award in 1971, the Jan Sibelius Award and the Prize of the Polish Composers Union in 1973, and the Polish State Award in 1978. In 1975 he was made corresponding member of the American Academy of Arts and Letters and, in 1976, a member of the Royal Academy of Music in London. In addition to an honorary doctorate in music from the Cleveland Institute in 1971, he received similar degrees from the University of Warsaw, Northwestern University in Chicago in 1974, the University of Lancaster in 1976, and the University of Glasgow in 1977. In 1979, the EMI record album, *Lutoslawski; Orchestral Works,* which he conducted with the Polish National Radio Symphony Orchestra, received the annual *High Fidelity*/International Record Critics Award. A four-day festival of Lutoslawski's music, conducted by the composer, who was publicly interviewed, took place in Montreal in April 1980.

MAJOR WORKS (supplementary)

Chamber Music—Sacher Variations, for cello solo; Epitaph, for oboe and piano.

Orchestral Music—Trois Poèmes d'Henri Michaux; Livre pour Orchestre; Concerto for Cello and Orchestra; Preludes and Fugue, for strings; Mi-Parti; Variations on a Theme of Paganini, for piano and orchestra; Novelette; Symphony No. 3.

Vocal Music—Les Espaces du Sommeil, for baritone and orchestra.

ABOUT (supplementary)

Maciejewski, B. M., Twelve Polish Composers; Nordwall, O., Lutoslawski; Varga, B. A., Lutoslawski Profile; Vinton, J. (ed.), Dictionary of Contemporary Music.

High Fidelity/Musical America, September 1971; Washington Post, January 27, 1980.

Gian Francesco Malipiero

1882–1973

For biographical sketch, list of earlier works, and bibliography, see *Composers Since 1900.*

Malipiero's opera, *Gli Eroi de Bona Ventura (The Heroes of Good Fortune)* (1968) caused a mild sensation when it was introduced at Piccola Scala in Milan on February 7, 1969 because of the unusual subject matter of the libretto (by the composer). It turned out to be a kind of autobiography in which the hero, Bona Ventura, is actually Malipiero himself who recalls past artistic and human experiences and summons past heroes from seven of his own operas written between 1935 and 1966. Changes of theme are made through newly written prologues and interludes. In a report to the New York *Times* from Milan, Everett Helm said: "Surprisingly enough, the device works. The result is not an anthology, but in effect an entirely new work containing some of the finest operatic music of this century."

On January 20, 1970, Malipiero's opera *Don Tartuffo Bacchetone* (1966), based on Molière, was introduced in Venice at La Fenice.

Malipiero's last two operas, *Uno Dei Dieci* and *L'Iscariota,* with his own libretti, were both completed in 1970, and introduced in Siena on August 28, 1971.

Gian Francesco Malipiero died of a heart attack in a hospital in Treviso, Italy, on August 1, 1973, in his ninety-first year.

A collection of Malipiero's essays was published in Turin in 1966 under the title of *Il Filo d'Arianna.*

MAJOR WORKS (supplementary)

Operas—Don Tartufo Bacchetone; Uno Dei Dieci; L'Iscariota.

Orchestral Music—Symphonies Nos. 10 ("Atrepo") and 11 ("Delle Cornamuse"); Piano Concerto No. 6 ("Della Machine"); Concerto for Flute and Orchestra.

ABOUT (supplementary)

Sadie, S. (ed.), The New Grove Dictionary of Music and Musicians; Vinton, J. (ed.), Dictionary of Contemporary Music.

Soundings (Cardiff, Wales), Autumn 1970.

Frank Martin

1890-1974

For biographical sketch, list of earlier works, and bibliography, see *Composers Since 1900*.

Martin's *Erasmi Momentum,* for orchestra and organ (1969), had its world premiere in Rotterdam on November 24, 1969. The composer was commissioned to write his Piano Concerto No. 2 for the opening of the Vienna Spring Festival in 1970, but the premiere had to be postponed because of the composition's formidable technical demands until June 1970 when it was performed in Scheveningen, the Netherlands, by Paul Badura Skoda (for whom it was written). Later in the same year it was finally brought to Vienna and Badura Skoda toured Europe with it, recorded it, and on April 7, 1972, performed it for the first time in the United States with the Cincinnati Symphony under the direction of Thomas Schippers. In this work, the composer combined the twelve-tone system with tonality. Eugene Hartzell reported from Vienna to *High Fidelity/Musical America:* "Surface brilliance is matched by depth of structure. Each section of the three movements has its own distinct character, its unmistakable rhythmic profile and motivic shape. ... This piece makes an immediate impression of strength."

Trois Danses, for oboe, harp, and string orchestra (1970) was premiered in Zurich, Switzerland, on October 9, 1970. During the summer of 1971 Martin visited Israel where he conducted a performance of his oratorio, *In Terre Pax* (1944) during the festival season. On his second visit to the United States in late 1971, he conducted the world premiere of *Poèmes de la Mort,* for three singers and three electric guitars whose text consists of philosophical reflections on death by François Villon. It was commissioned by the Chamber Music Society of Lincoln Center, which presented it at the Lincoln Center for the Performing Arts in New York on December 12, 1971. "Martin's score maintains a stark, vaguely threatening mood throughout," wrote a critic for *High Fidelity/Musical America.* "The rich modal harmonies for the voices evoke the Renaissance milieu of the poetry, while the death-rattle twanging of the electric guitars lends the music a strong contemporary flavor."

Martin's *Requiem,* for solo voices, chorus, and orchestra (1971-1972) received its first hearing in Lausanne, Switzerland, on May 4, 1973. One of Martin's last works was *Polyptyque: Six Images de la Vie du Seigneur,* for violin and string orchestra, written in 1972-1973, and dedicated to Yehudi Menuhin, who with the Menuhin Festival Orchestra introduced it in Lausanne on September 9, 1973, and in the United States on November 14, 1975, in New York. Inspired by medieval miniatures in Siena depicting episodes of the Passion, the solo violin assumes the role of Christ in this composition. "The music is clear, tonal and simple in the characteristic Martin manner, and wonderfully spiritual and intense," said John Rockwell in the New York *Times.*

Martin's last work, *Et la Vie l'Emporta,* a chamber cantata for small vocal group and instrumental ensemble, was completed by Bernard Reichel and premiered in Nyon, Switzerland, on June 13, 1975.

Since 1946, Martin, his wife, and six children have lived in a large cottage with a thatched roof, surrounded by numerous trees, in Naarden, west of Amsterdam. Martin chose to leave his native Switzerland for this secluded place because he felt the need for the solitude he could not hope to get in Geneva where he was so well known. Extraordinarily adept with his hands, he was well able to take care of the plumbing, electrical, and carpentry needs and he was also skillful in restoring paintings and old icons, cooking for special occasions, and repairing the toys of grandchildren.

Frank Martin died in Naarden, the Netherlands, on November 21, 1974. A collection of his writings—*Un Compositeur Medite Sur son Art* —was published posthumously in Lausanne in 1977.

MAJOR WORKS (supplementary)

Chamber Music—Ballade, for viola, harp, and harpsichord.

Choral Music—Magnificat and Stabat Mater, for soprano, violin, and orchestra; Requiem, for solo voices, chorus, and orchestra; Et la Vie l'Emporta, chamber cantata for small vocal group and instrumental ensemble (completed by Bernard Reichel).

Orchestral Music—Maria Triptychon, for soprano, violin, and orchestra; Erasmi Monumentum, for orchestra with organ; Piano Concerto No. 2; Trois Danses, for oboe, harp, and string orchestra; Polyptyque: Six Images de la Vie du Seigneur, for violin and double string orchestra.

Martino

Piano Music—Fantaisie sur des Rhythmes Flamenco.

Vocal Music—Poèmes de la Mort, for three men's voices and three electric guitars.

ABOUT (supplementary)

Martin, B., Frank Martin, ou La Realité du Rêve.

High Fidelity/Musical America, March 1972; New York Times, November 22, 1974; Schweizerische Musikzeitung (Martin Issue) September-October 1976.

Donald Martino

1931–

DONALD MARTINO

Donald James Martino was born in Plainfield, New Jersey, on May 16, 1931. James Edward Martino, his father, was born in New Jersey of Italian descent and was an accountant for the Public Service Electric and Gas Company in Plainfield; his mother, Alma Ida Renz Martino, of German descent, was a seamstress who grew up in sweatshops. Neither parent was musical, but both were accomplished ballroom dancers who, at one time, opened their own school of ballroom dancing. The musician in the family was Donald's grandfather, who had been a choral conductor in Switzerland.

His parents' ambition for Donald to become a dentist seemed to be realized, since he remembered, "I did nothing with music except for singing to my relatives who never listened anyway." His first interest in music surfaced when at nine years old he acquired a clarinet and took lessons at Evergreen Elementary School (it was out of trumpets and a clarinet was substituted). His first experience in a school band performance of the march, *Military Escort,* made him know that he wanted to become a musician. As a student at Plainfield High School, he occupied the first clarinet chair and he became solo clarinetist for the New Jersey All-State Band and Orchestra. While still in high school, he played the clarinet in the Plainfield Symphony Orchestra and he was beginning to do some composing. Until he was seventeen, his musical experiences were confined solely to the school band, the Symphony, and to popular music and jazz, all of which influenced his writing of music. As a high school

senior he was not impressed with Arnold Schoenberg's compositions.

Between 1948 and 1952 he attended Syracuse University on scholarship and his ambition to become a professional clarinetist had him studying composition with Ernst Bacon. He encouraged Martino to devote himself mainly to composition and, to a lesser degree, the clarinet. Under his tutelage Martino wrote *American Suite,* for clarinet and piano, in 1949; String Quartet No. 1 and *Folk-Song Suite* (for cello and piano), among other compositions in 1950; and, in 1951, a number of ambitious works including a Clarinet Sonata, a Piano Quartet, String Quartet No. 2, and a Piano Sonata. String Quartet No. 2 was first performed at Syracuse University on February 10, 1952, and received a Student Composers Award from BMI that year. Martino received his Bachelor of Music degree at Syracuse University in 1952.

The next significant influence in Martino's development as a composer came at Princeton University during two years of graduate work for his Master of Fine Arts degree in 1954. He entered Princeton on a fellowship to major in history, but soon switched to composition for a year with Milton Babbitt and a second year with Roger Sessions. Now a seminar with Sessions devoted to Schoenberg's String Trio aroused Martino's interest in the music of the 20th century master, although for quite a while thereafter he had no interest in becoming a twelve-tone composer. His admiration was obvious, when he described how Milton Babbitt taught him "to

---

Martino: mär tē nō

186

plot and plan a piece in advance . . . to prevision a work. Not that Babbitt demanded that. He's not academic or a pedant at all when he works with students. He tries to see what you're doing in music, what you're interested in, and sharpens you up in that language." Martino added: "If I had to single out any one encounter as the most decisive, I would probably say Milton Babbit, and yet my music least resembles his. So many of his views are important; so much of what he says is irrefutable. He is a true genius, and to come into contact with a man like him is to sharpen yourself."

In 1956, for Babbitt's fiftieth birthday, and on his own birthday, Martino composed a "musical birthday card" entitled *B,a,b,b,it,t* for B-flat clarinet, devising his own extensions which expanded the instrument's range to five octaves. He derived the music from the letters of Babbitt's name, the "t" signifying B-natural. The composer performed this piece at a special concert of the International Society for Contemporary Music in New Haven honoring Babbitt on May 21, 1966.

While attending Princeton, Martino married Mari Rice on September 5, 1953 and their only child, Anna Maria, was born in 1963. At Princeton, he completed several large-scale compositions, which were not stylistically affected by either Sessions or Babbitt but were mostly in a post-Bartókian idiom, sometimes with a touch of be-bop. His successful early compositions included the String Quartet No. 3 (1953), Cello Concerto (1954), Set for Clarinet (1954), and String Trio (1954). Arthur Bloom, clarinetist, introduced the *Set for Clarinet* at Princeton University in 1956 and since then, the work has received numerous performances. In *Musical America* (January 1957) David Epstein wrote: "Donald Martino's *Set for Clarinet* achieved the most difficult and elusive goal of solo pieces— making music that is interesting as well as virtuoso. The style was tonal and highly chromatic with traces of Bartókian mannerisms in the second piece and the drives and rhythms of jazz in the third. The long, lyrical line in the slow movement was skillfully shaped, varied rhythms avoiding what could be dull sequential extensions, and yet clearly growing from the basic melodic germs."

His reviews were beginning to be favorable and he was receiving a variety of honors: the Kosciuszko Scholarship in 1953–1954 and an award from the National Federation of Music Clubs, as well as a second Composer Award from BMI in 1954. He was also awarded the first of two Fulbright grants which enabled him to spend two years in Florence (1954–1956) to study with Luigi Dallapiccola, Italy's foremost serialist. Dallapiccola convinced him of the merits of composing in the twelve-tone system. Martino said, "In the Fifties, my music was getting out of hand, was getting *too* chromatic. The serial approach was a way to control it. It was a natural evolution for me. I didn't just say, hey, I'm going to write twelve-tone music. Twelve-tone music opened up so many possibilities for me. It became a way of sparking my ear."

Finding that he was well-suited to the technique, he wrote *Contemplations,* for orchestra (1957), which was commissioned by the Paderewski Fund but did not get a hearing until August 19, 1965, when Gunther Schuller conducted it at the Berkshire Music Center at Tanglewood, Massachusetts; *Quartet for Clarinet and Strings* (1957), introduced by Charles Russo, clarinetist, and the Knickerbocker Players in New York on February 15, 1958; *Piano Fantasy* (1958) which William Masselos introduced in New York on March 13, 1960; and *Trio,* for violin, clarinet, and piano (1959) which was heard first in New York on March 13, 1960. The two latter works demonstrated a further advance in the evolution of his style, in which a number of set forms are presented in a blending of fundamentally disparate instrumental colors. In the New York *Herald Tribune,* Eric Salzman described his results: "Donald Martino's *Trio* is based on a kind of careful serialism but elegantly worked out and purified into a kind of remarkable crystalline beauty." It was chosen to represent the United States at the International Society for Contemporary Music Festival in Amsterdam on June 13, 1963.

When he returned to the United States in 1956, Martino discovered that jobs for serious musicians were scarce and not lucrative. He did get a position as teacher of theory at the Third Street Settlement in New York for 1956–1957 and an instructorship in music at Princeton between 1957 and 1959. He, therefore, turned to popular music, played the clarinet in jazz bands, did arrangements, and wrote popular songs, hoping for a hit, so he could return full time to serious music. He wrote one song for Mario Lanza, who died before he could perform it, and another one for the Copacabana night club in New York, neither of which was successful. In 1958, he also wrote the score for the motion picture *The Lonely Crime,* that attracted little attention.

By 1959 he decided that popular music was not the way to prosperity and he would again concentrate on serious composition. In the meantime an appointment as assistant professor of music at Yale University in 1959 provided financial security. In 1966 he was promoted to an associate professorship and during the summers of 1965–1967 and 1969 he taught composition at the Berkshire Music Center. He left Yale to become chairman of the department of composition at the New England Conservatory from 1969–1980. He was also visiting lecturer at Harvard in 1971; Koussevitzky Composer-in-Residence at the Berkshire Music Center in 1973; and during the summer of 1978 he had a residency at the Composers Conference at Johnson State College in Vermont.

His compositions began to show maturity in the 1960s, beginning with *Two Rilke Songs,* for mezzo-soprano and piano (1961), in which he was influenced by the vocal music of Schumann, and although he did not imitate him, he composed the work in the tradition of the German lied. Neva Pilgrim introduced it at the Yale Divinity School in New Haven on February 25, 1963. The *Concerto for Wind Quintet* (1964), commissioned by the Fromm Music Foundation at Tanglewood, was premiered there by the Fromm Players on May 17, 1964. The five-sectioned work contains duos, trios, quartets, and quintets for flute, oboe, clarinet, French horn, and bassoon, and is framed by an introduction and coda composed principally of quintets. All of the sections are bridged by solo sections. As Eric Salzman noted in the New York *Times,* the work is "a complex twelve-tone piece of great intellectual integrity and honesty and is also long and demanding on everybody. The piece works partly because . . . there is real elegance and finesse to the conception, partly because . . . it grows out of the nature of the ensemble and the character of the instrument."

Parisonatina Al'Dodecafonia, for solo cello, was written at the request of the Brazilian cellist, Aldo Parisot, who introduced it at the Yale Summer School in Norfolk, Connecticut, on July 26, 1965. (Later in the summer he performed it again at the Festival of Contemporary American Music at Tanglewood.) The title, translated loosely, means "Sonatina for Parisot in a dodecaphonic (twelve-tone) style." The single movement of the work has four sections: the first one is a kind of passacaglia; the second, a rondo-like scherzo; the third, a tripartite song; and the fourth, a free cadenza. After hearing the work, Michael Steinberg, critic of the Boston *Evening Globe,* said: "Donald Martino is a thirty-five-year-old composer, certainly among the very best of his generation."

Martino's *Piano Concerto* is a work he often singles out as a favorite. "It is the one piece out of all these years that I really love. I have reservations about almost everything, but this piece I can sit and listen to and say 'I like it.' " The New Haven Symphony commissioned and performed it in March 1966 with Frank Brieff as conductor and Charles Rosen as soloist. Taking pieces of a piano work that he had abandoned in 1956, he completed the concerto in 1966. Instead of the single twelve-tone set in the original piece, he now presented a union of two different sets with an upper melody, a base line, and an internal accompaniment. He thought of the outer voices as the piano set and the others as the orchestra set. He explained: "As soon as I had perceived that, as soon as I got rid of the notion that I had to have one set, one and only one, as soon as I allowed myself to think of this union, I immediately wrote the piece."

Mosaic No. 3, for orchestra, is another favorite of the composer. He wrote it on commission from the University of Chicago for the Chicago Symphony which premiered it on May 26, 1967, with Jean Martinon conducting. A large orchestra of 104 players is employed, with many of its parts completely independent, although the entire work is controlled. The composer explained that the composition, is "a mosaic of mosaics. . . . One day, after having copied an immensely complicated score-page, I stood back, looked at my work, and was amazed by the mosaic-like network of tiny black notes. I then recalled that some years ago I had used the term 'mosaic' as a synonym for the more precise mathematical term 'partition' (in music this term implied that the set can be seen as the sum of its parts). At that moment I realized the special applicability of the word 'mosaic' to my composition. From the standpoint of technical means, the term 'mosaic' is particularly appropriate to the class of twelve-tone compositions of which *Mosaic* for grand orchestra is a member; the term is even more appropriate to my work which employs an additive 13-part form. The obvious historical model for such a structure can be found in the traditional variation form or, more analogously, in those variation-like piano pieces of Schumann which, at least superficially, do not exemplify the 'long line' concept so characteristic of the romantic sonata."

Martino felt that if he deserved a Pulitzer Prize in music at all it should have been for his *Piano Concerto* or the *Mosaic No. 3.* He won it in 1974 for *Notturno* which, he confessed, "does not mean much to me . . . not that I don't like it or that I would want to disclaim it. But in a way it seemed too routine to me. I guess I didn't go through enough torture over it. Virtually everybody said it was different for me, that I was getting mellow in my old age, that kind of thing, but I don't see it that way at all." The work, for flute, clarinet, violin, cello, piano, and percussion, was completed in 1973 on commission from the Naumburg Foundation and first heard on May 15, 1973, at a concert of Speculum Musicae, conducted by Harvey Sollerberger at the Lincoln Center for the Performing Arts in New York. Martino spent eight months writing this fifteen-minute composition which he described as showing "night mood rather than night sounds" (although a description he liked equally well was one made by Michael Steinberg of the Boston *Globe,* "a nocturnal theater of the soul"). David Noble wrote in the Boston *Herald American,* that the composition is "every bit . . . 'contemporary'. . . . But in melodic flow and rhythmic invention it suggests (without really sounding like) the most sweeping kind of romantic music."

The Pulitzer Prize climaxed numerous honors Martino had been gathering since the early 1960s: the Pacific Award in 1961 for his *Quartet,* for clarinet and strings; the Creative Arts Award in 1964 from Brandeis University in Waltham, Massachusetts; a Morse Academic Fellowship from Yale in 1965 enabling him to take a sabbatical leave from the New England Conservatory; a Guggenheim Fellowship in 1967 (another in 1973); and a grant from the National Institute of Arts and Letters in 1967.

In 1972, Martino departed sharply from his usual creative style by producing the whimsical and satiric *Augenmusik: A Mixed Mediocritique.* He described it as a "profane (X-rated) humorous offering." It was a tongue-in-cheek protest against the multi-media productions of the 1960s, calling for an actress, danseuse or female percussionist, and prerecorded tape. Around the same time he wrote *Seven Pious Pieces* for a cappella mixed chorus, to settings of poems by Robert Herrick, as a "penance" for *Augenmusik,* in response to a request for sacred music from the publishing house of E. C. Schirmer. While *Augenmusik* was written on weekdays, he composed each of the *Seven Pious Pieces* on seven consecutive Sundays in the winter of 1971–1972 and he dedicated the work to his first teacher, Ernst Bacon. His gesture of homage included a paraphrase of Bacon's chorale-style setting of Herrick's "The Soule." Lorna Cooke de Varon conducted the New England Conservatory in the premiere of the work in New York on April 4, 1976, and the John Oliver Chorale recorded it for New World Records. The liner notes for that recording, by Edwin London, said: "*Seven Pious Pieces* are highly personal sincere statements of artistic principle, religious in nature as well as in design, fully admissible for use in liturgical circumstances."

In 1974, on leave from the New England Conservatory, Martino began his most ambitious creative project, the *Paradiso Choruses,* with a text from *The Divine Comedy.* This work was commissioned by the Paderewski Fund in honor of Lorna Cooke de Varon who was choral conductor at the New England Conservatory for twenty-five years. Martino, long attracted to the Italian language and Dante, had contemplated writing a Berlioz-type orchestral work based on *The Divine Comedy.* He recalled, "Then I began to realize it would have to be visual in some sense. I thought about mime and about slides. When it finally became clear that this would have to be a three-act opera—no, a musical miracle play—I stopped, shivering, for four months." Instead, he mapped out a giant choral work (it might some day be the third act in an opera) which required an addition to the orchestra; large adult and children's choruses grouped into antiphonal sections; fourteen soloists; two electronic tapes (one of the altered voices of the Devil and the Souls of Hell, and the other of the Angels of the Ten Heavens). Following its world premiere in Boston on May 7, 1975, Richard Dyer, in the Boston *Evening Globe,* wrote that it was "some kind of masterpiece. His method here is eclectic. The piece is completely tonal, a new direction for him. There to be heard were fragments of medieval music in the sections from the Mass sung by the penitent souls in purgatory. People spoke of Debussy, of the Schoenberg of the *Gurrelieder,* of the Elgar of the oratorios, of the Mahler Eighth. . . . But all of these elements were disposed with . . . penetrating intelligence." A recording at the time of the premiere on the Golden Crest-NEC label won the *Record World* classical Critics Citation in 1976 as the "best record of contemporary music."

On December 12, 1976, Martino returned to his native Plainfield for the premiere of *Ritorno* by the Plainfield Symphony under Edward Murray. Of the title, "Ritorno," he said, "both as a noun form and as a first person singular of the verb "ritornare" it could evoke a very wide range of inflections of the emotions attending the experience of returning, recurring, repeating, giving, going and coming back." Returning home, and an undisclosed "tragic event in recent history whose effect on me was so powerful that I could not or would not pass it by," were the stimuli for composing *Ritorno,* which was charged with emotion, "a most ingenious, palatable and beautiful piece," said Michael Redmond in the Jersey *Star Ledger.*

In June 1968, his first marriage ended in divorce and on June 5, 1969, he married Lora Harvey who was a high school mathematics teacher; a son, Christopher James, was born in 1975.

Martino described his creative process as "a person who lives inside me. It's like a schizophrenic relationship. I'm not in control; it often controls me; it often does something other than what I want to do. When I want to do something, it refuses. I have stopped trying to dominate it. The way I work now is to be sensitive to it and follow its lead. Once you give your creativity its freedom, it begins to give you answers." What makes a composer, Martino added, "is the ability to find a middle fusion, to get together raw expression of feeling and raw expression of intellect, good or bad. Intellect is the servant of the emotions. It takes the composer's feelings and ideas and makes them into an ordered universe."

Martino works long and hard at composing, sometimes twelve hours a day, always seven days a week. Each major composition proceeds slowly, taking about eight or twelve months. He likes to begin working at 4:00 or 5:00 A.M. He

works in a basement studio which is a repository for his desk, upright piano, stacks of manuscript paper, audio equipment, books, and music. His home is in Newton, Massachusetts, and his favorite pastime is tennis, which he tries to play daily. Speaking of this passion and other diversions, he said: "One of the dangers for me is that I can elevate to a position of priority some wholly trivial project simply because it fascinates me."

"Martino is unassuming and soft-spoken, but at the same time amiable and witty," Joseph d'Ambrose wrote in a BMI brochure. "True to his Taurean demeanor, there lies within him an unshakable strength. On the surface, Donald Martino appears to be a man at ease. His easygoing consideration for others should not be confused with his feelings about himself: underlying much of his thought is caution and perhaps a streak of pessimism at odds with his accomplishment."

In 1980, Martino left the New England Conservatory to become professor of music at Brandeis University. He was elected to membership in the American Academy and Institute of Arts and Letters in 1981.

MAJOR WORKS

Chamber Music—3 string quartets; 2 Quodlibets, for solo flute; Quartet for Woodwinds; American Suite, for clarinet and piano; Folk Song Suite, for cello and piano; Sonata for Clarinet and Piano; Rhapsody, for violin and piano; Sonata for Violin and Piano; A Set for Clarinet; Prelude and Fugue, for brass and percussion; Three Dances, for viola and piano; Quartet, for clarinet and strings; String Trio; Sette Canoni Enigmatici, for various instrumental combinations; Trio, for violin, clarinet, and piano; Cinque Frammenti, for oboe and doublebass; Fantasy Variations, for violin; Concerto for Wind Quintet; Parisonatina Al'Dodecafonia, for cello solo; Strata, for bass clarinet solo; Notturno, for flute, clarinet, violin, cello, piano, and percussion; Solo Flute Pieces.

Choral Music—Portraits, secular cantata for mezzosoprano, bass baritone, chorus, and orchestra; A Virgin Most Pure; Carol Fantasy, for a cappella chorus; Seven Pious Pieces; Paradiso Choruses, for soloists, choruses, orchestra, and tape.

Orchestral Music—Fantasy; Sinfonia; Concerto for Cello and Orchestra; Contemplations; Concerto for Piano and Orchestra; Mosaic No. 3; Concerto No. 2 for Cello and Orchestra; Ritorno, for community orchestra (or concert band); Triple Concerto, for clarinet, bass clarinet, contrabass clarinet, and chamber orchestra.

Piano Music—With Little Children in Mind; Piano Sonata No. 1; Piano Fantasy; Pianissimo, sonata for piano; Impromptu for Roger; Fantasies and Impromptus.

Vocal Music—Separate Songs, for high voice and piano; My Silks and Fine Array, for soprano and piano (also orchestra); From the Bad Child's Book of Beasts, for high voice and piano; Three Songs to texts by James Joyce, for bass-baritone and piano; Two Rilke Songs, for mezzo-soprano and piano.

ABOUT

BMI, Many Worlds of Music, Issue 2, 1974; Boston Sunday Globe, May 12, 1974; High Fidelity/Musical America, September 1974.

Jean Martinon

1910–1976

For biographical sketch, list of earlier works, and bibliography, see *Composers Since 1900.*

After leaving his position as music director of the Chicago Symphony in 1969, Martinon assumed a similar one with the Orchestre National Français in Paris. He toured the United States with the orchestra on several occasions and recorded the orchestral works of Ravel, Debussy, and Saint-Saëns for Angel (the first ever made of the first two). In addition, he became principal conductor of the Hague Residentie Orchestra in Holland in 1974. These appointments did not preclude guest appearances with other major orchestras in the United States and in Europe.

In 1969, Martinon was the recipient of the Mahler medal.

Jean Martinon died in Paris after a long illness on March 1, 1976.

MAJOR WORKS (supplementary)

Chamber Music—5 additional sonatinas for violin and piano; String Quartet No. 2; Octet.

Orchestral Music—Vigentuor, for twenty instruments; Concerto for Flute and Orchestra; Concerto for Viola and Orchestra.

ABOUT (supplementary)

New York Times, March 2, 1976.

Bohuslav Martinů

1890–1959

For biographical sketch, list of earlier works, and bibliography, see *Composers Since 1900.*

Martinů's "opera film," *Trois Souhaits (Three Wishes),* written in 1929 for an orchestra including a jazz flute, saxophone, banjo, and accordion, received its world premiere posthumously, at Brünn, Czechoslovakia, on June 16, 1971.

A string quartet written in 1918 and then withdrawn was reconstructed by Jan Manus in 1972 with the addition of a newly discovered fourth movement.

In 1978 Martinů's six symphonies were recorded for the first time by Supraphon at a performance by the Czech Philharmonic, conducted by Václav Neumann.

Martinů's last opera, *The Greek Passion* (1956–1959) had its American premiere on April 4, 1981, in Bloomington, Indiana, by the University Opera Theater of Indiana University and the production was brought to New York on April 26, 1981. The Bloomington performance was filmed for cable television in May 1981.

In August 1979, Martinů's body was removed from Schoenberg, near Liestal, Switzerland, and brought back to Czechoslovakia for interment in the family grave in the composer's birthplace, Polička.

ABOUT (supplementary)

Halbreich, H., Bohuslav Martinů; Large, B., Martinů; Martinů, C., My Life with Bohuslav Martinů; Mihule, J., Bohuslav Martinů.

Pietro Mascagni

1863–1945

See *Composers Since 1900.*

Nicholas Maw

1935–

John Nicholas Maw was born in Grantham, Lincolnshire, England, on November 5, 1935. His father, Clarence Frederick Maw, assistant manager of a retail music shop and an excellent musician, had played the organ in a local church in his youth and received fine training as a pianist. Maw's mother, Hilda Ellen Chambers Maw, ran a dress shop. He recalled, "I first became really aware of my interest in music at a very early age, when I would stand for hours beside the piano listening to my father playing and turning over the pages for him. As a consequence of this, I can never remember a time when I could not read music. So the first body of music I got to know in detail was piano literature: the Bach *Well-Tempered Clavier,* the Beethoven piano sonatas, the Chopin Nocturnes. This would have been between the ages of seven and twelve." When he was eight he began piano lessons with his father and at eleven he continued them at Wennington School, a boarding school in Yorkshire. He confided: "I didn't enjoy playing the piano very much, largely owing to continual admonishments from my father about practising, so I took up the clarinet at about the age of fourteen. I became quite a good clarinetist."

When his academic education ended at Wennington School in 1954, he went to work in a bicycle factory. Several preludes for piano, composed at this time, got him admitted to the Royal Academy of Music in London in 1955, where he studied harmony and counterpoint with Paul Steinitz, composition with Lennox Berkeley, piano with Michael Head, and clarinet with John Davies. As a student, Maw composed *Six Chinese Lyrics,* for unaccompanied mezzo-soprano (1956), heard at a concert for the Promotion of New Music in London; *Sonatina,* for flute and piano (1957); *Requiem,* for soprano, alto, female chorus, string trio, and string orchestra (1958), performed by the Bach Society in London in the year of its composition; and *Nocturne,* for mezzo-soprano and chamber orchestra (1958), which received the Lili Boulanger Prize in 1959 and had its premiere at the Cheltenham

Maw: mô

NICHOLAS MAW

Festival in 1960 (where his *Chinese Songs,* for mezzo-soprano and piano, was also heard).

In 1958, he was awarded a French government scholarship which enabled him to go to Paris to study composition for a year with Nadia Boulanger and Max Deutsch. In 1960, he married Karen Graham, and they settled in London to raise a daughter and a son.

In London, Maw's career as composer went into full swing and his first significant compositions, in the late neo-Romantic style which he favored, were written in the first years of the 1960s. *Essay,* for organ (1961, revised in 1963), was given its first performance in 1961 at the Salisbury Cathedral by James Dalton. *Chamber Music,* for oboe, clarinet, horn, bassoon, and piano, was commissioned for the centenary of Southampton University where it was performed in 1962. Outstanding was *Scenes and Arias,* for soprano, mezzo-soprano, contralto, and orchestra (1961) which was commissioned by the B.B.C. for a Promenade concert in London where it was introduced on August 31, 1962, under the direction of Norman Del Mar. Its text was an anonymous poem written in or about 1300, entitled *Lines from Love Letters,* from a man to his mistress and her reply, in a mixture of old English and old French, with each couplet ending in a Latin expression as summation.

In *Scenes and Arias,* Maw crystallized his ideas on writing a symphony orchestra. As he told Raymond Ericson of the New York *Times:* "There's been a retreat from the orchestra. Even when it's been used, it's been used as a vast chamber ensemble in a Mahler tradition. I tend to think of it in a more traditional sense—a body of people playing together as opposed to their playing concomitantly. ... The orchestra is a simulacrum of our secret lives. It is a great product of Western civilization. It will develop and maybe change, but it will never die."

Maw revised *Scenes and Arias* in 1966, condensing the closing section and adding two orchestral interludes. The new version received its first performance in London on March 13, 1968, with Colin Davis conducting the B.B.C. Symphony and it has since been performed frequently in England and elsewhere. On September 26, 1974, it was premiered in the United States by the Philadelphia Orchestra under Eugene Ormandy, and the composer, on his first visit to the United States, attended that performance. Harold C. Schonberg said in the New York *Times*, "It is nothing if not an eclectic score. There are ... certain things in the writing that command respect—the powerful orchestration, the frequently unabashed romanticism, the canny mixtures of voices against the orchestral textures."

Maw's first opera, *One Man Show*, was written in 1964 and revised two years later. An opera buffa with text by Arthur Jacobs, it was based on a short story by Saki satirizing the pretentious and often artificial attitude toward modern art. It was commissioned by the London County Council for the opening of the Jeannette Cochrane Theater in London and introduced on November 12, 1964, with Norman Del Mar conducting. *Opera* (London) called it "a brilliant achievement. ... Musically it is what the theater needs today—a comedy that is not trivial or pastiche, but has real substance all through."

Maw's String Quartet, written a year later, was also well-received. It was commissioned for the first Harlow Arts Festival (with the help of the Aspen Fund) and performed in Harlow, Essex, on July 12, 1965, by the Alberni String Quartet. The report in the London *Sunday Times* was typical of the critical reaction: "Strength of thematic invention and impassioned ingenuity of treatment are the dominant features of this mature and deeply-considered quartet."

In 1965–1966 Maw taught composition at the Royal Academy of Music in London, and from 1966 to 1970 he was a Fellow Commoner in Creative Arts at Trinity College, Cambridge. In these years he wrote *Sinfonia,* for small orchestra (1966) which was commissioned by the Aspen Fund for the Northern Sinfonia and premiered at Newcastle–upon–Tyne on May 1, 1966. *The Voice of Love* (1966), a song cycle based on poems by Peter Porter, was introduced by Janet Baker in London on October 6, 1966. *Sonata for Strings and Two Horns* (1967), commissioned by the Bath Festival Society, was given its first hearing on June 7, 1967, with Yehudi Menuhin conducting the Bath Festival Orchestra. Referring to this Sonata, a critic for the London *Daily Telegraph* wrote: "The excellence of this combination of solidity and cleanness of sound is matched by the imaginative variations of texture, character, intensity and color."

In 1970, on commission from the Glyndebourne Festival Society, Maw completed a second opera, *The Rising of the Moon,* with a text by Beverly Cross. This romantic comedy, set in Ireland in 1875, was designed by the composer to give pleasure. It was produced at the Glyndebourne Festival on July 19, 1970, with Raymond Leppard conducting. Thoroughly entertaining, it also had a more serious side in character development through the music. The London *Observer* said, "The score has pace, variety and a sense of atmosphere which stems from an unusual combination of high spirits and sensuous warmth. He [Maw] has a knack of catching a physical gesture in music, and he is also adept at sustaining scenes with ideas that are developed and varied. The vocal writing is fluent, pointful—and singable." The *London Times* found that "Maw fertilized a lovely, saucy, ironical plot with sparkling agile music and some of the sensual heartfelt love music which has long been a specialty of his." The Glyndebourne Festival gave a second performance of the work in 1971, and there were other productions in Graz, Austria, and Bremen, Germany, in 1978.

In 1971, Maw left London for a new residence, "Home Farm," in Maperton, Wincanton, in Somerset. "I lived in an old farm house," he revealed to Raymond Ericson in 1974. "I needed the freedom to go out and walk around as much as I wanted to, and I needed the peace to work. The only drawback is being unable to visit the opera whenever I feel like it. I teach some classes at the University of Exeter, but I am largely self-supporting through my music. One skirts the thin edge financially sometimes, and it helps to have a friendly bank manager, but I don't worry about it too much."

Maw's principal works in the 1970s included *Five Irish Songs,* for chorus (1972), whose first performance took place at the Cork International Choral Festival in Ireland on May 4, 1973; *Life Studies,* a set of eight pieces for fifteen solo instruments (1973), commissioned by the Arts Council of Great Britain for the Cheltenham Festival, received its premiere on July 9, 1973, with Neville Marriner conducting; *Serenade,* for chamber orchestra (1973 and revised in 1977), was written on commission for the English Chamber Orchestra which performed it first in Singapore on March 31, 1973, with Andrew Davis conducting; *Personae,* for piano (1973), commissioned by the Greater London Council for the South Bank Summer Music Festival at Queen Elizabeth Hall (where Maw was composer-in-residence), was introduced on August 2, 1973, with Paul Crossley conducting; *La Vita Nuova,* a setting of Renaissance Italian poems for soprano and instrumental ensemble (1978) was premiered at the B.B.C. Promenade concerts in London during the summer of 1979; and *Odyssey,* a large-scale work for orchestra (1979), was commissioned by the London Symphony Orchestra for its seventy-fifth anniversary in 1980.

Since 1976, Maw has made his home in London. His interests aside from music include literature, painting, the theater, films, architecture, topography and landscape, wine, and good food.

MAJOR WORKS

Chamber Music—Sonatina, for flute and piano; Chamber Music, for oboe, clarinet, horn, bassoon, and piano; String Quartet; Double Canon for Igor Stravinsky (on his 85th birthday), for various instruments; Epitaph, canon in memory of Igor Stravinsky for flute, clarinet, and harp.

Choral Music—Five Epigrams, for a cappella chorus; Round, for children's voices, chorus, and piano; The Angel Gabriel, carol for a cappella chorus; Balulalow, a carol, for a cappella chorus; Corpus Christi Carol, arranged for sopranos and descant with piano; Five Irish Songs, for chorus; Te Deum, for treble, tenor, chorus, congregation, and organ; Reverdie, for male voices.

Operas—One Man Show, comic opera; The Rising of the Moon.

Orchestral Music—Scenes and Arias, for soprano, mezzo-soprano, contralto, and orchestra; Sinfonia, for small orchestra; Sonata for Strings and Two Horns;

Concert Music for Orchestra (derived from The Rising of the Moon); Life Studies, for fifteen instruments; Serenade, for small orchestra; Odyssey.

Organ Music—Essay; Trinitas.

Piano Music—Personae.

Vocal Music—Nocturne, for mezzo-soprano and orchestra; The Voice of Love, song cycle for mezzo-soprano and piano; Six Interiors, for tenor and guitar; Nonsense Songs for Children, twenty songs and rounds with piano accompaniment; La Vita Nuova, for soprano and chamber ensemble.

ABOUT

Foreman, L. (ed.), British Music Now; Whittall, A., Music Since the First World War.

Music and Musicians (London), May 1970; Musical Times (London), September 1962; New York Times, September 29, 1974.

Nicolas Medtner

1880–1951

See *Composers Since 1900.*

Peter Mennin

1923–

For biographical sketch, list of earlier works, and bibliography, see *Composers Since 1900.*

In spite of his administrative duties as the president of the Juilliard School of Music since 1963, Mennin has composed several major works. At the invitation of conductor Max Rudolf, Mennin composed *Cantata de Virtute,* for narrator, soloists, children's chorus, and orchestra (1969) for the Cincinnati May Festival. The text, based partly on *The Pied Piper of Hamelin,* was discussed by Mennin: "I reread the *Pied Piper* for the first time since childhood and found that in fact it was an austere morality tale. My interest grew . . . and . . . I found and read earlier source material from which Robert Browning had based his poetic text. This proved rewarding, for, as inevitably happens when one goes to the source, one finds variations and nuances which were not part of subsequent adaptations. . . . I realized that the medieval subject matter was pertinent to modern problems and pressures. Further thought also convinced me that the text of *The Pied Piper* alone would not be sufficient for the broad-scaled conception that had already been developing subconsciously. This led me to examine other materials which might support the concept I had formed, with the result that I have introduced the Latin text of Psalm 117, two thirteenth-century poems which elaborate on the basic conception and an adaptation of the Missa pro Defunctis. . . . Finally, in order to create a total context, several additions to and extensions of the contextual material have been made." The world premiere of *The Pied Piper* took place in Cincinnati on May 2, 1969.

On January 21, 1971, the Minnesota Symphony under Stanislaw Skrowaczewski, premiered *Symphonic Movements* (later called *Sinfonia*). Under the title *Sinfonia,* it was again performed by Skrowaczewski with the New York Philharmonic Orchestra, on March 25, 1971. A fifteen-minute composition in two movements, Harold C. Schonberg, of the New York *Times,* found *Sinfonia* to be "an attractive piece with a slow, mysterious first section, a cumulative build-up and a bang-up ending. . . . There is no deep message to the music: it is not that kind of piece. What it does is produce attractive sounds in a well-organized manner."

The first performance of Mennin's Symphony No. 8 (1973) was on November 21, 1974, with Daniel Barenboim directing the New York Philharmonic Orchestra. The entire work is unified by an underlying idea, each of four movements, inspired by a biblical text, unfolding along purely musical rather than programmatic lines. The movements are: I. "In the Beginning" *(In Principio);* II. "Day of Wrath" *(Dies Irae);* III. "Out of the Depths" *(De Profundis);* and IV. "Praise Ye the Lord" *(Laudate Dominum).*

Voices, for mezzo-soprano, percussion, piano, harp, and harpsichord, was commissioned and premiered on March 28, 1976, by the Chamber Music Society of Lincoln Center in New York with Frederica von Stade as soprano soloist. In four sections, the work sets to music four American poems: Thoreau's "Smoke," Melville's "Lone Founts," Whitman's "When I Heard the Learn'd Astronomer," and Emily Dickinson's "Much Madness Is Divinest Sense." The composer explained, "It was my intention to conceive musical settings that would bring out and strengthen the mystical and spiritual qualities of the metaphysical images." Donal Henahan of

the New York *Times* referred to *Voices* as "an often evocative piece," and a critic for *High Fidelity/Musical America* found the music "full of color and variety."

Because it is shorter and less formal in character than his earlier symphonies, Mennin was somewhat reluctant to identify his *Sinfonia Capricciosa,* for orchestra (1980), as Symphony No. 9. The work was introduced on March 10, 1981, in Washington, D.C., by the National Symphony Orchestra (which commissioned it), with Mstislav Rostropovich conducting. This work, in three short movements, requires twenty-one minutes of performance time. The last movement recalls the opening movement in rhythmic patterns reminiscent of Stravinsky. The following inscription appears at the beginning of the finale: "In Memoriam: I.S."

MAJOR WORKS (supplementary)

Choral Music—Cantata de Virtute, for narrator, vocal soloists, children's chorus, and orchestra.

Orchestral Music—Symphonic Movement, retitled Sinfonia; Symphony No. 8; Sinfonia Capricciosa (Symphony No. 9); Concerto for Flute and Orchestra.

Vocal Music—Voices, for mezzo-soprano, percussion, piano, harp, and harpsichord; Reflections of Emily, for a chorus of treble voices, piano, harp, and percussion.

ABOUT (supplementary)

High Fidelity/Musical America, March 1976 ; New York Times, March 21, 1971.

Gian Carlo Menotti

1911–

For biographical sketch, list of earlier works, and bibliography, see *Composers Since 1900.*

In addition to writing librettos for Samuel Barber *(Vanessa* and *Anthony and Cleopatra),* Menotti experimented as a playwright with *The Leper.* It was produced in Tallahassee, Florida, on April 22, 1970, for the opening of the Fine Arts Building of Florida State University where it was one of the main attractions of the Fine Arts Festival. Menotti originally planned to make *The Leper* an opera, but as he began to develop his subject he realized it was "too intellectual and philosophical" for musical treatment. However, a solo flute and some choral fragments are heard throughout. *The Leper* was a failure both in Florida and at its revival at the Spoleto Festival in Italy in the summer of 1980.

Menotti's *Triple Concerto a Tre* was performed at a concert of the American Symphony Orchestra conducted by Leopold Stokowski. It was commissioned as a tribute to the twenty-fifth anniversary of the United Nations, and introduced on October 6, 1970. Andrew DeRhen wrote in *High Fidelity/Musical America:* "Menotti obtains many delicate concerto-grosso effects, and his melodies are always agreeable—especially in the slow movement, which is built on one of those pliant, Italianate themes he knows how to write so well."

After an absence of several years from the opera stage, Menotti returned on March 12, 1971, with *The Most Important Man,* which was produced by the New York City Opera. Menotti's libretto concerns a black scientist in an apartheid community (South Africa) who creates a formula to make him the world's most powerful man and he meets death and the destruction of his formula. The critics were not kind to Menotti's new opera: George Movshon wrote in *High Fidelity/Musical America,* "This paper cut-out of a libretto was colored by numbers, with a wash of music to match, a sort of peanut-butter score, homogenized and utterly disposable." Irving Kolodin wrote in *Saturday Review,* "An opera lover . . . could not, for the most part, tell whether it is related to blacks and whites in South Africa or unhappy artisans in north Italy. Its method has more to do with *Tosca* than with the veldt, and leaves us hoping in vain for new tones, new tunes, new turns of Menotti inventiveness." Harold C. Schonberg wrote in the New York *Times,* "most of it is more soap opera than opera."

On his sixtieth birthday, an embittered Menotti dispatched a letter to the New York *Times* in which his resentment of the critics spilled over. "I hardly know of another artist who has been more consistently damned by the critics. Even those critics who have defended my music have done so (with two or three exceptions) condescendingly, or apologetically. Recently, a well-known New York critic wrote that he was 'ashamed' of liking my music. The insults that most of my operas had to endure through the years make a booklet as terrifying as Malleus Maleficarum." (Apparently, Menotti found no consolation in the fact that no other composer of the 20th century was performed more success-

fully and more frequently throughout the music world than he, and that on two occasions he had won the coveted Pulitzer Prize.)

Another untoward incident in 1971 involved his opera, *The Consul* (1950) which was scheduled for the 1972 May Music Festival in Florence, Italy, on the program with Luigi Nono's *Intolleranza.* Nono, Claudio Abbado (the famous conductor), and a group of left-wing intellectuals and musicians joined together to denounce Menotti's opera as "an expression of McCarthyism" and a "squalid product of the cold war of anti-Sovietism." They insisted that the opera be removed from the festival program. Amid the hostility, *The Consul,* in spite of objections, was produced at the festival on June 22, 1973.

Menotti thought of abandoning opera altogether, but when the Ninth International Congress of Anthropological and Ethnological Science asked him to write an opera for their Chicago convention, Menotti had a change of heart. He completed *Tamu-Tamu (Guests),* a two-act chamber opera, and its first performance took place in Chicago on September 5, 1973. The audience was most appreciative, rising to give Menotti and the cast a rousing ovation after the final curtain, but the critics again disagreed. In the Chicago *Sun-Times,* Peggy Constantine felt that the opera would have been a major achievement had his "concept been more poignant and sincere in execution." Karen Monson, of the Chicago *Daily News,* called the opera "a series of intriguing suggestions" but felt that "the silliness of *Tamu-Tamu*'s mundane moments undermines the seriousness of its most dramatic, philosophical segments." In the New York *Times,* Peter G. Davis commented: "It is a vulnerable piece, easily dismissed." The Oriental tinge in the music was criticized by the critics as "fake," to which Menotti replied, "It represents *my* version, *my* feeling of Oriental music."

In this opera Menotti's libretto explored the clash of cultures between a modern American couple in Vietnam and a war-ravaged Indonesian family marooned in a blizzard. While bonds between them were formed, broken, and reformed, the Indonesian family met death by the Vietcong and the Americans were spared. The Asian couple sang in Indonesian and the white couple sang in English.

The Lyric Opera Company commissioned Menotti to write an opera for the American

196

bicentennial celebration and Menotti wrote *The Hero,* a comic opera, which was produced by the Opera Company of Philadelphia (formerly the Lyric Opera Company) on June 1, 1976. The opera was set in a small town in Pennsylvania which became famous because a citizen had been sleeping for a record ten years. He was awakened by a kiss from his cousin who loved him and unhappy neighbors conspired to send him back to sleep. Menotti explained, "It's not actually a political satire. It's a gentle and good-humored indictment of contemporary society's self-satisfaction and greed, and of those leaders who, in order to protect their own interests, choose the mediocre, the expedient, and glorify the innocuous—the man who is asleep and thus cannot bother anyone. It is a plea to Americans to wake up to reality, to abandon self-congratulatory illusions and to return to their former rugged individualism. Nothing very serious, however. It is an opera buffa after all." While the plot unfolded, Menotti satirized the American scene. Donal Henahan reported in the New York *Times,* "*The Hero* is in the familiar idiom of other Menotti comedies. . . . A bit treadworn by now, but workable enough. The accompanied recitative that carries the action is generally supple and singable. There is a genuinely lyrical love duet in the second act curtain that is most welcome, though it relies a little too heavily on the knee-jerk cliches of the Puccini tradition. Several ensemble numbers are similarly effective." The first New York performance of *The Hero* was presented on December 10, 1980, by the Juilliard American Opera Center.

Shortly after this premiere, on June 17, *The Egg,* a one-act church opera, was performed at the Washington Cathedral in Washington, D.C. The magical egg in Menotti's libretto is supposed to provide the key to the meaning of life, and is owned by St. Simon Stylites who presents it to his nephew. In the Byzantine court, all attempts to break the egg prove futile, but when it is given in charity to a poor woman to feed herself and her child, the egg is broken. In *Opera News,* Charles Timbrell said that *The Egg* consisted of "a tedious succession of unaccompanied recitatives, interrupted only occasionally by innocuous punctuating ideas in the orchestra."

In 1976, there were premieres of two non-operatic Menotti compositions, including *Landscapes and Remembrances,* for chorus, four

vocal soloists, and orchestra, which was first performed by the Milwaukee Symphony and the Bel Canto Chorus on May 14, 1976. Menotti's own text was autobiographical and represented his impressions of life in the United States in nine sections: his arrival by ship in New York, a southern mansion, a Texas parade, a desert drive, a subway ride in Chicago, a picnic on the Brandywine, a trip to Wisconsin, a Vermont railroad station, and a flight from America at sunset.

The second work was Menotti's first symphony, entitled *The Halcyon,* in the key of A minor. Commissioned by the Saratoga Performing Arts Center in New York for the American bicentennial, it was introduced by the Philadelphia Orchestra under Eugene Ormandy on August 4, 1976. Menotti called it "The Halcyon," "because it recalls the most serene and optimistic days of my youth when the horizon shone unclouded." The work, in three classic movements, is tonal and assonant. The first movement is in sonata form, the second is a passacaglia, and the third is a rondo.

Another non-operatic work by Menotti which was heard on May 24, 1978, in New York is *The Trial of the Gypsy,* for treble voices and piano. The Newark Boys Choir commissioned and performed it. The text tells of a boy, raised and abandoned by gypsies, who is put on trial for vagrancy, theft, and sorcery, and outwits his accusers with bright answers. Allen Hughes of the New York *Times* described it as a "short, an unpretentious and deftly written work . . . at once simple and sophisticated."

When he was commissioned by the San Diego Opera to write a musical drama for Beverly Sills' fiftieth birthday, Menotti wrote *La Loca* in 1979. This was the first time Menotti chose an actual historic heroine and setting, Juana of Castile, daughter of King Ferdinand and Queen Isabella, in 15th century Spain. Three men with whom she is in love—her husband, her father, and her son, are involved in intrigues to get her to abdicate, and she is declared insane and imprisoned for thirty years. The world premiere of the opera took place in San Diego, California, on June 3, 1979, with Beverly Sills in the title role. Harold C. Schonberg reported in the New York *Times* that "*La Loca* is weak . . . Mr. Menotti has created a tearjerker with some pretense to Freudian psychology and, at the very end, a look at religion. . . . There are a few vague passes at

Spanish rhythms, but obviously Mr. Menotti was not interested in trying for an evocation of Medieval Spain. For the most part, the writing is pure 19th century opera, with harmonies that would not have disturbed any teacher at the Leipzig Conservatory in the 1950s." On September 16, 1979, the opera was produced at the New York City Opera.

On May 25, 1977, Menotti inaugurated the Spoleto Festival U.S.A. in Charleston, South Carolina, as an annual counterpart to his successful Festival of Two Worlds in Spoleto, Italy, which he founded in 1958 and of which he is president. In May 1981, the festival commemorated Menotti's seventieth year with performances of some of his most important works.

Menotti's opera, *Amahl and the Night Visitors,* originally written for television in 1951, was shown in an entirely new production (after a twelve-year absence) over the NBC-TV network on Christmas Eve, 1978.

In 1973, Menotti sold "Capricorn," the house he had shared for a quarter of a century with Samuel Barber in Mt. Kisco, New York. He divides his time between an apartment in New York and a fourteen-room baronial castle, Yester House, on seventy-two acres in Lothian, Scotland, which he shares with his legally adopted son, "Chip" (Francis Phelan). He said: "Having decided on a luxurious house, I wanted it to be *very* luxurious. . . . Yester House protects me from a world I have come to detest—a world of modern cities. Here, at least, I am close to nature. . . . Actually, this last gesture of mine is a foolish disregard for money and wealth because, although I live splendidly, I really live without a penny. Whatever I have, I spend immediately." He particularly enjoys Scottish weather because "I love to compose in cold weather. In the heat I become very lazy—my thoughts wander."

"I loathe to begin a new work," Menotti confided to his biographer, John Gruen. "Like Tobias I am always terrified by the prospect of my battle with the angel. Unconsciously, I keep postponing the day when I am to embark on a new project. Any excuse is good. I know that once I begin I am trapped. That is why I eagerly accept commissions or force myself into a position of having to accept a commission." He never sits at his work table for more than fifteen minutes at a time, frequently jumping up from his seat to pace the room nervously. As he works, he nibbles on nuts and dried fruits always at hand.

MAJOR WORKS (supplementary)

Choral Music—Landscapes and Remembrances, cantata for four vocal soloists, large chorus, and orchestra; Trial of the Gypsy, for treble voices and piano; O Pulchritudo, Mass for vocal soloists, chorus, and orchestra.

Operas—The Most Important Man; Tamu-Tamu; The Hero, comic opera; The Egg, one-act church opera; La Loca; Chip and His Dog, one-act opera for children.

Orchestral Music—Triple Concerto a Tre; Symphony No. 1, in A minor, "The Halcyon."

ABOUT (supplementary)

Gruen, J., Menotti: A Biography; Mordden, E., Opera in the 20th Century: Sacred, Profane and Godot; Tricoire, R., Gian Carlo Menotti: l'Homme et son Oeuvre.

New York Daily News, May 19, 1978; New York Times, September 16, 1973, April 14, 1974, June 5, 1977; New York Times Magazine, June 6, 1977; New Yorker, June 13, 1977; Opera News, May 1977.

Olivier Messiaen

1908–

For biographical sketch, list of earlier works, and bibliography, see *Composers Since 1900.*

Messiaen's oratorio, *La Transfiguration de Notre Seigneur Jésus Christ,* for solo voices, solo piano, solo cello, and orchestra (1965–1969) was introduced in Lisbon on June 7, 1969. Its American premiere was presented by the National Symphony under Antal Dorati in Washington, D.C., on March 28, 1972. The Latin text—from the Bible, St. Thomas Aquinas, and sundry Catholic liturgical writings—is a glorification and adoration of Jesus Christ as Light of the World. In fourteen movements, the oratorio is divided into two equal parts with seven movements each and four "gospel narratives" chanted at the beginning and in the middle of each half. In this work, as in so many of Messiaen's earlier works, he concentrates on the sounds of bird calls and on colors, harmonies, and sonorities which go, as he explained, "from blue striped green to black spotted with red and gold, by way of diamond, emerald, purplish-blue, with a dominant pool of orange studded with milky white." The work as a whole according to Harold C. Schonberg of the New York *Times,* "brings together a weird melange of musical and extra musical effects. It has liturgical chant, serial-sounding arrangements, massed dissonances next to triadic harmonies, derivations from classical Indian music, a stylistic adaptation of the chorale, polyrhythms, thick spatial relationships. . . . He has managed to work out a style peculiarly his own."

While on a visit to the United States in 1972, Messiaen gave the world premiere of *Méditations sur le Mystère de la Saint-Trinité,* a work for organ (1969), at the National Shrine of the Immaculate Conception in Washington, D.C., on March 20. This nine-movement work, Messiaen's first major organ composition in eighteen years, combines a Gregorian chant with rhythms of ancient India and bird calls; symbolism is blended with theology and color theories. Some parts, reported Allen Hughes in the New York *Times,* "are quite dazzling in their exotic sonorities and dramatic effect. . . . One of his great contributions has been to show that the instrument of Bach and Franck can do wonderful things those composers never dreamed of."

In 1973, Messiaen returned to the United States for a month in Parowan, Utah, where the scenic splendors of Cedar Breaks National Monument "inspired in me a feeling very close to awe." In a musical response, he completed a large work for orchestra, solo piano, and horn in 1974, entitled *Des Canyons aux Étoiles (From the Canyons to the Stars).* The world premiere took place in New York on November 20, 1974, by Musica Aeterna (which commissioned it) under Frederic Waldman. The three parts of the composition are subdivided into twelve sections, and in Messiaen's omnipresent mysticism, are suggestions of geography, geology, astronomy, bird calls (from eighty different birds), and color modes. Harriett Johnson said in the New York *Post,* "Messiaen has inflated his musical and literary ideas out of all proportion to their inherent value."

On November 1, 1973, two and a half weeks before the premiere of his *Des Canyons aux Étoiles,* Messiaen's wife, Yvonne Loriod, gave the first presentation of *La Fauvette des Jardins (The Warbler of Gardens),* for piano, at the Hopkins Center of Dartmouth College in Hanover, New Hampshire. Written in 1972 as a successor to the composer's *Catalogue d'Oiseaux* (1956–1958), it represents various times of the full day in the Dauphiné mountains in France beginning late at night to etch the colors and bird sounds of the mountains through daybreak, afternoon, and nightfall.

Messiaen's seventieth birthday celebrations began in the United States early in 1978 and were held all over Europe and Canada. On March 20, the Performers Committee for 20th Century Music presented a retrospective program of Messiaen's works in New York. On August 5, the citizens of Parowan (remembering his visit) held ceremonies in his honor (without his presence) and named a mountain after him, Mt. Messiaen. Prematurely, the New York Philharmonic Orchestra under Zubin Mehta honored Messiaen on November 9 by putting three of his compositions for orchestra on its program. Other American musical organizations joined in the celebration, frequently with Messiaen in attendance.

Messiaen received several distinguished awards since 1970: the Prix Erasme (1971), Prix Sibelius (1971), Grande Medalle d'Or des Arts, Sciences et Lettres (1972), Prix Ernst von Siemens (1975), Prix Sonning (1977) and Prix Ville de Paris (1977).

MAJOR WORKS (supplementary)

Choral Music—La Transfiguration de Notre Seigneur Jésus Christ, oratorio for solo voices, solo piano, solo cello, and orchestra.

Opera—St. Francis of Assisi.

Orchestral Music—Des Canyons aux Étoiles.

Organ Music—Méditations sur le Mystère de la Sainte-Trinité.

Piano Music—La Fauvette des Jardins.

ABOUT (supplementary)

Griffiths, P., A Concise History of Avant-Garde Music; Johnson, R. S., Messiaen; Mari, P., Olivier Messiaen, l'Homme et son Oeuvre; Nichols, R., Messiaen; Samuel, C., Conversations with Olivier Messiaen.

Music and Letters (London), April 1971; Music Magazine (Toronto) January-February 1979; Musical Times (London), September 1971; New York Times, June 20, 1971, November 20, 1974.

Miaskovsky

Nikolai Miaskovsky

1881–1950

See *Composers Since 1900.*

Francisco Mignone

1897–

For biographical sketch, list of earlier works, and bibliography, see *Composers Since 1900.*

Mignone's third opera, *O Chalaça*—his first opera in almost half a century—had its world premiere at the Teatro Municipal in Rio de Janeiro on October 22, 1976. "Chalaça," meaning "crude jest," was the nickname for Francisco Gomes da Silva who rose from barber to a power behind the throne during the reign of Pedro I. The libretto (by Mello Nobrega) deals with Donna Domitila de Castro, mistress of Emperor Don Pedro, and a power in the land until the emperor deserted her to marry Donna Amelia de Leuchtenberg. In a report to *Opera* (London), Antonio José Faro wrote: "The work is a succession of beautiful melodies, many of them based on the rhythms of the time [early 19th century]. ... The orchestration is rich and powerful, yet never drowns the singer but enhances the beauty and musicality of the Portuguese language."

In 1967, Mignone resigned from his position as professor at the National School of Music of the University of Rio de Janeiro.

MAJOR WORKS (supplementary)

Chamber Music—2 wind trios; 2 sonatas for flute and oboe; Sonata No. 3, for violin and piano; Sonata for Cello and Piano; Sonata for Trumpet Solo; Sextet No. 2, for wind quintet and piano; Sonata a Tre, for flute, oboe, and clarinet; String Quartet No. 3; Serenata a Dulcinéa, for string sextet; Preludio Coral para una Fuga, for piano quintet.

Choral Music—Sixteen Cantos Escolares.

Opera—O Chalaça.

Piano Music—Sonata No. 4; Sonata Humoristica, for two pianos; Rondo; 6½ Preludios.

ABOUT (supplementary)

Inter-American Music Bulletin, Special Mignone Issue, 1970–1971.

Darius Milhaud

1892–1974

For biographical sketch, list of earlier works, and bibliography, see *Composers Since 1900.*

Music for New Orleans, for orchestra, which was commissioned by the New Orleans Symphony, was never performed by that orchestra, but its world premiere took place instead at Aspen, Colorado, on August 11, 1968.

Commissioned by the Chamber Music Society of Lincoln Center in New York, Milhaud decided to write a trio for the traditional combination of violin, cello, and piano, the first of its kind for him in his vast chamber-music output. *Trio* received its world premiere in New York on October 31, 1968, and Peter Davis wrote in *High Fidelity/Musical America,* "This is a tough, muscular piece in four well-contrasted movements, harmonically astringent and rhythmically aggressive. The two slower movements have an agreeable impressionistic air about them, but here, too, the music possesses an urgency and forward driving tension. ... The Trio is a worthy addition to the large Milhaud catalogue."

Saint-Louis, Roi de France, an opera-oratorio set to a text by Paul Claudel, was given its first hearing on Italian Radio on March 18, 1972, before being performed on the stage on April 14 in Rio de Janeiro. This work was commissioned by the French government for the 700th anniversary in 1970 of the saint-king's death.

A ballet, *Vendanges,* which Milhaud wrote for the Paris Opéra in 1952 but which had never been performed (and never published), was revived in Nice on April 17, 1972, to honor Milhaud in his eightieth year. The libretto, by Baron Philippe de Rothschild, was based on his own poems and he explained, "Vendanges means harvest, in this case the wine harvest, and both plot and poem are a mingling of sensual human yearnings with the earthiness of the wine harvest in an evocation of nature's constantly self-renewing life cycle."

The premiere of Milhaud's last composition, *Ani Maamin* (I Believe), took place at Carnegie Hall, New York, on November 13, 1973. For narrator and chorus, its text is by Elie Wiesel who served as principal narrator at the premiere. The text is an affirmation of religious belief in the

200

face of the Nazi holocaust, God's seeming indifference to His People, and the failure of the Messiah to appear. Besides the narrator, there are three other biblical characters representing Abraham, Isaac, and Jacob. Milhaud's score contains a brief soprano solo and a series of brief choruses, one of which is whispered. "Some lovely melodies came and went (the pianissimo ending was especially effective)," wrote Harold C. Schonberg in the New York *Times.* "There were some powerful outbursts, and as a whole this proved to be a dignified and heartfelt addition to Jewish religious music."

In 1971 Milhaud resigned as professor emeritus and composer-in-residence at Mills College in Oakland, California. He had been on the faculty since 1940, and professor emeritus and composer-in-residence since 1962. At the same time he moved from the hilltop home built for him near Mills College, where he spent part of each year, to his apartment in Paris, which Ned Rorem described in *The Paris Diary,* as looking down "into the million wild lights of Pigalle's merry-go-round." Milhaud loved street crowds, lights, and noises and he had the ability to compose even with distractions of all kinds. He wrote swiftly—hence his vast output of over 450 compositions—never at the piano but at a desk, and rarely changing a note once he had put it down on paper.

Two years before his death, Milhaud left Paris for an apartment in Geneva, which reminded him of his residence in Oakland, California. A complaint against his native country came to light before his death. He said, "I did some statistics once, and calculated that 85 percent of my works had their premieres in other countries. . . . France covers me with honors, but does not perform my music."

Milhaud died at his home in Geneva on June 22, 1974, and was buried in Aix-en-Provence (the city of his birth) following a private prayer service conducted by Geneva's chief Rabbi, Alexander Satran, on June 25.

In remembrance of Milhaud's long association with Mills College, they presented a season-long festival of his music beginning on October 28, 1979, and twenty-five musical institutions in the San Francisco Bay area participated. A Milhaud professorship in music was established at the college in his memory, and its first recipient was Betsy Jolas, a former Milhaud student.

MAJOR WORKS (supplementary)

Ballets—Vendanges; 'Adame Miroir; La Rose des Vents; La Branche des Oiseaux.

Chamber Music—Piano Quartet; Piano Trio; Stanford Serenade, for oboe and eleven instruments; Musique pour Ars Nova, for thirteen instruments; Wind Quintet.

Choral Music—Cantate de la Croix de Charité; Cantate de l'Initiation, for chorus and orchestra; Invocations à l'Ange Raphael, for two women's choruses and orchestra; Cantate de Psaumes; Les Momies d'Egypt, choral comedy; Bar Mitzvah Cantata; Ani Maamin, for narrator, soprano solo, chorus, and orchestra.

Operas—Saint-Louis, Roi de France, opera oratorio; Jeux d'Enfants, short plays for children for voice and instruments.

Orchestral Music—Music for Boston, for violin and orchestra; Music for Prague; Music for Indiana; Music for Lisbon; Musique pour l'Universe Claudelien; Musique pour Graz; Music for San Francisco, with participating audience; Suite in G; Ode pour Jerusalem.

Piano Music—Ma Vie Heureuse.

Vocal Music—Adam, for vocal quintet.

ABOUT (supplementary)

Braga, A., Darius Milhaud; Palmer, C., Milhaud; Sadie, S. (ed.), The New Grove Dictionary of Music and Musicians.

New York Times, June 25, 1974.

Italo Montemezzei

1875–1852

See *Composers Since 1900.*

Douglas Moore

1893–1969

See *Composers Since 1900.*

Thea Musgrave

1928–

THEA MUSGRAVE

Thea Musgrave was born in Barnton, Midlothian, Scotland, on May 27, 1928, the only child of James P. and Joan Hacking Musgrave. Though she was musical from childhood, frequently finding amusement in making up her own melodies, her earliest ambition was to become a doctor so that she might help her fellow human beings.

After graduating from Moreton Hall, in Oswestry, England, in 1947, she enrolled in Edinburgh University for premedical studies. Still intensely interested in music, she decided to take advantage of the musical facilities of the University by studying harmony and musical analysis with Mary Grierson and counterpoint and the history of music with Hans Gál. By the time she had finished her music studies at the university, where she was awarded the Donald Francis Tovey Prize and received a Bachelor of Music degree in 1950, she put all thoughts of medicine out of her mind to concentrate on music, concluding that she could serve humanity just as well through it. With encouragement from pianist Clifford Curzon, she went to Paris in 1950 on scholarship for four years of postgraduate study with Nadia Boulanger. In Paris, she was drawn into twelve-tone and avant-garde music by becoming acquainted with and interested in the works of Schoenberg, Webern, Dallapiccola, Boulez, and Stockhausen.

During her last year of studies with Nadia Boulanger, Musgrave started composing—in a tonal style marked by diatonic lyricism. *A Suite o'Bairnsangs* for voice and piano, commissioned by the Scottish Festival at Braemar, and *Four Madrigals,* for a cappella chorus, and a one-act ballet, *A Tale of Three Thieves* (from a scenario based on Chaucer's *The Pardoner's Tale*) were all completed in 1953. She was awarded the Lili Boulanger Memorial Prize for the works, the first time such a prize went to a Scottish composer. In 1954, on commission from the B.B.C. (Scotland), she wrote *Cantata for a Summer Day* (with texts by Hume and Maurice Lindsay) for narrator, vocal quartet, and various instruments. It was successfully introduced by the Sal-

Musgrave: mŭs' grāv

tire Singers at the Edinburgh Festival in Scotland.

By 1955, Musgrave completed her first dramatic work, a one-act chamber opera, *The Abbot of Drimock,* for seven singers, violin, cello, piano, celesta, and percussion. The libretto, by Maurice Lindsay, was based on a Scottish Border tale (a version of the plot from Puccini's *Gianni Schicchi*). *The Abbot of Drimock* was heard first in London at a concert performance, in 1958, and was first staged in 1962 in London and revived in March 1977.

A gradual change in style became apparent as serial elements began to seep into Musgrave's writing in *Five Love Songs,* based on early English texts, for soprano and guitar (1955); in *Divertimento,* for string orchestra (1957); and in *Obliques,* for orchestra (1958), which was introduced on January 8, 1959, by the Scottish Symphony Orchestra, with Colin Davis conducting. The serial technique became more distinct in *A Song for Christmas* (1958), for voice and piano; and the String Quartet (1958) which was commissioned by the University Court in Glasgow. Not confining herself to strict serialism, Musgrave wrote *Scottish Dance Suite* (1959), for orchestra, premiered by the B.B.C. Scottish Orchestra on August 17, 1961, which was tonal. *Triptych,* for tenor and orchestra, (1959), with a text based on Chaucer, personalized her use of the serial technique with touches of lyricism and romantic feelings. *Triptych* was commissioned by the Saltire Society and introduced by the

London Symphony Orchestra under Meredith Davies on September 14, 1960.

From 1955 on, Thea Musgrave was active in England as a piano accompanist and she visited the United States for the first time in 1958 to participate in a program at Tanglewood in Massachusetts. From 1959 to 1965 she was extramural lecturer on music at London University at Teddington.

By 1960, Musgrave's compositions were written in a partly tonal style that was rich in romantic and lyric interest. She wrote *Sir Patrick Spens,* for tenor and guitar (1961), at the request of Peter Pears who introduced it with Julian Bream, guitarist, at the Aldeburgh Festival in June 1961 and Norman Kay described it as "a little gem" in *Music and Musicians; The Phoenix and the Turtle,* for small chorus and orchestra, based on Shakespeare (1962), was commissioned by the B.B.C. and introduced in London on August 20, 1962; *Marko the Miser,* "a tale for children to mime, sing and play' (1962); and *The Five Ages of Man,* for chorus and orchestra (1963), was commissioned by the Norfolk and Norwich Triennial Music Festival where it was performed on June 6, 1964.

Her rapidly expanding reputation brought her eight commissions for concert works and requests for music for films, television, and plays. Turning down all commercial requests, she preferred to devote her energies to a work she considered her most important one up to that time, the three-act opera *The Decision* (1964–1965). The libretto, by Maurice Lindsay, was based on a true incident in Scotland in 1935 in which John Brown, a miner, died after being entombed for twenty-three days in a cave-in, a tragedy which prompted government labor laws for new safety conditions in Scottish mines. The world premiere of *The Decision,* at Sadler's Wells in London on November 30, 1967, was a success.

The opera led Thea Musgrave in a new direction as a composer and to an instrumental style that she designated as "dramatic-abstract," signifying dramatic music without programmatic content. The first of these works was the Chamber Concerto No. 2, for five instruments (1965), a tribute to Charles Ives, in which each of the instruments is given independence, and the viola assumes a comedic role in an Ivesian way. Chamber Concerto No. 3, for string quartet, clarinet, bassoon, horn, and double-bass (1966) also emphasized the individuality of various instruments. As the composer explained, "It explores the virtuosic possibilities of the eight players who dominate the texture in turn." The second Chamber Concerto was premiered in Dartington in August 1966; the third in London on October 16, 1967.

In 1967, on commission from the Feeney Trust Fund, Musgrave wrote the single-movement Concerto for Orchestra, which was introduced on March 8, 1968 by the City of Birmingham Orchestra under Hugo Rignold. It was then performed by many British and European orchestras, recorded by the Scottish National Orchestra under Alexander Gibson, and its American premiere was heard on September 24, 1976, at a concert of the Philadelphia Orchestra conducted by Musgrave in her American conducting debut. This was the first time that the Philadelphia Orchestra was conducted by a woman performing her own work. Commenting on the solo performances, in the style of the concertino in the baroque concerto grosso, in this Concerto, Musgrave said, "It seemed to me that, to realize the full potential of the soloists, they would at times have to be independent of the bar line, and also at times independent of the conductor. I wanted them to have moments of freedom of expression without the texture of the whole lapsing into anarchy. I therefore evolved a system of intercueing the parts where the players play in relation to one another, occasionally giving each other leads. The players were quick to understand the principles involved, and I felt that the technique led to a more exciting musical interplay. At certain dramatic moments, I asked the soloists to stand, as I am convinced this encourages them to play with greater virtuosity and furthermore heightens tension, as their standing implies a certain defiance of the conductor. This confrontation became part of the dramatic form. Thus the Concerto for Orchestra is built essentially on the struggle between the solo and tutti forces, which gradually develops into a virtuoso piece for the orchestra."

In subsequent instrumental music, Musgrave developed the concept of "space play" in which the performer is allowed to move about the stage or in the hall, and when performing with orchestra is instructed from time to time to join different orchestral sections. "It's not a gimmick," Musgrave insisted, "not just the idea that 'wouldn't it be nice to have him walk around.' It grows out of the musical demand. In the Concerto for Clarinet and Orchestra (1968), for instance, the soloist plays with different small groups and they can't hear him unless he joins them." The *Clarinet Concerto* was written for Gervase de Peyer on commission from the Royal Philharmonic Orchestra of London; he introduced it in London on February 5, 1969. On November 10, 1975, it was heard at a concert of the New York Philharmonic devoted entirely to women composers and conducted by Sarah Caldwell.

"Space play" can also be found in *Night Music,* for chamber orchestra (1969) in which the sound colorations of two horns in the ensemble change even as do the positions the different performers assume on the stage. The B.B.C. Welsh Orchestra introduced it in Cardiff on October 24, 1969. In the Concerto for Horn and Orchestra (1971), which was written for Barry Tuckwell and commissioned by the Congress for the Arts at Dartmouth College in Hanover, New Hampshire, the soloist remains stationary on the stage in front of the orchestra while the horn players in the orchestra take positions behind the audience. Tuckwell gave the first performance in Glasgow on May 1, 1971, with the composer conducting the Scottish National Orchestra. *Space-Play,* for nine instruments (1974), was commissioned by the Koussevitzky Music Foundation. It was introduced by the London Sinfonietta on October 11, 1974, and performed first in the United States in 1975 by the Chamber Music Society of Lincoln Center in New York. In the Los Angeles *Times,* Martin Bernheimer described *Space-Play* as "an elegantly orchestrated squabble for nine strategically placed instruments [that] engage in a vital, multi-layered 'conversation' that spans polite discourse, inane chatter, witty interruptions, imitative competition and climactic hyperbole."

In the late 1960s Musgrave's creativity became less inhibited and enlarged to include electronic music, as in the ballet *Beauty and the Beast,* scored for chamber orchestra and magnetic tape. This work, completed in 1969, was introduced on November 19 by the Scottish Theater Ballet at Sadler's Wells. Musgrave told Shirley Fleming in an interview in the New York *Times,* "I had used it [magnetic tape] not just to enhance the score, but for theatrical purpose. It was the magic element, the spellbinder. I found it very interesting that tape can lift you to another level, that it has real dramatic force." When

Beauty and the Beast was performed later in 1969 in Edinburgh as a special Christmas production, Thea Musgrave made an unexpected bow as conductor, because the scheduled conductor was unable to perform. She recalled the incident: "They said I should do it and I said that's crazy—a little nuts. But I did it. It was jumping in at the deep end but it was a challenge and I enjoyed it."

Two other electronic works were written soon after: *Soliloquy No. 1,* for guitar and magnetic tape (1969) and *From One to Another,* for viola and magnetic tape (1970). Musgrave, however, refuses to consider herself an electronic composer or a serialist simply because she has written in the twelve-tone system.

In 1969, the B.B.C. in Scotland commissioned a composition for the Beethoven bicentennial celebration, and Musgrave wrote Memento Vitae: a Concerto in Homage to Beethoven (1969–1970) which depicted the conflict between the old and the new: she represented the old with quotations from Beethoven's works, and the new with orchestral improvisations. The premiere, by the B.B.C. Scottish Orchestra, was conducted by James Loughran on March 20, 1970. On September 6, 1974, Sarah Caldwell, in making her debut as symphonic conductor with the Milwaukee Symphony, presented the American premiere of *Memento Vitae.* A critic for *High Fidelity/Musical America* described it as "a one-movement piece of neo-Romantic program music during which the conflict of ideas swirled into a battle of the elements and resolved itself into an elemental battle in which the timpani fired the last shot."

In 1970, Thea Musgrave came to the United States as visiting professor of music at the University of Santa Barbara in California and has remained, filling a faculty position at the University's College of Creative Studies. At the university, she met another faculty member, a New York-born violist, Peter Mark, and she confessed, "I knew instinctively this was someone I'd like to know the rest of my life. While we were being introduced, I knew no introduction was necessary." Their interest in one another deepened when in 1970 Musgrave wrote for Mark, *Elegy,* for viola and cello and *From One to Another,* for viola and tape. They were married in London on October 21, 1971, and their permanent residence is divided between their Santa Barbara house overlooking the Pacific

Ocean, and Norfolk, Virginia, where Peter Mark is artistic director and conductor of the Virginia Opera Company.

On a return visit to London after their marriage, on August 13, 1973, they gave a joint recital, with Peter Mark as soloist and the Scottish Orchestra conducted by Musgrave in the world premiere of her Concerto for Viola and Orchestra (1973) which she had written for him on commission from the B.B.C. Musgrave was also invited to give a series of eight broadcasts on the B.B.C. Radio entitled "End or Beginning," exploring the potentials and possibilities of electronic music.

The success of the ballet, *Beauty and the Beast,* in 1969, led to a commission from the Royal Opera House and the Gulbenkian Foundation for a chamber opera for the English Opera Group, founded by Benjamin Britten. Her search for suitable dramatic material ended when she came upon Henry James's *The Last of the Valerii* which Amelia Elguera reshaped into a libretto. The three-act chamber opera, *The Voice of Ariadne* (1972–1973), involves the conflict of cultures between a rich Italian count and his American wife in a plot that tells of the Count who falls in love with a disembodied voice only to find out that his wife is the voice, Ariadne. The opera (dedicated to Britten) was first produced at Britten's Aldeburgh Festival in England on June 11, 1974. Its American premiere, on September 30, 1977, was performed by the New York City Opera. William Bender in *Time* called it "a potential classic. . . . Ariadne's music has the blush of innocent freshness to it. It floats from atonality to tonality and back with dramatic precision bringing to life the libretto's strange world and humanizing its perplexed cast of characters." In *The New Yorker,* Andrew Porter described Musgrave's music as "eloquent," and added "Her score is a natural flowering from the new freedoms, the adventurousness and the lyrical delight in sound and gesture which she showed in previous orchestral pieces. It is also very well written for the singers: the rightness in matching emotional pitch to actual tessitura, the sense of where in the voice to find a particular shade of feeling, the naturalness of the declamation, and the unstrained transitions from conversation to formal set pieces all tell of a born opera singer."

In 1974, Musgrave was awarded a Guggenheim Fellowship which enabled her to write *Orfeo II,* for solo flute and fifteen strings (1975), and required a solo flutist as Orpheus. When it was introduced by the Los Angeles Chamber Orchestra under the direction of Musgrave in 1976, Martin Bernheimer in the Los Angeles *Times* called it "a lovely work, full of ethereal shimmer and clever pathos."

Musgrave's opera, *Mary, Queen of Scots,* was commissioned by the Scottish Opera who presented it first at the Edinburgh Festival on September 6, 1977, with the composer conducting. The successful American premiere was held several months later, on March 29, 1978, by the Virginia Opera Association, with Peter Mark conducting. Musgrave's own libretto is based on a historical play by Amelia Elguera, in which Mary, eighteen years old, and already the widow of the King of France in 1561, returns to Scotland to assume the throne. She is sent away seven years later to England by her half brother, the Earl of Moray. Writing in *The Scotsman* in Edinburgh, Conrad Wilson said: "It moves with great theatrical pace and fire. . . . It is an eclectic score, but very alive, boldly drawn and uncommonly well written—there can be few modern operas in which the words cut through the orchestra so clearly." After the American premiere, Andrew Porter of *The New Yorker* wrote: "It is an interesting, affecting and important work, successful on many counts: as a poetic drama, as a presentation of characters and conflicts, as a study of history, as a long stretch of imaginative and excellently written music, and as a music drama in which words, sounds, spectacle and action conspire to stir a listener's mind and emotions. In short, it succeeds as a show, as a score, and as that fusion of both which created good opera."

Musgrave enjoyed substantial success with her first opera, written and premiered in the United States. *A Christmas Carol,* which the Virginia Opera Association commissioned and introduced in Norfolk on December 7, 1979, was based on the Charles Dickens classic. Musgrave wrote her own libretto, and her score called for twelve vocal soloists, an orchestra of fifteen, and an optional children's chorus at the end. Reviewing it is *Newsweek,* Annalyn Swan said that the opera "sparkles with Dickensian humor and good cheer. . . . To a remarkable degree, Musgrave . . . preserves the distinctive flow of Dickens' dialogue. . . . Musgrave's characteristic dissonance, with its echoes here and there of

Nabokov

Benjamin Britten, underscores Scrooge's misanthropy. But, as befits a sentimental theme, Musgrave has created the most melodic of her five operas. . . . Lyricism keeps breaking through—in happy dances; in quotations from 'Twinkle, Twinkle, Little Star' and 'God Rest You Merry Gentlemen' that are sprinkled throughout; in Tiny Tim's hauntingly simple 'God bless Us Every One.' "

In *Opera News,* Hans Heinsheimer characterized Thea Musgrave as "a tall, slim, casually but well-dressed woman with an exuberant personality, a quick-on-the-trigger mind, good looks and a persuasive smile." She objects to being referred to as a "woman composer." "Music is a human art, not a sexual one," Musgrave said. "Sex is no more important than eye color. The fight is not so much for women composers—but for composers and artists. Period."

Thea Musgrave was named honorary Fellow of New Hall, Cambridge, in 1973, and in 1976 she received an honorary doctorate from the Council for Academic Awards in England (presented to her by Prince Charles). She served on the central music advisory panel for the B.B.C., the music panel for the Arts Council of Great Britain, and on the executive committee of the Composers Guild of Great Britain.

MAJOR WORKS

Ballet—A Tale for Thieves; Beauty and the Beast; Orfeo.

Band Music—Variations.

Chamber Music—String Quartet; Colloquy, for violin and piano; Trio, for flute, oboe, and piano; Serenade, for flute, clarinet, harp, viola, and cello; Chamber Concerto No. 1, for nine instruments; Chamber Concerto No. 2, for nine instruments; Chamber Concerto No. 3. for eight instruments; Sonata for Three, for flute, violin, and guitar; Impromptu No. 1, for flute and oboe; Music for Horn and Piano; Elegy, for viola and cello; Impromptu No. 2, for flute, oboe, and clarinet; Space Play, a concerto for nine instruments.

Choral Music—Four Madrigals, for a cappella chorus; Song of the Burn, for a cappella chorus; The Phoenix and the Turtle, for small chorus and orchestra; Marko the Miser, "a tale for children to mime, sing and play"; The Five Ages of Man, for chorus and orchestra; Memento Creatoris, for a cappella chorus; Rorate Coeli, for a cappella chorus.

Electronic Music—Soliloquy No. 1, for guitar and electronic tape; From One to Another, for viola and electronic tape.

Operas—The Abbot of Drimock, chamber opera; The Decision; The Voice of Ariadne; Mary, Queen of Scots; A Christmas Carol.

Orchestral Music—Obliques; Scottish Dance Suite; Triptych, for tenor and orchestra; Sinfonia; Festival Overture; Nocturnes and Arias; Concerto for Orchestra; Concerto for Clarinet and Orchestra; Night Music, for chamber orchestra; Memento Vitae: A Concerto in Homage to Beethoven; Concerto for Horn and Orchestra; Concerto for Viola and Orchestra; Orfeo II, for solo flute and fifteen instruments.

Piano Music—Monologue; Excursions, for piano four hands.

Vocal Music—A Suite o' Bairnsangs, for voice and piano; Cantata for a Summer Day, for narrator, vocal quartet, string quartet, flute, clarinet, and doublebass; Five Love Songs, for tenor and guitar; A Song for Christmas, for voice and piano; Sir Patrick Spens, for tenor and guitar; Primavera, for soprano and flute.

ABOUT

Sadie, S., (ed.), The New Grove Dictionary of Music and Musicians.

High Fidelity/Musical America, September 1977, September 1978; Horizon, December 1979; New York Times, September 25, 1977; Opera (London), August 1977; Opera News, September 1977; Time, November 10, 1975, October 10, 1977.

Nicolas Nabokov

1903–1978

For biographical sketch, list of earlier works, and bibliography, see *Composers Since 1900.*

On January 3, 1972, Nabokov's *Prelude, Four Variations and Finale on a Theme by Tchaikovsky* was introduced by the Philadelphia Orchestra, with Mstislav Rostropovich conducting.

Nabokov's opera, *Love's Labor Lost,* "a comedy with music," was introduced at the Théâtre de la Monnaie in Brussels on February 7, 1973; the following September 13 it was performed during the Berlin Music Weeks in English by the Deutsche Oper. The Shakespearean comedy was adapted into a libretto by W. H. Auden and Chester Kallman, who did not hesitate to add their own poetry to Shakespeare's. What enchanted audiences and critics most, in Brussels and Berlin, was Nabokov's frequent digressions from the serious and the eloquent to levity and light-hearted satire. The score is sprinkled with spicy wit and gentle malice, through subtle takeoffs on the Weill–Brecht socially-oriented musical plays, the American popular song, the twelve-tone system, the neo-classical Stravinsky, and the Russian music of Mussorgsky and Tchaikovsky. Nabokov explained: "At the very end, I have a cello that is prepared like the instruments of John Cage, with paper and a loudspeaker. The orchestra always plays the same accompaniment as in Indian music, but the voices sing something very serious and very tragic."

In 1970, Nabokov married his fourth wife, Dominique Cibiel, a young photographer.

In 1970–1971, Nabokov was lecturer on aesthetics at the New York State University in Buffalo; in 1972–1973 he lectured on music at New York University; between 1970 and 1973, he was composer-in-residence at the Aspen Institute for Humanistic Studies in Colorado; and in 1973 he was decorated with the Commander's Cross of the German Order of Merit in West Germany. A second volume of his reminiscences—*Bagazh: Memoirs of a Russian Cosmopolitan*—was published in 1975.

Nicolas Nabokov died of a heart attack following surgery in New York on April 6, 1978.

MAJOR WORKS (supplementary)

Opera—Love's Labor Lost.

Orchestral Music—Prelude, Four Variations and Finale on a Theme by Tchaikovsky.

ABOUT (supplementary)

Nabokov, N., Bagázh: Memoirs of a Russian Cosmopolitan.

High Fidelity/Musical America, April 1, 1973; Intellectual Digest, April 1973.

Carl Nielsen

1865–1931

For biographical sketch, list of earlier works, and bibliography, see *Composers Since 1900.*

Nielsen's opera, *Maskarade* (1906) received its American premiere by the St. Paul Opera in Minnesota on June 24, 1972. Allen Hughes reported in the New York *Times:* "The music is of high quality throughout. Its lyric charm and beautiful orchestration offer one delight after another to the listener who cares about such things." When this opera was recorded by Unicorn and released in 1976, Abram Chipman, of

High Fidelity/Musical America, called it "a masterly work. ... There is never a suggestion of stasis, in the ebb and flow of movement, the sharp contrasts of sonority and density. If the basic manner is wide-eyed, noble lyricism, it is within the context that Nielsen again and again thrusts forth moments of the bizarre, the exotic and the sweepingly festive."

In 1972, Nielsen's only other opera, *Saul and David* (1898–1901) was conducted and broadcast by Thomas Jensen in Copenhagen in a recording made under the auspices of the European Broadcasting Union.

As a result of reawakened interest in Nielsen's music in the decades following World War II, all of his symphonies, concertos, and miscellaneous orchestral works were recorded in 1975 by EMI with the Danish Symphony Orchestra under the direction of Herbert Blomstedt.

ABOUT (supplementary)

Nielsen, C., Centenary Essays; Simpson, R., Sibelius and Nielsen.

New York Times, June 25, 1978.

Luigi Nono

1924–

For biographical sketch, list of earlier works, and bibliography, see *Composers Since 1900.*

In the latter half of the 1960s, the Italian Radio commissioned Nono to write a composition for a competition it was conducting. Nono wrote *Contrapunto Dialettico alla Mente* (1967–1968), a modern madrigal cycle for voices and naturalistic sounds on magnetic tape, with a text by Nanni Balestrini. The reproduced sounds came from a Venetian fish market, the bells of San Marco, the lapping of the waters in the Venetian lagoon, etc. The work was never submitted to the competition, but it was introduced at the Settimana Internazionale in Palermo in December 1968 where Andrew Porter of *The New Yorker* called it "a strong and beautiful composition."

Nono's *Ein Gespenst Geht um in der Welt* (1971), a setting for orchestra of the Communist Manifesto, received its world premiere in Cologne, Germany, on February 11, 1971.

On February 16, 1973, *Como Una Ola de*

Fuerza y Luz, which Nono completed in 1972 for singer, piano, magnetic tape, and orchestra, was performed for the first time in the United States by the Philadelphia Orchestra, under Claudio Abbado.

On commission from La Scala in Milan, Nono wrote the opera *Al Gran Sole Carico d'Amore,* whose first performance took place at Teatro Lirico in Milan in 1975. The title, from a poem by Rimbaud, can freely be translated as "in the great sun of blooming love." With no plot or characterizations, *Al Gran Sole* was identified by Nono as a "mural" which pictured class struggle from the Paris Commune of 1871 through the days of Czarist Russia, Cuba, Chile, Italy, to Vietnam. Peter Heyworth described the work in the New York *Times:* "Insofar as individuals enter this historical masque, it is in the shape of a quartet of women who march with determined tread from one revolutionary situation to another. . . . In its repetitiveness, *Al Gran Sole* has, at best, the impact of a political litany." La Scala produced the opera on February 11, 1978, in a revised version and it was also staged by the Frankfurt Opera, whose production was brought to the Edinburgh Festival in 1978, where Andrew Porter reviewed it in *The New Yorker:* "Nono's score is active and dramatic in itself, not merely illustrative. It does illustrate, as music readily can, such things as the crude massing of brute force, and opposition to it, in the form of revolutionary song. More subtly, it draws its listeners into a network of feelings about its central theme. . . . The work is tautly and potently constructed. It is composed for very large forces (several small male solo roles besides the major roles for women; semichorus of twenty; big full orchestra; four-track electronic tape projected through the theater) and employs a very wide range of textures and dynamics. . . . It made a strong impression."

A death in Nono's family and in the family of the concert pianist Maurizio Pollini, inspired one of Nono's most deeply emotional and touching instrumental works: *Sofferte Onde Serene,* for piano and magnetic tape, written in 1976 for Pollini who recorded it for Deutsche Grammophon. In her review of the recording, Karen Monson said in *High Fidelity/Musical America:* "The tape that runs along with and against the 'live' piano seems to represent death in both its inevitability and its quietude, and it gives . . . *Sofferte Onde Serene* ('sorrowful yet serene

waves') a feeling of motion and force. The taped sounds were derived from the piano, including such extra-musical noises as those made by depressing the pedals, but they have been altered and played with to the point where they have taken on supernatural qualities. The work has beautiful moments that echo the bells Nono hears from his house in Venice."

Long a member of the Italian Communist Party, Nono was elected to its central committee in 1975. In 1972, he precipitated a political and musical storm in Milan by withdrawing his one-act opera, *Intolleranza,* from the Florence May Music Festival, because it was also presenting Menotti's *The Consul,* which he regarded as a "squalid product of the cold war and of anti-Sovietism."

MAJOR WORKS (supplementary)

Electronic Music—La Fabbrica Illuminata, for voice and magnetic tape; Per Bastiana Tai-Yang Cheng, for electronic tape and three orchestral groups; Contrapunto Dialettico alla Mente, for voice and sounds on magnetic tape; Musica Manifesto No. 1, for voices and magnetic tape; Non Consumiano Marx, for electronic sounds; Y Entonces Comprendió, for voice and magnetic tape; Como Una Ola de Fuerza y Luz, for singer, piano, orchestra, and magnetic tape; Sofferte Onde Serene, for piano and magnetic tape.

Opera—Al Gran Sole Carico d'Amore.

Orchestral Music—2 piano concertos; Ein Gespenst Geht um in der Welt, for voice and orchestra.

ABOUT (supplementary)

Sadie, S. (ed.), The New Grove Dictionary of Music and Musicians; Stenzl, J. (ed.), Luigi Nono: Studien zu seiner Musik; Vinton, J. (ed.), Dictionary of Contemporary Music.

New York Times, April 27, 1975.

Vitězslav Novák

1870–1949

For biographical sketch, list of earlier works, and bibliography, see *Composers Since 1900.*

ABOUT (supplementary)

Lébl, V., Vitězslav Novák.

Gösta Nystroem

1890–1966

See *Composers Since 1900.*

Carl Orff

1895–

For biographical sketch, list of earlier works, and bibliography, see *Composers Since 1900.*

·*De Temporum fine Comoedia (The Play of the End of Time),* a monumental work by Orff for narrator, solo voices, a cappella chorus, a boys' chorus, orchestra, and magnetic tape, received its world premiere at the Salzburg Festival in Austria on August 20, 1973, with Herbert von Karajan conducting. The orchestra called for in the score is unusual in that it dispenses with all the violins and requires ninety-six percussion instruments, including many from Japan, Java, Egypt, and Latin America. The text, described by James H. Sutcliffe in *High Fidelity/Musical America,* "contrasts the Sibylline Prophesies of a fiery judgment day (I) with their vehement rejection by Nine Anchorites (II) who quote the third-century philosopher, Origenes, maintaining that 'the end of all things will be the forgetting of guilt.' A dream vision of that end (III) *Dies Illa* [symbolizes] the return of all creatures to pure spirit—this after the last human survivors have been hurled off the spinning earth, and Lucifer has been forgiven, becoming once again a naked, beautiful Angel of Light." Regarding the music, "it was Orff all over again: static tone clusters, shrieking piccolo trills, crashing climaxes of harmonically tame chords, endless ostinatos, ritually repetitious rhythms, word-groupings repeated three times in triplet accentuation (supposed to have the effect of magic incantation)." The Salzburg premiere performance was recorded by Deutsche Grammophon.

Orff's seventy-fifth birthday in 1970 was celebrated with performances of his works throughout West Germany. On that occasion he was awarded the Amadeus Mozart Prize by the University of Innsbruck, the Music Prize of the city of Salzburg, the Golden Honorary Medal of the city of Munich, and the Ring of the city of Salz-

burg. On his eightieth birthday, in addition to commemorative performances of his compositions, a motion picture presenting his masterwork, *Carmina Burana* (1937), was released in West Germany.

In addition, Orff was awarded the Mozart Prize of the Basel Goethe Foundation in 1969 and the Golden Medal of the City of Nuremburg in 1972. He received an honorary doctorate in music from the University of Munich in 1972 and was appointed honorary member of the Royal Academy of Sciences, Letters, and Beaux-Arts in Brussels in 1973. A sculptured bust of Orff is on view in the Munich National Theater.

MAJOR WORKS (supplementary)

Choral Music—Rota, for voices and instruments; De Temporum Fine Comoedia, for a cappella chorus, boys' chorus, orchestra, and magnetic tape.

ABOUT (supplementary)

Horton, J. (ed.), Some Great Music Educators; Sadie, S. (ed.), The New Grove Dictionary of Music and Musicians; Schmidt, H. W. (ed.), Carl Orff: Sein Leben und Sein Werk in Wort, Bild, und Noten; Thomas, W., Carl Orff, und Sein Werk.

Opera News, November 16, 1970; Saturday Review, July 26, 1969.

Andrzej Panufnik

1914–

For biographical sketch, list of earlier works, and bibliography, see *Composers Since 1900.*

On May 24, 1970, Leopold Stokowski conducted the world premiere of Panufnik's *Universal Peace* (1968–1969) at the Cathedral Church of St. John the Divine in New York. This work was set to Alexander Pope's poem, for four vocal soloists, chorus, three harps, and organ.

At the request of Yehudi Menuhin, Panufnik wrote the *Concerto for Violin and Strings* (1971), which Menuhin introduced as violinist and conductor of the Menuhin Festival Orchestra in London on July 18, 1972. The composer said, "I treated the violin as a singing instrument, so though keeping within my strict self-imposed discipline of sound organization, I constructed rather long and unbroken melodic lines. To further expose the solo part and keep it ever-prominent, as well as to achieve a specific color and texture, I chose to use an orchestra consisting only of strings."

Invocation for Peace, for treble voices, two trumpets, and two trombones (1972), with a text written previously, was originally intended as the finale of *Symphony of Peace,* which Panufnik abandoned. He rewrote the melodic line, scoring it for unison treble voices, two trumpets, and two trombones (though the composer says the instrumentation can be changed according to available resources, for example, strings and/or woodwinds). The work is religious in both text (by Camilla Jessel) and music, "an aspiration towards the unity of mankind," as the composer described it. The first performance took place in Southampton, England, on November 28, 1972, with Peter Davies conducting.

Discussing *Winter Solstice* (1972), for solo soprano, bass baritone, chorus, three trumpets, three trombones, timpani, and glockenspiel, and text by Camilla Jessel, the composer said: "When I was asked to compose a Christmas choral work, my mind could not help turning immediately towards the fascinating dualism between paganism and early Christianity, particularly the close parallel between the celebration of Christ's birth—the Son of God—and the pagan celebration of the birth of their god, the Sun, both events taking place at the same point of the year." This five-movement cantata had its world premiere at the Kingston-on-the-Thames Parish Church in England on December 16, 1972, with Louis Halsey conducting. The performers were divided into two well-separated groups, each with its own well-defined dramatic role and its own musical language. The Christians were represented by female voices and a baritone solo (St. Augustine), the trumpets, and timpani; the pagans were represented by male voices, solo soprano (Mother Earth), trombones, and timpani.

To celebrate the tenth anniversary of his marriage, Panufnik wrote *Sinfonia Concertante,* for flute, harp, and strings in 1973 as a token to his wife. The composer conducted its premiere with the Belgian Chamber Orchestra in London on May 20, 1974.

The *Sinfonia di Sfere (Symphony of Spheres)* was written in 1974–1975 and premiered in London on April 13, 1976, with David Atherton conducting the London Symphony Orchestra. Having no connection with the philosophy of Pythagoras ("music of the spheres") nor with

astrology, this work is abstract music, influenced by the beauty and mystery of geometry. Panufnik explained, "The concept of spheres gave me a double impetus: first and most essential, spheres of contemplative thoughts and emotions; and the secondary aspect, a group of spheres as a geometric figure which acts as a framework enclosing meticulously organized musical material in terms of spheres: "sphere of harmony," "sphere of rhythm," "sphere of dynamics," "sphere of tempo," and "sphere of general structure."

String Quartet (1976) was premiered in London by the Aeolian Quartet on October 19, 1976. The work is constructed like a triptych, consisting of a Prelude, a Transformation, and a Postlude and as in many other Panufnik works, the entire score is based on a single triad with its reflections and transpositions.

Sinfonia Mistica (1977), in six movements, was commissioned by the Northern Sinfonia which introduced it in London on January 20, 1978, with Christopher Seaman conducting. The "mystic" in this work applies, not to any religious order, but to the mysterious properties of numbers and geometry.

Metasinfonia (1978), for organ, strings, and timpani, is the composer's seventh symphony even though it is more of an organ concerto than a symphony. The composer explained: "Both parts of the title, *meta* and *sinfonia,* have equal significance. The prefix *meta* relates here to other words and ideas prefixed by *meta*—particularly *meta*morphosis, meaning change of shape, gradual transformation; the word *sinfonia* I used because the work has an extremely disciplined organ structure, even if its design goes rather far from the classical mold." In a single movement, the music represents a chain of meditative thoughts and expressions. *Metasinfonia* was commissioned by the International Festival of Organ Music, and its premiere took place in Manchester on September 9, 1978, with Geraint Jones as organ soloist, and the B.B.C. Northern Symphony conducted by the composer.

In 1980, Panufnik wrote *Concertino for Timpani, Percussion, and Strings* on commission from Shell (United Kingdom) Ltd. and their 1980 Music Scholarship for young percussion players. André Previn conducted the world premiere of the work in London in late January 1981, and the American premiere with the Pittsburgh Symphony Orchestra one week later (February 6). In writing the work, Panufnik aspired to take a fresh look at percussion, to emphasize the expressive, even singing, qualities of the instruments. For this reason, the second and fourth movements are entitled "Song"; the other movements are called "Entrata," "Intermezzo," and "Fine." The entire work is derived from one four-note cell introduced at the beginning of the composition by tubular chimes. It is carried as a catalytic agent throughout both melodically and harmonically, and at the end it is picked up by the orchestra. The composer explained: "Instead of writing a collection of already existing technical possibilities and various gimmicks for the performer, I wanted to compose a real test piece for his or her musicianship; to demonstrate quality of sound, precision, and above all, an understanding of the musical content of the work, its poetic element."

MAJOR WORKS (supplementary)

Ballet—Miss Julie.

Chamber Music—Triangles, for three flutes and three cellos; String Quartet; Prelude, Transformation, and Postlude, for string quartet.

Choral Music—Thames Pageant, for two choirs of treble voices and orchestra; Universal Prayer, cantata for four vocal soloists, chorus, three harps, and organ; Invocation for Peace, for treble voices, two trumpets, and two trombones; Winter Solstice, for solo soprano, bass baritone, chorus, and instruments.

Orchestral Music—Concerto for Violin and Orchestra; Sinfonia Concertante, for flute, harp, and strings; Sinfonia de Sfere; Sinfonia Mistica; Metasinfonia; Concerto Festivo; Concertino for Timpani, Percussion, and Strings.

Piano Music—Reflections.

ABOUT (supplementary)

Vinton, J. (ed.), Dictionary of Contemporary Music.

Horatio W. Parker

1863–1919

See *Composers Since 1900.*

Harry Partch

1901–1974

Harry Partch, the avant-garde composer who operated in a musical world of his own, which broke with traditional methods, means, instruments, and ideologies, was born in Oakland, California, on January 24, 1901. His father, Virgil Franklin Partch, was at one time a Presbyterian missionary and later became an immigration inspector. His mother, Jennie Childers Partch, had been a newspaper reporter, teacher, and a dedicated suffragette all her life. Both parents enjoyed music; his father collected and performed on various instruments, and his mother sang and played the organ. They came to California from China, where the father's missionary work was, bringing back with them a love for all things Chinese, including music. Harry Partch's earliest experiences in music were listening to his mother sing Chinese songs, and attending performances of Chinese operas at the Mandarin Theater in San Francisco. This Oriental influence helped to develop in him an attitude of musical iconoclasm in composing music.

The family moved to a homestead in Arizona near the Mexican border and his father found a job as an immigration officer. When Harry was about five or six, he learned to play the reed organ, mandolin, cornet, violin, and harmonica by ear with no formal training. His mother began teaching him to play the piano and to read and write music and he was composing by the time he was fourteen.

In his early adolescence the family moved to New Mexico where he continued music study with a number of private teachers. But his teachers were not sympathetic to his novel ideas in composing music and he abandoned all formal instruction, just as he had done academically, upon graduating from Albuquerque High School. Teaching himself, he read omnivorously and studied a variety of texts. Later, he listed the major influences on his cultural life as: Public libraries, Yaqui Indians, Chinese lullabies, Hebrew chants for the dead, Christian hymns, Congo puberty, Chinese music halls in San

Partch: pärch

211

Partch

HARRY PARTCH

Francisco, lumber yards, junk shops, and *Boris Godounov*.

In Albuquerque he supported himself by playing the piano and organ in silent movie theaters for a while, but in the 1920s he was forced to take any job he could find, such as schoolteacher, migrant fruit picker, proofreader for a newspaper. He was also writing music and by the time he was twenty-two he had already written a string quartet, an orchestral tone poem, a piano concerto, and about fifty songs. All of his compositions were in traditional form and he had become increasingly impatient with "the tyranny of tonality," and with the limitations imposed by established rules and precedents. He stopped writing music for six years, burned all his manuscripts, and began to write music again in 1930, with an entirely new approach. His retreat from tradition began with experimenting with microtones in the process of evolving a new scale of his own invention, and in fashioning his own musical instruments, "a man seduced into carpentry." Between 1928 and 1930 he built an "adapted" viola with an elongated neck that was played like a cello with thirty-seven tones to an octave. In the early 1930s he composed an Orientally-influenced microtonal composition for this new viola, *Seventeen Lyrics by Li-Po*, set to poems by an 8th century Chinese poet. The voice part consisted of a series of spoken or chanted incantations in pentatonic measure to the microtonal background of the adapted viola. Two other works at this time were similar: *Potion*

Scene from Romeo and Juliet and *By the Rivers of Babylon*.

In 1934 he spent a year in England on a grant from the Carnegie Corporation of New York studying the history of intonation at the British Museum. He came back to the United States during the depression (1935) to life as a hobo, traveling and learning first-hand about American geography, backgrounds, customs, peoples, culture, and social problems—collecting material for use in later compositions. He was also inventing musical instruments and in 1935, he adapted the Hawaiian-type guitar into an instrument with six to ten strings. Then in 1938 he began work on a seventy-two string kithara, a six-foot instrument shaped like an ancient Greek lyre, to accompany a work he wrote in 1941. It was entitled *Barstow* and had the subtitle "Eight Hitchhiker Inscriptions from a California Highway Railing at Barstow, California," with a text (graffiti scribbled by hitchhikers) which was chanted over an exotic instrumental accompaniment. This was a stage piece for solo voices and chorus as well as for his original instruments.

While he was employed as a lumberjack in the West in 1943, Henry Moe, executive director of the Guggenheim Foundation, became sufficiently impressed with his musical innovations to award him a Guggenheim Fellowship (extended for a second year in 1944). Partch turned once again to serious musical creativity, and his hobo experiences, when he wrote *U. S. Highball: a Musical Account of Transcontinental Life* in 1943, for solo voices, chorus, and instruments. The work had its world premiere in New York on April 22, 1944, on the same program with *Barstow*. His aim, he explained, was to point out the "disintegration of urbanic civilization and the pathos of the outcasts' search for the spring of life." The text, narrated or chanted by a hobo named Mac, is a litany of names of railway stations, slogans on billboards, and Partch's random thoughts while wandering around the country, and the background music from Partch's invented instruments recreated railroad noises, hillbilly music, and popular songs. (In 1950 Partch rewrote the work to include newly invented instruments.) In 1943, he also wrote *The Letter*, "a depressing message from a hobo friend," for voices and an instrumental ensemble.

Between 1944 and 1947, while Partch was a research associate on a grant at the University of

Wisconsin in Madison, he built more new instruments: Harmonic Canon I, with overlapping sets of forty-four strings and a movable bridge for each string, allowing all kinds of tonal patterns; two Chromo-melodeons, which were adapted reed organs with forty-three tones to the octave; and the diamond marimba, consisting of thirty-six spruce blocks over redwood resonators arranged in diagonal rows to permit the sounding of an arpeggio-like chord with a single sweep of the mallet. At the university, Partch wrote and published the book *Genesis of Music* (1949), elaborating on his new musical system and its goals. (It was reissued in New York in 1973.)

His third Guggenheim Fellowship was awarded in 1950. By the early 1950s, Partch perfected his tonal system, a forty-three microtonal scale, and his instruments were becoming increasingly esoteric, including: Cloud-Chamber Bowls made up of the tops and bottoms of Pyrex carboys (from the University of California Radiation Laboratory) were suspended from a six-foot high frame, and struck with a mallet to produce bell-like tones; Spoils of War, a percussion instrument, was made up of artillery shells, cloud-chamber bowls, bellows, a 1912 auto horn, and a "whang gun"; the Marimba Eroica consisted of four long wooden blocks on resonators, played with heavy padded mallets; the Boo (bamboo marimba) had sixty-four bamboo cylinders played with felted stick to give forth a dry, percussive sound with one enharmonic overtone; and a new type of kithara and Harmonic Canon. He endowed his instruments with picturesque names and adorned some of them with such decorations as African masks.

In 1951, Partch's interest turned to dramatic writing, in *Oedipus,* from the Yeats translation of the Sophocles drama, *Oedipus Rex.* Due to difficulty in finding actors with the necessary musical background, Partch abandoned microtonal writing for traditional scales and he noted precise tone, rhythm, and inflection of the speaking parts meticulously. He said, "The music is conceived as an emotional saturation that is the particular province of dramatic music to achieve. My idea has been to present the drama expressed by the language, not to obscure it, whether by operatic aria or symbolic instrumentation. Hence in the critical dialogue music enters almost insidiously as tensions enter." *Oedipus* was first produced on March 14, 1952, at Mills College in Oakland, California. Alfred

Frankenstein wrote in the San Francisco *Chronicle,* that "the score vastly enhanced the ominous tension of the tragedy." But *Time* found "mostly what Hollywood calls Mickey Mouse music—the tempo coinciding with movement—and speech. The orchestra produced cacophonous sounds sometimes reminiscent of a movie soundtrack for a Chinese street scene. The best thing about it, it seldom got in the actor's way."

On commission from the Fromm Music Foundation and the University of Illinois, Partch wrote a second dramatic work, the satirical *The Bewitched* (1955), modeled on the Japanese Kabuki Theater "Noh" play. In this work, Partch was "seeking release—through satire, whimsy, magic, ribaldry—from the catharsis of tragedy. It is an essay toward a miraculous abeyance of civilized rigidity." A group of lost clown musicians, as principal characters, destroys 20th century mechanization and intellectualism. "They are primitive," Partch explained, "in their outspoken acceptance of magic as real, unconsciously reclaiming an all-but-lost value for the exploitation of their perception." Episode titles provide a clue to the composer's dramatic intent: "A Soul Tortured by Contemporary Music Finds a Harmonic Alchemy," "The Cognoscenti Are Plunged into a Demonic Descent with Cocktails," and "Visions Fill the Eyes of the Defeated Baseball Team in the Shower Room." The score for *The Bewitched* calls for a number of Partchian instruments: Cloud-Chamber Bowls, Spoils of War, Marimba Eroica, Boo, Surrogate Kithara, Harmonic Canon, and Chromo-melodion. Eric Salzman reviewed the GRI recording for *Stereo Review:* "The musicians who play the instruments are not merely accompanists to the drama of the piece. They are protagonists. In addition to contributing to the visual impact of these extraordinary constructions by playing them on the stage, the instrumentalists also form a vocal Chorus of Lost Musicians who experience various uncommon misadventures of modern life." Salzman called the work "a remarkable example of Partch's ritual music theater. . . . He deals with the paradoxes and the banalities of contemporary life in terms of magical and spiritual transformation. And his theater, again like his music, is anti-specialized, anti-tragic and very much conceived as an antidote to the ills and woes of technological civilization." Partch spent six months training the students to play his instruments and *The*

Partch

Bewitched was presented on March 26, 1957, at the University of Illinois in Urbana; three years later it was produced at the Juilliard School of Music in New York. Reviewing that performance in the New York Herald Tribune, Jay Harrison wrote: "Mr. Partch's instruments give off a rainbow luminosity. The score itself is mainly incantational, an effect close to hypnosis being Mr. Partch's ultimate aim ... quite unlike any other music associated with the western world. Surprisingly, it all works, comes off with remarkable vibrancy. ... In the final analysis, it makes an authentic communication."

Revelations in the Courthouse Park (1960) is a contemporary version of Euripides' The Bacchae, set in a modern-day park instead of ancient Thebes. Dionysius is an Elvis Presley-type star called Dion, and the ritual of worshipping singing heroes is celebrated, Hollywood-style, in a parody on the popular song. Reviewer Peter Yates of High Fidelity was there when Revelations was performed at the University of Illinois at its premiere on April 11, 1961. He wrote, "The open-stage is dark, but we see at each side ... unusually shaped instruments ... the musicians enter ... and the lights go on among the instruments. ... At the rear of the hall, a brass band breaks out, and uniformed musicians march down the aisle led by four girls twirling batons. Here is the homecoming of Dion, the folk-hero from Hollywood. He is greeted with squeals and yells, and the whole chorus, gathering around him on the stage, breaks into a chant, song, shouting and dance, to the dark, heavy tones of the marimbas, the throb and glitter of the plucked strings."

On commission from the University of Illinois, Partch composed a fourth drama, the farcical Water, Water, described as an "American ritual." First produced on March 8, 1962, at the University of Illinois, this duet between man and nature takes place in eleven prologues and nine epilogues, separated by an intermission. On the left side of the stage stands a disk jockey, an alderman, a lady mayor, and a baseball commentator in an American city called Mystiana and on the right is open countryside. Man is symbolized by a huge dam which controls the water supply; Nature's ultimate victory is represented by torrential floods that destroy the city.

Commenting on the four dramas, Peter Yates concluded in High Fidelity that "This is a medium as distinct from the recitative and song opera as it is unlike the flat declamation or imitatively realistic speaking of the modern stage."

Delusion of the Fury: a Ritual of Dream and Delusion (1966) was judged by Tom Johnson in High Fidelity/Musical America to be the apex of Partch's writing for theater. "It is almost as if Partch's earlier works had been simply a preparation for this one. For here his many invented instruments, his ideas about the voice, his theatrical concepts and his highly sophisticated harmonic and textural devices all converge in one authoritative statement. ... It is hard to imagine that anyone who has ever heard Partch's masterpiece. ... could still believe that this is the work of a mere eccentric." Act I, whose hero is an enlightened ghost, is based on the Japanese Noh play; Act II, with a deaf, near-sighted judge as hero, is an adaptation of an Ethiopian folk tale. Partch elaborated: "Act I treats with death and with life despite death; Act II treats with life, and with life despite death." Introduced by an "Exordium" performed by several Partchian instruments, the work evokes the world of the Orient.

Partch's music found in motion pictures includes Windsong (1958), a study of nature, shown at the Brussels Exposition of 1958, and Rotate the Body in All Its Planes (1961), a film about gymnastics. Three films about Partch, himself, are Music Studio: Harry Partch (1958) which shows Partch performing on the ten instruments he used in Windsong; The Music of Harry Partch, produced by KEBS-TV, a television station at the San Diego State College in California; and a television film about Partch called The Dreamer Remains (1972).

Sporadic performances of Partch's works in the United States, and recordings of his music on his own label (Gate V) could not bring Partch sufficient recognition in America, outside of a small area in the West. But his reputation was enhanced in the East when on September 8, 1968, a concert of his works was given at the Whitney Museum of American Art in New York, in combination with an exhibition of his instruments. A cross-section of his work through the years gave the Eastern critics the opportunity to evaluate his work. Theodore Strongin reported in the New York Times, that "It was plain that Mr. Partch is fanciful, whimsical and a philosopher. ... It was even plainer

... that in the best sense he has never grown up. *Petals* and *Exordium* in particular have a kind of wide-eyed simplicity, a lack of disillusion that is unaffected by the oversophisticated musical practises." Referring to *And on the Seventh Day Petals Fell in Petalmuna* Strongin added: "Each episode seemed a segment of some far-off continuous music that reveals itself to us only at moments of hearing. It is an amiable, even funny piece."

Defending his innovations in disregard of tradition, Partch wrote: "The rebelliously creative act is also a tradition, and if our art of music is to be anything more than a shadow of its past, the traditions in question must periodically shake off dormant habits and excite themselves into palpable growth. Much has been said about expressing one's own time. Nothing could be more futile or downright idiotic. The prime obligation of the artist is to transcend his age, and therefore to show it in terms of eternal mysteries."

Harry Partch, however, remained aloof even from the mainstream of the avant-garde movement of the 1950s and 1960s. He regarded the serial technique as only a straitjacket for unbridled creativity and renounced the world of electronics (although occasionally he did try prerecorded taped sounds in his compositions). He said, "Electronic music is too impersonal. Music has validity for me only as a human expression. It must be corporeal. Man, not machine, is the ultimate instrument." He could see no value in "chance music," since "for me everything must make its own kind of logic, everything must be predetermined, systematically conceived."

Among Partch's awards was one from the National Institute of Arts and Letters in 1966, and the Nealie Sullivan Award from the San Francisco Art Institute. He spent his later years in his home in San Diego, California, where he enjoyed taking long walks, and his hobby, growing okra and watermelons. His iconoclasm, his disregard for the marketplace, his whimsy, fantasy, and absurdity in art, and even his appearance have caused him to be likened to Charles Ives. He, too, had a straggly beard, a lined and somewhat gaunt face, eyes that revealed the strength and determination of a prophet, and a partiality for rough clothes.

Harry Partch died of a heart attack in his apartment in San Diego on September 3, 1974.

MAJOR WORKS

Chamber Music—Barstow; Dark Brother; By the Rivers of Babylon; Potion Scene from Romeo and Juliet; The Wayward; San Francisco Newsboy Cries; Two Settings from Finnegan's Wake; 14 Intrusions; Plectra and Percussion Dances; Cloud-Chamber Music; And on the Seventh Day the Petals Fell on Petaluma.

Choral Music—U. S. Highball: A Musical Account of a Transcontinental Life.

Theater Music—Castor and Pollux; Even Wild Horses, dance drama for an absent drama; Ring Around the Moon; Oedipus; The Bewitched; Daphne of the Dunes; Revelation in the Courthouse Park; Water, Water; Delusion of the Fury: A Ritual of Dream and Delusion.

Vocal Music—17 Lyrics by Li-Po.

ABOUT

Ewen, D., Composers of Tomorrow's Music; Machlis, J., An Introduction to Modern Music; Partch, H., Genesis of a Music; Yates, P., 20th Century Music.

Hi-Fi/Stereo Review, February 1961; High Fidelity, July 1963; High Fidelity/Musical America, November 1975; New York Times, September 9, 1968, September 6, 1974; Saturday Review, November 27, 1971.

Thomas Pasatieri

1945–

Thomas Pasatieri was born in New York City on October 20, 1945, to Carmelo Thomas Pasatieri and Maria Lucia Carini Pasatieri. Neither parent was musical, nor were any of their Sicilian relatives as far back as they could remember. From his early days in Flushing, New York, Thomas was fascinated by both the theater and music. At St. Francis Prep School in Flushing (1958–1960) he participated in school productions. When he graduated from Sewanhaka High School on Long Island, in 1962, he single-handedly produced and directed Jerome Kern's musical, *Leave it to Jane,* as part of the graduation ceremonies. At the age of seven, he began his study of the piano with Vera Wels who was his teacher until 1961. He made such exceptional progress that within two years he was giving piano concerts in New York City, and between 1955 and 1965, he made numerous appearances besides filling in as conductor. He began to compose when he was fourteen without preliminary

---

Pasatieri: pä sä tyĕŕ ē

215

Pasatieri

THOMAS PASATIERI

instruction and within four years he wrote four hundred songs as well as some piano pieces.

At fifteen he cut classes in New York City to attend a lecture by Nadia Boulanger, the distinguished Parisian teacher of composition, after which he pushed a bundle of compositions into her arms, for advice and criticism. A few days later he heard from Boulanger who said that in studying the music, she was convinced he would become a composer, and she was ready to help him in any way she could. The only way she could teach him was through correspondence, and for the next year and a half, Pasatieri's manuscripts were dispatched to Boulanger in Paris and returned corrected, with appropriate comments.

In his sixteenth year, Pasatieri earned a scholarship in composition from the Juilliard School of Music where he sang in the chorus and gave recitals. He also studied composition with Vincent Persichetti and Vittorio Giannini, a successful American opera composer. Up to that time, Pasatieri had had no contact with opera but his love for the theater made him receptive to the idea of writing an opera of his own. Before Giannini would allow him to undertake such a project, Pasatieri had to study harmony, counterpoint, musical analysis, solfeggio, and music history and for exercise write as many as eighty fugues a month. Pasatieri recalled, "After all this exacting training, Giannini finally said to me, 'O.K. You are ready to write an opera.'" Pasatieri wrote a libretto and the music for *The Trysting Place,* based on a Booth Tarkington

story, and showed it to Giannini, who told him: "Fine. Now that you are an opera composer, let's learn how to write a *real* opera."

To master the techniques of writing for the voice, Pasatieri accepted various assignments coaching singers and playing the piano at vocal lessons. At the same time, under Giannini's guidance, he worked on a second opera, *The Flowers of Ice,* which was completed in 1965. Pasatieri told Peter G. Davis in an interview for the New York *Times Magazine,* "I learned from Giannini that the most important element of a successful opera is communication of the drama through an expressive vocal line—we analyzed every phrase in the libretto for multiple possibilities of expression before deciding on the most effective setting." Pasatieri later said: "Everything I see and experience—whether it's a child's puppet show, *Dark Victory,* an opera, a ballet, absolutely anything—affects my sense of the theater."

When he was nineteen, Pasatieri studied composition with Darius Milhaud in Aspen, Colorado, where he witnessed the first production of one of his three operas. *The Women,* a one-act opera to his own libretto, was produced at Aspen on August 20, 1965, and became the winner that year of the Aspen Festival Prize. Pasatieri told Peter G. Davis, "It all happened very quickly. One morning I woke up with a terrific idea for a libretto; it must have all come to me in a dream. I wrote the words down, finished the music in three days, the orchestration took another week, and right away it was performed by the other students. The audience reaction was tremendous and that hooked me on opera—the whole experience was exciting."

From then on, his operas came thick and fast, two or three a year. After study in Aspen, Pasatieri wrote a companion piece to *The Women,* a satiric one-act opera entitled *La Divina,* which was produced at the Juilliard School of Music (with *The Women*) in April 1966. *Padrevia,* also in one-act, was completed in 1966 and first performed at Brooklyn College, New York, on November 18, 1967. This opera completed a trilogy including *The Women* and *La Divina.* The three-act *Penitentes* had a libretto, written by Anne Howard Bailey in 1967, that told a grim story about a sect of New Mexican Indians who select a member of their tribe to reenact the Crucifixion. It did not reach the stage until seven years after composition, at Aspen on August 3, 1974.

Pasatieri received his Bachelor of Arts degree at Juilliard in 1965, his Master of Arts degree in 1967, and the first doctorate in music from Juilliard in 1969. He mentioned that as a Juilliard student (and even as a successful composer) he was often derided by fellow students for his conservative posture as a traditional composer who wrote tonal and singable melodies. "Once I was laughed out of composition class for writing such romantic music."

From 1967 to 1969, Pasatieri was on the music faculty of Juilliard, and from 1969 to 1971 on the Manhattan School of Music faculty. He has since taught master classes in composition at various American universities. By 1971 he had already given evidence that his interest and ability were in writing for the voice. Regarding his extensive study of singers and their techniques he said, "From Callas I learned what opera was all about, and from Tourel what a song is all about—how to make every nuance, every syllable in a text important. I am returning to bel canto. Not Bellini and Donizetti, of course, but I've always worked with singers and they always tell me that they are grateful for something written effectively for the voice. There is nothing like the voice." He was always ready to fashion a role to a particular singer, or to alter or reshape one of his melodies to suit a particular voice. Often he had a specific singer in mind when writing his music.

His skill at vocal writing drew the attention of Evelyn Lear and Thomas Steward, the husband-and-wife singers, who commissioned him, in 1971, to write something for them outside of opera. The commission resulted in a song cycle, *Héloïse and Abelard,* for soprano, baritone, and piano which Evelyn Lear and Thomas Stewart introduced in a joint recital in New York on December 11, 1971. The following April, Patricia Brooks selected four of Pasatieri's songs for her recital at the Lincoln Center for the Performing Arts in New York.

Pasatieri also attracted the interest of NET (National Educational Television) Opera which commissioned him to write an opera, the only commission it had ever given. The opera was *The Trial of Mary Lincoln,* which was first telecast on February 14, 1972. Anne Howard Bailey's melodramatic libretto was based on the trial at the Cook County courthouse in Chicago in May 1875 in which Mary Lincoln was declared insane. Adapted to the television medium, the opera made use of flashbacks, dissolves, voice-overs, and other devices not used on the stage, to portray the three-dimensional character of Abraham Lincoln's widow. The plan of the libretto, according to Harriett Johnson of the New York *Post,* "enables us to get psychological insight into Mary's personality in a way not possible in conventional opera. ... Witness her vanity, her experimental flights, her will to interfere and dominate . . . her temperamental flights, her conflicts of duty and devotion." Pasatieri's score combined soaring melody with dramatic song speech, always masterfully molded to the human voice. Irving Kolodin praised it in the *Saturday Review,* "It is the mark of an exceptional talent that Pasatieri was able to sustain a largely intellectual discussion over a period of nearly an hour. It is altogether possible that, in another dramatic situation, Pasatieri will attain an even greater realization of his latent abilities."

On another commission, from the Seattle (Washington) Opera, Pasatieri wrote *Black Widow* in 1972, with his own libretto based on Miguel de Unamuno's novella, *Dos Madres.* The Opera, which was produced on March 2, 1972, tells of a barren Spanish widow who is obsessed with the desire for a child. She forces her lover and his former sweetheart to marry and have a child, which she expropriates. Wayne Johnson of the Seattle *Times* called it "an intensely dramatic, richly lyrical work in which music and drama are effectively integrated to create a compelling musical-theater experience."

In Pasatieri's operas, critics found a kinship with Puccini's *verismo,* particularly his emotionalism and female characterizations, and also a similarity between Pasatieri's operas and those of Gian Carlo Menotti. Like Menotti, Pasatieri is concerned first and foremost with good theater and its impact on audiences, with making his music palatable through its lyricism, and on aiming to meet the demands of the stage and the singer. Pasatieri put it this way: "I am writing for an audience. I want to bring joy with my music. I would rather please a real audience than please five other composers sitting in a room." To charges that he was more of a showman than a creative artist (also a criticism of Menotti), Pasatieri countered with the statement: "I want to express myself in whatever way works, tonally or dissonantly. Because my music is tonal, I am accused of not being serious. What's avant-garde, what's conservative in the perspective of history?"

By the end of 1972, in spite of any disparaging criticism, Pasatieri was generally regarded as the white-haired boy of American opera and Hollywood offered him a contract to write for movies. He said, "Out there they offered me the whole thing—money, the big house, the swimming pool. But in the end I realized I did not need a swimming pool. You have to keep your artistic life as pure as possible."

He continued to write operas, such as the one-act *Signor Deluso,* to his own libretto based on Molière's *Sganarelle,* which was performed by the Wolf Trap Farm Company at Greenway, Virginia, on July 27, 1974. Donal Henahan of the New York *Times* called it "a good example of Pasatieri's facility and professionalism," while adding that it was also "a good example of a composer who has decided to aim at commercially safe targets."

Praise for *The Seagull* (1974) was unqualified. It was commissioned by the Houston Opera in Texas which introduced it on March 5, 1974, a day designated by the Mayor of Houston as Thomas Pasatieri Day. Confidence and courage were needed for Pasatieri to undertake an opera based on a text by Chekhov with pages and pages of dialogue and most of the drama offstage. Pasatieri recalled, "When I announced I was going to do it, people said I had gone off the deep end—that it [the play] was just talk, talk, talk. But I pointed out, look at what they are saying!" Kenwood Elmslie's workable libretto and Pasatieri's music met the challenge in *Seagull* with success. As Hubert Saal praised Pasatieri in *Newsweek:* "Chekhov is made of sturdy stuff and it is Pasatieri's reliance on that, along with his well placed faith that musical values will pinch hit for necessary abbreviations, that turns the opera into a splendid success. The young composer was born to write dramatic and vocal music. It pours out of him—for the orchestra, for the voices, in one diverse lyric outburst after another, tonal and atonal, aways suited to the characters who sing them." Other critics were also enthusiastic. In the *Dallas Times,* Olin Chism called it a "soaring piece of lyric theater." In her report to *High Fidelity/Musical America,* Shirley Fleming found in the opera "all the old-fashioned virtues, accessible to a first night audi-

ence and productive of a good deal of pleasure. . . . The opera as a whole is a warm and communicative work, and the music carried the emotional burden of the play."

One year later Pasatieri wrote *Ines de Castro,* a three-act grand opera commissioned by the Baltimore Grand Opera to celebrate its silver jubilee, and the first performance took place on May 31, 1976. Bernard Stambler's libretto was set in 14th-century Portugal, a tale of unrequited love, murder, and political intrigue. "Pasatieri has created a score with skill," Elliott W. Galkin reported in *High Fidelity/Musical America.* "It is, to be sure, well written in nineteenth-century vocal terms, but there is little in its language which escapes the prosaic, little in its effects which seems spontaneous."

To commemorate the American bicentennial, Pasatieri, on commission from the Michigan Opera in Detroit, wrote *Washington Square,* with a libretto by Kenwood Elmslie, based on Henry James's novel, *Portrait of a Lady.* The Michigan Opera produced it on October 1, 1976 and Robert Jacobson reported in *Opera News:* "The audience reacted with rapt attention and ovations, and it was obvious that the new piece exercised great appeal. . . . Pasatieri's writing had the virtue of simplicity, creating an emotional climax and propelling the action along. In the scoring for fifteen players, textures are kept lucid and generally delicate, even in big climaxes." In March 1979, *Washington Square* was presented in towns in South Carolina, Georgia, and Mississippi in a nine-performance tour by the Augusta (Georgia) Opera Company. A critic for *High Fidelity/Musical America* said, "Not only was the Southeastern premiere of Pasatieri's opera a success, but contemporary American opera is alive and well in this part of the country."

Before Breakfast is a one-act, one character opera written on commission from the National Endowment for the Arts for Beverly Sills but her retirement as a singer necessitated a change of cast. When the work received its world premiere at the New York City Opera on October 9, 1980, Marilyn Zschau assumed the role of the Woman. Frank Corsaro's libretto was based loosely on a one-act play by Eugene O'Neill about the Woman's unhappy marriage that ends with the suicide of her husband (offstage). One of the novel stage features of this little opera is a three-minute shimmy performed by the Woman in her underwear to a Duke Ellington recording. Donal Henahan reported in the New York *Times*, "Miss Zschau threw herself into all this with conviction, and she had herself a personal success but, unfortunately, could not carry a weak piece along with her."

Always faithful to the voice, Pasatieri turned to song literature, which had interested him in his early years. In 1974 he completed *Rites de Passage*, for voice and chamber orchestra, and *Three Poems of James Agee*, for voice and piano. The former work was introduced in Florida, in March 1974, by the Fort Lauderdale Symphony under Emerson Buckley and with Patricia McCaffrey as vocal soloist. *Three Poems of James Agee* was sung for the first time at the Lincoln Center for the Performing Arts in New York, in April 1974 by Shirley Verrett, whose voice Pasatieri had in mind when he wrote the music. On April 13, 1976, Catherine Malfitano was the soloist in the world premiere in Connecticut of *Permit Me Voyage*, a cantata for soprano, chorus, and orchestra with a text by James Agee. On February 25, 1979, Frederica von Stade was heard in *Day of Love*, a cycle for soprano and piano, set to poems by Kit Van Cleave, at the Lincoln Center for the Performing Arts in New York.

Describing his method of composing, Pasatieri told Peter G. Davis: "I make few changes when I get the notes down on paper because I've already made all the choices. First, I'll take any scene of a libretto and act it out myself to get the . . . motivation of the characters. Then I sit at the piano and just improvise the music. After that I go away and think it in my head." Pasatieri listed the composers who have had the most influence on him as Bellini, Puccini, Verdi, and Richard Strauss; and not only concert and opera singers who helped develop his vocal style, but also popular singers such as Barbra Streisand, Roberta Flack, and Dionne Warwick. Speaking of popular singers, he said: "It's fascinating to hear them work in the medium of a slow ballad. Their interpretation or bending a note is closer to Italian bel canto than anything being written today."

Pasatieri has received the Marion Freschi Prize, the Brevard Festival Prize, and the George A. Wedge Prize, among other honors. A bachelor, he has made his home, since January 1969, in an apartment in New York City.

MAJOR WORKS

Choral Music—Permit Me Voyage, cantata for soprano, chorus, and orchestra.

Operas—The Trial of Mary Lincoln, television opera; Black Widow; The Seagull; Signor Deluso, opera buffa; The Penitentes; Ines de Castro; Washington Square; Before Breakfast, one-act opera; Three Sisters.

Piano Music—2 sonatas; Cameos.

Vocal Music—Heloïse and Abelard, song cycle for soprano, baritone, and piano; Rites de Passage, song cycle for voice and chamber orchestra; Three Poems of James Agee, for voice and piano; Far from Love, for soprano and chamber ensemble; Ophelia's Lament; Day of Love, song cycle for soprano and piano.

ABOUT

High Fidelity/Musical America, March 1972; Newsweek, March 19, 1974; New York Times Magazine, March 26, 1976; Opera News, March 4, 1972.

Krzysztof Penderecki

1933–

For biographical sketch, list of earlier works, and bibliography, see *Composers Since 1900*.

As a foremost Polish composer since World War II, Penderecki has continued to be highly prolific, mostly working in grandiose designs and dimensions.

Utrenia can be classed as a religious work for the cathedral, although it was commissioned by the Philadelphia Orchestra. The composer told an interviewer: "I am fascinated with church acoustics. My music sounds much better there—not because of religious significance but because of the sound." His religious works are frequently written with specific cathedrals in mind, as was *Utrenia* (1970–1971). This large-scale two-part composition is scored for five solo voices, two choruses (one on the stage, the other in the rear of the church or in the balcony), a large orchestra, and an expanded percussion section including noisemakers. The first part of the work, "The Entombment," was first heard in the Altenberg Cathedral on April 8, 1970; the second part, "Resurrection of Christ," was heard in the Münster Cathedral on May 28, 1971. The Philadelphia Orchestra, with vocal soloists and the Temple University Choir, gave the first American performance of the entire work on September 29, 1970.

Penderecki

The word "utrenia" means "morning service." The text, in the old Slavonic language, consists of the Holy Saturday service in the Eastern Orthodox Church dealing with Christ's entombment. For this age-old liturgy, Penderecki provided music written in advanced 20th century techniques. "What he has evoked in his score," wrote Irving Kolodin in *Saturday Review* "are the atmosphere and excitement of such a service rather than the esthetic paraphrase of it. It thus leans more towards the 'photographic' rendering of the subject matter rather than to the esthetic transformation of it."

Cosmogony (1970) was commissioned for the twenty-fifth anniversary celebration of the United Nations and its premiere took place in the Great Hall on October 24, 1970; the first concert-hall presentation followed on October 29 in Carnegie Hall. On both occasions, the Los Angeles Philharmonic Orchestra and the Rutgers University Choir were directed by Zubin Mehta. The work is scored for soprano, tenor, and bass soloists, with chorus, large orchestra, and a large percussion section, and has a text derived from Genesis, Leonardo da Vinci, Ovid, Copernicus, and Sophocles, with quotations from Yuri Gagarin and John Glenn. *Cosmogony,* an avant-garde programmatic composition, describes man, space, and the universe. A critic for *High Fidelity/Musical America* said, "There are all sorts of sounds, some clearly descriptive, others less so, some from easily identifiable instrumental sources, others mysterious sounds emanating from the bowels of the orchestra."

De Natura Sonoris II (1971), a nine-minute study of sonority, was commissioned by the Juilliard School of Music in New York, and performed for the first time on December 3, 1971, by the Juilliard Orchestra under the direction of Jorge Mester. (The predecessor of this work—*De Natura Sonoris I*—written in 1965–1966, was first performed in Royan on April 7, 1966, and presented at the 22nd Warsaw Autumn Festival in mid-September, 1978.) Percussive sounds in *Sonoris II* were dominant, including some emanating from a heavy pipe hit with a hammer.

On commission for the fiftieth anniversary of the Eastman School of Music, Penderecki wrote the *Partita,* for harpsichord and orchestra, in 1971. The Eastman School of Music Orchestra introduced it in Rochester, New York, on February 11, 1972, with Felicja Blumenthal as soloist, before bringing it to New York four days

later. Although the principal instrument and the structure are baroque, the music is avant-garde and full of tone clusters, and it calls for controlled improvisation and such dadaistic effects as having two guitarists sit under the body of the harpsichord tapping their feet. Harriett Johnson described the music in the New York *Post:* "As in all Penderecki, there was drama; the drama of one tone moving to crescendos of tremolos, trills, fast passages, varied touches for strings, swirls up and down in the winds. There are fast chordal repetitions and virtuoso cadenzas for the harpsichord. There was an effective diversity of sounds including cowbells and triangle."

In Lisbon, on June 4, 1973, Penderecki's oratorio, *Canticum Canticorum Salomonis* (1972), for a sixteen-voice chorus, chamber orchestra, and two dancers, received its first hearing. The text, from Solomon's *Song of Songs,* was written in Latin and the score was typical of Penderecki in its use of tone clusters, portamentos, controlled aleatory processes, and the allocation of different material to each of the sixteen choristers.

Until 1973, Penderecki's compositions for orchestra were comparatively short pieces. His first large work for orchestra, Symphony No. 1, was written on commission from Perkins Engines, an English manufacturer of diesel engines which sponsors annual concerts for employees. The world premiere took place in the 12th century cathedral in Peterborough, England, on July 19, 1973, with the London Symphony conducted by the composer. The recording by EMI a few days later was also financed by Perkins Engines. On January 9, 1975, the American premiere was performed by the Los Angeles Philharmonic Orchestra under Zubin Mehta. In this Symphony a huge orchestra is required, with a greatly expanded percussion section (as well as the usual instruments) and including such items as a piece of train rail, cowbells, a vibra slap, small Japanese wood blocks, a whip, crotales, and congas. Twenty-four violins are not separated into first and second, for in many passages each of the twenty-four violins is asked to play its own material. There are so many special effects in the score that Penderecki had to devise special symbols to designate them. Although the music is not programmatic, there are machine sounds to remind the listener of the sponsor. The two movements are, in turn, divided into two parts: Part I—Arche I, Dynamis I; Part II—

Dynamis II, Arche II. "Arche" is the Greek word for "origin" and bears a relation to the first movement of the classical symphony in that basic elements of the symphony are introduced in it. Dynamis I is the slow movement, Dynamis II, the scherzo, and Arche II, the finale with coda. The entire symphony is built around the single pitch "A" and its harmonic series.

Als Jacob Erwachte, for voices and orchestra (1974), had its world premiere in Monte Carlo on August 14, 1974. The full title translates to: "Jacob awoke out of his sleep and said, 'Surely the Lord is in this place and I knew it not.'" What is unusual in the orchestration is that twelve ocarinas are used for the first time with serious musical intent. Notwithstanding such unorthodoxy, the music is deeply religious with touches of mysticism. Andrew Porter wrote in *The New Yorker,* "It is a solemn, striking composition for large orchestra, made like most of Penderecki's music, not of notes but of sounds— of evocative sonorities and timbres carefully laid out in time." When Penderecki first visited Israel during the summer of 1975 to conduct an all-Penderecki concert with the Jerusalem Symphony Orchestra on July 26 and 27, *Als Jacob Erwachte* was on the program with Symphony No. 1 and *Partita.*

Penderecki's *Magnificat* (1974), another one of his religious works, was premiered at the Salzburg Festival of 1974, on August 17. A massive work, it is scored for bass solo, a solo vocal group, two choruses, a boys' chorus, and orchestra. It was commissioned for the 1200th anniversary of the Salzburg Cathedral, where it was sung. When Robert C. Marsh reviewed the Angel recording for *High Fidelity/Musical America* he referred to the *Magnificat* as "important religious music, rising from the matrix of our own times ... something we must hear to understand our world and ourselves. ... He praises God in the manner of one who lives in darkness; it is a glorification that rises *de profundis.*"

In writing a violin concerto for Isaac Stern in 1977, Penderecki made concessions to the lyrical nature of the instrument by composing tonal and romantic music in a large-scale work with a single movement of about forty minutes. Isaac Stern introduced it in Basle, Switzerland in April 1977, before performing it in the United States in Minneapolis on January 4, 1978, as soloist with the Minnesota Symphony under

Skrowaczewski. "It is a big, often beautiful, undeniably serious work in a single, strongly tonal span," a critic for *High Fidelity/Musical America* wrote. "There is clearly more to this somber, affecting music than first meets the ear."

In 1973, the Chicago Lyric Opera began planning a commemorative production for the American bicentennial and called upon Penderecki for a new opera. Their choice of a Polish composer to write an opera celebrating an American observance (and his selection of Milton's *Paradise Lost* as text) raised criticism in American circles. Ezra Laderman, president of the American Music Center, published a letter in *Musical America* calling this an "all-too typical example of reverse chauvinism" and denounced the "apparent belief" of the Chicago Lyric Opera that "two hundred years of independence are insufficient for Americans to have produced a native composer equal to the occasion." Some other American musical organizations and composers joined in the protest, but the Chicago Lyric Opera refused to retreat; the Penderecki opera *Paradise Lost* (1974–1978) was to celebrate the bicentennial. However, it took Penderecki so long to write his opera that the bicentennial year came and went without its production. Cynics retitled the work "Paradise Postponed," and Penderecki explained: "Originally I thought the piece should run to about an hour and a half. The first plan was a short excerpt from Milton. But with the continued collaboration of Christopher Fry, who wrote the libretto, I began to realize we were involved in an enormous undertaking. I could not rush it. As I began to concentrate on it—I cannot work on several pieces at once—it became clear that this may turn out to be my most important work. I have spent four years on it, which for me is a lot. The deadline had to be ignored." The opera grew to monumental proportions, unequalled by anything Penderecki had ever written. A chorus of one hundred was supplemented by a children's chorus of thirty, the ballet corps called for five principals and forty others, and the elaborate scenery had to be transported to the theater by ten huge trucks. The chorus, in four-tier towers to the right and left of the stage, found the music so complex that they began rehearsing a half year before the premiere and the orchestra needed one hundred and ten hours of rehearsal time. The production lasted three and a half hours at a cost exceeding half a million dollars, an expenditure without precedent in opera. (Since this work was a cross between an opera and oratorio, Penderecki called it a *"sacra rappresentazione,"* a 17th century Italian form.)

As a highly publicized operatic event, the premiere—in Chicago on November 29, 1978—was awaited with considerable anticipation and critical reaction was disappointing. In *New York,* Alan Rich called it "strong, original, eloquent and flawed." In *Opera News,* Robert Jacobson found that Penderecki's music "per se is rarely uninteresting. . . . He keeps our ears alert and rewarded throughout a long evening. . . . His sounds and rhythms speak with true craft and immense variety, titillating the ears, fascinating the mind. . . . His writing for the singers [is] without distinction and unable to define character profiles, wearying in its sameness. Penderecki seems somewhat more conventional than he has been in the past, mixing Bergian serial techniques with the orchestral splendors of Strauss, turning to Bach (he quotes a Bach chorale) a *Dies Irae* for the vision of Man's wars and ending with a great D major tonal flourish." In *Time,* Annalyn Swan called it "a heavenly bore." In *The New Yorker,* Andrew Porter questioned Penderecki's decency in "making theatrical capital of scenes of sexual hysteria, purgation by enema, and prolonged torture." He found the score to be "much too heavy, portentous orchestral writing; long, long pedals; thumping drum figures to indicate that something important is going to happen; ponderous brass progressions; grandiloquent organ; clusters building up and then decaying. All the old tricky devices, and then some new ones. . . . When he misses the mark, the distance between aim and achievement produces an effect of bombast, even vulgarity." The European premiere of *Paradise Lost* took place at La Scala in Milan, on January 21, 1979, with the composer conducting.

The tendency found in the Violin Concerto, and in parts of *Paradise Lost,* to avoid avantgardism for a more traditional romantic and tonal style, was also evident in Symphony No. 2, "Christmas Symphony," whose world premiere took place on May 1, 1980, by the New York Philharmonic Orchestra conducted by Zubin Mehta, for whom it was written. Although Penderecki maintained that he was avoiding repeating himself, Nicholas Kenyon wrote in *The New Yorker,* that "the result of Penderecki's searching, if it is embodied in the Second Sym-

phony, is no more than a characterless echo of the past. . . . We are plunged into sounds of Brucknerian grandiloquence from the brass; contrapuntal strings scurry earnestly, arguing over Lisztian thematic fragments; they are swept away by trombone and brass again; and then there is revealed a conventionally harmonized fragment of the carol 'Silent Night,' quietly shimmering like the tinsel on a Christmas card. . . . The carol may have a deep significance for Penderecki, but he has not revealed it in this weak and sentimental reference. At any rate, the music rushes on; we pass through Shostakovich at his noisiest, Strauss at his emptiest, bells and tremolo strings, another haze of Christmas good will, and a recapitulation of the whole ghastly first section, and finish up with a pretty touching close."

Since 1970, Penderecki has been devoting a good deal of his time and energy to conducting because of dissatisfaction with some performances of his music. In making his first attempt at conducting and recording in the early 1970s, he noted, "I was pleased with it. It was my first contact with an orchestra. I think it is very important for composers to conduct—they can better understand their music and can make everything happen with the orchestra." His conducting debuts took place in Lisbon in the fall of 1972; and in America on November 14, 1973, with the St. Louis Symphony. Ever since, he has conducted throughout the world with as many as fifty to sixty engagements a year, only occasionally conducting works of other composers (Bartók, Shostakovich, Stravinsky).

Between 1966 and 1972, Penderecki was a member of the faculty of the Folkwang Hochschule für Musik in Essen, Germany; in 1970–1971 he served as adviser to the Vienna Radio in Austria; in 1973 he became part-time professor of music at Yale University and Rector of the Cracow Conservatory in Poland; in 1974, he was composer-in-residence at Florida State University; and in 1977 at Aspen, Colorado.

Penderecki has received awards from all over the world: the Gustav Charpentier Prize in 1971 and the Honegger Prize by the French Foundation in 1979, in France; an honorary doctorate from the Eastman School of Music in 1972; and he has been elected an honorary member of the Royal Academy of Music in London, the Arts Academy of West Berlin, the Arts Academy of the German Democratic Republic, and the Royal Academy of Music in Stockholm.

MAJOR WORKS (supplementary)

Chamber Music—2 string quartets; Capriccio per Siegfried Palm, for solo cello.

Choral Music—Utrenia, for vocal soloists, two choruses, and orchestra; Cosmogony, for soprano, tenor, bass, chorus, and orchestra; Ecloga VIII, for six a cappella male voices; Canticum Canticorum Salomonis, for sixteen-voice chorus, chamber orchestra, and dancers; Dimensions of Time and Silence, for forty-voice chorus, strings, and percussion; Als Jacob Erwachte, for voices, orchestra, and twelve ocarinas; De Profundis, for chorus and orchestra; Magnificat, for boys' voices, chorus, and orchestra; Te Deum, for solo voices, chorus, and orchestra; Lacrymosa, for soprano, chorus, and orchestra.

Electronic Music—Ekecheireia, for magnetic tape.

Opera—Paradise Lost.

Orchestral Music—2 symphonies; Capriccio No. 2, for piano and orchestra; Pittsburgh Overture, for wind ensemble; De Natura Sonoris II; Concerto for Cello and Orchestra; Actions, for jazz ensemble; Prelude, for winds, percussion, and doublebasses; Partita, for harpsichord and chamber orchestra (with electronically amplified solo instruments); Intermezzo, for twenty-four voices; Polymorphia, for 48 strings; Concerto for Violin and Orchestra.

ABOUT (supplementary)

Lisicki, K., Sketches About Krzysztof Penderecki; Maciejewski, B. M., Twelve Polish Composers.

High Fidelity/Musical America, December 1975; Music Journal, February 1977; New York Times, February 23, 1969; July 15, 1973, February 27, 1977; Opera News, November 1978.

George Perle

1915–

George Perle was born in Bayonne, New Jersey, on May 6, 1915, one of four children of Joseph and Mary Sanders Perlman who had emigrated from Russia shortly before World War I. His father, a house painter and paperhanger, wanted to be a farmer. When George was about six a new piano came into his house and his cousin began giving him lessons. Neither parent was a musician but both loved music; and hearing his aunt, a pianist, and his uncle, a violinist, perform at home left a vivid impression on him, as he

Perle: pĕrl

GEORGE PERLE

recalled, "the music put me into a strange and terrifying trance of which neither the performers nor anyone else—not even my mother—had the slightest inkling."

Piano playing did not prove to be his first love, but from his musical beginnings, he was more interested in composition, as he recalled, "I had to educate myself for a long time, with no sympathy from anyone except my mother. I analyzed the pieces I studied all by myself, and I can still recall my first discovery, very soon after my lessons started, the difference between a semicadence and a full cadence and their respective formal functions. This was one of the really memorable days in my life as a musician."

His family finally acquired a farm in Wisconsin where he attended a one-room schoolhouse. Then after settling in Chicago for several years, the family acquired another farm in northern Indiana between Michigan City and La Porte where his grammar and high-school education was completed. Piano lessons were resumed with various local teachers and the study of harmony was begun at the Chicago College of Music.

Between 1934 and 1938, Perle attended De Paul University in Chicago where he studied composition with Wesley La Violette; and then, after receiving his Bachelor of Music degree in 1938, he studied composition privately with Ernst Krenek (1939–1941). In 1942, Perle earned his Master's degree at the American Conservatory of Music in Chicago, before serving in the United States Army between 1943–

1946 in both the European and Pacific theaters of operation. Until the end of the war, he was with the army of occupation in Japan and was discharged in February 1946.

Almost everything Perle composed before 1939 was destroyed, with the exception of four pieces dating from 1937–1938: *Pantomime, Interlude and Fugue* and *Classic Suite*, both for piano, and *Triolet* and *Molto Adagio*, for string quartet. His initiation into the post-tonal music of Arnold Schoenberg and particularly Alban Berg in the late 1930s increased his dissatisfaction with what he had written. He recalled, "I was fully aware of the disintegration of the traditional harmonic and tonal system before I found out about the works of Schoenberg. My first five minutes with Berg's *Lyric Suite* at the piano was like a revelation (in the literal biblical sense). This was a thrill of discovery of the cyclic twelve-tone series on which my own theory of 'twelve-tone tonality' was based in 1939."

In 1939, Perle's composing began with a string quartet based on his new concept of the compositional technique, the twelve-tone row, but the problems of set structure prevented its completion. As he later wrote: "I considered the possibility of constructing special sets whose linear adjacencies would present a coherent pattern, sets more likely to suggest consistent harmonic procedures than does the general set." In *Grove's Dictionary of Music and Musicians* (6th edition), Paul Lansky explained: "Perle's approach does not define explicit procedures for composition but rather outlines a large and highly structured network of pitch-class and formal relations which can then serve as points of reference for compositional development." Beginning in 1969, several years of intensive collaboration between Perle and Lansky in developing a coherent system of twelve-tone harmony resulted in a radical and comprehensive expansion of the original theory.

Although most of Perle's compositions are based on his special method, he cannot rightfully or strictly be termed a twelve-tonalist or a serialist. The works in which Schoenbergian tone-rows or serial procedures are discernible are *Little Suite*, for piano (1939), *Piano Piece* (1945), String Quartet No. 3 (1946), and *Three Inventions*, for piano (1957). While Perle is not completely a tone-row or serial composer, he is a leading authority on the subject, and the author of a definitive study, *Serial Composition and Atonality* (1962).

His composing, Perle maintains, "reflects my preoccupation through all these years with something one might provisionally call 'post-diatonic tonality.'" The preoccupation led to the writing of a second book, *Twelve-Tone Tonality* (1977), propounding the thesis "that the seemingly disparate styles of post-triadic music share common structural elements, and that collectively these elements imply a new tonality, as 'natural' and coherent as the major-minor tonality which has been the basis of a common musical language in the past." One of Perle's earliest compositions demonstrating his special method was *Two Rilke Songs*, for soprano and piano, composed in 1941 and later recorded in 1979. Since 1969 all of Perle's compositions have been based on these principles. Going back to 1941–1969, there are a number of works that may be said to be "freely" or "intuitively" conceived, based neither on the conventional twelve-tone system nor on twelve-tone tonality. These works might represent an independent line of development that goes back to the so-called atonal music similar to that which preceded Schoenberg's formulation of his twelve-tone system in 1922–1923. However, Perle's music is much involved with tone centers and harmonic structure, and very different in its thematic and rhythmic character from the music of pre-serial "atonality." The most important of these other works is the Quintet, for strings (1958; San Francisco, February 19, 1960), one of Perle's finest chamber music works; the three Woodwind Quintets (1959, 1960, 1967); and a long list of pieces for unaccompanied solo instruments (flute, clarinet, violin, viola, and doublebass).

Perle began a long and eventful career as a teacher in 1948, serving first as lecturer on music at the College of the City of New York. In 1949 he joined the music faculty of the University of Louisville as instructor in composition and music history, and remained for eight years. Perle received his Ph. D. in musicology at New York University in 1956, after studying music history with Gustave Reese and Curt Sachs. Between 1951 and 1961 he was appointed to the music faculty of the University of California at Davis and in 1961 he was assistant professor of music at Queens College, New York, rising to associate professorship in 1963, and a full professorship in 1966. He was also affiliated with the Juilliard School of Music in 1963, the University of Southern California during the summer of 1965, Yale University in 1965–1966, and the Berkshire Music Center at Tanglewood during the summer of 1967. In addition, he was visiting professor at the State University of Buffalo in 1971–1972, at the University of Pennsylvania in 1976, and Columbia University in 1979. In 1966 he received the first of two Guggenheim Fellowships. While spending the summer of 1958 at the MacDowell Colony in Peterborough, New Hampshire, he met Barbara Phillips, an English-born sculptress. Having divorced his first wife, Laura Slope, in 1952, Perle married Barbara Phillips on August 11, 1958 and they raised two adopted daughters and Barbara's son by a first marriage.

On May 10, 1962, at a Composers' Showcase concert in New York, there were two world premieres of Perle's music: *Monody I,* for flute (1960), and *Serenade No. 1,* for solo viola and chamber orchestra (1962), one of Perle's most widely performed compositions. In *Stereo Review,* Eric Salzman described *Monody* as a "lively and engaging little masterpiece of the medium." When the *Serenade* was performed in Chicago, Donal Henahan wrote in the Chicago *Daily News* that it achieved "a variety in expression and sound that contemporary music too often ignores in its preoccupation with organizational techniques. . . . The composer enlivened matters at one point with a jazz interlude, then explored the varieties of musical experience inherent in the solo viola's insistence on one note, while the others went other more colorful ways." Perle himself explained that his *Serenade* was suggested by that 18th century form, "music written for an unstandardized ensemble of instruments and comprising a number of movements of varying character, a conception that lies somewhere between the symphony and the suite."

On June 14, 1963, Perle's *Three Movements,* for orchestra (1960), had its world premiere at the Festival of the International Society for Contemporary Music in Amsterdam. Reporting to the *Christian Science Monitor* from Amsterdam, Everett Helm wrote: "The piece displayed an admirable feeling for nicely balanced form, orchestral color, and texture. It was agreeable music, well written and expressive." *Three Movements* was premiered in the United States by the Chicago Symphony Orchestra under Jean

Martinon on March 7, 1965, and was recorded by the Royal Philharmonic, with David Epstein conducting.

When Irving Ilmer, violinist and violist, commissioned Perle to write a concert piece demonstrating his virtuosity, Perle wrote a five-movement *Solo Partita,* for violin and viola (1965), which Ilmer introduced in Chicago on April 23, 1965. The five movements in the work are: Prelude (viola), Allemande (violin), Courante (viola), Sarabande (violin), and Finale (violin).

Perle's String Quartet No. 5 was written in 1960, revised in 1967, and given its first performance at Tanglewood on August 13, 1967. "It was unconventional, first in its choice of a standard instrumental combination and in a kind of writing for that combination that showed no concern at all for showing how unlike their normal selves the instruments could be made to sound," said Michael Steinberg in the Boston *Globe.* "Its harmonic language with its chromatically flowing, gently dissonant triads, was wildly unconventional as well. . . . Perle's ear for such harmony is sensitive; he has a lively feeling for rhythm . . . ; he is altogether unself-conscious."

Serenade II, for chamber orchestra (1968), which was commissioned by the Koussevitzky Music Foundation for the Library of Congress in Washington, D.C., was introduced on February 28, 1969, with Arthur Weisberg conducting. This is a work described by Alan M. Kriegsman in the Washington *Post* as possessing "all the earmarks of modernity—a high dissonance quotient, unexpected sonorities, irregular rhythms, and so forth. . . . All told, an attractive, expertly crafted piece that seems blessedly free of cant."

On March 19, 1972, Robert Laneri, clarinetist, and the composer at the piano, premiered the *Sonata Quasi una Fantasia,* for clarinet and piano (1972). The Sonata is not only a demanding virtuoso piece with extraordinarily difficult rhythmic interrelations between the two instruments, but it also exploits multiphonics and harmonics for the clarinet solo.

Perle's String Quartet No. 7 (1973) is generally conceded to be his most significant chamber music work. It was commissioned by the Cleveland Quartet which introduced it in Buffalo, New York, on March 19, 1974. Paul Griffiths said in the *Musical Times* of London, "The main impression, thanks to the skill with which Perle balances phrase against phrase, section against section, is one of genial musical discourse."

One of Perle's rare ventures into choral writing—also one of his most distinguished works—is the *Songs of Praise and Lamentation,* for six solo voices, double chorus, and orchestra (1974), written in memory of Noah Greenberg, founder and director of the New York Pro Musica. In this three-part composition, the first part is set in Hebrew from the 18th Psalm, for solo singers, chorus, and orchestra. The second part, for a cappella chorus, uses four of Rilke's *Sonnets to Orpheus,* in German. The third part consists of three lamentations (collectively entitled *In Eius Memoriam*); the first two are in French, on the death of Binchois by Ockeghem and the death of Ockeghem by Josquin, and the third is in Latin, on the death of Josquin by Vinders. Perle's music, set to John Hollander's text, is in English with a Latin refrain. Renaissance choral music and a Gregorian chant are quoted in the final movement.

Songs of Praise and Lamentation was written by Perle during a year's absence from Queens College in 1974 made possible by a second Guggenheim Fellowship. Commissioned by the Dessoff Choirs (with grants from the New York State Council on the Arts, the Greylock Foundation, Joseph Machlis, and James Bond) it had its world premiere in New York on February 18, 1975. Writing in *New York,* Alan Rich commented that Perle uses "some Hebrew texts of lamentation and sets these texts in a manner free of both ethnic and atonal clichés. . . . four Rilke poems, marvelously sensitive and atmospheric pieces and again unique in their genre. But the crown of the work is the last movement, twenty minutes or so of sheer radiance." In *Musical Quarterly,* Bruce Saylor wrote: "With *Songs of Praise and Lamentation,* George Perle has praised and dignified famous men, brought to fruition a life's work, and given us an enduring monument of his own."

Six Etudes, for piano (1976), was premiered by Morey Ritt at a concert of the International Society for Contemporary Music in Boston on October 29, 1976, and described by Paul Hume in the Washington *Post* as "magnificent. Of dazzling technical virtuosity, they are of an intensity and concentrated content that should make them genuine popular favorites with both the public and those pianists able to master their pianistic and intellectual demands." Morey Ritt

played the etudes with a bleeding finger and announced, "I loved these etudes very much and I would like you to hear them played better." A proffered band aid enabled her to play the work a second time. "The audience had difficulty applauding her and Perle enough to show its great admiration," Hume added.

On June 19, 1978, at Princeton, New Jersey, Bethany Beardslee was accompanied by Morey Ritt at the piano, for the premiere of Perle's *Thirteen Dickinson Songs,* for soprano and piano (1978), where the motifs of remembrance, autumn, and death are recurrent. Perle's wife died soon after the premiere, and the subsequent recording of this performance was dedicated to her memory. Mark Swed said in *Keynote,* "One never loses Dickinson's voice as it moves from the awestruck emotions of childhood through wistful midlife sentiments to poignant thoughts about death. The music sets the mood, heightens the drama, underscores the emotion and subtly conforms to the poetic meter."

Perle's Concertino (1979), for chamber orchestra, had its initial hearing on April 21, 1979, in a Chicago performance by the Da Capo Chamber Players. In 1980, Perle wrote *A Short Symphony* for the Boston Symphony and its musical director, Seiji Ozawa, which was premiered at the Berkshire Music Festival in Tanglewood on August 16, 1980.

In addition to *Serial Composition and Atonality* and *Twelve-Tone Tonality,* Perle is the author of *The Operas of Alban Berg* (1980) as well as numerous magazine articles on the twelve-tone music in general and Schoenberg and Berg in particular. For his writings, he received the Deems Taylor Award from ASCAP (American Society of Composers, Authors and Publishers) in 1973 and 1978. Perle is regarded as an authority on the Viennese atonalist and some of his findings can be found in this Berg biography.

In 1978, Perle was elected to the American Academy and Institute of Arts and Letters. He is co-founder (1966) and now director of the International Alban Berg Society and from 1968 to 1970, he was president of the New York chapter of the International Society for Contemporary Music.

MAJOR WORKS

Band Music—Solemn Procession.

Chamber Music—String Quartets Nos. 5 and 7; 3 wind quintets; 2 solo-violin sonatas; Sonata for Solo Viola;

Three Sonatas, for solo clarinet; Hebrew Melodies, for solo cello; Lyric Piece, for cello and piano; Sonata for solo cello; String Quintet; Monody I, for flute; Monody II, for doublebass; Three Inventions, for bassoon; Solo Partita, for violin and viola; Sonata Quasi una Fantasia, for clarinet and piano.

Choral Music—Songs of Praise and Lamentation, for vocal soloists, chorus, and orchestra.

Orchestral Music—Three Movements; Serenade I, for viola and chamber orchestra; Six Bagatelles; Concerto for Cello and Orchestra; Serenade II, for chamber ensemble; Concertino, for piano, winds, and timpani; Short Symphony.

Piano Music—Little Suite; Piano Piece; Six Preludes; Sonata; Three Inventions; Short Sonata; Suite in C; Toccata; Six Etudes.

Vocal Music—Two Rilke Songs, for soprano and piano; Thirteen Dickinson Songs, for soprano and piano.

ABOUT

Machlis, J., Introduction to Contemporary Music; Vinton, J. (ed.), Dictionary of Contemporary Music.

American Composers Alliance Bulletin, September 1962; Musical Quarterly, April 1971.

Vincent Persichetti

1915–

For biographical sketch, list of earlier works, and bibliography see *Composers Since 1900.*

In 1969, Persichetti completed a major choral work, *The Creation,* an oratorio for four vocal soloists, chorus, and orchestra on commission from the Juilliard School of Music in New York for its opening concert of the season at the Lincoln Center for the Performing Arts. It is based on an assortment of texts from mythological, scientific, and poetic sources, "everything from the Maori and Mexican Indians to Haiku poetry of the Japanese," the composer said, and it includes such exotic traditions as Apache, Hittite, Quechua, Sanskrit, Xinca, and Zuni, as well as various translations of the Bible. On April 17, 1970, it was premiered by the Juilliard Orchestra and Chorus in New York with the composer conducting. The performance was repeated in Philadelphia, where Max de Schauensee reported in the Philadelphia *Evening Bulletin,* "The workmanship proves first class, as solos and choruses are masterfully integrated in the vast conception." In the Philadelphia *Enquirer,* Samuel L. Singer said: "Persichetti accompanies his text

with incisive orchestral comments, beginning when sound arises out of nothingness to depict effectively the Void before Creation. The composer uses precise colors in his scoring. The chorus is also employed effectively, sometimes singing in twelve parts with half-tone clusters, other times in unison."

Persichetti completed three works in 1970: *Sinfonia: Janiculum,* which the Philadelphia Orchestra under Eugene Ormandy introduced on May 5, 1971; *Night Dances,* for orchestra, first performed at Kiamesha Lake, New York, under Frederick Fennell's direction, on December 9, 1970; and a song cycle, *A Net of Fireflies,* performed for the first time by Carolyn Reyer at the Lincoln Center for the Performing Arts in New York on May 12, 1971. In her review in the New York *Post,* Harriett Johnson described *Sinfonia: Janiculum* as follows: "In one movement, *Janiculum* uses instruments and ideas in a most ingenious way while attempting to explore the concept of the god, Janus, after whom the hill is named. The *Sinfonia* consists of the two faces of Janus which symbolize opposites and conflicts of life. Is there a door of life opening or closing? Will man fail or conquer? Persichetti believes in the affirmative." Written during the year in which he received a second Guggenheim Fellowship while he was residing on the Janiculum in Rome, Persichetti was so impressed by the tolling chimes from the Chiesa di San Pietro and Gianicolo below that he incorporated the ringing chimes both at the beginning and the end of his composition. Harriett Johnson added, "In the same manner, he makes dramatic use of the timpani. Playing alone, for example, it links Section I and II and later it goes from pitch to pitch, a determined voice in a tumultuous contrapuntal fabric. There were thunderclaps with a purpose."

Early in 1973, Persichetti was invited to compose a work for the Presidential Inauguration, to be performed by the Philadelphia Orchestra under Eugene Ormandy, with Charlton Heston as narrator, which would incorporate the text of Lincoln's second inaugural address of 1865. Persichetti hesitated, feeling that it was impossible for a composer to complete such a work in three weeks and because, he said, "politically I was not interested in getting myself involved because of my personal convictions." However, when he read Lincoln's address, "I suddenly saw what I could do with it. And I felt that I could do it for anyone because this was a statement of my strong belief in my fellow human beings and also of my hope for peace." He completed *A Lincoln Address,* for narrator and orchestra, in eleven days, sometimes working around the clock. But a few days before the concert, the Inaugural Committee decided that the work would not be performed because Lincoln's address contained anti-war sentiments that might prove embarrassing. (The address read: "Both parties deprecated war; but one of these would make war rather than let the nation survive; and the other would accept war rather than let it perish. And the war came.") Such words could fan anti-Vietnam feelings prevalent in 1973. A letter from Persichetti to President Nixon seeking clarification did not clear the matter up and *A Lincoln Address* was introduced instead by the St. Louis Symphony under Walter Susskind, with William Warfield as narrator, on January 25, 1973, and repeated in New York on February 1. In the New York *Post,* Harriett Johnson found the work to be "somber in its tonal thought and in the dark color of its orchestration. It is poignant, often moving and beautiful."

Later in 1973, on February 28, at Penn State University, the Alard String Quartet premiered Persichetti's String Quartet No. 4 ("Parable X") which had been written for it. Then the Juilliard String Quartet presented it in New York on April 16, 1974. Persichetti described the quartet (with quoted material from earlier works) as a "one-movement story." In five sections, it is dissonant, with each of the four instruments developing its own melody. In the New York *Times* Harold C. Schonberg called it "a strong, assured, meaningful piece of considerable dignity."

On November 17, 1977, the New York Philharmonic commissioned, and presented under Erich Leinsdorf, with Thomas Stacy as soloist, the first performance of the Concerto for English Horn and Orchestra. Writing in the New York *Post,* Harriett Johnson reported that the Concerto was a "basically lyrical, conservative piece. ... The music is more sorrowfully reflective than tragic and ends with a short, dance-like section. ... Listening to the Concerto is a pleasant experience that shows off the instrument ... beautifully as song like or declamatory." The work received the first Kennedy Center Friedhelm Award for the best orchestral work premiered in the 1977–1978 season. On July 30, 1978,

Parable XVIII, for solo trombone, was introduced by Per Brevig at the meetings of the International Trombone Society in Nashville, Tennessee.

Persichetti's most extended work for the organ, *Auden Variations,* was premiered on July 14, 1978, at the International Contemporary Organ Music Festival in Hartford, Connecticut; with Leonard Raver as soloist. The "Auden" in the title refers to poet W. H. Auden, who wrote *For the Time Being,* the text on which the first hymn is based. The melody comes from Persichetti's *Hymn and Responses for the Church Year* (1955). Thirteen variations follow.

In 1973, Persichetti received a third Guggenheim Fellowship. Two years later he received the Creative Arts Award from Brandeis University. He has also been visiting composer-in-residence at numerous universities and colleges throughout the United States.

MAJOR WORKS (supplementary)

Band Music—O Cool Is the Valley, poem for band; Parable IX.

Chamber Music—Parable III, for solo oboe; Parable IV, for solo bassoon; Parable V, for carillon; Parable VII, for solo harp; Parable VIII, for solo horn; String Quartet No. 4; Parable XI, for solo alto saxophone; Parable XII, for solo piccolo; Parable XIII, for solo English horn; Parable XVI, for solo viola; Parable XVII, for solo doublebass; Parable XVIII, for solo trombone; Parable XX, for solo guitar.

Choral Music—The Creation, for soprano, alto, tenor, baritone, solos, chorus, and orchestra; Love for Women's Chorus; Glad and Very, five choruses.

Orchestral Music—Sinfonia: Janiculum; Night Dances; A Lincoln Address, for narrator and orchestra (or band); Concerto for English Horn and Orchestra.

Organ Music—Parable VI; Do Not Go Gentle; Auden Variations.

Piano Music—Parable XIX; Reflective Keyboard Studies; Mirror Studies; Mirrors; Three Toccatinas.

Vocal Music—A Net of Butterflies, song cycle.

ABOUT

Slonimsky, N. (ed.), Baker's Biographical Dictionary of Musicians (6th edition); Vinton, J. (ed.), Dictionary of Contemporary Music.

Ascap in Action, Spring 1980; Diapason, Spring 1979; Philadelphia Sunday Bulletin, April 12, 1970.

Gofreddo Petrassi

1904–

For biographical sketch, list of earlier works, and bibliography see *Composers Since 1900.*

Petrassi's *Otteto di Ottoni,* for four trumpets and four trombones (1968), received its first hearing during the summer of 1968 at the Hopkins Center Congregation of the Arts at Dartmouth College in Hanover, New Hampshire; it was then performed at the Juilliard School of Music in New York in 1970. The chamber oratorio, *Beatitudes,* for baritone and five instruments, written in 1969 in memory of Martin Luther King Jr., had its world premiere in Fiuggi, Italy on July 17, 1969. *Concerto No. 8,* for orchestra (1970–1972) was introduced by the Chicago Symphony Orchestra on September 28, 1972.

Petrassi's one-act opera, *Il Cordovano (The Man from Cordova),* written in 1944–1948, is a Cervantes farce about a May-December marriage in which the senior partner is impotent and the junior partner indulges in extra-marital affairs, and it received its New York premiere on April 22, 1976, by the New York City Opera.

Petrassi's seventieth birthday was celebrated in 1974 in Zagarolo, the city of his birth, with a concert of his music as well as a torchlight parade, speeches, a reception, and a ceremony in which the composer was presented with a medal. A Petrassi festival was held in Ravenna, Italy, between February 22 and 28, 1975, also to commemorate his seventieth birthday.

In 1974, Petrassi retired as professor of composition at the Santa Cecilia Academy in Rome. That year, he was made Grande Ufficiale Della Republica Italiana in Italy. He received an award from the American Academy and Institute of Arts and Letters in New York in 1977, and, in 1978, the Premio Internazionale "Feltrinelli" per la Musica Award. He was elected to membership in the Academy of Arts in West Berlin in 1975, the National Academy of Fine Arts in Buenos Aires in 1977, the American Academy of Arts and Sciences in Boston, and the Bavarian Academy of Fine Arts in Munich in 1978. The University of Bologna conferred an honorary doctorate in music on him in 1976.

MAJOR WORKS (supplementary)

Chamber Music—Otteto di Ottoni, for four trumpets

and four trombones; Soufflé, for one performer on three flutes; Elogio per un'Ombra, for solo violin; Nunc, for solo guitar; Ala, for flute and harpsichord; Quattro Odi, for string quartet; Fanfare, for three trumpets; Alias, for guitar and harpsichord; Grand Septuor, for clarinet, trumpet, trombone, violin, cello, guitar, and percussion.

Choral Music—Orationes Christi, for chorus, brass, eight violins, and eight cellos.

Orchestral Music—Concerto No. 8.

Piano Music—Oh! les Beaux Jours!; Petite pièce.

Vocal Music—Beatitudes, chamber oratorio for baritone and five instruments.

ABOUT

Bonelli, A. E., Serial Techniques in the Music of Goffredo Petrassi; Restagno, E., Storicità ed Attualità di Petrassi; Zosi, G., Ricerca e Sintesi Nell'Opera di Goffredo Petrassi.

High Fidelity/Musical America, January 1975.

Hans Pfitzner

1869–1949

For biographical sketch, list of earlier works, and bibliography, see *Composers Since 1900.*

Pfitzner's infrequently performed operatic masterwork, *Palestrina* (1917), was revived in a complete and excellent recording conducted by Rafael Kubelik, and issued by Deutsche Grammophon in 1973. Reviewing it in *Stereo Review,* Richard Freed remarked that it "is a resounding corrective to the notion that *Palestrina* is nothing more than a mummified object of somewhat localized veneration. The music . . . is always beautiful and frequently very moving, as well as being superbly crafted; the drama is well paced, invested with real vitality, and peopled with characters who are no mere symbols."

ABOUT (supplementary)

Abendroth, W. (ed.), Festschrift aus Anlass des 100 Geburtstag.

Opera News, December 13, 1969; New York Times, November 11, 1973.

Pierné

Gabriel Pierné

1863–1937

See *Composers Since 1900.*

Willem Pijper

1894–1947

For biographical sketch, list of earlier works, and bibliography, see *Composers Since 1900.*

ABOUT (supplementary)

Searle, H., and Layton, R., 20th Century Composers: Britain, Scandinavia, the Netherlands.

Key Notes, no. 3, 1976; Musical Quarterly, July 1976; Sonorum Spectrum, no. 30, spring 1967.

Walter Piston

1894–1976

For biographical sketch, list of earlier works, and bibliography, see *Composers Since 1900.*

In March 1973, Piston's *Fantasia for Violin and Orchestra* had its world premiere at the Hopkins Center Congregation of the Arts at Dartmouth College in Hanover, New Hampshire. In 1974, Piston was awarded the Mac-Dowell medal at a ceremony that he was too ill to attend and it was accepted for him by Michael Steinberg, the Boston music critic, who said: "The man and the music fit so beautifully together. It seems so cool and neat and so beautifully built that it takes a particular ear to become attuned to the quirks that give it the often witty and warm individuality that it has." Piston's last major work was the Concerto, for string quartet, wind instruments, and percussion, written on commission to commemorate the fiftieth anniversary of the Portland (Maine) Symphony Orchestra, which introduced it on October 26, 1976.

Walter Piston died at his home in Belmont, Maine, on November 12, 1976.

MAJOR WORKS (supplementary)

Orchestral Music—Concerto for Flute and Orchestra;

Fantasia for Violin and Orchestra; Concerto, for string quartet, wind instruments, and percussion.

ABOUT (supplementary)

Boretz, B., and Cone, E. T. (eds.), Perspectives of American Composers.

High Fidelity/Musical America, August 1974; New York Times, November 14, 1976; Stereo Review, April 1970.

Ildebrando Pizzetti

1880–1968

See *Composers Since 1900.*

Marcel Poot

1901–

For biographical sketch, list of earlier works, and bibliography, see *Composers Since 1900.*

Poot served as president of the Confédération Internationale des Auteurs et Compositeurs (C.I.S.A.C.) and as president of the Concours International Reine Elisabeth, both in Belgium.

MAJOR WORKS (supplementary)

Chamber Music—Légende, for four clarinets or saxophones; Quartet, for four horns; Mosaïque, for eight winds; Musique de Chambre, for piano trio; Concertino, for oboe and piano; Impromptu, for brass quintet.

Orchestral Music—Concerto Grosso, for piano quartet and orchestra; Suite En Forme de Variations; Danse Laudative; Cello Concertino; Symphony No. 4; Oboe Concertino; Symphony No. 5; Ballade Symphonique; Trumpet Concerto; Concerto No. 2, for piano and orchestra; Mouvement Concertante; Symfonische Ballade; Concerto for Clarinet and Orchestra.

Piano Music—Sonatina No. 2; Alla Marcia et Barcarolle.

Quincy Porter

1897–1966

See *Composers Since 1900.*

Francis Poulenc

1899–1963

For biographical sketch, list of earlier works, and bibliography, see *Composers Since 1900.*

Poulenc's one-character monodrama, *La Voix Humaine* (1958), was revived in New York by Magda Oliviero and the Little Orchestra Society under Thomas Scherman on November 2, 1971, and it was televised by the Public Broadcasting Service, starring Karen Armstrong, in 1979. On February 5, 1977, the Metropolitan Opera in New York presented its first production of *Les Dialogues des Carmélites* (1953–1956), and on February 20, 1981, it presented a rare revival in its first production of the one-act opera buffa, *Les Mamelles de Tirésias* (1947).

In 1980, EMI in France released a five-record album containing all of Poulenc's songs, performed by Elly Ameling, Nicolai Gedda, Gérard Souzay, and others. The album strengthened Poulenc's position as one of France's foremost songwriters, the 20th century's most eligible candidate to succeed Franz Schubert (according to Roger Nicholas in the *New Grove Dictionary of Music and Musicians*), and the creator of the finest songs by any French composer, Debussy and Fauré not excluded (in the opinion of Patrick J. Smith in *High Fidelity/Musical America*).

The French government issued a fifty-centime postage stamp bearing Poulenc's picture in July 1973.

ABOUT (supplementary)

Bernac, P., Francis Poulenc: the Man and His Songs; Gruen, J., Close-Up; Sadie, S. (ed.), The New Grove Dictionary of Music and Musicians.

New York Times, October 31, 1971; Opera News (Poulenc Issue), February 5, 1977; Stereo Review, January 1975.

Serge Prokofiev

1891–1953

For biographical sketch, list of earlier works, and bibliography, see *Composers Since 1900.*

The American staged premiere of Prokofiev's opera, *War and Peace* (1941–1952), in English translation by Edward Downes, took place on May 18, 1974. It was performed by the Opera Company of Boston and produced and conducted by Sarah Caldwell. On December 4, 1976, Prokofiev's earlier opera, *Love for Three Oranges* (1921), in English translation by Victor Seroff, returned to the city where it received its world premiere in 1921, in a production of the Lyric Opera of Chicago. On March 3, 1978, the Philadelphia Orchestra under Riccardo Muti presented the complete film score of *Ivan the Terrible* (1942–1945), arranged in oratorio form by Abram Stasevich. The oratorio had been introduced in Moscow in 1961, under Stasevich's direction, as part of a celebration commemorating Prokofiev's seventieth birthday; and it had its American premiere with the St. Louis Symphony on March 29, 1968; it was also recorded in the Soviet Union. The score (with additions from other music by Prokofiev) was used as background music for the ballet, *Ivan the Terrible,* choreographed by Yuri Grigorovich and presented by the Bolshoi Ballet in New York in April 1975. Commenting on the score as performed by the Philadelphia Orchestra on March 3, 1978, Harold C. Schonberg said in the New York *Times:* "If *Ivan the Terrible* does not rise to the great moments of *Nevsky,* it is still Prokofiev at his best, and for this Eisenstein film he contributed an exciting, even thrilling score."

In the late 1970s, the ample Prokofiev discography was added to by the first American recording of *Ivan the Terrible* (by the Philadelphia Orchestra under Muti for Angel), the first complete recording of the ballet *Romeo and Juliet,* in two different releases (London and Angel), and the first complete recording of Prokofiev's last ballet, *The Stone Flower* (Melodiya) in the Soviet Union.

In an interview with the New York *Times* on December 20, 1976, Prokofiev's first wife, Lina, denied being divorced from Prokofiev, casting some doubt on the legality of his marriage to Mira Alexandrovna Mendelson (long accepted as his legal second wife).

The collected works of Prokofiev in an 87-volume edition was issued by the Belwin-Mills Publishing Corporation in the United States in 1979.

ABOUT (supplementary)

Appel, D. (ed.), Prokofiev by Prokofiev: a Composer's Memoir; Samuel, C., Prokofiev; Schwarz, B., Music and Musical Life in the Soviet Union: 1917–1970.

Puccini

New York Times, December 20, 1976; Opera News, November 1976.

Giacomo Puccini

1858–1924

For biographical sketch, list of earlier works, and bibliography, see *Composers Since 1900.*

ABOUT (supplementary)

Ashbrook, W., The Operas of Puccini; Greenfield, H., Puccini: a Biography; Hopkinson, C., A Bibliography of the Works of Giacomo Puccini, 1858–1924; Jackson, S., Monsieur Butterfly: the Story of Giacomo Puccini; Weaver, W. and Hume, P., Puccini: the Man and His Music.

Henri Rabaud

1893–1949

See *Composers Since 1900.*

Sergei Rachmaninoff

1873–1943

For biographical sketch, list of earlier works, and bibliography, see *Composers Since 1900.*

The centenary of Rachmaninoff's birth in 1973 was commemorated by RCA with the release of *The Complete Rachmaninoff*, five albums comprised of fifteen records covering everything Rachmaninoff recorded between 1919 and 1942 as piano soloist, chamber-music performer, and conductor. Harris Goldsmith wrote in his review in *High Fidelity/Musical America* that in the records, "there is nary a mistake of voicing or timing. And even at its most violent, Rachmaninoff's tone—for all its mettle and metal—was pure velvet. His phrasing was unfailingly supple and authoritative, with an ability to be declamatory and flexible. In sum, one of the greatest of all pianists." The complete solo piano works of Rachmaninoff were recorded by Ruth Laredo for Columbia, and all Rachmaninoff songs by Elisabeth Söderström, with Vladimir Ashkenazy at the piano, for London.

ABOUT (supplementary)

Threlfall, R., Sergei Rachmaninoff: His Life and Music.

New York Times, April 1, 1973; Stereo Review, May 1873.

Maurice Ravel

1875–1937

For biographical sketch, list of earlier works, and bibliography, see *Composers Since 1900.*

In the early 1970s, the American musicologist, Arbie Orenstein, discovered six previously unknown and unpublished Ravel compositions in southern France. Orenstein had come to the French Basque country, where Ravel was born, to do research for a doctoral thesis on Ravel's vocal music. The results of Orenstein's inquiries to the heirs of the composer's estate were reported in the New York *Times:* "The heir, Alexandre Taverne, showed Mr. Orenstein the casually stored manuscripts and gave the researcher permission to have them all photographed. It was the first time they had been made available for scholarly research." Orenstein edited the scores for publication by Editions Arima of Paris: Sonata for Violin and Piano (1897), *Sérénade Grotesque,* for piano (1893), and four songs whose dates of composition ranged from 1893 to 1910. These pieces were heard for the first time at a Ravel centenary concert at Queens College, in New York, on February 23, 1975.

The centenary of Ravel's birthday inspired a three-week festival, *Hommage à Ravel,* by the New York City Ballet at the Lincoln Center for the Performing Arts in New York, between April 30 and June 20 of 1975. Three different ballet programs were presented, featuring such Ravel scores as his Concerto in G, *L'Enfant et les Sortilèges,* and *La Valse.* Orchestras, performing groups, and vocalists honored Ravel with performances of his works throughout Europe and the United States, and many new recordings of his music were issued.

On February 20, 1981, the Metropolitan Opera in New York presented its first production of *L'Enfant et les Sortilèges.*

ABOUT (supplementary)

David, J., Maurice Ravel: Étude Biographique; Fauré, H., Mon Maître, Maurice Ravel; Myers, R. H., Ravel:

His Life and Works; Nichols, R., Ravel; Orenstein, A., Ravel: Man and Musician.

High Fidelity, March 1975; High Fidelity/Musical America, August 1975; Musical Quarterly, October 1967; Music Forum 3, 1973; Stereo Review, November 1975.

Alan Rawsthorne

1905–1971

For biographical sketch, list of earlier works, and bibliography, see *Composers Since 1900.*

Alan Rawsthorne died in Cambridge, England, on July 24, 1971.

MAJOR WORKS (supplementary)

Chamber Music—Quintet, for piano and strings; Quartet, for oboe and strings; Suite, for flute, viola, and harp; Quintet, for piano, clarinet, horn, violin, and cello; Elegy, for solo guitar (completed by Julian Bream).

Choral Music—The God in the Cave, for chorus and orchestra.

Orchestral Music—Overture for Farnham; Concerto for Two Pianos and Orchestra; Theme, Variations and Finale; Triptych.

Piano Music—Theme and Four Studies.

ABOUT (supplementary)

Routh, F., Contemporary British Music: the Twenty-five Years from 1945 to 1970; Searle, H., and Layton, R., 20th Century Composers: Britain, Scandinavia, the Netherlands.

The Listener (London), December 30, 1971.

Gardner Read

1913–

For biographical sketch, list of earlier works, and bibliography, see *Composers Since 1900.*

After almost two decades, the world premiere of Gardner Read's Symphony No. 4 (1951–1958) took place on January 30, 1970. It was performed by the Cincinnati Symphony Orchestra under Erich Kunzel. In the Cincinnati *Enquirer,* Henry S. Humphreys wrote that it is "a very fine piece of music scored with skill . . . and replete with beautiful lyrical passages and soaring, powerfully buttressed climaxes." *Haiku Seasons* (1969–1970), a "musical mobile" for

four narrators and instrumental ensemble, is aleatory in that the audience participated in its first hearing on April 1, 1971, in Boston, with the composer conducting. The music is a setting of sixteen haiku verses by four renowned Japanese poets. Read's Concerto for Cello and Orchestra (1945) was performed publicly for the first time thirty years after its composition by the New Haven Symphony under Erich Kunzel, with Barry Sills as soloist, on October 14, 1975. The oratorio, *The Prophet* (1960), with a text by Kahlil Gibran, was given its first hearing in Boston on February 23, 1977, seventeen years after it was written.

Gardner Read retired as composer-in-residence and professor of composition at Boston University in 1978 after thirty years; he was named professor emeritus. His latest books are *Contemporary Instrumental Techniques* (1976) and *Modern Rhythmic Notation* (1978).

MAJOR WORKS (supplementary)

Chamber Music—Sonoric Fantasia No. 3, for five flutes, harp, and percussion; Conzone di Notte, for guitar; Hexadic, for six instruments; Invocation, for trombone and organ.

Choral Music—Christmas Ballad, for a cappella chorus; Songs to Sing, for a cappella chorus; Praise Ye the Lord, for a cappella chorus; As White as Jade, for chorus and piano.

Opera—Villon.

Orchestral Music—Haiku Seasons, for four narrators (two male, two female) and instrumental ensemble; Concerto for Piano and Orchestra.

Organ Music—And There Appeared Unto Them Tongues As of Fire; Sonoric Fantasia No. 4, for organ and percussion; Galactic Novae, for organ and percussion.

Vocal Music—The Hidden Lute, for soprano, alto, flute, harp, and percussion.

ABOUT (supplementary)

Slonimsky, N. (ed.), Baker's Biographical Dictionary of Musicians (6th edition); Vinton, J. (ed.), Dictionary of Contemporary Music.

Max Reger

1873–1916

For biographical sketch, list of earlier works, and bibliography, see *Composers Since 1900*.

ABOUT (supplementary)

Brand-Selter, E., Max Reger: Jahre der Kindheit; Röhring, K. (ed.), Max Reger 1873–1973; ein Symposion; Wirth, H., Max Reger in Selbstzeugnissen und Bilddokumenten.

High Fidelity/Musical America, May 1974.

Ottorino Respighi

1879–1936

For biographical sketch, list of earlier works, and bibliography, see *Composers Since 1900*.

To commemorate the centenary of Respighi's birth, the Caramoor Festival in Katonah, New York, inaugurated its 1979 season on June 16 with an all-Respighi program: a choreographed version of his orchestral suite, *The Birds*, and the American premiere of his last opera, *Lucrezia*. The scoring of the opera, unfinished because of the composer's death, was completed by his wife (and former pupil), Elsa Respighi. The world premiere took place posthumously at La Scala in Milan on February 24, 1937.

Elsa Respighi donated Respighi's manuscripts and library to the Fondazione Cini on the island of San Giorgio (Venice) as a memorial.

ABOUT (supplementary)

Opera News, June 1978.

Silvestre Revuletas

1899–1940

See *Composers Since 1900*.

Wallingford Riegger

1885–1961

See *Composers Since 1900*.

Knudåge Riisager

1897–1974

For biographical sketch, lists of earlier works, and bibliography, see *Composers Since 1900*.

The world premieres of Riisager's ballets *Galla Variationer* and *Svinedrengen* took place in Copenhagen; the former was produced by the Ballet Royal on March 5, 1967, the latter over Danish TV on March 10, 1969.

The following world premieres of Riisager's works were heard on Danish Radio in Copenhagen: *Stabat Mater*, for chorus and orchestra, on November 9, 1967; *Trittico*, for woodwinds, brass, doublebass, and percussion, on March 3, 1972; and *Bourrée-ballet Variations*, for orchestra, on March 2, 1977. *Entrada Epiloga*, and incidental music to *Apollon*, both for orchestra, received their first hearing on May 19, 1971, and November 11, 1973, respectively, in Copenhagen.

Riisager resigned as director of the Royal Danish Conservatory in 1967 the year his autobiographical memoir, *It's Amusing to be Small*, was published in Copenhagen; and an annotated catalog of his works was edited in Copenhagen by Sigurd Berg.

Knudåge Riisager died in Copenhagen on December 26, 1974.

MAJOR WORKS (supplementary)

Ballets—Galla Variationer; Svinedrengen.

Choral Music—Stabat Mater, for chorus and orchestra.

Orchestral Music—Burlesk Ouverture; Entrada Epiloga; Bourrée-ballet Variations; Trittico, for woodwinds, brass, doublebass, and percussion; Apollon, incidental music.

ABOUT (supplementary)

Riisager, K., It's Amusing to be Small.

Music and Education, September-October 1966.

Jean Rivier

1896–

For biographical sketch, list of earlier works, and bibliography, see *Composers Since 1900.*

MAJOR WORKS (supplementary)

Chamber Music—Duo, for flute and clarinet: Briliances, for seven woodwinds; Three Silhouettes, for flute and piano.

Choral Music—Dolor, for chorus and orchestra.

Guitar Music—Etude.

Orchestral Music—Résonances; Triade, for string orchestra; Climats, for celesta, vibraphone, xylophone, piano, and strings; Concerto for Bassoon and Orchestra; Concerto for Oboe and Orchestra; Concerto for Trumpet and Strings.

Piano Music—Sonata; Alternaces.

Vocal Music—Prière, for voice and piano (or organ).

George Rochberg

1918–

George Rochberg was born in Paterson, New Jersey, on July 5, 1918, the son of Morris Rochberg, a businessman, and Anna Hoffman Rochberg. He grew up in the nearby city of Passaic where the family moved when he was a year old, and he began taking piano lessons at ten by accident. The family acquired a second-hand upright piano for George's younger sister to take lessons some day. Since pianos fascinated George, he could not keep away from it so his mother decided to get him a piano teacher, Kathleen Hall, in 1928. A year later he made his first attempt at composition and his initial efforts, he said, "received varying degrees of disapproval or approval from teacher and parents, but which only I took seriously."

The years following, when he attended the Passaic public schools, graduating from the high school in 1936, were described by Rochberg as a time of "complete indirection." From the age of fifteen he played the piano in jazz groups and wrote popular songs with Bob Russell as his lyricist. Between 1937 and 1939, he wrote some piano music and art songs such as "There Was

Rochberg: rŏk′ bĕrg

GEORGE ROCHBERG

an Aged King," "With Rue My Heart," *"Warum sind Denn,"* "When I Am Dead," and *"Minnelied."* He attended Montclair State Teachers College, received his Bachelor of Arts degree in 1939, and found himself "so far from my ambition to become a composer that it seemed almost hopeless of realization."

In 1939, he met David Mannes, who provided the opportunity for him to enroll in his music school in New York City (renamed the David Mannes College of Music). He recalled, "This was the real beginning of my serious musical studies." He was at the David Mannes School until 1942, studying composition and theory with Hans Weisse, Leopold Mannes, and, during his last year, with George Szell. At this time, Rochberg wrote more songs and chamber and orchestral music among which was *Variations on an Original Theme* (1941), for piano, which Rochberg performed at the Mannes School in 1942.

On August 18, 1941, Rochberg married Gene Rosenfeld whom he met while both were attending Montclair State Teachers College and they moved to New York to live what Rochberg described as "a happy though precarious existence." To help with the finances, Gene taught English privately and worked in the book department of Macy's department store while George taught piano in Brooklyn and New Jersey. In 1944, their son, Paul, was born.

In 1942 (during World War II) Rochberg was inducted into the United States Army and as a second lieutenant, he served in Europe, was wounded in action, and earned a Purple Heart with Oak-leaf cluster. He said, "The war years were much more than an interruption in my musical studies. They taught me what art really meant because I learned what life really meant. The war shaped my psyche and precipitated my internal development. I came to grips with my own time."

After his army experience in the summer of 1945, Rochberg went on with music at the Curtis Institute of Music in Philadelphia studying composition with Rosario Scalero for one season and with Gian Carlo Menotti for two years after that. Rochberg admitted:"Though our musical interests differed, he had an uncanny sense for the weak points in my work; I valued this critical faculty of Menotti's and benefited from it greatly." During this period, Rochberg completed *Songs of Solomon,* for voice and piano, a tonal work of romantic character which was his first piece to be published and publicly performed (by the tenor David Lloyd in Philadelphia in 1947 and in New York a year later).

After receiving his Bachelor of Music degree at the Curtis Institute in 1947, Rochberg was appointed to the music faculty there in 1948, on Menotti's recommendation. Until 1964, he taught harmony and counterpoint, and initiated a new course in form and analysis for those instrumentalists about to graduate. Meanwhile, he attended the University of Pennsylvania from which he received his Master of Arts degree in 1949, submitting as his thesis Suite, for orchestra, written three years earlier.

His early compositions revealed a variety of influences: Trio, for horn, clarinet, and piano in 1947 (since withdrawn) was influenced by Hindemith; *Night Music* (1948) was influenced by Bartók, and four years later it won the Gershwin Memorial Award. In April 1953 it was introduced by the New York Philharmonic under Dimitri Mitropoulos; *Capriccio* (1949), for two pianos, was influenced by Stravinsky and Schoenberg; and Symphony No. 1 (1949) was influenced by Stravinsky and Hindemith. *Night Music* became the second movement in this five-movement symphony. However, in 1957, Rochberg revised it and removed *Night Music* and also a third movement. As a three-movement symphony, it was premiered on March 28, 1958, with Eugene Ormandy conducting the Philadelphia Orchestra.

In 1950, a Fulbright Fellowship and one from the American Academy of Rome, enabled Rochberg to live in Rome with his family, while he worked in a studio at the American Academy. He recalled, "Except for some occasional sightseeing in the city and environs, I kept up a rigid routine of work—from nine to five—for six crucial months; for during that time I came to the conclusions which affected the course of my music for years to come." He became aware of his artistic need for the kind of discipline serialism would impose upon him, and his interest in it increased through his personal associations with Italy's foremost dodecaphonic composer, Luigi Dallapiccola.

On his return from Italy, Rochberg became a music editor for the music publishing house of Theodore Presser (a position offered to him while he was in Rome), which he retained until 1960, and at the same time he continued teaching at the Curtis Institute. In 1952 (the year his daughter Francesca was born), he completed his first String Quartet, written in a Bartókian rather than Schoenbergian idiom. This quartet, which had its first performance in January 1953 by the Galimir Quartet, in New York, won the Society for the Publication of American Music award in 1956. In reviewing a CRI (Composer's Recordings Inc.) recording of the quartet by the Concord String Quartet, a critic for *High Fidelity/Musical America* said: "The string quartet is a beautifully made composition, rhythmically alive and contrapuntally engrossing."

In 1952, Rochberg also completed his first dodecaphonic work, a style he would favor for the next eleven years, with personal modifications. He introduced *Twelve Bagatelles,* for piano, in New York in 1953, and it became his first successful composition, a work favored by many pianists. Later Rochberg adapted the work for large orchestra, renaming it *Zodiac.* He explained, "I was interested primarily in the instrumental timbral possibilities which I had always felt were implicit in the original work. In some cases, no rewriting or recomposing was necessary, while in others I found it better to change things in order to take full advantage of orchestral color. The title of the work has no astrological significance that I am aware of. 'Zodiac' also implies a circle completed; and it was this conception which made me feel the term was appropriate. For the work is a twelve tone composition. . . . The twelve related sections of the work also, of course, have their association with the title." Max Rudolph conducted the Cincinnati Symphony in its first performance on May 8, 1965. Rochberg dedicated *Zodiac* to the memory of his son, Paul, who died of a brain tumor in 1964 at the age of twenty.

Chamber Symphony, for nine instruments (three woodwinds, three brasses, and violin, viola, and cello) was written in 1953. Its premiere took place in Baltimore in 1955 with Hugo Weisgall conducting. A critic for *High Fidelity/ Musical America,* in reviewing a recording of the work, described it as a "winning piece—a sturdy little symphony of neo-classical proportions." In 1954, Rochberg wrote *David, the Psalmist,* for tenor and orchestra, to a Hebrew text, and it was premiered eleven years later in Philadelphia by the University of Pennsylvania Orchestra conducted by Melvin Strauss.

In 1956, Rochberg completed Symphony No. 2. The four-movement work is played without interruption, and all of the movements are based on a single twelve-tone row. The first movement, "Declamando," is in the sonata form; the second movement, "Scherzo," is a contrasting trio; and in the third, "Molto Tranquillo," a chamber ensemble rather than the full orchestra is used, with solo instrumental writing predominating; in the finale, the full orchestra is called upon again to recall the opening movement. The Cleveland Orchestra under George Szell introduced it on February 26, 1959 and through a Naumburg Recording Award in 1962 it was recorded for Columbia by the New York Philharmonic Orchestra under Werner Torkanowsky. After the Cleveland performance, Frank Hruby wrote in *Musical America* that it stamped Rochberg "as one of America's leading contemporary men of music—serious, thoughtful, competent and uncompromising in the achievement of his goals." Hruby also found that the symphony was "unrelieved in its intensity, since Rochberg has seen fit here to link the movements together with interludes rather than giving the listener a chance to regain his equilibrium with between-movement breaks. Generally speaking, the work is predominantly fragmentary, with short angular motives tossed about in the various sections of the orchestra. Toward the close, Rochberg sweeps into an impassioned lyric section, overlaid with the earlier declamatory themes and finally the work draws to an end of resignation."

On a Koussevitzky Music Foundation commission, Rochberg completed *Dialogues,* for clarinet and piano, in 1956, and it was performed in New York by Eric Simon in 1958. Rochberg also wrote *Sonata-Fantasia,* for piano, in 1956, which was first performed in 1958 in New York by Harold Liebow. In this work, the composer quoted from one of his favorite compositions by Schoenberg, *Klavierstücke,* Op. 23, No. 1. Writing in *Music and Letters* (London) Peter Crump said that Rochberg's *Sonata-Fantasia* revealed the "wealth of material a note-row can yield. The range of invention compels admiration, as does the dazzling variety and ingenuity of the piano writing."

A Guggenheim Fellowship in 1956–1957 enabled Rochberg and his family to spend four months in Mexico, on leave-of-absence from Theodore Presser. During the next six years, Rochberg composed additional serial music including *Blake Songs,* a cycle of four songs for soprano and chamber ensemble (1957), to poems by William Blake, which was presented by the International Society for Contemporary Music in New York in 1961, with Shirley Sudock as soloist and Ralph Shapey as conductor. The *Cheltenham Concerto,* for small orchestra (1958), was commissioned by the Cheltenham Arts Center of Pennsylvania, and first heard at the Festival of the International Society for Contemporary Music in Rome; in the same year it won first prize in the Italian International Society for Contemporary Music competition. String Quartet No. 2, with voice (1959–1961), with the 9th Duinese Elegy of Rilke as text, was first heard on March 30, 1962, in a performance by Janice Harsanyi and the Philadelphia String Quartet. Alan Rich, in the New York *Times* wrote that the work was a "wholly superior testimonial to the continuing viability of the middle ground in the twelve-tone world." On a grant from the National Institute of Arts and Letters, String Quartet No. 2 was recorded by Janice Harsanyi and the Philadelphia Quartet for CRI.

Time Span I (1960), a symphonic movement commissioned by the Junior Division of the Women's Association for the St. Louis Symphony, was introduced there on October 22, 1960. A revised version, *Time Span II,* written four years later, was heard in New York on January 19, 1964, with the composer conducting the Buffalo Philharmonic Orchestra. Rochberg's last composition in a serial technique, *Trio,* for violin, cello, and piano—described by the composer as "a very passionate piece"—was written in 1963 for the Nieuw Amsterdam Trio who performed it in Buffalo, New York, in 1966.

In 1960, Rochberg was appointed chairman of the music department of the University of Pennsylvania, a position he held until 1968. From 1968 to 1978 he advanced from professor of composition and theory to composer-in-residence and first Annenberg Professor of the Humanities at the university in 1978. Meanwhile, in 1964, he was also Slee Professor at the State University of New York in Buffalo. In 1962, his Alma Mater, Montclair State College, awarded him an honorary doctorate in Humane Letters; in 1964 the Philadelphia Musical Society conferred an honorary doctorate in music on him.

The unexpected and tragic death of his son, Paul, so sapped Rochberg's strength and spirit that he almost lost the will to create. In 1965, he went back to his work, saying, "Right now composing is also a way of achieving integration and the means with which I can face existence. Without composing it would be well-nigh impossible." He ended his creative hiatus with *Contra Mortem et Tempus,* music for the magic theater. Then he wrote *Black Sounds* in 1966, a ballet score for winds, piano, and percussion, on commission from the Lincoln Center in New York for a "Special" telecast on September 24, 1966 by National Educational Television. *Black Sounds* was used as the music for *The Act,* a ballet choreographed by Anna Sokolow and the TV production received the Prix Italia that same year.

By the middle of the 1960s, Rochberg began to re-examine his musical goals and methods and in re-evaluating serialism he discovered that it had been restrictive of full freedom of expressivity, as he explained, "I saw that twelve-tone composition was another form of minimalism, a spiritual and psychological starvation. You reduce your palette, your scope, your variety. In the last fifty years we learned how not to be open or direct or simple. We hid behind complexity, what I call 'fancy footwork.' We were afraid that beneath the complexities there was nothing. Anyway, I was essentially a singer. And serialism didn't permit melody." Fond of the music of Gustav Mahler, he now began to feel that music was more than sound and structure; it was also the voice of human experience. He began to favor the neo-Romantic and emotional idiom, found in the music of the past, and started the

practice of quoting the music of past masters in his compositions. On a University of Chicago commission for a work for its seventy-fifth anniversary, he wrote *Music for the Magic Theater* in 1965. The music is a collage of quotations from Mahler (horn passages from Symphony No. 9), Mozart (virtually the entire Adagio from Divertimento in B-flat, K. 287), and even Edgard Varèse and Stockhausen. Its title and subject matter were suggested by Herman Hesse's *The Wolf of the Steppes.* The work was first performed in Chicago on January 24, 1967. In 1966, Rochberg wrote *Nach Bach,* a fantasy for harpsichord (or piano), for harpsichordist Igor Kipnis. As a "parody" of Bach's keyboard Partita No. 6 in E minor, Kipnis presented the first performance of *Nach Bach* at the University of Pennsylvania in January 1967.

In 1966–1967 Rochberg received a second Guggenheim Fellowship and in 1966 he appeared as guest composer at the Berkshire Music Center at Tanglewood, Massachusetts; in 1969 at Temple University College of Music; and in 1970 at the Oberlin Festival of Contemporary Music at Ann Arbor, Michigan.

Rochberg's creative evolution from serialism to romanticism and what he called "tonal gravities" became evident in *Tableaux* (1969), with a text based on *Silver Talons of Pietro Kostrov* by his son, Paul Rochberg, for soprano, two actors' voices, small men's chorus, and twelve players; and in *Songs in Praise of Krishna* (1970), a song cycle based on Bengali poems of Krishna's love for Radha. In both works Rochberg's writing is emotional; in the Krishna cycle, it is sensual and spiritual. The first performance of *Tableaux* was presented by the University of Washington Contemporary Group in St. Louis on October 31, 1969; the Krishna cycle was first sung by Neva Pilgrim at the University of Illinois in Urbana on March 16, 1971.

Rochberg's Symphony No. 3 (1966–1969), for double chorus, chamber chorus, vocal soloists, and large orchestra, was commissioned by the Juilliard School of Music where it was performed on November 24, 1970, with Abraham Kaplan conducting. In the symphony, there are extensive quotations from past composers' music. Rochberg regarded this Symphony as a "Passion According to the 20th Century," and James Felton of the Philadelphia *Bulletin* explained: "His idea of 'Passion' is the drama of man's struggle with his own nature. It is a confession of nostalgia for the lost peace of the Garden of Eden, a confession of hope that man will prevail in the present confusion. The line, 'Why do you persecute me?' is taken up by the soloists in turn, again and again and it becomes a question posed by a whispering chorus." The text, in Latin and German, is set from quoted texts by Heinrich Schütz and Johann Sebastian Bach as examples, and the music is quoted from Beethoven, Mahler, and Charles Ives in such baroque forms as fugues and chorales. Alexander L. Ringer observed in a review in *Musical Quarterly* that, "as with Mahler, the real issue is not whether everything hangs together properly but whether in the end it all adds up to an emotional experience the listener is unlikely to forget. Judging by the wildly enthusiastic response that it evoked at Tully Hall, the Third Symphony does accomplish what it sets out to do."

Similar in artistic intent and style—another "Passion of Medieval Jewry," Ringer said, is *Sacred Song of Reconciliation (Mizmor l'Piyus)* (1970), with text taken from the Bible (Moses, Isaiah, Genesis). Testimonium, a foundation in Jerusalem, commissioned it and its first performance took place there on January 5, 1971, with Gary Bertini conducting. Ringer added, "The composer decided to use the opening fragment, 'He has torn and He will heal us, He has smitten and He will bind it up,' as a refrain framing a dramatic piece that is divided into four principal sections accommodating the four biblical fragments. The initial words, '*Hu taraf*' ('He has torn') are belted out by the soloist in a deliberately raspy voice, while the chamber orchestra, reinforced by much percussion and two pianos, engages in violent motivic collision. The aural result literally tears at the innards and in so doing creates an intense craving for 'reconciliation!' that is offered as the piece proceeds tenderly and jubilantly, humbly and majestically, passionately and compassionately."

In the String Quartet No. 3 (1972) Rochberg simulates the styles of Beethoven, Brahms, Mahler, Bartók. This work, commissioned by the Concord String Quartet, received its first performance at the Lincoln Center in New York on May 15, 1972, at a concert sponsored by the Walter W. Naumburg Foundation. The recording by the Concord String Quartet for Nonesuch was singled out by *Stereo Review* as the record of the year. Rochberg described the Quartet as "primarily ironic in tone and spirit . . . a music

which left behind obvious modernisms, a music which relied almost entirely on basic, uncomplicated gestures" that "can, by regaining contact with the traditions and means of the past, re-emerge as a spiritual force with reactivated posers of melodic thought, rhythmic pulse and large-scale structure." Richard Freed noted, in reviewing the recording in *High Fidelity/Musical America,* that the composer "may sound a little stuffy, but after hearing the music one can only appreciate Rochberg's deep sincerity and welcome most heartily (and almost incredulously) a major contribution to the string quartet literature. This is not only a 'large-scale structure,' but one whose contents are both highly expressive and directly communicative (not always the same thing)—music that virtually reaches out and embraces the listener."

Borrowings and a different kind of simulation can be found in *Imago Mundi* (1973) for orchestra. The Baltimore Symphony commissioned and introduced it on May 8, 1974, with Sergiu Comissiona conducting. Not reaching into the musical past for his material but to the Orient, Rochberg recreated the sounds of the Japanese Gagaku, and the orchestral music of the 8th century Japanese Imperial Court, capturing the mystery, poetry, religion, and exoticism of the Orient. In the Baltimore *Sun,* Elliott W. Galkin described it as "an unusual conflict and brilliant resolution of styles, as fleeting as a musical dream—fairy-like and magical, and throughout tinged with an element of religiosity. . . . It is a unique work, truly gripping in its effect."

Phaedra (1973–1974), a monodrama for mezzo-soprano and orchestra, has a text by Rochberg's wife, Gene, taken from Robert Lowell's version of Racine's *Phèdre.* The New Music Ensemble of Syracuse, New York, with the assistance of the New York State Council on the Arts, commissioned the work, and Neva Pilgrim as soloist with the Syracuse Symphony under David Loebel, presented it on January 9, 1976. A critic for *High Fidelity/Musical America* called it "strong and forceful . . . an uncluttered work that is both appealing and accessible to a wide and diverse audience."

Rochberg's Concerto for Violin and Orchestra, composed during the spring and summer of 1974, was the first of seven works celebrating the American bicentennial on grants from the National Endowment for the Arts to be performed by seven major American orchestras. The commission for this concerto, however, came from the Pittsburgh Symphony Orchestra and its former musical director, William Steinberg, in memory of Donald Steinfirst, music critic of the Pittsburgh *Post-Gazette* who died in 1973. The work was intended for Isaac Stern, who, with the Pittsburgh Symphony conducted by Donald Johanos, presented the world premiere on April 4, 1975. A revised version has since been performed by Stern with major orchestras in the United States and Europe.

Rochberg characterized the concerto as "an elegiac work—even romantic in spirit." He consciously set out to work in the violin-concerto traditions that began with Mozart and continued through Bartók and Schoenberg, saying "I turned my back on the 20th century. I adapted this tradition to my own needs and interests. Basically, my concerto is a tonal work, with occasional excursions into atonal chromaticism." Romantic in spirit, and sometimes beautifully lyrical, it is completely assimilable. The work's five movements are divided in two: Part I consists of three movements: an Introduction, Intermezzo, and Fantasia; Part II contains a second Intermezzo and an Epilogue. A *Time* critic stated: "What makes it fresh and exciting is Rochberg's willingness to be unafraid of the past. He wants to be able to use any device, technique or idea he likes. . . . Ranging in mood from innocent to the diabolic, from the elegiac to the ecstatic, Rochberg's thirty-eight-minute score seems sure to become a favorite with violinists, conductors and their audiences."

On a grant from the National Endowment for the Arts, Rochberg wrote the Piano Quintet for pianist, Jerome Lowenthal, and the Concord String Quartet in 1975. The first performance took place at the Lincoln Center in New York on March 15, 1976. In *Newsweek*, Hubert Saal described it as a "wonderfully singing piece that effectively blended diverse musical materials and passionately explored the extremes of human emotion."

To celebrate his sixtieth birthday in 1978, Rochberg completed three string quartets (Nos. 4, 5, 6) to be played in sequence in a single concert. Because they were intended for the Concord String Quartet (which recorded his previous three successful quartets), this trio of chamber-music compositions is known as the *Concord Quartets*. Mannerisms in string-quartet writing from Haydn to Schoenberg are explored

and quotations from Beethoven's String Quartet in G Major, Op. 18, No. 2 and Pachelbel's familiar "canon," both in the last movement of the sixth quartet link it to the past. Traditional structures, such as fugues, rondos, fantasias, and serenades, combine to achieve Rochberg's self-stated aim "to ensure maximum variety of gesture and texture and the broadest possible spectrum I could command, from the purest diatonicism to the most complex chromaticism." Hubert Saal said in *Newsweek:* "His new quartets seesaw eloquently back and forth between harshness and atonality and the sweetness of tonality. Sometimes that tension itself becomes musical material. In the spirited opening movement of the new Fourth Quartet, aggressive dissonance and lofty lyricism clash head-on and the work ends not in a reconciliation but in an uneasy truce. The Fifth Quartet is merry, nonaggressive, energetic. The final movement of the Sixth and the last, with its classical allusion, answers the questions inherited from the Fourth. It ends with unequivocal affirmation of melody, the unconditional surrender of the atonal adversary, and a true musical peace."

The Concord String Quartet introduced the *Concord Quartets* at a festival of Rochberg's chamber music at the University of Pennsylvania on January 20, 1979. The Quartet then took the three works to New York on January 22, and to the Santa Fe Chamber Music Festival in July 1979, where both the Quartet and George Rochberg were in residence. In 1979, the fourth quartet received the Kennedy Center Friedhelm Award in Washington, D.C., as the year's best chamber music work.

In addition to being composer-in-residence at the Sante Fe Festival in 1979, Rochberg was also in residence at the Aspen Conference on Contemporary Music during the summer of 1972 and the Grand Teton Festival in Wyoming during the summer of 1977.

"The pursuit of art," Rochberg said, "is much more than achieving technical mastery of means or even a personal style; it is a personal journey toward the transcendence of art and of the artist's ego. . . . Every time you write a serious work you are in effect laying your life on the line. But I can't think about that or what my message is. My job is to convince the performer, his job is to convince the audience."

Rochberg's wife, Gene, wrote the libretto for his first opera, based on *The Confidence Man*, by

Herman Melville, which was commissioned by the Sante Fe Opera for production during the summer of 1982. The Rochbergs reside in Newton Square, Pennsylvania. His hobbies include reading and occasional painting.

MAJOR WORKS

Ballet—Black Sounds.

Chamber Music—7 string quartets (including the 3 Concord Quartets); Duo Concertante, for violin and cello; Chamber Symphony, for nine instruments; Serenate d'Estate, for six instruments; Dialogues, for clarinet and piano; La Bocca della Verità, for oboe and piano (also violin and piano); Music for the Magic Theater, for fifteen players; Piano Trio; Music for The Alchemist, for eleven players with incidental soprano; Contra Mortem et Tempus, for violin, flute, clarinet, and piano; Fifty Caprice Variations, for violin and piano; Electrikaleidoscope, for flute, clarinet, cello (all amplified), piano, and electric piano; Ricordanza, soliloquy for cello and piano; Ukiyo-e, Pictures of the Floating World, for solo harp; Piano Quintet; Slow Fires of Autumn (Ukiyo-e II), for flute and harp; Septet, for winds and strings, and piano; Octet, A Grand Fantasia for flute, clarinet, horn, piano, violin, viola, cello, and doublebass.

Choral Music—Three Psalms, for chorus; Passions According to the 20th Century, for soloists (singers and speakers), chorus, and instruments; Tableaux, for soprano, two actors' voices, small men's chorus, and twelve players; Behold My Servant, for a cappella chorus.

Orchestral Music—4 symphonies; Night Music; Cantio Sacra, for small orchestra; David the Psalmist, for tenor and orchestra; Cheltenham Concerto, for small orchestra; Time Span II; Zodiac, circle of twelve pieces (orchestral version of Twelve Bagatelles for piano); Sacred Song of Reconciliation, for bass baritone and chamber orchestra; Imago Mundi; Phaedra, monodrama for soprano and orchestra; Transcendental Variations, for string orchestra; Concerto for Violin and Orchestra.

Piano Music—Variations on an Original Theme; Twelve Bagatelles (also for orchestra under the title of Zodiac); Sonata-Fantasia; Arioso; Nach Bach, fantasia for harpsichord (or piano); Prelude (on Happy Birthday); Carnival Music; Partita-Variations; Book of Contrapuntal Pieces, for keyboard instrument.

Vocal Music—Book of Songs, for voice and piano; Songs of Solomon, for voice and piano; Blake Songs, for soprano and chamber ensemble; Songs in Praise of Krishna, for voice and piano; Fantasies, for voice and piano; Songs of Inanna and Dumuzi, for alto and piano.

ABOUT

Musical Quarterly, October 1966, January 1972; Newsweek, February 19, 1979; New York Times, May 28, 1972; New Yorker, February 12, 1979.

Joaquín Rodrigo

1901–

Joaquín Rodrigo was born in Sagunto, Valencia, Spain, on November 22, 1901. (Most music encyclopedias give 1902 as the year of his birth. But a plaque on the house of his birth and a confirmation from Rodrigo himself give 1901 as the correct date.) Neither his father, Vicente Rodrigo Peirtas, a businessman, nor his mother, Juana Vidre Ribelles, was musical. When Joaquín was three, a diphtheria epidemic broke out in Sagunto claiming the lives of many children and severely damaging Joaquin's eyesight. A year later, he underwent an unsuccessful operation which left him totally blind. The child began to seek solace in music, at first by listening to the organ at the Santa Maria Church in Sagunto. In his fifth year, Rodrigo's family settled in Valencia and he began learning to play the piano without instruction. Although he was not a prodigy, he showed enough aptitude for music and made sufficient progress in playing the piano to attract the interest of local musicians who gave him his first formal lessons in 1917. His most notable teachers were Enrique Goma, Edouardo Lopez Chavarri, and Francisco Antich. Chavarri, besides being a composer, was an eminent folklorist who began transferring his enthusiasm for Spanish folk music to his young pupil, who carried it over in his own music years later. Antich gave him a sound training in harmony and composition.

Joaquín's first compositions were written in 1923: a five-movement baroque-like suite for piano, *Berceuse de Otono; Ave Maria,* for a cappella chorus; and his first work for orchestra, *Juglares.* The last of these was performed in 1924 by the Orquesta Sinfonica de Valencia and was received favorably by the Valencia press.

In 1927, Rodrigo went to Paris, where for five years he attended the École Normale de Musique studying composition with Paul Dukas. Dukas's influence on Rodrigo was far-reaching in that it helped him to refine and sensitize his style of composition. In addition, his personal association with such important Spanish contemporaries in Paris as Manuel de Falla and the pianist Ricardo Viñes, strengthened his

---

Rodrigo: rō drē′ gō

241

Rodrigo

JOAQUÍN RODRIGO

resolve to write music rooted in Spanish folklore, and descriptive of Spain and its background. His friendship with Andrés Segovia interested him in writing Spanish music for the guitar. In Paris, too, he met Victoria Kamhi, a Turkish concert pianist who had graduated from the Paris Conservatory and whom he would marry in Valencia on January 19, 1933. (A daughter, Cecelia, was born to them in 1941.)

In 1934, Rodrigo was appointed professor of music at the Colegio di Ciegos in Madrid. That same year, the premiere of his tone poem for orchestra, *Per la Flor del Lliri Blau* (1934), was presented at the Circulo de Bellas Artes in Valencia. The Conde de Cartagena Scholarship was awarded to Rodrigo in 1934 by a unanimous decision of the jury and enabled him to study music for two more years in Paris: musicology with Maurice Emmanuel at the Paris Conservatory and music history with André Pirro at the Sorbonne. He was in Paris in 1935 when Paul Dukas, to whom he was very attached, died, a tragedy that led Rodrigo to write the *Sonada de Adios* for piano, in Dukas's memory.

During the Spanish Civil War years (1936-1938), Rodrigo traveled in France, Germany, and Austria, and lived in Freiburg, Salzburg, and Paris, where in October 1938, he completed writing the work that made him internationally famous: the *Concierto de Aranjuez,* for guitar and orchestra, probably the most celebrated guitar concerto ever written. In this colorful work, Rodrigo is successful in evoking the mysticism and poetry of Spain in his music. Without any

direct quotes from authentic Spanish folk music, Rodrigo's composition is melodically and rhythmically Spanish to the core. Aranjuez in the title refers to a royal palace on the banks of the Tagus near Madrid, once the favorite home of Charles I and Philip II. In his music, Rodrigo draws a portrait of this beautiful setting, where, he explained, "there linger the fragrance of the magnolias, the singing of the birds and the gushing of fountains ... dreams hidden beneath the foliage of the park surrounding the baroque palace." He added that his concerto was "a synthesis of the classical and the popular in point of form and sentiment." At its world premiere (in Barcelona, on November 9, 1940, with Regino Sainz de la Maza as soloist), this concerto was so spectacularly successful that it made Rodrigo a leading exponent of the nationalist movement in Spain like Manuel de Falla. V. Albéniz stressed this in *Hoja del Lunes* when he wrote: "Since the first performance of Manuel de Falla's *Nights in the Gardens of Spain* there has not been such an important musical event as this. This date makes history." In *A B C,* Gerardo Diego declared: "*Concierto de Aranjuez,* that's the name of a new masterwork." And in *Alcazar,* Conrado del Campo called the three movements of the concerto "three etchings most deliciously clad in the vernacular flavor of the past. ... Through them, springing in dreamy gentleness, come images of gallant pageants, perfumes, sways and echoes of distant dances. The delicious plucking of the solo guitar is admirably concerted with the varied colors of the orchestration, resulting in three movements of intense poetic climate." The American premiere took place on November 19, 1959, with Rey de la Torre as soloist, and the Cleveland Orchestra conducted by Robert Shaw. In 1973, almost twenty years after its writing, Rodrigo adapted the Concerto for harp and orchestra at the request of the distinguished harpist, Nicanor Zabaleta, who performed it with major orchestras in Europe and the United States and recorded it for Philips.

Concertos for instruments other than the guitar gave a wider dimension to Rodrigo's creative accomplishments. *Concierto Heroico (Heroic Concerto),* for piano and orchestra (1942), received the National Prize in Spain in 1942, and was then introduced by Leopoldo Queroi (to whom it was dedicated) in Lisbon on April 5, 1943. The composer intended this work to be a four-movement study of four different aspects of heroism, with the piano assuming the role of the hero. *Concierto de Estio (Concerto of Summer)*, for violin and orchestra (1943), reflected Rodrigo's lifelong fascination for the music of the 18th century in returning to the baroque concerto form of Vivaldi; its three movements are entitled "Prelude," "Siciliana," and "Rondino." Rodrigo wrote it for the violinist Enrique Iniesta, who gave its first performance in Lisbon on April 11, 1944. (It was also one of the compositions featured at the First Festival of American Music in Madrid on October 28, 1964.) *Concierto Galante* (1949), for cello and orchestra, was premiered by Gaspar Cassadó in Madrid on November 4, 1949. *Concierto Serenata,* for harp and orchestra (1952), was written for Zabaleta who performed it extensively. It presents two images of Spanish life: in the first movement, "Estudiantina," is the 16th century Spanish custom of having students parade through the streets playing mandolins and guitars, and a haunting Intermezzo is followed by the finale, "Sara," a gala Madrid festival. *Concerto Madrigal* for two guitars and orchestra (1966), was premiered by Pepe and Angel Romero at the Hollywood Bowl in Los Angeles on July 30, 1970. *Concierto Andaluz* (1967) was written for four guitars and orchestra. In 1978, Rodrigo completed *Concierto Pastoral,* for flute and orchestra, written for James Galway, who premiered it in London in October 1978 at a concert of the Philharmonia Orchestra, with Eduardo Mata conducting.

Rodrigo's other important works besides concertos included *Dos Pieras Caballerescas,* for cello and orchestra (1945); *Cuatro Estampas Andaluzas,* for piano (1946); *Cuatro Madrigales Amatorios,* a cycle of four songs for voice and piano (1947); *Cuatro Madrigales Amatorios* (1948), another work for voice, with orchestra, which had been commissioned by the Louisville Orchestra in Kentucky; and *Auscencias de Dulcinea (Absences of the Dulcinea)* which he wrote in 1948 to celebrate the fourth centenary of the birth of Cervantes. The last of these compositions, scored for bass, four sopranos, and orchestra, described Don Quixote's ceaseless search for Dulcinea, the lady of his dreams. In the year of its composition, *Ausencias* was awarded the Cervantes Prize. It was performed at the Teatro Colón in Buenos Aires in 1949 during the Joaquín Rodrigo festival when the composer first visited South America. On May 25, 1963, it was heard at the Festival of the International Society for Contemporary Music in Madrid.

In 1939 Rodrigo became affiliated with the music division of the National Radio in Madrid and in 1944, he was appointed director. Between 1939 and 1949 he wrote music cricitisms for various publications and in 1946 he was named professor of music history at the Faculty of Philosophy and Letters at the University of Madrid, remaining there for the next three decades. He traveled extensively as lecturer and pianist in Europe, North Africa, North and South America, the Middle East, and the Orient, and his first appearance in the United States in May 1957 was in a joint concert with Andrés Segovia in New York. It was during this visit that Segovia commissioned and presented the world premiere of Rodrigo's *Fantasia Para un Gentilhombre* (1954), in San Francisco on March 5, 1958. As with *Concerto de Aranjuez,* the work became basic to the guitar repertory, having been performed by leading guitarists everywhere and recorded more than ten times. It was inspired by little dance tunes and other melodies written in 1667 by Gaspar Sanz. Rodrigo explained, "My ideal is that if Sanz could hear the work he would say 'It isn't me but I can recognize myself.' "

In 1963, Rodrigo taught courses in music history at the University of Puerto Rico and in 1978 he conducted a master class on his own music for the Houston Classic Guitar Society in Texas.

With Manuel de Falla's death in 1946, Rodrigo was generally acknowledged to be Spain's foremost living composer and he was so honored. He was appointed to the Royal Academy of Fine Arts in San Fernando in 1950, and decorated with the Grand Cross of the Order of Alfonso X in 1953. For a Rodrigo festival in Barcelona he was commissioned to write the cantata *Musica Para un Codice Salamtino* (with a text by Miguel Unamuno), for bass, mixed chorus, and instruments for the seventh centennial celebration of the founding of the University of Salamanca; the premiere performance of the cantata was presented on October 12, 1953. In 1964 he was awarded an honorary doctorate in music by the University of Salamanca; in 1968 he was decorated with the Grand Cross of the Merito Civil in Spain; in 1974 a street in Madrid was named after him, and two years later a street in Málaga too. He was also honored outside of

Rodrigo

Spain: he was named Officier des Arts et des Lettres in 1960 and a Chevalier of the Legion of Honor in 1963, in France; Mexico decorated him with the Espuela de Plata in 1975; and Belgium elected him to membership in the Academy of Science, Letters and Beaux Arts in 1978. Rodrigo festivals were held in Ankara, Turkey, in 1972 and in Tokyo and Osaka in 1973.

Other major compositions in Rodrigo's later years included a ballet, an opera, and a symphonic work. The ballet, *Pavana Real* (ca. 1955) has a scenario written by Victoria Kamhi based on a work by Luis de Milan. It had successful performances in Barcelona, at the Teatro Colón in Buenos Aires, in Chile, and elsewhere. The opera *El Hijo Fingido,* is a lyric comedy introduced in Madrid in December 1964. It has a libretto by Victoria Kamhi and Jesus M. Arozamena, which is based on a work by Lope de Vega. *In Search of the Beyond (A la Busca del Mas Alla),* a symphonic work, was commissioned by the Houston Symphony in honor of the American bicentennial in 1976.

In his biography of Rodrigo, F. Sopeña was complimentary in writing about Rodrigo: "Although in a sense Rodrigo belongs strictly to the school of Falla and Turina, his artistic scope is extraordinary. Aside from his achievements as a mature musician with a perfect command of the musical media, he is also a distinguished writer, an excellent pianist and a talented lecturer. His comments as music critic over a period of ten years have done much to promote vital inquiry and exploration into the newest trends of esthetics. His influence on contemporary Spanish cultural media has been decisive, an influence seen in his scholarly guidance of the younger generation ... at the University of Madrid. Never before has a Spanish musician occupied such an important position in Spain's cultural life."

Rodrigo served for more than two decades as vice president of the International Society for Contemporary Music and as head of the music division of the Spanish National Organization of the Blind. His home is in Madrid.

MAJOR WORKS

Ballets—Pavana Real; Juana y los Calderos.

Chamber Music—Dos Esbozos, for violin and piano; Siciliana, for cello and piano; Impromptu, for harp solo; Rumaniana, for violin and piano; Capriccio, for violin solo; Sonata Pimpante, for violin and piano; Sonata la Breve, for cello and piano.

Choral Music—Ave Maria; Yo Tin un Burro; Triste Estaba el Rey David; Dos Canciones Sefardias del Siglo XVI; Villancicos y Canciones de Navidad; Musica Para un Condice Salmantino, cantata for bass, chorus, and instruments; Humanos Nupciales, for three sopranos and organ; Himnos de los Neofitos de Quamram; Himno a los Santo Patronos de Sagunto; Himno a la Virgen del Castillo de Cullera; Himno a la Virgen de Jerez.

Guitar Music—Zarabanda Leajana; En los Trigales; Entre Olivares; Por Tierras de Jerez; Tiento Antiguo; Bajando de la Meseta; Jupto al Generalife; Invocation et Danse; Hommage à Manuel de Falla; Sonata Giocosa; Trois Petites Pièces; Elogio de la Guitarra; Sonata a la Española; Tres Piezas Españolas; Parajos de Primavera; Tonadillo, for two guitars; Dos Preludios.

Opera—El Hijo Fingido, lyric comedy.

Orchestral Music—Juglares; Canconeta, for violin solo and strings; Cinco Piezas Infantiles; Preludio Para un Poema a la Alhambra; Tres Viejos Aires de Danza; Zarabanda Lejana y Villancico; Per la Flor del Lliri Blau; Dos Berceuses; Homenaje a la Tempranica; Concierto de Aranjuez, for guitar and orchestra; Concierto Heroico, for piano and orchestra; Concierto de Estio, for violin and orchestra; Dos Piezas Caballerescas, for an orchestra of cellos; Cuatro Madrigales Amatorios, for voice and orchestra; Ausencias de Dulcinea, for bass, four sopranos, and orchestra; Concierto en Modo Galante, for cello and orchestra; Soleriana; Fantasia Para un Gentilhombre, for guitar and orchestra; Sones en la Giralda, for harp and orchestra; Concierto Madrigal, for two guitars and orchestra; Concierto Andaluz, for four guitars and orchestra; In Search of the Beyond; Concierto Pastoral, for flute and orchestra.

Piano Music—Suite; Berceuse de Otono; Bagatela; Pastoral; Preludio al Galla Mananeor; Zarabanda Lejana; Berceuse de Primavera; Air de Ballet Sur le Nom d'une Jeune Fille; Serenata Española; Sonata de Adios; Cinco Piezas del Siglio XVI; Tres Danzas de España; Gran Marche de los Subcreatrios, for piano four hands; A l'Ombra de Torre Bermeja; El Album de Cecioia; Cuatro Estampas Andaluzas; Cinco Sonatas de Castilla con Toccata a Modo de Pregon; Danza de la Amapola; Atardecer, for piano four hands; Sonatina Para Dos Manecas, for piano four hands; Preludio y Ritornello, for harpsichord.

Vocal Music—(unless otherwise designated, all are for voice and piano)—Cantia; Muy Graciosa Es la Doncella; Romance de la Infantina de Francia; Serranilla; Album de Canciones; Coplas del Pastor Enamorado, for voice and guitar; Cuatro Madrigales Amatorios, for voice and piano; Romance del Commendadore de Ocana; Folias Canrias, for voice and guitar; Doce Canciones Españolas; Adela, for voice and guitar; De Ronda, for voice and guitar; Tres Villancicos, for voice and guitar; Le Espera; Duermete Niño, for soprano, baritone, and piano; Dos Poemas de Juan Ramon Jiménez; Homenaje a Debussy; La Grotta; Quatro Canciones Sefardies.

ABOUT

Iglesias, A., Joaquín Rodrigo; Pla, V. V., Joaquín Rodrigo: su Vida y su Obra; Sopeña, F., Joaquín Rodrigo.

Ned Rorem

1923–

For biography, list of earlier works, and bibliography, see *Composers Since 1900.*

Rorem's Piano Concerto No. 3 was commissioned by the Music Association of Aspen, Colorado, for Jerome Lowenthal, and introduced on December 3, 1970 by the pianist and the Pittsburgh Symphony under William Steinberg. Reviewing a later performance by Lowenthal with the Chicago Symphony under Irwin Hoffman, James Roos reported to the Miami *Herald* that the work was "agreeable to the ear from the start [showing] off the orchestra and piano to equal virtuoso advantage and [making] a friend of melody, while remaining essentially twentieth century in sound. ... The music is never academic. It has an impressionistic quality." Although the work itself makes no attempt at being programmatic, the titles of the six movements are: "Strands," "Fives," "Whispers," "Sighs," "Lava," and "Sparks."

To celebrate Rorem's fiftieth birthday, two concerts of his works were presented at the Lincoln Center for the Performing Arts in New York on November 25 and 26, 1973. The works included, *Day Music* (1971; Ames, Iowa, October 15, 1972) and *Night Music* (1972; Washington, D.C., January 12, 1973), each a set of eight short pieces for violin and piano, and *Ariel* (1971; Washington, D.C., November 26, 1971), a cycle of five songs to poems by Sylvia Plath, all first New York performances. *Bertha,* a one-act opera with text by Kenneth Koch, had its world premiere at the same concert. The performers were Koch as narrator, Beverly Wolff as principal vocal soloist, and the composer at the piano, with the Concert Ensemble conducted by James Holmes. *Bertha,* a satire on politics and war, consists of ten blackout scenes describing the exploits of a mad and quixotic Norwegian queen who leads her kingdom to war and disintegration. "The writing is typical Rorem—often consonant, very vocal and good to the voices of all the singers," wrote Speight Jenkins in the New

York *Post.* "More important, he has not lost his touch; no one can catch better the nuance of a word in vocal writing than he."

To celebrate the American bicentennial, Rorem was commissioned to write seven works: the orchestral tone poem, *Assembly and Fall,* composed for the North Carolina Symphony which introduced it with John Gosling as conductor on October 11, 1975 in Raleigh; *Book of Hours,* an eight-part piece for flute and harp, based on prayers for different times of the day, which was premiered in New York on February 29, 1976, by Ingrid Dingfelder, flutist, and Martine Geliot, harpist; *Eight Etudes,* for piano, was commissioned by the Washington Performing Arts Society with a grant from the Edyth Bush Charitable Foundation for pianist, Emanuel Ax, who introduced it in Washington, D.C., on March 13, 1976; *Serenade* (based on five English poems by Shakespeare, Tennyson, Thomas Campion, and Gerard Manley Hopkins) for voice, viola, violin, and piano, was commissioned by Walter and Virginia Wojno, for its first performance at the Akron (Ohio) Art Institute on May 23, 1976; *Sky Music,* for solo harp, was first performed in Albuquerque, New Mexico, on June 24, 1976; *Women's Voices,* a song cycle, was introduced by Joyce Mathis on November 4, 1976; and, most important, *Air Music,* for orchestra, was winner of the Pulitzer Prize in Music in 1976.

Air Music was commissioned by Thomas Schippers and the Cincinnati Symphony Orchestra with a grant from the National Endowment for the Arts for the bicentennial. It was premiered in Cincinnati on December 5, 1975, and performed again in the same month in Washington, D.C., and New York. The composer discussed the work: "Why *Air Music?* Because I'd already composed *Water Music* as well as *Day Music* and *Night Music.* And because when the piece was finished, I came upon this apt quote from Wilhelm Heinse (1749–1803) which stands as an epigraph on the title page: 'Music touches the nerves in a particular manner and results in a singular playfulness, a quite special communication that cannot be described in words. Music represents the inner feeling in the exterior air. ... *Air Music* could have been subtitled 'Chamber Music for Orchestra' since much of it is for intimate groups, yet groups obtainable only when a symphony is at hand. The overall tone is of understatement, an immense miniature. Form, however, and not color, is the unifying force, and so I subtitled the piece 'Ten Variations.' The term variations is used as dancers use it: the variations are on each other rather than on an initial statement, for there is no theme proper. The movements share traits (shapes, hues, rhythms, tunes) but their resemblance is more that of cousins than siblings."

The work, played without pause, is in three sections for full orchestra and seven small instrumental groups. Writing in *Musical America,* Bruce Saylor called the work "a big, bold set of ten etudes for orchestra, which shows not only the imagination and skill of this established composer, but also demonstrates effectively and intelligently a way to integrate the musical language of the 1960s and the 1970s into one's own musical style. . . . *Air Music* left its mark on the memory of the listener."

Surprised by the Pulitzer Prize, Rorem recalled: "That day I was feeling fatalistic in a negative sort of way, and had some Haagen Dasz ice cream to lift up the spirits. There was a telegram under the door, but before I had a chance to open it, the phone rang and it was a music critic in Cincinnati asking me how I felt winning the Pulitzer Prize. . . . I do like attention for I am both self-confident and very insecure. To have won the Pulitzer Prize has been totally satisfying. It's a once-in-a-decade refashioner, carrying the decree that bitterness is henceforth unbecoming. And if you die in shame and squalor, at least you die Official."

In composing *A Quaker Reader,* for organ solo, in 1976, Rorem produced Quaker music, attempting to reconcile his profession with his religious background. The work, a ten-movement suite, is modeled somewhat on Jessamyn West's book of the same title. Each movement, headed by an epigraph from Friends' writings (John Greenleaf Whittier, William Penn, Robert Barclay, and George Fox), interprets their moods and thoughts. *A Quaker Reader* was introduced on February 2, 1977, by Leonard Raver at the Lincoln Center for the Performing Arts and was recorded by Raver for CRI.

Sunday Morning, an eight-part suite for orchestra, was commissioned by the Saratoga Performing Arts Center in New York for the Philadelphia Orchestra under Eugene Ormandy. The world premiere took place in Saratoga on August 25, 1978. The composer explained that the music "is a non-literal dreamlike recollection of Wallace Stevens' long poem, *Sunday Morning,* written in 1915. . . . The words are not expressed through a human voice but through the colors of instruments, alone and together. . . . The subtitles are explained by the music." The parts are entitled I. ". . . green freedom" (full orchestra); II. "passions of rain" (six horns and strings); III. "indifferent blue" (clarinet and cello solos with harp and muted strings, also a flute, an oboe, a bassoon, and one horn, one trumpet, and one tuba); IV. ". . . birds before they fly" (three flutes and muted strings); V. "death is the mother of beauty" (full orchestra); VI. ". . . our insipid lutes" (full orchestra with mandolin solo); VII. ". . . a ring of men" (timpani solo with full orchestra); VIII. ". . . to darkness on extended wings" (two solo violas against the full orchestra). In the Philadelphia *Evening Bulletin,* James Felton wrote: "He brings everything off with mastery of tone color blending in kaleidoscopic dazzle and a strong, sure sense of direction and handling of material at all times. Each section faithfully reflected the mood of the key words.'

As composer-in-residence at the Santa Fe Music Festival in New Mexico, during the summer of 1980, Rorem completed (on commission from the Festival) *The Santa Fe Songs,* for baritone, piano, and string trio. It was premiered by William Parker, baritone, and introduced by him in New York on August 25, 1980. In *The New Yorker,* Andrew Porter called the song cycle, set to twelve poems by Witter Bynner, "music of eloquence, unself-conscious charm, and fine, inventive workmanship. . . . His familiar virtues—unforced rhythmic variety of declamation, naturalness of pace, quick response to verbal colors, and command of a decisive cadence—are everywhere apparent. So is the sovereign virtue: expressive melody."

Rorem gave his reasons for being a composer: "Less from self-expression than because I want to be an audience to something that will satisfy me. The act dispels the smoke screen between my ego and reality. However my gifts may seem a luxury to others, I compose for my own necessity, because no one else makes quite the sound I wish to hear. I am never *not* working, yet I never catch myself in the act. At the end of each year, I've somehow produced around an hour of music, and that hour is not a few sheets of pencilled whole notes but hundreds of pages of inked orchestration. Work is the process of com-

246

posing—making it up as it goes along, which is the only precise description since Homer. The action is at once so disparate and so compact that the actor is unaware (which is doubtless why I never find myself). I don't consider as work the post-compositional drudgery (often pleasant) of copying instrumentation, rehearsal, letter-writing, or dealing with publishers, though all this is time-consuming. Nor do I consider as work the compiling of my books which is the assembling of rewritten fragments. I do not consider as work the answering of this question—'when do you work?'—since it concerns, like musical composition, the placement of motion into order. As to when, and is it daily, I notate when I have a commissioned deadline and don't when I don't; the goal is functional and its approach makes me scribble ten hours a day. Between commissions, months are eaten up looking at soap operas."

Since 1970, Rorem has added to his fame as an author with four new books: *Critical Affairs* (1970), *Pure Contraption* (1974), *The Final Diary: 1961–1972* (1974), and *An Absolute Gift: a New Diary* (1978). He received the ASCAP-Deems Taylor award in 1971 for *Critical Affairs* and again in 1975 for *The Final Diary*.

He also accompanies Donald Gramm and Phyllis Curtin on concert tours in programs of American songs, half of which are his own. Long recognized as America's foremost composer of art-songs, Rorem once provided the following three mottos for song writing: "Use only good poems—that is, convincing marvels in English of all periods. Write gracefully for the voice—that is, make the voice line as seen on paper have the arched flow which singers like to interpret. Use no trick beyond the biggest trick—that is, since singing is already such artifice, never repeat words arbitrarily, much less ask the voice to groan, shriek or rasp. I have nothing against special effects, they are just not in my language. I portray the poet by framing his words, not by distorting them."

Rorem spends winters at his apartment in New York City; summers, on his farm in Nantucket, which was acquired in 1974. Wherever he is, he practices twenty minutes of yoga before breakfast while listening to news broadcasts. Then he gets down to work at his piano, which he calls "jumping headlong into the orchestra pit," and he added, "If the phone rings at this point I take it as the worst possible insult. If my

friends drop in on me my day is wrecked." He makes it a point never to socialize before 1:00 P.M.

In 1978, Rorem was awarded a second Guggenheim Fellowship; and in 1979 membership in the American Academy and Institute of Arts and Letters. In reviving its undergraduate composition department in 1980 (after four years), the Curtis Institute appointed Rorem as co-director (with David Loeb).

MAJOR WORKS (supplementary)

Chamber Music—Day Music, for violin and piano, eight pieces; Night Music, for violin and piano, eight pieces; Book of Hours, for flute and harp; Sky Music, for solo harp; Romeo and Juliet, for flute and guitar; After Reading Shakespeare, for solo cello; Quintet, for clarinet, bassoon, violin, cello, and piano.

Choral Music—Gloria; Seven Unaccompanied Canticles; Little Prayers, for chorus, two soloists, and orchestra; Missa Brevis; Three Motets, for mixed chorus and organ.

Opera—Bertha, one-act satirical opera for one mezzo-soprano, various other voices with piano; Hearing, five scenes for four singers and seven instrumentalists.

Orchestral Music—Piano Concerto No. 3; Assembly and Fall, tone poem; Air Music; Sunday Morning; Double Concerto, for cello, piano, and orchestra.

Organ Music—A Quaker Reader.

Piano Music—Eight Etudes.

Vocal Music—War Scenes, for baritone and piano; Ariel, for soprano, clarinet, and piano; Last Poems of Wallace Stevens, for soprano, cello, and piano; Serenade, for mezzo-soprano, violin, viola, and piano; Women's Voices, for soprano and piano; Santa Fe Songs, cycle for baritone, piano, and string trio.

ABOUT (supplementary)

Rorem, N., An Absolute Gift: a New Diary; Rorem, N., Final Diary: 1961–1972.

Ascap Today, Spring 1978; High Fidelity/Musical America, August 1976; New York Times, May 30, 1976; Opera News, December 8, 1973; People, August 21, 1978.

Hilding Rosenberg

1892–

For biographical sketch, list of earlier works, and bibliography, see *Composers Since 1900*.

In 1967, Rosenberg was commissioned to write a cantata to celebrate the 300th anniversary of Lund University. He composed *Hymn to*

Roussel

a University, for baritone solo, chorus, and orchestra to a text by H. Guilberg and E. Tegner, and it had its premiere in Lund on June 13, 1968.

Two major Rosenberg works were performed on Stockholm's radio and TV facilities in 1968: the ballet, *Babels Torn,* written for the Culbert Company, and shown on TV on January 8; and Symphony No. 7, heard on radio on September 29. On May 24, 1970, Rosenberg's opera, *The House with Two Doors,* based on Calderón's *Casa Con Dos Puertas,* was produced in Stockholm on May 24, 1970. The opera's score contains music previously written for theater productions of Calderón's play in 1934 and 1950.

In 1971, Rosenberg extensively revised his Symphony No. 1 (1917) which is one of his favorite works. His Symphony No. 8, for chorus and orchestra, subtitled "In Candidum," was written in 1974 for the fiftieth anniversary of the Malmö concert hall, where it was introduced on January 24, 1975.

Rosenberg was awarded the Christ Johnson Music Prize and a medallion for "services to music" in Stockholm in 1962. Three years later he became the first composer since Ludvig Norman in the 19th century to receive the Swedish Academy Gold Medallion. In 1969 he was the recipient of an honorary prize from the city of Stockholm.

MAJOR WORKS (supplementary)

Ballets—Salome; Sönerna; Babels Torn (music also used for Symphony for Wind Instruments).

Chamber Music—2 additional violin sonatas; Symphony for Wind and Percussion (music from the ballet, Babels Torn); Six Moments Musicaux, for string quartet; Alone in the Quiet of the Night, for string quintet and tenor solo.

Choral Music—Hymnus, cantata for children's choir, two choruses, organ, and instruments; Hymn to a University, cantata for baritone solo, chorus, and orchestra.

Opera—The House with Two Doors.

Orchestral Music—2 additional symphonies; Metamorfosi Sinfoniche, Nos. 1–3.

ABOUT (supplementary)

Bergendal, G., 'Hilding Rosenberg' in 33 Svenska Komponister; Connor, H., 'Hilding Rosenberg' in Samtal med Tonsättare; Searle, H. and Layton, R., Twentieth Century Composers: Britain, Scandinavia, the Netherlands; Yoell, J. H., Nordic Sound.

Albert Roussel

1869–1937

See *Composers Since 1900.*

Edmund Rubbra

1901–

For biographical sketch, list of earlier works, and bibliography, see *Composers Since 1900.*

Rubbra's Symphony No. 8 (1966–1968) was introduced in London on January 5, 1971 and was followed by a large-scale choral work, *Sinfonia Sacra,* Symphony No. 9 subtitled "Resurrection" (1971–1972) for soprano, baritone, narrator (contralto), mixed chorus, and orchestra. The music in the latter work is continuous and develops so symphonically that Rubbra decided to call it Symphony No. 9. The long narrative line (Authorized Version) begins with the Crucifixion and continues with events leading to the Ascension. To break it up, Rubbra intersperses the narrative with new settings of four traditional Latin hymns for chorus and orchestra, thus delocalizing the events in a more specifically spiritual vein. The work ends in a triumphant affirmation of faith. *Sinfonia Sacra* was performed for the first time in February 1973, by the Liverpool Philharmonic Choir and Orchestra directed by Sir Charles Groves.

Sinfonia da Camera is Rubbra's Symphony No. 10 (1974). In one continuous movement, its four sections approximate the movements of the classical sonata form. Commissioned by the Northern Sinfonia, and dedicated to the memory of Sir Arthur Bliss, the symphony was first heard on January 8, 1975, in London, with Rudolf Schwarz conducting.

A concert overture, *Resurgam* (1975), was commissioned by the Plymouth Symphony Orchestra to celebrate its centenary, and first performed in November 1975 in London under the direction of David Cawthra. The composer discussed the origin of the title: "It was taken from the single word found on a piece of wood nailed over the remaining doorway of a church destroyed in a bombing raid during World War II, and I used it to signify the birth of a new city.

The desolation of the music at the beginning of the overture (with the sea in the background) gradually changes to a mood of optimism and hope."

Other Rubbra premieres of later works include his String Quartet No. 4 (1976–1977), performed in Oxford by the Amici Quartet in November 1977, and the *Fantasia on a Chord,* for treble recorder, harpsichord, and viola da gamba (1977), which Carl Dolmetsch, Joseph Sasby, and Marguerite Dolmetsch introduced in London in March 1978.

In 1978, Rubbra was awarded an honorary doctorate in letters by Reading University.

MAJOR WORKS (supplementary)

Chamber Music—Piano Trio No. 2; String Quartet No. 4; Fantasia on a Chord, for treble recorder, harpsichord, and viola da gamba; Transformations, for harp.

Orchestral Music—4 additional symphonies; Resurgam, concert overture.

Piano Music—Four Studies.

Vocal Music—Fly Envious Time, for low voice and piano; Four Short Songs, for mezzo-soprano, baritone, and piano; Three Greek Folk Songs, for soprano, alto, tenor, and bass.

ABOUT (supplementary)

Foreman, L. (ed.), Edmund Rubbra: a Symposium.

Carl Ruggles

1876–1971

For biographical sketch, list of earlier works, and bibliography, see *Composers Since 1900.*

On February 2, 1971, the National Orchestral Association conducted by John Perras presented the world premiere of the orchestrated version of Ruggles' *Evocations,* originally for piano. The orchestral version, discovered just before his death, was reported by Donal Henahan in the New York *Times:* "The translation from keyboard to orchestra served to emphasize the strength and Yankee directness of the 94-year-old composer's style."

Carl Ruggles entered a nursing home in Bennington, Vermont, in 1966 and died there on October 24, 1971. Soon after his death, his home in Arlington, Vermont, was designated as a musical landmark.

A retrospective concert of Ruggles' music was presented by the Committee for 20th Century Music at Columbia University on February 18, 1976. At that time, the composer's paintings were exhibited for intermission viewing. The complete works of Carl Ruggles were recorded by the Buffalo Philharmonic conducted by Michael Tilson Thomas for CBS Masterworks, and released in 1980.

MAJOR WORKS (supplementary)

Orchestral—Evocations (also for piano)

ABOUT (supplementary)

Thomson, V., American Music Since 1910.

New York Times, October 26, 1971; Perspectives in Music, vol. 16, no. 1, 1978.

Harald Saeverud

1897–

For biographical sketch, list of earlier works, and bibliography, see *Composers Since 1900.*

For the eleven-hundredth-year jubilee of the city of Bergen, Norway, in 1970, Saeverud wrote *Sonata Jubilata* and *Fanfare and Hymn,* both for orchestra. Saeverud also contributed *Overtura Monumentale* for the opening of the new Edvard Grieg Hall during the Bergen Festival in 1978, and at the same festival, his *Pastorale,* a set of variations for cello solo, was also introduced.

"From time to time," Saeverud wrote, "I have been asked whether I try to write typical music. My answer is, as a rule, that I write straight from the heart, and my heart, I hope, is Norwegian. But perhaps I had better express it in this way: I write down what Nature suggests to me."

As a tribute to Saeverud on his seventy-fifth birthday, Giles Easterbrook wrote: "What impression is left of this wonderful and, to us, slightly elusive figure? We see a man who is thoroughly imbued with the spirit of Western Norway, with majesty, brilliance, fantasy, poetry and quirks of his own—a truly Norse composer who makes no effort to imitate the mere sound of folk-music effects, but nevertheless one who writes from a deep personal inspiration and love of his country. We see him, therefore, as, de facto, the thoroughly Norwegian composer par excellence."

In 1973, Saeverud was decorated as Knight of the Yugoslav Flag, and in 1977 he was made

Satie

Commander of St. Olav Order in Norway. He was appointed member of the Slovene Academy of Sciences and Arts in Ljubljana.

MAJOR WORKS (supplementary)

Chamber Music—3 string quartets; Serenades for the Two Rivals, for string quartet; Pastorale, variations for solo cello.

Orchestral Music—Sonata Jubilata; Fanfare and Hymn; Mozart-Motto Sinfonietta; Overtura Monumentale.

Piano Music—Fabula Gratulatorum.

ABOUT (supplementary)

Searle, H. and Layton, R., 20th Century Composers; Britain, Scandinavia, the Netherlands.

Erik Satie

1866–1925

For biographical sketch, list of earlier works, and bibliography, see *Composers Since 1900*.

In May 1979, all of Satie's works were performed in two six-hour alternating sessions in Paris. The event, called "Intégrale Erik Satie," required the services of hundreds of performers, including singers and dancers from the Paris Opéra, the Ars Nova Ensemble, actors from the Comédie Française and the boulevard theaters, the Brussels Marionettes, and gymnasts from the Paris Fire Department.

Satie's masterpiece, the ballet *Parade* (1917), was added to the repertoire of the Metropolitan Opera House on February 20, 1981.

ABOUT (supplementary)

Harding, J., Erik Satie; Rey, A., Erik Satie; Wehmeyer, G., Erik Satie.

Henri Sauguet

1901–

For biographical sketch, list of earlier works, and bibliography, see *Composers Since 1900*.

In 1971, Sauguet was awarded the Grand Prix de la Société des Auteurs et Compositeurs Dramatiques in Paris. He was elected to the Académie des Beaux-Arts four years later.

MAJOR WORKS (supplementary)

Chamber Music—Sonatine aux bois, for oboe and piano; Un Soir à Saint-Emilion, for bassoon and piano; Sonatine en Deux Chants, for clarinet and piano; Alentours Saxophoniques, for alto saxophone, wind ensemble, and piano; Oraisons, for four saxophones and organ.

Choral Music—Chant Pour Une Vieille Meurtrie, oratorio for solo vocal voices, chorus, and orchestra; Cantate Sylvestre, for female chorus, viola, and piano; Elisabeth de Belgique, la Reine aux Cheveux d'Or, for low voices and six instruments.

Opera—L'Impositeur, ou le Prince et le Mendiant.

Orchestral Music—Symphonie de Marches (Symphony No. 3); The Garden's Concerto, for harmonica and orchestra; Symphony No. 4, Du Troisième Âge.

ABOUT (supplementary)

Bril, F.-Y., Henri Sauguet.

Florent Schmitt

1870–1958

See *Composers Since 1900*.

Arnold Schoenberg

1874–1951

For biographical sketch, list of earlier works, and bibliography, see *Composers Since 1900*.

In 1952, a year after Schoenberg's death in the United States, a street in Vienna was named after him—Schönberg-platz (the Austrians adhered to the Germanic spelling of his name rather than the American spelling which Schoenberg preferred in later years). The centennial of his birth was commemorated in Vienna in 1974 in a variety of ways. On June 5, his ashes, buried in the United States for twenty-three years, were reinterred in Vienna's Central Cemetery. A Schoenberg Congress was convened in Vienna between June 4 and 9, which was highlighted by a Schoenberg exhibition at the Secession Museum. On June 6, his Viennese home in Mödling was dedicated as a Schoenberg museum and research center, with an appropriate plaque on the building. A course on Schoenberg's string quartets was offered in Vienna between August 24 and September 13 under the direction of Rudolf Kolisch and Rudolph Stephen. The Schoenberg centennial was also celebrated in the United States by the University of Southern California in Los Angeles in September. A site was dedicated on campus for a Schoenberg Institute which was opened on February 20, 1978, as a repository for Schoenberg manuscripts (6,000 items), books (2,000 volumes), scores, and various other memorabilia. A Schoenberg concert, as part of the dedication ceremony, was held in the Institute's exhibit hall.

ABOUT (supplementary)

MacDonald, M., Schoenberg; Newlin, D., Schoenberg Remembered: Diaries and Recollections (1938–1976); Reich, W., Arnold Schoenberg: a Critical Biography; Rosen, C., Arnold Schoenberg; Stein, E. (ed.), Letters of Arnold Schoenberg; Stein, L. (ed.), Style and Ideas (Selected from Schoenberg's writings); Stuckenschmidt, H. H., Arnold Schoenberg, His Life, World and Work.

High Fidelity/Musical America, September 1974, August 1977; Stereo Review, September 1974

Franz Schreker

1878–1934

For biographical sketch, list of earlier works, and bibliography, see *Composers Since 1900.*

Franz Schreker's fame, which declined in the years following his death, was partially restored at the Berlin Festival on the occasion of the hundreth anniversary of his birth in 1978. Between October 12 and 15, several of his works were performed and there was a symposium on his music. The world premiere of his last opera, *Christophorus,* was presented by the Freiburg City Opera on October 1. The opera, written between 1925 and 1929, was scheduled for a premiere in Freiburg in 1933, but because of the composer's half-Jewish heritage, the Nazi regime cancelled the performance. Although Schreker's daughter got the opera manuscript out of Germany, little was known about it until the long-delayed premiere. The text (by the composer) was about the unsuccessful attempt by a music student to compose an opera about the legend of St. Christopher. It was set in Berlin in the 1920s and Schreker used jazz and other fashionable musical styles at that time in a cabaret scene reminiscent of Berlin's night life. Report-

ing from Freiburg to *High Fidelity/Musical America,* Christopher Jailey wrote: "Schreker uses a variety of musical means to underscore his drama. In *Christophorus* he developed a musical-dramatic style embracing the full declamatory range from spoken dialogue, recitative, *Sprechgesang,* to arioso and lyric bel canto passages in order to articulate the levels of dramatic action and differentiate his characters. ... In his orchestra, Schreker achieves utmost transparency. ... Schreker's musical language ranges freely from sections of nontonal dissonance to purest tonality and modality. Thus, through a conscious application of heterogeneous musical and dramatic means, Schreker sharply focuses the essentials of his drama."

At this time there was a successful revival of Schreker's third opera, regarded by some as his masterwork, *Die Gezeichneten,* by the Frankfurt Opera in Germany on January 20, 1979. Schreker described his libretto as "the tragedy of an ugly man," a hunchback Renaissance nobleman who is frustrated in his desire to achieve beauty and love, and ends up mad. Paul Moore reported from Frankfurt to *High Fidelity/Musical America,* that "the music, thoroughly tonal and easily assimilable at first hearing, evokes late Mahler and early Schoenberg, with an unusually extensive palette of tonal color."

Gunther Schuller

1925–

For biographical sketch, list of earlier works, and bibliography, see *Composers Since 1900.*

Schuller's opera for children, *The Fisherman and His Wife,* was commissioned by the Junior League of Boston as "a gift to the children of Boston." It was produced by the Opera Company of Boston and conducted by the composer on May 7, 1970. John Updike, a distinguished writer, adapted the familiar Grimm fairy tale to a libretto about a magical fish that can grant wishes, and an avaricious fisherman's wife whose mounting requests end up with her wishing to be God. Raymond Ericson wrote in the New York *Times,* "In a few scenes the music develops character—a lyrical area for the wife, a charming duet for the cat and fish ... a jazz background for royalty, and an impassioned aria

Schuller

for the wife when being a Pope fails to satisfy her."

Museum Piece, a composition for a solo ensemble of Renaissance instruments and a modern symphony orchestra, was introduced by the Boston Symphony Orchestra under William Steinberg on December 11, 1970. Schuller's compositions in 1972 included *Capriccio Stravagante,* for orchestra, which was commissioned by the San Francisco Symphony for its sixtieth anniversary and performed in December 1972, with Seiji Ozawa conducting. The work is a "fun piece" in the style of "capriccio stravagante," invented by Carlo Farina in the 17th century. *Tre Invenzione,* for twenty-five players was commissioned by the Fromm Music Foundation for its twentieth anniversary and it was premiered on August 8, 1972, at the Festival of Contemporary Music at Tanglewood in Massachusetts. In the work twenty-five instrumentalists are divided into five corresponding quintets (with no strings), made up of one each of high woodwinds and high brass, one each of low woodwinds and brass, and one keyboard quintet (plucked and struck).

Schuller's works had two world premieres in 1975 of special interest. *Triplum II,* for orchestra, was commissioned and performed by the Baltimore Symphony on February 26, with Sergiu Comissiona conducting. In the form of a Baroque Sinfonia Concertante, this work skillfully combines serialism and aleatory procedures with romanticism within a classical scructure. Elliott W. Galkin wrote in the Baltimore *Sun* that the composition "reveals in its pages a unique gift of writing music which, no matter how dissonant, possesses immediately accessible tonal tensions and inevitabilities." The other premiered work, *Four Soundscapes,* was introduced by the Hudson Valley Philharmonic in Poughkeepsie, New York, with the composer conducting, on March 7, 1975.

For the American bicentennial, Schuller wrote the three-movement Concerto No. 2, for orchestra, on commission from the National Symphony Orchestra of Washington, D.C., and its conductor Antal Dorati. The first performance was given in Washington on October 12, 1976. After having written an organ piece for the American Guild of Organists that was performed in Boston's Old West Church to inaugurate a new Fisk organ, the composer thought that writing for the organ taught him "so much

about sonority and harmonic constructions that it gave me a whole new orientation, a new vision of how the orchestra can be used. So the Concerto for Orchestra is kind of special, a new departure . . . a step forward for me in a direction that fascinates me." Paul Hume in the Washington *Post* said that the Concerto "commands attention for its imaginative fertility, the complete exploitation of the orchestra in new yet masterful resourceful ways." In the Washington *Star,* Irving Lowens wrote that "Schuller exploits the resources of the modern orchestra with more imagination and ingenuity than anyone would believe possible." Two months earlier, Zvi Zeitlin had introduced Schuller's Violin Concerto with the Lucerne Festival Orchestra in Switzerland, with the composer conducting (August 25, 1976).

On commission from the Boston Symphony Orchestra, Schuller wrote *Deaï,* for two orchestras, and it was premiered on March 17, 1978, in Tokyo by the Boston Symphony and the Tokyo Symphony with Schuller and Ozawa conducting; the American premiere followed on August 4, 1979, at the Festival of Contemporary Music at Tanglewood. In the work, the orchestra is divided into three groups, one on the stage and one on each side of the audience, which gradually disband and join the main orchestral body. Donal Henahan explained in the New York *Times* that "The composer fancied that this could symbolize the trend in recent decades for Oriental musicians to 'infiltrate' Western orchestras. The ultimate merging of the groups he interpreted as a 'symbolic handshake' between East and West."

In June 1978, Schuller's Horn Concerto No. 2 had its premiere in Budapest, with Mario di Bonaventura conducting and Ferenc Tarjani as soloist. The Contrabassoon Concerto (the first ever written for that instrument) was first performed on January 16, 1979, at a concert of the National Symphony Orchestra in Washington, D.C. (which commissioned it); Mstislav Rostropovich was the conductor, and Lewis Lipnick was the soloist. The Octet, for winds and strings, commissioned by the Chamber Music Society of Lincoln Center in New York was premiered on November 2, 1979. It was influenced in its instrumentation by Schubert's Octet. Harold C. Schonberg of the New York *Times* wrote: "It has color, mood and recognizable melody. There are beautiful moments in the piece. The introspective, moving ending of the second movement is one, and the scherzo has a nice, perky, humorous quality. . . . The Octet is a handsome work."

From 1967 to 1977, Schuller was the president of the New England Conservatory in Boston; from 1969 to 1972 he was co-artistic director of musical activities at the Berkshire Music Center at Tanglewood and, in 1972, became its artistic director. He has been just as active as conductor as he has been as educator and composer, appearing in guest performances in the United States and Europe in traditional and contemporary programs of music. Schuller also formed the New England Conservatory Ragtime Ensemble, comprised of twelve (later sixteen) Conservatory students, who perform ragtime classics such as Scott Joplin's *Red-Back Book*. The group makes many public appearances and they also recorded two best-selling Scott Joplin albums. The first, The *Red-Back Book*, sold more copies in the United States in six months than any other classical release; in 1973 it won a "Grammy" from the National Academy of Recording Arts and Sciences. The ragtime concerts and recordings added to the momentum of the ragtime revival in the early 1970s. Schuller also orchestrated Joplin's opera, *Treemonisha,* and conducted it with the Houston Grand Opera on May 25, 1975, and later at the Kennedy Center for the Performing Arts in Washington, D.C. and the Uris and Palace theaters on Broadway.

In 1970, Schuller received the Alice M. Ditson Conducting Award from Columbia University for his "unselfish championship of fellow composers through the conducting of their orchestral works here and abroad." In 1971 he was presented with the Rodgers and Hammerstein Award and in 1980, membership in the American Academy and Institute of Arts and Letters. He received honorary doctorates in music from Northeastern University (1967), the University of Illinois (1968), Colby College (1969), Williams College (1975), the New England Conservatory (1978), and Rutgers University (1980). His book, *Early Jazz: Its Roots and Musical Development* (1968), received the ASCAP-Deems Taylor Award in 1970, and was acclaimed a definitive musico-analytical history of the early jazz movement.

In 1975, Schuller founded Margun Music for the purpose of not only publishing works by contemporary composers, young and old, who have been overlooked, but also to circulate works in the areas of ragtime, jazz, and other vernacular or ethnic modes of expression of past and present, including medieval and Renaissance compositions.

MAJOR WORKS (supplementary)

Chamber Music—Four Moods, quartet for tubas; Concerto da Camera, for nineteen instruments; Octet, for winds and strings.

Choral Music—The Power Within Us, oratorio for narrator, baritone, chorus, and orchestra; Poems of Time and Eternity, for chorus and nine instruments.

Opera—The Fisherman and his Wife, a fairy-tale opera.

Orchestral Music—Shapes and Designs; Consequents; Museum Piece, for Renaissance instruments and orchestra; Contrasts, for woodwind quartet and orchestra; Tre Invenzioni; Capriccio Stravagante; Three Nocturnes; Four Soundscapes; Triplum II; Concerto No. 2 for Orchestra; Concerto for Violin and Orchestra; Concerto No. 2 for Horn and Orchestra; Concerto for Contrabassoon and Orchestra; Sonata Serenata, for chamber orchestra; Deaï, for two orchestras; Concerto for Trumpet and Orchestra.

Organ Music—Triptych

Vocal Music—Six Early Songs after Li-Po, for soprano and piano.

ABOUT (supplementary)

BMI, Many Worlds of Music, Winter 1976; High Fidelity/Musical America, April 1976; New York Times, September 6, 1970, May 29, 1977.

William Schuman

1910–

For biographical sketch, list of earlier works, and bibliography, see *Composers Since 1900.*

Schuman's Symphony No. 9, *Le Fosse Ardeatine* (The Ardenite Caves) was Schuman's first symphony with programmatic intent, though it makes no effort to be realistic. The work is a tribute to the 355 Romans (Christian and Jews) who were murdered by the Nazis in the Ardeatine Caves in reprisal for the killing of 32 Germans by the Italian underground. Schuman and his wife visited those caves in 1967 during the Easter-Passover season, and he recalled:"Somehow, confrontation with the ghastly fate of several hundred identifiable individuals was more shattering and understandable than the reports on the deaths of millions which, by comparison, seem abstract statistics. The mood of my symphony, especially in its opening and closing sections, is directly related to the emotions engendered by this visit. But the entire middle section, too, with its various moods of fast music, much of it far from somber, stems from the fantasies I had of the variety, promise and aborted lives of the martyrs." The symphony, in three parts, is played without interruption beginning with an "Anteludium," continuing with an "Offertorium," and ending with a "Postludium." Composed in 1967–1968, the work was scored in Rome after a second visit to the monument. The Friends of Alexander Hilsberg for the Philadelphia Orchestra commissioned the symphony which had its premiere on January 10, 1969, by the Philadelphia Orchestra under Eugene Ormandy.

When Ben Shahn, the American artist, died in 1969, several friends commissioned Schuman to write a work in his memory. Schuman wrote *In Praise of Shahn: a Canticle for Orchestra* in which he made an attempt to catch something of the artist's personality. Schuman said, "The music I have created reflects two prominent characteristics of his nature. Shahn, it seems to me, combined a contrasting yet wholly compatible duality—unabashed optimism and a searching poignancy." Eastern European and Jewish music was introduced because of Shahn's feeling for it. The New York Philharmonic Orchestra under Leonard Bernstein performed it first on January 29, 1970. "It is indeed a hymn of praise, a celebration, somewhat noisy but impressive . . .," commented Raymond Ericson in the New York *Times.*

At the request of Donald McInnes, violist, with a commission from the Ford Foundation, Schuman composed *Concerto on Old English Rounds,* for solo viola, women's chorus, and orchestra in December 1973. On November 29, 1974, the Boston Symphony, the Radcliffe Choral Society, and Donald McInnes as viola soloist, performed it for the first time in Boston with Michael Tilson Thomas as conductor. The work was inspired by four English rounds from the late 17th century. Schuman himself explained: "All the music of the Concerto stems in one way or another from the impetus engendered from these rounds. . . . The rounds are treated in a variety of ways, sometimes far from their origi-

nal simplicity, other times virtually in their original forms, and in still others with musical concepts that might seem to the listener to have no direct bearing on the rounds at all but to the composer the seminal relationship is ever present." The movements include: "Amaryllis" as introduction and in variations in the first movement (where the chorus not only sings the words but also accompanies the melody with "la-las") and it returns in the finale. Solo chimes lead to "Great Tom Is Cast." After that comes a fast movement, "Who'll Buy Mi Roses" and the quiet, pastoral "Come, Follow Me." In his review in the New York *Times,* Harold C. Schonberg wrote: "There are some beautiful things in this viola concerto, especially at the quiet opening and closing. Here and there, there is a modal feeling or a deliberate archaism, but Mr. Schuman has not set out to be quaint. . . . It is when Mr. Schuman was in repose that he created the memorable moments of the score."

Schuman's prominence among living American composers made him a natural choice for the American bicentennial celebration. Between 300 and 400 performances of 20 different works by Schuman were performed, including six symphonies and the ballets *Undertow* (1945) and *Night Journey* (1947). A work written for the bicentennial commemoration was Symphony No. 10, "American Muse," commissioned by the National Symphony Orchestra of Washington, D.C., and its music director, Antal Dorati, for a premiere on April 6, 1976. Schuman subtitled the Symphony "American Muse" because, as he explained, "it is dedicated to our country's creative future." In looking at one of his old choral works, *Pioneers!* (1937), based on a poem by Walt Whitman, Schuman said, "Recalling *Pioneers!* and experiencing again its optimism was precisely what I needed to get me started on the symphony. . . . To be sure, the spirit of optimism one expresses in his middle sixties is as removed from that of the middle twenties as are today's complexities from those of colonial times. The symphony reflects these differences. Between the outer movements is the large contemplative second movement, and while the variegated facets of the first and third movements surely cannot be described as exclusively optimistic, I trust that, over all, the music emerges as an expression of affirmation." The work opens and closes with the theme from Schuman's early work.

Two other Schuman works were premiered by the National Symphony Orchestra on April 6, 1976. *The Young Dead Soldiers,* based on a poem by Archibald MacLeish, is scored for soprano, French horn, eight woodwinds, and nine strings. Schuman described it as a "lamentation." Raymond Ericson of the New York *Times* described it as "basically simple, the intertwining vocal and horn melodies being generally supported by the string and wind chords of a rich density. . . . It is written with unerring taste, evoking a strong sentiment but never sliding into sentimentality." The third work that evening was a "baseball cantata" entitled *Casey at the Bat,* for soprano, narrator, chorus, and orchestra. This was a new concert version of the three-scene opera, *The Mighty Casey,* written between 1951 and 1953.

In 1976 Schuman changed the setting of the old English round, "Amaryllis," used in his *Concerto on Old English Rounds,* and in his string trio (1964). *Amaryllis,* "variants for strings on an old English round," was introduced in the summer of 1976 by the Philadelphia Orchestra conducted by André Kostelanetz.

Schuman wrote *In Sweet Music: Serenade on a Setting of Shakespeare* in 1978 on commission from the Chamber Music Society of Lincoln Center for its tenth anniversary. This was Schuman's third musical setting of Shakespeare's poem, "Orpheus with his Lute" from *Henry VIII:* it was also used as a song for voice and piano (1944) and as a fantasy for cello and orchestra entitled *A Song of Orpheus* (1961). The new work, scored for soprano, flute, harp, and viola, takes its main theme from the 1944 Schuman song, and is heard at the beginning and end of the composition, and in variations in between. The world premiere took place at Lincoln Center in New York on October 29, 1978.

On January 24, 1980, the New York Philharmonic Orchestra under Zubin Mehta presented the world premiere of Schuman's *Three Colloquies,* for French horn and orchestra, which it had commissioned for Philip Myers, its first horn player. Harold C. Schonberg said in the New York *Times,* "In many respects, it is a 'color piece.' Mr. Schuman . . . seems intensely interested in contrasting sonorities. The first movement is full of block harmonies set against violent percussion, against which the horn breathes long-phrased notes. The second movement is typical Schuman—bracing, with peppery rhythms and a hint of jazz. The finale has the horn in long, quiet melodies, ending with a chorale in almost traditional harmonies."

In 1969, Schuman resigned as president of the Lincoln Center for the Performing Arts to devote more time to composing. Since then he has been involved in numerous activities: as consultant to various projects; as director of the Chamber Music Society of Lincoln Center, the Film Society of Lincoln Center, the Koussevitzky Music Foundation, the American Academy and Institute of Arts and Letters, the Naumburg Foundation, and the Ives Society; as chairman of the board of the MacDowell Colony, and the Norlin Foundation which awards excellence in music. He regards the time since his retirement from administrative duties as "one of the richest and most rewarding of my professional life."

In 1971, at the presentation of the medal of the MacDowell Colony to Schuman "for exceptional contributions to the arts," Aaron Copland said of his music: "Whenever I think of it, I think of it as being the work of a man who has an enormous zest for life . . . and that zest informs all his music. . . . His music represents big emotions! In Schuman's pieces you have the feeling that only an American could have written them. . . . You hear it in his orchestration which is full of snap and brilliance. You hear it in the kind of American optimism which is at the basis of his music."

Schuman was elected to membership in the American Academy and Institute of Arts and Letters in May 1974 and he was awarded doctorates of music from the Peabody Conservatory in Baltimore in 1971 and the University of Rochester in 1972, and a doctorate of fine arts from the University of the State of New York in Buffalo, in 1974. He received the Boston Symphony Horblit Award in 1980.

Schuman's seventieth year was celebrated in 1980 with performances of his major works by America's leading symphony orchestras, choral groups, and bands. Festivities began on his birthday, August 4, 1980, with a concert of his music and a celebration at the Aspen Festival in Colorado where he was composer-in-residence that summer.

Schuman maintains a home in Greenwich, Connecticut, and an apartment in New York City. A habitual early riser, he does his main composing in the morning.

Schwantner

"I am a romantic," he told Shirley Fleming in an interview for *High Fidelity/Musical America* in 1980. "To be anti-romantic is to be anti-person. Romanticism is fulfillment of self—you have to be able to work with intrinsic restraints but without extrinsic restraints. By that I mean you shouldn't shackle yourself to a system but you must have control over your mind and spirit. You can't do anything without self-discipline—Robert Schumann was just as disciplined as Mozart. Part of being a romantic is to come to an understanding of your strengths and weaknesses. You must find joy in your strengths. And as for your weaknesses, if you haven't made mistakes, you haven't lived."

MAJOR WORKS (supplementary)

Band Music—Dedication Fanfare; Be Glad Then, America.

Chamber Music—In Sweet Music: Serenade on a Setting of Shakespeare, for flute, mezzo-soprano, viola, and harp.

Choral Music—Haste, a round for a cappella chorus; Mail Order Madrigals; Declaration Chorale, for a cappella chorus; To Thy Love, choral fantasy on old English Rounds; Casey at the Bat, a baseball cantata for vocal soloists, chorus, and orchestra; Time to the Old.

Orchestral Music—2 additional symphonies; In Praise of Shahn; Voyage for Orchestra; Concerto on Old English Rounds, for solo viola, women's chorus, and orchestra; Prelude for a Great Occasion, for brass and percussion; The Young Dead Soldiers, for soprano, French horn, and seventeen instruments; Amaryllis, variants for strings on an old English Round; Three Colloquies, for French horn and orchestra.

ABOUT (supplementary)

Lichtenwanger, W. and C. (eds.), Modern Music—Analytic Index.

BMI, Many Worlds of Music, Winter 1976; High Fidelity/Musical America, August 1980; New York Times, January 28, 1970, November 28, 1975, August 31, 1980; Stereo Review, June 1974.

Joseph Schwantner

1943–

Joseph Schwantner was born in Chicago on March 22, 1943, to Joseph Schwantner (a tool maker) and Mary Jean McElvain Schwantner. While neither parent was particularly musical,

---

Schwantner: shwänt'ner

JOSEPH SCHWANTNER

even though his mother had studied piano when she was young, Schwantner recalled, "For as long as I can remember I have been attracted to music. Just as some kids had baseball, I had music." He was about eight when he first became interested in music and was given lessons in classical guitar by Robert Stein. An early stimulus for Schwantner's interest in music was Adeline Anderson, his grade-school music teacher at the Warren Palm School in Hazlecrest, Illinois, where he played in the school band. In 1957, he entered Thornton Township High School in Harvey, Illinois and played the tuba (also with Adeline Anderson) in the high school band, the guitar with a jazz combo, and he started to write and arrange music. After graduating from high school in 1961, he enrolled in the Chicago Conservatory College, majoring in composition under Bernard Dieter, and received his Bachelor of Music degree in 1964. He completed his first work for orchestra, *Sinfonia Brevis* in 1963 and went on to postgraduate education at Northwestern University School of Music in Evanston, Illinois, majoring again in composition, with Alan Stout and Anthony Donato. In 1966 he was awarded the William T. Faricy Award for Creative Music, his Master's degree in music in 1968, and his doctorate in music two years later.

Early compositions at Northwestern University were written in serial form and included *Nonet* (1964); *Concertino for Alto Saxophone and Three Chamber Ensembles* (1964) which earned him his first BMI Student Composers Award in

1965 at its first university performance in May 1965; *Diaphonia Intervallum,* for alto saxophone, flute, piano, and six strings (1965), which also received a BMI Student Composers Award in 1966 and the Bearns Prize from Columbia University in 1967; and *Chronicon,* for bassoon and piano, which won a third BMI Student Composers Award in 1968, at its first hearing at the Festival of Contemporary Music at Tanglewood, Massachusetts, in August 1968. It was performed the same year at the International Rostrum of Composers in Paris.

On August 21, 1965, Schwantner married Janet Elaine Rossate, an executive secretary in Riverdale, Illinois, and they had a son and daughter. From 1968 to 1969 he was on the music theory and composition faculties at both the Chicago Conservatory College and the Pacific Lutheran University in Tacoma, Washington. In 1969–1970 he was assistant professor of theory at Ball State University in Muncie, Indiana, and guest composer and lecturer at Miami-Dade Junior College in Miami, Florida in 1971. Since 1970 he has been on the faculty of the Eastman School of Music in Rochester, New York, as assistant professor of composition and theory (1970–1973); assistant professor of composition (1974–1975); associate professor of composition since 1975; and chairman of the composition department since 1979. In 1975, while on leave from the Eastman School, he was Lecturer in Music at the University of Texas at Austin and guest composer and lecturer at the University of Houston, Texas.

In later compositions, Schwantner revealed a renewed interest in tonal material. *Consortium I,* for five instruments (1970), which contained aleatory passages, was written for Boston's Musica Viva which introduced it in Cambridge on September 23, 1970. The work opened and closed the first half of the program. Reviewing it in the Boston *Evening Globe,* Michael Steinberg described it as "breezily virtuostic, with a delightful surface . . . and quite enough individuality and substance to make the second hearing as persuasive and engaging as the first." *Consortium II,* for six instruments (1971), was also written for Boston's Musica Viva, which premiered it in Cambridge on February 7, 1972 and then performed it successfully in London, Hamburg, and Cologne in June 1973.

In Aeternam (1973), for cello and four players, requires the players to play their own instruments and a large variety of percussion and sound generators as well. It was written for Musica Viva, in a twelve-tone technique and its premiere took place in Cambridge on February 26, 1973. *In Aeternam* achieved unusual, and at times beguiling, sonic effects through novel innovative means—such as slipping wet fingers across the rim of crystal goblets, using pencils to strum on piano strings, dropping a sonorous gong in a tub of water, or playing metallic percussion instruments with the bow of a violin or cello. Louis Snyder of the *Christian Science Monitor* reported that "It is full of related textures that seem to have been logically and purposefully woven together, not just by chance, and it is mercifully free of the old avant-garde instrumental fits and starts that used to trade on their shock value. Mr. Schwantner is admittedly writing about 'forever,' so that the sounds of flutes, far-off bells, cymbals touched with string bows, sunken bells and singing water-goblet rims . . . suggest the echoing of the far-offness of eternity." *In Aeternam* is one of Schwantner's most frequently performed compositions; in one year (1974–1975), it was performed more than forty times by the Contemporary Chamber Ensemble in the United States, Switzerland, England, Finland, Spain, and the Netherlands.

Twelve-tone series with unusual sonic effects also characterize *Shadows II,* for baritone and eight players (1973). Set to Kenneth Rexroth's *One Hundred Poems from the Japanese,* the work was written for the Boston Musica Viva who premiered it in Cambridge on March 4, 1974, again playing it twice on the program. Novel effects in the work are achieved by lowering vibrating triangles into buckets of water and a pretape. In *Musical Quarterly,* Arthur Custer commented: "The texts, by Kenneth Rexroth, are a series of images limning the simplicity and wonder of the natural world. They are richly evocative, full of allusions to drifting petals, hanging raindrops, evening mist, rustling leaves. Schwantner brings these images palpably to life. Feelings are reflected in sound; music is a shadow (the derivation of the title?) of reality."

Schwantner completed two important compositions in 1974. *Elixir,* for flute and five players (required to double on other instruments) was composed for the Boston Musica Viva, and its premiere took place at Simon's Rock College in Great Barrington, Massachusetts, on October 3, 1975. In this work, too, crystal-glass rims

rubbed by wet fingers and small cymbals (crotales) played and struck by string bows were
again the means to produce novel, and at times
haunting, sonic effects. When it was performed
later in New York in April 1977, *Elixir* was
commended by Raymond Ericson in the New
York *Times* for its "jewel-like ... craftsmanship
and its mysterious ringing sounds. Delicate brilliance is the result, and a magical power suggested by the title." Musica Viva performed the
work in 1976 on a European tour to Germany,
Holland, England, and Denmark. In addition,
the United States section of the International
Society for Contemporary Music selected it for
a performance at the ISCM World Music Days
in Helsinki, Finland, on May 9, 1978, which
Schwantner and his wife attended, courtesy of
the Martha Baird Rockefeller Foundation.

Schwantner's second major work in 1974 was
Autumn Canticles, for violin, cello, and piano,
which was commissioned for the Western Arts
Trio by the William Robertson Coe American
Heritage Foundation Commission in American
Music, and written under a grant from the Creative Artists Public Service Program of the New
York State Council on the Arts. The title refers
to five ancient Chinese poems dealing with various aspects of autumn, which provided the inspirational and creative impetus for the work.
Although the work is not programmatic, each
poem relates to one of the five movements or
sections and lends a rich reservoir of moods,
feelings, and ideas which stimulate and intensify
the work. It was premiered at the Western Arts
Festival of the University of Wyoming in Lara-
mie in July 1974 and the Western Arts Trio
featured it extensively on its European tour in
1976.

Canticle of the Evening Bells was commissioned by Conductor Arthur Weisberg and the
Contemporary Chamber Ensemble and written
in memory of the distinguished Italian dodecaphonist, Luigi Dallapiccola. Scored for a flute
pitted against a highly diverse instrumental ensemble of twelve players, it was introduced at
the Lincoln Center for the Performing Arts in
New York on February 19, 1976, and performed
by that group on its State Department tour of
Asia later in the year.

On commission from the Naumburg Foundation, Schwantner composed *Wild Angels of the
Open Hills,* for soprano, harp, and flute, with a
poetic text by Ursula LeGuin, for the Jubal Trio.

Donal Henahan of the New York *Times* called
it "the high-water mark" of the concert in which
it was first heard on February 2, 1977, at Lincoln
Center. He added: "Mr. Schwantner handles the
merger of words and tones with lapidary precision" while bathing the poems "in strange but
apt sonorities. ... There are plenty of ghostly
whistles, half-heard murmurings and disembodied tones of tuned water glasses, and a heavy
reliance on string harmonics."

On February 28, 1977, in Rochester, New
York, Schwantner's *and the mountains rising nowhere,* for amplified piano, wind, brass, and percussion, was introduced by the Eastman Wind
Ensemble under Donald Hunsberger on a grant
from the National Endowment for the Arts. In
this work, too, the wind instrumentalists are
called upon to sing, whistle, and play the glass
crystals, watergongs, antique cymbals, tam-
tams, and vibraphones in addition to performing
on their own instruments. They are joined by the
percussion choir, with its wide diversities of instrumental and sonorous possibilities, and the
amplified piano. The composition's title is from
a line in a poem by Carol Adler, the composer's
friend. On March 9, this composition also highlighted a concert of the College Band Directors
of Maryland in College Park.

Schwantner was awarded the Pulitzer Prize
for music in 1979 for *Aftertones of Infinity,* for
orchestra (1978). Commissioned by the American Composers Orchestra, its world premiere,
under Lukas Foss's direction, took place at Lincoln Center for the Performing Arts on January
29, 1979. Schwantner derived his basic musical
material for this work from his earlier *Wild Angels of the Open Hills* and again the woodwind
players double on musical glasses while various
other orchestral members vocalize with a "pure,
delicate child-like quality ... like a distant
ethereal choir." According to the composer, the
title is a line from his own poem which acted as
"a kind of 'creative generator' for the work,
[providing] a wellspring of extra-musical images
and ideas to which [he] attempted to find appropriate musical analogs."

In *Sparrows,* for soprano, instruments, and
percussion (1979), the composer uses as text hai-
kai by Issa which begins and ends with a reference to sparrows. The verses and the music
create a series of "dream states" which drift
from one to another throughout the composition, and from time to time, six instrumentalists

provide a wordless background chant. The first performance was heard in Washington, D.C., on March 18, 1979, and Paul Hume wrote in the Washington *Post,* "He achieves his purpose in music of exquisite sounds and images."

Through Interior Worlds, commissioned by the Chamber Music Society of Lincoln Center in New York, received its premiere performance on April 3, 1981.

In 1978, Schwantner was awarded a Guggenheim Fellowship and in April 1979 he was composer-in-residence at Wolf Trap Farm for the Performing Arts in Vienna, Virginia. Besides for *and the mountains rising nowhere,* he received grants from the National Endowment for the Arts for *Sparrows* in 1972, for *Shadows II* in 1974, and for *Elixir* and *Canticle of the Evening Bells* in 1975.

Schwantner resides with his family in Rochester, New York, and when he is not involved with academic or creative pursuits, he seeks relaxation in astronomy, poetry, and reading nonfiction.

MAJOR WORKS

Chamber Music—Nonet; Diaphonia Intervallum; Chronicon, for bassoon and piano; Enchiridion, for violin and piano; Consortium I, for violin, viola, cello, flute, and clarinet; Consortium II, for flute, clarinet, violin, cello, piano, and percussion; In Aeternam, for cello and four players; Shadows I, for piano quartet; Autumn Canticles, for violin, cello, and piano; Elixir, for flute and five players; Canticle for the Evening Bells, for flute and twelve players; Etherea, for flute, horn, piano, percussion, and contrabass; Gossamer Song, for amplified contrabass and amplified piano; Music of Amber, for flute, clarinet, violin, cello, and piano; Through Interior Worlds.

Orchestral Music—Sinfonia Brevis; Concertino for Alto Saxophone and Three Chamber Ensembles; August Canticle, for twelve flutes, twelve strings, three percussionists, piano, and celesta; and the mountains rising nowhere, for amplified piano, wind, brass, and percussion; Aftertones of Infinity.

Organ Music—In Aeternam II.

Vocal Music—Music for Soprano, Brass, and Percussion; Entropy, for soprano, saxophone, bass clarinet, and cello; Shadows II, for baritone and eight instrumentalists; Wild Angels of the Open Hills, for soprano, harp, and flute; Sparrows, for soprano and eight instrumentalists.

ABOUT

BMI, Many Worlds of Music, Winter 1976, Issue 2, 1979; High Fidelity/Musical America, December 1979; Who's Who in America 1980–1981.

Cyril Scott

1879–1970

For biographical sketch, list of earlier works, and bibliography, see *Composers Since 1900.*

A Cyril Scott Society was formed in England in 1962 to promote performances and recordings of his major works. It was launched with an all-Scott concert in Duke's Hall at the Royal Academy of Music in which John Ogdon, Peter Pears, and Edmund Rubbra were among the performers.

Scott was the recipient of an honorary doctorate in music from the Chicago Conservatory of Music in 1959 and a decade later he was honored by the Royal Academy of Music in London.

A second volume of his reminiscences, *Bone of Contention,* was published in 1969.

Cyril Scott died in Eastbourne, England, on December 31, 1970.

ABOUT (supplementary)

Scott, C., Bone of Contention: Life Story and Confessions.

Alexander Scriabin

1872–1915

For biographical sketch, list of earlier works, and bibliography, see *Composers Since 1900.*

From the 55 pages of musical fragments and sketches of Scriabin's monumental "Mystery" which he did not live to complete, Alexander Nemtin created a large-scale work for orchestra entitled *Universe, Part I,* between 1970 and 1972. It had its world premiere in Moscow on March 16, 1973, with Kiril Kondrashin conducting.

ABOUT (supplementary)

Bowers, F., The New Scriabin: Enigma and Answers; Bowers, F., Scriabin: a Biography of the Russian Composer; MacDonald, H. J., Skryabin.

Humphrey Searle

1915–

Humphrey Searle was born in Oxford, England, on August 26, 1915, to Humphrey Frederic Searle, an English government employee, and Charlotte Mathilde May Schlich Searle who was of German descent. The paternal side of the family were musicians in Devonshire; his grandfather was a trained organist. Neither one of Humphrey's parents was musical but they saw to it that he received piano lessons during his early years in Burma where his father was employed. Humphrey showed little interest in music until, at the age of thirteen, he attended Winchester College, and was introduced to such 20th century works as Stravinsky's *Rite of Spring* and Honegger's *Rugby* and *Pacific 231,* and his ambition to become a composer was aroused. At college, George Dyson began giving him harmony lessons, and Searle wrote his first piece which was performed by the school orchestra.

After college, although he knew he wanted to become a composer, he continued studying the classics and philosophy for the next four years (1933–1937) on a classical scholarship to New College, Oxford. During this time he was receiving further instruction in harmony from Sydney Watson, the college organist. He recalled, "My chief revelation at Oxford was the first English performance of *Wozzeck,* given by the B.B.C. under Sir Adrian Boult, which knocked me absolutely sideways. I determined to try and find out more about this kind of music." The arrival at Oxford of Theodor Wiesengrund-Adorno, a refugee from Nazi Germany who had been a pupil of Schoenberg and Webern, made it possible for young Searle to learn more about the Viennese school of twelve-tone composition.

While at Oxford, Searle also attended the Royal College of Music in London where for a while he studied composition with John Ireland. Sir Hugh Allen, professor of music at the College and Oxford, was sufficiently impressed with several of his compositions to arrange for him to be given a traveling scholarship after receiving his Master's degree at Oxford in 1937. The scholarship enabled Searle to study privately in

HUMPHREY SEARLE

1937 with Anton Webern while attending the Vienna Conservatory for courses in conducting and musical history and to hear performances of the Vienna State Opera almost nightly. When his scholarship ran out, he left Vienna for London, just two weeks before Hitler's troops invaded Austria.

Searle reentered the Royal College of Music where he studied counterpoint with R. O. Morris and conducting with Gordon Jacob. Since his father insisted that he enter the civil service, Searle's allowance was stopped, thus abruptly cutting short his musical training at the college. He received no further instruction in music after that.

To support himself, Searle found a position as librarian for the B.B.C. where his job, he said, "consisted mostly of carting two hundred and fifty copies of the *Messiah* around London and distributing them to members of the B.B.C. Chorale." He had stopped writing music just before he went to Vienna because he felt the need for a radical change of style, but he began to compose again in 1939 with what he described as a piece in "hybrid style" which was introduced in London in April 1939 at a concert of the London String Orchestra under his own direction. He recalled, "This concert showed me that I was not very experienced either as a composer or a conductor, but nevertheless I went on writing music in my spare time and finished . . . a set of piano variations and a string quartet during 1939."

When World War II broke out in Europe, the

Searle: sĕrl

B.B.C. moved to Bristol and Searle went along. In March 1949, after joining the army, he spent time in Bristol with the Gloucestershire Regiment, was transferred to the Intelligence Corps in a remote part of the Scottish Highlands, and he trained paratroopers in southern England. He rose to the rank of captain, and in 1946 was stationed at the Rhine Army Headquarters in Germany where he helped H. R. Trevor-Roper do research for his book *The Last Days of Hitler.*

While in uniform, Searle continued writing music. Suite No. 1, for string orchestra (1942), designated as Op. 1 (all prior works were discarded), was performed in London in 1943 with Walter Goehr conducting. *Night Music,* for string orchestra (1943) was written to honor Webern on his sixtieth birthday. Searle also wrote *Vigil,* for piano (1944), Concerto No. 1 for Piano and Orchestra (1944), Quintet, for bassoon and strings (1945), and *Nocturne No. 2,* for chamber orchestra (1946) which was inspired by the tragic accidental death of Webern on September 15, 1945. All of the compositions were atonal, occasionally written in the twelve-tone technique which he was using only tentatively and experimentally. They were all first performed in London, with the exception of the Quintet, for bassoon and strings, which was introduced in Australia, and all of the works were heard within a year of their composition.

After being discharged from the army in 1946, Searle went back to the B.B.C. as producer of musical programs. He was instrumental in bringing to British radio the music of leading dodecaphonists in spite of opposition from higher-ups.

A performance of Searle's *Nocturne No. 2* in London was presented as an interlude in a ballet performance at Sadler's Wells and attracted the interest of René Leibowitz, a leading figure in French twelve-tone music. At Leibowitz's suggestion Searle embraced the twelve-tone technique more completely in *Intermezzo,* for eleven instruments, in 1946. He dedicated the work to Webern and it was introduced at a Festival of Contemporary Music in Paris conducted by Leibowitz early in 1947. This was his first twelve-tone work, and he remained a strict dodecaphonist, influenced more by Schoenberg than by Webern. (However, in the mid-1950s he made an aborted attempt to write in a free atonal style, without any series.)

Between 1947 and 1949, Searle was employed as general secretary of the International Society for Contemporary Music. In 1948, he left the B.B.C. to devote more time to composition and after 1949 supported himself by teaching and lecturing. He was professor of composition at the Royal College of Music from 1949 to 1959 (an honorary associate of the College since 1966). He was also active in organizations promoting new music in England, such as the London Contemporary Music Center, the Society for the Promotion of New Music, and the Composers Guild. From 1950 to 1962 he was honorary secretary of the Liszt Society, and from 1951 to 1957 he was a member of the advisory panel of Sadler's Wells Ballet. On August 26, 1949 he married Margaret Lesley Gillen Gray.

As a mature twelve-tone composer, he wrote *Put the Flutes Away* (1947), for voice and six instruments, to a poem by W. R. Rogers which expressed anti-war sentiments. It was presented at the International Society for Contemporary Music in Amsterdam on June 8, 1948, after having previously been introduced in London. *Fuga Giocosa,* for orchestra, was first presented in London in 1948 and then at the ISCM Festival in Palermo, Italy, on April 26, 1949. His most ambitious work up to this time, *Gold Coast Customs,* with a text by Edith Sitwell, for narrators, male chorus, and an orchestra made of winds, brass, two pianos, a good deal of percussion, and only the lower strings, was written in 1949. It was first performed in May of that year, with Edith Sitwell and Constant Lambert as narrators; it was repeated twice in the year by the B.B.C. *Passacaglietta in Nomine Arnold Schoenberg* (1949), for string quartet, was written to honor Schoenberg's seventy-fifth birthday and had its first hearing in Israel. *Poem,* for twenty-two strings, was completed in 1950 and performed that year as a wedding gift for his wife at the Darmstadt Summer School under the direction of Hermann Scherchen. It was heard again at the Festival of the International Society for Contemporary Music in Salzburg, Austria, on June 24, 1952.

Becoming interested in Searle through the *Poem,* Scherchen sponsored the Düsseldorf premiere of *The Riverrun,* for narrators and orchestra (1951), with a text from the final passage in James Joyce's *Finnegan's Wake.* Scherchen repeated the performances in Liverpool and London in 1955. (*The Riverrun* was the second of a trilogy of works for narrators and orchestra; the first was *Gold Coast Customs* with male chorus and the last was *The Shadow of Cain,* with male chorus, performed at the Palace Theater in London in 1952 with Edith Sitwell and Dylan Thomas as narrators.) Scherchen asked Searle to write his first Symphony. It was completed in 1953, and its premiere was conducted by Scherchen in Hamburg in 1954.

Searle's financial situation became greatly improved in the late 1950s through various commissions, but he suffered a personal tragedy when his wife died of cancer on Christmas Day of 1957. He found solace in work, and in 1958 he wrote Symphony No. 2, the *Variations and Finale* for chamber orchestra, and his first opera, *The Diary of a Madman.* The one-act opera was written at Scherchen's request for a short musical-stage composition for the Berlin Music Festival in 1958. Searle, himself, adapted Gogol's novel into a libretto, and used electronic effects to describe in music the maniacal fantasies and delusions of the demented government clerk. The world premiere of the opera was given in Berlin on October 3, 1958, and in 1960 it received the UNESCO Radio Critics Prize. On November 5, 1960, Searle was married for a second time, to Fiona Elizabeth Anne Nicholson.

On September 3, 1960, Searle's Symphony No. 3 (1960) was introduced at the Edinburgh Festival by the Royal Philharmonic under John Pritchard. It was inspired by a visit to Agamemnon's palace in Mycenae, Greece. Symphony No. 4 (1962), commissioned by the Feeney Trust for the City of Birmingham Orchestra, was introduced there on November 8, 1962. The source for Symphony No. 5, written in a three-month period in 1964, was found in the life of Webern as told in Friedrich Wildgan's biography. The Hallé Orchestra in Manchester, under Lawrence Leonard, presented the premiere performance on October 7, 1964. Between the fourth and fifth symphonies, Searle wrote *Dualites,* a ballet (1963), introduced in Wiesbaden, Germany, on May 31, 1963, and his first full-length opera, *The Photo of the Colonel* (1964), commissioned by the B.B.C. for radio and first performed on March 8, 1964. It received its first stage presentation on June 3 of the same year in Frankfurt, Germany. The opera is based on Ionesco's play *The Killer,* which is about a maniacal murderer who terrorizes the people of a small town.

While in Africa in 1964 Searle completed *Song of the Sun,* for unaccompanied chorus, which was based on pre-Aztec Mexican poems translated by Irene Nicholson. In 1964, he came to the United States for the first time to serve as composer-in-residence at Stanford University in California for a year. He returned later in 1967 as guest composer at Aspen, Colorado.

Searle's next full-length opera, *Hamlet,* was written at the request of Rolf Liebermann, general manager of the Hamburg Opera. It took Searle three years to complete both libretto and score, and the opera was produced in German in Hamburg on March 6, 1968. Though Peter Heyworth, of the New York *Times,* objected to the way Searle distorted Shakespeare, he did find merit in Searle's twelve-tone score. "It is clearly written in a coherent idiom. As in so much of Searle's music, it shows a gift for atmosphere and evocative orchestral color. And when the action finally starts to move with Laertes' return to avenge his father, Polonius, it also reveals a lively sense of theatrical excitement."

After *Hamlet,* Searle's principal works included *Labyrinth,* for orchestra, written in 1971 and introduced that year in London; *Kubla Khan,* for tenor solo, chorus, and orchestra, based on Coleridge, was completed in 1973 and performed in Santa Barbara, California, four years later; *Fantasia on British Airs,* a wind symphony, was written in 1976; *Dr. Faustus,* written in 1977, was a cantata for soloists, chorus, and orchestra based on the novel by Thomas Mann, and it was performed in London in 1979; and *Music for the Oresteia of Aeschylus,* for chorus and orchestra, was written in 1978 and performed in London one year later.

Humphrey Searle discussed his method of composing: "In writing twelve-tone works I have not used classical forms to any great extent, except in the first symphony; I have tried to derive the form from the idea behind the work. I do however still use themes, which many modern composers have given up. I probably work more now with short fragments than long melodies—I have done this particularly in the fourth symphony—but I am against works being constructed entirely out of blocks of color."

Searle is the author of *Schoenberg: Structural Functions of Harmony* (1954), *The Music of Liszt* (1954), *20th Century Counterpoint* (1954), *Ballet Music, an Introduction* (1958), and *20th Century Composers: Britain, Scandinavia, the Netherlands,* the last written in collaboration with Robert Layton (1972). Searle is also the editor and translator of *Berlioz: Selected Letters* (1966) and English translator of biographies of Schoenberg by H. H. Stuckenschmidt and of Webern by Wildgans and Kolneder.

In 1968, Searle was made Commander of the Order of the British Empire, and in 1969, Fellow of the Royal College of Music. He was guest professor at the Staatliche Hochschule für Musik in Karlsruhe, Germany, between 1968 and 1972, and visiting professor of music at the University of Southern California in Los Angeles in 1976–1977.

MAJOR WORKS

Ballets—Noctambules; The Great Peacock; Dualities.

Chamber Music—Quintet, for bassoon and strings; Intermezzo, for eleven instruments; Quartet, for violin, clarinet, viola, and bassoon; Passacaglietta in Nomine Arnold Schoenberg, for string quartet; Gondoliera, for English horn and piano; Divertimento, for flute and piano (or strings); Suite, for clarinet and piano; Three Movements, for string quartet; Sinfonietta, for nine instruments; Divertimento, for clarinet ensemble; Fantasia, for cello and piano; Five for Guitar, for guitar solo; II Pensoroso e L'Allegro, for cello and piano.

Choral Music—Song of the Sun, for a cappella chorus; The Canticle of the Rose, for a cappella chorus; I Have a New Garden, for a cappella chorus; Kubla Khan, for tenor, chorus, and orchestra; Rhyme Rude to My Pride, for a capella male chorus; Skimbleshanks, the Railway Cat, for baritone, chorus, and orchestra; My Beloved Spake, for chorus and organ; Dr. Faustus, cantata for vocal soloists, chorus, and orchestra.

Operas—The Diary of a Madman, one-act opera; The Photo of the Colonel; Hamlet.

Orchestral Music—5 symphonies; 2 suites for chamber orchestra; 2 piano concertos; Night Music, for chamber orchestra; Nocturne No. 2, for chamber orchestra; Fuga Giocosa; Gold Coast Customs, for narrators, male chorus, and orchestra; Overture to a Drama; Poem, for twenty-two strings; The Riverrun, for narrators and orchestra; The Shadow of Cain, for narrators, male chorus, and orchestra; Concertante, for piano, strings, and percussion; Aubade, for horn and strings; Variations and Finale, for chamber orchestra; Scherzi, for small orchestra; Oxus, for voice and orchestra; Jerusalem, for narrator, tenor, and orchestra; Zodiac Variations, for small orchestra; Labyrinth; Tamesis.

Organ Music—Toccata alla Passacaglia; Fantasy and Toccata.

Piano Music—Vigil; Ballade; Threnos and Toccata; Sonata; Suite; Prelude on a Theme of Alan Rawsthorne.

Vocal Music—Two Songs of A. E. Housman, for voice and piano; Put the Flutes Away, for voice and instruments; Three Songs of Jocelyn Brooks, for voice and

chamber ensemble (also piano); Counting the Beats, for voice and piano; Ophélie, for voice and piano; Donkey, for voice and piano; Les Fleurs du Mal, for voice, horn, and piano; Contemplations, for mezzo-soprano and chamber orchestra.

ABOUT

Routh, F., Contemporary British Music; Schafer, M., British Composers in Interview; Searle, H., and Layton, R., 20th Century Composers; Britain, Scandinavia, the Netherlands.

Roger Sessions

1896–

For biographical sketch, list of earlier works, and bibliography, see *Composers Since 1900*.

Sessions was commissioned to write Symphony No. 8 (1967–1968), for the 125th anniversary of the New York Philharmonic Orchestra. Its world premiere took place on May 2, 1968, with William Steinberg conducting. Sessions' *Rhapsody,* for orchestra, was also written on commission, for the Baltimore Symphony which introduced it on March 18, 1971. In a review of an Argo recording of both works, a critic for *Stereo Review* wrote that they were "good examples of the intense, personal lyric expression of his [Sessions'] recent music. . . . They are squarely in the great [Classic/Romantic] tradition of Western music, close to Berg and Schoenberg but reaching back to the traditions of Brahms and at the same time synthesizing elements of American neo-classicism." Of the two works, the critic regarded the two-movement Symphony as more rewarding "with its very deeply felt slow movement and a lively, distinctive fast finale—a Sessions trademark." Writing in *High Fidelity/Musical America,* Royal S. Brown said: "While the latter [the Symphony] has the quality of an exceptionally beautiful meditation, the *Rhapsody* seems to have more dramatic implications that culminate in the third section in a grim, explosive episode that has somewhat the quality of a frenzied march."

The cantata, *When Lilacs Last in the Dooryard Bloom'd,* for vocal soloists, chorus, and orchestra (1967–1970), which had its premiere at the University of California in Berkeley on May 23, 1971, with Michael Senturia conducting, is one of Sessions' most profound compositions, a masterwork, according to some critics. Written to the poem by Walt Whitman, it was commissioned by the university to commemorate the hundreth anniversary of its founding. Andrew Porter, of *The New Yorker,* called it "an inspired and stirring composition, one to set beside Delius' *Sea-Drift* (1903) and Vaughan Williams' *Sea Symphony* (1910) for its large, visionary presentation, with large forces, of Whitman's thought, and one to set above them for the way it makes music of the sounds and the movement of Whitman's actual lines. In Sessions' cantata we find the rapture, tenderness and poignancy of *Sea-Drift* and the energy, grandeur and mystical contemplative calm of the *Sea Symphony* together with a quality that can be more easily described than analyzed as American."

Sessions wrote *Three Biblical Choruses,* for chorus and orchestra (1971), on commission from Amherst College for its sesquicentennial in 1971. Its premiere was delayed until February 8, 1975, when it highlighted the weekend Sessions festival of lectures and concerts at Amherst. The *Choruses* has texts from the Psalms and Isaiah, and is scored for an orchestra of twenty-five performers including a pianist, percussion, and chorus. *High Fidelity/Musical America* reported; "It is less lyrical than some audiences might like, but it does have the continuity of musical line, without a loss of musical detail. ... The third movement is particularly effective in presenting an energetic and powerful rush of words and music toward the final 'Praise Ye the Lord.' " After the intermission, the composition was repeated to a standing ovation.

The Syracuse Symphony, conducted by Frederick Prausnitz, commissioned Sessions to write Symphony No. 9, which was premiered in January 1980. In *The New Yorker,* Nicolas Kenyon reported: "It is a tough, dense score, and, as with so much of Sessions' music, difficult to like at first hearing. ... The most striking aspect of the music is its constant state of flux, its perturbed restlessness."

A retrospective concert of Sessions' music covering half a century was performed at a concert at Columbia University in New York on February 7, 1973. Eight years later, on March 28, 1981, Sessions' eighty-fifth birthday was commemorated by the Continuum Concerts in New York with still another retrospective concert spanning fifty years.

In 1974, Sessions was awarded a special citation by the Pulitzer Prize Committee for "his life's work in music." His opera, *Montezuma,* which had been introduced in Berlin in 1964, received its American premiere on March 11, 1976, by the Opera Company of Boston under the direction of Sarah Caldwell.

In 1966–1967, Sessions was the Ernest Bloch Professor of Music at the University of California in Berkeley, and in 1968–1969, the Charles Eliot Norton Professor at Harvard University. Sessions has also taught composition at the Juilliard School of Music.

Sessions is the author of *Questions About Music,* published in Cambridge, Massachusetts, in 1970. His collected essays, *Roger Sessions on Music,* edited by E. T. Cone, was published in Princeton in 1979.

MAJOR WORKS (supplementary)

Choral Music—When Lilacs Last in the Dooryard Bloom'd, cantata for vocal soloists, chorus, and orchestra; Three Biblical Choruses, for chorus and orchestra.

Orchestral Music—Rhapsody; Concerto for Violin, Cello, and Orchestra; Concertino, for chamber orchestra; Symphony No. 9.

Piano Music—Five Piano Pieces.

ABOUT (supplementary)

Boretz, B. and Cone, E. T. (eds.), Perspectives of American Composers.

BMI, Issue 2, 1974; High Fidelity/Musical America, July 1976; Newsweek, May 13, 1968; New Yorker, May 16, 1977; Time, May 10, 1968; New York Times, March 21, 1981.

Arthur Shepherd

1880–1958

For biographical sketch, list of earlier works, and bibliography, see *Composers Since 1900.*

ABOUT (supplementary)

Loucks, R., Arthur Shepherd: American Composer.

Dmitri Shostakovich

1906–1975

For biographical sketch, earlier list of works, and bibliography, see *Composers Since 1900.*

Shostakovich's Symphony No. 13 had its American premiere in January 1970 when it was performed by the Philadelphia Orchestra under Eugene Ormandy. This Symphony, introduced in Moscow on December 18, 1962, has as its text the provocative poems by Yevutchenko entitled "Babi Yar," which at one time brought Shostakovich temporarily into conflict with Soviet officialdom because of Yevutchenko's indictment of Soviet anti-Semitism. Irving Kolodin wrote in the *Saturday Review* that "It is a work that rings with sincerity and speaks an intelligible message." A year later, in January 1971, the Philadelphia Orchestra under Ormandy again offered the American premiere of a new Shostakovich Symphony, the fourteenth, which was first performed on September 29, 1969, in Leningrad. In this eleven-sectioned Symphony, the voice is used prominently in a text comprised of eleven poems with death as a common theme by Lorca, Apollinaire, Rilke, and Küchenbecker. Raymond Ericson remarked in the New York *Times,* "It is almost as if the composer were writing his own requiem—the first four notes make up the 'Dies Irae' theme—and it is an extraordinary mixture of the elegiac, anguish, anger and consolation."

Shostakovich's last Symphony, No. 15 (without voices), was introduced by his son, Maxim, in Moscow on January 8, 1971. It proved to be notable because it is the only symphony in which Shostakovich wrote a twelve-tone passage, in spite of the fact that he had frequently expressed disdain for dodecaphony. (He had, however, used twelve-tone rows in his String Quartet No. 12 and his Violin Sonata, both written in 1968.) In an interview with Royal S. Brown in *High Fidelity/Musical America,* Shostakovich explained: "I have a very negative attitude towards this kind of approach. But if a composer feels that he needs this or that technique he can take whatever is available and use it as he sees fit. It is his right to do so." Another unusual thing about the Symphony No. 15 is that it quotes from Rossini's *William Tell Overture* and the "Fate" motive from Wagner's *Ring* cycle. At its

Moscow premiere the Symphony was extraordinarily successful and Tilhon Khrennikov, head of the Composers Union, called it "one of Shostakovich's most profound works ... filled with optimism, affirmation of life, and trust in man's inexhaustible strength." However, when the Philadelphia Orchestra under Ormandy presented the American premiere in New York on October 2, 1972, Harold C. Schonberg of the New York *Times* called it "a pastiche," "unconvincing," and "parodistic." Brown of *High Fidelity/Musical America* concluded that "the work can perhaps be best understood in the light of Shostakovich's entire *oeuvre,* on which it seems to offer a kind of stream-of-consciousness commentary."

Shostakovich's last major works were the String Quartet No. 15 (1974) and the Sonata for Viola and Piano (1975). The Quartet is elegiac in tone, with six adagios, one of which is a funeral march. A critic for *High Fidelity/Musical America* described it as "grim stuff, with no ray of light, no redemption, no affirmation of the spirit." It was thought that it was the music of a man aware of the passing of his life.

Shostakovich had been ill, on and off, since suffering a heart attack in 1966, but other afflictions such as a broken leg and crippling arthritis made it difficult for him to play the piano, write or walk. In spite of physical distress, he visited the United States in 1973 to receive an honorary doctorate of Fine Arts from Northwestern University. Stephen E. Rubin interviewed him for the New York *Times* and described his condition as tenuous with "continuous twitches and tics. ... He rarely smiles, and his quivering lips appear permanently drawn in an unhappy frown. When talking, he tends not to look in the listener's eye, and therefore seems remote."

Shostakovich was hospitalized in Moscow from July 9 to August 1, 1975 for a heart ailment, readmitted on August 4, and died on August 9, 1975. The first news of his death in America was announced at the Berkshire Music Festival at Tanglewood in Massachusetts on August 9 where, as it turned out, Rostropovich, who was deeply affected by his death, was conducting a concert that included Shostakovich's Symphony No. 5 with the Boston Symphony Orchestra. Sieja Ozawa, the festival's music director, made the announcement at the concert and requested the audience to stand in silent tribute. The composer laid in state in the Grand

Hall of the Moscow Conservatory while from a nearby balcony his music was sung and played along with the music of Schubert's *Unfinished Symphony,* Chopin's *Funeral March,* and the Soviet national anthem. He was buried in the Novodevichy Cemetery in Moscow.

In 1971, Shostakovich had been decorated with the Order of the October Revolution, and a complete catalog of his works was edited by Malcolm MacDonald and published in London in 1974. A stamp bearing his photograph and an excerpt from his Symphony No. 7 was issued posthumously in the Soviet Union for his seventieth birthday. In 1976, the publication of all of Shostakovich's works, amounting to forty-two volumes, was initiated in the Soviet Union and is expected to be completed by 1984.

Music quoted from several of Shostakovich's symphonies, from his film score for Hamlet, and other works were used as background music for a three-and-a-half hour ballet, *The Idiot.* Introduced in West Berlin on June 15, 1979, it was based on the Dostoyevsky novel and choreographed by Valery Panov.

Shostakovich's *Suite on Poems of Michelangelo,* for bass voice and orchestra, received its American premiere on December 12, 1980. John Sirley Quirk was the soloist with the Cincinnati Symphony Orchestra under the direction of John Nelson.

Forty-seven years after its premiere in Leningrad in 1934, Shostakovich's opera *Katerina Ismailova* (originally entitled *Lady Macbeth of Mzensk*) reached the stage of the Bolshoi Opera in Moscow, on December 25, 1980. It was produced by Boris A. Pokrovsky, conducted by Gennady Rozhdestvensky, and Nina Fomina was in the title role.

The reputed memoirs of Shostakovich, which were smuggled out of the Soviet Union in 1977, were edited by Solomon Volkov and published in the United States in 1979 under the title of *Testimony: The Memoirs of Dmitri Shostakovich.* Because of the book's indictment of the Stalin regime (the composer had been held in highest esteem by the Soviet authorities in his closing years), it was denounced as spurious by Soviet musical officials, including Maxim Shostakovich, the composer's son. But some American critics found in it the torment of a dissenting artist who had to pay lip service for political expediency.

Maxim Shostakovich and his son Dmitri defected to the West in April 1981, originally seeking political asylum in West Germany. Two weeks later, Maxim Shostakovich renounced his Soviet citizenship to seek permanent residence in the United States and American citizenship. "I want to stress," he said, "that our departure is a profoundly conscious step, a sign of protest, a sign of disagreement—my spiritual legacy from my never-to-be-forgotten father, who devoted his entire life, all his creativity, to the great humanitarian ideals of mankind." The young conductor's first professional appearance in the United States took place on May 25, 1981, when he conducted the National Symphony Orchestra in Washington, D.C., in a special Memorial Day concert.

MAJOR WORKS (supplementary)

Band Music—March of the Soviet Militia.

Chamber Music—5 additional string quartets; Sonata for Violin and Piano; Sonata for Viola and Piano.

Choral Music—Faith, ballad-cycle for men's a cappella chorus.

Orchestral Music—Symphony No. 15.

Vocal Music—Spring, Spring, a cycle of six songs to Pushkin's poems, for contralto and chamber orchestra; Suite on Poems of Michelangelo, for bass and piano (also for orchestra); Four Verses by Captain Lebyadkin to texts by Dostoyevsky, for bass and piano; Six Songs to Poems by Marina Tsvetayeva, for mezzo-soprano and piano.

ABOUT (supplementary)

Sabinina, M., Shostakovich, the Symphonist; Shneerson, G. (ed.), Dmitri Shostakovich; Shostakovich, D., Testimony: The Memoirs of Dmitri Shostakovich, as related to and edited by Solomon Volkov.

High Fidelity/Musical America, October 1973, November 1975; New York Times, June 28, 1970, June 24, 1973, August 11, 1975.

Jean Sibelius

1865–1957

For biographical sketch, list of earlier works, and bibliography, see *Composers Since 1900.*

Sibelius's little known one-act ballad opera, *Jungfrun i Tornet,* or *The Maid in the Tower* (1896), had a rare revival in Helsinki on January 28, 1981, in a performance by the Helsinki Radio Symphony. "Much of it is beautiful in his Scandinavian vein," reported Inge Laure to

Opera News, "not at all in the somber Finnish *Kalevala* mood, and gives evidence that he could have been a prominent opera composer."

Sibelius' widow, Ainö Sibelius, died in Helsinki in June 1969 at the age of ninety-eight.

ABOUT (supplementary)

Levas, S., Sibelius: a Personal Portrait; Tawastsjerna, E., Sibelius.

Elie Siegmeister

1909–

For biographical sketch, list of earlier works, and bibliography, see *Composers Since 1900.*

Siegmeister's opera, *The Plough and the Stars,* with a libretto by Edward Mabley based on Sean O'Casey's drama, had a premiere at the Louisiana State University School of Music on March 16, 1969, and a world premiere in French at the Grand Theatre in Bordeaux, France, on May 13, 1970. "Siegmeister and his librettist have produced a strong, sharp, tormented, extremely theatrical work," wrote Jean-Louis Cassou in *Opéra,* a French publication. "The musical writing is healthy but far from tame, evoking Gershwin in its rhythms, or Kurt Weill in its atmosphere. It is nonetheless personal and of great intensity, with bravura pieces, such as the magnificent finale." *The Plough and the Stars* was revived by the New York Lyric Opera Company on October 19, 1979.

Symphony No. 4 (1967–1970) was introduced by the Cleveland Orchestra under Lorin Maazel on December 6, 1973. Siegmeister said: "In the ten years between the completion of my Third Symphony and the first sketches of the Fourth, my music underwent some kind of transformation. I had been occupied in the earlier days with finding my own language, and then spent years trying to perfect it, searching for a pithy, concentrated and yet as lyrical a style as I had it in me to find. In the last ten or twelve years, my work, it seems, has taken on a certain wildness, intensity and fantasy as well as a rugged, firmly grounded architecture (why else write symphonies?)." The four-movement Symphony opens in unorthodox fashion with a long, sustained episode for solo cello. Siegmeister notated this free, wide-ranging melodic piece in October 1967

without any intention of using it for his symphony, but later realized that it could be the first theme of his symphony, however unconventional it was. When Maazel conducted it in New York with the Cleveland Orchestra on February 13, 1974, a critic for the Long Island *Press* reported that it "is conceived on a grand scale with a sombre opening and a stirring finale, a sardonic scherzo and a soaring Andante of special power and beauty." In her review in the New York *Post,* Harriett Johnson said: "Siegmeister has poured his past into the symphony—jazz, a touch of ragtime, a touch of origins, a children's song, polyrhythms, polyharmonies—all adding up to immense sophistication."

Symphony No. 5, "Visions of Time," was written a year later, on commission from the Baltimore Symphony which introduced it at the Interamerican Music Festival at the Kennedy Center in Washington, D.C., on May 2, 1977, with Sergiu Comissiona conducting. The Symphony was inspired by reflections of Thoreau, George Bernard Shaw, Thomas Mann, and Faulkner on the nature of time. Its form is unconventional, with two short opening movements followed by two somewhat longer ones—a "symphony quasi una fantasia" as the composer described it. A brief quotation appears at the head of each movement. Thoreau's "time is but the stream I go a-fishin' in" from *Walden* appears in the opening movement; then Shaw's "A lifetime of happiness! No man alive could bear it; it would be hell on earth" introduces the slightly ironic second movement; the opening lines from Mann's *Joseph,* "Very deep is the well of the past. Should we not call it bottomless?" precede the meditative slow movement; and William Faulkner's "It was not a monument: it was a footprint. A monument only says 'at least I got this far,' while a footprint says 'this is where I was when I moved again' " leads the finale. But, as the composer explained, these inscriptions occurred to him *after* the Symphony was completed. "They are in no sense an interpretation of the music but rather mottos of a kind, reflecting my 'visions of time.' " Elliott W. Galkin of the Baltimore *Sun,* wrote: "With its novel neo-impressionistic passages, the textures light and airy, the sound of the various percussion instruments bright and shimmering, there are also some wonderful melodic moments, surprisingly expressive in Nineteenth Century romantic terms—epic passages written for unison celli, and poignantly eloquent lines for the French horn combined with the English horn. The symphony is also a magnificent exercise in rhythmic variety, for the musical motion seems to be in an incessant state of flux, constantly modified in its metrical transformations."

The Concerto for Piano and Orchestra (1973–1974), commissioned by the National Gallery of Art in Washington, D.C., was first performed in Denver by Alan Mandel (the composer's son-in-law) and the Denver Symphony under Brian Priestman on December 3, 1976. The material, according to the composer, is a mingling of opposites, "On the one hand a tumultuous freely bounding energy—what Walt Whitman called 'a wild, barbaric yawp'—and on the other, lyricism —a reflective or intense inner quality." A critic for *High Fidelity/Musical America* wrote the following description: "The piano enters in aggressive syncopation, a trumpet wails in counterpoint, a flute enters and the entire first movement, Moderato con moto, continues to flail at this pace. The second movement gains in repose, but it soon becomes frenetic and involved. In the finale, materials get sorted out more interestingly, particularly in the difficult piano cadenza."

Poems by Norman Rosten, Langston Hughes, and Lawrence Ferlinghetti provided the text for the cantata, *A Cycle of Cities* (1974), for chorus, solo soprano, solo tenor, and orchestra. Written on a grant from the National Endowment for the Arts, the poems and music reflect various aspects of city life—the poetic, comic, romantic, erotic, and violent, and the seven sections are entitled: "Harbor at Night" (Rosten), "57th Street" (Rosten), "Childhood Memories" (Hughes), "Fortune Has Its Cookies" (Ferlinghetti), "Pegasus on 10th Avenue" (Rosten), "Big Fat Hairy Vision of Evil" (Ferlinghetti), and "Life Is Fine" (Hughes). The work was first heard on August 8, 1974, at Wolf Trap Farm Park in Virginia, under the direction of Murry Sidlin and choreography by Anna Sokolow.

In 1974, Siegmeister received three commissions from the Shreveport Symphony Orchestra in Louisiana for the commemoration of the American bicentennial: a work for orchestra, a ballet, and an opera. The orchestral work is *Shadows and Light: Homage to Five Paintings* (1974–1975). Siegmeister explained, "The work starts [first movement] in the dim light of Albert Ryder ('Night Ship,), rises [third movement] to the flashing brilliance of Fernand Léger ('The

Great Parade') and culminates [fifth movement] in the starlight and moonlight darkness of Van Gogh ('Starry Night'). The second movement was inspired by Paul Klee ("All around the Fish"), and the fourth by Edgar Degas ("Blind Woman Arranging Flowers"). The Shreveport Symphony under John Shenaut premiered it on November 9, 1975. The Cleveland Orchestra under Lorin Maazel programmed *Shadows and Light* on October 25, 1979.

The second commission was for the ballet *Fables from the Dark Wood,* a scenario based on five symbolic fables from a book of Creole folk tales compiled by Alcée Fortier in 1895. The Katherine Posin Dance Company and the Shreveport Symphony under Shenaut presented it on April 25, 1976. "Siegmeister's ballet score . . . is terse, witty, radiant with orchestral color and full of meter changes and biting dissonances," wrote Mark Nelson in the Shreveport *Times.*

The opera, in three acts, is *Night on the Moonspell* (1974–1976), with a libretto by Edward Mabley freely based on Shakespeare's *A Midsummer Night's Dream;* its premiere took place in Shreveport on November 14, 1976, with John Shenaut conducting. Harlan Snow wrote in *Opera News,* "Siegmeister's score is an ingenious composition of beautiful sonorities, powerful and illuminating effects and solid dramatic integrity. The composer possesses a Puccinian sense of the dramatic, his score complementing the drama so well that the stage is impelled by the orchestra. Music and drama have a cohesion that frees the auditor to become immersed."

When Isidore and Anne Saslav commissioned a "light-hearted work, one suited for a summer night outdoors, and American in character," Siegmeister wrote *An Entertainment for Violin, Piano and Orchestra* (1976) for the American bicentennial. It was played at the opening of the Baltimore Festival in the Merriweather Post Pavilion in Columbia, Maryland, on June 25, 1976, with Sergiu Comissiona conducting the Baltimore Symphony Orchestra and Isidore Saslav (concertmaster of the orchestra) and his wife, Anne, as soloists. In four movements, the violin is the solo in the first ("Song for One"), the pianist is the solo in the second ("Dance for Another"), and there is a free-for-all entertainment for both soloists and the orchestra in the last movement ("Three for All").

In 1973, Siegmeister detailed five characteristics of his compositions: "For me, melody is still the core of music. No matter how interesting the composer's ideas may be, in the long run they become dry and lifeless without melody. Curving, sweeping, jagged or freely flowing lines—these are what the composer has to work with, today as in the past (although obviously today's melodies are different from the older ones). . . . After lyricism, a kind of wildness might be seen as a balancing force—a craggy, harsh feeling that appears in violent rhythms and biting harmonies. . . . An improvisatory quality often appears in my orchestral music. . . . The fourth element in my music is architecture. The freer a work becomes, the more vital, I believe, are its structural underpinnings. With all the dazzling possibilities of sonority and texture available to the contemporary composer, form remains more important than ever. To find the precise structure and texture is often a bitter struggle but essential if the work is to survive a few hearings. Not unexpectedly, the fifth characteristic of my music is the dramatic. For me, no gulf exists between the world of the theater and that of concert music—although each, of course, has its special requirements. The dramatic principles that make a successful opera or ballet are also found in a good string quartet and symphony. Symphonic techniques, conversely, function with equal power in the theater."

On March 16–17, 1978, the eighth annual Contemporary American Composers Festival, presented by the music department of the University of Bridgeport in Connecticut, devoted four concerts entirely to Siegmeister's works beginning with 1927 and ending chronologically with two 1977 works which received their world premieres on March 17: *A Set of Houses,* for piano, and a song cycle, *City Songs,* to poems by Norman Rosten. In addition to the concerts, Siegmeister gave several lectures and conducted a student master class in composition at the Festival. During the summer of 1978, Siegmeister was composer-in-residence at the Brevard Music Center in North Carolina where in addition to concerts of Siegmeister's music, he was a lecturer on contemporary composition and conductor of master classes in composition. Previously, from 1966 to 1976, he had been composer-in-residence at Hofstra University in Long Island, New York.

In 1978, Siegmeister received an award in recognition of his creative work in music from the American Academy and Institute of Arts and Letters plus a sum to pay for recording one of his works. That year, he also received a Guggenheim Fellowship in composition for the first time and remarked wryly, "I have been applying for Guggenheims for forty years. My students used to get them, but I never did. When I would fill out recommendations for them, I would kid them about giving *me* a recommendation. Well, if you live long enough. . . ."

In celebration of Siegmeister's seventieth birthday the Metropolitan Music School in New York presented a program of his music on January 16, 1979.

Siegmeister is a member of the board of directors of the American Society of Composers, Authors, and Publishers (ASCAP), on the executive board of the Kennedy Center Black Music Colloquium and Competition, and the founder and chairman of the Council of Creative Artists, Libraries, and Museums.

He is the editor of *The New Music Lover's Handbook* (1973).

MAJOR WORKS (supplementary)

Ballet—Fables from the Dark Wood.

Band Music—Ballad for Band; Front Porch Saturday Night; Celebration.

Chamber Music—Sonata No. 4, for violin and piano; Sonatina No. 5, for violin and piano; String Quartet No. 3, on Hebrew themes; Declaration for Brass and Timpani; Summer, for viola and piano.

Choral Music—A Cycle of Cities, for solo soprano, solo tenor, chorus, and orchestra.

Operas—Night of the Moonspell; The Marquesa of O.

Orchestral Music—2 additional symphonies; Concerto for Piano and Orchestra; Shadows and Light; An Entertainment, double concerto for violin, piano, and orchestra; Concerto for Violin and Orchestra.

Piano Music—On This Ground—A Set of Houses; Sonata No. 3.

Vocal Music—Five cummings Songs, for soprano and piano; Six cummings Songs, for baritone and piano; Songs of Innocence, for soprano and piano; City Songs, for voice and piano; Three Minute Songs; Ballad of Adam and Eve, for voice and piano; Life is Fine, for voice and piano; Songs of Experience, for voice, viola, and piano; Brief Introduction to the Problems of Philolosphy, for voice and piano.

ABOUT (supplementary)

Shneerson, G., Portraits of American Composers; Siegmeister, E. (ed.), The New Music Lover's Handbook (contains an autobiographical sketch).

New York Times, January 7, 1979; Newsday, January

26, 1972; Opera News, March 14, 1970; Washington Post, June 23, 1976.

Christian Sinding

1856–1941

See *Composers Since 1900.*

Charles Sanford Skilton

1868–1941

See *Composers Since 1900.*

Leo Sowerby

1895–1968

See *Composers Since 1900.*

Robert Starer

1924–

Robert Starer, born in Vienna, Austria, on January 8, 1924, was the second child of Nison Starer and Erna Gottlieb Starer. He revealed, "My father owned a textile factory; my mother was emancipated and studied psychoanalysis with Alfred Adler. The Vienna home of my childhood had many political upheavals, often accompanied by considerable violence, some of which I saw from the windows of our centrally located home."

A governess who taught the Starer children French and good manners discovered that the child Robert had absolute pitch, and gave him his first piano lessons when he was about four. After the governess left, a regular piano teacher was engaged. In his thirteenth year, Robert Starer entered the State Academy where he studied piano with Victor Ebenstein. He confided, "My mother insisted that I practice every day but

---

Starer: stärer

ROBERT STARER

luckily for me her ears were more attuned to the psyche than to music and she could not tell what I was playing. I much preferred improvising to practicing, and she never knew. That may be why I became a composer and not a pianist."

While studying music at the Academy, Starer attended high school for four years of Latin and Greek; he did well both in his studies and in the game of soccer, his favorite sport. Since his father was a Zionist, though not religious, young Starer was also given private instruction in colloquial Hebrew. Starer recalled the Nazi occupation and annexation of Austria, in the spring of 1938. "I stayed up all night and watched the German troops enter Vienna." The Starer family was now in peril, but fortunately for Robert, he played for Emil Hauser, founder of the original Budapest String Quartet and director of the Jerusalem Conservatory, who accepted him for admission to that institution.

Starer remembers that in August 1938, at fourteen, he was separated from his family to take refuge in Palestine. "The Jerusalem to which I came was a rather strange place in which Jews from different European countries and Arabs lived in varying degrees of disharmony under British rule." At the Conservatory, he studied composition with Joseph Tal who introduced him to the music of Hindemith and Schoenberg, and with Oedoen Partos, who acquainted him with the music of Bartók. Starer was on a scholarship from Mailamm, an American organization which required the study of near-Eastern music, so he had to combine his

Conservatory studies with lessons on the oud (an Oriental predecessor of the lute) from a Jewish musician from Bagdad. Improvisations of his teacher so fascinated him that he put many of them on paper and after two years he wrote a composition himself for oud and orchestra, "a rather crude attempt at synthesis of two styles," he said. Western-style composition was begun in earnest in his late teens.

To support himself Starer worked as a staff pianist for the Palestine radio between 1941 and 1943, and at eighteen, he married Johanna Herz, a soprano who also attended the Conservatory on March 27, 1942. A year later, Starer enlisted in the British Royal Air Force because he felt that fighting Hitler was more urgent than studying music. "The Germans were to the north of us in Syria and at El-Alamein in Egypt. But my own participation in the fighting was both minimal and uneventful. While I traveled about a great deal, most of my activities in the air force were musical. The British supplied good classical music to their troops and I played a great many concerts in some very unlikely places."

In uniform Starer wrote *Fantasy for Strings* (1945) in a neo-romantic idiom and the style of early Schoenberg. It was performed by the Palestine Philharmonic Orchestra under George Singer on March 11, 1947. Max Brod, the Czech writer, composer, and music critic, wrote in a Palestine journal that the *Fantasy* "showed that he [Starer] creates from the very depths of his soul" and is "one of the most talented young composers of our country." When the composition was performed in New York in 1949, Noel Straus described it in the New York *Times* as "rich textured, deeply expressive music that has something to say, and said it with fervor, originality and conviction."

On being discharged in May 1946, Starer got a scholarship to resume music study either in London, Paris, or New York and he chose New York. He took entrance examinations at the Juilliard School of Music in August 1947 and was immediately put on a post-graduate level. (Consequently he never earned a college degree, but did get a post-graduate diploma from Juilliard.) In 1949, he joined the faculty of Juilliard until 1975 and he became an American citizen in 1957.

He supplemented his income in New York by accompanying singers and instrumentalists, but he said, "My chief and only interest was compo-

sition, to which I gave every free moment." Under Frederick Jacobi, his composition teacher at Juilliard, he wrote chamber music and his first composition for orchestra, *Prelude and Dance* (1949), which was performed by the Juilliard Orchestra under Dean Dixon on April 29, 1949. Starer's first symphony, written in 1950, was never performed, but his one-movement Symphony No. 2 (1951) was introduced in Tel Aviv by the Israel Philharmonic Orchestra under Erich Leinsdorf on May 7, 1953. A large choral work—*Kohelet (Ecclesiastes),* for soloists, chorus, and orchestra—was premiered at the Juilliard School of Music in New York on February 20, 1953.

Starer felt that his Piano Concerto No. 2 (1953) was a milestone in developing a personalized style, modern harmonic and rhythmic writing in a classical structure. David Bar-Illan gave the first performance of the Concerto with the Cincinnati Symphony under Thor Johnson, on July 17, 1956. This work of only fourteen minutes' duration is actually a concerto in three movements. It was repeated in New York by Bar-Illan with the Brooklyn Philharmonic Orchestra under Siegfried Landau, and Paul Affelder described the performance in the Brooklyn *Eagle:* "Its statements are brief and to the point, and its mood is light. The first of its three movements has a martial character; the second is reflective, contrapuntal, and at times polyharmonic; the finale is a gay and tuneful rondo with a catchy principal theme and a syncopated subsidiary one."

On November 22, 1954, the Little Orchestra Society under Thomas Scherman gave the first performance in New York of *Concerto a Tre* (1954) in which the three solo instruments (clarinet, trumpet, trombone) play against the main orchestra much in the style of the baroque concerto grosso. Ross Parmenter of the New York *Times* reported, "The solo strands were skillfully interwoven with the music of the strings." In the New York *Post,* Harriett Johnson noted: "There was an intensity and compulsion about his ideas which arrested the attention." In 1955 Starer wrote *Prelude and Rondo Giocoso,* for orchestra, and *Ballade,* for violin and orchestra. The former work was premiered on October 27, 1956, at a concert of the New York Philharmonic under Dimitri Mitropoulos, and the latter in New York on October 15, 1957, with Zvi Zeitlin as soloist, and the

Symphony of the Air conducted by Izler Solomon.

In 1957, Starer was awarded a Guggenheim Fellowship which enabled him, his wife, and their three-year-old son, Daniel, to travel in Europe. Returning to the city of his birth, Starer composed a four-movement Concerto for Viola, Strings, and Percussion in an apartment that was so cold that he had to wear gloves while composing. It was first performed in a radio broadcast in Geneva on July 3, 1959, by the Orchestre de la Suisse Romande, with Ron Golan as soloist. Its later American premiere on December 10 of that year was by William Lincer, soloist, and the New York Philharmonic Orchestra under Leonard Bernstein. Reviewing that performance, Howard Taubman of the New York *Times* cited the jazz, although the work was in more classical traditions. "There is a touch of it in the second movement and the use of the percussion in other places calls up not only familiar orchestra exoticism but also a feeling of jazz. Starer is fundamentally a lyricist in the late romantic spirit. His first movement sings broadly, and the third has a grave simplicity."

In 1959–1960 Starer taught composition at the New York College of Music and in 1962–1963 he served on the music faculty of the Jewish Theological Seminary in New York. Between 1962 and 1964 he was a member of the board of directors of the American Music Center. He was awarded a second Guggenheim Fellowship in 1963, the year he was appointed professor of music at Brooklyn College in New York. In 1964 he earned a Fulbright predoctoral research grant.

By 1960, Starer, branching out, was singularly successful in writing ballet music. On March 15, 1960, Anna Sokolow danced to his music for *The Story of Esther* on CBS television. In the same year, on September 20th, his full-length ballet, *The Dybbuk,* was introduced in Berlin by Herbert Ross and Nora Kaye. He also contributed music for several ballets for Martha Graham and her group: *Samson Agonistes* (originally entitled *A Visionary Recital*) on April 16, 1961, and *Phaedra* on March 4, 1962, both produced in New York; *Secular Games* (set to his *Concerto a Tre*), was danced in New London, Connecticut, on August 17, 1962; *The Lady of the House of Sleep* in June 1968, and *Holy Jungle,* on April 27, 1975, were danced in New York. Walter Terry's review of Starer's music for *Phaedra* in the New York *Herald Tribune* could apply to his other ballet music as well: "Mr. Starer's score served the dramatic needs of this powerful drama . . . handsomely."

Starer described the ideal artistic collaboration between choreographer and composer. "The idea or concept for the work must be the choreographer's. He speaks about it to the composer, who must decide whether he is suitable for the subject or whether he should decline. In my own case, my reaction is absolutely immediate as it is—incidentally—to the written word. . . . Most of the musical ideas for *Phaedra* came to me as I heard Martha Graham speak about it one weekend on Shelter Island. After listening, I always ask a good many questions chiefly in order to find out whether my conception corresponds to that of the choreographer. I believe that timing should be discussed, but only in general terms. After that, the composer should be left alone to create what he considers suitable music for the subject outlined by the choreographer. If the musical timing of a work is unsound, the best choreography will not save it."

Seven years after writing the ballet score for *Samson Agonistes,* Starer rewrote it as a symphonic work and the Cincinnati Symphony Orchestra under Max Rudolf performed it on May 8, 1965. Starer explained that the music "does not attempt to describe pictorially the external events of Samson's life. To me, Samson is not just the well-known biblical figure but represents 'man' in the widest sense." The work, in five sections, is played without interruption and uses two twelve-tone rows so freely and flexibly that some of the thematic material is hardly derived from them. Winthrop Sargeant wrote in *The New Yorker,* "Mr. Starer succeeds in conveying something to his audience. What he conveys is largely a mood of gloom and frustration, but the frustration has not turned him into a cynic. He is serious about his gloom; he is even eloquent about it. After listening to his work, I felt that for the first time in many months a composer was asking me to share an experience. And that to me is the sign of a composition of real significance." The dodecaphonic technique is also used in *Mutabili, Variants for Orchestra,* which was first performed by the Pittsburgh Symphony Orchestra under William Steinberg on October 28, 1966.

The atonal and the twelve-tone music of Schoenberg and Berg influenced Starer's first full-length opera, begun in 1967 and completed five years later. *Pantagleize,* with a libretto by the composer, was adapted from a play by Michel de Ghelderode about a hero who makes an innocent remark about the weather, inadvertently signaling the outbreak of an uprising. The opera was produced by the Brooklyn College Opera Theater, with Karoly Kope conducting, on April 8, 1974. Andrew Porter reported in *The New Yorker:* "Starer has done more than set a good and unusual play to music. Ghelderode's *Pantagleize* now seems to have been reshaped by Starer in musical form ... Starer has a happy knack for scherzo inventions that match the farce, for pregnant snatches of melodic motif that can assume many tempers while keeping their audible identity, and for music in which grotesquerie and sadness are mingled."

Starer revealed another facet of his creativity in Concerto for Violin, Cello, and Orchestra (one of few such works since Brahms' *Double Concerto*) in 1967. Departing from the twelve-tone technique, he concentrated on the virtuosity of the two solo instruments and their capabilities for lyric expression within a tonal framework. James Oliver Russell, violinist, and Michael Grebanier, cellist, were soloists when the concerto was first performed on October 11, 1968, by the Pittsburgh Symphony Orchestra under William Steinberg.

In Symphony No. 3 (1969)—premiered by the Pittsburgh Symphony under William Steinberg, on October 30, 1970—Starer departs from the traditional concept of the symphony in terms of key relationships. He explained, "What it did retain from the classical concept is the principle of statement of ideas, development, transformed re-statement and conclusion—a logical structure not limited to a brief period in the history of music." Starer also retained the four-movement structure, each movement representing a basic human mood or attitude: I. Introspective, dramatic, intense; II. Light, humorous, jocose; III. Lyrical, contemplative; IV. Dance-like, rhythmically straightforward.

Piano Concerto No. 3 (1972) successfully amalgamates stylistic elements identified with Bartók, Berg, and Stravinsky, arriving at a truly personal style. Elliott W. Galkin, in the Baltimore *Sun,* described it as "individual and impressive, gently kaleidoscopic in its contrast of brilliance and intimacy in contemporary terms ... Mr. Starer, at fifty years of age, has produced

a major work for the piano." David Bar-Illan (for whom the Concerto was commissioned) was the soloist with the Baltimore Symphony Orchestra under Sergiu Comissiona when the work was introduced on October 9, 1974.

In *The Last Lover* (1974), Starer wrote a musical morality play, with a libretto by Gail Godwin based on the legend of St. Pelagia. In the legend a courtesan in the fourth century decides to become a monk rather than a nun, is accused of having impregnated a nun, and is banished to the mountains and death. Scored for three singers accompanied by a woodwind quintet which also takes part in the stage proceedings, the work is mostly neo-classical, and at times highly dissonant. Joanna Simon, Richard Fredericks, Linda Phillips, and the Dorian Wind Quintet were the performers at its premiere on August 2, 1975, at the Caramoor Festival in Katonah, New York.

Gail Godwin also wrote the text for *Journals of a Songmaker,* for baritone, soprano, and orchestra, written in 1975 on a grant from the National Endowment for the Arts. Starer denies autobiographical intent in his treatment of different women in a composer's life as found in entries in a diary. A critic for *High Fidelity/ Musical America* said, "The jaunty music ebbed and swelled with excellent ideas and scoring. . . . This is a healthy, dignified and well-crafted expression." The work was premiered on May 21, 1976, a sentimental occasion for both William Steinberg, who marked the end of a twenty-five-year tenure as musical director of the Pittsburgh Symphony, and Starer himself, since Steinberg, as he said, "was the most important conductor in my life." The work was commissioned for Steinberg's farewell.

Robert Starer wrote *The People, Yes,* for chorus and orchestra, in 1976 on commission from the Broome County, New York, Bicentennial Commission and the Binghamton Junior League. The Chorus of the State University at Binghamton and the University Harpur Symphony under David Buttolph presented the world premiere on December 4, 1976. The text used excerpts from Carl Sandburg's epic poem of the same name. A critic for *High Fidelity/ Musical America* wrote "Starer responds warmly to the poem, as his music shows. . . . The score sets tonalities, wanders and returns, demanding both subtle dynamic nuances and sudden shifts from the performers. It is well mated to the moods and word-sounds of the poetry."

Still

Starer, separated from his wife in the early 1970s, lives in Woodstock, New York. He does his basic composing in the morning, leaving details of orchestration for later hours but when he has a deadline, he resumes composing in late afternoon. After a lunch with wine and a nap, he continues to work far into the night. Having no hobbies, he said, "I make music, because it is what I enjoy the most."

MAJOR WORKS

Ballets—The Story of Esther; The Dybbuk; Samson Agonistes; Phaedra; The Lady of the House of Sleep; Holy Jungle.

Band Music—Stone Ridge Set.

Chamber Music—String Quartet; Concertino for Two, for violin and piano (or two voices); Five Miniatures for Brass; Duo, for violin and viola; Variants, for violin and piano; Trio, for clarinet, cello, and piano; Colloquies, for flute and piano; Piano Quartet; Profiles in Brass.

Choral Music—Kohelet (Ecclesiastes), for baritone, soprano, chorus, and orchestra; Ariel (Visions of Isaiah), for soprano, baritone, chorus, and orchestra; Joseph and His Brothers, for narrator, soloists, chorus, and orchestra; Sabbath Evening Service; I'm Nobody, for a cappella female voices; On the Nature of Things, for chorus; Images of Man, for soprano, mezzo-soprano, tenor, baritone, mixed chorus, and instruments; The People, Yes, for chorus and orchestra.

Opera—The Intruder, one-act; Pantagleize; The Last Lover, musical morality play; Apollonia.

Orchestral Music—3 symphonies; 3 piano concertos; Fantasy, for strings; Prelude and Dance; Prelude and Rondo Giocoso; Concerto a Tre, for clarinet, trumpet, trombone, and strings; Ballade, for violin and orchestra; Concerto for Viola, Strings, and Percussion; Samson Agonistes, symphonic portrait; Mutabili, Variants, for orchestra; Concerto for Violin, Cello, and Orchestra; Six Variations with Twelve Notes; Journals of a Songmaker, for baritone, soprano, and orchestra; Voices of Brooklyn, for narrator, vocal soloists, and symphonic band.

Piano Music—2 sonatas; Fantasia Concertante, for piano four hands; Sketches in Color.

ABOUT

Vinton, J. (ed.), Dictionary of Contemporary Music.

New York Philharmonic Program Notes, April 25, 1968; New York Times, April 1, 1973; Pittsburgh Symphony Program Notes, October 11, 1968.

William Grant Still

1895–1978

For biographical sketch, list of earlier works, and bibliography, see *Composers Since 1900.*

At an all–Still concert in Oberlin, Ohio, on November 9, 1970—a salute to the composer's seventy-fifth birthday—the Oberlin Orchestra under Robert Baustian presented the world premiere of Still's Symphony No. 5, "Western Hemisphere," which he composed in 1937 (as Symphony No. 3) and revised in 1970. A programmatic work, more like a four-movement suite than a symphony, it depicts, according to a note in the score: "1. the vigorous, life-sustaining forces of the Hemisphere (briskly); 2. the natural beauties of the Hemisphere (slower, with utmost grace); 3. the nervous energy of the Hemisphere (energetically); and 4. the overshadowing spirit of kindness and justice in the Hemisphere (moderately)." The Symphony was also performed at an all-Still program by the Detroit Metropolitan Orchestra under Charles Sumner, on February 25, 1973.

On November 15, 1974, Opera/South in Jackson, Mississippi, presented the world premiere of Still's *A Bayou Legend* (1941). The libretto, by Verna Arvey (Still's wife), was based on an authentic legend from Biloxi about a man who falls in love with a spirit. Frank Hains reported to *High Fidelity/Musical America* that "Still's music has a quality distinctly his own, marked by an extraordinarily rich orchestral palette whose complexities are superbly controlled in juxtaposition to a direct lyrical line. . . . Aria and recitative are skillfully interwoven." When *Bayou Legend* had its West Coast premiere in Los Angeles on February 13, 1976, as part of the observance of Black History Week and the American Bicentennial Year, Daniel Cariaga wrote in the Los Angeles *Times:* "Beauties abound in the score. . . . His skills at writing for the voice, creating colorful but uncluttered orchestrations and fashioning a balanced and tight superstructure are considerable."

On December 3, 1977, Opera Ebony, a national organization providing opportunities for black singers, revived Still's two-act opera, *Highway 1 USA,* in New York.

Still's eightieth birthday was celebrated in Los Angeles by the University of Southern California School of Music with a program of his works on May 14, 1975. On September 22, 1976, in Beverly Hills, the American Society of Composers, Authors, and Publishers (ASCAP) presented Still with a scroll honoring him for his "extraordinary contributions to the literature of symphonic music, opera, ballet, chamber music, songs and solo works" and for personifying "greatness both as an artist and a human being." A new arts center, the William Grant Still Community Arts Center, a facility of the Municipal Arts Department, was dedicated in Los Angeles on March 11, 1978.

Long suffering from a heart ailment, failing eyesight, and several strokes, Still was confined to a nursing home in Los Angeles toward the end of his life, where he died on December 3, 1978. A memorial concert of Still's compositions was presented at the University of Southern California School of Performing Arts in Los Angeles in May 1979.

Howard Hanson wrote, "William Grant Still's place in music as the dean of America's Negro composers is assured. It is a proud distinction, but it is not enough. For Still is, above all, an American composer, interpreting the spiritual values of his own land through his own particular genius." In 1971, Still received an honorary doctorate in music from the University of Arkansas.

In 1974, Columbia Records released a new recording of Still's Afro-American Symphony (1931), and on June 15, 1981, his opera *A Bayou Legend* (1941) was telecast over the Public Broadcasting Service network by the Opera/South Company of Jackson, Mississippi.

MAJOR WORKS (supplementary)

Choral Music—We Sang Our Songs.

Orchestral Music—Miniature Overture; Threnody: In Memory of Sibelius; Choreographic Prelude.

ABOUT (supplementary)

Haas, R.B., (ed.), William Grant Still, and the Fusion of Cultures in American Music; Southern, E., Music of Black Americans: a History.

ASCAP Today, Winter, 1975; Black Perspective in Music, Spring 1974, May 1975; High Fidelity/Musical America, March 1975.

Karlheinz Stockhausen

1928–

For biographical sketch, list of earlier works, and bibliography, see *Composers Since 1900.*

Stockhausen's *Stimmung (Tuning),* for six vocalists, was commissioned by the Rhenish Music Schools in Cologne, Germany. It was written in 1968 while Stockhausen was in the United States, and on December 9, 1968, it was introduced on the Paris Radio in a concert promoted by the Centre Culturel Allemand, the Goethe Institute, and the Groupe de Recherche Musicale. In performing the work, each singer holds a microphone which is attached to six spherical loudspeakers placed around the auditorium. The seventy-five-minute score in B-flat, and its overtones, contains interpolations of text consisting of names, words, the days of the week (in German and English), and excerpts from German and Japanese poetry. During the World's Fair in Osaka, Japan, in 1970, *Stimmung* was performed 72 times in the German pavilion and at a performance on June 2, 1969, at the Palais Chaillot in Paris which Stockhausen regarded as the perfect setting for his work. The Collegium Vocale of Cologne presented it in New York in November 1971, and Irving Kolodin reviewed it in *Saturday Review:* "Stockhausen has brought together an experience not unrelated to the music of India in its suspension of time, its aspiration to a condition of Nirvana in which one responds to the *effect* of the sound rather than to its *meaning.* But it is so skillfully organized, so craftily constructed that it caters also to the European-conditioned listener's need for contrast, variety and an attention-holding factor. . . . In pursuit of his poetic purpose—which can be simply defined as hypnotizing, tranquilizing or merely mood-inducing—Stockhausen utilized all the possible permutations of six voices together, five together, four with two silent, etc."

In 1970, Stockhausen was invited to give a lecture on the composer for a Beethoven centennial celebration. Stockhausen explained, "My spontaneous reaction was to propose an evening of meditating on Beethoven's music." To accomplish this Stockhausen wrote *Opus 1970* for piano, electric viola, electronium, and tam-tam. Quotations from Beethoven's works were paraphrased electronically, while the text of his Heiligenstadt Testament was read.

Early in February 1971, two Stockhausen concerts were held in New York within a three-day period. On February 25, the New York Philharmonic Orchestra under Stockhausen devoted its entire program to *Hymnen* in a three-hour performance. Scored for orchestra and electronic sounds, *Hymnen* (1966–1967) is an elaborate collage of national anthems which Stockhausen de-composed and then re-composed into a single anthem embracing the universe. It was first performed in Cologne, Germany, on November 30, 1967. As the composer explained, his aim was "to realize the divine mission of ONE united world." Three days after the first American performance, a program of Stockhausen's works was presented at Tully Hall at Lincoln Center by the New and Newer Music series.

Two of Stockhausen's later major works were premiered in the United States. *Zodiac* (1975–1976), "twelve melodies of the star signs for melody and/or keyboard instruments" was introduced in New York by the Berlin Octet on April 13, 1977. This work had originally been scored two years earlier for music clocks or music boxes, but Stockhausen decided to rewrite it for formal instruments. The twelve melodies (corresponding to the signs of the zodiac and taking about thirty seconds to perform) were assigned to single instruments or to an ensemble. The melodies began and ended with the zodiac sign for the date of performance or the birthday of the person to whom it was dedicated. John Rockwell in his review in the New York *Times,* wrote: "Each tune has been carefully constructed according to both musical and mystical respects, and some of them had an appeal on both these levels. But the end effect seemed static and stiff."

Sirius (1975–1977), for soprano, bass, trumpet, clarinet, and electronic sounds, is a cantata which the Federal Republic of Germany commissioned as a gift to the United States for its bicentennial celebration. Dedicated "to American pioneers on earth and in space," a part of *Sirius* was introduced at the Smithsonian Institution in Washington, D.C., on July 18, 1976, and the complete work was first performed on August 8, 1977, at Aix-en-Provence, France, and in the United States on January 13, 1978, in Houston, Texas, during a week-long Stockhausen festival. The mystical text is a mixture of

astronomy, astrology, seasonal cycles, space travel, global unity and diversity, human relationships, and universal peace. The soloists represent master musicians who come to earth from the Dog Star to celebrate the cycle of the seasons. In commenting on *Sirius,* Stockhausen said: "Every musical composition is linked to the rhythm of the stars, the time of the year and day, the elements and the existential differences of the living beings. The music which I have composed . . . transfers some of these principles of musical form and creation onto our planet." Reporting on the Washington premiere to the New York *Times,* Peter G. Davis wrote: "The main problem with *Sirius* . . . is that the music never turns out to be as interesting as the concept behind it. . . . Despite its elaborate space-age paraphernalia and intricate musical processes, *Sirius* still sounds very much bogged down in the stale, dry-note anonymity of the 1950 s serialism. The constant simultaneity of complex events, the unrelenting jagged surfaces and unvaried dynamic levels eventually cancel one another out."

Stockhausen's mysticism and spirituality also pervade *Licht,* a work the composer believes will be his life's *Meisterwerk,* for he began writing it in 1977 and expects to continue working on it for the rest of his life. While *Sirius* celebrates the seasons of the year, *Licht* involves the seven days of the week, and Stockhausen hopes to have it performed on seven successive evenings. The huge dimensions of this opus can best be measured by the scope of the first completed work, "Thursday," which consists of three acts: I. *"Michaels Jugend"* (first performed in October 1979 in Jerusalem); II. *"Michaels Reise"* (performed in Paris in 1978); III. *"Michaels Heimkehr"* (premiered at the Holland Festival in June 1980). "Thursday" is concerned with "the progress of the innocent and rather insipid Michael, a watered-down 20th century Siegfried, toward maturity and universal knowledge," reported Nicholas Kenyon in *The New Yorker.* "The journey is set against the background of astrological symbols, spirits and deities special to the day of the week: for Thursday, the special symbol is plants and the special character is wisdom. . . . The music Stockhausen has provided for this extraordinary farrago is not without interest. In *'Jugend'* it is intricate and sometimes striking; a ceaseless flow of complex recitative-type declamation, which seems to lose its way from time to time. In *'Heimkehr,'* however, it is static and ritualistic, built on high sustained string lines and solid, monolithic chords for chorus and orchestra over which the soprano soloist soars. . . . At present, it is a most ambitious piece of music-theater, full of arresting ideas but in grave danger of collapsing under the weight of its metaphysical pretentions."

In discussing his overall aim as a composer, Stockhausen said: "The constant goal of my searches and efforts: the power of transformation—its operation in time, in music. Hence, a refusal of repetition, of variation, of development, of contrast. Of all, in fact, that requires 'shapes'—themes, motives, objects to be repeated, varied, developed, contrasted, to be dismembered, rearranged, augmented, diminished, displayed in modulation, transposition, inversion or retrograde. All this I renounced. . . . For me there followed . . . a series of metamorphoses tending to no visible end. Never is the same thing heard twice. Yet one had the clear feeling that an immutable and extremely homogeneous continuity is never abandoned. There is a hidden power of cohesion, a relatedness among the proportions; a structure. Not similar shapes in a changing light. Rather this: different shapes in a constant, all-permeating light."

Since 1964, Stockhausen has toured the world, including the near East and Far East, with an instrumental ensemble performing the live electronic music which he founded, for which he wrote some of his later compositions, and with which he has made recordings.

In 1966–1967, Stockhausen was visiting professor of music at the University of California in Davis; in 1968, he conducted a seminar of new music in Bratislava, where his music was performed. In 1970, he monitored performances of his music at Expo '70 in Osaka, Japan, and in 1971 he was appointed professor of composition at the State Conservatory in Cologne, Germany. He was decorated with the Grosser Kunstkreuz des Landes Nordhein-Westfalen in 1968 and the Bundesverdienstkreuz, first class, in 1974. In 1979 he was elected to honorary membership in the American Academy and Institute of Arts and Letters and also to membership in the Academy of Free Arts in Hamburg, the Academy of Arts in Berlin, and the Royal Swedish Academy in Stockholm.

On April 3, 1967, Stockhausen married Mary Bauermeister, a painter, in San Francisco and they make their home in Cologne with their two children.

MAJOR WORKS (supplementary)

Chamber Music—Alphabet for Liège, thirteen musical pictures for soloists and duos; Hebstmusik, for four players; Musik im Bauch, for six percussionists and music boxes; Zodiac, twelve melodies of the star signs for melody and/or keyboard instruments; Harlekin, for clarinet; Amour, five pieces for clarinet; In Freundschaft, for flute, or clarinet, or oboe, or trumpet, or violin or viola.

Choral Music—Breathing Gives Life, choir-opera with orchestra (or tape).

Electronic Music—Opus 1970, for piano, electronic viola, electronium, and tam-tam; Sirius, cantata for soprano, bass, trumpet, and electronic sounds.

Orchestral Music—Fresco, for four orchestral groups; Für Kommende Zeiten, seventeen texts for intuitive music for small ensemble; Sternklang, park music for five groups; Trans; Ylem, for nineteen or more players or singers; Inori, adorations for one or two soloists and orchestra; Jubiläum; Der Jahreslauf, for dancers and orchestra; Michael's Trip Around the World, for trumpet and orchestra.

Piano Music—Mantra, for two pianos.

Theatre Music—Thursday, and Tuesday, two parts of *Licht.*

Vocal Music—In the Sky I Am Walking, twelve American-Indian songs; Mondeva, for tenor and basset horn.

ABOUT (supplementary)

Cott, J., Stockhausen; Conversations with the Composer; Griffith, P., A Concise History of Avant-Garde Music; Harvey, J., The Music of Stockhausen: an Introduction; Heikinheimo, S., The Electronic Music of Karlheinz Stockhausen; Maconie, R., The Works of Karlheinz Stockhausen; Wörner, K.H., Stockhausen: Life and Work.

Musical Quarterly, January 1975; Newsweek, April 16, 1973; New York Times, February 21, 1971; New Yorker, August 25, 1980; Observer (London), April 25, 1971; Perspectives of New Music, vol. 16, no. 1, 1979.

Richard Strauss

1864–1949

For biographical sketch, list of earlier works, and bibliography, see *Composers Since 1900.*

It was fifty-three years before Strauss's opera, *Intermezzo* (1923), described in the score as "a bourgeois comedy with symphonic interludes in two acts," was staged in the United States. It was finally performed on February 25, 1977, in Philadelphia, by the Curtis Institute of Music at the Walnut Street Theater. Strauss's libretto is based on an episode in his life in which a mis-directed love letter creates a misunderstanding between him and his wife. John Rockwell of the New York *Times* described the music as "fas-cinating. The whole idea of this conversational libretto was for it to float over the music, which skitters along illustratively in the most brilliant-ly clever manner, then broadens out to suggest depths of emotion that the words never convey."

In 1976 Vanguard Records again released the recording (1944) of the Vienna Philharmonic Orchestra playing five of Strauss's tone poems, reminding many of his significance as a conduc-tor. In reviewing the record, Irving Kolodin said in *Stereo Review:* "This may be the most compel-ling effort ever recorded by a composer in his own behalf. . . . The result is the rarest kind of musical experience; an outpouring of pure artis-tic essence, unmarred by mannerisms, ego or intrusive counterproductive 'personality.' "

ABOUT (supplementary)

Abert, A. A., Richard Strauss: die Opern; Jefferson, A., The Life of Richard Strauss; Kennedy, M., Rich-ard Strauss; Krause, E., Richard Strauss.

New York Times, July 24, 1977.

Igor Stravinsky

1882–1971

For biographical sketch, list of earlier works, and bibliography, see *Composers Since 1900.*

From 1967 on, Stravinsky's health underwent a rapid process of deterioration including ulcers, circulatory problems, and lung congestion, which weakened his condition and convinced him to sell his home in Beverly Hills, California in 1969 and abandon Los Angeles. He estab-lished residence in New York on October 14, 1969, at the Hotel Essex and attempted to con-tinue working on the orchestration of two of Bach's Preludes and Fugues from the *Well-Tem-pered Clavier.*

In her book, *And Music at the Close: Stra-vinsky's Last Years,* Lillian Libman described his attempt: "I saw him sitting at his piano, hunched over, arms pressed against his body, his gaze fixed on a piece of white pencil-marked

paper that he had set against the open score of Bach's *Well-Tempered Clavier.* He stared and stared at the paper for fully five minutes without moving a muscle or uttering a sound. Then he placed on the piano ledge a pencil he had been holding, took the paper and carefully tore it in half; and then he placed the two pieces together and tore them again in half, dropping the pieces on the floor."

In Stravinsky's last year, his eyesight and hearing were failing and he could hardly walk. His bedroom at the Essex House resembled a hospital room. After spending time at Lenox Hill Hospital for heart and kidney complica-tions, he was able to go for a rest cure in Evian, France, in the summer of 1970. Back in New York, while waiting for a new apartment, he was back in the hospital for pulmonary edema be-tween March 18 and 30. One week after occupy-ing his new home he died of a heart attack, on April 6, 1971. A Russian Orthodox service was held in New York and, as he requested, his body was transported to Venice for burial on the is-land of San Michele. The strains of his last work, *Requiem Canticles* (1966) were sounded at his grave and memorial concerts of his works were given throughout the world.

Pierre Boulez said, "The death of Stravinsky means the final disappearance of a musical gen-eration which gave music its basic shock at the beginning of this century and which brought about the real departure from Romanticism. Something radically new, even foreign to West-ern tradition, had to be found for music to sur-vive, and to enter our contemporary era. The glory of Stravinsky was to have belonged to his extremely gifted generation and to be one of the most creative of them all."

An editorial in the New York *Times* said "By common consent Igor Stravinsky was the great-est living composer. . . . Stravinsky was a semi-nal figure, and that alone attests to his strength and assures his immortality. No minor compos-er in history has ever put his mark on the age. Only the major ones do."

Between June 18 and 25, 1972, the New York City Ballet presented a Stravinsky festival in New York in which thirty-two productions were danced (twenty-one were premieres) to Stra-vinsky's scores. A week-long Haydn-Stravinsky "Celebration," in which Stravinsky's chamber-music works were featured, was conducted by the Chamber Music Society of Lincoln Center in

New York between September 13 and 20, 1981. Even more monumental was the two-month Stravinsky festival held in London in October 1979 at which all the orchestral, chamber and instrumental solo compositions of Stravinsky were heard in eleven concerts, including music rarely heard.

ABOUT (supplementary)

Craft, R., Stravinsky: The Chronicle of a Friendship, 1948–1971; Dobrin, A., Igor Stravinsky: His Life and Time; Horgan, P., Encounters with Stravinsky: a Personal Record; Libman, L., And Music at the Close: Stravinsky's Last Years, a Personal Memoir; MacLeish, K., Stravinsky; Routh, F., Stravinsky; Stravinsky, I., and Craft, R., Retrospectives and Conclusions; Stravinsky, T., Catherine and Igor Stravinsky: a Family Album; Stravinsky, V., and Craft, R., Stravinsky; Stravinsky, V., and Craft R., (eds.), Stravinsky: In Pictures and Documents; White, E. W., Stravinsky: The Composer and His Works (2nd edition).

Intellectual Digest, August 1972; Musical Quarterly, July 1979; Opera News, October 10, 1970; Saturday Review (Stravinsky Issue), March 29, 1971; Stereo Review, November 1972.

Morton Subotnick

1933–

Morton Subotnick, an avant-garde composer, was born in Los Angeles on April 14, 1933. Both of his parents—Jack and Rose Luckerman Subotnick—were merchants by profession and amateur musicians by avocation. His father's performances on the mandolin stand out as Morton's earliest musical experiences, and are reflected in the composer's later use of the mandolin, or mandolin-like sounds, in several compositions. His mother, who only played the piano slightly, gave him his first music lessons. When he was seven, Morton decided to learn to play the trombone because he liked the way it looked, and forgetting its name, he tried to locate it on a non-illustrated list of instruments. He finally chose a clarinet because, as Joan La Barbara revealed in Notes on the Arts, "it sounded like his mental image of the trombone." Not until many years later—after studying the clarinet with Fred Stokes (1947–1951)—did he confess that the clarinet was not the instrument he originally intended to study.

Subotnick: soō bôt nĭk

MORTON SUBOTNICK

He taught himself the theoretical aspects of music by reading biographies of great composers, poring through their scores, and copying their works note by note to master their harmonic and contrapuntal practices. While attending Canfield Elementary School in Los Angeles between 1940 and 1945, Subotnick began to write piano music and compositions for chamber music combinations with whom he performed. Joan La Barbara said, "He described putting notes on a page as a sensual experience he always enjoyed, capturing the sounds, placing them on paper, and then throwing them out into the air to be enjoyed anew as an aural sensation."

He also taught himself to play other woodwind instruments, in order to alternate from one instrument to another in the orchestras of the University High School (1948–1949) and North Hollywood High School (1949–1951). He was initiated into avant-garde music at North Hollywood High School by Joel Harry who instructed him in the twelve-tone technique. For high school graduation, Subotnick wrote a score for a stage production using such techniques as polytonality, polyrhythm, and unresolved discords, very much in the style of Charles Ives whom he admired and who influenced him.

After passing the preliminary placement examinations in 1951, he entered the University of Southern California in Los Angeles on scholarship and he had his first formal composition lessons with Leon Kirchner. Then he went to Denver for two years (1951–1953), as a member of the Denver Symphony Orchestra. In 1953, he was inducted into the United States Army and stationed at the Presidio in San Francisco, where he was able to continue studying composition with Kirchner and also clarinet with Mitchell Lurie (1953–1954).

After being discharged from the army in 1956, he entered Denver University where he majored in English and received his Bachelor of Arts degree. On a graduate fellowship he went to Mills College in California in 1957 where he continued studying composition with Leon Kirchner and Darius Milhaud and earned a Master of Arts degree in 1959. From time to time, he was a substitute player with the San Francisco Symphony Orchestra.

From 1959 to 1962, Subotnick was professor of music at Mills College where he co-founded the Mills College Performing Group which was organized to present new music of young composers. As the musical director of the Ann Halperin Dance Company in San Francisco in 1961–1967, he became actively involved in the musical avant-garde movement there, in helping to program concerts for the International Society for Contemporary Music—League of Composers which provided hearings for his young and little-known contemporaries. Also involved with electronic music, Subotnick became the co-founder and director of the San Francisco Tape Music Center from 1959 to 1965 when it was absorbed by Mills College.

Subotnick's personal composing style gave evidence of creative maturity. Two serenades, the first for flute, clarinet, vibraphone, piano, and mandolin (1959), and the second for clarinet, horn, piano, and percussion (1959), revealed an inclination toward post-Webern techniques. The second serenade was presented at the Biennale Festival in Venice on April 16, 1963, after being introduced in San Francisco a year earlier. Electronic music and multi-media productions lured him away from serialism to new concepts, methods, and instrumentations of his own. Finding the concert scene decadent, he sought to create a new art form that would create a closer bond between composer and audience: one which utilized traditional instruments with electronic music; combined electronic music with films and abstract theatrical forms; and introduced game elements and audience participation. Such works included *Mandolin* (1962), scored for viola, tape, and film; and a score set to Bertolt Brecht's *The Caucasian Chalk Circle*, which was produced by the Actor's Workshop in San Francisco in 1963 and called for percussion, mandolin, narrator, solo voice, and three choristers. *The Tarot* (1963)—for ten instruments and magnetic tape—requires a "choreographed conductor"; it was first heard in 1963 at Mills College.

Between 1964 and 1966 Subotnick completed four electronic compositions collectively entitled *Play!: Play! 1* (1964) was for woodwind quintet, piano, tape, and film; *Play! 2* (1964) was for orchestra and magnetic tape; *Play! 3* (1965) required a mime and film as well as magnetic tape. The most ambitious of the series was *Play! 4* (1965), a multi-media production for four players in four successive "games," four musicians, two conductors, magnetic tape, and two films. In this work Subotnick extended the boundaries of music by combining musical sounds with cinema, theater, games, light shows, and various rituals, at times becoming aleatory.

In 1967 Subotnick returned to New York as musical director of the Lincoln Center Repertory Theater at the Lincoln Center for the Performing Arts for its initial season. Between 1967 and 1969 he served as Master Artist at the School of Arts at New York University, and as director of electronic music at the Electric Circus Discotheque in Greenwich Village, for which he wrote *Realities 1–2* (1967) and other electronic pieces.

Strange new sounds attracted many visitors to the studio on Bleecker Street in Greenwich Village where Subotnick was producing a modular electronic synthesizer designed by Donald Buchler of San Francisco. One visitor was Jack Holtzman, producer of Nonesuch Records, who commissioned Subotnick to write the first piece of electronic music solely for a recording, *Silver Apples of the Moon* (1967). Following its release, it achieved considerable publicity, becoming an early classic in electronic music and in background ballet music for the Netherland Ballet Company, the Ballet Rambert of London, and the Glen Tetley Dance Company. Subotnick produced other electronic pieces for recordings, including *The Wild Bull* (1967), *Touch* (1969), *Sidewinder* (1970), *Four Butterflies* (1971–1972), and *Until Spring* (1974). In *Electronic Music,* Elliott Schwartz described *Silver Apples of the Moon* as a "fascinating interplay of overlapping ostinati patterns (using the sequencer most delicately) and percussive noise-filtered sonorities, which alternate with a succession of lyric, often bell-like, arias. ... The general mood is quiet, restrained even in its most vigorous passages, and spacious in timbre." Schwartz said *The Wild Bull* was "far more forceful in its timbral and dynamic contrasts."

Irving Kolodin of the *Saturday Review* wrote about *Touch:* "I hear deep silences and mysterious paddings-about on an electronic marimba-like phrase. There is a disquiet and alarm and even a gigantic climax succeeded by an even more gigantic one. Then, finally, deep silence."

While he was in New York, Subotnick completed a "concert," for wind quintet, tape, lights, and the film entitled *Misfortunes of the Immortals* (1969), which was shown at the Smithsonian Institution in Washington, D.C., during the 1969–1970 season. In this work electronic sounds are combined with reminders of more traditional music, quotations from Mozart, Beethoven, Pergolesi, and Rossini. *A Ritual Game Room* (1970), a multi-media production for tape, lights, dancer, four game players, "and no audience," was premiered at the Walker Art Center in Minneapolis in 1970. This piece—and its companion pieces, *The Balance Room* and *The Game Room,* collectively named *2: Game for Two Players*—was circulated in museums and art galleries rather than concert halls. Even more off-beat is electronic music conceived by Subotnick in 1969 for a New York office building *(Music for Twelve Elevators)* and a New York toy store (no title) in which the public participated in sound production.

Subotnick was visiting professor of music at the University of Maryland in 1968–1969 and at the University of Pittsburgh in 1969–1970. In 1969, he returned to the California Institute of the Arts in Valencia as associate dean, and as director of electronic music and head of the composition department since 1972. In 1975 he was awarded a Guggenheim Fellowship.

Subotnick produced a series of compositions in which the butterfly—with its three-stage form of larva-cocoon-butterfly—serves as a basic aesthetic and philosophic metaphor, and he described his theory as follows: "The butterfly is viewed as: 1. a symmetrical form—WING-BODY-WING; 2. a metaphoric process—larva, pupa, and imago (butterfly)—the idealized image of the larva. The symmetrical view provides all the external and internal 'shaping' qualities. The metaphoric view essentially says

that at all levels the three-part form (wing-body-wing) will progress in such a way that the first wing will be larva-like, the body will be pupa-like (transformations will be taking place but hidden from the viewer), and the final wing will be the butterfly or imago—the idealized self image of the original material."

Four Butterflies and *Until Spring,* already listed as recordings, belong in the metaphoric butterfly category as well as his two most ambitious and prestigious compositions for orchestra which follow. On a grant from the National Endowment for the Arts he spent seven months in 1974 writing *Two Butterflies for Amplified Orchestra* which was introduced by the Los Angeles Philharmonic under Zubin Mehta on April 17, 1975. This work is in two principal sections: "Butterfly 1" consists of WING A—BODY ("noise" transformed) and WING B; "Butterfly 2" is made up of WING A (identical performance but transformed by the addition of ten violins fitted with contact microphones)—BODY ("music" transformed)—WING B (again, an identical performance transformed by the addition of the violins). The composer explained: "The butterfly metaphor provides a pre-compositional set of guide lines or 'rules' which eventually have a strong effect on the compositional process and, finally, the end produced which will be experienced by the audience." The orchestra is divided into several groups of instruments, some amplified, others modifying the amplified sound in various ways (such as altering up or down in pitch from a sixteenth of a tone to a minor third). In reviewing the premiere for *High Fidelity/Musical America,* Melody Peterson said: "One admired the adroit ordering and coloristic display of amplified and timbrally modified instruments, of violas and cellos tuned at a quarter tone variance from one another, of claps and whispers, delicate trilling, bow tapping, key clicking and the like."

In commemoration of the American bicentennial, Subotnick was one of six major American composers commissioned by the National Endowment for the Arts to write compositions for performance by America's six leading orchestras. In fulfilling this commission, Subotnick returned to his "butterfly" metaphor in *Before the Butterfly* (1974–1975) in which he aspired to capture, as he explained, "the idea of emergence, or more precisely, the moment before emergence —the moment before transformation—the moment before breaking free—before change—*Before the Butterfly.*" The world premiere of the work took place in Los Angeles on February 26, 1976, with Zubin Mehta conducting the Los Angeles Philharmonic Orchestra. Later it was performed by the Chicago Symphony, the Boston Symphony, the Cleveland Orchestra, the New York Philharmonic, and the Philadelphia Orchestra. The composer discussed the three distinct sections of the work: "Each of the three sections makes its own move 'to become' and each draws from the preceding movement the most emergent qualities as its basis or starting point. In composing the work, I referred to the three as: the sea of G; the scherzo of chaos; and the wilderness/echoes of reunification. ... (a suggestion of reunification)." In contrasting this work with its predecessor, *Two Butterflies,* Melody Peterson noted in *High Fidelity/Musical America:* "*Before* utilizes electronically modified instruments in a manner far more coloristically concise and formally chiselled than its predecessor. Although seven minutes longer (for a total of about twenty minutes), the three sections of *Before* pass quickly and produce results that are not only more interesting but more likeable than *Two Butterflies.*" Joan La Barbara, also of *High Fidelity/Musical America,* described *Before the Butterfly* as follows: "Here is a composition that approaches the orchestra as a unit as well as a compendium of technically proficient individuals, and it makes use of modern electronic technology with delicacy. Beginning with a single tone in the violin ... the sound begins to expand gradually, utilizing close tuning to create beats (the vibrations caused by colliding sound waves), tasteful electronics to emphasize this rhythmic character, and shimmering sounds with quiet percussive pops and taps from the cellos. Some particularly beautiful moments included the plucked harp tones that caused lovely rippling sounds, the strings descending glissandos with bounced bows causing a gentle tap at the end of this slide, the highly effective rapid pulsing tones (synthesizer enhanced or induced) and the charming visual effect of the entire violin section strumming their instruments like mandolins.... One is left with the anticipation of the miracle of the butterfly's emergence, something just on the brink of occurring without ever reaching the event itself."

In the late 1970s, Subotnick turned to writing "ghost pieces" for solo instruments and tape, in which, as we learn from a press release from Subotnick's publisher, the Theodore Presser Company, that "the tape contains no audible sound—it is a 'ghost score' containing recorded information which triggers other electronic equipment ... that modifies instrumental sounds as they are played—the soloist providing, in a sense, his own electronic accompaniment. The electronic modifications include the capacity to change the pitch, timbre, volume, and directionality of the sounds; the electronic tape specifies its own set of attacks and rhythms, adding another whole dimension to the sound of the instrument or voice."

One of these "ghost pieces," *Liquid Strata,* for piano (1977)—described as a "response to Newton's insights about fundamental realities of nature"—was written for Ralph Grierson who introduced it on June 11, 1977, at the Ojai Music Festival in California. It is a three-part composition comprised of a fantasy, toccata, and postlude. Daniel Gariaga in the Los Angeles *Times* wrote, "Each demands from the solo pianist extreme digital control and concentration. The tape, whether one considers it distortion or enhancement—and in actuality it is both—is the strongest unifying element here, yet it is subordinate to the composer's vision of the total. The toccata—fast, furious and as exciting as a fistfight—is the focal point, but the real sonic messages of the piece are contained in the silence-dotted-outer sections."

Other "ghost pieces" include *Wild Beasts,* for trombone and piano, *Passages of the Beast,* for clarinet, *The Life Histories,* for voice and clarinet, all written in 1978, and *The Last Dream of the Beast,* for voice (1979), which was sung by Joan La Barbara for the first time on March 2, 1979, in New York, in a concert devoted exclusively to Subotnick's "ghost" music.

Subotnick received a $4,000 award from the American Academy and Institute of Arts and Letters in 1979. At his home and studio in Santa Monica, he takes a three-mile morning run in a park overlooking the Pacific Ocean before beginning the day's work. All of his time belongs to music and art, and raising a son and daughter from his first marriage to Linn Pottle. Subotnick's second marriage to Doreen Nelson, in 1976, also ended in divorce two years later.

MAJOR WORKS

Chamber Music—Serenade No. 1, for flute, clarinet,

vibraphone, cello, piano, and mandolin; Serenade No. 2, for clarinet, horn, piano, and percussion.

Electronic Music—The Tarot, for flute, oboe, trumpet, trombone, three percussion, piano, viola, bass, magnetic tape, and "choreographed conductor"; Serenade No. 3, for flute, clarinet, violin, piano, and tape; Silver Apples of the Moon; The Wild Bull; Realities 1–2; Touch; Sidewinder; Two Life Histories, for clarinet, voice, and electronic "ghost" score; The Wild Beasts, for trombone, piano, and electronic "ghost" score; Until Spring; Passages of the Beast, for clarinet and electronic "ghost" score; Ice Flow; Parallel Lines, for piccolo and electronic "ghost" score; A Sky of Cloudless Sulphur; The Last Dream of the Beast, for voice and electronic score; Axoltol, for cello and electronic "ghost" score.

Multi-Media—Mandolin, for viola, tape, and film; Play! No. 1, for woodwind quintet, piano, tape, and film; Play! No. 3, for mime, tape, and film; Play! No. 4, for four game players, two conductors, four musicians, tape, and two films; Misfortune of the Immortals, A Concert, for woodwind quintet, lights, films, and tape; A Ritual Game Room, the Balance Room, the Game Room, three game pieces for four game players, electronic sounds, lights, dancer, and "no audience."

Orchestral Music—Play! No. 2, for orchestra, conductor, and tape; Laminations, for orchestra and electronic sounds; Two Butterflies, for amplified orchestra; Before the Butterfly; Place.

Piano Music—Prelude No. 3, for piano and electronic sounds; Prelude No. 4, for piano and electronic sounds; Liquid Strata, for piano and electronic "ghost" score.

ABOUT

Schwartz, E., Electronic Music; A Listener's Guide; Thomson, V., American Music Since 1910; Vinton, J. (ed.), Dictionary of Contemporary Music.

Musical Journal, January 1970.

Joseph Suk

1874–1935

For biographical sketch, list of earlier works, and bibliography, see *Composers Since 1900*.

Suk's complete works for the piano were recorded in a five-disk album by Pavel Stepan, and released in 1979 by Supraphon.

Carlos Surinach

1915–

Carlos Surinach was born in Barcelona on March 4, 1915, where his father, Luis Surinach, of Catalan extraction, was a stock broker; his mother, Ascension Wrokovna Surinach, was of Austro-Polish background. She was an excellent pianist who had been awarded first prize in piano at the Royal Conservatory in Madrid, and she became his first piano teacher until he was thirteen. She also took him to performances of operas and ballets (but not to concerts) in Barcelona and he became acquainted with and fascinated by the symphony orchestra. His father tolerated his musical activity providing he received good marks in his academic studies. Since Carlos was an excellent student in elementary school and, later, as baccalaureate, there was no paternal interference with his continuous musical training.

When Carlos was fourteen, he entered the Caminals Academy of Music where his piano teacher was José Caminals, a former pupil of Granados. Surinach recalled, "He was a good teacher and a good music-father, but he was fascinated by two wonder children he had as piano students whose shadows became my nightmares. Nevertheless I continued to study at the Academy for seven years where the influence on me of my fellow students replaced that of my mother. We learned from each other by freely exchanging opinions and ideas."

He emerged from the Caminals Academy as an excellent pianist and musical theorist, and went on to study composition privately with Enrique Morera, director of the Municipal Conservatory in Barcelona for three years. Surinach avoided military action in the Spanish Civil War by doing office work for the army in uniform. After his day's office work, he studied musical scores and composed one of his earliest works, *Tres Canciones,* for voice and piano (or small orchestra). It was based on texts by Federico García Lorca and Antonio Machado and became his first composition to be published. This effort to compose revealed the far-reaching influence of Spanish music on his creativity.

Morera advised Surinach to continue his

Surinach: soo͞' re̅ näk

Surinach

CARLOS SURINACH

musical education in Germany despite the fact that Nazi Germany was at war, telling him, "Hitler will collapse, Germany will survive, and if you go, the musical education you get there will be yours forever." Surinach went to Düsseldorf in November 1940 on an Alexander von Humboldt Fellowship to study with Hugo Balzer and other teachers at the Robert Schumann Conservatory who prepared him for admission to the Academy of Fine Arts in Berlin. At the Academy, he became a *"Meisterschuler"* in composition with Max Trapp, under whose guidance he composed three works: a Sonatina for piano; a Quartet for Piano and Strings; and *Sinfonia-Passacaglia* for large orchestra. In these pieces he unconsciously used the eight-note flamenco scale. Many years later, the Quartet was performed in New York, and Virgil Thomson reviewed it in the New York *Herald Tribune:* "Clarity and tenderness are his especial gift, brilliancy and instrumental imagination are his charm.... His Piano Quartet ... has a structural integration rare in Spanish music and a loveliness of sentiment rare in any."

The musical environment of Berlin was rich and varied even in wartime and he attended concerts by the Berlin Philharmonic, recitals by Gieseking, Bakhaus, and others, and became acquainted with such new works as Carl Orff's *Carmina Burana,* Heinrich Sutermeister's opera *Romeo and Juliet,* and older ones such as Richard Strauss's *Salome* and *Elektra,* enriching his musical background.

Surinach returned to Barcelona in the spring of 1942, and found employment as assistant conductor of the Gran Teatro del Liceo Opera House and conductor of the Barcelona Philharmonic Orchestra in 1944. At one of his orchestral concerts, he introduced his *Sinfonia-Passacaglia* on April 8, 1945. When the war ended, he had such a busy conducting schedule in Western Europe that composition dwindled, but the small handful of compositions included a ballet, *Monte Carlo,* whose scenario described fickle fortunes at the gaming tables. The ballet was produced by the Ballets de Paul Goubé at the Teatro Coliseum in Barcelona on May 2, 1945; a one-act opera, *El Mozo que Casó con Mujer Brava (The Bridegroom Who Married a Wild Woman),* which was introduced in Barcelona on January 10, 1948; and Symphony No. 2, which had its world premiere in Paris on January 26, 1950, by the Orchestre Nationale de la RTF, with the composer conducting. Surinach said that in his Symphony, "my aim of writing new Spanish music that was at once more primitive and more advanced was set. This was elemental music, sophisticated music, whose basis was the Flamenco scale. It was partly homophonic, partly polyphonic, with a good deal of motor energy."

From 1947 to 1950, Surinach lived in Paris where he conducted several orchestras and became a friend of such famous French composers as Poulenc, Auric, Honegger, and Messiaen.

By 1950, Surinach was on his way to becoming the conductor of the Quito Symphony in South America, and stopped off in New York, where he found a lucrative occupation writing jingles for television commercials. He conducted two concerts of contemporary chamber music at the Museum of Modern Art in May 1952 and on May 5 he premiered his *Ritmo Jondo,* for clarinet, trumpet, tamburo, xylophone, timpani, and hand clappers. On April 15, 1953, *Ritmo Jondo,* revised and enlarged, accompanied the ballet, *Deep Rhythm,* with choreography by Doris Humphrey. Commissioned by the Bethsabee de Rothschild Foundation, it was presented by José Limon and his company. Later, in 1953, *Tientos,* for harpsichord, English horn, and timpani, was commissioned by the harpsichordist Sylvia Marlowe, and heard in New York on November 11. *Sinfonietta Flamenca* (1954) was premiered in Louisville, Kentucky, on January 9, 1954, with Robert Whitney conducting. It was commissioned by the Louisville Orchestra, under a

Rockefeller Foundation grant. Reviewing *Sinfonietta* in *Musical Quarterly,* Henry Cowell called it the cream of the crop of Louisville Orchestra commissions. "The work is traditionally Spanish in its use of frenetic color and fantastic melismas, with contrasts between overwhelmingly piercing rapid highs and lyrically Oriental lows. . . . For the most part, he goes directly to the historical mainstream of melody and rhythm as sources for very skilled and sophisticated development, the result of which pleases and excites the layman, for it is not abstruse; yet it offers plenty to provoke interest in the most erudite musicians."

Looking back at the first performances in the United States, Surinach said: "My American career had begun." He has remained in America ever since, establishing permanent residence in New York City and becoming an American citizen in 1959, with new successes. The *Concertino for Piano, Strings and Cymbals* (1956) was commissioned by MGM records and received its first hearing on February 9, 1957, by the MGM Orchestra under the composer's direction, with William Masselos as soloist. The music was then used in two successful ballets: *La Sibila,* performed by the John Butler Dance Company at the Festival of Two Worlds in Spoleto, Italy, on July 3, 1959, and *Celebrants,* with choreography by Robert Cohen, which was produced by the Bath-Sheba Dance Company of Israel in Tel Aviv on November 25, 1963. *Sinfonia Chica* (1957) had its premiere by the Musical Arts Society Orchestra of La Jolla, California (which commissioned it) on August 6, 1957, with the composer conducting. In 1958, Surinach provided the score for the first of several ballets choreographed by Martha Graham and danced by her company. On commission from the Bethsabee de Rothschild Foundation he wrote the music for *Embattled Garden,* presented by the Martha Graham Dance Company in New York on April 3, 1958; since the premiere, this ballet has enjoyed over five hundred performances. *Paeans and Dances of Heathen Iberia,* written in 1959 on commission from the American Wind Symphony of Pittsburgh for the bicentennial celebration of the founding of the city of Pittsburgh, was first performed on June 15, 1959, with Robert Austin Boudreau conducting. The Pittsburgh *Post-Gazette* described the performance as "by turns fiery, vigorous and wholly vital. . . . He is a master of effects also, and his choice of orchestral dispersal is admirable. . . . The dances are vigorous and buoyant, and their carefree and virile open-air attitudes are wholly ingratiating."

Discussing Surinach's early works in *The Music of Spain,* Gilbert Chase wrote: "Sharply etched lines, dissonant clashes, emphasis on the sheer primitive power of rhythm, and strong reliance on percussion, give Surinach's music a 20th century accent that contrasts with the post-impressionistic language prevalent in most contemporary Spanish composition. . . . He has made the 'Flamenco Kingdom' his musical domain."

In subsequent works, the Spanish influence in Surinach's writing remained persistently pronounced, invariably structured on the eight-tone Flamenco scale. Surinach explained, "Unlike the twelve-tone row, this scale allows for modulation, cadences or points of rest; arrival or conclusion—although these are not like cadences of the tonal system."

Since 1958, Surinach has continued to be an outstandingly gifted and successful composer for ballet and he has often said (quoting Cervantes): "If you are born Italian, you sing, if German, you play, if Spanish, from the moment you are out of the womb you dance." He wrote three additional scores for Martha Graham, beginning with *Acrobats of God* (1960), which was performed by the Martha Graham Dance Company in New York on April 27, 1960, and five hundred more performances since. In reviewing the work in the New York *Herald Tribune,* Walter Terry singled out Surinach's music for special attention. "The specially commissioned score by Carlos Surinach which involved the presence of three mandolinists on the stage has both Spanish color and a gay theatrical exuberance perfectly suited to Miss Graham's joyful scheme." *Chronique,* in which Martha Graham's choreography is based on poems by St. John Perse, was produced in New York on April 19, 1974. *The Owl and the Pussycat,* based on the famous poem of Edward Lear, with Miss Graham's choreography, was introduced in New York on June 26, 1978. Even in the score of this work, the Spanish influence is present, since it includes a tango.

Surinach provided ballet scores for other dance groups as well. *David and Bath-Sheba,* commissioned by CBS-TV, with choreography by John Butler, was presented on the television network on May 15, 1960. (The same score was used for still another ballet: *A Place in the Desert,* with choreography by Norman Morrice, and the Ballet Rambert presented it at Sadler's Wells in London on July 25, 1961.) *Apasionada* was commissioned by Pearl Lang and performed by her company in New York on January 5, 1962. *Feast of Ashes,* written on commission from the Rebekah Harkness Foundation, was first performed on November 30, 1962, by the Robert Joffrey Ballet Company (with choreography by Alvin Ailey) in Lisbon, Portugal. (Less than a year later, it was presented eighteen times by the Joffrey Ballet troupe in the Soviet Union.) *Venta Quemada* was premiered by the Harkness Ballet at the Festival of Dance in Cannes, France on March 12, 1966, with choreography by George Skibine; it was also commissioned by the Rebekah Harkness Foundation. The Paul Taylor Dance Company presented *Agathe's Tale,* with Paul Taylor's choreography, in New London, Connecticut, on August 12, 1967, after being commissioned by the Dance Festival of Connecticut College. *Suite Española,* with choreography by José de Udaeta, was commissioned by the Rebekah Harkness Foundation and presented in Barcelona on October 6, 1970, by the Harkness ballet. *Bodas de Sangre,* based on a stage drama by García Lorca, with choreography by Miguel Terekhov, was written for the Oklahoma University School of Drama, Department of Dance, and performed in Norman, Oklahoma, on April 25, 1979.

Surinach has been equally active and successful in writing for the concert stage. *Symphonic Variations* was introduced by the Phoenix Symphony Orchestra under Guy Taylor in Arizona on May 25, 1963. The Detroit Symphony, under Sixten Ehrling, performed *Melorhythmic Dramas,* a seven-movement orchestral suite, at the Meadow Brook Music Festival (which commissioned it) in Rochester, Michigan, on August 16, 1966. Howard Klein reported to the New York *Times* that the work "caught fire. . . . The audience cheered for fifteen minutes." *Missions of San Antonio,* a symphonic canticle in five parts for orchestra and male chorus with texts in Latin from medieval Spanish prayers, was performed on January 25, 1969, by the San Antonio Orchestra under Victor Alessandro before being televised nationally by CBS the following June 15. (CBS and the San Antonio Orchestra together commissioned it.) *String Quartet,* commissioned by the Grand Rapids Symphony Society

of Michigan, was heard at the Canary Islands Music Festival in Las Palmas on May 21, 1975. *Piano Concerto,* written for Alicia de Larrocha, was premiered in Grand Rapids, Michigan, on November 13, 1974, with the Minnesota Symphony under Stanislaw Skrowaczewski. *Concerto for Harp and Orchestra* was performed first in Michigan on February 15, 1979, by Nicanor Zabaleta and the Grand Rapids Symphony under Theo Alcantara.

In 1955, Surinach transcribed seven pieces for orchestra from Albéniz's *Iberia,* suite for piano which Eugene Ormandy and the Philadelphia Orchestra performed in 1956.

Surinach, who is a bachelor, lives in an apartment in New York City, frequently traveling to Europe to conduct its major orchestras. He conducted the orchestra at the Festival of 20th Century Music in Rome when Leontyne Price made her Italian debut, and the orchestra at the world premiere on August 19, 1961, of Peggy Glanville-Hicks's opera, *Nausicaa,* in Athens. In 1966–1967 he was visiting professor of composition at the Carnegie-Mellon University of Pittsburgh and, from 1974 to 1976, adjunct professor of music at Queens College of the City University of New York. In 1969 he received the Arnold Bax medal in Great Britain, and in 1972 he was named Knight Commander of the Order of Isabella I of Castile by the Spanish government.

MAJOR WORKS

Ballets —Monte Carlo; Ritmo Jondo; Embattled Garden; Acrobats of God; David and Bath-Sheba; Apasionada; Feast of Ashes; Los Renegados; Venta Quemada; Agathe's Tale; Suite Española; Chronique; The Owl and the Pussycat; Bodas de Sangre.

Chamber Music—Quartet, for piano and strings; Tres Cantos Berberes, for flute, oboe, clarinet, viola, cello, and harp; Tientos, for harp (or harpsichord), English horn, and timpani; Flamenco Cyclothymia, for violin and piano; String Quartet.

Choral Music—Cantata of St. John, for chorus and percussion; Songs of the Soul, for a cappella chorus; Missions of San Antonio, symphonic canticle for men's chorus and orchestra; Via Crucis, for chorus and guitar; Celebraciones Medievales, for chorus and symphonic band.

Guitar Music—Sonatina; Una Rosa en Cada Galata, for two guitars.

Orchestral Music—Passacaglia-Symphony; Symphony No. 2; Sinfonietta Flamenca; Doppio Concertino, for violin, piano, and chamber orchestra; Concertino, for piano, strings, and cymbals; Feria Magica, overture; Fandango; Madrid 1890, suite; Sinfonia Chica; Concerto for Orchestra; Paeans and Dances of Heathen

Iberia, for band symphony; Symphonic Variations; Drama Jondo, overture; Melorhythmic Dramas; Las Trompetas de los Serafimes, overture; Concerto for Piano and Orchestra; Concerto for Harp and Orchestra.

Piano Music—Sonatina; Flamenquerias, for two pianos; Tales from the Flamenco Kingdom, children's suite; Trois Chansons et Dances Espagñoles.

Vocal Music—Romance Oracion y Saeta, for voice and piano (also for orchestra); Flamenco Meditations, for voice and piano; Prayers, for voice and guitar; Tres Cantares, for voice and piano, also for orchestra; Tres Canciones, for voice and piano, also orchestra.

ABOUT

Chase, G., The Music of Spain; Vinton, J. (ed.), Dictionary of Contemporary Music.

BMI, Many Worlds of Music, Winter 1976.

Heinrich Sutermeister

1910–

For biographical sketch, list of earlier works, and bibliography, see *Composers Since 1900.*

As the dean of Swiss composers, Sutermeister's premieres for most of his later major works took place in Switzerland, including *Sérénade pour Montreux,* for two oboes, two horns, and string orchestra (1970), performed at the Montreux Festival on September 17, 1970, by the chamber orchestra of the Paris Radio under the direction of André Girard; *Ecclesia,* for vocal soloists and orchestra (1972–1973), was performed in Lausanne on October 19, 1975, under the direction of Robert Mermond with Herrat Eickel and Etienne Bettens as soloists; Concerto No. 2 for Cello and Orchestra (1971), performed in Geneva by Esther Nyffeneger, soloist, and the Orchestre de la Suisse Romande conducted by Wolfgang Sawallisch on November 27, 1974; *Te Deum,* for soprano, chorus, and orchestra (1975), performed in Zurich on November 25, 1975, with Hans Erisman conducting and Kari Lovas as soloist; *Quadrifoglio* (1977), a concerto for flute, oboe, clarinet, bassoon, and orchestra, was performed in Bern on December 1, 1977, with Charles Dutoit conducting the Bern Orchestra; and *Consolatio Philosophiae,* dramatic scene for high voice and orchestra (1979), was performed in Geneva on February 21, 1979, with Wolfgang Sawallisch conducting the Or-

chestre de la Suisse Romande and Peter Schreier as soloist.

Between 1963 and 1975, Sutermeister taught composition at the Hochschule für Musik in Hanover. In 1977, he was elected to membership in the Bavarian Academy of Fine Arts.

MAJOR WORKS (supplementary)

Chamber Music—Modeste Mignon, for ten wind instruments.

Operas—La Croisade des Enfants, TV opera; Der Flaschenteufel, TV opera; Maikafer-Komödie, TV opera.

Choral Music—Der Kaiser von China, for male chorus; Drei Lieder, for children's chorus; Omni ad Unam, for baritone, chorus, and orchestra; Ecclesia, for vocal soloists, chorus, and orchestra; Te Deum, for soprano, chorus, and orchestra.

Orchestral Music—Sérénade pour Montreux, for two oboes, two horns, and string orchestra; Concerto No. 2, for cello and orchestra; Concerto for Clarinet and Orchestra; Quadrifoglio, Concerto for flute, oboe, clarinet, bassoon, and orchestra.

Piano Music—Winterferein.

Vocal Music—Consolatio Philosophiae, dramatic scene for high voice and orchestra.

ABOUT (supplementary)

Larese, D., Heinrich Sutermeister.

William Sydeman

1928–

For biographical sketch, list of earlier works, and bibliography, see *Composers Since 1900.*

Sydeman's *Malediction,* for tenor, speaking actor, string quartet, and tape, with a text derived from Laurence Sterne's *Tristram Shandy,* was introduced in New York on February 5, 1971.

MAJOR WORKS (supplementary)

Chamber Music—Trio, for bassoon, bass clarinet, and piano; Duo, for horn and piano; Duo, for percussion; Duo, for violin and double bass; Trio Montagnana, for clarinet, cello, and piano; Five Movements, for winds; Duo, for two clarinets; Fugue, for string quartet; Duo, for two horns; Eighteen Duos, for two violins; The Last Orpheus, for two flutes; Duo, for clarinet and saxophone; Duo, for xylophone and vibraphone.

Electronic Music—Projections No. 1, for amplified violin, tape, and slides; Malediction, for tenor, speaking actor, string quartet, and tape.

Szymanowski

Orchestral Music—Texture Studies.

Vocal Music—Full Circle, for three solo voices, clarinet, trombone, percussion, and organ.

ABOUT (supplementary)

Reich, N. B. (ed.), Catalog of the Works of William Sydeman; Vinton, J. (ed.), Dictionary of Contemporary Music.

Karol Szymanowski

1882–1932

For biographical sketch, list of earlier works, and bibliography, see *Composers Since 1900.*

In 1978, the simultaneous release of four recorded albums of Szymanowski's music attracted attention to Poland's foremost 20th century composer. The records included: the complete recording of the opera *King Roger* (Qualiton Records); the two violin concertos (Qualiton Records); Symphony No. 2 (Qualiton Records); and *Symphonie Concertante,* for piano and orchestra, with various solo piano compositions (Unicorn Records).

Szymanowski's opera, *King Roger* (1918–1924), received its American premiere on May 10, 1981, in a concert performance by the St. Louis Symphony Orchestra, with Leonard Slatkin conducting.

The publication of all of Szymanowski's compositions, in 26 volumes, took place in Cracow in 1966.

ABOUT (supplementary)

Chylińska, T., Szymanowski; Rubinstein, A., My Young Years; Sadie, S. (ed.), The New Grove Dictionary of Music and Musicians.

Toru Takemitsu

1930–

Toru Takemitsu, who was born in Tokyo, Japan, on October 8, 1930, is primarily self-taught in music. While attending the Keikwa Middle School in Tokyo, from which he was graduated in 1948, he briefly studied composition privately

---

Toru Takemitsu: tô rōo tä kä' mǐt sōo

TORU TAKEMITSU

with Yasuji Kiyose, the sole formal instruction in music he ever received. Kiyose was the director of a progressive musical group of which Takemitsu was a member between 1950 and 1952. At one of its concerts in December 1950, *Lento for Piano* (1950), a dissonant composition by Takemitsu, became his first work to be given a public performance.

In 1951, Takemitsu helped found and became a member of an avant-garde group called "Experimental Work Shop," which was made up of composers, painters, poets, and musical performers. For the group, he composed *Pause Uninterrupted I,* for two pianos (1952), in which he experimented with dissonances, irregular rhythms, and the absence of bar lines. This work was followed by *Chamber Concerto,* for thirteen instruments (1955) which was novel in its use of sonority.

Takemitsu became involved in electronic music in 1955, beginning with such experimental works for magnetic tape as *Static Relief* (1955) and *Vocalism A-I* (1956). Both works were performed in New York in March 1961 by the United States section of the International Society for Contemporary Music.

The first Takemitsu composition to draw international attention was *Requiem,* for strings (1957). It was introduced on June 20, 1958 by the Tokyo Symphony Orchestra conducted by Masashi Ueda. Its European premiere took place on May 17, 1963, in Hamburg, Germany, where it was performed by the North German Radio Orchestra. An American premiere followed on July 18, 1963, at the Ravinia Festival in Chicago, with Seiji Ozawa conducting. *Requiem* has no text, nor does it have the customary subdivisions of the traditional liturgical requiem Mass. The one-movement orchestral elegy in three parts was described as follows by Edward Downes in program notes for the New York Philharmonic concert under Ozawa on March 21, 1965: "The opening and closing sections correspond in mood and thematic material. For the most part, the string choir is subdivided into anywhere from ten to a dozen sections. An almost impressionistic mood is established in the opening page with the entire muted string choir sounding dissonant, in part polytonal harmonies. . . . The middle section . . . is played without mutes and is slightly more vigorous, although it rarely rises above a mezzo forte. The *Requiem* is rounded off with a return to the themes and the muted mood of the opening, dying away to silence in the end."

Winning a number of awards during the next few years added further to Takemitsu's fame in Japan. In 1958 he won first prize at the Contemporary Music Composition Competition organized by the Institute of 20th Century Music in Japan, for *Le Son Calligraphie I* (1958), a four-minute (thirty-one measure) piece for two string quartets. *Requiem,* for strings, won first prize at the Tokyo Contemporary Music Festival in 1960. In 1961, *Ring,* for lute, flute, and guitar (1961) won the German Ambassador's Prize at the fourth Contemporary Music Festival in Osaka. Outside Japan, *Coral Island* (1962), for soprano and orchestra, with a poem by Makoto Ooka as text, won the fifth citation of the International Rostrum of Composers (UNESCO) at its introduction in Paris by the Japan Philharmonic under Akeo Wantanabe, with Mutsumi Masuda as soloist, in 1963.

In the *Requiem, Le Son Calligraphie I and II,* and several works from the 1950s such as *Tableau Noir,* for narrator and orchestra (1958) and *Solitude Sonore* for orchestra (1958), Takemitsu was influenced both by the atonality of Berg and Schoenberg and the harmonic and rhythmic vocabulary of Messiaen. In his principal works of the 1960s and thereafter, he successfully brought about a union between Japanese modalities and melodic features, and sometimes between traditional Japanese instruments and ultra-modern techniques of Western music. He called for a native Japanese instrument, the biwa

(a lute), for the first time in his score for the Japanese film *Seppuku* (1962) which was selected as the best screen music heard at the Mainichi Music Festival in Tokyo. His first concert work for Japanese instruments was completed four years later: the widely performed and highly acclaimed *Eclipse* (1966) for biwa and shakuhachi (bamboo flute). His works, whether for Western or Japanese instruments, demonstrate the importance of silence as well as sound, as he indicated: "To make the voice of silence live is to make the infinity of sounds. Sound and silence are equal."

In 1964, Takemitsu was invited by the East-West Center of the University of Hawaii to lecture at the Festival of Arts of the 20th Century in Hawaii. His composition *Textures,* for piano and orchestra, commissioned by the Koussevitzky Music Foundation, was introduced by the French Radio Orchestra in October 1965 and won first prize from the Tribune of Composers of UNESCO in Paris. When *Dorian Horizon,* for two string ensembles (1965), was premiered by the San Francisco Symphony under Aaron Copland in February 1967, it was awarded the Music Critics of the West Coast prize; it was also performed at the Festival of the International Society for Contemporary Music in Warsaw on September 9, 1968.

In 1967, Takemitsu was invited by the Rockefeller Foundation to spend six months in New York. On commission from the New York Philharmonic Orchestra to commemorate its 125th anniversary, Takemitsu wrote *November Steps,* a double concerto for the biwa, shakuhachi, and orchestra; it was introduced on November 9, 1967, with Ozawa conducting, and became the composer's most frequently played composition. *Asterism,* for piano and orchestra, with aleatory and improvisational passages, was written in 1968 on commission from RCA, and its first performance was by the Toronto Symphony Orchestra under Ozawa on January 14, 1969. At that concert of Takemitsu's works, *Green (November Steps II),* written in 1967, was also introduced. Both new works, and the older *Dorian Horizon* and *Requiem,* were recorded for RCA at this time by the Toronto Symphony under Ozawa.

In 1968, Takemitsu was guest composer at the Canberra Festival in Australia; in 1970, he was called upon to design the "Space Theater," a hall equipped with laser beams and 800 speakers, at

Takemitsu

Expo '70 at Osaka, and to organize and direct the "Music Today" concert series there; in 1971 he, Stravinsky, and Stockhausen were invited as visiting composers to the International Contemporary Music Week (Semaines Musicales Internationales) in Paris, and he was visiting composer at the Marlboro Festival in Vermont where Leon Kirchner conducted several of his works; in 1972, he participated in "The Encounter Series" at the California Institute of Technology; and in 1973 he became artistic director and organizer of the "Music Today" festival in Tokyo.

He wrote *Cassiopeia,* for solo percussion and orchestra, in 1970 on commission from the Ravinia Festival in Chicago where it received its first hearing on July 8, 1971; it was performed again on the 28th by the Boston Symphony under Ozawa at the Berkshire Music Festival in Tanglewood, Massachusetts. In 1974, a Takemitsu Festival was held at the Nissei Theater in Tokyo to celebrate the centenary of the Nissei Music Series. *Gitimalya,* for marimba and orchestra (1975), was commissioned by Michiko Takahashi, who performed it in November 1975 with the Rotterdam Philharmonic Orchestra conducted by Edo de Waart. *Quatrain,* for violin, clarinet, cello, piano, and orchestra, which was commissioned by the Tokyo radio station, was introduced by "Tashi" and the New Japan Philharmonic with Ozawa conducting on September 1, 1975, and it was awarded the Odaka Prize as the best new orchestral work heard in Japan that year.

When the San Francisco Symphony under Edo de Waart introduced *A Flock Descends Into the Pentagonal Garden* (1977) on November 30, 1977 (commissioned for the orchestra by Dr. and Mrs. Ralph L. Dorfman), it received, according to Alfred Frankenstein in *High Fidelity/Musical America,* a "wildly enthusiastic reception." The program notes, by Heuwell Tircuit of the San Francisco *Chronicle,* referred to Takemitsu as "probably one of the five top composers of the present day." Frankenstein added that "the work is a study in the use of pentatonic modes—five of them. It moves slowly, with quiet grandeur, occasionally attaining a quasi-Wagnerian symphonic utterance, as does the music of Debussy himself. But it is considerably more dissonant than Debussy, and since de Waart laid down the baton for a considerable stretch during the course of this twenty-minute work, part of it

must be aleatory. The orchestration uses Debussy's greyed pastel colors with, of course, much emphasis on the solo oboe."

Two of Takemitsu's subsequent major works were also commissioned. For the tenth anniversary of the Tokyo String Quartet, Takemitsu wrote his first string quartet (1980), in a single movement. It bears the subtitle "A Way a Lone," inspired by the following line from James Joyce's *Finnegans Wake:* "The keys to Given! A way a lone a last a long the." The Tokyo String Quartet presented the world premiere in New York on February 23, 1981, and Donal Henahan wrote about it in the New York *Times:* "Mr. Takemitsu's piece concentrates, like most of his music, on playing with sonorities in extremely refined and sensitive ways. ... The notation is precise and fully spelled out (no aleatory ad libbing allowed in this one) and much use is made of the plaintive and eerie whistle of string harmonics. The music, while systematically atonal and charged with a muted but suffocating intensity, makes a strong and immediate appeal."

A musical group in Tokyo, the Minsh Ongaku Kyokai, commissioned *Far calls. Coming far!,* for violin and orchestra (1980). Ida Kavafian (for whom it was written) performed the premiere with the Tokyo Metropolitan Orchestra, on May 24, 1980, with Tadaaki Odaka conducting. The American premiere followed in February 1981 at a concert of the San Francisco Symphony Orchestra, with Edo de Waart conducting, and Ida Kavafian as soloist again.

Takemitsu has also written music for more than seventy Japanese films, the most famous of which are *Hara Kiri, Kwaidan, Woman in the Dunes, Silence,* and *Empire of Passion.* Between February 23 and March 8, 1981, the Japanese Film Center in New York presented thirteen Japanese films with Takemitsu's music. Simultaneously, RCA released a ten-disk album containing the thirteen scores.

In 1977, a concert devoted exclusively to Takemitsu's works and directed by Morton Feldman, was presented by the Creative and Performing Arts Center at the State University of New York in Buffalo. A year later, an "Evening of Takemitsu's Works" was performed by the Tokyo Metropolitan Orchestra under Iwaki in Tokyo.

In 1975, Takemitsu was visiting professor of composition at Yale University; in 1976 he was invited to tour China; and in 1978 he served on the jury for the International Competitions for Excellence in the Performance of American Music, in Washington, D.C. He was also artistic adviser for the Festival d'Automne in Paris where eighteen concerts of Japanese music were presented.

Takemitsu said, "I would like to develop in two directions at once, as a Japanese in tradition and as a Westerner in innovation. Deep within myself, I would like to keep two music genres, both of which have their own rightful form. Making use of these incompatible elements at the heart of many processes in composition is, in my view, only the first stage. I don't want to resolve this fruitful contraction; on the contrary, I want to make the two blocks fight each other. In this way I avoid isolating myself from tradition whilst advancing into the future with each new work. I would like to achieve a sound as intense as silence."

MAJOR WORKS

Chamber Music—Chamber Concerto, for thirteen instruments; Le Son Calligraphie I, II, and III; Landscape, for string quartet; Ring, for flute, guitar, and lute; Sacrifice, for flute, lute, and vibraphone; Valeria, for violin, cello, guitar, electric organ, and two obbligato piccolos; Seasons, for one or four percussions; Voice, for solo flute; Distance, for oboe or oboe and shō; Stanza III, for solo oboe, or oboe and shō; Munari by Munari, for percussion; Voyage, for three biwas; Folios, for solo guitar; Garden Rain, for four trumpets, three trombones, bass trombone, tuba, and bassoons (divided into two groups); Waves, for clarinet, horn, two trombones, and percussion; Bryce, for flute, two harps, marimba, and percussion; Quatrain II, for clarinet, violin, cello, and piano; Waterway, for piano, clarinet, violin, cello, two harps, and two vibraphones; String Quartet, "A way a lone."

Choral Music—Crossing, for twelve female voices, guitar, harp, piano, vibraphone, and two orchestras; Wind Horse, for female chorus.

Electronic Music—Static Relief; Vocalisms A-1; Water Music; Cross Talk for two bandoneons and magnetic tape; Toward; Stanza II, for harp and magnetic tape.

Orchestral Music—Requiem, for string orchestra; Tableau pour Noir, for narrator and orchestra; Solitude Sonore; Ki No Kyoku; Coral Island, for soprano and orchestra; Corona, for strings; Arc; Textures, for piano and orchestra; Dorian Horizon, for seventeen strings; November Steps, for biwa, shakuhachi, and orchestra; Green (November Steps II); Asterism, for piano and orchestra; Eucalyptus I, for flute, oboe, harp, and strings; Cassiopeia, for percussion solo and orchestra; Winter Gemeaux, for oboe, trombone, and two orchestras (with separate conductors); Autumn, for biwa, shakuhachi, and orchestra; Gitimalya, for

marimba and orchestra; Quatrain I, for violin, cello, clarinet, piano, and orchestra; Marginalia, for two harps, celesta, piano, five percussion, and strings; A Flock Descends into the Pentagonal Garden; Far calls. Coming far!, for violin and orchestra.

Piano Music—Two Lentos; Pause Uninterrupted I, for two pianos; Undisturbed Rests; Piano Distance; Corona for Pianists; Far Away.

Vocal Music—Stanza I, for piano, guitar, harp, vibraphone, and female voice.

ABOUT

Slonimsky, N., (ed.), Baker's Biographical Dictionary of Musicians; Vinton, J. (ed.), Dictionary of Contemporary Composers.

New York Times, February 13, 1981; San Francisco Program Notes, November 30, 1977, February 1981.

Joseph Tal

1910–

Joseph Tal (originally Gruenthal) was born on September 18, 1910, in Pinne, near Posnán, Germany (now Poland), where his father was a rabbi. While Joseph was still very young, his family moved to Berlin where he grew up and was educated, academically and musically. After receiving private instruction in piano, he entered the Berlin High School for Music in 1928, to study piano with Max Trapp, composition with Heinz Tiessen and Paul Hindemith, harp with M. Saal, and music history with Curt Sachs. Berlin in those years, as he recalled, "was the center of artistic activity in the world. Everybody of importance in the arts came to Berlin, and I was privileged to see and hear all the great masters." On completing his studies at the Berlin High School, he found employment at a Berlin radio station and he made a number of appearances as a concert pianist.

In 1934, a year after the rise of the Third Reich, Tal emigrated from Germany to Palestine. "Why Palestine and not to the United States or some European country?" he was asked by Martin Bookspan in an interview for *Opera News,* and he replied: "I cannot give a rational answer. I knew well that at that time there was virtually nothing in my field in Palestine—a desert. I think I looked upon that as a challenge. I wanted to start at the beginning and

Tal: tăl

JOSEPH TAL

(1946), a choreographic poem for baritone solo and orchestra inspired by a dance poem by Deborah Bertonoff on the biblical story of the Exodus, which was premiered in Tel Aviv on December 14, 1947, by K. Salmon and the Palestine Symphony Orchestra under Bernardino Molinari; and in *The Mother Rejoices* (1949) a symphonic cantata for chorus, orchestra, and piano solo, which was performed in 1950 in Jerusalem with the composer conducting the Kol Israel Orchestra. The subject of the latter work was the Maccabean legend of Hannah who sees her seven sons murdered by a ruthless king because they refuse to bow before the Cross. The cantata, *Succoth,* for chorus, solo voices, and small orchestra (1955), with a text by E. Kallir, was heard in 1955, with the composer conducting the Kol Israel Orchestra again.

Two of Tal's most important works in the early 1950s were Symphony No. 1 (1953) and Concerto for Viola and Orchestra (1954). The Symphony, in a single movement, is in three uninterrupted parts, as the composer described it: "I have used an ancient Persian-Jewish Lamentation . . . [which] actually furnished the entire motivic material for the symphony. In its beginning, small melodic turns of the song are developed; new musical themes are created through enlargement and variation. After a slow introduction in the spirit of the Lamentation, there follows an air of rebellion. In the second section the ancient tune appears in its original form followed by simple variations. . . . The third section returns to the material of the opening." In 1953 Heinz Freudenthal conducted the Israel Philharmonic in the premiere of the Symphony in Tel Aviv.

When the Concerto for Viola and Orchestra was performed for the first time on June 3, 1954, in Haifa, at a concert of the Festival of the International Society for Contemporary Music, with Gideon Roehr as soloist and the Kol Israel Orchestra conducted by Freudenthal, a critic for the Jerusalem *Post* wrote: "With his grand new viola concerto, Joseph Tal once more proved to be one of Israel's most serious composers. From his uncompromisingly atonal origins, he has developed a style that is less rigid but remains harmonically bold. The form is concentrated, the rhythm is assertive, and the work discloses a neo-romantic yearning for melody." The Concerto was awarded the South African Prize.

In many of his works written in the 1950s, Tal

try to express myself rather than go to other places with existing traditions and assimilate myself. My best friends, even my parents, were against my going to Palestine; they thought it was just an adventure. But I did it. As the events of history unfolded, my mother died a natural death but my father was one of those millions deported by the Nazis. We don't know when or where he died."

Arriving in Palestine, Tal at first found little need for his music, being one of the first pianists to emigrate to Palestine. He traveled from one kibbutz to another and finally settled in the Kibbutz Gesher, where he contributed time and manual labor in helping to build a new nation. After two years he became convinced that the place for him was Jerusalem, and he went there in 1936.

In 1937, he found a job as piano and composition teacher at the Music Academy in Jerusalem where he served as director from 1948 to 1952. He also worked for the Palestine Broadcast Service, and married Paula, a sculptress, in 1940, with whom he had two sons (one was killed during the Six-day War).

The early influence of the modern German-Austrian school on his first large works was carried over into his new Palestine music. His writing was dissonant, at times atonal, and sometimes derived from the twelve-tone row as in Concerto No. 1, for piano and orchestra (1944), which was introduced by the Palestine Symphony Orchestra under George Singer with H. Schlesinger as soloist, in 1947; *Exodus* turned to the Bible and Jewish legends for inspiration, as with *Exodus.* This was also true of the "opera-concertante" *Saul at Ein-Dor* (1957), introduced by the Ramat Gan Orchestra under Michael Taube in 1957. The biblical influence can also be found in non-theatrical works, such as his Second and Third Piano Concertos, completed in 1953 and 1956 respectively. The Piano Concerto No 2, featured at the Festival of the International Society of Contemporary Music in Vienna on June 18, 1961, was based on the traditional modal cantillations of Jeremiah's lament and developed along serial lines. In abstract music, Piano Concerto No. 3, with tenor solo, is based on a Hebrew poem by Eleazar Hakalir from the early Middle Ages describing allegorically the revolt of the Maccabeans. This Concerto was introduced in Jerusalem in 1956, with the composer as soloist and the Kol Israel Orchestra with Michael Taube as conductor.

In 1950, Tal became a lecturer at the Hebrew University in Jerusalem where, in 1965, he established a department of musicology which he directed until 1971. In 1957–1958 he researched electronic music on a UNESCO Fellowship in studios in Paris, Cologne, and Milan. Electronic music began to play an all-important role in his creativity, and in 1961 he was appointed director of the Institute for Electronic Music at Hebrew University in Jerusalem, a position he has retained ever since. His electronic compositions include Piano Concerto No. 5 (1964) scored for solo piano, electronic tape, and orchestra, one of his earliest major electronic works to be heard in the United States. After its introduction in 1964 at the Berlin Festival, it had its American premiere, sponsored by Composers Showcase, at an all-Israeli concert on March 10, 1965, at the Lincoln Center for the Performing Arts in New York. Harold C. Schonberg wrote in the New York *Times:* "It is an avant-garde work. Some sections are exciting. ... Where the concerto falls down is in the problem of relating piano to tape. Once in a while, there was a mesh, where the instrument integrated with tape in an intriguing manner. For the most part, though, the taped sounds had little to do with the piano sound."

Another electronic work is the oratorio, *The Death of Moses* (1967), whose world premiere took place in Jerusalem on September 3, 1967. Written in the style of a modern miracle play in which history is combined with mysticism, Tal

scored this large work for solo voices, orchestra, and electronic generators. It received the Israeli State Prize in 1971.

But Tal did not confine himself to writing electronic music exclusively. In 1960 he completed Symphony No. 2 on commission from the Israeli Philharmonic, and it was premiered in Jerusalem in 1961 by the Kol Israel Orchestra under S. Ronly-Riklis. The work was included in an all-Israeli program by the Israel Philharmonic under Zubin Mehta in Carnegie Hall, New York, in October 1973. At that time, Raymond Ericson wrote in the New York *Times* that it is a " 'sound' piece more effective for its sonorities, percussive rhythms and color than for its formalism and musical ideas."

In 1966, Rolf Liebermann, the general manager of the Hamburg Opera, commissioned Tal to write a full-length opera for his company. It took Tal three years to write *Ashmedai,* which the Hamburg Opera staged in October 1971. As the first Israeli opera to be produced outside Israel, it enjoyed a huge success. The text by Israel Eliraz is derived from the Talmud and involves a king who makes a wager with the devil to rule his country in order to spend a year with his mistress without official obligations and duties. In the course of a year, former peace-loving farmers become fanatical warriors, their country is ruined, and the one-time king is killed by his son. Thus, evil triumphs over good and, as the librettist noted, Tal was not only indicting the Nazis but also "any fascistic regime or any regime in which there is a confrontation between the people and their music."

Tal's expressive score, praised for its consummate craftsmanship and dramatic impact, employed electronic sounds as well as the twelve-tone technique. On April 1, 1976, *Ashmedai* (in English) had its American premiere by the New York City Opera, directed by Harold Prince. It was Prince's first opera production and also the first time an Israeli opera was produced in the United States. In reviewing *Ashmedai* in the New York *Times,* Harold C. Schonberg noted that it is a "modern opera in which the play is much more important than the music. There are a few arias and ensembles, but for the most part the vocal line is declamation while most of the music comes from orchestral background effects. ... *Ashmedai* ends up much more heavily weighted as drama than as music. It is a thoughtful piece of work with a telling

Tal

libretto." In *High Fidelity/Musical America,* Patrick J. Smith felt that the merit of the music was "in its very self-effacement, for it allows the text to be clearly understood."

In his next opera, *Masada 967* (1972), Tal dispensed with an accompanying orchestra and relied exclusively on electronic sound and notated vocal parts. Trudy Groth, reporting from Jerusalem to *High Fidelity/Musical America,* said the sound added "greatly to the drama unfolding on the stage. Far from being the kind of conglomeration of noises and background provisions which some may still associate with the term 'electronic music,' the score is a composition with distinct sonorities and expressive aspects." Israel Eliraz's libretto dramatically recalls the historic three-year Roman siege of the Masada fortress in 73 B.C., which ended in the suicide of every man, woman, and child preferring death to Roman rule. The opera had its world premiere in Jerusalem on July 21, 1973, and highlighted the Israel Festival that summer.

Tal collaborated again with Israel Eliraz in another opera, *Die Versuchung (The Temptation),* commissioned by the Bavarian State Opera in Munich for its summer festival. Written in 1973–1974, it was produced in German on July 26, 1976. In the libretto, six disallusioned young people attempt to remold a male mute, who is totally innocent of the ways of civilization, by teaching him the ways of the outside world. In a materialistic society, he becomes a ruthless dictator who destroys the young people who fashioned him. Herbert E. Reed, reporting from Munich to *Opera News,* said Tal "has achieved his goal of seamless coordination between music and stage, applying everything from *Verfremdung* of a Bach chorale to jazz sax and the occasional electronic touch. The result: a lot of pointed musical illustration, but no really absorbing sense of cumulative musical development."

In July 1979, the Israel Philharmonic commissioned and presented the premiere of Tal's Symphony No. 3 (1978) in Tel Aviv, under Zubin Mehta, who also conducted the New York Philharmonic American premiere on November 2, 1979.

Discussing his own music, Joseph Tal said: "One of the main stimuli in my art is experiment. Quality is measured by intelligence of the experiment and the experiment is an integral part of the artistic invention. My style has changed with each period of my life which is a way against a type of national music. Since you live in a community, you unconsciously express its values in your music."

Tal lives in Jerusalem and makes numerous appearances in Israel, Europe, and the United States as pianist, conductor, and lecturer. In 1971 he served as director of an international course on contemporary music at the Eduard van Beinum Institute in the Netherlands and he was also made Fellow of the Berlin Academy of Arts.

MAJOR WORKS

Chamber Music—3 string quartets; Sonata for Oboe and Piano; Sonata for Violin and Piano; Sonata for Viola and Piano; Duet for Viola and Piano; Woodwind Quintet; Piano Trio.

Choral Music—The Mother Rejoices, symphonic cantata for chorus, piano solo, and orchestra; Succoth, cantata for chorus and orchestra; With All My Soul, for baritone chorus, boys' voices, and orchestra.

Electronic Music—3 piano concertos for piano, orchestra, and magnetic tape; Exodus, electronic ballet; Ranges of Energy, electronic ballet; Concerto for Harpsichord, with magnetic tape; The Death of Moses, oratorio, for vocal soloists, chorus, small orchestra, and magnetic tape; Concerto for Harp with electronic sounds; Masada 967, opera for voices and electronic sounds; Michael, the Wooden Horse, cantata for vocal soloists, chorus, and electronic sounds.

Operas—Saul at Ein-Dor, opera concertante; Amnon and Tamar, one-act opera; Ashmedai; The Temptation.

Orchestral Music—3 symphonies; 3 piano concertos; The Exodus, choreographic poem for baritone and orchestra; Reflections, for string orchestra; Concerto for Viola and Orchestra; Festive Vision; Concerto for Cello and Orchestra; Concerto for Violin, Cello, and String Orchestra; Concerto for Harp and Orchestra; Shape, for chamber orchestra; Concerto for Flute and Concerto for Two Pianos and Orchestra.

Piano Music—Sonata No. 1; Six Sonatas; Three Preludes; Inventions, Five Instructive Compositions in Dodecaphonic Technique; Five Densities.

Vocal Music—Else, chamber scene for mezzo-soprano, narrator, and four instruments; Na'ari, for soprano and clarinet.

ABOUT

Gradenwitz, P., Music and Musicians in Israel; Vinton, J. (ed.), Dictionary of Contemporary Music.

Musical Quarterly, January 1965; Opera News, May 1976.

Louise Talma

1906–

Louise Juliette Talma was born on October 31, 1906, in Arcachon, France, to American parents, both of whom were musicians. Her father, Frederick, was a trained pianist who died when Louise was an infant, and her mother, Alma Cecile Garrigues, sang in opera in Europe as well as at the Metropolitan Opera in New York. As Louise's first important influence, she gave her daughter her first piano lessons when she was five, and took her regularly to concerts (as many as eight a week) and, as Louise Talma revealed, she "was always supportive in anything I wanted to do and instilled in me the values which have guided me throughout my life." Louise attended the New York public schools, graduating from Wadleigh High School in 1922. From 1922 to 1930 she went to the Institute of Musical Art in New York, where she studied theory with George Wedge, ear training with Helen Whiley and Franklin Robinson, counterpoint and fugue with Percy Goetschius, and composition with Howard Brockway. At the Institute, she was awarded the Isaac Newton Seligman Prize in 1927, 1928, and 1929 for three student chamber-music works. The National Federation of Music Clubs presented her with first prize in an Eastern interstate piano competition in 1927. Academic undergraduate work was completed at New York University and she earned her M.A. at evening sessions at Columbia University between 1923 and 1933. During the summers of 1926 and 1927 she studied the piano with Isidor Philipp at Fontainebleau, France.

In spite of her talent in music, Talma seriously considered specializing in chemistry for she excelled in the subject at Columbia University. She could not make it her lifework, however, because at twenty-one, her mother fell seriously ill, making it essential for her to support herself and her mother, by teaching piano. At the same time, she pursued music study assiduously.

Returning to Fontainebleau during the summer of 1928, she continued piano study with Isidor Philipp and entered Nadia Boulanger's class in harmony, counterpoint, fugue, and composition. She studied with both teachers each summer until 1935 when Nadia Boulanger, who was impressed with one of her student composi-

LOUISE TALMA

tions, advised her to concentrate solely on composition for several more summers. She received the Stovall Prize for composition at Fontainebleau in 1938 for *The Hound of Heaven,* for tenor and small orchestra, and in 1939 for *In Principio Erat Verbum,* for chorus and organ.

Nadia Boulanger, the second dominant influence in Talma's musical development, also influenced her spiritual life profoundly. During a lecture, Boulanger listed professions in order of their importance, and Talma was shocked that religion took precedence over music and she wondered, "She was so brilliant, I didn't understand how she could be religious." Following Boulanger's example, she spent three years in intensive reading in religion, and after being born a Protestant and living as an atheist, she converted to Catholicism at twenty eight. She said, "Today, religion is the basis of my life."

Talma's teaching experience was extensive: between 1926 and 1928, she taught theory and ear training at the Manhattan School of Music in New York; in the summers of 1936 and 1938 she taught solfège at the Fontainebleau School in France, the only American on the faculty; and in 1928 she became a member of the music faculty at Hunter College of the City of New York where, from 1952 on, she served as professor of music, and, since September 1976, as Professor Emeritus and Distinguished Visiting Professor. While she was at Columbia, in 1932, she earned the Joseph H. Bearns Prize of $1,200 for her composition, *La Belle Dame sans Merci,* a setting of Keats's poem for baritone solo and women's chorus.

Talma began composing in earnest when she was thirty-three with *In Principio Erat Verbum,* for chorus and organ (1939), whose text was derived from St. John. It was first performed by the Juilliard Chorus conducted by Robert Hufstader. *Four-Handed Fun,* for piano four hands (1939), was performed at the MacDowell Colony in New Hampshire (Talma frequently spent summers composing there) in August 1943, with the composer and Lukas Foss at the piano. She presented the premiere of her Piano Sonata No. 1 (1943) at a concert of the League of Composers in New York on January 21, 1946; and in 1947 she was awarded the North American prize of $1,000 for it. Her first orchestral work was *Toccata* (1944), which the Baltimore Symphony Orchestra under Reginald Stewart introduced on December 20, 1945.

Some of her most ambitious compositions in the 1940s were *Terre de France,* a song cycle for soprano and piano (1945) to poems by Charles Péguy, Joachim de Bellay, Charles d'Orléans, and Pierre de Ronsard, and the oratorio, *The Divine Flame* (1946–1948) with a text from the Bible and the Missal, for chorus, orchestra, and mezzo-soprano and baritone solos. The former work was a loving tribute to France expressing nostalgic yearnings to return by those living in far-away places. It was introduced in New York over radio station WABF on January 27, 1946, and the solo portions of it were performed at Harvard University in Cambridge, with the composer at the piano, on February 14, 1950.

In 1946, Talma received her first Guggenheim Fellowship and she recalled, "I had applied without too much hope because I'd composed so little at the time. Yet I was chosen over applicants with better credentials. It was mysterious." When she received a second Guggenheim Fellowship a year later, she became the first women ever to receive two. In 1951, the French government awarded her the *"Prix d'Excellence de Composition"* for her work in general, on the recommendation of Nadia Boulanger.

Louise Talma's composition style in the 1940s was neo-classic, tonal in character, and contrapuntal. However, there was a turning point in her creativity in 1952 when she first became interested in twelve-tone music. That year she heard a dodecaphonic string quartet by Irving Fine and recalled later: "I was so struck by the beauty of that piece that I decided if anyone could make beauty from it I had to use it. We went into correspondence in which he taught me how to use the twelve-tone idiom." But the adoption of the twelve-tone technique did not preclude tonality: "I like to use serialism as a tool and to incorporate it with the other modes in music. I see no reason for chopping off what has developed simply because something new has come along. I believe in using all the tools available." A work which combines tonal and serial elements in a single composition is the Piano Sonata No. 2 (1955) which Paul Harelson performed for the first time on February 13, 1959, at the American Music Festival in New York on the municipal radio station, WNYC.

In 1952, Talma first became acquainted with Thornton Wilder, the distinguished novelist and playwright, at the MacDowell Colony where Wilder told her how greatly he admired her five-minute piano piece, *Alleluia in the Form of Toccata* (1945). Within two weeks, Wilder suggested collaboration on an opera and Talma accepted. "I never found out why he decided to write an opera with me. Everybody was after him to write librettos. He merely said, 'Louise, we're going to write a grand opera together. No holds barred. Twelve principals, a big chorus, a big orchestra!'" She worked on material the playwright outlined for her, they corresponded for about a year, and then the matter dropped. Later, after listening to a reading of Wilder's play, *The Alcestiad,* Talma was inspired: "As Wilder described Hercules emerging from the land of Hades with Alcestis, I could hear a very lonely thread-like melody. Then I knew that this was the play I wanted to set to music." Wilder wrote a special libretto from the play for use in the opera and Talma composed her score in three years and orchestrated it in two with no prospect of production. Ten of the months of composition were spent in Rome on a Senior Fulbright Research Grant.

At a Century Club luncheon, Wilder confided to the director of the Frankfurt Opera in Germany that he had an opera waiting to be staged. The director became interested and Louise Talma became the first American woman to have an opera premiered by a major European company. The Frankfurt Opera premiered *The Alcestiad* in German, with Wolfgang Rennert conducting, on March 1, 1962. Seven additional performances followed in March and April, and at curtain time, the audience responded with a twenty-minute ovation, and calls for "Louise! Louise!"

In *Music Magazine,* Ruth Berges wrote: "Miss Talma's music, strong and straightforward, enhances its dramatic power. The opera builds with ease. Although each act is a complete playlet in itself, the work, as a whole, has unity. There are no overtures or preludes. Each act plunges directly into the action. The vocal line is fluent, and the choruses are used effectively." Talma's score is tonal and partly derivative of the dynamism of Stravinsky and Bartók, and utilizes the twelve-tone row. *Time* reported that it was "aglow with curving lyric lines but avoided any hint of romantic lushness. . . . The lightly modern music at no point obscured the text, but at many points sharply illuminated it." Talma received the Marjorie Peabody Award from the National Institute of Arts and Letters for *The Alcestiad.* Other honors in 1963 included the Sibelius Medal for Composition from the Harriet Cohen International Awards in London (the first time it was awarded to a woman); the National Association for American Composers and Conductors Award "for outstanding service to American music"; and the National Federation of Music Clubs Award "for advancing national and world culture through distinguished service to music." On May 20, 1966, Talma was also given a $7,500 sabbatical leave grant by the National Endowment for the Arts.

In 1963–1966 on commission from the Koussevitzky Music Foundation, Talma wrote *All the Days of My Life,* a cantata for tenor, clarinet, cello, piano, and percussion. It was based on a biblical text and a quatrain found in a trench in Tunisia in 1943. The Contemporary Chamber Ensemble under Arthur Weisberg, and Charles Bressler, tenor, introduced it at the Library of Congress in Washington, D.C., on November 25, 1966, before repeating it in New York the following December 10. Michael Steinberg of the Boston *Globe* described the text as "a contemplation of the frailty of life, the inevitability of death, and of belief in God as the only true source of light," and he wrote that Talma's musical language was "essentially Stravinskyan, marked by precisely articulated rhythms, irregular metrics and clear-cut contrasts between quick and slow movements. . . . She has devised a powerful text declamation for the solo tenor voice, and has effectively surrounded and punc-

tuated that declamation with busy but unfailingly careful writing."

On December 12, 1965, the Buffalo Philharmonic under the direction of Lukas Foss, and Grant Johannesen as piano soloist, were heard in the premiere of *Dialogues for Piano and Orchestra* (1963–1964). On May 11, 1968, *A Time to Remember,* for three choruses and orchestra (1966–1967) was presented by the Hunter College Choirs under Ralph Hunter. With a text derived from speeches by John F. Kennedy and biblical and literary quotations, the work is made up of five sections entitled: "First Day," "A Time for Every Purpose," "The Way of Peace," "Last Day," and "Invocation" played without pause.

The Tolling Bell, a triptych for baritone and orchestra (1967–1969), with a text based on three poems dealing with death by Shakespeare, Marlowe, and Donne, was commissioned by the MacDowell Club of Milwaukee. The Milwaukee Symphony Orchestra under Kenneth Schermerhorn, with William Metcalf as vocal soloist, premiered it on November 29, 1969. *Summer Sounds* (1969–1973), for clarinet and string quartet, is programmatic in content and written in serial form. The call sounds of two thrushes are simulated in the initial measures of the opening movement ("Dawn"), expanded into a twelve-tone row, and found again in the closing of the fourth section ("Night"). *Voices of Peace,* for chorus and strings, was inspired on January 28, 1973, when news of peace in Vietnam was announced. It uses material from the Bible, the Missal, St. Francis of Assisi, and Gerard Manley Hopkins. Talma was expressing "the resurgent and universal yearning of the human soul for peace on this earth." The first performance of the work took place in Philadelphia at the Civic Center Museum, with Louis Salemno conducting, on February 10, 1974.

Talma wrote *Textures,* for piano (1977), on commission from the International Society for Contemporary Music for the seventieth birthday of Beveridge Webster, pianist. The work, in five brief sections, was first performed on March 17, 1978, at a ISCM concert in New York.

For Talma's fiftieth anniversary as a teacher at Hunter College, her colleagues and friends arranged a program of her music at the Hunter College Playhouse in New York on February 4, 1977. Her seventieth birthday was commemorated with a reception and a program of her music at the Maison Française at New York University. Her Alma Mater honored her by making her a member of the President's Club at Hunter College and in 1979 the international music sorority, Sigma Alpha Iota, presented her with an Award of Merit and a citation reading: "To Louise Talma in recognition of her long and distinguished career as one of our foremost women composers and her dedication as a most eminent teacher, thereby touching and enriching many lives throughout the United States and the world."

Talma's honors in the 1970s included election to the National Institute of Arts and Letters in January 1974 (the first woman thus honored) and a $3,750 fellowship grant from the National Endowment for the Arts in 1974. In March 1975 Talma was Clark Lecturer at Scripps College in Claremont, California, and in March 1976 she was made Samuel Simons Sanford Fellow at Yale University and presented with a medallion and a concert of her music at Yale's Sprague Hall in New Haven.

Talma, who never married, lives in New York in an apartment whose walls are covered with photographs of musicians, including one of her mother in the costume of Susanna in *The Marriage of Figaro.* Since 1950, Talma has been a member of the board of directors of the League of Composers and of the Fontainebleau Arts Association; since 1963, she has been a corporate member of the Edward MacDowell Association and charter member of the Society of University Composers; since 1978; she has been a member of the board of directors of the American Music Center; and between 1970 and 1973 she was a member of the board of directors of the International Society for Contemporary Music. She is also the author of *Harmony for the College Student* (1966) and *Functional Harmony* (1970) with James S. Harris and Robert Levin.

MAJOR WORKS

Chamber Music—Song and Dance, for violin and piano; String Quartet; All the Days of My Life, cantata for tenor, clarinet, cello, piano, and percussion; Sonata for Violin and Piano; Three Dialogues, for clarinet, two violins, viola, and cello; Diadem, for tenor, violin, cello, flute, clarinet, and piano.

Choral Music—In Principio Erat Verbum, for chorus and organ; The Divine Flame, oratorio for mezzo-soprano and baritone solos, chorus, and orchestra; The Leaden Echo and the Golden Echo, for double chorus, soprano solo, and piano; Let's Touch the Sky, for chorus, flute, oboe, and clarinet; La Corona, for a cappella chorus; A Time to Remember, for chorus and orchestra; Voices of Peace, for chorus and strings; Celebration, for women's chorus and small orchestra; Psalm 84, for a cappella chorus.

Opera—The Alcestiad.

Orchestral Music—Toccata; Dialogues, for piano and orchestra; The Tolling Bell, triptych for baritone and orchestra.

Organ Music—Wedding Piece.

Piano Music—2 sonatas; Four-Handed Fun, for piano four hands; Alleluia in Form of Toccata; Pastorale Prelude; Six Etudes; Three Bagatelles; Passacaglia and Fugue; Soundshots, twenty short pieces; Textures.

Vocal Music—One Need Not be a Chamber to be Haunted, for soprano and piano; Carmina Mariana, for two sopranos and piano; Terre de France, song cycle for soprano and piano; Leap Before You Look, and Letter to St. Peter, two songs for soprano and piano; Two Sonnets, for baritone and piano; Birthday Song, for tenor, flute, and viola; Rain Song, for soprano and piano; Have You Heard? Do You Know?, divertimento for soprano, mezzo-soprano, tenor, and chamber ensemble.

ABOUT

Goss, M., Modern Music-Makers; Contemporary American Composers; Vinton, J. (ed.), Dictionary of Contemporary Music.

New Haven Register, March 14, 1976; New York Post, March 1, 1974; New York Times, February 4, 1977; SoHo News, January 25, 1979.

Alexander Tansman

1897–

For biographical sketch, list of earlier works, and bibliography, see *Composers Since 1900.*

On commission from the Denver Symphony Orchestra, Alexander Tansman wrote *Diptyque,* for orchestra (1969), which was introduced with Vladimir Golschmann as conductor in November 1969. In 1970, Tansman's *Hommage à Erasme,* for orchestra (1969), which was commissioned by the Rotterdam Philharmonic, was premiered under Jean Fournet. A third commission, from Affaires Culturelles in Paris, led in 1972 to the writing of *Stèle: In Memoriam Stravinsky,* which was premiered in Paris on November 14, 1973, by L'Orchestre Nationale under the direction of Maurice Suzan.

Georges Dandin, an opéra-comique based on Molière's comedy, was produced at the Festival de Sarlat in France on July 7, 1974. *Élégie,* for orchestra, written in 1976 in memory of Darius Milhaud, was performed for the first time in 1977 at the Spring Festival in Posnań, Poland, by the Posnań Philharmonic under the direction of Renard Czajowski. *Apostrophe à Sion,* for chorus and orchestra, with a text from a psalm discovered in the grotto of Kumran in 1977, was commissioned by the Testimonium of Jerusalem for the Jerusalem Festival of Contemporary Music in 1979.

Tansman's eightieth birthday was celebrated in 1977 with Tansman festivals in several European cities. In 1977, he was elected to the Royal Academy of Sciences, Letters, and Beaux-Arts in Belgium.

MAJOR WORKS (supplementary)

Chamber Music—Musique à Six, for string quartet, clarinet, and piano.

Choral Music—Apostrophe à Sion, for chorus and orchestra.

Guitar Music—Hommage à Chopin; Variations on a Theme of Scriabin.

Opera—Georges Dandin, opéra-comique.

Orchestral Music—Hommage à Erasme; Diptyque; Concertino for Flute and String Orchestra; Stèle: In Memoriam Stravinsky; Élégie (in memory of Darius Milhaud); Sinfonietta No. 2.

Piano Music—Hommage à Rubinstein, two pieces.

ABOUT (supplementary)

Le Courier Musical de France, No. 63, 1978.

Deems Taylor

1885–1966

See *Composers Since 1900.*

Alexander Tcherepnin

1899–1977

For biographical sketch, list of earlier works, and bibliography, see *Composers Since 1900.*

Tcherepnin's cantata, *The Story of Ivan the Fool,* based on Tolstoy's play, was introduced by the B.B.C. Radio in London on December 24,

1968. In 1971, a concert of Tcherepnin's cello works was given by Paul Olefsky, with the composer at the piano, at the Lincoln Center for the Performing Arts in New York. His last major work was *Musica Sacra,* for chamber orchestra, whose world premiere took place at the Festival of Lourdes, in France, on April 28, 1973.

Tcherepnin continued making appearances in the United States and Europe both as conductor and pianist performing his compositions up to the time of his death in Paris on September 29, 1977.

In 1968, Tcherepnin was made Chevalier Arts et Lettres by the French Minister of Culture, and in 1974 he was elected to membership in the National Institute of Arts and Letters.

MAJOR WORKS (supplementary)

Chamber Music—Quintet, for two trumpets, horn, trombone, and tuba; Quintet, for woodwinds; Duo, for two flutes.

Choral Music—Baptism Cantata, for chorus and orchestra.

Orchestral Music—Russian Sketches; Musica Sacra, for chamber orchestra.

ABOUT (supplementary)

Thomson, V., American Music Since 1910.

New York Times, October 1, 1977; Tempo (London), January 1960.

Randall Thompson

1899–

For biographical sketch, list of earlier works, and bibliography, see *Composers Since 1900.*

The Place of the Blest, a cantata for treble voices and chamber orchestra (1969), had its first performance on March 2, 1969, at St. Thomas Church in New York. *Fare-Well,* for a cappella chorus (1973), was first heard on March 4, 1973, at St. John's Lutheran Church in Merrick, New York. *A Concord Cantata,* for mixed voices and orchestra, was introduced in Concord, Massachusetts, on May 3, 1975 and *The Morning Stars,* for chorus and orchestra, was premiered in Lexington, Kentucky, on March 18, 1976. *Five Love Songs,* for baritone solo, mixed voices, and string quintet, received its first hearing on August 6, 1978, at the Rocky Ridge Music Center in Estes Park, Colorado.

Thomson

MAJOR WORKS (supplementary)

Chamber Music—String Quartet No. 2; Music for a Wedding in Rome, for string quartet.

Choral Music—The Place of the Blest, cantata for treble voices and chamber orchestra, or piano; Two Herbert Settings: Bitter Sweet and Antiphon, for a cappella voices; Fare-Well, for a cappella chorus; The Eternal Dove, for a cappella chorus; A Hymn for Scholars and Pupils, for treble voices and chamber orchestra; A Concord Cantata, for chorus and orchestra; The Morning Stars, for chorus and orchestra, or piano, or band; Five Love Songs, for baritone solo, chorus, and string quintet.

Organ Music—Twenty Chorale Preludes; Four Inventions and Fugues.

ABOUT (supplementary)

Thomson, V., American Music Since 1910; Vinton, J. (ed.), Dictionary of Contemporary Music.

Virgil Thomson

1896–

For biographical sketch, list of earlier works, and bibliography, see *Composers Since 1900.*

For Thomson's seventy-fifth birthday in November 1971 New York City presented him with the Handel Medallion, the highest award for achievement in the arts that the city could bestow; New York University also conferred an honorary doctor of music degree on him. On this occasion, there were performances of Thomson's music in his honor throughout the United States, notably at the University of Bridgeport in Connecticut where a series of concerts provided a large cross-section of his creativity and a revival of his opera, *Four Saints in Three Acts* (1928). As a further tribute for his birthday, his opera, *The Mother of Us All* (1947), was revived in New York City on November 25, 1971. Although countless performances of the opera were given in early years by opera workshops and college music departments, it was not until the summer of 1976 when it finally received a professional production by the Santa Fe Opera Company in New Mexico, with Raymond Leppard conducting. This performance was recorded in its entirety by New World Records, and was selected as record of the year in 1978 by *Stereo Review.*

On April 20, 1972, the Juilliard American Opera Center in New York presented the world premiere of Thomson's three-act opera, *Lord Byron* (1968–1971), with Gerhard Samuel conducting. At Thomson's request Jack Larson wrote the libretto, taking direct quotes from Byron. Originally the opera was commissioned for the Metropolitan Opera by the Ford and Koussevitzky Music Foundations and four major scenes were auditioned by Rudolf Bing, the general manager, and others at the Metropolitan Opera in April 1968. Thomson recalled, "Mr. Bing seemed to like it at the moment, but on the next day he changed his mind about producing it—or, at least, producing it immediately. So the Met did not do it although they never decided not to do it. They gave no reason. They had no obligation to give reasons."

In place of the usual first-act overture of an opera there is a choral elegy in which Londoners in Westminster Abbey mourn the body of Byron returning from Greece. Then, flashbacks provide glimpses into Lord Byron's life, as a poet and social celebrity. As friends and relatives beseech Dean Ireland to permit him to be buried there without success, other poets including Shelley joyously welcome him to their midst. The text touches on the burning of Byron's memoirs by those close to him. Andrew Porter wrote in *The New Yorker,* that the score "limns sentiments with sure, easy strokes and does not aim to stir emotion in the listeners. The music is distinguished, above all, by the peculiar justness of word setting. ... Thomson has the gift to declaim English lines in melodies that not merely are fitting in rhythm and pitch inflections but make a music in which words and musical contour seems indissolubly joined. ... Thomson has the gift to be simple; his notes come down where they ought to be, in the place just right. But his simplicity is that of a master, not a naif. The music is not artless but careful, refined, purified by a process that has not destroyed its zest."

Of his later works, Thomson is partial to *Lord Byron* and to *Cantata on Poems of Edward Lear* (1973), five settings of poems by Lear for two sopranos, a baritone solo, chorus, piano, and chamber orchestra. Thomson wrote the Cantata for Towson State College in Baltimore and it was introduced in Maryland on November 18, 1973. This work posed a creative problem for Thomson, as he explained: "The verses of Edward Lear are clearly nonsense poetry, and their humor is overt. How to neutralize their comic intent in marrying them to music did present, I must admit . . . a problem. A cantata is, after all, a concert work, not a patter piece for actors working in character and wearing funny costumes. It must be rendered straightforwardly. At the same time, Lear's texts must be projected. My attempted solution has been to put these jingles into musical conventions so far removed from the poetic ones involved that the contrast is itself a joke, another joke, if you will, but one which does not ask for laughter. Adding, for instance, to 'The Owl and the Pussycat' a piano rag, or canonic textures to a rhymed alphabet, or a tango to 'The Akond of Swat' is so willfully inappropriate that the very shock of it, one hopes, may tend to immobilize the poetry.'' When the Cantata was heard in New York in April 1975, Raymond Ericson of the New York *Times* described it as "at once innocent and sophisticated, and it is all delightful. . . . The underpinning of popular dance rhythms avoids the obvious, and the vocal line is always side-slipping into unexpected turns."

On commission from the American Brass Quintet, Thomson wrote *Family Portrait,* in 1974, and it was first performed on March 24, 1975, in New York. This work continues a series of "portraits" Thomson started in 1927: drawing personal tonal portraits from life in the sitter's presence and scoring them for various instruments or instrumental combinations. By 1974, Thomson had written about 150 of these compositions including *Family Portrait,* which consists of five portraits, four of a single family in Aspen, Colorado, and a fifth stranger or guest in New York. All were "posed" in 1972, and scored for brass quintet in Jerusalem two years later, in 1974. Thomson's score called for unusual instruments: two alto trombones and two piccolo trumpets in high F. Regarding his portraits, the composer explained, "Beneath all the diversities of character and mood, there seems to be the kind of resemblance that is common to people spending lots of time together. The visitor, on the other hand, has clearly another background, another life style. He is from another part of the country, too, and quite certainly has other things on his mind."

A ballet, *Parson Weems and the Cherry Tree,* for chamber orchestra, with choreography by 'Erick Hawkins, purports to tell the true story of young George Washington chopping down the cherry tree. Commissioned by the Foundation for the Modern Dance with a grant from the National Endowment for the Arts, it was first produced at the University of Massachusetts in Boston on November 1, 1975.

As a salute to Thomson on his eightieth birthday, he received the Town Hall awards of a silver bowl and a silver tray in New York, on November 14, 1976. On the same occasion, the American Symphony Orchestra under Aikyama presented the world premiere of his Symphony No. 3 on December 26, 1976, in New York. This work is actually an orchestration of Thomson's String Quartet No. 2 (1932) which was orchestrated in 1972 for the dream sequence in his opera *Lord Byron.*

On January 6, 1979, a retrospective concert of Thomson's music was presented in New York. Kansas City honored him on his eighty-fourth birthday in October 1980 with a week-long festival of performing his principal works. On this occasion, a television documentary of his life was previewed, prior to its release by the Public Broadcasting Service in New York on November 25, and nationally on December 27.

Alan Rich described Thomson as "a radical conservative" and analyzed his music in the *American Record Guide:* "Thomson's music is the work of a conservative; it was recognized as such when it was new, and it remains that today. But the important thing is the wonderful amount of taste, wit and fancy with which he has always operated. He has done some terribly daring things within his chosen musical language—some wonderfully cheeky, genuinely funny things, and some that are totally endearing. . . . Thomson has never been afraid of borrowing ideas, or whole chunks of music from other composers. He has done it in a way that is much too obvious to be dismissed as mere plagiarism; it's more like a kind of tribute. . . . But the ideas that Thomson himself has dreamed up are, for the most part, as good as the ones he borrowed. There is a great, soaring power to his lyrical gifts."

In an interview with John Gruen of the New York *Times,*Thomson insisted that in old age he has "not really changed very much. I do the same things I've always done. I lecture some, I conduct some, I write music and I sometimes write about music. I have friends in to dinner and occasionally I cook a bit. . . . I don't think too much about being alone, and I don't think too much about my past. . . . There are people who, I have reason to suppose, don't like me very much. I avoid them. And there are people whom I don't particularly like, whom I sometimes avoid. But there's hardly anybody I don't speak to, or who doesn't speak to me. . . . One thing I don't do very much anymore is to go out to hear music. It isn't so much because of my lack of toleration for musical experience as that the slight decay of my auditory nerve has rendered musical sound somewhat less than pleasant. The bloom is off the rose, so to speak. To me, music is not as intoxicatingly delicious as it used to be. But I adore writing music, because I hear it all in my head, and that sounds wonderful."

Since 1969, Thomson has been heaped with an accumulation of honors in addition to those already mentioned in conjunction with his birthdays. He received an honorary Doctorate of Fine Arts from the University of Missouri (1971), a Doctorate in Music from Columbia University (1978), a Doctorate of Humane Letters from Johns Hopkins University (1978), and an honorary Doctorate in Music from the Kansas City Conservatory (1980). He was presented with the Henry Hadley Medal by the National Association for American Composers and Conductors (1972), was elected to the American Society of the French Legion (1973), was named to the Board of American Academy and Institute of Arts and Letters (1977), and was awarded the Edward MacDowell Award (1977). He was also made a member of the ASCAP Board of Directors and corresponding member of the Academia Nacional de Bellas Artes in Buenos Aires, in 1977.

Thomson was composer-in-residence at the University of Bridgeport (1972), at Trinity College in Hartford, Connecticut (1973), at Claremont College in California (1974), at Dominican College in San Rafael in California (1974), at Otterbein College in Westerville, Ohio (1975), and at the University of California in Los Angeles (1976). In 1975 he was artist-in-residence at the California State University in Fullerton.

Among his latest books is *American Music Since 1910* (1971).

In 1979, Thomson presented a huge collection of his autographed scores and letters to the music school of Yale University. This acquisition was celebrated at Yale with a two-day Thomson Festival on April 22 and 24. Previously, he had donated his library of books on music, paintings, and recordings to Johns Hopkins Uni-

versity, New York University, and the Manhattan School of Music.

MAJOR WORKS (supplementary)

Ballet—Parson Weems and the Cherry Tree.

Band Music—Edges; A Portrait of Robert Indiana; Study Piece; Portrait of a Lady; Metropolitan Museum Fanfare.

Chamber Music—Family Portrait, five pieces for two trumpets, French horn, and two trombones.

Choral Music—Cantata on Poems of Edward Lear, for two sopranos, one baritone, chorus, piano, and chamber orchestra.

Opera—Lord Byron.

Orchestral Music—Symphony No. 3 (orchestration of String Quartet No. 2).

Vocal Music—From Sneden's Landing, variations for soprano and piano.

ABOUT (supplementary)

Sadie, S. (ed.), The New Grove Dictionary of Music and Musicians; Thomson, V., American Music Since 1910 (Chapter X).

ASCAP Today, January 1972; High Fidelity/Music America, November 1971; Intellectual Digest, October 1972; New York Times, March 21, 1971, January 9, 1972, April 9, 1972, April 25, 1976; New York Post, December 17, 1971; New Yorker, January 17, 1977; Opera News, July 1976.

Sir Michael Tippett

1905–

For biographical sketch, list of earlier works, and bibliography, see *Composers Since 1900*.

Sir Michael Tippett was commissioned by Covent Garden in London to write his third opera, *The Knot Garden* (1966–1969), with his own text as in two previous operas. It was produced on December 2, 1970, with Colin Davis conducting. The setting of the opera is a garden—specifically, an intricate, formal, maze-like Elizabethan one known as a "knot garden," which is symbolic of the complex modern world in which seven characters, each representing a different facet of modern society, are enmeshed. They include a civil engineer and his wife; a gardener; their teenage ward who feels she is being pursued by her adoptive father; her sister, a freedom fighter; a Negro writer and a white musician who are homosexuals; and a magician representing a present-day psychiatrist. They meet, develop complex and tense relationships, reveal their true inner selves, and enact their fantasies with the aid of the magician in a kind of group therapy. Tippett's score, as Martin Cooper wrote in the London *Daily Telegraph,* is filled "with an extraordinary variety of attractions. Much of the music consists of gestures—brass fanfares and percussive cannonades of explosions—whose primary function is theatrical, but there are some set pieces that will stand comparison with the best thing in the earlier operas." At times, Tippett wrote in jazz and the blues (the orchestra includes an electrified guitar and a jazz combo), a quotation (a Schubert song—*Mein Schatz Hat Grün So Gern*), and a fragment from "We Shall Overcome." William Mann wrote in the London *Times* that "Tippett's music . . . is violent, discreet, bitter and deeply loving, brilliant and satirical." As in his two earlier operas, Tippett's writing for orchestra and voices is masterful, and a strong and rhapsodic lyricism is combined with dramatic declamations.

When *The Knot Garden* had its American premiere at Northwestern University in Evanston, Illinois, on February 22, 1974, it became the first opera by Tippett to be produced in the United States. The first professional performance was on February 4, 1978, by the Minnesota Opera in St. Paul.

A piece from the second act of *The Knot Garden* was combined with other material from the same opera for *Songs for Dov* (Dov is one of the opera's characters), for tenor and small orchestra with a text by the composer. The work was written in 1969–1970 on commission from the Music Department of the University College in Cardiff with financial assistance from the Welsh Arts Council, and it was performed in October 1970 by Gerald English and the London Sinfonietta conducted by the composer. A critic for *High Fidelity/Musical America* wrote, "The most attractive musical elements of the *Song for Dov* lie in the transparent song forms which provide a welcome cohesiveness and some of the instrumental passages, such as the haunting accompaniment at the beginning of the first song."

Blues, and a quotation from a great musical master of the past, are also part of the texture of the Symphony No. 3 (1970–1972) for soprano and orchestra, with a text by the composer. It was commissioned by the London Symphony which premiered it on June 22, 1972. The Sym-

phony has two parts: The first is exclusively instrumental, beginning with a dynamic and robust part which the composer likened to "an explosion of energy, like a jet engine." This part is joined to a meditative Lento which the composer explained as follows: "You might think of it as a windless night sky, the sounds are up in the air." In the second part the soprano is heard in a sequence of four blues and there is a seven-measure quotation from Beethoven's Ninth Symphony. (In his text, Tippett questions whether Schiller's "Ode to Joy" that ends the Beethoven symphony, and the concept of brotherhood of man, are applicable to modern times.) The Symphony ends with the words: "We sense a huge compassionate power to heal, to love."

When the Symphony No. 3 had its first American performance on February 15, 1974, by the Boston Symphony under Colin Davis, Michael Steinberg said in the Boston *Globe:* "It is music of large ambition, technically and spiritually. The spirit speaks powerfully because the technique is so well in hand—and, of course, because Tippett's maverick fantasy, daring and originality are as large and generous as his ambition. Also, the urgency of his address is overwhelming. . . . The orchestral conception is brilliant, the harmonic perception rich (what an ear for the right notes) and the prodigality of detail in all dimensions is a wonder on and on." Tippett attended this concert, on his first visit to the United States since 1965. In his two-month stay, his Symphony No. 3 was performed seven times in Boston, New York, and Chicago, with Tippett himself appearing as conductor in Chicago. He was also at the American premiere of *The Knot Garden* in Evanston and the New York Philharmonic performance of his early *Double Concerto* (1939). The frequency of Tippett performances in America was commented on by Hubert Saal in *Newsweek:* "Right now, England's Michael Tippett may be the most popular contemporary composer in America."

Tippett's fourth opera, *The Ice Break* (1973–1976), was commissioned by Covent Garden where it was first performed on July 7, 1977, under the direction of Colin Davis. It is Tippett's first opera with a contemporary setting, though its plot is allegorical (the libretto is his own). A program note explained that its theme is "stereotypes—their imprisoning characteristics—and the need for individual rebirth." The plot deals with problems of the generation gap within a family, the racial gap between blacks and whites, and the drug scene. In the New York *Times,* John Rockwell explained that *The Ice Break* "is actually a sort of operatic compendium of the 1960s symbols, from political protest to racial confrontation to flower-child celebrations to a psychedelic trip." In the Edinburgh *Scotsman,* Conrad Wilson called it "a powerful, thrilling and moving work. . . . So concentrated and so teeming with life is Tippett's writing that there is no actual sensation of brevity. Not one of the acts lasts more than half an hour . . . but the dramatic tension is so strong, with thrust and repose held in perfect balance, that the work creates its own satisfactory form. Musically, with its heavy pounding figures, its exultant outbursts of energy, its vivid tributes to jazz, pop and European tradition (with, at one point, a symbolic confrontation between two rival gangs, one led by a jazz clarinetist, the other by a classical violinist), its dancing exuberance and color, and its tranquil, infinitely touching moments of lyricism, it is a characteristically cornucopian score which will demand to be heard again and again." *The Ice Break* had its first American performance by the Opera Company of Boston under Sarah Caldwell, on May 18, 1979. In *Time,* Christopher Porterfield wrote: "Tippett's score—dense, compact, intricate—rumbles darkly with violence and glistens with unexpected color. The choral scenes capture the shout of the mob. The solo lines sometimes soar in daring melismas, sometimes settle into softly swooping lyricism." Reporting to the New York *Times,* Joseph Horowitz wrote: "The general quality of the writing . . . and the interplay of text and music, are simply superb—in recent decades, perhaps a handful of composers have exercised the craft of opera-writing with comparable knowhow and imagination."

The world premiere of Tippett's String Quartet No. 4 (1977–1979) was an attraction at the Bath Festival in England, when it was performed by the Lindsay String Quartet on May 20, 1979. The London premiere of this quartet, on January 2, 1980, was one of several performances of Tippett's works in England celebrating his seventy-fifth birthday.

Tippett returned to the United States in 1976 to give a series of lectures on fine arts at the University of Austin in Texas and returned again a year later, when six leading American orchestras performed his works. Tippett con-

ducted in several cities as well as with the Minnesota Opera in American performances of *The Knot Garden.* He was in Cleveland, between October 16 and 23, when Michael Tippett Week was proclaimed by the mayor and a wide range of his creativity was displayed in numerous concerts, including one by the Cleveland Orchestra when he shared the podium with its music director, Lorin Maazel.

An important event during his 1977 visit was the world premiere of his one-movement Symphony No. 4 (1977) which was commissioned and performed by the Chicago Symphony under Sir Georg Solti on October 6, 1977. Meirion Bowen, who wrote the program notes with Tippett's advice, explained that the Symphony "essays yet another recipe for balancing the abstract and dramatic elements in his music. The work relates more to the tradition represented by the symphonic poems of Liszt, Strauss and Elgar. . . . The symphony falls into seven sections which are dovetailed together to produce a continuous unfolding of musical ideas and argument." Tippett described the work as a "birth-to-death piece" in the style of Richard Strauss's *Ein Heldenleben.* He told of being inspired by the memory of a film he had seen many years earlier about a fetus growing in the womb of an animal. Karen Monson wrote in the Chicago *Daily News* that "The person who walks, tiptoes, skips and dances through this musical portrait—surely the composer himself—is a clever chap who demands attention. Although Tippett's portrayal of life is in no way naive or infantile, it is full of hope, beauty and fun." In *High Fidelity/Musical America,* Karen Monson added: "It sings—with long, lithe solos for flute, oboe and cellos among others. In contrast to this lyricism stands a tart scherzo, a well-bred fugal section, a clip-clop horse-and-carriage ride, and contrapuntal passages more intricate than have been the recent Tippettian rule."

On commission from the London Symphony, Tippett wrote his Triple Concerto, for violin, viola, cello, and orchestra in 1980. Its world premiere took place at a Promenade concert at the Royal Albert Hall on August 22, 1980, with Sir Colin Davis conducting. The North American premiere followed on September 30th in Toronto with Andrew Davis directing the Toronto Symphony Orchestra. In this work, the composer was not striving for the concerto grosso form, nor did he conceive of his work in the romantic tradition, but, instead, each soloist retains his own individuality. "I don't provide material for any of the solo instruments that at all belongs to the others," he explained. Writing in *The New Yorker,* Andrew Porter said: "At the start, each in turn establishes a separate character in an exuberant, rapturous, cadenza-like outpouring. Then the three join in a stretch of tranquil music derived from the coda of Tippett's Fourth String Quartet. . . . Although the three lines are quite independent, they conspire to create a single mood, serene and radiant. . . . The concerto is a work of abundant lyricism and invention, and very beautiful."

In his book *Moving into Aquarius,* Sir Michael Tippett wrote: "I am a composer. That is someone who imagines sounds, creating music from the inner world of the imagination. The ability to experience and communicate this inner world is a gift. . . . Like every creative artist, my days are spent pondering, considering, wrestling in my mind with an infinite permutation of possibilities. I must create order out of chaos. The act of imagination is sometimes of great intensity, sometimes more wayward and always for a big piece of music, prolonged. I am, as it were, possessed, taken over by the creative drive from within, and even when I put away the manuscript paper, I find it almost impossible to switch off the inner activity. . . .

"I have been writing music for forty years. During those years there have been huge and world-shattering events in which I have been inevitably caught up. Whether society has felt music valuable or needful, I have gone on writing because I must."

When Alan Blyth interviewed Tippett for *High Fidelity/Musical America* in 1974, he found that "despite his sixty-eight years and perhaps because of his predominantly open-air upbringing [Tippett] remains as youthful as his mind. Indeed, he is still in some ways unnervingly boyish and enthusiastic, or perhaps 'questioning' would be the better word, ever seeking new solutions to matters musical and philosophical. . . . His long, expressive hands and his eagle-like, concentrated eyes (which have sadly been giving him much trouble of late so that he has had to compose with large characters on very big sheets of stave paper, a cruel handicap that he carries lightly) add to the portrait of a sensitive, joyful, inspiriting man whose personality is well represented in his music."

Up to 1970, Tippett lived in a Victorian home near Bath, and since 1970 he has occupied a house on a hilltop in Wiltshire, a hundred miles from London. He used to enjoy playing Monopoly and croquet, and he remained an omniverous reader until failing eyesight made reading difficult. From 1969 to 1974 he was the artistic director of the Bath Festival in England. In the summer of 1978 he was composer-in-residence at Aspen, Colorado and in January 1973 he was elected to honorary membership in the American Academy of Arts and Letters in recognition of his contributions to the arts. The citation read: "Michael Tippett composes in a style which is peculiarly his own and has expressed this individuality in a variety of forms. . . . What attracts one most in his music is the vibrancy and exuberance it gives off, the feeling it communicates of a richness of temperament and of humanity." In 1979 he was named Companion of Honor in Great Britain. His seventy-fifth birthday in 1980 was commemorated with extensive performances of his works in Great Britain, Canada, and elsewhere.

MAJOR WORKS (supplementary)

Chamber Music—In Memoriam Magistri, for flute, clarinet, and string quartet; String Quartet No. 4.

Opera—The Knot Garden; The Ice Break.

Orchestral Music—2 additional symphonies; Songs for Dov, for tenor and small orchestra; Triple Concerto, for violin, viola, cello, and orchestra.

Piano Music—Sonata No. 3.

ABOUT (supplementary)

Kemp, I., Tippett: a Study of his Music; Matthews, D., Michael Tippett: an Introductory Study; Sadie, S. (ed.), The New Grove Dictionary of Music and Musicians; Searle, H., and Layton, R., 20th Century Composers: Britain, Scandinavia, the Netherlands; Sternfeld, F. W., Music in the Modern World; White, E. W., Tippett and his Operas.

Cleveland Orchestra Program Notes, October 20, 1977; High Fidelity/Musical America, February 1974; Music Magazine (Toronto), October 1980; New York Times, February 17, 1974, October 30, 1977; New Yorker, September 19, 1977; Records and Recordings (London), January 1975; Stereo Review, March 1974; Sunday Times Magazine (London), March 7, 1977.

Ernst Toch

1887–1964

For biographical sketch, list of earlier works, and bibliography, see *Composers Since 1900.*

Toch's *The Shaping Forces of Music* was reprinted in New York in 1977 and it contains a detailed biography of Toch by Lawrence Weschler and a completely new listing of his works.

An Ernst Toch Archive, to house his manuscripts, letters, books, and memorabilia, was established at the University of Southern California in Los Angeles in 1974.

ABOUT (supplementary)

Weschler, L., Ernst Toch, 1887–1964: a Biographical Essay Ten Years After his Passing.

LESTER TRIMBLE

Vincenzo Tommassini

1878–1950

See *Composers Since 1900.*

Lester Trimble

1923–

Lester Albert Trimble was born in Bangor, Wisconsin, on August 29, 1923. His father, John Lester Trimble, was a research and development chemist for corporations that supply the baking industry. Though he never played an instrument, the elder Trimble is a lover of good music, as is Lester's mother, Clara Frieda Piske Trimble, a former schoolteacher who plays the piano. Lester's first experience in music came when he was two from the family phonograph which introduced him to the joys of concert and popular music. The family had moved to Milwaukee when Lester was four and he was particularly affected by the weekly radio broadcasts of children's concerts by Walter Damrosch, which were part of the elementary school curriculum. He began to be involved in making music in his childhood years by singing solos at Christmas church programs, and taking piano lessons

when he was seven, and violin lessons two years later. When, in 1933, the Trimble family left Milwaukee for Pittsburgh, Lester continued to study the violin with Robert Eicher, first violinist of the Pittsburgh Symphony Orchestra. By the time he was fifteen, he was sufficiently advanced in violin and viola playing to become a permanent member of Robert Eicher's string quartet. Evenings and weekends were spent at Eicher's home in what Trimble recalled as an "orgy of music making" and Trimble became familiar with practically every important work in chamber-music literature, including works of "moderns" (Bartók, Hindemith, and Ravel). Trimble's experience as a violinist in a chamber orchestra directed by Eicher taught him about the concerto grosso and string orchestra literature as well.

Auditioning successfully for a violin scholarship at Duquesne University, Trimble was awarded a four-year full tuition scholarship. But after one semester in the depression years, he was forced to give it up and find a job in a music shop to help out with family finances.

Trimble began composing when he was sixteen and he wrote some pieces for violin and piano, a few movements for string quartet and, in 1942, a full-length string quartet without ever having any formal instruction in theory or composition. The only knowledge of composing he had was from reading several theoretical treatises, all "equally bad" as Trimble recalled.

In 1942, during World War II, Trimble served in the Army Air Force for a year as a teacher.

Then, stricken by rheumatoid arthritis in 1943, he spent ten months in a hospital in Salt Lake City and later in Tucson, Arizona. He said, "It was during this period that I realized my hopes of a career as a violinist had probably ended." On a sudden impulse, he wrote a letter, enclosing a few of his compositions, to Arnold Schoenberg, who was teaching at the University of California in Los Angeles. "It was the most audacious act of my life. I knew nothing about Schoenberg except that I adored his *Verklaerte Nacht* and that he was in California which seemed relatively near to a Wisconsian lying in a hospital bed in Arizona." Schoenberg answered, encouraging Trimble to pursue a composing career and giving him advice and guidance. The letter can be found in Erwin Stein's collection of Schoenberg's correspondence.

Returning to Pittsburgh as a civilian "in a semi-crippled condition," Trimble enrolled in 1944 as a violin major at the Carnegie Institute of Technology. Fortunately, he was there during the one semester when Nikolai Lopatnikoff, eminent composer, joined the composition faculty and he decided, "At that point, and without hesitation, I changed my major to composition." He was Lopatnikoff's student during his entire undergraduate period which ended in 1948 when he received his Bachelor of Arts degree and a Phi Kappa Phi key. He continued to study with Lopatnikoff while he was fulfilling requirements for a Master of Fine Arts degree, which he received in 1949. While still an undergraduate, he was also drawn to literature, and he wrote part of a novel which won the Dial Press Award in New York merely for the excerpt. Although the novel was never completed, Trimble was encouraged by Frederick Dorian with whom he studied musicology at the Carnegie Institute, to assume the position as associate music critic on the Pittsburgh *Post-Gazette*.

During the summer of 1947, after receiving his Bachelor of Arts degree and before his Masters, Trimble studied composition with Darius Milhaud at the Berkshire Music Center at Tanglewood in Massachusetts. Earlier that summer, on July 5, he married Mary Constance Wilhelm, whom he met at the Carnegie Institute where she was an art student.

After receiving his Master of Arts degree, Trimble taught for two years at the Pennsylvania College for Women (now Chatham College) in Pittsburgh. Having discarded all his earlier efforts at composition, he began composing anew. In 1950 he wrote his first string quartet, which was introduced in New York in 1954 and selected for publication by the Society for the Publication of American Music in 1956, and his first symphony, the *Symphony in Two Movements*. It received its world premiere almost a decade and a half after it was written—on April 14, 1964, in New York—by the National Orchestral Association with John Barnett as conductor. John Gruen reviewed it in the New York *Times* as follows: "The symphony is a model of clarity and invention, making its various points with a minimum of orchestral trappings and evolving its ideas through means that are both economic and musically interesting. ... What emerges is an accessibility that is seldom predictable and a maneuvering of thematic material that never palls. In short, it is a music that engages one's emotions as well as one's mind."

In 1951, Trimble took a leave of absence from his teaching post at Pennsylvania College for Women to go to Paris with his wife for additional musical training. He attended the École Normale de Musique to study composition with Arthur Honegger, attended Milhaud's composition classes at the Paris Conservatory, and studied privately with Nadia Boulanger. He recalled, "I had planned to stay in Paris for at least two years, studying. But I was in a precarious state of health and the weather in Paris was insistently inclement. I realized that I could not stand another year of such weather, especially under living conditions which quite literally were those of 'la vie Bohème.' "

He returned to the United States, settled in New York, and in 1952 on invitation from Virgil Thomson whom he met in Paris, he joined the staff of the New York *Herald Tribune* as music critic for eight years. At the same time (1956–1961), he was music critic of the weekly liberal journal, *The Nation,* and he contributed numerous articles on music to other publications and newspapers. Between 1968 and 1972 he was making significant advances in performances of his compositions. *Concerto for Winds and Strings* (1952) was premiered at a concert of the Young Composers League in Copenhagen, Denmark, on September 26, 1956; *Sonic Landscape,* for orchestra (1957), originally called *Closing Piece,* was commissioned by the Pittsburgh Symphony for the tenth anniversary of the International Music Fund and introduced under William Steinberg on February 7, 1958. The work was revised in 1968 with a new title, *Sonic Landscape,* and its first performance took place at the Fourth Inter-American Festival in Washington, D.C., on June 30, 1968, with Walter Hendl conducting the National Symphony Orchestra; *Four Fragments from the Canterbury Tales,* a cantata for soprano, harpsichord, clarinet, and flute (1958), won an award and citation from the American Academy and Institute of Arts and Letters in 1961, and it had been introduced in New York on April 21, 1958. When it was recorded by Columbia, Robert Sabin described the work in *Musical America:* "Trimble opens his cantata with an excerpt from Chaucer's Prologue in which we hear the spurs of the pilgrims jingling, smell the sweet earth and see the bright colors of the train of travelers. The idiom is modern, the rhythms definitely contemporary, yet he so perfectly mirrors the character of the text that one feels no jar of worlds. This is even truer of the three portraits that followed—of the Knight, the Squire and the Wife of Bath. . . . The vocal lines are finely spun in a highly organized texture." On a grant from the Alice M. Ditson Fund, Trimble wrote an opera, *Boccaccio's "Nightingale"* (1958–1962), with a text by George Maxim Ross which was based on the *Decameron.*

In 1959, Trimble was invited to serve as composer-in-residence and lecturer at the Composers Conference at Bennington College in Vermont. For two years (1960–1962), he was general manager of the American Music Center and editor of its newsletter and in 1963 he was appointed professor of composition at the University of Maryland, for five years. He was also a contributing music critic to the Washington *Star* (1963–1966), head of the composition department of the Bennington Composers Conference (summer of 1965), lecturer and senior composer at the Composers Conference at Duke University in Durham, North Carolina (1967), and recipient of a Guggenheim Fellowship in 1964.

Compositions in the 1960s not only enhanced his growing reputation in American music, but brought his creative style to full maturity. Shunning fads and fashions, trends, and provocative "schools," he followed his own inclinations by "maintaining his own ideas of compositional logic, expressivity and structure with unusual independence and conviction," as Oliver Daniel noted in a brochure published by Broadcast Music Inc. (BMI). Although Trimble occasionally would employ such advanced techniques as serialism, chance music or electronic devices (after having spent 1969–1970 learning the techniques of electronic music at the Columbia-Princeton Electronic Music Center), he retained his own creative profile consistently. He described his style as "an American amalgamation of the Germanic (Beethovenian) concept of thematic, motivic and formal unity and the French sense of instrumental color (also harmonic color) and elegance of execution."

To Alan Kriegsman, Washington *Post* critic, the greatest skill of Trimble's *Five Episodes,* for orchestra (1961), "lies in the scoring, which generates an amazingly varied palette of instrumental color. It is not, however, color for color's sake. Each separate complex of timbres has its own expressive and thematic function. Each of the episodes has its own 'thing,' a specific texture and cellular idea which is carefully nursed but not overworked." The work was commissioned and premiered by Henry Mazer and the Florida Symphony Orchestra in Orlando, Florida, on February 15, 1962. The composer wrote it as a solo piano piece which Zita Carno performed at an all-Trimble concert in Town Hall, New York, on March 30, 1962.

In Praise of Diplomacy and Common Sense, for baritone, male speaking chorus, two speaking soloists, and orchestra (1965), was first heard at a "Music in Our Time" concert in New York on March 26, 1965. Its text is made up of news items touching on current events such as the Kennedy assassination, the atrocities in the Congo and De Gaulle's edicts, either recited or sung against a percussion background. A critic for the Washington *Post* described it as "not so much a composition as a sonic happening. As it progresses, the various dimensions of word and tone more and more overlap, *à la Ives.* The percussion backdrop reminds one of Varèse. The verbal techniques hark back to the 'newsreel' devices of Joyce and Dos Passos. This listener found himself drawn into the muddle and indefinably stirred." *In Praise of Diplomacy and Common Sense* received a Martha Baird Rockefeller recording grant in 1970.

One is reminded of John F. Kennedy again in *Duo Concertante,* for two solo violins and orchestra (1968), which is subtitled "To a Great

American." In this work Trimble quoted the original Irish folk tune, "Hail to the Chief" remembering President Kennedy's Irish heritage and he composed an abrupt and violent ending to symbolize the sudden ending of the President's life. Commissioned by the Meadow Brook Festival in Rochester, Michigan (summer home of the Detroit Symphony), the work was introduced on August 10, 1968, with Sixten Ehrling conducting the Detroit Symphony and Mischa Mischakoff and Gordon Staples as soloists. In the Detroit *Free Press,* Collins George called it "a work of great strength and beauty."

Trimble's most ambitious orchestral work is his Symphony No. 2 (1968), commissioned by the Koussevitzky Music Foundation. It was introduced as a principal attraction at the weeklong American Music Festival in Lisbon by the Orquesta Sinfónica de Emissora Nacional under Igor Buketoff on April 25, 1969. Lisbon's leading critic, Joao de Freitas Branco, believes that "Trimble's Second Symphony is a work far above the many just 'well written' works; it is well constructed and shows a solid grasp of the art of composing. Trimble has nothing in common with any of the earlier composers in his treatment of tonal poles, the formation and sequence of harmonies, or in the super-positions of harmonic formations. We think this work will make a fine career."

In 1969, Trimble was the beneficiary of a three-year grant from the Thorne Music Fund. In the 1970s he produced a series of abstract compositions for various combinations of instruments called *Panels* which are made up of numerous, independently composed episodes or "modules" or (in Trimble's word) "events," juxtaposed and overlaid to create a steady flow of sound. His method is similar to that of Jackson Pollock who superimposed lines on his abstract canvases. Trimble devised this developmental method as an alternative to the traditional musical structures, he said, because "I thought if I heard another fugal movement I'd scream." At the same time he did not want to be restricted by any rigid system such as serialism. A critic for *High Fidelity/Musical America* further described Trimble's process: "Each module remains essentially unaltered during its career through the final synthesis, except for changes in its dynamic levels and its sonorous neighborhood—the mix of other modules (or panels) sounding at the same time. Two features obvi-

ously must characterize every such composition, and do so by design: enormous rhythmic energy generated by the hurling together of Trimble's disparate 'events' . . . and a complete absence of thematic or harmonic development." *Panels I,* for ten players (1969), was introduced in New York in March 1971 before it was conducted by Gunther Schuller at a festival of American music at Tanglewood in Massachusetts on August 16, 1972; it was recorded with a Ford Foundation Recording Grant. *Panels IV,* for sixteen players (1973–1974; New York, October 27, 1978), and *Panels V,* which is actually String Quartet No. 3 (1974–1975) were commissioned by the National Endowment for the Arts. *Panels IV* was greatly expanded in 1976 into *Panels for Orchestra,* whose premiere was on December 17, 1976, by the Milwaukee Symphony Orchestra under Kenneth Schermerhorn.

On a Rockefeller Foundation grant, Trimble was composer-in-residence with the New York Philharmonic in 1967–1968, after being selected by Leonard Bernstein. Since 1971, Trimble has been on the faculty of the Juilliard School of Music where he teaches composition, orchestration, and theory. In 1973, he was the first composer selected to be in-residence at Wolf Trap Farm in Virginia and in 1974 he received the Creative Artists Public Service Award from the New York State Council on the Arts.

Lester Trimble and his wife make their home in New York City. He wrote, "I'm afraid I have no hobbies. My interests lie strongly in the area of world affairs; sociological happenings and developments; psychological thinking, writing and research; and literature. I am very 'nature oriented' (both human and non-human). I respond strongly to the elements of 'plant-nature' as exemplified in growing things—both field and mountain—and to 'elemental nature,' as exemplified by the ocean and the winds and the sun. I love to swim and I am a devotee of yoga exercise (without any mystical connection, however). I don't have a mantra (and don't want one)."

MAJOR WORKS

Band Music—Concert Piece; Serious Song.

Chamber Music—3 string quartets; Duo, for viola and piano; Solo for a Virtuoso, for solo violin; Panels I, for ten players; Panels II, for thirteen players; Panels III, for six players; Panels IV, for sixteen players; Music for Solo Trumpet; Panels VI, "Quadraphonics," for percussion quartet; Panels VII, serenade for nine players; Fantasy, for solo guitar.

Choral Music—Allas, Myn Hertes Queene, for a cappella male chorus or male chorus and instruments; In Praise of Diplomacy and Common Sense, for baritone, male speaking chorus, two speaking soloists, and percussion; A Cradle Song, for a cappella women's chorus; Psalm 93, for a cappella chorus; Credo, for a cappella chorus.

Opera—Boccaccio's "Nightingale."

Orchestral Music—2 symphonies; Concerto for Winds and Strings; Sonic Landscape; Five Episodes; Kennedy Concerto, for two violins and chamber orchestra; Notturno, for chamber orchestra; Duo Concertante, for two solo violins and orchestra based on the Kennedy Concerto; Concerto for Violin and Orchestra; Two Panels; Concerto for Harpsichord and Orchestra.

Piano Music—Five Episodes; Portrait of Juan de Pareja.

Vocal Music—Petit Concert, five interludes and arias for soprano, harpsichord, violin, and oboe; Four Fragments from the Canterbury Tales, for voice and instruments; Nantucket, for voice and piano; The Mistress of Bernal Frances, for voice and piano; A Whitman's Birthday Broadcast with Static, for soprano and piano.

ABOUT

Slonimsky, N. (ed.), Baker's Biographical Dictionary of Musicians (6th edition); Vinton, J. (ed.), Dictionary of Contemporary Music.

Joaquin Turina

1882–1949

See *Composers Since 1900.*

Edgard Varèse

1883–1965

For biographical sketch, list of earlier works, and bibliography, see *Composers Since 1900.*

Varèse's principal works were revived in New York on April 17, 1981, by the Orchestra of Our Time conducted by Joel Thome with Lucy Shelton (soprano) and Sue Ann Kahn (flutist) as soloists in a program entitled "A Musical Tribute to Edgard Varèse."

ABOUT (supplementary)

Boretz, B., and Cone, E. T. (eds.), Perspectives of American Composers; Charbonnier, G., Entretiens

avec Edgard Varèse; Jolivet, H., Varèse; Ouellette, F., Edgard Varèse; Thomson, V., American Music Since 1910; Varèse, L., A Looking Glass Diary; Vivier, O., Varèse; Wehmeyer, G., Edgard Varèse.

Ralph Vaughan Williams

1872–1958

For biographical sketch, list of earlier works, and bibliography, see *Composers Since 1900.*

The centennial of Vaughan Williams's birth was commemorated in Great Britain with concerts of his major works and performances of some of his operas. On this occasion, England issued a postage stamp bearing Vaughan Williams's likeness, the first musical subject for a stamp.

ABOUT (supplementary)

Day, J., Vaughan Williams; Douglas, R., Working with R.V.W.; Hurd, M., Vaughan Williams; Lunn, J. E. et al., Ralph Vaughan Williams: a Pictorial Biography; Ottoway, H., Vaughan Williams Symphonies; Sadie, S. (ed.), The New Grove Dictionary of Music and Musicians.

Heitor Villa-Lobos

1887–1959

For biographical sketch, list of earlier works, and bibliography, see *Composers Since 1900.*

Following Villa-Lobos' death, the Brazilian government, in a unanimous decision of the judges, gave Arminda de Almeida the legal right to call herself Señora Villa-Lobos. She had lived with Villa-Lobos from 1936 until 1959 but was unable to marry him because Brazil law forbade divorce; Villa-Lobos was legally separated from his wife.

On August 12, 1971, Villa-Lobos' opera, *Yerma* (1955), whose performance had been held up because of litigation over Villa-Lobos' estate, was finally produced in New Mexico, by the Sante Fe Opera. Reporting to the New York *Times,* Robert Sherman wrote: "By no means an unflawed masterpiece, *Yerma* is nonetheless a strong, serviceable, compelling piece of operatic theater sparked by many moments of striking beauty and others of high dramatic tension."

The opera is unusual in that its libretto is a word-for-word setting of a play by Frederico García-Lorca entitled *Yarma.*

In commemoration of Villa-Lobos' ninetieth birthday, BMI issued an album of ten LPs covering twenty-two of his compositions, including all the *Bachianas Brasileiras,* with the composer conducting.

A Villa-Lobos Museum, established in Rio de Janeiro in 1960, contains his works, portraits, photographs, medals, and various other memorabilia. It is supervised by scholars who provide information about the composer and his music.

ABOUT (supplementary)

Guimaraes, L., Villa-Lobos; Visto de Platéia e Na Intimidade; Peppercorn, L. M., Heitor Villa-Lobos, Leben und Werk der Brasilianischen Komponisten; Pereira da Silva, F., Villa-Lobos.

Opera News, December 10, 1977.

Sir William Walton

1902–

For biographical sketch, list of earlier works, and bibliography, see *Composers Since 1900.*

Walton's *Improvisations on an Impromptu by Britten,* for orchestra, had its world premiere in the United States on January 14, 1970, with Josef Krips conducting the San Francisco Symphony Orchestra.

On March 2, 1972, in Perth, Australia, the Academy of St. Martins-in-the-Fields Orchestra, directed by Neville Marriner, presented the premiere of Walton's *Sonata for String Orchestra.* An adaptation of an earlier Walton composition, the String Quartet, is in A minor (1947). During 1972, there were two more Walton premieres: *Jubilate Deo,* for chorus and organ, performed by Christ Church Cathedral Choir conducted by Simon Prestin, in Oxford, England, on April 22, during the English Bach Festival; and *Five Bagatelles,* for guitar, performed by Julian Bream (for whom it was written), in Bath, England, on May 27. Several years later, Walton orchestrated the work under a new title, *Varii Capricci,* and it received its first performance on May 4, 1976, with André Previn conducting the London Symphony Orchestra. Previn also conducted the Pittsburgh Sympho-

ny in the American premiere on September 26, 1980.

Cantico del Sole, for a cappella mixed voices, was commissioned by Lady Mayer for the 1974 Cork International Festival where it was premiered on April 25 by the B.B.C. Northern Singers under Stephen Wilkinson.

A month-long William Walton Festival was held in Georgia, by the Atlanta Symphony under Robert Shaw in May 1974, which was climaxed by performances of *Belshazzar's Feast* (1931), the Cello Concerto (1957), and the *Partita,* for orchestra (1958).

In 1972, Walton was made an honorary member of the Royal Manchester College of Music. He was also a member of the Royal Swedish Academy of Music and of the Santa Cecilia Academy in Rome.

A thematic catalog of Walton's works, edited by Stewart R. Craggs, was issued in London in 1977.

MAJOR WORKS (supplementary)

Band Music—Miniatures (arrangement of Music for Children), for orchestra.

Choral Music—Jubilate Deo, for chorus and organ; Magnificat and Nunc Dimittis, for mixed chorus and organ; Cantico del Sole, for a cappella mixed chorus; Antiphon, for chorus and organ.

Guitar Music—Five Bagatelles.

Orchestral Music—Capriccio Burlesco; Improvisations on an Impromptu of Britten; Sonata for Orchestra (orchestration of String Quartet in A minor); Anniversary Fanfare, for trumpets and trombones; Varii Capricci (orchestration of Five Bagatelles).

Vocal Music—Beatriz's Song, for voice and guitar.

ABOUT (supplementary)

Lichtenwanger, W. and C. (eds.), Modern Music . . . Analytic Index; Searle, H. and Layton, R., 20th Century Composers: Britain, Scandinavia, the Netherlands.

Robert Ward

1917–

For biographical sketch, list of earlier works, and bibliography, see *Composers Since 1900.*

In celebration of the American bicentennial and also the twenty-fifth anniversary of the Oratorio Singers of Charlotte (North Carolina) Ward wrote his Fifth Symphony—*Canticles of*

America—with grants from the Mary Reynold Babcock Foundation, the Mary Duke Biddle Foundation, and Mr. and Mrs. Marcus E. Yandle. The text and the narration, written jointly by the composer and his wife, were taken from peoms by Walt Whitman and Henry Wadsworth Longfellow, and history books and biography. The composer's aim in the work was to express through words and music important developments in the spirit of America, as he described it: "The *Canticles of America* follows the traditional form of the classical symphony in having four contrasting movements, the first an extended sonata form, the second a lively part song in place of the traditional scherzo, the third, a meditative Adagio, for soprano solo with violin obbligato, and the last a more massive movement combining a fugue and a broad processional-like march tune." The world premiere of the Symphony took place in Charlotte, North Carolina, on May 1, 1976, and proved, as Richard Maschal reported in the Charlotte *Observer*, "a triumph."

Although Ward's opera, *Claudia Legare*, was commissioned by the New York City Opera, its world premiere was presented by the Minnesota Opera in St. Paul on April 14, 1978. Bernard Stambler's libretto was an adaptation of Ibsen's *Hedda Gabler* in a different setting and time, Reconstruction in America following the Civil War. New American names, from old Charleston city directories, were assigned to the characters and the rivalry for a university professorship in Ibsen became a conflict over restoring the economy of the South. Except for these changes, the libretto followed the original Ibsen plot. The score included a southern Civil War song, "The Bonnie Blue Flag," the words of the hymn, "No Surrender," and several duets and set pieces. The style was mostly declamatory as in previous Ward operas. John H. Harvey wrote in the St. Paul *Sunday Pioneer Press* that "Ward has written vocal lines which are by turns attractive and well charged dramatically and always are eminently singable. The orchestral writing skillfully and effectively creates atmosphere, heightens the dramatic moments, and also is unobtrusively supportive when the focus is on the vocal lines."

For the opening of Andrew Jackson Hall, the new home of the Nashville Symphony in Tennessee, Ward was commissioned to write *Sonic Structures*, for orchestra, in 1980 which was premiered on September 13, 1980.

An early Ward opera—originally introduced in 1956 under the title of *Pantaloon*, and then produced three years later by the New York City Opera as *He Who Gets Slapped*—was revived in New York in January 1972 by the Encompass Theater with the title *Pantaloon; He Who Gets Slapped*. For the revival, Ward reorchestrated the score for an intimate theater, requiring only six instrumentalists (flute, clarinet, trumpet, piano, cello, and percussion) instead of a full orchestra.

In 1967, Ward resigned as vice president and managing editor of Galaxy Music Corporation and Highgate Press to become Chancellor of the North Carolina School of the Arts, a position he held until 1975. From 1975 to June 1977 he taught composition at the School; in 1978 he was visiting professor at Duke University in Durham, North Carolina; and in April 1980 he was guest composer at the American Festival at DePauw University in Greencastle, Indiana, where several of his works for orchestra, chorus, and band were performed.

In 1972, Ward received an honorary Doctorate of Fine Arts from Duke University and, in 1975, he received an honorary Doctorate in Music from the Peabody Conservatory in Baltimore. The state of North Carolina presented him with its Fine Arts Award in 1975. He was named as a member of the board of directors of the American Symphony League and of the board of trustees for the National Opera Institute, in 1977, and to the board of trustees of the Moravian Music Foundation in 1978.

MAJOR WORKS (supplementary)

Band Music—Abstractions.

Opera—Claudia Legare.

Orchestral Music—Fifth Symphony—Canticles of America; Sonic Structures.

Organ Music—Three Celebrations of God and Nature.

ABOUT (supplementary)

Thomson, V., American Music Since 1910; Vinton, J. (ed.), Dictionary of Contemporary Music.

BMI, Many Worlds of Music, Winter 1976; New York Times, September 30, 1973.

Anton Webern

1883–1945

For biographical sketch, list of earlier works, and bibliography, see *Composers Since 1900*.

Webern's *Six Bagatelles,* for string quartet (1913), and *Five Pieces for Orchestra* (1913), were choreographed by Rudi von Dantzig and presented by the Netherlands National Ballet in Holland as *Moments* in the late 1960s. The ballet was introduced in the United States in January 1969 when that company appeared in New York.

Between 1962 and 1978, six international Webern festivals were held in Europe and the United States. Webern's complete works were recorded by Columbia under Pierre Boulez's direction. The first volume, containing Op. 1 through Op. 31, received the French Grand Prix du Disque in 1978.

ABOUT (supplementary)

Moldenhauer, H., and R., Anton von Webern: a Chronicle of His Life and Work; Rostand, C., Anton Webern, l'Homme et son Oeuvre.

American Record Guide, December 1979; New York Times, June 10, 1979, January 11, 1981.

Kurt Weill

1900–1950

For biographical sketch, list of earlier works, and bibliography, see *Composers Since 1900*.

On March 4, 1970, Kurt Weill's opera, *The Rise and Fall of the City Mahagonny,* with a text by Bertolt Brecht, received its American premiere in New York forty years after its introduction in Leipzig, Germany. Clive Barnes of the New York *Times* wrote: "It is a great and lovely work, one of the masterpieces of the 20th century lyric theater, with ironically sentimental music that with all its sweetness and bitterness will stay with you as long as you live." On December 10, 1979, the opera was added to the repertory of the Metropolitan Opera and a performance of it was telecast live from the Metropolitan Opera stage on November 17, 1979.

Another Weill opera, *Happy Ending,* which failed when first produced in 1929, received a rare revival on April 6, 1972, in Brooklyn, New York, by the Chelsea Theater Center before its Broadway revival on May 16.

On October 1, 1972, *Berlin to Broadway with Kurt Weill,* a staged anthology of some of Weill's best music for the theater, was presented in New York. *A Kurt Weill Cabaret,* an evening of Weill songs, was brought to Broadway in November 1979 after touring night clubs and campuses for a decade. The Greenwich Philharmonic, under David Gilbert, offered an entire program of Weill's rarely heard concert music, including the American premiere of his Symphony No. 1 (1921) and the New York premiere of *Quodlibet,* for orchestra (1924) on October 27, 1978, at the Lincoln Center for the Performing Arts. Weill's Symphony No. 2 (1934) was revived in New York on November 25, 1979, with Julius Rudel conducting.

The hundredth anniversary of the premiere of *The Threepenny Opera* was commemorated with revivals throughout Germany in 1978, testifying, as Elizabeth Forbes commented in *Opera News,* "to the vitality of a piece conceived for a particular place—Berlin—and a particular time —the 1920s—but universal in its application and appeal."

In a review of the revival of *Street Scene,* which returned to the New York City Opera in 1978 after an absence of a dozen years, Andrew Porter of *The New Yorker* reappraised Weill's art: "In much the way that Handel can be claimed as Britain's greatest opera composer, Kurt Weill might be claimed as America's: a master musician, master musical dramatist, and large soul who found song for the people of his adopted country, learned its idiom, joined them to his own, and composed music of international importance." *Street Scene* was telecast live from the stage of the New York City Opera on October 27, 1979.

On March 20, 1980, the New York City Opera presented the first staged production of the opera, *Der Silbersee (Silverlake),* whose text by George Kaiser was revised by Hugh Wheeler. This was the first production since its disastrous opening in Germany in 1933 when it had to close down after one performance due to Nazi opposition. Weill's "ballet-chanté," *The Seven Deadly Sins* (1933), was premiered in Paris on June 7, 1933, and revived on June 4, 1980, by the Opera Theatre of St. Louis.

Weinberger

ABOUT (supplementary)

Kowalke, K. H., Kurt Weill in Europe; Sadie, S. (ed.), The New Grove Dictionary of Music and Musicians; Sanders, R., The Days Grow Short: the Life and Music of Kurt Weill.

ASCAP Today, March 1970; New York Times, March 16, 1980; New Yorker, November 18, 1978; Opera News, December 1, 1979.

Jaromir Weinberger

1896–1967

See *Composers Since 1900.*

Hugo Weisgall

1912–

For biographical sketch, list of earlier works, and bibliography, see *Composers Since 1900.*

The failure of Weisgall's opera, *Nine Rivers from Jordan,* caused primarily by poor production when it was introduced by the New York City Opera on October 9, 1968, proved so traumatic to the composer that he could not undertake the writing of another opera for eight years. He asked George Gelles in an interview for the New York *Times:* "Do you know what it is to have a major failure at the New York City Opera?" and he provided his own reply: "You feel dirty, you feel you've conned everybody, you feel guilty. I don't mind the bad reviews. But when you know that you've bored everybody, that the audience hates your music because they're bored, then you really take stock of yourself and say, maybe, this isn't my business at all."

For a number of years he concentrated on smaller creative projects, including *Fancies and Inventions,* a song cycle for baritone and five instruments, whose text was Robert Herrick's *The Hebrides.* It was introduced in Baltimore, Maryland, on November 1, 1971. A month later, at an all-Weisgall concert sponsored by Composers in Performance, it was first heard in New York on December 9, 1971. On November 17, 1974, another song cycle, *End of Summer,* for tenor, oboe, and three strings with a text by Po-Chu-I and George Boas, had its world premiere in Baltimore.

To celebrate the hundredth anniversary of the founding of Johns Hopkins University, Weisgall wrote the cantata *A Song of Celebration,* for soprano, tenor, chorus, and orchestra on commission. It was introduced by the Baltimore Symphony and the Goucher College Chorus in Baltimore on February 20, 1976, with Sergiu Comissiona conducting.

Weisgall wrote his first opera in eight years, *Jenny/or the Hundred Nights,* in one act, with a libretto by John Hollander which was based on a Japanese Noh play by Yukio Mishima. It was presented by the Juilliard American Opera Center in New York on April 22, 1976. The plot, involving a ninety-nine-year-old courtesan, who dooms her lover, takes place in Kensington Gardens in London at the turn of the century. Alan Rich of *New York* called the opera "a small but important masterwork. . . . It is an atmospheric piece, but it is built on beautifully realized characters whom Weisgall's music fleshes out with a sweeping lyricism and a skillfully managed leavening wit. I think the opera is a work of considerable emotional power."

The premiere of *The Golden Peacock,* a seven-song cycle adapted from Yiddish songs, was sung in New York on January 23, 1978, by Judith Raskin and proved so popular with the audience that it was repeated. Peter G. David wrote in the New York *Times:* "Without changing any important particulars in the vocal lines off these traditional melodies, the composer has created a witty, moving, inventive and quite original song cycle by means of the ingeniously devised piano accompaniments."

After being awarded an honorary Doctorate in Music by the Peabody Conservatory in 1973, Weisgall became W. Alton Jones Professor there in 1974–1975. In 1975, he was elected to membership in the National Institute of Arts and Letters and awarded an honorary Doctorate of Humane Letters by the Jewish Theological Seminary in New York in 1976. He was also named Distinguished University Professor at Queens College, in New York, in 1980.

MAJOR WORKS (supplementary)

Choral Music—A Song of Celebration, cantata for vocal soloists, chorus, and orchestra.

Opera—Jenny/or the One Hundred Nights, one-act opera; The Gardens of Adonis.

Vocal Music—End of Summer, for tenor, oboe, and three strings; Fancies and Inventions, for baritone and five instruments; The Golden Peacock, seven popular songs from the Yiddish, for soprano and piano; Liebeslieder, four songs for voices with interludes.

ABOUT (supplementary)

Musical Quarterly, April 1973; New York Times, April 18, 1976.

Richard Wernick

1934–

Richard Frank Wernick was born in Boston on January 16, 1934, to Louis Wernick, an antiques dealer, and Irene Prince Wernick. A boyhood musical experience that was so unforgettable that it made him resolve to become a composer was hearing Bartók's Concerto for Orchestra when he was nine. A year later, at the urging of an uncle and aunt, he began taking piano lessons, but, he confessed, "I didn't do terribly well at it."

In his boyhood, the family moved from the Dorchester section of Boston to Newton where he attended Newton High School and studied theory with Henry Lasker. Already composing music, Wernick's interest was increasing to the point where at eighteen he made a personal commitment to devote himself solely to music. Lasker advised him to study composition with Irving Fine, a member of the music faculty at Brandeis University in Waltham, Massachusetts. Thus, he disregarded his father's desire for him to go to Harvard, entered Brandeis University in 1951, and studied composition and theory not only with Irving Fine but also with Arthur Berger and Harold Shapero. Wernick described Fine: "He was incredibly erudite, and I think the most important thing was that he instilled in me a sense of the elegance in music." He subsequently strived for "elegance" in writing a string quartet (since withdrawn) in 1953, which was introduced in Boston in March 1953; and in Four Pieces, for string quartet, written in 1955 and performed for the first time in April of that year at Brandeis University.

The summers of 1954 and 1955 were spent at the Berkshire Music Center in Tanglewood, Massachusetts, where Wernick continued to study composition with Aaron Copland, Ernst

Wernick: wer′ nĭk

RICHARD WERNICK

Toch, Boris Blacher, and conducting with Leonard Bernstein and Seymour Lipkin.

After receiving his Bachelor of Arts degree from Brandeis in 1955, Wernick enrolled at Mills College in Oakland, California, for a year as a teaching fellow in score-reading and figured bass while he continued to study composition with Leon Kirchner who introduced him to the world of atonality and twelve-tone music. He recalled that "Boston had been so neo-classic that all the time I was there I didn't know anything about Schoenberg and Webern." At Mills College Wernick had his first conducting experience in directing Britten's incidental music in a stage production of This Way to the Tomb in November 1955, and Pergolesi's opera buffa, La Serva Padrona, in April 1956. In 1956, Wernick received his Master of Arts degree, and as part of his thesis, he submitted a Divertimento, for viola, cello, clarinet, and bassoon, which was performed by the Mills College Chamber Players in May 1956. A month later, his From Tulips and Chimneys, for baritone and orchestra (whose text was several poems by e.e. cummings) was performed at a symposium of western colleges at the University of Utah in Salt Lake City.

On July 15, 1956, Wernick married Beatrice Messina, a bassoon student at the Berkshire Music Center where they met. Wernick served as the coordinator of the Brandeis University Festival of Creative Arts in 1957 and as music director and composer-in-residence for the Winnipeg Ballet in Canada in 1957–1958. He conducted a full season of performances of the standard and modern repertory, and, on commission, he composed scores for the ballets *The Twisted Heart* (1957) and *Fête Brilliante* (1958), whose premieres he conducted on November 27, 1957, and January 13, 1958, respectively. As music director and composer-in-residence for the Canadian Broadcasting Corporation he directed performances of thirteen ballets, and composed music, on commission, for two television ballets: *The Emperor's Nightingale* (1958) and *Queen of Ice* (1958) which he conducted in April and May 1958. Wernick also wrote a concert piece, *Duo Concertante,* for cello and piano, which was commissioned in 1957 by Gerald and Susan Kagan, who performed it first in May 1960 at the University of Wisconsin, and the following September in New York.

The Wernicks left Canada in 1958 to establish a six-year residence in New York City and he recalled "I had the notion that a composer could make it on his own. I did films, mostly documentaries and industrial films; scores for television; background music for the old 'Play of the Week' TV series; and incidental music for several Off-Broadway plays. It was exciting. A producer would call you Thursday and want a score by Tuesday."

In 1959, Wernick was commissioned by Brandeis University to collaborate with Irving Fine and Gertrude Norman in writing an opera, *Maggie,* based on Stephen Crane's novel, *Maggie: a Girl of the Streets.* The opera, however, was abandoned after completion of the first act. *Music for the Nativity: Ballet for Television,* commissioned by the CBS Public Affairs Department, was televised over the network on January 1, 1961, with choreography by John Butler. Trio, for violin, clarinet, and cello, commissioned in 1961 by the department of music at Brandeis University was performed by the Brandeis Players on December 7, 1962, and repeated two days later at the Institute of Contemporary Arts in Cambridge.

In New York, Wernick also did a considerable amount of private teaching and from 1959 to 1962 he was a member of the theory and composition department of the Metropolitan Music School, a community music school in New York City. From 1962 to 1964, with grants from the Ford Foundation, he wrote music for the Bay Shore, Long Island schools, where he recalled, "I had my own timetable but had to write music

playable by student instrumentalists." He wrote *Hexagrams,* for chamber orchestra (1962), whose premiere he conducted at Bay Shore High School and subsequently at the Annual Directors Conference of the New York State School Music Association in Kiamesha Lake, New York, on December 4, 1962; and String Quartet No. 1 (1963) was first performed on December 5, 1963, by the Bay Shore High School String Quartet.

Realizing that he was not fulfilling himself as a composer by writing functional music, he decided to write music solely for his own satisfaction while earning his living by teaching music at universities. In his first position as instructor of music at the State University of New York in Buffalo (1964–1965) where he coordinated the Department of Music and the Center of the Creative and Performing Arts, he was working 120 hours a week. "It consumed me," he recalled. In 1965–1966 he was instructor of music at the University of Chicago, and rose to assistant professor between 1966 and 1968; he was conductor of the University of Chicago Symphony Orchestra from 1965 to 1968. In 1968 he was appointed assistant professor of music at the University of Pennsylvania in Philadelphia, became associate professor in 1969, chairman of the department of music from 1969 to 1974, and full professor in 1976. Between 1968 and 1970 he also conducted the University of Pennsylvania Symphony Orchestra.

Wernick regards 1964 as the real beginning of his mature style which is basically tonal, but makes full use of 20th century harmony, counterpoint, rhythm, and lyricism. The first examples of his mature style can be found in *Music for Viola d'Amore* (1964), commissioned by Walter Trampler, who performed it twice in New York in April 1965, and *Stretti,* for clarinet, violin, viola, and guitar (1964), commissioned by Sherman Friedland, clarinetist, who performed it first on April 25, 1965, in Buffalo, and again in New York two days later. *Lyrics from I x I* and *Aevia,* were both written in 1966. The first work, for soprano, vibraphone, and marimba, to poems by e.e. cummings, was commissioned by the Ars Nova Consort in Buffalo and it was performed by the Contemporary Chamber Ensemble of the University of Chicago in December 1966. *Aevia,* for orchestra, was commissioned by the University of Chicago as part of its seventy-fifth anniversary celebration, and its first performance took place in December 1966 by the University of Chicago Symphony Orchestra. It was then performed on Chicago television in July 1967 before being distributed nationally by Eastern Educational Television.

Two compositions written in the latter half of the 1960s were *Haiku of Bashō,* for soprano, various instruments, two percussionists, piano, and magnetic tape which was first performed on March 1, 1968, by the Contemporary Chamber Players of the University of Chicago, and later in New York and at the Ravinia Festival in Illinois. The second composition was *Moonsongs from the Japanese,* for soprano and two prerecorded tracks of the soprano voice, which Neva Pilgrim commissioned in 1969. It was performed for the first time in spring of 1969 at the University of Pennsylvania.

Several of Wernick's later works were ethnically oriented, including *A Prayer for Jerusalem* (1971) for mezzo-soprano and percussion in Hebrew, set to five verses from Psalm 122. The music is based on the opening phrase of Bach's chorale, *"Es ist Genug."* It was premiered at the University of Pennsylvania by Jan DeGaetani and Matthew Hopkins in the spring of 1972. In *The New Yorker,* Andrew Porter described it as a "poignant, quietly passionate invocation." In 1976, the composition won the Naumburg Recording Award.

One of Wernick's most deeply moving and personal compositions was inspired by the anger and frustrations aroused in America by the Vietnam War. *Kaddish-Requiem, A Secular Service for the Victims of Indo-China,* was written in 1971 on commission from the Philadelphia Composers Forum where it was introduced in the same year. The text is partly Hebrew (the "Kaddish," the Hebrew prayer for the dead, intoned by a cantor on magnetic tape) and partly the traditional Latin Requiem Aeternam, sung by a mezzo-soprano. A few notes from the "All Flesh is like Grass" section of Brahms's *A German Requiem* are quoted to emphasize the horrors of napalm bombing and defoliation and two instrumental interludes quoting the Orlando de Lassus motet *"Sancti Mei"* are played against the Kaddish tape. The mezzo-soprano part closes the composition, while Palestrina's *"Veni Spiritus"* is quoted. The *Kaddish-Requiem* was performed at the Santa Fe Chamber Music Festival in July 1978, when Wernick was composer-in-residence. In the Albuquerque *Journal,* Allan

Pearson wrote: "Wernick's *Kaddish-Requiem* is an example of protest music which works and will endure. It does so because it captures a universal emotion of lament, a contrast of violence and serenity in musical language that can be understood on many levels."

The funereal tone found in *Kaddish-Requiem* also prevails in *Songs of Remembrance,* a cycle for mezzo-soprano and instruments (1973–1974), since it was inspired by the death of the young daughter of one of Wernick's close friends. With texts by Pythagoras, Horace, Virgil, and Robert Herrick, the work was commissioned by the singer, Jan DeGaetani, as a birthday gift to her husband, Philip West. He performed at times on a medieval instrument preceding the oboe called the "shawm" and Wernick wrote the work for this instrument (as well as the English horn and oboe) for the accompaniment.

In 1976, Wernick received a Guggenheim Fellowship and a year later gained national prominence when he was awarded the Pulitzer Prize in music for *Visions of Terror and Wonder,* for mezzo-soprano and orchestra. Its text was taken from the Koran and the Old and New Testaments. The Aspen Music Festival commissioned it (with a grant from the National Endowment for the Arts) and it was performed on July 19, 1976, in Arabic, Hebrew, and Greek by Jan DeGaetani with Richard Dufallo conducting. Following its New York premiere on March 18, 1979, Joseph Horowitz explained in the New York *Times* that the music's "inspirational mainspring is an escatological sequence found in the Scriptures of all three major Western religions: first, a purifying obliteration of the existing order, then the wondrous creation of a 'new heaven and a new earth.' " As for the music, Horowitz added: "Although it generally dispenses with tonality and motivic repetition, the new work seems relatively traditional in terms of instrumentation and texture."

Introits and Canons, for chamber ensemble (1977) is a three-movement composition in modern polyphonic writing. It was first performed at the Juilliard School of Music in New York on January 13, 1978. Its score calls for a string quartet (violin, viola, cello, and doublebass) on the conductor's left; a wind quartet (flute, clarinet, horn, and bassoon) on his right; and a row of percussion instruments (performed by a single player) lined up in the back. Structurally this work contains a variety of forms such as canon, chaconne, passacaglia, scherzo, cadenzas, and an isorhythmic obbligato. Joseph Horowitz noted in his review in the New York *Times* that "It is the work's broad Romantic gestures that make the most striking first impression. . . . Mr. Wernick's canons are . . . in the nature of surface events. . . . More conspicuous are recurrent motivic elements chiefly associated with the 'introit' sections. . . . These are developed toward a closing statement in which the polyphonic wandering of the whole seems to congeal into stirring homophony. . . . Mr. Wernick skillfully uses instrumental color to reinforce the shifting moods."

On January 20, 1980, the Society for New Music in New York presented the world premiere of *A Poison Tree,* with sardonic overtones and occasional parodic passages, and whose text is the William Blake poem of the same name.

Since 1968, Wernick has been the conductor and music director of the Penn Contemporary Players. In the spring of 1979 he was conductor of the Swarthmore College Orchestra in Pennsylvania and in May he was guest conductor of the Philadelphia Orchestra in performances of George Crumb's *Star-Child.*

Wernick received an award from the National Institute of Arts and Letters in 1976 and he was awarded a second grant by the National Endowment for the Arts in 1979.

The Wernicks and their three sons make their home in Media, Pennsylvania. Aside from being an avid reader, Wernick has no interests or hobbies outside music.

MAJOR WORKS

Chamber Music—2 string quartets; Music for Solo Viola d'Amore; Stretti, for clarinet, violin, viola, and guitar; Cadenzas and Variations, for viola and piano; Cadenzas and Variations II, for solo violin; Cadenzas and Variations III, for solo cello; Partita, for solo violin.

Choral Music—Beginnings; Kee El Asher.

Orchestral Music—Hexagrams, for chamber orchestra; From Tulips and Chimneys, for baritone solo and orchestra; Aevia; Visions of Terror and Wonder, for mezzo-soprano and orchestra; Introits and Canons, for chamber ensemble.

Vocal Music—Lyrics from I x I, for soprano, vibraphone, marimba, and doublebass; Haiku of Bashō, for soprano, flute, clarinet, violin, doublebass, two percussion, piano, and magnetic tape; Moonsongs from the Japanese, for soprano and two pre-recorded tracks of soprano voice; A Prayer for Jerusalem, for mezzo-

soprano and percussion; Kaddish-Requiem, A Secular Service for the Victims of Indo-China, for mezzo-soprano, chamber ensemble, and magnetic tape; Songs of Remembrance, four songs for mezzo-soprano, shawm, English horn, and oboe; Contemplations of the Tenth Muse, Book I, for soprano and piano; A Poison Tree, for soprano and chamber ensemble; Contemplations of the Tenth Muse, Book II, for soprano and piano; And on the Seventh Day, a Sabbath evening service for cantor and two percussion.

ABOUT

High Fidelity/Musical America, August 1977; New York Times, May 8, 1977.

Ermanno Wolf-Ferrari

1876–1948

See *Composers Since 1900.*

Charles Wuorinen

1938–

Charles Wuorinen was born in New York City on June 9, 1938. Both of his parents—Charles Peter and Alfhild Kaiijarvi Wuorinen—are of Finnish descent; the father was professor of history, and later chairman of the history department at Columbia University in New York.

Charles Wuorinen first revealed his interest in composition at five, when he started scribbling musical notes on paper. Except for some early piano lessons from neighborhood teachers, he never received any intensive formal instruction on the piano, but he did study composition privately with Jack Beeson and Vladimir Ussachevsky. One of Wuorinen's compositions won him the New York Philharmonic Young Composers Award when he was fifteen.

He received his academic schooling at the Trinity School in New York and graduated in 1956. By that time he had composed numerous works for solo piano, for percussion, and for organ, and *Te Decet Hymnus* in 1954, a composition for mezzo-soprano, bass, mixed chorus, two pianos, and timpani, and two compositions for orchestra, *Into the Organ Pipes and Steeples*

Wuorinen: wûr′ ĭnen

CHARLES WUORINEN

(1956) and *Music for Orchestra* (1956). In 1956, Wuorinen enrolled at Columbia University where he studied composition with Otto Luening. His undergraduate work was subsidized by an Alice M. Ditson Fellowship in 1959, an Arthur Rose Fellowship in 1960, and mainly by working as a piano accompanist, a recording engineer, and a countertenor with church choirs.

During his undergraduate years he was highly productive creatively, completing about thirty compositions including *Triptych,* for violin, viola, and percussion (1957); a piano sonata (1958); three symphonies (1958, 1959, 1959); and a large variety of chamber music, piano music, and vocal compositions. His musical style, at this time, which was strongly influenced by Stravinsky and Varèse, was aggressive and at times, dramatic or turbulent. When Symphony No. 3 (1959) was introduced in New York in 1959, Jay Harrison, of the New York *Herald Tribune,* called it "a hulky blockbuster of a piece," and when it was recorded three years later, Alan Rich, of the New York *Times,* described it as "tremendously energetic." On three occasions, Wuorinen was awarded the Bearns Prize at Columbia (1958, 1959, 1961). He was also awarded the first of four BMI Student Composition Awards in 1959, and the first of two Lili Boulanger Memorial Awards in 1961.

He was awarded the Phi Beta Kappa key and his Bachelor of Arts degree at Columbia in 1961. For the next two years he pursued graduate studies at Columbia, on a Regents College Teaching Fellowship, earning his Master of Arts

degree in 1963. In 1964 he was appointed lecturer of music at Columbia, rising to assistant professor a decade and a half later. In addition to teaching assignments, Wuorinen and Harvey Sollberger founded the Group for Contemporary Music in 1962, to present concerts of 20th century music and works of young and still comparatively little-known composers who needed exposure. This was probably the first campus-based contemporary music ensemble in the United States, and it served as a model and inspiration for many similar groups in colleges throughout the country.

While teaching at Columbia, Wuorinen was visiting lecturer at Princeton University in 1967–1968, at New England Conservatory in Boston in 1968–1969, and at the University of Iowa in Iowa City in 1970. He was awarded a Guggenheim Fellowship in 1968, the Ingram Merrill Fellowship in 1969, and the Creative Arts Award Citation in Music from Brandeis University in Waltham, Massachusetts in 1970. Paterson State College in Wayne, New Jersey, conferred an honorary Doctorate in Music on him in 1971.

In the early 1960s, Wuorinen began to write music in serial form and his first serial works included *Piano Variations* (1963), *Flute Variations* (1963), and *Chamber Concerto,* for flute and ten players (1964), which was commissioned by the Fromm Music Foundation for a modern music festival at Tanglewood in Massachusetts. In the Boston *Globe,* Michael Steinberg called it "an extraordinary virtuoso vehicle for the newly extended flute technique . . . strong and gripping music."

Through Vladimir Ussachevsky, Wuorinen became interested in electronic music and his first electronic compositions were *Consort from Instruments and Voices,* for magnetic tape (1961), and more important *Electronic Exchanges,* for orchestra and tape (1965). When the work was introduced at the French-American Festival of the New York Philharmonic on July 30, 1965, with Lukas Foss conducting, Raymond Ericson said in the New York *Times:* "The work opposes taped music, used to 'display certain musical relationships' and orchestral music thought of as 'performed' commentary on the taped music. Since the taped music keeps more or less to normal orchestral sounds, the work has more homogeneity than most such mixtures." John Gruen described it in the New

York *Herald Tribune:* "A series of aural explosions formed imaginary abstract shapes—each of them organized by the composer with brilliant forethought and invention."

In 1968, Nonesuch Records commissioned Wuorinen to write an electronic composition suitable for a single LP. For a year, he worked at the Columbia-Princeton Electronic Music Center in NewYork with the RCA Mark II Synthesizer (Milton Babbitt used it for many of his electronic compositions). He completed *Time's Encomium* (1969) for synthesized sound and processed synthesized sound, and he explained his title: "Because I need it, I praised time. . . . Because it doesn't need me, I approach it respectfully, hence the word 'encomium.' " Sometimes the electronic sounds simulated those of the piano, organ, harpsichord, or other traditional instrument, but most of the time the sounds were well beyond their capabilities of the instruments. Reviewing the Nonesuch recording in *High Fidelity/Musical America,* Alfred Frankenstein wrote: "This is a wonderful work . . . a genuinely mighty score, full of new worlds and galaxies of sound, magnificent in its size, its spacious implications and the grandeur of its form." In 1970, *Time's Encomium* was awarded the Pulitzer Prize in music, the first time the award was given for a composition on a recording. Wuorinen later rescored the composition for orchestra.

Wuorinen resigned his professorship at Columbia University in 1971 with considerable controversy and press coverage. Denial of tenure and university withdrawal of its support for the Group of Contemporary Music were basically his reasons for leaving, as he explained in the New York *Times:* "The ruling circles of the Music Department are—through accidents and retirement, resignation and the like—overwhelmingly musicological. Perhaps by concentrating so much on the past, they have developed a hostility to the present, and to those who advocate it in music. Perhaps, also by allowing their own active practice of the art to atrophy into scholarly sedentariness, they have likewise come to fear those who compose and perform. . . . The same contempt for individual accomplishment for which the university has become well known now presides over the atrophy of the compositional scene at Columbia." Although he could have stayed on at Columbia for two additional years without tenure, he preferred to join the music faculty of the Manhattan School of Music

in 1971, and he took the Group of Contemporary Music with him. He was subsequently presented with a second Guggenheim Fellowship (1972), the Phoebe Ketchum-Thorne Honorary Award (1973), the Creative Artists Public Service Award (1976), and the Arts and Letters Award of the Finlandia Foundation (1976).

The Pulitzer Prize helped to increase his stature in contemporary American music. String Quartet (1971), commissioned by the Fine Arts Quartet, was performed in New York in the winter of 1973 and *Speculum Speculi* (1972; New York, February 21, 1973), for a small chamber group, was commissioned by the Naumburg Foundation for the Speculum Musicae ensemble. Both works demonstrated increasing originality in his serialist methodology, and both were scored solely for traditional instruments, but other major works called for electronic resources. Two concertos which utilized electronic amplification for their solo instruments were *Concerto for Amplified Violin and Orchestra* (1972), which was commissioned by the Fromm Music Foundation for the Festival of Contemporary Music at Tanglewood and introduced by Paul Zukofsky and the Boston Symphony Orchestra under Michael Tilson Thomas on August 4, 1972. In *Newsweek,* Hubert Saal described the work: "In mood it's harsh, a blitzkrieg in attack, deadly serious and much more thoughtful than the gimmicky idea of an amplified violin suggests. Its chaos is like children let loose. At the end, the meeting is called to order and the children's playground turns out to be Pandemonium, the violin Lucifer himself, the orchestra his fellow fallen angels." A year later, Wuorinen applied the amplification idea to his *Concerto No. 2,* for piano and orchestra. He composed it on a grant from the National Endowment for the Arts, and its world premiere took place in New York on December 6, 1975, with Erich Leinsdorf conducting the New York Philharmonic Orchestra and the composer as the soloist. Although the entire work is constructed on a twelve-tone set, the row is never explicit and the music is written entirely in 4/4 time without a single alteration of the meter. Antiphonal effects are produced by scattering loudspeakers throughout the auditorium.

In later compositions, Wuorinen modified his approach to twelve-tone music further by aiming for the abolition of the dichotomy between tonal and twelve-tone procedures. Keeping in mind that Stravinsky had similar aims in his last works, Wuorinen wrote *A Reliquary for Igor Stravinsky* (1975), in which the last fragments on which Stravinsky was working at the time of his death became the basic material, combined with Wuorinen's own. In the closing coda, the style emulates Stravinsky's endings in *Symphony of Psalms* and *Requiem Canticles*. Commissioned jointly by the Buffalo Philharmonic and the Ojai Festival in California, *A Reliquary for Igor Stravinsky* was premiered at the Ojai Festival in California on May 30, 1975.

In 1975, Wuorinen wrote his first opera: the "baroque burlesque," *W. of Babylon*, with a text by Renaud Charles Bruce, and set in 17th century France. Older operatic styles and practices are alluded to in the opera but it never resorts to outright parody. Several scenes from the opera were first heard on December 15, 1975, in a performance by the Group of Contemporary Music in New York.

The *Tashi Concerto* (1975) acquired its name from the fact that Wuorinen wrote it for the distinguished American chamber-music ensemble called Tashi. The composer wrote two versions of the composition. The first one was scored for clarinet, violin, cello, and piano, and it was introduced by Tashi on February 18, 1976. The other one is for the same four instruments and an orchestra. The Cleveland Orchestra, with the composer conducting, and the Tashi group as soloists, presented the work first in Cleveland on October 13, 1976.

With a second grant from the National Endowment for the Arts, Wuorinen wrote *Percussion Symphony* in 1976 for the New Jersey Percussion Ensemble which introduced it at Somerset County College in Somerville, New Jersey, in January 1978 and then recorded it. As the composer's most extended percussion composition, requiring twenty-four players, there are three sections, with contrasting "entr'actes" in between. For the "entr'actes" Wuorinen transcribed "*Vergine Bella*," a chanson by the 15th century master Guillaume Dufay twice, each one differing in tempo, instrumentation, and "key." The purpose of the two "entr'actes" the composer explained is "to provide the relief afforded by light-textured and simple (but sophisticated) diatonicism as a contrast and foil to the denser, louder contrapuntalities of the main movements."

In *Two-Part Symphony* (1978) which was premiered on December 11, 1978, in New York by the American Composers Orchestra under Dennis Russell, Wuorinen reverts to the neo-Stravinsky style of *A Reliquary for Igor Stravinsky*. Donal Henahan commented in the New York *Times,* that it "strode along in percussive strides. As the second movement drove towards its conclusion, it built up a good head of propulsion that managed to combine both simple urgency and metrical complexity." In 1980, the Symphony represented the United States at the International Rostrum of Composers UNESCO in Paris.

Wuorinen was commissioned by the Handel Oratorio Society of Augustana College, in Rock Island, Illinois, to write the sacred oratorio, *The Celestial Sphere,* for chorus and orchestra (1980) in celebration of the hundredth anniversary of the college's founding. The oratorio was introduced on April 25, 1981.

In discussing contemporary music in general, Wuorinen said: "We should be able to say, 'this music means nothing to me' and still know it's the future. If a worker in science comes up with something, we embrace it. I'd like to know how many well-funded scientific projects amount to anything. They are measured by their successes and we by our failures." About himself he said: "In many ways I think my life is more difficult than that of my contemporaries because I have always been driven to compose all the time. That is what I do for the most part. . . . Composing is a strenuous activity and one at times grows weary in its pursuit. In any case, I've always felt that perhaps the best contribution as an individual composer to the overall health of the compositional trait is to attempt to demonstrate a certain possibility of independence for the artist."

Wuorinen, who has never married, owns a brownstone house in Manhattan. Donal Henahan wrote about him in the New York *Times:* "The Charles Wuorinen who sits in his Spartanly furnished bachelor digs . . . discussing the teachings of Lao-Tse, the legendary founder of Taoism, is hard to reconcile with the angry young scientist-artist. This is a non-violent, positively gentle man, assured but not pedantic, a collector of old books, a philosopher unenamored of the easy putdown, the facile paradox and the intellectual shibboleth. . . . A dabbler in Chinese philosophy for some years, Wuorinen recently opted for total immersion and began formal study of the language." The ancient art of calligraphy has long delighted him. "Calligraphy is the only visual art I really can appreciate because of my weak eyesight," Wuorinen said.

MAJOR WORKS

Chamber Music—3 trios, for flute, cello, and piano; 2 string quartets; 2 sets of Cello Variations; 2 sets of Flute Variations; Triptych, for violin, viola, and percussion; Spectrum, for violin, brass quintet, and piano; Concertante No. 3, for harpsichord, oboe, violin, viola, and cello; Trio Concertante, for oboe, violin, and piano; Musica Duarum Partium Ecclesiastica, for brass quintet, piano, organ, and timpani; Sonata, for flute and piano; Turetzky Pieces, for flute, clarinet, and contrabass; Eight Variations, for violin and harpsichord; Consort, for four trombones; Octet, for flute, clarinet, horn, trombone, violin, cello, contrabass, and piano; Chamber Concerto, for cello and ten players; Composition, for violin and ten instruments; Chamber Concerto, for oboe and ten players; String Trio; String Quartet; Canzona, for twelve instruments; Harp Variations, for harp, violin, viola, and cello; Bassoon Variations; for bassoon, harp, and timpani; Violin Variations; On Alligators, for eight instruments; Speculum Speculi, for flute, oboe, bass, clarinet, contrabass, piano, and percussion; Grand Union, for cello and drums; Arabia Feliz, for flute, bassoon, violin, electric guitar, vibraphone, and piano; Fantasia, for violin and piano; Tashi, for clarinet, violin, cello, and piano; Hyperion, for twelve instruments; The Winds, for eight wind instruments; Fast Fantasy, for solo cello; Archangel, for bass trombone and string quartet; Wind Quintet; Six pieces, for violin and piano; Joan's, for instruments; Archaeopteryx, for bass trombone and instruments.

Choral Music—Te Decet Hymnus, for mezzo-soprano, bass, chorus, two pianos, and timpani; Be Merry All that Be Present, for chorus and organ; The Prayer of Jonah, for chorus and string quintet; Super Salutem, for male voices and instruments; Mannheim 87, 87, 87, for women's chorus and organ; An Anthem for Epiphany, for chorus, trumpet, and organ; The Celestial Sphere, sacred oratorio for chorus and orchestra.

Electronic Music—Consort from Instruments and Voices, for magnetic tape; Orchestral and Electronic Exchanges, for orchestra and tape; Time's Encomium, for synthesized sounds and processed sounds; "ng. c".

Operas—The Politico of Harmony, masque; W. of Babylon.

Orchestral Music—3 symphonies; 2 piano concertos (one for amplified piano); Concertante No. 1, for violin and orchestra; Alternating Currents, for chamber orchestra; Concertante No. 2, for violin and orchestra; Concertante No. 4, for violin, piano, and orchestra; Concertone, for brass quintet and orchestra; Grand Bamboula, for string orchestra; Concerto for Amplified Violin and Orchestra; A Reliquary for Igor Stravinsky; Tashi, orchestral version; Percussion Sym-

phony, for twenty-four players; Ancestors, for chamber orchestra; Two-Part Symphony.

Piano Music—2 sonatas; Piano Variations; Harpsichord Divisions, for harpsichord; Making Ends Meet, for piano four hands; Twelve Short Pieces; Self Similar Waltz.

Vocal Music—Wandering in This Place, for mezzo-soprano and piano; The Door in the Wall, also On the Raft, for two mezzo-sopranos (or one mezzo-soprano and one soprano) and piano; Madrigale Spirituale, for tenor, baritone, two oboes, two violins, cello, and double-bass; Six Songs, for two voices, violin, and piano; Symphonia Sacra, for tenor, baritone, bass, two oboes, two violins, double-bass and organ; A Message to Denmark Hill, for baritone, flute, cello, and piano; A Song to the Lute in Musicke, for soprano and piano.

ABOUT:

Machlis, J., Introduction to Contemporary Music (revised edition); Thomson, V., American Music Since 1910.

The Boston Phoenix, April 24, 1973; BMI, Many Worlds of Music, Winter 1976; Esquire, July 1973; High Fidelity/Musical America, September 1970; New York Times, June 7, 1970; August 8, 1971, February 13, 1977.

Iannis Xenakis

1922–

Iannis Xenakis, one of Europe's most prestigious avant-garde composers, was born on May 29, 1922, in Braïla, Rumania. His father, Charcos Xenakis, was a wealthy businessman; his mother was Fantins Parlou Xenakis. When Iannis was ten, his family brought him to Greece where he was raised and educated in elementary school and at the Greek-English College in Spetsai. As a boy, he was fascinated by unpitched sounds (or "sound events" as he would later identify them). He recalled: "As a boy I used to go camping, and I remember hearing the locusts at night—thousands of disconnected sounds coming from all directions. For me it was so beautiful. It seemed music to me, but nobody in those days could see it as music."

By 1934, Xenakis decided to divide his time and energy between music and the sciences. He began to receive training in composition from Aristotle Koundourov, a former pupil of Ippolitov-Ivanov. In 1940, he successfully passed

---

Xenakis: zä nä′ kǐs

IANNIS XENAKIS

his entrance examinations for the Polytechnic Institute in Athens from which he was graduated in 1947 with an engineering diploma.

His schooling years were a time of stress and anguish, as for most Greeks, for on October 28, 1940, Italian troops invaded Greece. Xenakis joined the anti-Nazi resistance movement in Greece and, in 1941 became the secretary of a Resistance group at the Polytechnic Institute, and he was jailed and tortured several times. On January 1, 1945, his face was disfigured and permanently scarred with complete loss of vision in one eye when he was struck by a tank during street combat in Athens. Sought by the Italian military police and faced with death as a terrorist, he fled from Greece with a forged passport in September 1947, entering France illegally as a stateless person and a political refugee. (In 1951, a war counsel in Greece sentenced him, in absentia, to ten years' imprisonment as a deserter.)

In Paris, Xenakis became interested in architecture. After studying with Le Corbusier, one of France's highly esteemed architects, Xenakis became his assistant and closest collaborator for a number of years in planning ambitious structures in Europe and elsewhere. Music was not forgotten and although in 1948 he was turned down by both Nadia Boulanger and Arthur Honegger as a pupil in composition, he managed to get advice and criticism from Darius Milhaud. From 1950 to 1962 Xenakis attended the Paris Conservatory, and studied composition with Olivier Messiaen. In 1953, Xenakis married

Françoise, a successful novelist, and a former heroine in the French resistance movement during World War II who had been decorated several times for saving the lives of underground fighters. They have one child, a daughter.

In 1954, Xenakis began to develop his own method of musical composition which has come to be called "stochastic" (from the Greek root meaning "straight aim"), in actuality involving controlled improvisation. As a mathematician he evolved his method from the laws of mathematical probability, symbolic and mathematical logic, probability calculus, and set theory—his music was worked out according to the probabilities of certain notes, rhythms, and sonorities recurring in a given work. Jan Maguire, a French journalist, described the Xenakis method: "Instead of thinking in terms of harmony, as musicians for many centuries have done, Xenakis thinks in terms of sound entities which possess the characteristics of pitch, intensity and duration, as associated to each other by and within time." The stochastic method, as further detailed by Bernard Jacobson in the *Dictionary of Contemporary Music,* "is related to Jacques Bernoulli's Law of Large Numbers, which says that as the number of repetitions of a given chance trial (such as flipping a coin) increased, the probability that the results will tend to a determinate end approaches certainty. A stochastic process, then, is one that is probabilistic in the sense of tending toward a certain goal. . . . His aim is nothing less than the expression in music of the unity he sees as underlying all activity, human and nonhuman, artistic and scientific . . . and, finally, to order the results of calculation and transcribe them into musical notation." Xenakis commented on his own method: "There exist in a given space musical instruments and men; there is no cause or organization to produce sounds. But given a sufficiently long period of time, it is probable that there will be a fortuitous generation of some sounds of certain length, certain colors, certain speeds and so forth. . . . These are sound events, isolated sounds. They could be melodic figures, cellular structures, agglomerations whose characteristics are ruled by the laws of chance." For almost all of his compositions, Xenakis used Greek titles to point up the fact that modern science and art were derived from the ancient Greeks. To some of his electronic pieces he has given symbols rather than titles.

Xenakis

Xenakis's first important composition in his stochastic method (he did not arrive at his own avant-garde language, as so many others did, by way of serialism) was *Metastasis,* or *Transformation* (1953–1954), for an orchestra of 61 instruments, each required to play its own music. The work created a scandal when it was introduced on October 15, 1955, at the Donaueschingen Festival in Germany, conducted by Hans Rosbaud. It begins with several measures on the note G sustained in the strings, while gliding glissandi in the rest of the orchestra and expanding dynamics help to create an eerie effect and to arrive at a dramatic climax. In this work, and in his second work, *Pithoprakta,* or *Actions by Means of Probabilities* (1955–1956), for an orchestra of fifty musicians, whose first performance took place in Munich on March 8, 1957 under Herman Scherchen's direction, he explored the possibilities of simulating or even outclassing electronically produced sounds and sonorities with conventional instruments. The composer himself described the work as a "dense cloud of sonorous material movement." All kinds of sounds are produced by the string instruments, such as tapping the bodies of the instruments, an unusual use of bow and plucked strings, and glissandos in the trombones. Textures are dense and sonorities overpowering. Xenakis insisted that his music was not programmatic and should be listened to solely for the experiences in sound it provides, but he did say that in both *Metastasis* and *Pithoprakta* "there is all the agony of my youth, of the Resistance and the aesthetic problems they posed with the huge street demonstrations, or even more, the occasional mysterious deadly sounds of those cold nights of December '44 in Athens." For these two compositions, Xenakis was awarded the Geneva Prix de la Fondation Européenne pour la Culture in 1957. Both compositions were later used by the New York City Ballet in 1968 for a ballet choreographed by George Balanchine entitled *Metastasis and Pithoprakta.*

Xenakis's earliest experiment with electronic music on magnetic tape was in 1957 with *Diamorphoses,* developed in the studios of the Groupe de Recherche Musicale de la Radio-Television Française in Paris. His interest in electronic music increased after meeting Edgard Varèse at the Brussels World Exposition in 1958. Xenakis had helped Le Corbusier design the Philips Pavilion where Varèse's *Poème Électronique* on magnetic tape was regularly projected through some 400 speakers. He also wrote a short electronic piece for magnetic tape, *Concret PH,* intended as a welcoming piece at the Philips Pavilion.

Xenakis went from magnetic tape to computer—the IBM 7090—finding the computer valuable in stochastic calculations. *ST/4,* for string quartet, *ST/10* for ten instruments, and *ST/48* for forty-eight musicians playing forty-eight different parts were produced between 1956 and 1962. (ST represents Stochastic; the adjoining number is the number of instrumentalists required.) The liner notes to an Angel recording of these pieces read: "Basically, the program is a complex of stochastic laws by which the composer orders the electronic brain to define all the sounds one after the other in a previously calculated sequence. First comes the occurrence date, then the tonal class (arco, pizzicato, glissando, etc.), the instrument, the height, the glissando pitch if there is any, the length of time, and the dynamic form of the emission of sound." *ST/10* actually bears the longer title of *ST/10, 1,080262* (the first digit, "1," indicates that it is Xenakis's first stochastic work for ten instruments; the rest of the digits represent the date when the calculations for this composition had been completed—February 8, 1962. *ST/48* bears the longer title of *ST/48, 1,240162* (Xenakis's first stochastic work for forty-eight instruments, completed on January 24, 1962). Lukas Foss led the premiere performance in Paris on October 21, 1968. *ST/4* is the string-quartet version of *ST/10.* Reviewing *ST/48* for *High Fidelity/Musical America,* a critic noted that bowed glissandos were used so extensively "that the ear soon became saturated with this device. . . . The work has enough activity to occupy one's attention at the first listening. But the novelty fades upon repeated exposure." *Atrées,* or *The Law of Necessity* (1956–1962), for ten instruments and written in homage to Pascal, was also programmed and calculated on the IBM 7090.

Another area in which Xenakis experimented was that of "games." *Duel* (1959)—first performed in October 1971 by Radio Hilvershum in Germany, was a competitive "game" for two orchestras with two conductors, each playing different music mathematically devised from a single theory; and the audience had to decide who the winner was. *Stratégie* (1962), similarly had two orchestras and two conductors competing with one another. When it was introduced at the Venice Festival on April 23, 1963, the orchestra conducted by Bruno Maderna won over that of Konstantin Simonovic.

In 1960, Xenakis gave up architecture to devote himself exclusively to music. "I have no time to be an architect," he explained. "Architecture is a business and I don't like business. I like research."

In 1962, the year in which he was awarded the Prix Manos Hadjidakis in Athens, Xenakis visited the United States for the first time, at the invitation of Aaron Copland, to teach composition at the Berkshire Music Center at Tanglewood, Massachusetts. Later in the same year, Xenakis served as artist-in-residence in Berlin at the invitation of both the Ford Foundation and the West Berlin Senate.

Eonta, or *Beings* (1963–1964), for piano and brass choir, was premiered at the Domaine Musical in Paris in October 1964, with Pierre Boulez directing. It was described by Roy McMullen in *High Fidelity/Musical America* as a "violent stochastic combat between a piano and a sounds lab created by four trumpets and six trombones. It did not, as the French say, leave you different." On instructions from the composer, the brass moves about the stage from time to time and blows into the strings of the piano. Theodore Strongin reported in the New York *Times* when *Eonta* was performed at Tanglewood in 1968: "The piano provides the motor energy, the brass harness it. This result is a handsome, musical no-nonsense piece of music." Similar controlled power is generated in *Akrata*, or *Pure* (1964–1965), for 15 wind instruments and vibraphone, commissioned by the Koussevitzky Music Foundation. Its world premiere took place in Paris in 1965, and then it was presented at the English Bach Festival in Oxford, England, on June 28, 1966. Leonard Altman described it in *Stereo Review:* "It is a striking piece, full of enormous color, dynamic contrast, intensely dramatic moments, clean-sounding and of an almost transparent quality despite its sometimes massive sonorities." Two compositions—in 1965–1966 and in 1967–1968 —require the musicians of the orchestra to be scattered among the unsuspecting audience while a variety of sonorities are unleashed, including noise elements. They were *Terretektorh*, or *Action of Construction*, and *Vamos Gamma*,

or *Law Gamma*. Both works were introduced at the Royal Festival of Contemporary Music in France on April 3, 1966 and on April 3, 1969, respectively. A program note at the *Terretektorh* premiere advised: "If desired, a rain of hair can surround each of the listeners, or perhaps a murmuration of a pine forest, or any other atmosphere or linear concept, static or in motion. The individual listeners will then find themselves as though sailing on a frail boat on a turbulent sea, or in a pointillistic universe of sonorous sparks moving in cumulus or isolated clouds."

The first Xenakis Festival took place at the Salle Gaveau in Paris in 1965. A year later the composer was invited to participate in the Musicological Congress in Manila and to be present at the Japanese premiere of his *Stratégie* at the Festival of Contemporary Music in Tokyo. In 1966, Xenakis founded the Équipe de Mathématique et Automatique Musicales, in Paris, which, four years later, received official recognition and accommodation in the Centre de Recherche Nucléaire of the College de France. For Expo '67 in Montreal, Xenakis conceived and realized a light and sound spectacle entitled *Polytope de Montréal* for the French Pavilion. In 1967, Xenakis was named associate professor of music at Indiana University in Bloomington where he founded and directed a new Center for Mathematical and Automated Studies in Music for five years.

When the Canadian Arts Council commissioned a Xenakis ballet to open a new auditorium in Ottawa on June 2, 1969, he wrote not only the music but also his own scenario. *Kraanerg (Perfected Energy)* takes place in the year 2069 when youth control the world and decree that anybody over the age of thirty must be exterminated. The score for magnetic tape and orchestra—Xenakis's first original score for a ballet—was called by Clive Barnes in the New York *Times* "a wonderful piece of music, enthralling, and one that grips the mind and the heart. Indeed, even at a single hearing, I would feel inclined to say that it is one of the major ballet scores of the century. ... Mr. Xenakis' music, with its gushes and rushes of sound, its architectural buildups into aural space, its strange and chilling sonorities, its curious interplay between taped sound and orchestral musicians, is wonderfully exciting."

The Composers Showcase in New York provided an evening of Xenakis music on May 11,

1971, with the composer providing comments. One of the pieces performed *Bohor I,* for magnetic tape (1962), created the strongest unfavorable response. Donal Henahan reported in the New York *Times,* "As the piece . . . roared and jangled and howled madly toward Armageddon, people who had listened intently up till then began to defect in gross lots. One woman . . . screamed throughout the final few minutes and —incredibly—made herself heard." While in the United States in 1971, Xenakis was scholar-in-residence at the Aspen Institute in Colorado. In 1973 he was guest professor both at Columbia University and Barnard College in New York. Major festivals of Xenakis music were held in Tokyo in 1973, in Bonn in 1974 (covering twenty-seven of his works in ten concerts), and in Paris between November 28 and December 21, 1977.

Cendrées, for chorus and orchestra (1974), was commissioned by the Gulbenkian Foundation in Lisbon for its late spring-early summer festival in 1974. The work is for a wordless chant and was introduced on June 20. *Erikhthon,* for piano and orchestra (1974), was introduced in May 1974 by Claude Helffer and an orchestra directed by Michel Tabachnik in Paris. On October 16, the same year, Sir Georg Solti led the Orchestre de Paris in the premiere of *Noomena,* for large orchestra (1975). On June 29, 1975, at the La Rochelle Festival in Paris, *Empreintes,* for orchestra (1975), had its first hearing; on January 28, 1976, *Phlegra,* for eleven instruments (1975), was premiered in London; and on December 20, 1976, *Retours—Windungen,* for twelve cellos (1976), was premiered in Bonn. When Zubin Mehta and the New York Philharmonic Orchestra presented the American premiere of *Empreintes,* or *Imprints,* on October 16, 1980, Nicholas Kenyon, writing in *The New Yorker,* described it as follows: "It explores one idea—the 'image of waves erasing the footprints of men and animals on the beaches.' A single note, fluctuating in volume, penetrates its texture; around it, murmurs of string sound come and go, but the single note survives. . . . After about seven and a half minutes, the texture suddenly thins and then diversifies (the effect is electrifying). Little staccato blobs in the winds take over, while the single note whistles high on piccolo. A grunt from the contrabassoon, and it's all over."

In addition to honors already mentioned,

Xenakis was the recipient of the Bax Society Prize in London in 1968, the Maurice Ravel gold medal in Paris in 1974, the Grand Prix National de la Musique in Paris in 1976, and the Prix Beethoven in Bonn in 1977. In 1972 he was made an honorary member of the British Computer Art Society and, in 1975, an honorary member of the American Academy and Institute of Arts and Letters. The Sorbonne conferred an honorary Doctorate in Humane Letters and Sciences on him in 1976. Recordings of Xenakis music earned numerous awards in Europe, including the Grand Prix du Disque in Paris (several times), the Nippon Academy Award in Tokyo, and the Edison Prize in Amsterdam.

Xenakis is the author of *Musique Formelle* (1963, translated into English as *Formalized Music* and published in the United States in 1971) and *Musique Architecture* (1976), in addition to numerous articles on stochastic and electronic music for French publications.

Since 1947 he has made his home in Paris, becoming a French citizen in 1965. In 1974 he was finally permitted to return to Greece, his first visit since 1947 and he was given a hero's welcome.

In the New York *Times,* Donal Henahan described Xenakis: "Though he speaks like a scientist, Xenakis looks the part of an ex-Resistance street fighter. . . . A facial scar . . . lends him a Bogartish toughness, and he can turn on an askew grin that is pure Sam Spade. For his stop in New York, he wore brown suede desert boots, electric blue socks, brown suede jacket, crumpled pants, and a tieless white shirt, rolled up carelessly at the sleeves. . . . His English, spoken with agonizing care, has an odd musical lilt that suggests Peter Sellers playing an Anglo-Indian."

MAJOR WORKS

Ballets—Kraanerg; Antikhthon.

Chamber Music—Analogiques A & B, for nine string instruments; ST/4, for string quartet (an adaptation of ST/48); ST/10, for ten instruments; Morsima-Amorsima, for piano, violin, cello, and double-bass; Atrées, for ten instruments; Eonta, for piano and five strings; Anaktoria, octet; Persephasa, for six percussionists; Charisma, for clarinet and cello; Aroura, for twelve strings; Mikka, for violin solo; Linaia-Agon, for horn, tenor trombone, and tuba; Phlegra, for eleven instruments; Psappha, for solo percussion; Theraps, for solo double-bass; Retours-Windungen, for twelve cellos; Epeï, for English horn, clarinet, trumpet, two trombones, and double-bass; Mikka S, for violin solo;

326

Dmaathen, for oboe and percussion; Akanthos, for nine instruments; Kottos, for viola solo.

Choral Music—Polla ta Dhina, for children's choir and small orchestra; Hiketides, stage music for female chorus and instrumental ensemble; Oresteia, suite for chorus and chamber orchestra; Nuits, for twelve a cappella voices; Medea, stage music for male chorus and instrumental ensemble; Cendrées, for chorus and orchestra; Hélène, stage music for female chorus and two clarinets; À Colonne, for male chorus, horn, trombone, and double-bass.

Electronic Music—Diamorphoses, for magnetic tape; Concret PH, for magnetic tape; Orient-Occident, for magnetic tape; Bohor I and II, for magnetic tape; Hibiki-Hana-Ma, for twelve-channel magnetic tape; Polytope II, for magnetic tape and lighting; Diatope, for magnetic tape.

Multi-media—Poiytope de Montréal; Persepolis; Polytope de Cluny; La Légende d'Er.

Orchestral Music—Metastasis; Pithoprakta; Achoripsis, for twenty-one instruments; Duel, "game" for two orchestras; Syrmos, for eighteen or thirty-six string instruments; ST/48; Stratégie, "game" for two orchestras; Akatra, for sixteen wind instruments; Terretektorh; Nomas Gamma; Synaphai, for piano or two pianos and orchestra; Eridanos, for eight brasses and two horns, two tubas, and strings; Erikhthon, for piano and orchestra; Noomena; Empreintes; Jonchaies.

Organ Music—Gmeeoorh.

Piano Music—Evryali; Herma; Khoai, for harpsichord.

Vocal Music—N'shima, for two mezzo-sopranos, two horns, two trombones, and cello; Akanthos, for soprano, flute, clarinet, two violins, viola, cello, double-bass, and piano.

ABOUT

Bois, M., Iannis Xenakis, the Man and His Music; Fleuret, M., Xenakis; Rostrand, C., Xenakis; Sadie, S. (ed.), The New Grove Dictionary of Music and Musicians.

Music and Musicians (London), April 1972; New York Times, March 17, 1968, November 10, 1968, April 21, 1976; Saturday Review, June 24, 1967.

Eugene Zador

1894–1977

For biographical sketch, list of earlier works, and bibliography, see *Composers Since 1900.*

The world premiere of Zador's *Studies for Orchestra* (1970) was performed by the Detroit Symphony Orchestra under Sixten Ehrling on November 12, 1970. Each of its eight sections

has its own personality but the work as a whole is marked by vivid contrasts in tempo, instrumentation, and musical style, and it includes an Allegro in a jazz idiom. In the Detroit *News,* Jay Carr praised Zador for his "great skill as an orchestrator" and described the studies as "pleasantly unpretentious picture postcards."

Forty-three years after it was written, Zador's opera, *The Inspector General* (1928), finally had its premiere in Los Angeles on June 11, 1971. With a libretto by the composer based on the famous satirical novel by Gogol and an English version by George Mead, the opera reveals "a charming and intuitive originality of its own," according to Orrin Howard in the Los Angeles *Times,* with solos and ensembles of "soaring grace and lyric warmth. Much of the opera's strength lies in the colorful, apt commentary of Zador's orchestration."

In celebration of Zador's eightieth birthday, his opera, *The Scarlet Mill* (1967), had its West Coast premiere at the University of Southern California in Los Angeles on February 6, 1974.

A new Zador opera (his thirteenth), *Yehu,* a one-act Christmas piece, was introduced in Los Angeles on December 21, 1974. Anna Együd's libretto portrays those who provided shelter for the birth of Jesus; the simple people who permitted Mary and Joseph to use their stable for the Holy Birth. Their son who is one of Herod's soldiers and suffers from leprosy is assigned to murder the infant, but he is incapable of it and is miraculously cured of his disease. Henry Reese wrote in *Opera Journal,* that "It is a straightforward, unpretentious libretto, but thoroughly dramatic. Zador's music supports, elevates and intensifies it. . . . It is a relief to hear Zador's music *sing* in an extension of human speech."

A cancer victim for several years, Eugene Zador died in his sleep at the Hollywood Presbyterian Hospital in Los Angeles on April 4, 1977. Just before his death, he said, "I have had it all."

MAJOR WORKS (supplementary)

Chamber Music—Suite, for woodwind quintet; Brass Quintet.

Choral Music—The Judgment, for solo voices, women's chorus, brass ensemble, and percussion; Song of the Nymph Called Echo, for women's chorus and orchestra; Cain, for solo voices, women's chorus, brass ensemble, and percussion.

Zador

Opera—Yehu, one-act Christmas opera.

Orchestral Music—Rhapsody for Cimbalon and Orchestra; Fantasia Hungarica, for double-bass and orchestra; Duo Fantasy, for two cellos and string orchestra; Studies; Concerto for Accordion and Orchestra; Suite, for horn, strings, and percussion; Concerto for Oboe and String Orchestra.

Vocal Music—Silence, for voice and piano; Lullaby, for voice and piano; Lullaby to Peter, for voice and piano.

ABOUT (supplementary)

Zador, L. (ed.), Eugene Zador: a Catalogue of His Works.

Picture Credits

Herbert Ascherman, Jr., Erb; *C. Bailey*, Argento; *Studio Alfred Bernheim, Ricarda Schwerin*, Tal; *BMI Archives*, Partch; *Boosey and Hawkes*, Druckman; *East Anglican Daily Time and Associated Papers*, Alwyn; *European-American Music (U.S. & Canadian agent, Universal Edition, publisher)*, Birtwistle; *Nicolette Hallett*, Maw; *Les Productions J. Raney*, Xenakis; *Lidbrooke*, Hamilton; *Robert Maplethorpe*, Glass; *Ongaku No Tomo Sha Corp.*, Takemitsu; *Louis Ouzer*, Schwantner; *Pach Bros. Inc.*, Imbrie; *C.F. Peters Corp.*, Feldman; *Barbara Pflaum*, Haubenstock-Ramati; *Theodore Presser Co.*, Subotnik; *David Stevens*, Ligeti; *Bruce Stromberg Photograph*, Wernick; *Carol Vitz*, Andriessen.

2051